SPLIT IMAGE

CHARLES WINECOFF

SPLIT IMAGE

THE LIFE OF ANTHONY PERKINS

A DUTTON BOOK

In memory of Christopher Isherwood (1904–1986)
and
Robert S. Freedman (1955–1992)
Thanks for believing in me.

DUTTON
Published by the Penguin Group
Penguin Books USA Inc., 375 Hudson Street, New York, New York 10014, U.S.A.
Penguin Books Ltd, 27 Wrights Lane, London W8 5TZ, England
Penguin Books Australia Ltd, Ringwood, Victoria, Australia
Penguin Books Canada Ltd, 10 Alcorn Avenue,
Toronto, Ontario, Canada M4V 3B2 Penguin Books (N.Z.) Ltd, 182–190 Wairau Road,
Auckland 10, New Zealand

Penguin Books Ltd, Registered Offices:
Harmondsworth, Middlesex, England

First published by Dutton, an imprint of Dutton Signet,
a division of Penguin Books USA Inc.
Distributed in Canada by McClelland & Stewart Inc.

First Printing, September, 1996
3   5   7   9   10   8   6   4   2

REGISTERED TRADEMARK—MARCA REGISTRADA

LIBRARY OF CONGRESS CATALOGING–IN–PUBLICATION DATA:
Winecoff, Charles.
Split image : the life of Anthony Perkins / Charles Winecoff.
p.   cm.
Includes bibliographical references and index.
ISBN 0-525-94064-2 (alk. paper)
1. Perkins, Anthony, 1932–.   2. Actors—United States—Biography.   I. Title.
PN2287.P388W56   1996
791.43'028'092—dc20
[B]   96-6783
CIP

Printed in the United States of America
Set in Bembo

Designed by Jesse Cohen

This book is printed on acid-free paper. ∞

CONTENTS

AUTHOR'S NOTE

"WHY TONY PERKINS?"

I've heard that refrain ad nauseam since I began this project, usually put forth enthusiastically, sometimes suspiciously, by someone who was supposed to be answering questions for me. Many times during the interviewing process I had the ironic feeling that I was the one under scrutiny. None of Perkins's friends, colleagues, or lovers knew me, and they were perplexed. Who was I? Had I known Tony? I'll answer again, once and for all.

I grew up around the corner from Tony Perkins—two blocks away, to be exact, but still around a corner—in the downtown Manhattan neighborhood of Chelsea. I can't claim to have been a fan, but he was the first movie star I ever saw in the flesh, just passing on the street, and he fascinated me. As a boy I was a walking encyclopedia of horror film trivia, and I knew he was the star of *Psycho*, the movie so shocking it couldn't be shown on television. When, at age twelve, I finally did see it, late one night after prime time and butchered for broadcast, it didn't horrify me nearly as much as it left me feeling unsettled. Norman Bates embarrassed me. I was too young to appreciate how superb Perkins's portrayal was, but on a visceral level I felt a connection with the shy motel keeper who spent too much time alone or at home with his mother—a connection that I didn't like. It was as if Tony Perkins were playing me. I felt exposed.

At fourteen, on the reluctant verge of full-blown pubescence, I saw *On the Beach* (again on television, that reassuring atomic age baby-sitter). Perkins's strange, gangly, shifty-eyed performance in the film, so inappropriately awkward for his role as a young family man, seemed to mirror the overwhelming confusion and guilt I was experiencing both sexually and familywise at the time (my parents were separating). Things were happening to me that I didn't fully understand, and Perkins embodied my disharmony. Again, watching him I felt ashamed.

Consequently, seeing him on the street, a walking manifestation of all my suppressed and tangled feelings, became even more disturbing. We passed each other many times over the years. He seemed to be everywhere I went, my doppelgänger. When I was eighteen and rebellious, staying out all night at discos, I saw him one Sunday morning on Ninth Avenue wearing mirrored glasses, leather pants, and a white T-shirt. He looked like he was just getting home, too.

When I fled to Los Angeles in 1980 to go to college, he was already there. Away from home for the first time, my scary familiar was still with me; he and his family now lived around the corner from a friend of mine in Laurel Canyon. There were times I actually wondered if he was following me.

We spoke only once, in 1983. He came into the Unicorn Bookstore in West Hollywood, where I happened to be working the cash register part-time, and made a beeline for the adult section at the rear of the store. I remember being surprised that he was so open about the several porn magazines (all-male) he brought to the counter a few minutes later. I glanced up at him, he smiled and looked me straight in the eye. "Hi, how are you?" he said, and asked me my name. I didn't think he recognized me, and answered perfunctorily. But the moment he walked out of the store onto Santa Monica Boulevard, as I watched him disappear on the other side of the plate-glass window, I remember feeling sad that I hadn't said more. That was the last time I saw him. I never imagined that a decade later I would be writing a book about him.

He continued to haunt me from beyond the grave. The Monday after he died was a particularly dreary one for me. I was still mourning the death of a close friend of mine from AIDS a few months earlier, a friend in whose miraculous recovery and heartbreaking decline I had been deeply involved. I still felt numb as I sat on the subway going to work that morning and noticed Perkins's obituary in a fellow rider's newspaper. I didn't know he had passed away. The news stunned me, but not nearly as much as the statement he had made just before dying, about his "great adventure" in the world of AIDS and the love and compassion he had come to know only since his illness. It seemed so unlike the cagey image of Tony Perkins I'd always held. At a new and very sobering time in my own life, he still managed to echo my innermost thoughts and feelings. What had happened to *him* over the years to bring out such astonishing openness and humanity at the end? His moving farewell made me want to know.

Undertaking this book has been an odyssey for me, a precarious journey back to a darker time that many gay men have lost sight of in the wake of AIDS and that the public at large has generally been oblivious of. I am grateful to a good number of people whose kindness helped open various doors to the past.

For sharing with me their personal, often intimate memories of Perkins's life and work, I offer my sincere thanks to: Elaine Aiken, Joe Alaskey, Robert Altman, Dale Amlund, Donna Anderson, Robert Anderson, Alan Arkin, Don Atkinson, Don Bachardy, Ben Bagley, Jenelle Bailey, Conrad Bain, Bob Balaban, Roger Bentley, Ted Berkman, Richard Bernstein, Ron Bernstein, Noel Black, Raphael Blau, David Blewitt, George Bloomfield, Paul Bogart, William Bogert, Haskell Boggs, Abba Bogin, Peter Bonerz, Robert Borod, Michael Brandman, Scott Bromley, Hilyard Brown, Robert Alan Browne, Abbe Miller Buck, Henry Bumstead, Ray Burchett, Terence Burk, Bart Burns, Carter Burwell, Mario Busoni, Dyan Cannon, Charmian Carr, the late Lee Cass, Harry Chandler, William Chapman, Stephen Cheng, Susan Clark, Buddy Clarke, Maurice Class, Patience Cleveland, Ira Cohen, Richard Colabella, Alvin Colt, Carole Cook, Linda Cook, Saralou Cooper, Gretchen Corbett, Jeff Corey, Charles Correll, Warren Crane, Dean Cundey, Keene Curtis, Gwen Davis, Shelly Davis, Jean DeBaer, David DeCoteau, William De Silva, Lydia Dorsett, Dortha Duckworth, Richard Dunlap, Dominick Dunne, Jonathan Dunn-Rankin, Richard Earle, Ben Edwards, Hector Elizondo, Roger Englander, Joe Eula, Jeff Fahey, Mia Farrow, Mary Fickett, Ruth Ford, Robert

Forster, Charles Forsythe, Conard Fowkes, Richard Franchot, Anne
Francis, Richard Franklin, Michael Frazier, Burry Fredrik, Bruce Jay
Friedman, Sideo Fromboluti, Cary Fuller, Yvonne Furneaux, Art Gar-
funkel, Beverly Garland, Lee Garlington, Lannie Garrett, Mick Garris,
John Gavin, Hugh Gillin, Kenneth Gilman, James Glennon, Billy
Goldenberg, Osanna Gooding, Sidney Gordon, Stuart Gordon, Mor-
ton Gottlieb, William A. Graham, Sabin Gray, Hilton Green, Jane
Greenwood, Jess Gregg, Georgia Gresham, Kay Griffith, Tammy
Grimes, Nicholas Guest, the late Dolly Haas, Jacques Haitkin, Wynn
Handman, Joseph Hardy, Margery Gray Harnick, Wally Harper, Curtis
Harrington, Phil Harrington, Eric Harrison, Peter Haskell, Rex Hauck,
Howard Hays, Don Hellerman, Jerome Hellman, Buck Henry, Arthur
Hill, George Roy Hill, Pat Hingle, Rose Hobart, Tom Holland, Mor-
gan Holman, Bob Hoover, Barbara Howard, Tab Hunter, Robert
Hussong, Joe Hyams, Frances Hyland, Louis Ingram, Rob Iscove,
Mitchell Jason, Robert Jiras, Page Johnson, Robert Juergens, Joseph
Justice, Joseph P. Kahn, Elia Kazan, E. K. Kerr, John Kerr, Leland
Kimball, Robert Kirk, Edgar Knapp, Michael Knue, Stanley Kramer,
Richard Lamparski, Lionel Larner, Andrew Laskos, Piper Laurie, David
Lawlor, Kerry X. LeBre, Jack Lee, Jennifer Lee, Sondra Lee, Janet
Leigh, Richard Lesneski, Barbara Poe Levee, Willard Levitas, Susan
Loesser, Eileen Lottman, Lance Loud, Betty Low, Al Lowman, Sidney
Lumet, George Lymburn, Ellen McCown, Keith McDermott, Roddy
McDowall, Bill McGaw, Donna McKechnie, Christopher Makos,
Gerard Malanga, Karl Malden, Delbert Mann, Martin Manulis, Barney
Martin, Gaylord Mason, Pam Matteson, Walter Matthau, Roberta
Maxwell, Deborah May, the late John Megna, Marian Mercer, the late
Melina Mercouri, Iris Merlis, Natalie Merritt, Sylvia Miles, John Mil-
ius, Stuart Millar, George Miller, Josh Miller, Mark Miller, David
Mitchell, Donna Mitchell, Michael Monroe, Bill Moor, Mary Tyler
Moore, Norma Moore, Gabor Morea, Greg Mullavey, Robert Mulli-
gan, Michael Mullins, Rory Murphy, Rosemary Murphy, Joseph Nas-
sif, Jacques Natteau, Steve Neilson, Gary Nelson, Lois Nettleton, Carl
Nicholas, James Noble, Thomas Norden, Maila "Vampira" Nurmi,
Michaela O'Harra, Gerald Olson, Conrad Osborne, Bibi Osterwald,
Holly Palance, Stephen Paley, Pat Patterson, Robert H. Pearce, Gre-
gory Peck, Austin Pendleton, the late Frank Perry, Nehemiah Persoff,
Lenka Peterson, Louis Peterson, Charles Pogue, Henry Polic, Helen

Pond and Herbert Senn, Derek Power, André Previn, Pat Proft, Dotson Rader, Remak Ramsay, John Randolph, Robert Fitz Randolph, Shirley Finkle Rane, Herman Raucher, Virginia Raymond, David Redding, John Rich, William Richert, Peter Mark Richman, Sara Risher, Adam Roarke, Curtis Roberts, Gerald Robinson, Charles Rodgers, Fred Rogers, Wayne Rogers, Clayton Rohner, Bob Rosengarden, Herbert Ross, Philip and Steven Ross, Alan Rudolph, Barbara Rush, Paul Sand, Barry Sandler, Mia Sara, Henry Scammell, Diana Scarwid, George Schaefer, Joel Schumacher, Bernard Schwartz, Marian Seldes, Kevin Sessums, Robert Shaye, Alan Shayne, James Sheldon, Henry Silva, Karl Silvera, Jack Simmons, Jean Simmons, Stanley Simmons, Neil Simon, George Skaff, Bernard Slade, George Sluizer, Michael T. Smith, Stephen Sondheim, Leonard South, Alan Spencer, Maureen Stapleton, Joseph Stefano, Frances Sternhagen, Harold Stevenson, Venetia Stevenson, Arthur Storch, C. J. Strawn, Peter Strongwater, Alan Sues, Florence Sundstrom, Bruce Surtees, Elaine Swann, Kristoffer Tabori, Maggie Task, Leigh Taylor-Young, Stephanie Terrazas, Joan Tewkesbury, Morton Thaw and Ed Robak, Ernest Thomas, Jennifer Todd, Jo Van Fleet, Gus Van Sant, Gore Vidal, Annie Walker, William Walsh, Ray Walston, Tony Walton, Skip Ward, Wisner Washam, Mary Webster, Alan Weeks, Yale Wexler, "William," Adam Williams, Van Williams, Charles Williamson and Tucker Fleming, Perry Wilson, Ellery Woodworth, Teresa Wright, Jane Wyatt, Catherine Wyler, Michael York, and everyone else who asked to remain nameless.

For curing me of my library phobia, I bow to Sam Gill and his congenial staff at the Margaret Herrick Library of the Academy of Motion Picture Arts and Sciences in Beverly Hills; the days I spent working there were shockingly pleasant. Likewise, Stuart Ng at the University of Southern California library made perusing the Warner Brothers Film Archives easy. Thanks are also due to: Charles Silver at the Museum of Modern Art Film Study Center; Marty Jacobs at the Museum of the City of New York; the staff of the Performing Arts Research Center of the New York Public Library at Lincoln Center; Trudi Laframboise and Kate Reich at the Rollins College Department of Archives, Special Collections and Records Management; Beth Jacobson and Deborah Kelsey at the Buckingham Browne and Nichols School; Mary Ellen Jobson at the Candlelight Dinner Theatre

AMERICAN FAIRY TALE

CAPE COD, AUGUST 1973

RING YOUR CAMERA. We're going to get married."
It was typical Tony Perkins: teasing, in a terse kind of way. No invitations, no church, no ostentatious ceremony. Just a few surprise phone calls to a few close friends, and the forty-one-year-old movie star was set to wed twenty-five-year-old socialite and photographer Berry Berenson. No one had expected it. At least no one in Tony's crowd. After eight months of living with Berry, who had moved into his Chelsea brownstone in January, and publicly proclaiming their shared indifference to social convention, the aging actor, whose bachelorhood had been a source of gossip on both coasts for nearly two decades, was abruptly tying the matrimonial knot. And he was doing so in a secluded setting that could not have been farther away from the smiling opportunism of Hollywood, which he shunned, or the fierce modishness of New York that his bride thrived on.

Their love affair, which had begun less than a year before, had been a great source of publicity for Perkins, the likes of which he had not enjoyed since the shocking success of Alfred Hitchcock's *Psycho* in 1960, the film which had put him on the iconographic map, for better or for worse, as Norman Bates, Hollywood's first cross-dressing, serial-killing boy next door (and a character whose life held uncanny similarities to his own). Since *Psycho*, his career had slid inexorably downhill with a series of artistically promising but disappointing European films in which he'd been repeatedly cast as the neurotic, almost effeminate young love interest opposite actresses like Ingrid Bergman and Melina Mercouri, professional tigresses who had seemed to devour him right onscreen. (Ironically, offscreen he allowed himself to be dominated by a series of strong women as well.) For more than ten years, American audiences and critics had found it impossible to take Tony Perkins seriously as a leading man.

He still looked good; he exercised constantly, even compulsively. But he was too old to be a teen idol any longer—in 1956 he had been foisted on a grieving public as Paramount's answer to the late James Dean—and he still found it hard to shake the "wounded adolescent" persona that had gotten him through so many obstacles in his early career. At this point in his life, as an actor and as a man, he desperately needed a transition, some event to carry him to the next plateau. He had tried stage directing and screenwriting, to some acclaim, but even so had left those projects with more personal questions and self-doubts than he'd had going in. The phone was not exactly ringing off the hook with job offers. That he had worked with some of the greatest directors in the history of film—George Cukor, William Wyler, Alfred Hitchcock, Orson Welles—meant nothing in the aftermath of the socially volatile sixties. Tony Perkins may have smoked his share of mind-expanding dope, but his career was still a product of the old Hollywood studio system, a regime that had fallen years ago, taking his crown as a major romantic star down with it.

But there was hope. Now that he was marrying the Berenson girl, darling of the fashion world—Diana Vreeland's protégée, who just happened to be both the granddaughter of legendary haute couturiere Elsa Schiaparelli and the "ugly duckling" sister of jet-setting supermodel Marisa Berenson—Perkins was back in the spotlight with a vengeance. He was playing the romantic lead in real life.

According to newspaper and magazine reports, Perkins and Berenson had met completely by chance the previous fall, at a party thrown by actress Ruth Ford for the cast of Tony's latest film, *Play It As It Lays*, based on the novel by Joan Didion. As an infatuated twelve-year-old growing up in European boarding schools, Berry had kept an avid fan's scrapbook of Tony Perkins clippings. But, she told the press, she'd never dreamed that she'd ever actually meet him.

In fact, she had met him before, on the Nevada desert location of *Play It As It Lays*, where she had flown with a friend, deliberately to meet Perkins. Still, it was just after their reintroduction at Ruth Ford's that Berenson asked to interview Perkins for Andy Warhol's *Interview* magazine, where she worked on the covers with her fiancé, artist Richard Bernstein. The assignment ultimately served as the clincher for their relationship. It almost destroyed Bernstein.

Though no one questioned Berry's near-obsessive love for Tony—she had taken him by storm with a flood of tears and good intentions, her modus operandi—there were those who had doubts about Tony's feelings for her. "What we have today is as good as a marriage," Berry had told *Women's Wear Daily* in May. "We're in love, and that's something I wouldn't lie about." By August the bride-to-be was already three months pregnant.

That in itself had been a surprise. "I was using a coil," she claimed. "The baby was a mistake." To prevent her lover from feeling cornered she'd offered to have an abortion, but, she said, "He was thrilled." So were her glamorous sister and her illustrious grandmother (who had always favored Berry). But her mother, Gogo Berenson di Cacciapuoti, had been horrified, urging her "degenerate" daughter to get married fast.

"We had very distinctly planned *not* to be married and *not* to have a baby," Tony told reporters.

"Of course," Berry admitted years after the fact, "there was no way we were not going to have that child."

On Thursday morning, August 9, 1973, the couple, accompanied by their friend photographer Stephen Paley, paid an unnoticed visit to the justice of the peace in Tony's beloved summer town of Wellfleet, Massachusetts, to acquire a license. Strangely enough, after years of flashbulb-lit publicity dates with studio starlets, all of which had been contrived to make Tony appear the ladies' man he most definitely was not, no reporters were present for this watershed in his real life.

At high noon, a small service was held in the misty seaside garden of playwright Michaela O'Harra, the longtime female companion of Tony's mother, Janet Perkins, who was also there to act as a witness. Michaela and Jane, as Janet was called, were a well-known, if unlikely, couple in Wellfleet: Michaela with her no-nonsense, almost glumly masculine manner; Jane with her fashionable suits and incessant, chattering charm. Jane had never remarried after Tony's father, legendary stage actor Osgood Perkins, had passed away suddenly thirty-six years before, leaving her with nothing but a child to raise. Fortunately, she had always been a self-sufficient woman. Tony referred to her wryly as "the Mysterious Lady."

Berry's friend actress Lucy Saroyan, daughter of author William Saroyan, had taken time out from her run in the stock production of Neil Simon's *The Gingerbread Lady,* which Tony was directing, to serve as the other witness. Paley and his camera were also there, as were Mr. and Mrs. Joseph Schoonejongen, a local couple whom Tony had helped out financially over the years.

None of Berry's family were present.

At Michaela's behest, the Reverend Ernest Davis Vanderburgh, a local Episcopal clergyman and social worker, presided. "My God, what if he sees that I'm pregnant?" Berry asked Jane before the ceremony.

"What if he does?" Mrs. Perkins staunchly reassured her. "It's none of his business." Jane was more attentive to needy Berry than she had ever been to Tony. After the abrupt wedding announcement, which her son had expected would fill her at long last with maternal pride, Jane had instead cut him down with the retort of a lifetime: "I only hope you're good enough for her."

Tony and Berry walked up the driveway to the garden, where they exchanged traditional vows to the strains of Ennio Morricone's lush score from the Arctic adventure film *The Red Tent* (one of Tony's favorites, played on a portable cassette deck); it was appropriate accompaniment for a couple embarking on their own expedition into equally uncharted territory. He was dressed with virginal simplicity in white shirt and slacks, with fifteen-year-old white bucks on his feet; she was barefoot, wearing layers of pastel pink, blue, and green to hide their future son. She giggled tearfully, nervously—almost hysterically—through the entire procedure.

"All the time I wanted to kill myself," Tony later said of that day. "My life had come to a stop. . . . I wanted to walk into the ocean and dive to the bottom."

Conspicuously absent were several key people in Tony's life.

Choreographer Grover Dale, the man with whom he had shared his home for six years prior to Berry, was off building a new identity for himself as the husband of redheaded actress Anita Morris, whom he'd married just ten days before—a coincidence that raised eyebrows all over Manhattan. Long known around town as a couple, Perkins and Dale, it seemed to friends, had made a pact to "straighten" themselves out. Both had been seeing the same analyst, Mildred Newman, for years; Dale had even bought a country home near hers. Perhaps for both men this new sexual twist in their lives was a last grasp at some much needed professional respectability. Whatever the case, Grover and his new wife were now living on a mattress in the basement of Tony's town house.

Even more noticeable was the absence of Helen Merrill, Tony's longtime protector, known variously, and not always affectionately, as the Witch of Belsen, the Watchdog, or the Dragon Lady. An older German immigrant with whom he had shared a home for more than a decade as a rising young star, Merrill had forfeited her own career and identity as a photographer to support and maintain his.

Palpably present, in spirit if not flesh, was Mildred Newman—now Berry's analyst too, as well as many of their friends'—who had, with her husband, Bernard Berkowitz, coauthored the slight but massively best-selling *How to Be Your Own Best Friend*, the original "me-generation" bible that precipitated an avalanche of self-help imitations. There was no doubt that the Jewish, earth-motherly, self-promoting Newman had been instrumental in altering Tony and Grover's life together. Her maxim for clients was prosperity, to get the most success out of life, and obviously that meant playing by society's rules. For Newman, who was widely considered the Dolly Levi of the psychoanalytic community, mainstream meant marriage. Perkins would later admit that they'd had many a knock-down-drag-out argument during their sessions over his feelings (or lack thereof) toward the opposite sex. Newman had called him "repressed." And she was relentless. The matrimony-minded shrink had lots of gay clients—including writers Larry Kramer and James Kirkwood, to whom she also "proselytized" the virtues of conventional marriage—but none as malleable as the otherwise sharp-witted *Psycho* star. As he had always done, Tony relinquished control of his life, perhaps gratefully, to someone with whom he was emotionally entangled, offering himself up in full submission.

"I'd never really had girlfriends before," he'd confessed just three months before the wedding. "I knew a lot of girls, but I had a sort of suspiciousness about them. I must admit I was unfair toward them. But for years now, I've been working through analysis to raise my unconscious and make it conscious. . . . Sometimes, unconsciously, you don't think you deserve something, so you make a deal where you settle for much less. Or you settle for something else."

"It was total disaster," said Berry. "There I was, pregnant and about to be married. My friends had mixed reactions about the baby, but they all did cartwheels when they heard Tony and I were married. I guess it is what everybody wants."

For "Lonely Tony Perkins," as he had always been touted in the fan magazines, things were going to be very different.

Norman Bates was about to become a family man.

Immediately after the wedding, he asked Stephen Paley to call Sue Mengers, his agent, and get her advice on how to best publicize his impromptu fairy-tale wedding. Mengers was not forthcoming. If Tony Perkins could have seen into the future, perhaps he would have realized how little it would matter. He would soon be a father, with a devoted wife who would sublimate much of herself to help him build the kind of home they had both been denied as children, a home he could always return to no matter how many times he strayed.

But there would be a price to pay for "normalcy." Soon, the actor best remembered as a raving homicidal transvestite would become an offscreen self-parody, wielding New Age slogans and "family values" instead of a butcher knife to keep his past at bay. Burned too many times, for too long, by the puritanical expectations of the American public and the demands of his Hollywood career, now Tony Perkins was searching for answers, alternatives, a way out, where he had never dared look before.

But reinvention, or denial, would be harder than he naively hoped; old lusts and dreams don't die so easily. Without the camouflage of greasepaint or youth, the middle-aged actor would soon find the image of his own ravaged face a painful reminder of the promising, untouchable young man he'd once been. The troubled teenager he had poignantly embodied for the cameras years ago—so exalted and yet so threatening to the skin-deep values of 1950s America—had grown into a grotesque adult.

"Face it, gang," he would tell his friends, "I *am* Norman Bates."

For Tony Perkins, who had lived his life trying to please a fickle and uncomprehending public, there had never been any other choice.

1

ABSENT FATHER

I AM AN EXHIBITIONIST," Osgood Perkins declared in early 1937. "All actors are exhibitionists. And like most actors, I'm a bit mad."

On September 20, as the curtain in Washington's National Theatre fell on the first pre-Broadway performance of *Susan and God*, the new comedy-drama by Rachel Crothers about a socialite who misguidedly tries to reform her alcoholic husband with religion, Perkins (as the husband) basked as usual in deafening applause. Despite the odd lethargy he'd been feeling all week, the tall, dark, spindly actor, who was as famous for his whip-quick line delivery as he was for his cartoonishly villainous looks, had no idea this would be his last moment of glory.

"Thank God we'll never have to go through that again," he commented to his flamboyant British costar, Gertrude Lawrence, as they walked off the stage. It had been an especially strenuous night for Perkins, who had missed rehearsals the week before, including the final run-through, due to a persistant ache he'd dismissed as grippe. Luckily, no one in the audience had detected any strain onstage; the reception was indeed thunderous, for both of them. After thirteen years of astoundingly steady work on Broadway, crowned by his portayal of ruthless newspaper editor Walter Burns in the 1928 hit *The Front Page*, and appearances in several films, most notably Howard Hawks's *Scarface*,

Osgood Perkins could do no wrong. The public and the critics loved him equally.

But tonight there would be no celebration. Fatigue and a little heartburn still lingered; Osgood wanted to rest. Janet, his wife of fifteen years, met him backstage, and together they walked to the Willard Hotel, stopping once at a drugstore for something to ease the pain in his chest. "I like that role," he told her. "I hope the play never closes."

Later in bed, he couldn't sleep; the pain kept him awake. At approximately 2 A.M. he rose and went into the bathroom for some more medicine. Jane immediately heard a thud, and rushed in to find her husband lying unconscious on the floor. The house physician, Dr. Ernest Mitchell, was summoned, but it was too late. Osgood Perkins, star of stage, screen, and radio, had died of heart failure at age forty-five. (His older brother, G. Gerritt B. Perkins, vice president of the Perkins Glue Company in Philadelphia, had died of the same, at the same age, five years before.)

"I was born with a terrific theater sense," Osgood had proclaimed just a few months earlier. "I am convinced that timing can't be taught." Later that morning, the reviews for *Susan and God* came in, glowing. Osgood had been a smash.

Gertrude Lawrence, suffering from a combination of exhaustion and remorse, didn't want the show to go on without him. But of course it had to; Perkins's understudy, Paul McGrath, who had read his lines while he was out sick, replaced him for New York.

"Oggie had every actor's dream of his own death," says actress Rose Hobart, a close friend of the Perkinses who later played a supporting role in the film version of *Susan and God*. "Opening in a play, getting the best notices of his life, and then his obituary, side by side in the papers. They were side by side. It was such a shock to everybody."

The theater world was indeed stunned, and a tremendous outpouring of love and remembrance filled the columns in the following weeks. "It is safe to say that no one who ever saw him on a stage will ever forget him," proclaimed one critic. "His loss is nothing less than a great disaster to the American theater." The *New York Times* wrote: "Wiry, nervous, unerring in the accuracy of his attack, he could energize a play enormously by the mental and physical vitality of his playing." Critic and columnist John Mason Brown observed, "There was also a sense of sadness about him. It was a cosmic melancholy; a disillusionment born of a search for something he could not seem to find but which pity and compassion had sent him questing for."

"[The] deepest sorrow in Perkins' life," contended the *New York World Telegram,* "was that he had not been asked to portray the managing editor in the film version [of *The Front Page*]. Hollywood entrusted that part to Adolphe Menjou." Osgood's wife and son probably would have agreed.

Five-year-old Anthony Perkins was asleep at home in New York when his father collapsed on that bathroom floor, without the consolation of having seen the show that came before the final curtain. "He became a mythic being to me," the adult Anthony would say, "to be dreaded and appeased."

James Ripley Osgood Perkins entered the very ordinary world of West Newton, Massachusetts, on May 16, 1892. There were no other actors in his Episcopalian family. His father, Henry Phelps Perkins, was a physician. His mother, Helen Virginia Anthony Perkins, originally of New York, was a housewife with a passion for the theater. His older brother grew up to run a glue factory.

No doubt at Helen's urging, young Osgood was given violin lessons and enrolled in the class of a local vocal coach, in whose annual recital he made his debut as a boy soprano (Anthony would later have a surrogate "Helen" to guide him as well). Mother-son theatrical outings further encouraged the boy, the first occurring when he was eight: a Saturday matinee performance of William Young's circuslike *Ben-Hur,* based on the Lew Wallace novel, at Boston's Colonial Theater. The most lavish of several popular religious dramas at the time, it featured 120,000 square feet of scenery and a vivid chariot race created via an ingenious combination of treadmills, horses, chariots, a fan to blow wind in the drivers' faces, and a speeding backdrop. "[She] had thought it would be a great treat for me," Osgood later recalled. "It was not. It was the beginning of a new life for me; the beginning of an entirely new me. From that moment on I was an actor. Nothing was real. If I labored hard at mowing the lawn, I was a galley slave, chained to the oar. If I rode my bicycle swiftly down a country lane . . . I was a conquering hero, driving a chariot drawn by white horses."

Sarah Bernhardt's internationally acclaimed vehicle, *Camille,* which was packing them in at the Boston Theater shortly thereafter, further captivated the boy. Tickets cost his mother ten dollars each, but such was her determination, and the drawing power of Bernhardt's name, that she couldn't resist. The performance was given entirely in French, which, while incomprehensible to little Oggie, left an indelible impression on him. He loved the sound of the language, became almost obsessed with it, and vowed one day to make it his own. (Decades later, Anthony Perkins would be a bigger star in France than his father had ever been.) Osgood's own theatrical training began in his family's Episcopalian church, where he produced, directed, and sometimes accompanied amateur plays on his violin.

In 1910, after completing his curriculum at Newton High School, he was accepted into Harvard. Despite the fact that he was by then entertaining the idea of a career in medicine, he took part in the university's Hasty Pudding Club and Pi Eta productions. In an original Brahmin musical comedy, *The Legend of Loravia*, the real world first noticed him. As the juvenile lead, an impudent young American in Europe for the first time, Osgood stole the show. "With the possible exception of [Robert] Benchley, J. R. O. Perkins is the best comic actor Harvard has had for years," said the *Harvard Crimson*. From March 29 through April 24, the show toured Cambridge, Boston, New York, Philadelphia, and Baltimore. Osgood's comic songs were singled out by the *New York Times*. It was 1914, his senior year.

"At Harvard," Osgood later told the *New York American*, "they were most indifferent about preparing young men to make a living." The theater was simply not a proper profession for an upstanding young Bostonian. With his A.B. degree (in French) firmly in hand, he went to New York to look for work, where, after several misfired attempts (tutoring, copywriting), he was struck with the inspiration to enlist in the army. He landed in his beloved France in 1915 as an ambulance driver for the American unit of the Lafayette Escadrille. Like many young men, Osgood considered travel the key to self-discovery. Returning to the States in 1916, he did training as a shoe salesman for a firm that intended to do business in Russia. But when America entered the war, Osgood reenlisted and went back to France the following year, this time as a second lieutenant of artillery with the Twenty-sixth and Eighty-ninth Divisions.

At the front north of Toul, an incident occurred that not only put an end to his military career, but proved to have a lasting effect on his future life as an actor. Dan Bartlett, who served in the same regiment, later recounted: "[Osgood] had a tough time. . . . He was thin faced, sharp nosed, tight lipped, with a thin black mustache, heavy black Mephistophelian eyebrows, sleek black hair parted in the middle, spoke with a Bostonese accent, and carried a violin." The musical lieutenant got caught in some artillery fire and, after some digging, was quickly found buried under a pile of rubble. "He had what was called a case of shell shock. He couldn't control his hands; his eyebrows, eyelids, lips, and the other muscles of his face were in a constant twitch. . . . Whether it was for shock or flu, I don't know; but we finally shipped him to a hospital." Osgood would eventually incorporate these stress symptoms into a personal and unique acting style; the eloquent way he used his hands and his nervous, expressive facial twitch would, in fact, become his theatrical trademarks. (A traumatic run-in with the military years later during the Korean War would also augment the performance style of his son.) On the day of the armistice, he was still infirmed in Vichy, France.

After the war, Osgood was running out of options. Rapidly approaching age thirty, he had nothing to lose by giving acting a try, so he started making the rounds of New York's cruel casting offices. With beginner's luck, he ran into Frank Tuttle, an aspiring director and Yale grad, who was starting up a film production company with several other Ivy League spawn; Tuttle needed someone who could look villainous, and the prematurely craggy-faced shell shock victim more than fit the bill.

In 1922, the Film Guild, as Tuttle's company was soon known, began shooting a string of low-budget melodramas at the old Pyramid Studios in Astoria, Queens. It was there that Perkins, dressed as Pierrot, took his professional bow before the camera as a deranged circus clown who almost kills his tightrope-walking lady love—a part not hard to imagine his post-*Psycho* son playing. Written and directed by Tuttle, *The Cradle Buster* was not an auspicious debut for anyone involved (though Tuttle would eventually go on to direct *This Gun for Hire*, the first film noir to pair Alan Ladd and Veronica Lake).

That same year, Osgood married Janet Esselstyn Rane, two years his junior, whom he had met while sharing a small apartment with struggling writer Torrey Ford. Originally from Morgantown, West Virginia, Jane, as she preferred to be called, was a graduate with top honors from Wellesley College, where her own academic interest in the theater had led her to participate in the Shakespeare Club. A staunchly independent young woman of the liberated twenties, she was working as a private secretary when she met her husband-to-be. The two were wed in New York's ornate but quaint Little Church Around the Corner, off Fifth Avenue on East Twenty-ninth Street.

"Osgood Perkins . . . steals the picture from Glenn Hunter and pretty Mary Astor," *Film Daily* proclaimed of the Guild's *Puritan Passions*, based on *The Scarecrow*, a little-known play by Percy MacKaye about the complications that ensue when black magic turns a sack of hay into a desirable young man. Even so, when the Guild lost handsome Hunter to Paramount, it also lost its distributor, the W. W. Hodkinson Releasing Company. Artistic merits aside, Osgood's forgotten early film work would ultimately put him in professional contact with the likes of Clara Bow, Rod LaRocque, Louise Brooks, Morton Downey, and even Tallulah Bankhead (in George Cukor's *Tarnished Lady*, her 1931 film debut; Anthony Perkins would later make his screen debut under Cukor).

As the theater recoiled under the weight of the new visual technology, a purer, indigenous American voice began to emerge on Broadway. Eagle-eyed playwrights and directors like George S. Kaufman, George Kelly, and Philip Barry wrote incisive, often wisecracking, satires of American life and its values, replacing the sentimental fluff that had previously been popular. In one such play, *Beggar on Horseback*, Kaufman and Marc Connelly's expressionistic comedy about the uneasy relationship between commerce and art, Osgood got his first big break: the minor but hilarious role of Homer Cady, a wealthy, art-hating hypochondriac. *Beggar* opened at the Broadhurst Theater on February 12, 1924, and was a hit, winning Perkins several laudatory mentions in the press for his small but flashy performance.

More important, producer Jed Harris, then a press agent, noticed him. "It was a grand show, with lots of good actors," Harris later wrote, "but for me the best thing in it was the moment when . . . Osgood Perkins pointed his finger at another character in the play. I have never forgotten that gesture. It was malign, sardonic, contemptuous, weird and altogether funny. His forefinger seemed at least a foot long and I had the uncomfortable feeling that it was being poked into me. . . . I left the theatre with vague designs on this Mr. Perkins."

The following year, Harris indeed cast Perkins as a hypocritical preacher in his debut production, *Weak Sisters*. The play was a flop, but Osgood's performance was vivid enough that, much to his dismay, he found himself typecast as a cleric in two subsequent plays. He broke that mold as a gigolo in Brock Pemberton's 1926 comedy, *Loose Ankles*—only to find himself typecast again, this time as a heavy. *Love 'Em and Leave 'Em*, a film with Louise Brooks, and the legendary play *The Front Page* (produced by Jed Harris and directed by George S. Kaufman) both served to solidify the new image. "After *The Front Page* closed [276 performances later]," Harris wrote, "Osgood was being offered all the most maniacal parts on Broadway—'screwey guys,' eccentrics, lunatics that wanted that 'Perkins touch.' He was getting pretty sick of those, too." Years later, young Tony Perkins would find himself in the exact same actor's trap, but in Hollywood, where artistic latitude was not an option.

Osgood dealt with the theater's nearsightedness by fighting back. To undermine the one-note casting mentality of Broadway, he didn't work onstage for a year, refusing all the "toughies" that were offered him in spite of the catastrophic stock market crash that had already devastated so much of the country and drastically cut the number of plays produced. "That's when I learned to wash dishes," he said. "My wife and I did all our own housework!" Finally, at Osgood's suggestion, Harris brought an old-fashioned revival of Chekhov's *Uncle Vanya* to the Cort Theatre in April of 1930, giving the actor the chance to play more introspective comedy opposite movie great Lillian Gish.

Queer People, a film project for Howard Hughes based on a comic novel by Carroll and Garrett Graham, brought Osgood and Jane to Hollywood for the first time in 1931. Because of casting problems, the production never got under way, but Osgood landed another job, as a gangster in Hughes's production of *Scarface* starring Paul Muni. It is still Osgood's portrayal of spineless mobster Johnny Lovo for which he is best remembered today. "I always had the theory that heavies had beady eyes," said the director, Howard Hawks, "and Osgood certainly had them." As shockingly violent for its day as *Psycho* would be three decades later, the film so glamorized the world of organized crime that the Hays Production Code stiffened its rules, demanding several recuts before it could be released. As for the Perkinses, they made the rounds of Hollywood parties. According to one relative, Osgood, who had been around sexually liberated theater folk for a decade now, delighted in teasing his wife with rumors of which actresses were lesbians. He may have sensed something restless—unfulfilled—about his own wife.

Back in New York, Janet Perkins no longer needed to work. She handled Osgood's money (as she would later handle Tony's) and accompanied him on business, but after nearly ten years of dedication to his career, she wanted a career of her own, this time as a mother. The prospect of a child did not excite Osgood, who feared that the responsibility might distract him just when business was finally going his way.

"He was basically an actor, his whole life was centered in acting, even though he started it very late in life," recalls Rose Hobart, who'd also been whisked off to Hollywood in 1930 to star in a film version of *Liliom*, re-creating the stage role made famous by the notorious Eva LaGallienne. "He and Jane were totally different types of people. She was warm and outgoing and modern as hell—I mean, anything that she wanted to try, she tried—whereas Osgood was sterner. He was like his face, actually, which was kind of sharp. But as far as anybody knew, they were fine together as a couple. Except after Tony was born.

"As a matter of fact, Osgood accused me of being the reason he and Janie had Tony. I'd seen quite a lot of Janie when they were out on the coast, and I think he thought I talked her into it. He always said to me, 'You started this.' Because they were both getting on in age, and in that era you didn't suddenly have children in your thirties or forties."

Osgood was in the midst of rehearsals for a play called *Foreign Affairs* with Jean Arthur, Henry Hull, and Dorothy Gish, when Jane gave birth to a son on April 4, 1932. He was named Anthony, most likely after Osgood's mother, Helen Anthony Perkins, rather than actress-director Antoinette Perry, as is popularly believed. Jane was then thirty-eight years old.

"I had a woman obstetrician who believed that a woman shouldn't have any unpleasant recollections of childbirth," she told *Good Housekeeping* in 1959. "She gave a combination of drugs which meant, as a result, that I had absolutely no recollection whatsoever of the birth. . . . From the start, I had a detached feeling about Tony."

The ever present Hobart describes mother Jane as "the attentive type, without being soppy about it."

Life for the matriarch of the unorthodox little Perkins family (which would become even less conventional after the untimely death of her husband) consisted of strolling Tony through Gramercy Park ("Practically the ghetto in New York at that time," according to Hobart), taking occasional exercise classes with a lady friend, then putting Tony to bed at night so Osgood could entertain the bawdy, sophisticated crowd he enjoyed reigning over. Hobart, Antoinette Perry, Jed Harris, Brock Pemberton, actress June Walker, Franchot Tone, Kenneth MacKenna, and his wife, Mary Phillips, were regulars at the Perkinses' two-bedroom penthouse, which was brimming with books and music and culture, and decorated in an elegant bohemian style thanks to Osgood's famous hand-painted murals (Jane and Osgood's ornate marriage bed, for instance, was a fake—a mere box spring gaily surrounded by an original faux headboard applied directly to the wall behind).

At these gatherings, after a few drinks, Osgood would succumb to what friends affectionately referred to as "mantel disease," his penchant for leaning on the fireplace and launching into a sardonic tirade on any topic—the state of theater, art, philosophy, politics (Osgood himself, it should be noted, always voted a very *un*bohemian straight Republican ticket). He was constantly performing, addicted to the release of adrenaline that the spotlight—anywhere, anytime—provided.

"Osgood resented Tony because he took up more of Janie's attention that he was used to getting," Hobart remembers clearly more than fifty years later. "He was very unfatherly. He really wasn't around much. Oggie was a very private person you never had a feeling you really knew. But he was a great storyteller, and was fun to be with." As for Jane, "she never talked *about* Tony or Osgood; she just *was* so good with them that you knew everything was fine. Or at least you assumed. She was a very self-possessed woman."

There were occasional getaways to France for Osgood and Jane—success in the States had not abated his Franco fever—and on one of their trips they even brought back a French housekeeper, Jeanne, to watch after Tony (who consequently learned French almost as well as he did English). But Osgood's career continued to become more and more demanding. *Foreign Affairs* closed before the end of April, and by the end of May, he was already back onstage at the Selwyn Theatre in *A Thousand Summers* with Franchot Tone and Josephine Hull. Even the summer was spent thesping in a breakneck series of plays at Connecticut's Westport Country Playhouse, under the direction of the Theatre Guild's Theresa Helburn, with an ensemble cast that included June Walker, Jane Wyatt, Elisha Cook, Jr., and the young Elia Kazan (also the assistant stage manager), who would later be instrumental in the advancement of Tony's career.

"[Osgood] was the definition of the word 'professional,'" Kazan proclaimed in his 1988 memoir, *A Life*. "There was no 'take a minute' technique with him; in fact, there was no emotion. Only skill. In every aspect of technical facility, he was peerless. . . . He stood for a whole other side of theatre art than the one I'd learned from [Lee Strasberg and Harold Clurman]." The inner acting technique advocated by Strasberg and Clurman's Group Theatre, which they'd founded in 1931 with Cheryl Crawford in the hope of establishing a native ensemble company that would present new, socially significant American plays, was not part of Osgood's artistic vocabulary. He came from the old, broad school that built character from the outside in, relying on costumes and mannerisms to find motivation and emotion. Anthony, whose career would soar at the peak of the Method's popularity and influence in the 1950s, would always cherish his father's brand of physical preparation, while uncovering his own, very personal (if erratic) approach to finding a character.

One of the Westport plays, Rose Albert Porter's *Chrysalis*, opened on Broadway in mid-November with Osgood, Margaret Sullavan, and Humphrey Bogart. It closed December 3. But before the year was out, Osgood managed to score one of his biggest successes in the Allan Scott–George Haight comedy *Goodbye Again*, which featured the young James Stewart in a small role. Hollywood, too, was calling more often. In 1934 alone, Perkins would appear in William Dieterle's frothy *Madame Du Barry* with Dolores Del Rio and Anita Louise, *Kansas City Princess* with Joan Blondell and Glenda Farrell, and William Wellman's *The President Vanishes* with Rosalind Russell and Jason Robards (Sr.).

By today's standards of sex appeal, it's hard to imagine the bony, severe-looking Osgood, with his long, delicately gangling arms (which his son inherited), as anything more than a character actor. But in the 1920s and 1930s, the simple fact of his dark, lean appearance and machine-gun line delivery was enough to make female theatergoers swoon, as they had occasionally done during the run of *Loose Ankles*, his first incarnation as a gigolo. Of course, Osgood was famous and glamorous, and that in itself was appealing to women. He was not immune to temptation.

"Jane and Osgood, in their heyday, were great freethinkers," one relative says. "Jane used to laugh about all the ingenues that would fall in love with Osgood and just drive him crazy. When they'd start clinging, he would bring them home to her and say, 'Jane, get her loose from me!' "

Rose Hobart remembers one potentially damaging liaison in particular. "There was a time when Osgood was seeing an awful lot of a gal who took him over, was going to do things for him. She was a publicity woman. Everybody began thinking that Janie should do something to stop her from monopolizing Osgood, but Jane paid no attention. 'Oh, come on,' she'd say, 'I can handle bits like that.' She allowed Oggie to be who he was without ever trying to change him. Maybe it was because she was not that interested in him physically anymore. When he went around with that girl, she let it go. Then he came back, and everything was fine again." The arrangement of their lives fell back into place.

In 1936, the Perkinses enrolled their four-year-old son in Miss Carden's School, a liberal-minded kindergarten located in a brownstone on East Sixty-seventh Street, "a progressive place for unmanageable kids like me," as Tony would later describe it. Mae Carden, the founder, had caused some controversy in the academic world for her phonetic approach to reading, but the school was nevertheless popular among show people who had offspring, legitimate or otherwise, and convenient for the Perkinses, who were now living fashionably uptown at 21 East Sixty-sixth Street. Tony's classmates included Nora Johnson, the daughter of writer Nunnally Johnson, and June Walker's son, John Kerr.

"Tony was a strikingly good-looking little boy," remembers Kerr, whose acting career would later run neck and neck with Tony's, "but he was shy." While attending the Carden school, Tony began to stutter badly, but was "cured" when Jane and his teacher stopped forcing him to use his right hand. Left-handedness was still considered an abnormality, a portent of freakishness, even perversity, and Jane wanted Tony to change—an oddly conservative desire given Jane's liberal nature.

"I'd probably have wound up in reform school," Tony told *Modern Screen* with tongue in cheek in 1957, "if it hadn't been for French." Of course, he was already fluent in the language, but the lessons served to animate his dormant theatrical genes. "I used to play dumb in that class, pretending to learn. Then at the end I'd cut loose and finish in a blaze of glory." Hating to be read to by Miss Carden, he learned to read at home so that he could do it independently. To further distinguish himself, skinny Tony could, and would, run more swiftly than any of the other kids during recreational outings. "He usually won races when we went to Central Park," Kerr recalls. "He was very fast." He had to be; he already had a lot to run away from. Life as a star's son wasn't easy. The star was never around.

In a watershed interview for *People* magazine that scandalized his family and friends nearly fifty years later, Tony Perkins painted an unsparingly bleak picture of his ostensibly illustrious childhood. "I became abnormally close to my mother," he confessed, "and whenever my father came home I was jealous. It was the Oedipal thing in a pronounced form. I loved him but I also wanted him to be dead so I could have her all to myself." An uncannily similar sentiment is echoed in the scripted emotions of Norman Bates ("a boy's best friend is his mother"), the poignantly disturbed killer in Alfred Hitchcock's *Psycho*, the role that would eventually make Tony Perkins a legend.

When the boy turned five in April of 1937, Osgood, typically, was off in California headlining a road tour of Robert E. Sherwood's *Tovarich* with Bela Lugosi. That summer, however, most likely at Jane's insistence, Osgood took an uncharacteristic hiatus and rented a cottage for his family on the glorified sandbar known as Fire Island, then an almost deserted getaway for New York's bohemian crowd. (By the time Tony would be old enough to enjoy it on his own, it would be a resort of a very different kind.) It was there that Osgood made his first, and last, effort to get to know his son. After years of almost nightly curtains to meet, days and weeks of rehearsals and matinees, and endless trains to catch, Osgood took time out to deal with his slim, watchful little boy. Together, they walked the sandy shores, fished, boated, and swam. Jane was pleased when her workaholic husband expressed satisfaction with the way his son had actually turned out.

There were few serious distractions that summer. As a concession to his career, Osgood did four radio programs back in town, three of them with the brilliant comic actress Ina Claire, and he and Jane took occasional theatrical excursions to enjoy the summer-stock productions of other people for a change. One of the last plays they saw together was *Honor Bright*, starring Rose Hobart, which they attended in early September at Matunuck, Rhode Island. A promising *Children's Hourish* melodrama about the perilously passionate friendship that develops between a schoolteacher and her young female pupil, it marked the theatrical (and semiautobiographical) debut of an aspiring twenty-four-year-old playwright from northern California (who also claimed to be a distant relative of outlaw Jesse James), Miss Michaela O'Harra. She and Jane and Osgood were introduced backstage.

"Osgood was very impressed with [the play]," O'Harra claims, "and asked me to write one for him, which I was doing when he died." The backstage meeting would ultimately prove most fruitful for the two women, who ten years later began a deep partnership, living together almost until Jane's death in 1979. Meanwhile, before the month was out, *Honor Bright* was hailed by *Variety* as the Shubert brothers' "first flop" of the season. It did not proceed to Broadway, and O'Harra never finished the play she had started for Osgood.

As for Tony, he read and daydreamed away the last days of summer. His father had to get back to the city to start rehearsals for *Susan and God*, and with the end of summer in sight, Tony did something that perhaps hints at how much those rare days together as a family had really meant to him. He buried his favorite marbles in some small boxes underneath the Fire Island boardwalk, vowing to himself that he would return as a man of thirty and exhume them.

When the widow Perkins returned home from Washington, she was faced with the task of explaining the meaning of death to her five-year-old boy. Against the advice of theatrical friends, who recommended that she simply tell Tony his father was away on a permanent tour, she took her son into the privacy of her bedroom and told him the truth, while the ever present Rose Hobart waited in the outside room.

"[It] must have been the greatest shock he'd ever experienced," Mrs. Perkins told *Photoplay* in 1958, "but there were no tears." Much to her frustration, the boy merely nodded and said nothing.

"I was horrified," Tony revealed only in 1983, after more than a decade of psychoanalysis. "I assumed that my wanting him to be dead actually killed him. I prayed and prayed for my father to come back. I remember long nights of crying in bed. For years I nursed the hope that he wasn't really dead."

As a young man, Tony would tell friends how Jane had taken him out on a small boat and, to his complete surprise, casually dumped Osgood's ashes into the water with no warning or ceremony at all. It seemed to the boy that she might as well have flushed his father down the toilet.

On Friday, October 15, at four o'clock in the afternoon, a memorial service was held at the Little Church Around the Corner, where Osgood and Jane had been married fifteen years before. Jane was ill and could not attend, but Tony had insisted on going. He was accompanied by his aunt, Osgood's sister, Leslie Perkins. Jane's mother, Elizabeth Bailey Rane of Boston, known as "Mimi" to her family, was also there, along with three hundred of Osgood's friends and associates, including Brock Pemberton, Worthington Miner, Sidney Phillips, and Jo Mielziner. The Reverend Randolph Ray, rector of the church and first vice president of the Episcopal Actors Guild (of which Osgood had been elected a vice president in 1936), presided.

Actor Kenneth MacKenna spoke on behalf of the Actors' Equity Association (hyperactive Osgood had been a first vice president there since 1934). If Tony had come hoping to find some of the summertime love his father had shown him just two months before, MacKenna's speech must surely have disappointed and enraged the boy, who sat counting and recounting the change in Mimi's purse as he listened.

Outwardly directed at Tony as a "way to find an expression for us all," MacKenna's well-intentioned but insensitive monologue read like a litany of Osgood's spread-thin intentions and attentions: Not only was Osgood a father to Tony but he was also a father to "all the young actors" he knew; not only had he taught his son precious things (Tony would later say that all Osgood ever showed him was how to tie his shoelaces), but he had taught his fellow players so much via his "unselfish devotion" and his "high professional ethics and high artistic standards"; a pillar of "strength and wisdom" to all his colleagues, Osgood was loved by Tony, naturally, but "we also shared in that."

Osgood Perkins had never really belonged to Anthony Perkins at all.

MacKenna wrapped up with a pretentious promise to fan the flame of Osgood's memory, "as a symbol of all the beautiful things [he] stood for both as a man and as an artist."

"When my father died," Tony told *Photoplay* years later, "dozens of people kept hugging me and picking me up and clucking at me. I wanted to run away and I couldn't. I don't know whether I really pushed them away or not, but I wanted to."

After the ceremony, walking down the aisle, Leslie Perkins offered her nephew a consoling hand to hold, but her gentle grasp was abruptly shaken away. Her young charge, his head held defiantly high, walked out of the church on his own. Words like "artistic standards" and "professional ethics" usually mean little to the adults who speak them; they mean nothing to a hurt little boy.

MOTHER'S LOVE

NSURANCE WAS NOT THE NATIONAL PASTIME that it is now," Tony later said of Osgood's monetary legacy. Despite the fact that at the time of his demise Perkins *père* had an income of about $40,000 a year, a hefty sum in 1937, he had been a flagrant spendthrift when it came to his theatrical cronies. He had obviously not been intending to leave the stage so soon. His estate was valued at $10,000, and there was $55,000 in insurance. "I have made no provision for such of my needy friends and relatives as I have helped financially from time to time," Osgood's will read, "as I feel confident that my wife . . . will, of her own accord, continue to extend such assistance to them as may be warranted by the size of my estate. This is merely an expression of hope on my part and shall not be construed as imposing any obligation on my wife, Janet." Jane never shared her husband's openhandedness when it came to cash, and if she had ever pretended to, all that was about to change.

Five-year-old Anthony remained passive, numb in the wake of his father's death. He may have been surrounded by gabbing theatrical types, but at home the Perkinses were still WASPs. So inexpressive was Tony that Jane began to worry her son was headed for a nervous breakdown. Her instinct proved right when, three months later, he collapsed, physically exhausted. He would not eat, he was losing

weight, and his breathing was labored. But it wasn't grief; it was tuberculosis, from which he did recover, only to be stricken with an even
worse case of scarlet fever. That winter, out of necessity more than
anything else, Jane took him to Florida to recuperate, and to plan their
uncertain future.

Down south, the boy became fascinated by astronomy, enthralled
by the twinkling array of real stars that were never visible on murky
New York nights. Perhaps he thought his famous father was up there
among them. (As a budding young actor in New York, Tony would
continue to sleep with painted stars on the ceiling and his name in
Christmas lights just above his head.) In any case, his infatuation with
the heavens was just one in a long list of dreamy, introspective hobbies,
topped by reading, that were the escape of a sickly, left-handed boy—a
boy whose solitary nature concerned his already overburdened mother.

Like most single mothers, Jane worried about the lack of a masculine influence on her son's dawning identity, and urged Tony to take
up an outdoor sport. She pushed baseball, of which Osgood had been
a fan. Tony hated it; he was scared of the ball. Aside from that, the act
of tossing a leather object back and forth held little intellectual stimu-
lation for the boy's critical eye. But Jane persisted. As trivial as it may
seem, this very predicament, the tyranny of sports and the pressure to
conform in the lives of American men, would play a huge part in
young Tony's future career, first on Broadway in *Tea and Sympathy*
and later, with stinging results, in the psychological baseball film, *Fear
Strikes Out.*

But whether Tony played baseball or not, Osgood's memory was
kept alive at home with frequent stories, and visits from old colleagues
like June Walker and her son, John Kerr. "I remember they had a little
dog named Medor, a Boston terrier," Kerr says. "They spoke French to
it, and it responded to commands in French." Perhaps if baseball had
been played in France, Tony would have been more receptive; he remained a withdrawn boy, content to live in a fantasy world, strangely
sheltered given the sophisticated milieu in which he'd been raised.

Though she maintained her ties to the theater, Jane, who described
herself as "the administrative type," got a job with the Women's Civil-
ian Defense Corps. Tony was left largely on his own while his mother
worked. "After the death of my husband," she told *Cue* in 1956, "I was
afraid of overprotecting Tony. So I made sure he'd get away from any

possibility of too much mothering." Though she never spoke directly to her son about finances, Jane's increasingly puritanical attitude toward money was such that Tony felt obliged to hand over any small change that he made (shoveling snow, for example). He would continue the habit well into his prime as a film star.

In 1942, before moving to Boston, where Jane intended to share living expenses with her mother, she and Tony spent the summer in Los Angeles at the home of Kenneth MacKenna, who was now an executive at MGM. There, Tony saw his first movie studio, and also got his first glimpse of his father's real legacy: *Scarface* had been rereleased, and he sat through it several times before curtly pronouncing Osgood "rather shorter than I expected him to be."

"Because loving my mother was connected in my mind with killing my father," a fifty-one-year-old Tony told *People* years later, "it became dangerous to love my mother." It didn't help that Jane was, and would always be, her son's harshest critic.

Back east, Jane and Tony moved into an apartment at 1120 Beacon Street in Brookline, Massachusetts, a posh suburb just outside of Boston. Jane's father, the late Francis Rane, had started the Boston Gardening Company, a farm operation in nearby Waban, which was now run chiefly by his widow, Mimi, and Jane's brother, Ainsworth. The agreement was that Mimi would live part of the year with Jane and Tony, and the other part in Palm Beach, Florida, where the Ranes seemed slowly to be migrating.

More important, Jane's theatrical contacts had garnered her a position with the American Theatre Wing's Boston Stage Door Canteen. For Jane, it was the next best thing to actually being in the military, an active lifestyle that was appealing to many of the largely invisible gay women of the era. Now that men were away in the front lines, women from all over were flocking to the cities to take advantage of wartime opportunities, form new communities, and enjoy the thrill of unexpected autonomy. Suddenly it was acceptable for a woman to be single, to think for herself, and even to wear pants—which the widow Perkins did not, though she did wear a uniform. The war effort allowed women like Jane to camouflage their sexuality behind an easy mask of public service and duty, and it brought them together like no other twentieth-century event until the feminist and lesbian movements of the 1960s and 1970s.

Stage Door Canteens were already booming in New York, Philadelphia, Washington, Cleveland, and San Francisco; in mid-1943 Boston became the sixth American city to open its generous doors to servicemen. Jane was in on the ground floor of planning. Run primarily by local socialites and wealthy wives, the SDC offered free entertainment, tickets to sporting events, ballroom dancing, art classes, and "tea dances" for the war boys. Tony occasionally helped Jane punch tickets at the door. The Boston SDC accommodated approximately 508 visitors a night, with more than 2,300 alternating girls from colleges and private homes acting as junior hostesses—one girl for every three servicemen. However, no liquor was served, the Canteens shut down promptly at midnight, and hostesses were forbidden to leave with any of the patrons.

Jane flourished in this environment, her administrative bent blooming amid the needy chaos of bureaucracy and entertainment. When the Boston building commissioner shut down the SDC at its first location near Copley Square, Jane was made executive director of the new site at 48 Boylston Street. She tore into her duties with missionary zeal, raising funds, organizing benefits (her Fall Fashion Revue of 1944 was a huge success), and bringing in performers like Helen Hayes, Diana Barrymore, radio MC Louise Morgan, and bandleader Guy Lombardo.

Tony, meanwhile, was more than glad to have the attentive Mimi around, with whom he played endless word games like Scrabble and anagrams, pastimes he would love until the day he died. On most weekends, at least when his grandmother was there, Tony's Uncle Ainsworth and Aunt Shirley, a newspaper reporter, and his first cousin, Stephanie, would visit Beacon Street for Sunday dinner. Mimi alone was the drawing card that kept the Waspish Ranes in touch. Otherwise, according to one relative, "we never got together for family reunions or anything of that nature. Jane was more involved with the theater, and her metropolitan type of life."

"We weren't brought up to be close," confirms Stephanie, who was six months Tony's junior. "The only cohesive element was Mimi. We all adored her. Tony and I sort of vied for her favoritism. It was unspoken. But she was very fair-minded. I thought he was so lucky to have Mimi stay with him for long periods of time."

At these small get-togethers, while the grown-ups sat around with their after-dinner drinks, it was up to Tony to entertain his younger cousin. "He just hated it," Stephanie recalls. "I was just a dumb girl and he was, from the time he was born, very precocious and intellectual, and had a hell of a sense of humor, even if it was a little macabre." He was also extremely insecure about being loved, and hence extremely territorial. There was a pond behind the apartment building, and Tony would frighten Stephanie with tales of its engulfing, bottomless depths.

"There was also a beautiful, old caged elevator in their apartment building, similar to the one Olivia de Havilland had in that marvelous movie, *Lady in a Cage*. One time, Tony told me, 'You know, we have a mad janitor down there who has dismembered cats and dogs and God knows what else. You must be careful not to look him in the eye.' We got on the elevator, he punched it to go down, and then he jumped off—and I didn't know how to operate the elevator! He sent me down to the basement by myself, and he just laughed. I was petrified. Finally, he let me back upstairs. Later, when I saw him in *Psycho*, I thought, 'Perfect.' "

More than anything, young Perkins wanted attention. And when he didn't get any in the overcrowded public school where Jane had placed him, he rebelled, as he had even at Miss Carden's, by being lazy. According to his teachers he was a "gifted drifter," who simply did not bother to expend the energy to learn what they wanted him to. "[Tony] sorely lacked discipline and regimentation," admitted Jane. "I felt that he could get it only with an association of men and other boys." The answer? Boarding school.

The Brooks School, located on the unspoiled shores of Lake Cochichewick in North Andover, Massachusetts, forty minutes outside of Boston, was a preparatory boarding school fashioned after the public schools in England; teachers were addressed as "masters" and there was a strict uniform. Founded in 1926 by the Reverend Endicott Peabody, headmaster of the prestigious Groton School, Brooks was named after a onetime bishop of Massachusetts, Phillip Brooks, and maintained a strong affiliation with the Episcopal Church. It boasted a strong athletic agenda, primarily football, and a commitment to the Judeo-Christian ethic. Surely Osgood would have been proud of Jane for choosing such a place to toughen up their passively unruly son.

Tony deeply resented her for sending him away.

The year 1944 would mark a turning point in young Tony's life: the first time he would be singled out for being different—for not being athletic, not a jock or a joiner—and hated for it. It would be his first taste of the fear that can sometimes come simply from being who you are, a fear that would be his longtime companion in the public eye.

In the Brooks School's Old Whitney dormitory Tony lived in a small, single-windowed cubicle with no ceiling and a curtain for a door. To Tony, it was a nightmare. Behind his flimsy portal, he could listen to the shouting and roughhousing of the other boys along the echoing hall and in the common room, and the inevitable approach of boisterously mean-spirited feet. Names were shot through the curtain, accusations, insinuations. Tony was scared, and very much alone. But again, he did not respond; instead his stony coldness hardened, he became inscrutable.

For the first time in seven years, he began to stutter again, and spent much of his time feeling sick or feigning sickness so that he could be placed in the safety of the infirmary, where he silently read under the covers—mostly Dickens, his favorite author, whose bleak childhood appealed to his sense of drama.

Jane, meanwhile, was still harping on baseball, on sports in general, trying to convince Tony to participate, as if the mere act of tossing or catching a ball would magically endow him with the right stuff necessary to become a conventional all-American boy. Tony was too introverted, too smart to think baseball could change anything; even so, the guilt he felt was undoubtedly intense. He was not great like his father, nor was he a "normal" boy. He hated baseball. He seemed to have no place in the world, such as it was.

Once, after he had unintentionally missed a school ball game, a group of boys came into his space and proceeded to verbally and physically harass him. He wrote to Jane, begging her to let him transfer to another school. She replied with a crushing note telling him to straighten up and fly right. She also sent a gift, which may have cheered Tony for a moment—until he opened it. The product of Jane's motherly compassion was a brand-new leather baseball glove. Perhaps her urgency was in part a reaction to her own undeniably emerging, and possibly frightening, sexuality.

"She wasn't ill-tempered or mean," Tony told *People* years later.

"Just a strong-willed, dominant, New England kind of woman. She controlled everything about my life, including my thoughts and feelings. . . . She felt she was taking responsibility, but she was really taking control." As much as he despised Jane's delicate iron grip, an insidious, irresistible pattern of domination and submission—of love and trust via acquiescence—had begun, paving the way for a string of strong, often manipulative women to rule his life.

"His mother was unliving, unloving, stark," says novelist Gwen Davis, one of Tony's first friends in Hollywood, who was madly infatuated with him for years. "He was unbelievably wounded that she never acknowledged anything about him."

He came down with scarlet fever again his second year, and was sent home to recover. But by the next term he was back in savage North Andover. At this point, Tony was at the absolute bottom of his class gradewise, so Jane made him a deal: if he worked harder his third year and improved his marks, she would let him complete his schooling back home in Boston. Needless to say, he applied himself, and rose to the top third of his class, determined to escape.

"Tony Perkins is considerably more mature than most of his contemporaries," wrote Dr. Frank Ashburn, headmaster of the Brooks School, "and is impatient with many of their schoolboy interests."

One evening during his last week at Brooks, Tony was about to retire to his cocoon when he heard the usual fracas moving past his curtain toward the common room. But this time, instead of burying his head in the pages of a book, he walked down the hall, stopped for a moment to listen to the ever present jeering, then stepped into the room. "I'm not coming back next year," he said calmly, and for the first time took a seat among the dumbfounded mob.

After three vicious years, he'd had enough. "[Brooks] taught me not to run away from any issue," Tony claimed when he was in Hollywood ten years later, in the midst of a surprisingly similar crisis of machismo. "After my time there, I could face—and can still face—any eventuality with complete control." The stage was set for him to take control through acting.

It was Jane who pushed him to do so, though Tony would later claim she did everything to stop him from acting while he was a teenager. "As Tony grew older and saw other boys with their fathers," she recalled, "he badly missed his own father. And the only identification he could have with his father was through the theater. . . . I began to realize that he was acquiring an unusual interest in [performing]. By the time he was fifteen, I was certain. A friend was running a summer-stock company, and I approached him to ask whether Tony might play some small parts." The friend agreed, if Jane would accompany him and run the box office.

At the Brattleboro Summer Theater in Vermont, Tony would have the opportunity to play small roles in such tried-and-true strawhat circuit pieces as *Junior Miss, Kiss and Tell,* and *George Washington Slept Here,* and to earn twenty-five dollars a week as the company's gofer or, as he put it, "summer slave." Slavery, though, would get him an Equity card.

His official stage debut took place on June 30, 1947, in the season opener, *Junior Miss.* Despite the play's wafer-thin plot about a teenage girl's efforts to gain the respect of her father, Tony's part did not go off hitchless: he missed his entrance cue, an offstage doorbell ring. Brattleboro's *Daily Reformer* singled Tony out as the progeny of the late great Osgood Perkins.

The next month he fared better as the kid brother in F. Hugh Herbert's *Kiss and Tell,* which boasted Lois Wilson and Eddie Nugent as the stars. "Tony was very right for the role," recalls Theodora Landess, a fellow apprentice with whom Tony took acting lessons in the morning, worked rehearsals in the afternoon, and performed onstage at night. "He got it up quickly like a professional. We all thought he was good because he came from a theatrical family." This time the *Daily Reformer* almost raved: "Perkins, aged 15, was good for a laugh everytime he stepped on the stage."

On August 4, Tony appeared more fittingly as the juvenile lead in the Moss Hart–George S. Kaufman comedy *George Washington Slept Here.* As a neglected brat who is pawned off on his aunt and uncle while his parents settle their divorce, he had some acerbic lines to fling about his character's promiscuous mother and the dubiousness of his father's identity, stingers that Tony, with a little transference, no doubt enjoyed delivering.

As Jane had promised, that fall Tony began his seventh grade at the Browne and Nichols School in Cambridge, a nonboarding prep school for boys that was just a short commute from Brookline. Like Brooks, the student body had a high percentage of football players, but also, because of the war, slightly older veterans who were trying to complete their truncated educations. Unlike at Brooks, however, the seemingly frail Tony, his confidence healed by the applause of the summer, wasted no time in marking his boundaries.

"As a student, Tony played the role of rebel to the hilt," said his classmate and longtime friend, Henry Scammell. "He flouted authority with real daring and enormous self-control."

But Don Hellerman, a B&N football star and wrestler who had been in the Marine Corps before returning to school, still remembers Tony's famously poor posture, slicked-down hair, ill-fitting suits, and his touching desire to please. "He was withdrawn, very delicate in his demeanor, even though he was tall. He was ingratiating to people he was intimidated by, fearful of. He was very solicitous of me—sort of like my pet." Hellerman also recalls Tony as often seeming "encumbered and burdened."

Even so, with less than thirty boys per grade in the upper school, the classes at Browne and Nichols were small, allowing Tony the opportunity to shine as an individual if not as a student. He quickly became known as the class magician and also got praise for his piano playing, which he usually launched into during recess as a more acceptable way to avoid the humiliation of contact sports. "It was a small enough school that differences weren't always liabilities," remembers Henry Scammell. "The fact that Tony was different made him interesting."

His frequent caustic arguments with his French instructor, on class time, were enjoyed by all—perhaps Tony was hypercritical when it came to the only tangible legacy Osgood had left him—and he enjoyed the flamboyant teaching style of "Doc" Walters, the science professor, and Edgar Knapp, the English teacher and football coach. All of Tony's assignments and papers were signed with a picture of an Indian tepee (for T.P.), his own way of initialing his work. (The same rebus would later serve as the name of Perkins's production company, Wigwam.)

Knapp remembers young Perkins as a B-minus student whose "marvelous ear and voice for the English language" occasionally raised his grade. In class, Tony would "take off" with Hamlet's opening soliloquy, "O, that this too too solid flesh would melt,/Thaw, and resolve itself into a dew!" "It always seemed to me that he was so good with the Bard's lines that he should have been a Shakespearean actor at some point in his life. But I don't think he ever was." Perkins's total disregard for the classics over the course of his forty years in show business was something that would always vex his friends and colleagues.

For the first time in his life, Tony found a social circle of his own, namely Henry Scammell and Serge Boutourline, the three of whom, as one student recalls, "used to bum around Harvard Square making asses of themselves in a typically teenage way that didn't include the rest of us." Like Tony, Henry and Serge came from less-than-wealthy families and were in some way distanced from their parents. Henry had lost his father when he was twelve, and had also suffered from rheumatic fever as a child, which had impaired his athletic ability. Occasionally, Tony and Henry would walk to the cemetery where Henry's father was buried. Serge, the "Class Genius and Scientist" as he was voted their senior year, was the son of two grindingly poor Russian immigrants; for him, life at home was a constant tug-of-war between the old world and the new. He later committed suicide. But when they were together, the three boys spurred each other on intellectually, and shared a sense of humor and a love of practical jokes. Tony and Henry especially enjoyed writing (Scammell went on to become a novelist).

Tony knew by now how to make the most of his infirmities and idiosyncrasies. For instance, he taught Henry how to fake tuberculosis: smoke a cigarette dipped in iodine, puff it from the other end, and it leaves spots in your lungs that look like TB. But he pointedly did not participate in cheap bragging about sexual experiences—he didn't have any, beyond petting with the daughter of a Harvard professor—and without sports, there was little masculine bravado for him to indulge in. "He didn't drink at all," Scammell says. "He really didn't feel his metabolism was up to it. I think he always thought of himself as being fragile." Tony's mind and tongue were becoming his best defenses.

One of Tony's trademarks in the halls of B&N was his Roddy McDowall impersonation, a lisping, mincing caricature that he frequently acted out both in an attempt to be one of the guys and to deflect attention away from the painful truth about himself. "By pretending to be something, he was clearly disclaiming it," notes Scammell. Ironically, years later, McDowall would be one of Tony's closest friends in the industry.

Such an open display should come as no surprise given the fact that Tony was probably feeling cornered, both by his own burgeoning pubescence and some striking events in the literary world. In early 1948, the *Kinsey Report's Sexual Behavior in the Human Male* shocked the nation with its declaration that 37 percent of adult American men had had homosexual experiences; alternate sexuality was suddenly on America's mind as it had never been before. The same year also saw the publication of a cluster of high-profile gay novels, including Gore Vidal's *The City and the Pillar,* Truman Capote's *Other Voices, Other Rooms,* and James Baldwin's *Giovanni's Room.* (Vidal and Baldwin would also later become friends of Tony's, in Hollywood and Paris.) There can be no doubt that in an academic setting these books were joked about by the testosterone-laden students, despite the fact that the very subject of homosexuality was still taboo in "polite" society.

"Tony differed from the other boys in the school," Henry Scammell wrote in 1957. "He simply didn't have the resilience that is necessary to face the every day limitations of prep school life. Where others would bend, Tony would harden. Yet he retained an acute sensitivity which quite often made adults feel uncomfortable with him. He was quickly aware of their motives and deceits. People felt naked with him."

The summer of 1948, Jane found employment as business manager of the Robin Hood Theatre in Arden, Delaware, and enlisted Tony to manage the box office and gain more stage experience. Newly founded by director Windsor Lewis and a small troupe of actors, the Robin Hood strove trendily to be economically cooperative, with everyone, from the gofers to the performers, working for an equal base salary—rejecting the "star packages" that were the norm for many summer companies. Many of Lewis's recruits came from the Martin Beck Theatre in New York, where he had recently stage-managed the Katharine Cornell and Guthrie McClintic production of *Antony and Cleopatra.*

The people of Arden, almost all of whom were involved in one way or another with the theater, offered single rooms in family homes to the incoming theater folk. Jane and Tony stayed in separate lodgings, probably because that was all they could get. "Jane was very quiet, very dignified," recalls Pat Patterson, with whose family Tony lived for two seasons. "She was older than we all were, and was very much her own person. She wasn't one to enter into things. Tony lived his life and we all lived together. She was a good mother, in that respect. She allowed him to be himself." (Tony would later reveal that he and his mother were anything but detached, that they were, in fact, unnaturally close.) With all the responsibilities of single motherhood, and perhaps because of her own awakening sexual identity, Jane seemed to have conflicting ideas about her role as a parent.

Actress Betty Low, who was there with her own five-year-old son, remembers Mrs. Perkins as "quite prim, but anxious about Tony, far more anxious about him than anything else. He was her lamb, and I think she had suffered a great deal with the family, her in-laws. Whether they helped or not, I have no idea, but she was watching Tony constantly, very anxious about him." Another company member describes Jane as "elegant, and a little forbidding."

Pat Patterson, who had two small children of her own, remembers that with Tony in the house, "it was like having a grown son all of a sudden"—who was deathly afraid of flying insects. "He lived in a den, which is off the living room, and one evening he came tearing out as if the most terrible thing were happening," Patterson recalls. "It was just a June bug that was flying from beam to beam. But Tony was frantic, he was terrified. He had gathered some newspapers to try and hit it, and as tall and gangly as he was, it was quite a sight. He was just desperate."

But Tony's behavior was usually impeccable. "He had very rigid, almost old-fashioned ideas and feelings about how one should conduct oneself," Patterson says. Never voluntarily displaying *any* emotion off-stage, he only let his guard down once, when his landlady was late coming home after the theater one night: "I had visited a friend who wanted some company and Tony suddenly started scolding me. *'Where have you been?!* Do you think it's right leaving Mr. Patterson *alone* all evening?!' Well, I became very apologetic in front of this big boy, who was very upset."

He may have had good reason to be; the other members of the company, put off by his age (at sixteen he was the youngest) and his lineage, had greeted him with an antagonism bordering on cruelty. Low recalls that "they all looked down their nose at him. 'Osgood Perkins's son? Oh come on.' He naturally sensed that, and so he put on an air that he had a long stage tradition from his father that nobody else had. He was arrogant because he was scared, and he was young, with his father's name treasured in his memory. He was quite lofty, which was his protection."

Perhaps because he identified with her as a single mother—safely, as someone *else*'s mother—Tony liked Betty Low. At dinnertime, the two of them and her son, who was also named Tony, were banished to the small children's table in the dining hall. Low had been a dancer, and she and Tony shared a love of "emotional, wonderful music" by early twentieth-century composers like Ravel, Stravinsky, and Copland. Tony made regular excursions to Maeson's Record and Television Center in Wilmington, where he bought recordings that he thought would please his surrogate mom.

"After rehearsals and performances, he and I would sit in the empty theater together and choose music to play during the intervals of the next production," Low remembers. "I was just about the only person he really talked to, or chummed around with, if you could use that term. He was moody. The only times he really relaxed were during our long sessions listening to music in the dark theater. I don't think he was getting on with his mother. It was a period of growth and thrashing about, dying to get into the theater, and leave Mom behind. Perfectly normal, at that point."

The unlikely friends were cast as nonidentical, nearsighted twins in *Sarah Simple*, a now forgotten drawing room comedy by A. A. Milne that had been popular in London (with Gertrude Lawrence), but had lost something in crossing the Atlantic. While Betty and Tony worked, Jane kept her distance, "closeted away with the box office," according to Low, "even during our rehearsals." Tony could rarely get her attention or approval.

Jane did turn out to see her son's debut, which took place on the evening of June 29, in ninety-degree heat, to a meager crowd. "*Sarah Simple* wasn't such a great play," Low maintains, "and Tony was never even really noticed."

Maybe not from the wings, but from across the footlights, something was there. Charles Williamson, who was in the audience that summer and later joined the Robin Hood as an actor, recalls that "he made an impression on the whole company. He was only sixteen at the time, and had great charm."

Before they parted at the end of the season, Tony gave Betty's five-year-old son, Tony Pageant, a farewell gift: a book of fairy tales that he claimed Osgood had given him at the same age. "He trusted children," Low recalls. "He knew they were not snide or against him or sizing him up. He was overly sensitive about the world—well, who isn't at sixteen?"

"To Tony P. from Tony P." read the inscription, like a schizophrenic wish that his father's legacy had been a joy rather than a disappointment and now a burden.

"Since he'd gone and died on me," Tony said many years later, "I decided to pay him back by outsucceeding him."

The following June Tony was shipped off to Ontario to work at the Peterborough Summer Theatre, while Jane took a job alone with the Cohasset Theatre outside of Boston. Perhaps she needed some time by herself after years of juggling career and son. Whatever the reason, it was there that she became reacquainted with Michaela O'Harra, who had come to see one of the plays. Soon Jane would move back to New York to share living quarters with the young playwright. But in the meantime, they spent weekends together in New York while Michaela worked on her proposal for the New Dramatists Committee, an organization that would provide a finance-free breeding ground for struggling playwrights like herself. (O'Harra's career never recovered from the derailment of *Honor Bright*, but the New Dramatists is still active today.)

Tony's cousin Stephanie, who remained close to Jane until her death, admits there was speculation within the family about the nature of the relationship—though Jane never discussed it, and none of Jane's family ever met O'Harra. "I'm sure Jane had affairs before she met Osgood because she was a freethinker, a pioneering woman. She was so crazy about Osgood. She told me when they slept together that they curled up like one person, that they turned over together, that she had the most wonderful life with him.

"As far as she and Michaela went, Jane never told me they were lovers, so I can't say that they were. But looking back on it, if you live with somebody for twenty years you would certainly have to have, if not a sexual relationship, an awfully wonderful platonic one." Whether Jane was lesbian or bisexual, her widowhood provided the kind of socially acceptable cover that no gay man could enjoy.

"I don't think Jane ever had any specific beliefs that anybody was anything but a person," O'Harra maintains today. "All this business about declaring oneself one thing or another seems to me is beside the point of being a person. It's nobody's business. It just seems to me there's too much emphasis put on feminism, for instance, or being one thing or another of any kind. You're a person or you're not a person. Sooner or later, I'm sure that the human race will come to that. It's just too bad that they haven't come to it yet."

Meanwhile, the repertoire in Canada proved fruitless for Tony; if his previous stock experiences had been fraught with the tension of a watchful mother and jealous colleagues, this summer's was simply hard labor and a bore. There were no roles for teenagers, and less than a decade later all memory of the wearisome season would be erased from his mind.

That September he immersed himself in school activities with a vengeance. As a senior, he joined the varsity tennis team (Osgood had also loved tennis), became a member of the glee club, and was made co–literary editor with Henry Scammell of the school's paper, *The Spectator*. Tony wrote much of its contents himself. In fact, he enjoyed writing almost as much as acting, but not quite. "Acting was just memorizing lines, and I was good at that," he later told a reporter with typically flippant aplomb. "Writing was harder and required more work."

So did certain classes, such as physics, which Tony simply could not bring himself to fathom. Only when it came to a public contest like the Browne and Nichols Science Fair, in which the boys of the chemistry and physics departments competed for first prize (a chance to have an exhibit at the statewide MIT Science Fair), did Tony become inspired. He built an absurd, theatrical-looking contraption that was supposed to create water from the hydrogen and oxygen in the air.

"Tony's project was scientific bullshit," remembers classmate Peter Haskell, who later became a popular television actor, "but it was so clever. I had done something with ferns and spores and stuff like that. But Tony had rigged almost a movie set with arcs and wires and electricity traveling down in waves like a bolt of lightning in a Frankenstein movie." His elaborate invention was not-so-secretly attached to an ordinary tap, from which his "magic" water flowed. When a local minister passed and asked Tony if his exhibit was legitimate, his reply was a smiling, "Father, would I lie to a man of the cloth?"

Serge Boutourline won first place in the fair, but nobody forgot Tony's bogus exhibition, which was designed more than anything else to attract attention. Instead of failing miserably, which he clearly foresaw, Tony knew instinctively how to raise himself above a situation with humor, and look down at the results.

Finally popular as a senior, inside Tony harbored a defeating suspicion about his sexuality. He had at last arrived socially, but to guard against being found out he mocked the very situations he longed to be a part of. He easily got the upper hand in any conversation with his peers. "He was very conscious of both his intellect and his talent," Haskell confirms. "But he could be borderline cruel if he thought you were being dumb. He was quick to flay you."

By January of 1950, the B&N boys were required to start thinking about college. Most of them had been preparing to go to Harvard, but Tony knew his grades were too low and didn't even bother to apply. It was one way of separating himself from the standard set by his father.

When John O. Rich, the young, newly appointed director of admissions at Rollins College in Florida, paid Browne and Nichols a visit to drum up some business, not a single student turned out to hear his sales pitch—until the headmaster sent Tony in to see him. Rich didn't know of Tony's background, barely knew who Osgood Perkins was, and the two talked for a while as equals. Rollins, Tony learned, was far away from the winters of New England, which no doubt appealed to his iconoclastic side, and offered an extensive theater arts program. More to the point, the college operated on a pass-fail grade system. That was all it took to interest Tony.

If summer stock had given Tony confidence, then his appearance that spring in B&N's coproduction (with Boston's all-girl Brimmer and May School) of Gilbert and Sullivan's *Yeoman of the Guard* must have made him feel as American as apple pie. Overnight, he became the star of his class, despite the fact that, as one classmate put it, "he did not have a singing voice, all efforts to make him into a musical performer to the contrary." Nevertheless, Tony's quirky, over-the-top performance in the small role of Shadbolt left an indelible impression on everyone who saw it.

With a hollow-eyed, almost cadaverous face—his own makeup creation, self-applied—Tony brought an almost tragic intensity to his characterization of the buffoon. More than forty years later, classmate Ellery Woodworth, who headed the cast, still remembers Tony's interpretation as being "more psychopathic than the role suggests. Shadbolt is the fool who gets hoodwinked constantly. Tony played it with a serious psychological overtone, the weird side as opposed to the fool side—he overplayed the deranged aspect of it. It was pretty heavy."

On the morning of June 7, 1950, in sweltering heat, Tony graduated from B&N at almost the very bottom of his class. "Great natural charm and ability to amuse," wrote one of his teachers. He didn't care; his prep school days were over, and he had places to go.

He went back to Delaware that summer, again without Jane who was preoccupied for the season with young Michaela O'Harra on Cape Cod. By now the Robin Hood was one of the most successful and important summer theaters in the country. Tony, still the youngest member of the company, was now considered a veteran and was better accepted by the group. He, in turn, was more extroverted, and more curious about the lives of the other players; he loved gossip, something that would become a lifelong, vicarious fascination.

"He liked to draw you out about your background as an actor and where you'd worked," recalls Gaylord Mason, who appeared in several of the plays, and whose performance as a psychopathic handyman in Mel Dinelli's *The Man* Tony especially admired. "He wanted to know all about everybody, and how they lived." Charles Williamson, who was now a player as well (on his way to the Yale Drama School), remembers Perkins being amused by the fact that one of the actresses, Marguerite Morrissey, was madly in love with the "aggressively heterosexual" director, Windsor Lewis, who was not reciprocating because of the presence of another actress, Barbara Bel Geddes, whom he had just met and would soon marry (Morrissey later became a nun).

Tony and Charles lunched together almost every day and often enjoyed a quick swim just before the nightly performances. Williamson remembers that although his friend read movie magazines voraciously, "it was a stage career that he wanted. He loved the theater, and got on particularly well with the older people in the company." Character actor Ivan Simpson was a special favorite, as was the scenic designer, Jack Knisely. And everyone loved the Robin Hood's gutsy star, Cynthia Rogers, a middle-aged actress who had made a name for herself both as an ingenue on Broadway, most notably in the 1933 production of *Mary of Scotland* with Helen Hayes, and as the "mistress" of homosexual stage producer Dwight Deere Wyman. Now mainly a star of the New England circuit, her blush had faded; she smoked, drank, and indulged in fleeting liaisons. According to Williamson, "she loved younger people," and it was not uncommon for her to jokingly promise a summer apprentice that she'd be his first. "Cynthia was interested in getting to know Tony better, and me better." Eager Tony, however, was merely interested in what Rogers could tell him about the theater of the previous two decades, which probably just made her feel older.

No matter how small or superficial his parts, Tony always wanted his performances evaluated in detail, and he barraged Williamson incessantly with questions about his work; the acclaim didn't mean as much to him at this point as did his desire to achieve a sense of control and accomplishment over what he was trying to project onstage, and probably off. According to Williamson, "He never expressed his homosexuality during the summer of 1950. He did not act on it at all. At that time, I was very much in the closet and repressed. We both shared that."

There wasn't much choice. Unlike most summer companies, the tone at Arden was set by the well-known homophobia of Windsor Lewis. Homosexuality would not be tolerated in the midst of his new liaison with Bel Geddes, despite the fact that gays and bisexuals were, and have always been, a staple of the theatrical workforce. "One time during that summer someone had come down—an assistant scene designer or some such thing—and he left very suddenly within a couple of weeks," Williamson recalls. "There was word of some overt activity, because I remember Tony saying to me, 'You know, that guy's going back to New York. He's *queer*.' He had obviously ruffled some feathers in the company."

In their tacit understanding Tony developed a secret crush on his friend, who was several years older than himself. "Let's go swimming" or "Let's go to the movies" were his constant refrain—and always just the two of them; Tony never wanted the intrusion of anyone else on their excursions. Sometimes he'd suggest they take a forty-five-minute drive just to get a hamburger and a milk shake.

Only in the darkness of the movies would Tony dare to rest his head on Chuck's shoulder—"in a very youthful, charming way,"

Williamson says. "Both of us were at a stage where we would never have made any overture other than just an affectionate gesture. I picked up on it, but I was not about to do anything about it."

Understandably. Just a few months earlier and a few miles away, beyond the relative rural innocence of Arden, several Republican senators, most notably Joe McCarthy, had begun witch-hunting "perverts" and "subversives" along with Communists within the State Department. If homosexuals had been invisible before, in the current climate they were rapidly becoming targets.

On August 22, 1950, Tony stepped into the slight role of Fred Whitmarsh in Ruth Gordon's autobiographical comedy, *Years Ago*. As the guileless young suitor to Marguerite Morrissey's stagestruck teenage Ruth, Tony was mentioned in the *Wilmington Journal* for his "outstanding" work. He felt an almost proprietary attachment to the paper-thin part, which consisted of little beyond the boyish mannerisms that would become his trademark. Just two years later, his conviction about Fred would prove strong enough to land him his first job in Hollywood.

With the Arden season over, Tony joined his mother in Truro, Massachusetts, where she and Michaela had rented a small apartment overlooking the Pamet River. It was his first time on Cape Cod, which would become his private getaway, and his first time meeting his mother's friend. "I don't think he'd ever really been on the Cape at all," O'Harra recalls, "but that summer he fell in love with it."

But he did not fall immediately in love with Jane's new domestic situation. There was some tension at the start. According to O'Harra, Jane's son arrived with a mandolin, "which was about as big as he was. The apartment where Jane and I were living was just a room, and he was so big and the mandolin was so big that it took up the whole place. I've forgotten where we had him sleep. There was one bedroom, just big enough to have two beds in it, and Jane and I were sleeping in there. None of us had any money.

"I was writing plays at the time, and the landlord was a retired painter who let me work in his studio, so I was out of the house during the day. But in the evenings, there was just no room for all of us, and Tony and I began to get on each other's nerves. Jane worried that we were going to start fighting any minute, so she went to see if she could find a room for Tony, which she did. But then, both of us being very tight about money, we refused to have anything to do with it! So Tony stayed there, and we didn't spend the money on the room."

To keep him inoculated with a healthy dose of male companionship, and out of Michaela's way, Jane introduced Tony to Joseph Schoonejongen, a local fisherman who was old enough to be his father. Out on his boat, Schoonejongen taught Tony how to bass fish and offered the now six-foot-two boy a father's caring ear. Tony would never forget the kindness. He remained a friend to the Schoonejongen family, the only real family he had ever known, for life, long after he'd given up trying to win his mother's love.

EXTRACURRICULAR ACTIVITIES

P ROSPERITY AND FAMILY were America's rigidly optimistic values in the decade following the war, the time when Tony Perkins was just emerging as an actor and as a young man. All too soon he would find himself having to assume, even personify, many of those dreams. By September 1950, there was already suffocatingly little room for anything else.

In Washington a Senate subcommittee had been appointed to investigate Senator Joseph McCarthy's accusations that the United States government employed "red sympathizers." That, of course, meant anyone even remotely "subversive," and for McCarthy in particular "subversive" meant "homosexual." "Perverts," as gay men became known under his regime, were considered high security risks ostensibly because of their vulnerability to blackmail. In April the *New York Times* quoted Republican national chairman Guy George Gabrielson: ". . . as dangerous as the actual Communists are the sexual perverts who have infiltrated our Government in recent years." The preposterous link between homosexuality and Communism leaked down into the media and the popular consciousness; *Coronet* magazine referred to homosexuality as "that new menace," and even as late as 1964, *Life* magazine would ask, "Do the homosexuals, like the Communists, intend to bury us?"

In this shrill climate, few places could have seemed farther away from the madness than Florida's oldest institution of higher learning, Rollins College, a $1,600-a-year, Christian-based, all-American, athlete-filled "country club" school, tucked away on the sunny shores of Lake Virginia in wealthy Winter Park. Lying just outside the unassuming, pre-Disney city of Orlando (population then a mere sixty-two thousand), the campus lodged fewer than seven hundred students, most of them the sons and daughters of rich Yankees who found Rollins a convenient baby-sitter. With not a single African American student in sight to mar the school's smug uniformity, trouble must have seemed like a Civil War myth. But Rollins had rumblings of its own.

There was increasing dissent among faculty over the progressive educational philosophy of the school's handsome new president, Paul A. Wagner, a vital, charismatic man who was, at age thirty-one, the youngest college president in the country. Deeply opposed to what he termed "the Prussian pedantic system" of teaching—the typical method whereby students robotically memorize lessons by rote—Wagner advocated modern "audiovisual" teaching techniques. As he declared at his inauguration ceremony: "If our teachers intend to compete with movies, television, and comic books, they will have to use the tools of our times."

Surely Wagner's spry, egalitarian stance would have appealed to Tony. Unfortunately, the faculty was already bristling behind closed doors. Their conservatism would soon come out of the closet, manifesting itself in much crueler ways—in a mini–witch-hunt, in fact, fashionably in line with the national trend.

After so many summers of acting on makeshift stages in renovated barns, the school's ornate, whitewashed, Spanish-style Annie Russell Theatre, surrounded by palm trees, flowers, and hanging moss, must have seemed to Tony more like an exotic cathedral than a playhouse. It would indeed prove a luxurious escape from the otherwise sports-oriented campus, popularly known for its crew, golf, water-skiing, swimming, and tennis facilities. The catalogue promised "practically every wholesome activity found in a large university." Not so much as whispered was the fact that it also offered the chapel towers and remote boathouses where horny young men who were so inclined could go to relieve themselves.

In this relentlessly bright, healthy new environment, at least Tony was tall. As fellow student Robert Newton Peck recalls, "He was the most uncoordinated young man I've ever seen—a gangling, skinny, unmuscular, unathletic youth who was sort of like a dog in a pet shop window, always wanting to be adopted."

Again, Tony made his idiosyncrasies work for him. Fred Rogers, who graduated from the Rollins Conservatory of Music in 1951, and eventually went on to achieve fame as television's Mister Rogers, remembers Tony as "musical" rather than athletic. "I had a piano in my room because I was a composition major, and Tony used to stop by and play every once in a while. He must have been able to play by ear."

For musical boys like Tony, who were sexually ambiguous or simply slow to blossom (in Hollywood, Rock Hudson and his friends were using the word "musical" as a code word for identifying other gay men), the theater arts department offered refuge. For one thing, the class and rehearsal schedule kept them aloof from regular school and social activities; when most students were getting together at the end of the day for beer and cramming, Tony, like an early-rising vampire, would just be heading for the Annie Russell or the Fred Stone (the school's small auditorium), taking in the perfumed glow of the evening. Theater arts also offered close proximity to girls, but the kind of girls who loved the nonthreatening attention of "musical" boys.

"He was interested in the theater, and that's about it," one student recalls. "From up North, down there in a little Southern school, he just looked sad all the time. I do not remember Tony dating anyone, ever. We attributed it to shyness. That could have been our naivete."

Tony wasted no time losing himself in activity, curricular and otherwise. On November 1, 1950, the theater department kicked off its season in the Fred Stone with *A Dream for Marjorie*, an original play by two Rollins graduates, Frank Weber and Marge Humpfer. Louis Ingram, who lived down the hall from Tony on the first floor of Chase Hall, the freshman dorm, took the lead in this semicomic story of two San Francisco families pondering the meaning of life in the atomic age. Tony appeared in the minor role of a philosophy-spouting cop. The *Orlando Morning Sentinel* praised Ingram's performance, and merely pigeonholed Tony as the "son of the late noted actor."

With Ingram, Perkins cowrote the annual freshman variety show, which was performed later that month in the Annie Russell Theatre. The three-act result was *As Thousands Jeer* (Tony's title), the format of which was a series of "auditions" for a pair of klutzy twin-brother theatrical producers (played by the writers). President Wagner loved the show, and sent its creators a personal note afterward, praising their work. Tony, unaware that Wagner was on his way out, must have been pleased.

In early December, Tony appeared with Louis Ingram, Fred Rogers, and Robert Peck, among others, in Jean Giraudoux's *The Madwoman of Chaillot*, directed by Howard Bailey, an ex–New York actor who was now enjoying personal success as the head of the theater arts department. Professor Bailey, who some students felt favored Tony, remembered the young Perkins as having an "electric quality that came over the footlights. He had a little boy quality, too, like Henry Fonda, that made people want to mother him. Perhaps that was the secret of his charm. But I don't think it was deliberate; it was inherent in his personality."

Not everyone was so impressed. "He was always difficult," says Roger Bentley, who met Tony in Chase Hall and worked with him in several college shows. "Because of his background he was always setting himself apart from everybody else. He was very professional, very arrogant, very lonely. Underneath it all, there was the desire to be loved, but he didn't know how to go about it."

One way Tony tried to go about it, with little success, was to pledge the Kappa Alpha fraternity. The KAs, also known as the "Knights of Alcohol," represented everything that Tony Perkins was not, a household of popular party animals and jocks who made an occasional allowance for a game bookworm. The three-story brick KA house, with its white columns, open porch, quarter-acre green lawn, and fountain in back, must have seemed like a childhood dream to Tony: the ideal, picture-perfect home, full of the brothers and fathers he'd never had, enough to get lost in.

Unfortunately, the brothers had some reservations about his masculinity, his general aloofness and apparent indifference to the opposite sex, and his pledge was rejected. Jane, at least, was relieved; she hadn't wanted him to join in the first place.

But despite his reputation among peers as an uppity loner, and among his elders as a little boy lost, male companionship was far from lacking in Tony's new life. In Chase Hall, he had become intimately involved with a unique group of young men, thanks to his roommate, Barclay Powers, a handsome, blond-haired boy from Coral Gables. In personality and style, Powers was every inch Tony's opposite, and an anomaly for the 1950s: an almost defiantly open queer, who had been conscious even in high school of what he was, and had never been afraid to admit it. "He was very good-looking," one dormmate remembers, "and always had somebody buzzing around him."

Barclay quickly introduced Tony to his friends, ★Stanley Howell, ★Dick Baker, and Bill Hamilton, who was the older brother of actor George Hamilton and later became a successful interior decorator. Baker and Hamilton were already something of an item on campus—everyone noticed the two striking young men who were always together. They spent much of their time *off*-campus, romantically involved at Hamilton's apartment. It didn't take long for things to get complicated.

Amid the social and academic pressures of life away from home, Tony found easy sexual release with the rather demure and accessible Stanley, who lived directly across the hall; together they enjoyed occasional relief sex, which consisted mostly of kissing and masturbation. But Tony's eye was really on the more strapping Dick Baker, who was dark and handsome like his lover Bill, but edgy, always claiming that he really preferred girls. Tony made no bones about the fact that he wanted Dick. Luckily for him (much to Dick's private regret), Bill Hamilton was not a possessive lover.

Tony got his wish. An intense sexual relationship started up between the two tall, watchful young men, who, of the five friends, had the most in common. Both were Yankees who came from poorer backgrounds than either Stanley, whose family owned land in another Southern state, or Bill Hamilton, whose mother was a popular Palm Beach socialite. Dick's father was just a small-town Illinois minister, and Tony's a memory. Neither of them had much confidence socially, both were nagged by self-doubt. To escape their woes, which for Dick meant his disappointing relationship with Hamilton, the two outsiders lost themselves in sexual trysts at the deserted Rollins beach house, or away from prying eyes down at Daytona Beach.

How sexually experienced Tony was at this point in his life is hard to say. At Rollins, he certainly seemed to be making up for lost time.

★Names preceded by a star have been changed.

But according to Stanley, Tony was no virgin. Quite probably, Tony's first sexual experience had happened in a car, for he had always been an enthusiastic hitchhiker, and living with Jane did not allow much privacy. If one reads between the lines in this 1958 *Photoplay* article, written by Jane and cunningly titled "He Still Baffles Me," it's easy to imagine the lengths to which her boy had to go for sex: "I remember when we were living in Cambridge . . . and Tony was attending high school. He'd go out with the other boys in the evenings, but he would always phone me, saying where he was going and when he would be home. One time, he didn't call and he didn't show up all night. Naturally, I was worried sick.

"Later, I learned what had happened. Tony and some of his pals had gone to a café a few miles out of town. The fellows sat around, drinking Cokes and playing the jukebox. When Tony noticed it was getting late, he suggested they leave. But the others weren't ready to go. Tony ambled off by himself and, not having a car, thumbed a ride. The auto broke down and Tony tried to help the man fix it. Finally, they phoned for a mechanic, but by the time the car was repaired and Tony had arrived within the city limits, it was two o'clock in the morning. Tony rang a school friend's doorbell and bunked at his house that night.

" 'Mother,' Tony explained the next morning, 'I didn't want to come in so late and wake you.' " A likely story. Hitchhiking—in Arden, in Ontario, on the Cape—provided easy sexual contacts without the shameful hindrance of being identified as the son of a deified actor. On his own with his new friends at Rollins, Tony could at last assert who he was with no wrenching reminders of who he was supposed to be in the name of his father.

Shortly before the Christmas holidays, the boys' arrangement met an unexpected and brutal demise.

One afternoon Barclay, Bill, and Stanley all received frantic phone calls from Dick, whose mom and dad were in town, asking them to come to his parents' hotel room right away. Tony was most likely busy with a rehearsal. Stanley and Bill Hamilton agreed to meet Barclay there.

When the two boys arrived at the hotel and started down the hall toward the Bakers' room, something they heard froze them dead in their tracks. They heard screams, Barclay's screams—"No! Nooooo!"—loud enough not to be missed down a hallway from behind a closed door. Someone was violently beating their friend. Stunned and terrified, Bill and Stanley fled.

Behind that door, in his parents' hotel room, Dick Baker and his father, who was by profession a man of God, were viciously pounding pretty Barclay Powers into a bloody, swollen pulp—a bonding, father-son battering that sent the "bad" boy to the local hospital. Exactly what provoked the assault is unknown, but it's probable that the Reverend Mr. Baker had stumbled upon a clue about his son's true private life—a love letter, a magazine—and confronted him with it. Dick, who was high-strung to begin with, had in turn pointed an hysterical, accusing finger at his own circle, at the "queers" who had lured him into their degenerate ways. By doing so, he also unleashed his vendetta against his lover Bill Hamilton, whose indifference had hurt him deeply.

Charges were brought not against the violent preacher and his son, who were seen as having acted justifiably, but against the gay students. Bill and Stanley denied everything; Barclay, whose mother came to sit by his hospital bed, could barely speak. Stanley Howell remembers being interrogated by Arthur Enyart, the dean of men, a rabid football fan (who resigned when President Wagner dropped football from the curriculum as a budget cut). Many of Enyart's insinuating questions hinged on Stanley's friendship with the sophisticated Bill Hamilton, who had become the prime suspect in the ordeal.

"Did you visit Bill Hamilton's apartment? Did you spend the night?"

As for Tony, he seemed to have vanished as soon as the trouble hit, though his name was definitely included as one of the accused. Almost paralyzed with fear, he had turned immediately to his older allies for help, adults having always been the most easily manipulated by his boyish charms. To John Rich, the director of admissions, whom he trusted, the young actor claimed complete innocence, maintaining that he hadn't done anything, that his friends were trying to drag him down with them.

In the safety of Rich's office, Tony allowed himself to be distraught. "They were my friends," he kept repeating, sometimes tearfully. He felt betrayed and ashamed, as well as horrified that his first college friends were being ripped away from him by the administration. But after a lifetime of lonely neglect, self-preservation understandably came first for the boy who had heretofore only found acceptance on the stage. It is not known whether Tony ever dared to visit his unfortunate roommate in the hospital. The accused quickly went their separate ways, and never saw one another again. (Barclay Powers died of AIDS in 1993.)

Naturally, the administration tried to keep things as hush-hush as possible. Beyond those directly involved, the students at large sensed nothing major amiss. "Queers," except for uppity ones like Barclay Powers, were invisible anyway. "It was all very clandestine," recalls one former student. "There were rumblings, but nobody really knew anything and nobody really wanted to talk about it, back in a time when such things were looked upon aghast. We were all in the closet." (In the early 1960s, another gay witch-hunt would sweep the school, resulting in several student suicides.)

"Social probation" was what the expulsion of Barclay Powers, Bill Hamilton, and Stanley Howell was politely coined. In 1950, there was no place for their kind amid the healthy, wealthy student body of a Christian campus like Rollins. Fortunately for everyone involved, their timing had at least been good; the Christmas holidays arrived, giving them all a phony white blanket under which to slip and never reappear, no questions asked.

How Tony avoided official implication in the scandal is another mystery. Probation of any kind would have prevented him from participating in any more theater productions, so it's possible that the theater arts department stepped in on his behalf (though Howard Bailey's wife denies it). In any case, he quietly took the train back up to Boston, where he spent the holiday with his mother and Michaela O'Harra, who had come up from New York. He didn't breathe a word of what had happened, but he would never forget it.

Four years later, the experience, as frightening and painful as it was, would serve him well for his Broadway debut as Tom Lee, the sensitive schoolboy accused of homosexuality in Robert Anderson's *Tea and Sympathy*.

Thirty-two years later, on a return visit to Rollins to accept an honorary degree, Tony Perkins would have his revenge.

In early January, Tony apprehensively returned to the scene of the crime—typically, Jane had given him enough money for a berth on the train, but her frugal son economized by traveling in a coach seat—to find, to his complete surprise, that one of his more socially acceptable fantasies had come true: he'd been removed from Chase Hall and reassigned to a room in the Kappa Alpha house. Just how he ended up there isn't entirely clear, but it's probable that the Rollins authorities placed him there to save face; Perkins was one of the school's needier cases (he received a partial scholarship his second year and a full one his junior year), and it would have looked bad for a sponsored student to be expelled. Instead, Tony was relocated to what must have seemed to all eyes a healthier environment. It probably seemed that way to Tony too. At least at first.

Most of the boys roomed on the second floor of the old brick house, but Tony was placed out of the way on the first floor. Nevertheless, he could not have helped but notice the handsome young man who lived in one of two rooms on the third floor, the big blue-eyed, crew-cut John Boyle, a popular member of the varsity crew whose "claim to fame," as one KA put it, "was that he could balance anything and everything on his chin," usually large objects, such as canoes (the wood-and-canvas kind) and T-crossed wooden planks lined with Coke bottles (of which he reportedly never broke a single one). "John wasn't muscular per se," remembers KA Richard Colabella, who roomed next door to Boyle, "but he was strong as an ox."

Of all the frat brothers, John was the one most talked about by the small inner circle of KA homosexuals, who wasted no time in befriending their theatrical new housemate. For Tony, Boyle's appeal was only enhanced by the fact that he suffered from what was delicately referred to as "a touch of epilepsy," the poignant chink in an otherwise impenetrable all-American facade. For now, however, wary Tony could only watch from the sidelines; the suffering of the previous semester was still palpable.

Thanks to the fatherly guidance of Howard Bailey, Tony quickly got wrapped up in his work, which he surely perceived as a kind of public redemption. Every free moment was spent at the Annie Russell Theatre, building the scenery—or rehearsing lines for his first leading role, in Fay Kanin's *Goodbye, My Fancy*, directed by Bailey's second in command, Wilbur Dorsett, a flamboyant, rotund man described by one student as "a Dom DeLuise type."

As Matt Cole, the love interest to the play's wistful leading lady,

Tony had some improbably macho lines ("[She's] the only reporter I ever knew who could sit in a poker game, win the biggest pot and still have every guy wondering what she'd be like in bed"), but he delivered them with such knowing, hammy boyishness, that in his own way he renounced the very meaning of the words. Clearly Tony's technique had less to do with content than with self-promotion. But for Tony, behaving like a boy meant no one could hate him, a modus operandi that would, as he got older, lend his performances an unfortunate air of grotesquerie.

His preposterous role in *Goodbye, My Fancy* was followed a month later by the walk-on part of *Miss* Johnson in *Harvey*, the comedy made popular the year before by the Jimmy Stewart film. So intent was Howard Bailey that Tony remain onstage that the character's sex was changed to fit the circumstances. Tony did his best, mugging his bit as the maid.

In March, he fared better as Theseus, the romantic lead in Julian Thompson's faux classical satire about the war between the sexes, *The Warrior's Husband*. As the Greek hero who woos and wins the Amazon princess Antiope, Tony paraded about the Annie Russell stage in a parody of masculine behavior, wearing a scanty Greek kilt, carrying a shield, and ultimately ending up in a clincher with the Rollins Players' pretty star, Cynthia Crawford. Only his poor posture betrayed any misgivings; his neck slouched forward in guilty discomfiture, a stance it would take years for him to shake.

By now, the campus was in an uproar and morale at an all-time low as a stifling school debt (half a million dollars) and poor enrollment projections caused President Wagner, "the boy wonder of education," to dismiss 30 percent of Rollins's already small teaching staff. Though he had done so with trustee approval, the fact that the casualty list included some tenured faculty stirred up a backlash worse than his cutting of the football program.

The student body protested loudly, and even Tony's new home, the Kappa Alpha house, threatened to secede entirely unless Wagner resigned. A taunting FOR SALE sign was hammered into the ground in front of Wagner's home, and he was publicly ostracized by people who had formerly been his friends. In the provincial world of academia, Wagner was being made to pay for his nonconformity. Even the college chaplain piously lamented, "I never knew that so much evil could flow."

In 1951, nineteen-year-old Tony knew; if you were different, hatred was a fact of life. He began spending more time alone, often fishing by himself out on Lake Virginia, a soothing reminder of his quieter days on the Cape with Mr. Schoonejongen. There was turmoil all around him, and within him as well. The handsome boy upstairs was causing him considerable private pain. But out there on the lake, apart from the noise and laughter of the water-skiers and speedboaters, he could allow his defenses to drop, his anxieties to subside, his thoughts and his sadness to fill him up, and float there for a while, before submerging them again for the inevitable return to real life.

On campus, when he wasn't at the theater, he spent more time with John Rich, his other father, or brother figure, usually in Rich's office. At these times, he poured out his feelings for John Boyle, spoke of how deep his "urges" were, and how he was coping with them. He was very much in love with Boyle, and wanted desperately to keep his affections under control. And always, like an incantation, Tony would ask Rich, "Do you think I'm queer?"

Back in Arden, Delaware, that summer, heartsick Tony, who by now had the honor of being the Robin Hood's juvenile lead, kept smiling in a series of comedies with Cynthia Rogers, John Drew Devereaux (a cousin of the Barrymores), and a wholesome young newcomer named Barbara Rush, whose arrival had been anticipated not without some excitement. Rush, who was then married to screen hunk Jeffrey Hunter, was under contract to Paramount Pictures, where she had just starred in the science fiction film *When Worlds Collide*. In a few short years, Tony would also find himself at Paramount, as the floundering studio's unlikely answer to James Dean.

Meanwhile, he enjoyed the familiarity of the company, and the fleeting moments of adulation on stage. Conrad Osborne, an apprentice that year, remembers Tony as being big brotherly, and offering generous criticism to the younger performers. "Beyond that, he struck me as someone who was very hard to get to know," Osborne says. "He was very flip, almost to the point of arrogance." Occasionally, Tony let his defenses down enough to appear depressed, but would inevitably slough it off as concern over the production at hand.

Barbara Rush saw a different side of her costar. "It was like working with Mickey Rooney in the Andy Hardy films. Tony was the most joyful, giggliest, silliest person you ever met in your life." With the pretty young actress, Tony found some respite from his self-worries. They rode bikes together, which surely gave him the appearance of boyish normalcy, and he taught Rush, who was from California, how to catch fireflies. She recalls Perkins as "not the least bit interested in movies. He never thought about anything but going to New York."

In the last play of the season, Noel Langley's *The Walrus and the Carpenter*, Tony was singled out by the local paper for his amusing performance as a theater student in the throes of first love. Obviously, it was a role he could act with some conviction, and it allowed him the opportunity to express at least some of the feelings and frustrations he normally had little outlet for. If he closed his eyes, he could see John Boyle instead of a girl. "He was tall, rangy, and a mass of bones," Rush later recalled. "In the love scenes, I'd get bruised because his elbows and shoulders were so sharp. I could feel his ribs in a close embrace."

Tony officially pledged the KA house again that September and was accepted as a brother, despite the fact that he was unathletic and didn't even drink beer. By now he was enough of a star on campus to pass as one of the guys (one of his sponsors within the house was John Boyle). But Jane was still adamantly against the idea of her son joining, fearing it would disrupt his studies.

"It always seemed so strange to me that they took Tony in, because he was more like a lost soul," recalls Kay McDonnell, a theater arts major who dated John Boyle for several years in college. "He really didn't fit in with those wild party boys, and he didn't go out of his way to try to fit in. He just seemed to like the camaraderie and the warmth and the friendship. John thought Tony needed a friend."

Boyle, for all his bravado, must have needed one too. His epilepsy, like Tony's homosexuality, gave him a sense of difference. "It was pretty easy to pick up that he was ashamed of it," one fraternity brother says, "that it made him more introverted than a lot of us. He was laboring under the misapprehension that he was a lesser man than most of us—that was the prevailing feeling at that time with *any* malady. You would never say the word 'cancer.' You wouldn't even say 'pregnant,' you'd say 'with child' or something. To be an epileptic and say it? You wouldn't do that. You felt ashamed and you stayed quiet." It was Boyle's shame and modesty that appealed to Tony. Tremendously attractive and perfectly coordinated at any sport—a school hero—Boyle nevertheless suffered the occasional public seizure. No one who witnessed one of these attacks could fail to be moved.

With Tony's newfound acceptance came new living quarters. Richard Lesneski, a pledge who roomed with Tony briefly, remembers their first meeting: "I was shown to a room in which there was a double bunk bed, and there on the bottom sat a tall, lithe figure, wearing sandals, shorts, and strumming a guitar as he sang a plaintive song. Tony was a quiet, rather shy individual who spent a lot of time seemingly dreaming." (A more precise description of Tom Lee, the role in *Tea and Sympathy* that would soon catapult Tony to Broadway stardom, could only be found in the pages of Robert Anderson's script.) Shortly thereafter, Tony moved to the more remote third floor to share a room with his handsome sponsor. Pretty soon he was balancing a canoe on his chin as well, a trick he later demonstrated in countless studio publicity photos.

Tony pretty much played it straight, and even started lifting weights on the back porch in a rather hopeless effort to build up his scrawny physique to something more desirable, along the line of John's (as he got older, Tony would become obsessed with physical fitness and his own body image). In the basement, he occasionally played pool with older brother Bill McGaw, who went on to become an Oscar-winning documentary filmmaker, and indulged in fantasies about their futures in show business.

"I remember he was short on money," McGaw says, "and he was going to see about getting a job in a restaurant. He played guitar and sang, and he had a pretty good voice. He went around from table to table and did some background playing and chatting with the diners. He did it primarily for tips. I thought that was awfully courageous of him because he surmounted a basic shyness to do it. The need for the extra money was pretty acute. He didn't have much to live on or play with as most of the other students at Rollins did." Tony also took jobs baby-sitting and reading to elderly Winter Park residents.

The Annie Russell Theatre, however, continued to be his retreat, where he could prove himself, improve himself, lose himself. It also offered him direct access to Kay McDonnell, who was the next best thing to John Boyle. Jealous, but thrilled to be near someone with whom he secretly shared so much, Tony could safely ply Kay with questions about her beau. "He didn't like to talk about himself," she remembers. "It was just casual conversation about classes—*and* his roommate, which was my favorite topic at the time. I used to tease Tony a lot. He was very shy until he got onstage, and then he was dynamic."

But even at the theater, Tony's reserve was common knowledge. "We could never persuade Tony to have a drink with the rest of the crowd," said Howard Bailey's daughter, Lynn. "He just shook his head and disappeared. One night, quite by accident, we discovered him in town, talking to two street urchins—about eight or ten years old. They had a dog and a bicycle. He was riding the bike and playing with the dog." Animals and small children weren't likely to hurt anyone.

In early December, the Rollins Players put on a play in which Tony made the most of the small but scene-stealing role of an expectant father. The *Orlando Post* declared him "responsible for the main body of laughs." Closing night the cast decided to get back at Perkins for upstaging them all, and reblocked the show so that it would be practically impossible for him to face the audience. In retaliation, he swiped the champagne glasses for the cast party. He didn't drink, anyway.

By now, Jane had left Boston and was living with Michaela O'Harra in New York. Mimi had moved permanently to Florida, so Jane needed someone new to share her expenses. Michaela, who was struggling with the New Dramatists Committee and her own lethargic writing career, did too. Together, they made an unlikely pair, but no one blinked at two "war widows" splitting the cost of living at the start of a new decade. They set up house in a cold-water flat at 300 East Fifty-first Street, near Second Avenue. Michaela rented a room outside to work on grant proposals and try to write.

"I never could really understand why Jane was attached to Michaela, except that it started out as someone she wanted to help," says a longtime friend of the widow Perkins. "They seemed like the oddest couple in the world. Unlike Jane, Michaela just didn't make an effort with people. She didn't know how to reciprocate." But she was younger, more than twenty years Jane's junior, and artistic—an irresistible combination for Mrs. Perkins, who was rapidly developing a soft spot for youthful creative types (she would later befriend many of Tony's teenage fans).

How Tony reacted to his mother's new living situation during the Christmas holidays is anybody's guess. F. Clason Kyle, a KA who was visiting New York that season, recalls that Tony would only meet him on neutral territory. John Kerr, who visited Jane's new flat with his mother, June Walker, recalls, "I knew Tony was gay, and I also had the sense that his mother was gay. But I never heard anyone speak disparagingly of Jane or that relationship. Probably every child brought up by a single parent, like Tony, is going to be a little more self-protective."

To escape, Tony spent a lot of time at Cynthia Rogers's place in the East Seventies, where he played it very straight. Wonderful at entertaining young people, Rogers always had an open bar—and loved to ply her innocents with martinis.

That winter, according to Rogers herself, who tended to brag about such things, Tony lost his virginity, heterosexually speaking, with her—not, as would be publicized years later, while on a desert location with starlet Victoria Principal, but in a swank Upper East Side apartment with an aging actress. At least Rogers was a friend. One can only imagine Tony's embarrassment, perhaps even disappointment, when "the phase" he was going through, as homosexuality was invariably dismissed, did not magically cease.

At this time, Tony dallied with the notion of becoming a Catholic (later spiritual quests and fads would prove more cerebral, such as the I Ching, Bahaism, and the philosophy of Krishnamurti). Compared to the relatively loose world of his upbringing, the sententious mysticism of the Catholic Church must have seemed passionate and surefire to Tony, whose faith in himself was at best wobbly. His cousin Stephanie recalls that Jane "was very upset that he had looked into becoming Catholic. He was searching, and then decided that maybe he'd become Episcopalian. He took instruction from some Episcopalian minister, and Jane said he'd told her that in the final analysis the guy had disillusioned him.

"She was angry that this man had left Tony with nothing. She couldn't believe how some people can be given positions of authority in religion, and then diminish all hope for others. She was just thunderstruck. Then she was always trying to get Tony into metaphysics."

Since 1946, Jane, who had been raised a Congregationalist and didn't think much of organized religion, had been a devoted advocate of the then-new Church of Religious Science (also known as the Science of Mind or simply "metaphysics"), a philosophical conglomerate of the "universal truths revealed in all the world's religions," the positive-thinking movement of its day. "She was a very strong person just in terms of her beliefs," says Cary Fuller, an avid Tony fan whom Jane befriended. "Religious Science really affected her and also rubbed off on him. She believed if she got a cold or something that she could will it away herself. If Tony was working and caught cold, she would suggest he go to a church 'practitioner' to be cured."

One can imagine the tension in the eccentric Perkins household: Jane, with her chirpy enthusiasm; Tony, with his sullen moods; and rational Michaela, with her silent skepticism. ("Michaela's religion was probably Freud or something," says actress Perry Wilson, who knew the women from the Cape, and later acted with Tony in both *Fear Strikes Out* and *The Matchmaker*.)

"Jane was very sold on the theories of metaphysics," O'Harra confirms. "She talked about it whenever Tony or I were in any kind of trouble." If Jane had known how distressed her son really was that Christmas, she probably never would have shut up.

Kenneth MacKenna, who was in town from Los Angeles for the holidays, offered Tony the chance to come to California the following summer, promising to secure him a job as a messenger boy at MGM. The possibility of a whole summer far away from Jane and her new friend—a vacation with a *man* who had known his father—was too good to turn down. He would return to the dusty frontier where Osgood had made *Scarface*. The Robin Hood Theatre could wait.

But Rollins could not; he had another semester to get through before he could escape. Although he was by now also a member of Theta Alpha Phi, the National Honorary Dramatic Fraternity, the winter was a slow season. Tony had no choice but to content himself with coursework.

Things were not going so well back at the KA house either. His relationship with his roommate had become strained. Though John Boyle liked Tony and had done a lot to support him, Tony's constant hanging around and wanting to be included had begun to make Boyle distinctly uncomfortable. "John felt crowded," says Richard Colabella, who lived in the room next door. Whether Tony openly expressed any of his true feelings for Boyle is unknown, but Kay McDonnell remembers John's main feeling for Tony quickly turning to one of annoyance. (John Boyle declined to be interviewed for this book.)

Without a new role to keep him occupied, Tony turned to writing. That fall the first of three fraudulent pieces about his golden days at the Brooks School was published in Rollins's literary magazine, *The Flamingo*. "Brooks Revisited" offered a wistful look back at lost school days, irretrievable childhood—just the sort of harmless sentiment that would impress an elderly English professor. "Gone, gone," wrote Tony, "the clatter of many shoes through the halls at noon bell. The shouts and smiles of friends of other years. And all the way down the darkening poplar-lined drive to the road, the pleas enticed him back, of familiar voices, long remembered, long forgotten." A parody of a school essay, "Brooks Revisited" won a not insubstantial monetary award of twenty-five dollars. If Tony couldn't bowl them over with his boyish sensitivity onstage, he was sure to do it in print, so strong was his need to project an acceptable public image. Rewriting the past was one way to cope with his very real confusion and fear.

Fanning his idle frustration was an item that caught his eye while thumbing through the *New York Times* in the library: MGM had bought the rights to Ruth Gordon's comedy *Years Ago*. "Since I had played it in Vermont," Tony inaccurately recalled years later (he'd done it in Delaware), "I felt it was reasonable that I should get the part in the movie. To me, it seemed just like common sense."

Howard Bailey, sensing Tony's dejection, got him a winter job in the Central Florida Drama Festival, kicking off the role of the teenage son in the W. Somerset Maugham–Guy Bolton comedy *Theatre*, which was to go on to tour from there. The story of an aging actress's desperate but meant-to-be-hilarious attempts to prove herself still sexually attractive to her husband (played by Bailey) and employers alike, *Theatre* was a vehicle almost too brutally close to home for its star, Kay Francis. One of Hollywood's most glamorous and highly paid actresses during the 1930s (when she was briefly married to actor Kenneth MacKenna), she had worked for Paramount in pictures such as Ernst Lubitsch's *Trouble in Paradise*, then moved to Warner Bros., where she'd gradually been eclipsed by Bette Davis. Francis was demoted to B pictures, and when Warners dropped her, she coproduced three low-budget vanity films at Monogram (*Divorce, Allotment Wives,* and *Wife Wanted*) before banishing herself to summer stock, where her name still had some drawing power.

Author Jess Gregg, who reviewed *Theatre* on opening night, remembers: "Something terrible happened in the last act. I knew the play, I'd seen Cornelia Otis Skinner do it on Broadway and I'd read the book, and all of a sudden Kay had stopped playing the scene and was improvising. She was a very funny, savvy woman, and she was being marvelous, but it was obviously improvisation, and I realized she was covering for someone. It went on and on, and I thought, 'They've got to bring down the curtain,' and then suddenly Tony made his entrance—but looking very different. He had no makeup on." Tony had mistakenly thought his role was done, and the stage manager had hustled him onto the stage at the last minute for the climax of the play.

Kay Francis later told Gregg it had been the worst five minutes of her life. And she kidded Tony about it mercilessly, but kindly, from then on. She had to be kind in the face of talent. "He's very raw in many ways," she confided to Gregg, "but you watch him. He's going to be big."

Tony turned down the opportunity to tour New England in June, opting to stick with his original plan. He boarded a bus for Hollywood—but not for long. Preferring the freedom of the open road and its observable, potentially seduceable strangers, Tony scrambled off the bus and thumbed his boyish act the rest of the way to the Coast.

He'd never had any intention of working as a studio gofer; he spent his summer trying to see various MGM casting directors and producers to convince them he should play the role of Fred Whitmarsh. It wasn't difficult; his father's name still meant something to most of the executives, and MacKenna knew lots of people in the industry. One of the stars MacKenna introduced him to was Humphrey Bogart, who had also known Osgood. Tony would later impress his friends back at school with his tale of visiting Bogart, who walked around the house, drink in hand, getting "a buzz on."

Tony's tenacity eventually paid off. "I hung around the casting gate all summer," he recounted in 1972, "running errands and picking up sandwiches for the guards. One day they were testing Margaret

O'Brien [who, at that point, was neck and neck with Debbie Reynolds for the lead role] and they needed the back of someone's head. They didn't know who to use. Then someone piped up and said, 'How about that kid that's always hanging around here? We could use the back of *his* head!'

"They called me in and I stood right in front of the camera, almost obliterating poor Margaret O'Brien's face and causing a director to say, 'Please move a little to the left.' When he said this, I turned around and said, 'Who, *me?*' and I was in the test." (O'Brien, who was five years Tony's junior, had already retired from the screen the previous year with her withering laurels as MGM's child star of the 1940s; she would not get this or any other comeback role.)

Meanwhile, Tony had to wait to find out if he had actually got his foot in the proverbial door. Reluctantly, he returned to Rollins via New York, uncertain about his future as a film star, but certain he needed to take a more professional approach to his efforts. That meant photos. Jane suggested he go see a young woman named Helen Merrill, who had been the assistant to Marcus Blechman, a popular portrait photographer of the 1930s and 1940s. Blechman had taken many shots of Osgood in his day, and even of Tony as a young child.

Merrill was now a struggling photographer in her own right. Fourteen years Tony's senior, she had been active in the German underground with her father, an American socialist who was married to a German. When the United States entered the war, Helen had left Germany, alone. A strong, proud young woman used to conquering obstacles, she had arrived in New York with nothing in her pockets, and after several disappointing job leads, settled on photography as a trade and an art. In her apartment at 127 West Fifty-sixth Street, where the living room doubled as a studio, Merrill took theatrical photographs for young actors who were struggling like she was. She also rented rooms to them, at an affordable price that included meals. The whole small building, in fact, was made up almost entirely of immigrants like herself; none of them had anything, and consequently money was no status symbol. Merrill was direct, down-to-earth, with an agreeably wry sense of humor. She didn't call everyone "darling" the way Jane did.

Tony was fascinated by the stripped-down, bohemian, but undeniably homey atmosphere of her studio. It was no-nonsense artsy, full of activity and a sense of striving and individuality. He may not have known it then, but he would be back.

Life went on as provincially as usual in Winter Park, especially now that President Wagner had been replaced by art professor Hugh McKean (who just happened to be married to one of Florida's wealthiest philanthropists). John Boyle was still friendly, but cautious. Tony stage-managed a production of Truman Capote's *The Grass Harp*, directed by Professor Dorsett, in mid-November. Miraculously, at the end of the month, a cryptic telegram arrived from MGM demanding that he report to the studio for wardrobe fittings.

Further inquiries revealed that Fred Whitmarsh was indeed Tony's role (much to the delight of Ruth Gordon, a friend of Tony's late father, who many feel championed Tony to be in the film), and that glamorous Jean Simmons had beat out Margaret O'Brien as his leading lady. Spencer Tracy and Teresa Wright had been cast as Gordon's parents, and the maestro would be no less than legendary women's director George Cukor, who had guided Garbo through her exquisite performance in *Camille*, and introduced moviegoers to Tallulah Bankhead in *Tarnished Lady* with Osgood Perkins. An auspicious debut seemed imminent. Tony could see destiny unfolding before his starstruck eyes. *Years Ago* would be shot over the Christmas holidays and into January.

The always supportive Howard Bailey granted Tony a special leave of absence to follow his dream, feeling that it would be the best thing for the boy—knowing, really, that he had no choice but to let him go. Tony was released from his scheduled role in the upcoming production of *Gramercy Ghost*, which was to open on December 9.

If Tony's theater arts cronies were jealous, his brothers at the KA house were genuinely ecstatic and relieved, none more so than John Boyle. In a touching gesture, they took up a contribution among themselves to buy their "poor man's Carleton Carpenter" the bus fare to Hollywood (even though the studio was supplying his air ticket).

Before he left, Tony said good-bye to John Rich. "I'm heading for Hollywood now," he declared, "and I'm still a virgin." Perhaps he was referring to Fred Whitmarsh.

FAME AND FORTUNE

UTH GORDON'S *YEARS AGO* was a small period script that
MGM did not want to make. It had no hook—no wide screen,
no 3-D, no special effects, no all-star cast, no battle scenes, not
even color—no gimmick with which to pull increasingly reticent
audiences into the theater to see it. The advent of television had
caused the major movie studios to think twice about mere artistic
quality; receipts were too far down. What a movie needed in the
1950s was a lure, something grand and flashy that the public couldn't
get from a primitive black-and-white living-room tube. MGM had recently placed high hopes on two big-budget period spectacles, *Ivanhoe*
and *Quo Vadis?*. *Years Ago* offered no opportunity to feed anyone to the
lions. Except maybe Dore Schary.

Schary, a literate man who had worked as a journalist and playwright and had shared a 1938 Academy Award for his screenplay of
MGM's *Boys Town*, had been head of production since 1948, when
he'd replaced the legendary taskmaster, Louis B. Mayer. *Years Ago*,
which the studio had at one time been enthusiastic about, remained
Schary's pet project. But through no fault of his own, or George
Cukor's, the picture ended up costing him considerable professional
credibility.

Tony's first film, which was quickly given the working title *Fame
and Fortune*, was shot entirely in Culver City (budget cuts precluded the

originally intended location photography in New England), with a twenty-four-day production schedule.

Jean Simmons recalls that "suddenly, on the set one day, came this wonderful, sort of gawky, very slim young man. He was supposed to be gawky, you know, with the sleeves too short and all that stuff." Gawkiness was something Tony came more than prepared to play. "He wasn't all that at ease," says Teresa Wright, who had been chosen over both Shirley Booth and Dorothy McGuire to play her first character role as Ruth Gordon's mother. "He was a little bit stiff. But then, as a young boy it was almost rather natural."

"I was so ambitious, nothing was going to stop me," Perkins remembered twenty years later. "I wanted to become a movie star and I would become one. [Spencer Tracy, Jean Simmons, and Cukor] were all a clique, but it didn't bother me; I was too taken up with myself to care." Cukor, never easily manipulated, would have none of Tony's shtick, which he referred to on the set as his "Ogunquit gestures," meaning his broad summer-stock style. The fact that he'd worked with Tony's father on the Tallulah Bankhead vehicle *Tarnished Lady* didn't matter. "Mr. Cukor kind of gave him a bad time," Simmons remembers. According to Wright, "That was just George's way."

As Tony himself described it the following year in *Seventeen* magazine, "Cukor would let me go through my scenes, praise everyone else involved and then he would holler out, 'Tony, you were terrible.' I'd want to sink through the floor! 'Now,' he would go on, 'let's drop that "Aw, shucks, Ma!" school of acting, and try it *this* way.' " In the scene where Tony and Simmons talk in the parlor while her parents are preparing for bed, "I started out to play Fred for laughs as a sheepish, ill-at-ease young fellow the way I was directed in summer stock. Cukor straightened me out."

So did Tracy, whose irascibility was almost as famous as his acting. "I remember saying, 'Good morning, Mr. Tracy' every morning until one day Tracy said, 'Good morning, good morning, good morning, good morning, good morning, good morning, good morning—now that should last you for a week.' " Tony was so put off that he began hiding behind the scenery at lunch break for fear no one would want him at their table.

Nevertheless, he deeply enjoyed the experience of his first film and developed a rapport with Simmons, with whom he shared almost all of his scenes. "They were very dear together and they both had very good singing voices," Teresa Wright recalls. "Tony seemed very shy at first, but when he and Jean would sing, he kind of opened up."

Invited to dine at home with Simmons and her husband, Stewart Granger, Tony distinguished himself with his flair for charades. "He was very funny, with a lovely sense of humor," the actress remembers. "It was very subtle, rather like a Dorothy Parker sense of humor. If you weren't paying attention, you'd miss it."

By February Tony had returned to Florida, "and when people asked me how I spent my Christmas vacation," he later told a *New York Times* reporter, "I got great pleasure out of saying, 'Oh I went to Hollywood and made a movie.'" In a letter to Cukor dated February 5, 1953, Tony politely thanked the director for his firm, minimalist advice, adding bluntly that he hoped he could work for him again sometime. That would never happen. (By 1986, after years of psychoanalysis, Tony would remember Cukor, like his mother, with less generosity: "He had other fish to fry on that film. He treated me with scorn and had only contempt for my lack of experience. He took pleasure in pointing out my weaknesses. . . . After that I left California and erased myself so thoroughly from the Coast that, when I came back, my first screen credit [in *Friendly Persuasion*] read 'Introducing Anthony Perkins,' even though it wasn't quite kosher to introduce an actor who'd already been seen.")

"I gave Anthony Perkins his first big break," Cukor was later quoted. "But don't blame me—that's Hollywood, folks!"

Meanwhile, Tony had to content himself with the Rollins Players, and, on short notice, the lead role of Algernon Moncrief in Oscar Wilde's "trivial comedy for serious people," *The Importance of Being Earnest,* which ran for five performances starting on February 17. Because of his work in Hollywood, now more than ever he was treated as a major asset to the Annie Russell stage. "People *made* him different because they knew he'd been in the movies," one student says. "He was given top billing over other capable people because he would have a draw." But the attention, while gratifying, now bored Tony. With his professional sights set higher, he no longer cared about impressing his amateur colleagues.

"When he came back from Hollywood," Jess Gregg recalls, "he was thought to be much different. People would kid about his clothes, which were a little bit too short for him. He had high-water trousers and cuffs that didn't quite cover his wrists. He was making a real thing of being a gawky young kid, but he hadn't dressed that way before."

Jenelle Bailey, Howard Bailey's new wife, observed that "he didn't open up easily to other people. In fact, I couldn't see that he really related terribly well to the other students. But onstage, of course—all business." Classmate Roger Bentley also remembers the "new" Tony as being "a different person onstage than he was in real life. He was cordial to people, for one thing. When he got offstage he'd just walk away like he'd turned off a switch. His handshake was like a limp dishrag. There was no warmth to him at all."

Rehearsals for *The Importance of Being Earnest* were not the easiest. Tony and Louis Ingram, who played John Worthing, "were very difficult to handle together," says Mrs. Bailey, who was the stage manager. Ingram claims that Tony "would do things that were really calculated to upstage someone else."

Part of the problem was Tony's lack of affinity for the play. "He felt very uncomfortable in a period piece, and really only wanted to do parts where he could be Tony Perkins," Mrs. Bailey says. Her husband felt that the boy needed training in the classics, but Tony was not interested in his role. He continued to slouch forward, as he would for years, and Bailey had a hard time just getting him to stand up straight and act in a more formal way suitable to the drawing-room comedy. To prevent him from constantly putting his hands in his pockets, which had become a lazy habit (the period trousers were not supposed to have pockets), Bailey had Tony's pants stitched up. The classics required too much work for the instant gratification Perkins was used to. He just wanted the adulation he felt he'd earned and deserved—the love he'd worked so hard to get, that he'd missed as a boy.

"You had the feeling that a large part of his drive came from his deep sorrow of having lost his father," says John Rich, who probably knew him better than anyone else at the time.

Despite everything, the performances went off without a hitch, except one. "There was an extra performance on Sunday night which was attended by dignitaries visiting the college," Louis Ingram remembers. "Tony and I got to the theater early and were sitting in the green-room, and this kitten was outside, so we brought it in. Tony said, 'Wouldn't it be fun to bring it onstage?' So we contrived a number of lines that were very Oscar Wilde-ish, sort of arch. I made my entrance with the cat on my lapel, and Tony turned to his butler and said, 'Here, take this kitten that Mr. Worthing has brought us and put it with the lame parrot he brought last week.' But when we tried to take the cat off my lapel, it had dug its claws in and wasn't going to be removed with anything approaching ease—it was like a rubber band that would just elongate every time we tried to pull it off! Tony was one of the most controlled people onstage, but he actually broke down and laughed out of character probably for thirty seconds. It was the only time I'd ever seen him break up."

The show was well received by all but one school critic who shrewdly admonished, "Mr. Perkins, *The Importance of Being Earnest* is a play; not an exercise in putting across the boyish personality."

On March 13, 1953, MGM previewed *Fame and Fortune* at the Encino Theatre in the San Fernando Valley, where nearly three hundred preview cards were distributed to an audience consisting mostly (and most inappropriately) of teenagers. Predictably, male viewers found the film draggy and ambiguous, while female viewers were more enthusiastic. Each performance was rated either "excellent," "good," "fair," or "poor." The three stars garnered a majority of "excellents," while Tony's balance lingered in the "good." Among the female comments were several saying, "Would like to see more of Anthony Perkins."

From March 31 through his twenty-first birthday on April 4, Tony made what would be his last stage appearance at the Annie Russell, in Valentin Kataev's *Squaring the Circle,* a bedroom farce set in "red" Moscow, which made fools out of Communists and their ideology. It was perfect fare for 1953.

"He would always come in with his lines perfectly memorized the first day of rehearsal," cast member Richard Lesneski recalls, "but he'd always sit by himself. He didn't mingle with the rest of us. We were always joking around, laughing; he was very aloof. If you asked him something, he was quite approachable, friendly. But he didn't volunteer any information." Making a movie, which had so thrilled him and had seemed to promise so much, proved instead to have been a fickle, isolated event. Now that he was back in real life—still the same, still mortal, unchanged—the feeling of disappointment and boredom drained the old activities of any excitement or purpose. Sitting alone, pondering the drear of the amateur, Tony plotted his inevitable next move.

The announcement that he was transferring to New York's Columbia University to be near theaters and agents caused some resentment within the department. Though no one said anything, the feeling was that Tony had known exactly what he was doing months before, when he'd first convinced Howard Bailey to let him go to Hollywood. Forty years later, the refrain at Rollins College remains bitter: "He never really came back."

Actually, Tony had no intention of going to Columbia either. New York meant the theater, not more school. Nor did he have any intention of living with Jane, not that he could have with Michaela around. Jane's apartment had never really been his home. Instead, Tony went directly to photographer Helen Merrill's door on West Fifty-sixth Street, and, munching on a box of cookies, asked, with all his calculated charm, for a room.

She said no.

Merrill didn't want any unemployed actors around, and she already had one young actor living with her, Richard Franchot, who was John Kerr's understudy in the new Elia Kazan production, *Tea and Sympathy*.

But something about Tony hooked her. Perhaps it was the fact that he was so obviously a child in need of love, perhaps it was the fact that her own daughter, Bambi, was far away in Germany with Helen's ex-husband. Maybe it was the cookies. Whatever the reason, Helen made Tony a deal: if he promised to enroll at Columbia, she would give him a room, at a rent of fifty-five dollars a month (Franchot had been paying eighty dollars), which included breakfast, use of her phone, laundry, and utilities. Tony happily agreed; John Kerr was also at Columbia studying Russian, so why not.

The Actress, as *Fame and Fortune* had been flatly retitled, much to everyone's chagrin, premiered on Sunday, October 11, at the Trans-Lux Sixtieth Street Theatre with a benefit screening for the American Theatre Wing. Tony, Jane, and Michaela were there, along with many of Jane's old theatrical friends.

Despite some laudatory reviews—critic Bosley Crowther praised

Tracy and Simmons, adding, "In our enthusiasm, we have almost over-looked the wonderful quietness yet firmness with which Teresa Wright plays the mother . . . and the amusing gaucherie of Anthony Perkins in the role of a high-collared beau"—the film was not the same one that George Cukor and authors Garson Kanin and Ruth Gordon had set out to make. The lackluster teenybopper preview cards had caused MGM and producer Lawrence Weingarten to demand major recutting and redubbing of the final picture; in a changing market, the studio had no confidence in the genre. As Teresa Wright recalls, "MGM didn't know what to do with it, I suppose because it was quiet and didn't have music or a big man-woman schmaltzy vehicle thing. The sad thing was that MGM did absolutely nothing with it, they didn't adver-tise it—we thought they weren't even going to release it! They finally just sort of put it out, you know. You'd think they'd have had the sense to realize they had something with a Spencer Tracy film directed by George Cukor. But they didn't. That's the kind of mentality the big studios had then." Consequently, *The Actress* ended up being one of MGM's worst box-office flops of the year. Surely Tony had heard the old adage that you're only as good as your last picture. This was his first. Later, he would remember *The Actress* as "a flop for everyone, es-pecially me."

Nevertheless, his performance as Fred Whitmarsh, so full of promise, remains one of his freshest and most natural appearances onscreen, with not a hint of the pinched, side-talking mannerisms that would mar so much of his later work. In his sole piece of publicity generated by the picture, he told *Seventeen* magazine that "more than school, more than getting married, more than a play on Broadway, more than a mil-lion dollars," he wanted to make another movie. He already knew just what to say.

HOME

27 WEST FIFTY-SIXTH STREET was smack in "the heart of the dance belt," as that part of the theater district was unofficially (and lewdly) coined. Right down the street from the backside of Carnegie Hall, and directly across the street from the City Center theater, it was surrounded by the landmarks of culture that New York in the 1950s was still known for. At that time, it was not uncommon to see living icons like Arturo Toscanini or Marlon Brando having a cup of coffee at the Carnegie Tavern on the corner of Seventh Avenue. It was the perfect location for an ambitious young actor like Tony Perkins.

"Ours was a building of eccentrics," remembers Mario Busoni, who lived with his musical family, direct relatives of the composer Ferruccio Busoni, two flights up from Helen Merrill. "It was absolutely New York in that respect." Directly above Merrill was an older single lady, the Busonis over her, an Italian mafioso (or so the other tenants thought) on the fourth floor, and a struggling painter and his wife in the garret. In the basement was a greasy spoon luncheonette, known fondly as Steve's after its owner, even though the actual name of the place was something else entirely. The neighbors rarely spoke to one another, except in passing to complain when a bathtub overflowed, or to toss grumbling suspicions about one another back and forth. Mario, who was sixteen at the time and whose family had lived in the building for years before Helen Merrill moved into the first floor, only met his downstairs neighbor when she invited him in from the street to see her photographic darkroom, which she had set up in the small space under the stairs.

"She'd come here as a young woman and had really gone through the school of hard knocks," Busoni recalls fondly. "She was almost a street kid who'd made it, a tough cookie without being tough. She had tenacity, not toughness. But her real vocation was being the confidante of young people."

To accommodate Tony, Helen moved Dick Franchot out of Bambi's room, where he'd been staying, and into the living room, part of which served as Helen's studio. Tony was then given the bedroom, which was small and spare, almost cell-like, with a white bed, a white dresser, a white chair, and child's stars painted on the blue ceiling, stars that may have reminded the boy of his Florida days after Osgood's death. Franchot remembers that Tony kept his new room "absolutely neat, very orderly. It was that of a person who thought things through very carefully." They all shared one bathroom.

"One was immediately charmed by Tony even though at the same time he was ill at ease," Busoni recalls. "It was a strange combination." For Helen, it was an irresistible one. "I guess I didn't have the emotional need that Helen was looking for in somebody," Franchot muses, "so she took on, almost as a career, Tony Perkins. I think Helen would have liked to have kept Bambi, that she was looking for other children to raise. I fell into that category, as did Tony. But I was more independent of her than he was."

Helen and Tony quickly developed a comfortable camaraderie, and a private language that helped him communicate more easily. "Tony just became part of the house," Busoni remembers. "He loved the sound of language. Helen and I both spoke German, and we would make up nonsense phrases in German, and he would banter them about." Every evening Helen, Tony, and whoever else in the extended family was around would take Punky, their stray dog (or "boy," as Helen referred to canines), which Tony had named after the cat in *The Actress*, outside to "make Belsen," which was the ugliest expression they could come up with barring "shit." Other words in their homey vernacular were "Mr. Winker" (the local butcher, who used to wink at Helen), "singing" (urination), and "the Delanceys" (diarrhea, due to the fact that Tony had gotten the runs once from some food down on the Lower East Side). "Subway" became "*suppen veg*," the way an immigrant might say it, and one never said "good-bye"—that was always just "okay," or rather the informal German expression "*ok-nak.*"

Everything was twisted around or had a little German added to it, and Tony especially liked to use umlauts. Helen became "Hüly," and Tony, in turn, became "Töne Bönes," or just "Bönes" for short, due partly to his huge, thin physique, and partly to the fact that he would regularly joke that his cheek-*bönes* were his best asset. "When they're gone," went the refrain, "I'm finished." (Later, in Hollywood, he would have some molars removed to make his cheekbones even more pronounced.) He and Dick Franchot called each other "Tone" since Franchot was a first cousin of actor Franchot Tone.

One of Tony's favorite pastimes was sketching caricatures of Hüly, which depicted needs and fulfillments that could never be resolved in life. "Helen said she would love to do photography forever," Mario Busoni recalls, "if she didn't have to deal with the customers—*that* she couldn't stand. So he drew Helen leaning back, looking through a periscope-like device attached to other things that went on and on and on forever, and at the very end was the client being photographed. The character of Helen would be grotesquely accurate, drawn with all the insecurity she felt about her face." Helen's hawklike nose had been broken once, and her chin protruded upward. According to Busoni, "She looked like a Punch-and-Judy puppet, but with real character. She used to joke about it." Both her daughter and her sister, who worked as a model in Europe, were beautiful leggy blonds, an irony that became part of the repertoire as well; Helen enjoyed relating the fact that her sister worked modeling coffins, posing as a beautiful corpse.

Like a watchful parent, Merrill took Tony's drawings seriously, even framing some of them. She worried that her new charge, who seemed to have so many natural gifts—drawing, writing, painting, even singing—would become a dilettante. As a general studies student at Columbia, Tony read ravenously—Shakespeare, Nabokov, Updike, Lawrence Durrell—and Helen encouraged him in that. He was bright and quick, and as wary of empty pleasantry as she was, but his lack of discipline concerned her.

For all her idiosyncrasies, Helen was social and made friends of some of her clients. It was not uncommon for Judy Garland, Jack Palance, or Elia Kazan to stop by for a visit. "She laughed easily and was a good listener, an appreciative listener," Busoni says. "And she remembered everything about you."

Tony wasn't quite as easygoing. Though he was an avid Garland fan, he always vanished when company arrived. According to Busoni, "Tony would go immediately into hiding and knock on the pipe, which meant 'Help, bring something to read.' I'd go down the fire escape from the third floor and hand him a magazine or whatever, and he'd be in there an hour, sometimes three, depending on how long it took for the company to leave. I would have thought the interest in meeting these theater people might overrun the shyness, but it didn't." It was also Tony's own way of telling Helen he wanted his new home, his first real home, to be his alone.

If he wasn't hiding, he liked to talk. Busoni remembers clearly the "funny whimsy in the room when he was around. You could never tell what little joke might start something going. He was very shy and yet very social, caustic yet friendly. The dichotomy was constant. The way he spoke had a definite rhythm—a halting, strange, amused yet insecure rhythm. That scene in *Psycho* where he's describing why the motel isn't doing well anymore is not acting. That's how Tony was."

"He was able to lavish tremendous love and affection on the dog, Punky," Dick Franchot concurs, "but with people he was very private, very withdrawn. His relationship at that time consisted of Helen Merrill, and he seemed to be limited to that. His life was with her."

Despite the fact that Jane was just a few blocks away on the East Side, her visits to West Fifty-sixth Street were infrequent. "She'd breeze in, affecting a conspicuous nonchalance," Busoni recalls. "I took one look at her and knew she was the hardest, coldest bitch in the world. She seemed not to care a damn about him." Jane and Helen tolerated each other, but Helen found her a frightened woman, uncomfortable even with her own child. Dutifully, Tony scheduled regular dinners with his mother, usually over at her apartment on East Fifty-first Street. "He didn't allow himself to lose his temper with her," observed writer Louis Peterson, who had lived in Bambi's room before Franchot and still dropped in for an occasional visit. "But according to Tony, she was a pain in the ass."

Once in a while, someone would be invited along to dine with

Jane. Franchot remembers one such dinner: "It was lovely. There was no antagonism, no animosity. If she was domineering, it was very subtle. It was not apparent to me. Helen was domineering. Jane was totally willing to turn him over to her.

"The deepest conversations Tony and I had were about Osgood Perkins. He stated many times that he wanted to be as good an actor as his father, and how important that was to him. I mean, his goal was to exceed the fame of his father. If anything, that was a standard against which it was very hard to measure up. It was a major drive, and a major obstacle."

Contrary to what he would later tell reporters ("I hardly remember him"), Tony secretly knew every part his father had played, word for word. He wanted to be a star, and he told Helen that if he didn't make it by the time he was twenty-four, he'd go back to school and become a physicist. Much to Helen's regret, acting was not something he studied; instead, he practiced signing his autograph and worried that the name "Anthony" was too long for a marquee. He readily admitted that he dreamed of having his name in lights and spelled out on a dressing-room door. To support and humor him, Helen had a box made in which Tony's name was arranged in Christmas lights. She put it on a shelf over his bed. The weight of the box scared Tony, who was always afraid it would come crashing down on him during the night.

As much as young Perkins liked to pretend he was not his father's son, Osgood's name opened the doors to casting agents. It was an old friend of Osgood and Jane's, June Walker, who arranged for Tony to meet Edith Van Cleve, who had worked with Osgood as an actress on Broadway and was now an agent at the powerful Music Corporation of America (or MCA). Van Cleve took him on. "Tony wanted work and was willing to try anything," she told *McCall's* in 1957. "I've never handled a boy with such an intense drive to be in show business."

New York was then the center of live television as well as the legitimate theater, and Van Cleve felt certain she could find Tony work in the new medium. The networks were making great use of young talent; actors like James Dean, Susan Strasberg, and Grace Kelly all appeared in early television productions before going on to Broadway or Hollywood. But for Tony, with his too tall, too thin, cranelike physique, the going was slow. He wasn't macho enough for the Method era, when surly Marlon Brando, the Actors Studio's neurotic hulk, was the be-all and end-all of acting.

Dick Franchot remembers Tony being even more quiet than usual back at Helen's during the late fall of 1953. Charles Williamson, too, recalls Tony being very discouraged over his future as an actor, and threatening, "If I don't act, I'll be a writer." At his lowest point, Tony reportedly walked into Van Cleve's office and announced, "Now I've heard them all. I got turned down for a part because the director said I was too good-looking."

At last, Tony broke through the casting barrier with a small part on the popular television show *You Are There*. Unfortunately, no record exists of the episode or even what historical moment Tony might have reenacted. Early television, despite its moniker as "the golden age," was sadly underdocumented. Some kinescopes, which were made for broadcast in the western time zones, are still around, but for the most part live television was just that, a series of electric moments that flashed and vanished. Nevertheless, Tony managed to appear on shows such as *Studio One*, *The U.S. Steel Hour*, *General Electric Theater*, and *The Big Story*, among others, which offered him the chance to act opposite the likes of Eli Wallach, Susan Strasberg, and even legendary movie monster Boris Karloff. He was soon announcing himself to Van Cleve as "the busiest actor in television."

Tony's clean, quiet, almost fey introspection—his own personal brand of Method acting, free of dogma—which had at first been a detriment to his career, became an asset once directors had worked with him. Richard Dunlap, who produced and directed *Kraft Television Theatre*, recalls Perkins as "so different from Jimmy Dean, who was often so sullen and angry. Tony was thoughtful and cooperative. He also wasn't so involved in the 'Technique'—at least he didn't bring it to the studio. He was a cooperative young actor to work with, and in those days that was not the norm." Word quickly got around that Tony was a good boy, a refreshing throwback to an earlier theatrical era, who wouldn't mumble before the cameras and slow up production with tedious preparation and angst.

He generally charmed those he worked with, especially if they were older. The late Dolly Haas, who costarred with him on an episode of NBC's *Armstrong Circle Theater*, remembered him as "a most sensitive, wonderful young actor." During rehearsals for a *Theatre Guild on the Air* with Barbara Baxley, Jessie Royce Landis, and Walter Matthau, Tony played catch with Matthau on the street during rehearsal breaks, actually tossing a baseball back and forth and catching it with a dreaded mitt, something he had never done as a real boy. Cigarettes hanging out of both their mouths (it was chic to smoke then), Tony insisted upon calling Matthau "Dad," claiming that the older actor resembled the long-gone Osgood. The resemblance is hard to see, but clearly Tony enjoyed acting out the father-son relationship.

Director James Sheldon, who had also directed the difficult Dean, remembers Tony as funny and feisty. When he broached the subject of whether Tony had considered taking any young actresses around town for publicity, Tony responded, with surprising vitriol, that if a pill existed that could make him like women, he'd grind it into the ground with his foot. An actor could get away with statements like that in the more permissive theater community of New York, but not in Hollywood, as Tony would soon discover for himself.

During the week it took to rehearse his *Kraft Theatre* episode, "The Missing Years," which starred Osgood's old friend Mary Astor and aired on February 3, 1954, Tony only asked for special treatment once, when he asked Richard Dunlap for an extra hour off during lunch. The answer was no. But when Tony explained that it was the only time "Mr. Kazan" could read him for the replacement cast of *Tea and Sympathy*, Dunlap agreed.

Just about every movie magazine since has declared that Elia Kazan gave Tony the role in *Tea and Sympathy* as a consolation prize for losing the lead in the film *East of Eden* to James Dean. "That's bullshit," Kazan maintains today. "I never saw Tony. I met him because I needed a replacement for whoever it was who was playing the part [in *Tea and Sympathy*] he finally played. I knew his father well and liked him very much, and then I met the boy a few times and liked him personally, but not like I liked his father. I had great respect for Osgood."

"I told Kazan about Tony," said John Kerr. "I'd never seen him act, but physically he was very right."

He was more than right; he'd already lived the part of the guitar-strumming, poetic college boy who prefers music to football and is accused of homosexuality because of it. But in Tony's real-life case there was no beautiful housemother to step in and heterosexualize him at the final curtain. There was just hawk-faced Helen, who had no illusions about such things, and mother Jane, whose only comment when he told her he'd got the part was, "You'll never be as good as John Kerr."

Tea and Sympathy was Robert Anderson's first play, and the first unqualified triumph of the Playwrights Company, which had been founded in 1938 by Maxwell Anderson, S. N. Behrman, Sidney Howard, Elmer Rice, and Robert Sherwood as a vehicle for presenting their own works (Robert Anderson and Kurt Weill joined later). By early December 1953, *Tea and Sympathy*, which had just opened at the Ethel Barrymore Theatre on September 30, had paid back its entire sixty-thousand-dollar investment and had even earned a profit of more than twelve thousand dollars. This was due largely to the drawing power of British beauty Deborah Kerr (no relation to John), who had starred in several popular films, including *Black Narcissus*, *The Hucksters*, *Quo Vadis?* and 1953's *From Here to Eternity*. In her Broadway debut as the man-saving faculty wife, Laura Reynolds, Kerr had won the hearts of the New York critics.

But the play's appeal went deeper than that. Dramatically taut and well crafted, and meant as a liberal reproach of American machismo, *Tea and Sympathy* was nevertheless a seductive reflection of the prevailing postwar puritanism, which had run like wildfire through the American psychiatric community, that homosexuality (or "sissyhood") could be cured by the proverbial "right woman." For theatergoing gay men, it was the only Broadway offering that even approached dealing with the pain and shame they were feeling in the 1950s. Unfortunately, the play's denouement—a "sensitive" cliffhanger which suggests that the young protagonist and his house mom are about to jump into bed together and save his reputation—smugly reinforced the societal stance that homosexuality didn't *really* exist, or at least wasn't a viable option. Noel Coward denounced the play as "a mixture of naïveté and dishonesty . . . treated untruly and lasciviously."

"It was the best part ever written for a young guy," Tony maintained without irony almost twenty years later. "I felt so involved with that particular play. In many ways I *was* Tom Lee."

His reading, onstage at the Barrymore with Deborah Kerr, was difficult. But it didn't matter; Kazan cast him anyway, despite his feeling that Tony was "quite unsure of himself . . . off-beat. But he had something that I recognized as talent—sensitivity, perhaps."

The next morning, Tony systematically obliterated himself from Columbia University. Just a month short of graduating, he opted instead for rehearsals. "I couldn't do both," he told *The Saturday Evening Post*. "And rather than go to the registrar's office and get in a big deal, I just picked up my books, took my name off my locker and went to as many classrooms as possible and erased my name off the seating plan. I thought I'd get a kind of kick out of seeing how completely I could vanish without leaving a trace."

Poet and photographer Ira Cohen, who had met Tony in Professor Ernest Brennecke's Shakespeare course (which they had both dropped from boredom), remembers running into his former classmate on the street: "I asked him what he was doing and he said, 'Oh, I have a part in a play.' I was not even aware that he was an actor. I asked what play it was, and, little by little, he volunteered that it was *Tea and Sympathy*. So I asked him if he had a speaking part, and he said, in a very shy way, averting his eyes slightly, 'Yes.'

" 'What kind of part is it?' I asked.

" 'Well, I play the boy.' I'll never forget how sweetly he said it."

Tony was set to replace John Kerr, who was leaving for Hollywood, on May 31, 1954. Deborah Kerr would also be leaving the show that week to star in a film of Graham Greene's novel *The End of the Affair*, before taking *Tea and Sympathy* on national tour. There was talk that she would be replaced by Viveca Lindfors, who, along with Geraldine Page, had been one of the original choices for the role. But it was soon announced that Oscar-winning film star Joan Fontaine would make her Broadway debut as Laura Reynolds.

To prepare her for New York, Kazan's friend, actor Karl Malden, who had actually cast *Tea and Sympathy* when *On the Waterfront* had demanded the director's presence elsewhere, rehearsed Fontaine for two weeks on the Warner Brothers lot in Burbank, California, where he was under contract. Tony came, too, and stayed with Malden and Kazan in the Hollywood Hills home of Margo and Eddie Albert. Tony and Malden rarely saw Kazan, who was again occupied with other business.

One week into rehearsal, Kazan asked to see what they'd done, so Malden, Fontaine, and Perkins arranged to give a performance for the director at Fontaine's home. Afterward, Kazan told Malden, "You're doing great with Tony, but she's taking the easy way out. Push her a little. She's so used to playing her personality, push her a little."

"The second week," Malden recalls, "I started to push her a little more, and she rebelled, in a very nice way. She just said, 'I feel ill, I'm going home.' She left, and I said to Tony, 'She's not ill. She doesn't like what I'm doing.' We laughed, and I told him, 'I don't give a shit. It's her fight and she's going to have to do it. I'll concentrate on you.' So I did. It was as much his play as hers. He was man enough not to say anything. She walked out, but he wanted to rehearse, he wanted to work. So I promised him we'd work like mad, and we did. Joan rebelled because she thought Kazan was going to direct her. When she didn't see that, she was teed off.

"To make it even more difficult, Kazan went home by plane, but he put us on a train. So I had three more days with them to rehearse lines, meanings. And I didn't give her anything, my whole effort went to Tony. I tried to get him to let go. I'd say, 'Even if it's wrong, try it.' He was afraid to make that step, of being laughed at. Later on, as he got older, I think he didn't care. But at that time, he worried about it."

Back home, with Tony's debut looming, Helen asked Dick Franchot, who was now understudying both John Kerr and Tony, to move out. "Helen said she didn't feel it would be good for the star and the understudy to be living in the same place," Franchot remembers. "That was fine with me, I was ready to move out." With her new boy on the ascent, Merrill was restrategizing her camp. "Helen was very manipulating—that's such a negative word, but it's true—very controlling," says Franchot. "I heard somebody refer to her as the Witch of Belsen. As years went by, she began to take on the role of Tony's protector."

"Helen was maybe the weirdest woman in Christendom," recalls Gwen Davis, who met Tony in Los Angeles just a few years later. "She was like dealing with a dragon keeping the gate. It was horrible. I was frightened of her. Tony did that deliberately, he chose a dragon to hide behind."

According to Henry Scammell, Merrill "ran interference" for Tony, screening his phone calls and keeping old friends at bay. That was one thing she had in common with Jane, says Scammell, the view "that Tony's life was set apart, that he shouldn't dawdle too long at the starting gate with people he'd known in pasture."

But Helen could not help Tony at rehearsals, which at first went badly. Kazan and Robert Anderson were both, according to the actor, "in despair" over his performance. At one point, during an extra rehearsal, Kazan was overheard saying, "Well at least he *looks* good up there."

"Tony had an oddness about him that Jack Kerr didn't," recalls Anderson. "Jack was a very straightforward young man. Tony always had an edge to him, and that's what made him a big movie star. All of his movements were angular or abrupt, sort of like a large crane. I guess we just thought that Jack was a little less strange. That's why we'd picked him. We just felt in his nature that he was more solid."

Kazan readily admits that "there wasn't much [direction]. I was busy, and Tony followed what what's his name—Johnny Kerr—was doing. He listened attentively and did his best, but I didn't have much time for him."

Problems continued, too, with Joan Fontaine, who was by all accounts difficult. A top Hollywood star throughout the 1940s, with a list of prestige pictures to her credit that included Alfred Hitchcock's *Suspicion*, Robert Stevenson's *Jane Eyre*, and Max Ophuls's *Letter from an Unknown Woman*, Fontaine's star had begun to fade with the advent of younger celluloid beauties such as Elizabeth Taylor and Jean Simmons. By the time she took on *Tea and Sympathy*, she had been reduced to acting in more pedestrian flicks like the Bob Hope vehicle *Casanova's Big Night*. Whereas the two Kerrs had conveyed an unmistakable sexual tension on stage, Fontaine and Perkins had no rapport at all.

"I'd envisioned her as the frail ladies she'd played in films, and found that she was a lot less of a lady than Deborah Kerr," recalls Yale Wexler, an understudy who eventually took over the part of Tom Lee's roommate, Al (originally played by *Bewitched*'s Dick York). "She was full of rather vile language."

Alan Sues, who played the bullish Ralph and later achieved stardom as a regular on TV's *Laugh-In*, concurs that Fontaine was "the complete opposite of anything you'd ever seen on screen. She was a broad, and that was a shocker to everybody. She was a really big party girl, just going a mile a minute. Once I saw her come to a matinee wearing a fur coat, and she took it off and underneath she had on a two-piece bathing suit with sand all over. She'd been at the beach, and they'd flown her in to get her there on time. She put her costume on right over that, took a swig of brandy, went out and was fine in the show.

"Tony was the total opposite of that. He wanted you to think that he was preparing for the part. She'd go, 'Oh, Tony, get off it.' She wouldn't pretend that they were making great art. He didn't like her because she would say, 'Hey, why don't we all go out and get drunk?' and he was looking at it completely as a career move. That was the friction."

Mary Fickett, who understudied both Kerr and Fontaine, remembers that Fontaine "wasn't Tony's kind of actress. She approached things from the outside in, the things that concerned her had more to do with the external. That would never have been true of Tony, who was all internal. She was more of a posturer."

Tony so disliked his costar that one night after the show he reportedly complained to Jane, "I can't work with that woman! I can't! I won't!" To which she coolly retorted, "Are you a boy or an actor?"

Differences aside, Tony and Joan Fontaine received good notices from the press. "Miss Fontaine gives a forceful and thoughtful performance," Brooks Atkinson wrote in the *New York Times* on August 15. "She is personally modest and professionally able. . . . Still, something is missing. Call it the luminous quality that Miss Kerr brought to the part. There was a delicacy about her acting that gave the play a grace of spirit which is lacking now. . . . Miss Fontaine's acting is equally gallant but more rational. Her Laura seems to know exactly what she is doing. . . .

"Mr. Perkins' Tom is softer and shyer. A gangling, frowning, sweetly humorous lad, he is winning and disarming, perhaps a little more helpless than he was originally. . . . He gives a mature performance of an immature role."

As Tony's confidence gradually grew, so did his ego; despite his success, it was generally felt that he was not pleased to be playing the second cast. "I think Tony got the idea that I wasn't fond of him because we'd picked John first," Robert Anderson says. "He sat deliberately in this strange, dark little dressing room. I guess it must have been Jack's room, too, but boy, it was just . . . You went upstairs, 'Hi, Tony, how are things?' 'Oh, you here again?' Very curt. He was always very defensive with me, not expressed, but very clear. He was always strumming his guitar or doing various things, and I got a feeling of inhospitality. I never even had a meal with him."

Of all the people in the cast, it was Alan Sues whom Tony chose to be most friendly with; the comic's humor relaxed the self-conscious star. "I was funny, and I wasn't a threat to him," Sues explains. "I watched Tony, and I wished a lot of times that I had the knack for manipulating people that he did. Because he did manipulate them very well. You know, if you play that kind of sensitive, I-don't-know-if-I-can-get-through-this sort of thing, people come to you. His approach was that he was suffering, that stuff was going on inside him, and I don't think it was. His strong suit was knowing how to project an image. He created a charisma about himself. Who knows whether that's really being an artist.

"He was always sort of conning you. After a while, it got to me, and I didn't want to see him as much because he would always say things like, 'I just can't do it. I just can't do it.' I'd ask, 'What?' 'I want the newspaper. Would you go and buy it for me?' He would do that to everybody. He was very friendly, if you wanted to play his games."

With his newfound success and the adherent paycheck, Tony's tightfistedness, which he had inherited from Jane, took on bigger dimensions as well. "Helen Merrill used to mend his T-shirts until they were like lacework," Sues recalls. "One time, he came to my apartment in July, and he was wearing a tweed suit. I said, 'Jesus, Tony, it's so hot!' And he said, 'Well, it'll be cool in a couple of months.' He was so tight with money."

Despite their friendship, Alan was never invited to Tony's home. "That was his world with Helen Merrill. She spooked me. She didn't want anybody near Tony. I'm sure she had a sort of love affair going on in her head, 'This is my boy' or whatever, and I'm sure he said things to her to make that world continue. She felt she was in control, but I'm sure he really was."

Around this time, Fred Rogers, who hadn't seen Tony since his freshman year at Rollins, ran in to him on the street: "I was working in New York and had gotten married in '52. Joanne and I were walking down Fifth Avenue, and all of a sudden we saw this person in sneakers on a bicycle. It turned out to be Tony, and I hailed him.

"He was just thrilled to see us. He got off his bike and said, 'Come on! Let's go to the top of this building.' I don't remember what building it was, but we went to the roof, he made paper airplanes, and we threw them off the top of the building. That was so typical of Tony and his enthusiasm.

"I wish that we'd been able to stay close after that. But his was a very different life from the one that I had chosen."

The general consensus backstage was that Tony had no romantic liaisons. To Yale Wexler, he seemed "more asexual than homosexual." Indeed, the very nature of the play that was putting Perkins's name on the Broadway map and training him as an actor must have been paralyzing him personally.

"I would never let myself go long enough to become another person. I'd be afraid I might not get back," Tony said of his own approach to acting. But Tom Lee wasn't another person. Every night, on the stage of the Ethel Barrymore Theatre, Tony relived the nightmare of his first semester at Rollins, and every night the audience applauded him, poured out their love for him, as the final curtain fell on the redemptive fantasy ending. *Tea and Sympathy* gave Tony a public forum which allowed him to come perilously close to revealing the truth about himself, then pull back and, with the help of his lady savior, "lick this thing."

> TOM: *Everything I've been doing all my life makes me look like a fairy. . . .*
> LAURA: *. . . one day you'll meet a girl, and it will be right. (Tom turns away in disbelief.) Tom, believe me.*
> TOM: *I wish I could. But a person knows—knows inside.*

Night after night, Tony rewrote his past, denying his homosexuality and acting out his renouncement for all the world to see. The fact that, for the first time in his life, he was making real money (about four hundred dollars a week) and being publicly praised for "straightening" himself out probably brainwashed him as well as any psychiatrist at the time could have.

> LAURA: *You men think you can decide on who is a man, when only a woman can really know.*

"Tony was not a demonstrative person in any way, on any level of emotional experience in his private life," observed Dick Franchot. "He saved it all for his performances. As far as I could tell, he totally ignored [his sexuality]. So therefore it was an area of obvious discomfort."

"I don't know what his love life was then," Alan Sues admits, "but whatever it was, I imagine it was fleeting. At that time, there was never a gay bar you didn't go down an alley to get to, and you were always worried that there might be a raid. I don't think Tony would've taken a chance like that. He was always guarded. Nothing was going to get in the way of his career."

Tony's nocturnal habit of disappearing after performances, as he had at Rollins, continued. "Every night, Tony would go down to Forty-second Street until two or three in the morning to see any old film that he could," Yale Wexler recalls. "Most New York actors in those days weren't interested in films, even declined offers to go to Hollywood because their friends who were contract players had no control over their careers." But Tony loved the old films of directors like Fritz Lang, John Ford, and Howard Hawks.

Going to the movies, however, served another purpose, depending on the time of day. Fifties gay men met wherever they could, wherever they would be most invisible, and his forays into dark movie houses probably offered an easy sexual outlet to help him wind down from the continuous pressure of the show. Certain legitimate movie theaters were notorious in the silent gay community as secret sexual meeting places, tacitly known to be active on different days, at different times. Tony was a regular at the Loews Fifty-first Street (now the Loews New York Hotel) and the RKO Fifty-eighth Street on Third Avenue (long since replaced by a McDonald's fast-food franchise).

According to one daytime participant, who wishes to remain anonymous, "Both theaters had these enormous staircases that went up to the very top balcony, and there were shows on the stairs that were better than what was on the screen. This was usually early in the day, during the first show, from about noon to three o'clock.

"I remember a guy who was a salesman, always dressed in a suit and tie. He was rather short, five foot seven, and very, very attractive. He was an exhibitionist. People used to wait for him. He would put down his attaché case, loosen his tie, and whip out this humongous dick, which would draw an incredible crowd—including yours truly and Mr. T.P. He would never let anyone touch it, but we could all watch.

And, of course, everyone would get so hot watching this guy masturbate that one thing would lead to another.

"Everyone knew each other's faces, but nobody talked. Tony and I would nod, acknowledge each other's presence, but we would never speak. It was totally anonymous. I did not know who he was until five or six months after the initial contact. Then, after he became a star, I never saw him on the staircase. There were other actors who were there, but not him."

In the collective American mind, Tony's kind didn't really exist. And Tony, who now existed as a big Broadway star, had nowhere else to go—until one hot August night when an idealistic young man who had seen him from across the footlights came backstage to say hello.

6

PROMISE

ILLIAM, A HARVARD SCHOLAR originally from the Midwest, had been in New York just over a month when he accompanied a friend to see *Tea and Sympathy*. Forty years later, he still remembers the evening well: "We had a fine time, although the play itself seemed dishonest, even to our fifties ears. If it was wrong to persecute the boy because 'it' wasn't true, did that mean it would be all right to persecute him if 'it' *were* true? In any case, that night I fell in love with the actor who was now the boy upstairs. I was twenty-four, just out of the army, a graduate student at Columbia, and it didn't even occur to me not to try my luck."

The next night, dressed in head-to-toe Brooks Brothers, he arrived at the stage door and asked to see Mr. Perkins, dropping the name of a mutual acquaintance. He was admitted to Tony's dressing room, where "the scene which followed, while romantic at the time, seems comic in retrospect." Hardly a professional actor, he pretended to be interested in getting work with the road company of *Tea and Sympathy*, and Tony, who had nothing to do with the casting, feigned interest in helping him. William was smaller than Tony, slim and boyishly pretty—exactly the type that would later become an addiction for the star.

"It was pretty obvious that we were actually interested in each other," William recalls. "I smoked several nervous cigarettes, although he had no ashtray and clearly disliked the smoke in his dressing room. He closed the door, 'so we could hear better,' and managed to let his dressing gown fall open so I could see he was naked except for his jockey shorts." It was a carefully executed move. The star already had plans that night, so they agreed to meet in his dressing room again the following week and go for a drink from there, ostensibly to discuss business.

As neither of them were drinkers, they ended up having sandwiches and tea at a nearby restaurant. William was staying in a sublet on the East Side, and invited Tony over, "just to see where I lived." Perkins agreed, but had to walk his dog first; if William would help him do that, he'd gladly come by for more tea. He'd been working so hard, he said, it would be fun to just sit and talk.

On Fifty-sixth Street, William was told to wait outside while Tony went in to get Punky; they then walked to Central Park, around the lake, and back. "I had the impression that Tony lived alone," William remembers, "but that later proved to be false." Without the dog, they went to William's place.

"We sat on the sofa beside the fire and did the excruciating dance of the fifties, moving toward each other without admitting we were doing it. Finally, we grabbed each other and began kissing. At some point, we stopped to look at each other, and I said, 'I'm looking for someone.' He said, 'I am too.' That was the end of the conversation." They spent the night together.

Tony never made more than a few cryptic mentions about his earlier love life, but William remembers him "showing me a photograph of a suntanned, swimsuited Florida boy. In any case, it was quite clear on our first night together that he was sexually experienced, probably more so than I."

Later that week, they saw each other again, and began the closeted ritual of meeting in the greeting card section of a nearby Broadway drugstore instead of at the theater. From there they would go to Fifty-sixth Street and walk Punky, then return and indulge in "lengthy kissing in the foyer of his house. Apparently, Tony was quite sure no one would come down the stairs. I didn't understand why he didn't ask me in, but I didn't want to push anything." They agreed to spend Saturday night together at William's so they could sleep late and enjoy each other's company on Sunday.

Two things happened on Sunday, however, that nearly frightened skittish Tony off. "Having slept late, we were lounging about the apartment, enjoying being nude together. Suddenly, Tony decided to make scrambled eggs. He pulled on his jockey shorts, saying he wasn't going to expose his essential parts to the hazards of a hot stove, and proceeded to cook scrambled eggs and toast, all the while doing an impromptu comic monologue which combined teaching me how to cook with sexual innuendos.

"Just as he was dishing up the two plates, we heard a key in the lock of the hallway door, and in walked the apartment's owner. He saw us, was astonished, recognized Tony, was even more astonished, apologized profusely for disturbing us, and made a bumbling exit. After his departure, we ate breakfast and tried to recapture the happy, intimate mood. But it was a strain. Tony's comment was, 'Well, I guess you can't live in the closet all your life.' "

That afternoon, as they were strolling around the deserted Broadway area, they ran into Morton Gottlieb, *Tea and Sympathy*'s company manager (who, decades later, would produce *Romantic Comedy*, starring Tony and Mia Farrow). Gottlieb began a conversation with Tony, who did not bother to introduce William. Afterward, Tony was clearly upset. Confronted with the possibility of exposure as a gay man, he became "opaque" and immediately withdrew into himself. "I walked him home," William recalls, "and as we parted he said he needed some time to think about all this. I said okay, quite stunned, and he said goodbye—meaning *goodbye*—and disappeared into his building. I didn't even know his telephone number."

(Tony would always be phobic about openly gay male couples, even long after he'd taken on the safe role in real life of husband and father. When Cynthia Rogers told him that Charles Williamson had brought his live-in lover to meet the troupe at Arden the previous summer, Tony confided to her that he was shocked Charles would dare to live *openly* with another man. One can only imagine how he felt about his mother's relationship, or the double standard that allowed women to live more freely together than men. Because of his career in the public eye, Tony would never be able to fully relax into that kind of relationship, though he would eventually give it a try with choreographer Grover Dale.)

Meanwhile, William wasn't about to give up so easily. Buoyed by the passion of youth, he did something which was quite dangerous and illegal even at the time. "That Monday night, knowing theaters were dark and he wouldn't be working, I went to West Fifty-sixth Street, determined to find out what was happening. From the street, I could see there were no lights on in the front of the first-floor apartment." William entered the foyer to find the building dead silent. (There was no lock on the street door at 127 West Fifty-sixth; Helen and young Mario Busoni both felt that they shouldn't need a key to get into their own home and always removed the locks, which a puzzled landlord continually had to replace.)

"I tried the door of Tony's apartment," William recalls. "It was un-locked, so I pushed it open. All was dark inside, but I could hear music very faintly. Thinking Tony lived alone, I assumed he had gone out and left the radio playing. I was determined to see where he lived, no matter what." Frightened but resolved, he made his way through the shadowy rooms that he would later know as the studio, the office, the kitchen, the hallway, the living room, and the bedroom. All empty. The music grew gradually louder as he ventured farther in. It was one of Handel's concerti grossi.

"Off the bedroom was the last room, with a window on the alley. A candle flickered in the room. I entered, and seated on the window ledge, fire escape behind him, was Tony, wearing a T-shirt and shorts. I was struck dumb, both by the eerie quality of the moment and the possibility that he might call the police. I gasped, but could find noth-ing to say. Tony, on the other hand, did not seem very surprised to see me at all."

"Sometimes I get hungry for this music," the actor said as the record came to an end. "Sit down. Do you like Handel?"

William loved Handel. They sat together on the bed and Tony put on another concerto. "We looked at each other in the candlelight for a while. Then we embraced, and made love without making love, by holding each other. The bond was made. Later I learned that Tony lived in this apartment with an older woman—and that all of the events of our meeting had been made possible by the fact that she was out of town that week."

The young men began seeing each other regularly, several times a week, and in the process William became friendly with Helen. "She was a woman of powerful personality and strange appearance," he remembers.

"She was his mentor, housemate, friend, cook, and housekeeper. But something else as well. They lived together like two survivors of a terrible catastrophe, now doing very well, thank you.

"Soon after I met Helen, she was obviously assessing me. She suddenly said, 'Let me see your hands!' I showed her my hands, palms up, and she examined them with great interest. Then she nodded and smiled as though satisfied, and I was accepted. My first thought was Gypsy fortune-telling, but something she said on another occasion made me realize that she was gauging my class and money. From her background in Germany, she assumed that workers had rough hands, while wealthy people had soft hands. I passed because I did indeed have soft hands.

"I wanted to discuss the 'Handel concerti' experience with Tony, and come to some conclusion about it. It seemed to me that he, sort of like a princess in a tower, had almost expected me to break in, and that I had passed a crucial test by finding him in his lonely room. But it was not his way, then at least, to talk about things. We were together, and such deep matters were accepted, not discussed."

William's sublet was up at the end of August, and with Tony's help he found an inexpensive two-room apartment located more conveniently in nearby Hell's Kitchen. Though they both loved the new apartment, "the question of Tony's moving in with me never arose. He continued his show and his home, and I was gradually fitted in. But I had joined him and Helen; he and I were not forming a new unit." Their lives settled into a cozy routine.

"Most nights I met Tony at the drugstore on Broadway after his show. We walked home, ate something, and took Punky to the park, usually with Helen. When she went in, we necked in the hallway, even occasionally went up to the roof and made love under the stars. Then I would visit or just say good night, and go home." Occasionally, they would go straight to William's, having arranged for Helen to walk the dog. Saturday nights, if nothing interfered, they would sleep together (always at William's), then have part of Sunday together, sometimes with Helen.

Sunday nights on Fifty-sixth Street meant Scrabble and *The Ed Sullivan Show*. Tony often entertained by doing monologues, or imitations of the other actors in *"Tea and Schlup,"* as he called it—or an elaborate Judy Garland impersonation made up of several songs he had memorized from her records, accurate right down to the arm gestures. "Oddly enough, it was not faggy," William says. "It wasn't so much an imitation of a woman as much as an imitation of an icon. The emphasis was on *his* personal charm rather than a fake femininity. It wasn't like drag, it was just immensely charming." On the roof, when they weren't sexually engaged, Tony enjoyed the popular New York diversion of peeping on neighbors with a telescope. Sometimes he would bring his guitar and sing a love song to his friend, usually Martini's "Plaisir d'amour," Tom Lee's plaintive song from the show.

Despite the pleasantry of these visits, overnight stays on Fifty-sixth Street were strictly verboten. "It was clearly accepted by Helen that Tony and I were lovers," William recalls, "but we didn't act like lovers in her presence, more like students in the presence of a headmistress. This was not something she imposed on us; we imposed it on ourselves. That's how we thought we were supposed to behave. Within the circumstance of our love affair, it was a love affair; but to anyone else, we were 'college buddies.' Gay lovers who acted like gay lovers were something that only existed in the Greek isles or someplace, certainly not in the streets of New York. I was hardly ever introduced to other friends of his, if he had any, except at the apartment by Helen. This was the fifties, a public person could not go public, even if he wanted to. And Tony didn't want to."

William's presence at the theater, however, did not go unnoticed. While paying a visit to the new cast, John Kerr remembers seeing William, whom he recognized from Harvard, hanging around the stage door. Tony's school chum Henry Scammell was even introduced to William once backstage. It brought back memories of Tony's Roddy McDowall impersonation: "He was far more extravagant a parody of a gay man than anything Tony had ever contrived. He minced endlessly and flounced everywhere, and just whined and whimpered and did all the things that Tony and I had done in parodying that kind of thing. I was so amazed that Tony would have a life with somebody like that."

Nevertheless, Tony did arrange for William to meet his mother, whom he had taken to calling the "Mysterious Lady." The boys dressed up and went to her place for dinner. Michaela was conspicuously absent. For dessert Jane made snow pudding, a frothy lemon concoction that was Tony's favorite. "It was obvious that I was being presented and

approved," William remembers, "although *as what* I can't say. I seemed
to pass the test, and all went well. But it never happened again."

That fall was marked by a fleeting but devastating crisis in Tony's life
that no one but William was privy to: "He called me one morning, said
he had to do something very difficult, and asked if I would meet him
that afternoon at my apartment, so he would have something to look
forward to afterward. I said certainly, thinking it was a dentist appointment or something of the sort.

"Sometime after lunch, Tony rang my bell, ran up the stairs, burst
in the door, and threw himself on the bed in the bedroom. I went to sit
with him, and was astonished to find that he was shaking all over and
crying."

Tony grabbed William tight and told him what had happened: he
had been ordered to report to the Selective Service for examination.
"Without consulting me or Helen or his mother, he had determined
that he would not go into the army. There was no war on, he was not
really needed, but he feared it would stop his career cold. He had even
consulted a psychiatrist. But the doctor had pointed out that he could
only sign a medical exclusion if Tony became his regular patient." Finally, Tony had decided to avoid the draft simply by admitting he was
homosexual.

That morning he had gone for the examination, and had told the
truth. "Something very unpleasant had happened," William says. "I never
learned what had actually been said and done at that examination—I
would guess verbal abuse, mocking, and unnecessary penis and rectum
examinations—but whatever it was, Tony experienced it as intensely hu-
miliating and painful, and never forgot it." Perhaps on some level Tony
was trying to relive the witch-hunt at Rollins, and rewrite his own cow-
ardly part in it. Only this time, there had been no authority figure like
John Rich or Howard Bailey to turn to for protection.

"After telling me all this, he continued to tremble and cry, and then
changed into a very strange behavior that I'd never seen before. He began to whimper, like an injured dog. He was also sweating and feverish.

"By now, I was quite worried. I took off all his clothes, dried him
with towels and massaged him all over, held him as he quieted down,
and finally, at his request, made love to him. He went to sleep, and

slept until it was time to go to the theater for his half hour. I walked him there, and by that time he seemed to have recovered."

Typically, Tony seldom, if ever, mentioned the experience again, though he and his lover were then "as close as we would ever be. Anytime military matters came up, I saw by the look in his eyes what he was thinking about."

William was somewhat shocked when, just a few weeks later, Tony incorporated the painful whimpering sound into his performance as the persecuted Tom Lee.

Christmas 1954 was a high time for all on West Fifty-sixth Street. The unlikely trio decorated the whole apartment and the tree—William remembers Tony looking around like a Dickensian orphan, and innocently asking, "We all have something to do, don't we?"—and played lots of holiday music (including Handel). Helen cooked a delicious family dinner, and then the foursome (including Punky) exchanged gifts. William gave Tony a gold watch, Swiss, that he had inherited from his grandfather, with his grandfather's name etched out and a star with the initials "AP" engraved in. Tony's gift to him was an original oil painting he'd done, of a strange, lone harlequin taking a bow on a surreal stage.

Life went on as usual, and although Tony and William's relationship was good, it showed no signs of moving beyond the threesome it had become with Helen. "I remember Tony frequently shaving and washing in the bathroom off the hallway, with the door open, wearing nothing but his jockey shorts," William says, "and I wondered at the degree of intimacy between him and Helen.

"The room I called 'the bedroom' was at the back of the apartment. This served as Helen's bedroom at night, and as a second living room, music room, Tony's painting room during the day. Tony's bedroom was next to it. Helen slept next to the wall of Tony's room, and the door was always open. She could hardly have failed to hear all the sounds of his private life. At least before me."

In Helen's presence, Tony's behavior oscillated from little-boy innocence to the edge of raunchiness. "On one occasion, we were eating and Tony was describing a visit that day to his dentist. Suddenly he gave me a very mischievous smile and said that the dentist had noticed a change in the overall appearance of his teeth and gums. The dentist, he claimed, wanted to know if there had been a change in the kinds of liquids and foods he was taking in. Tony then gave me a half-joking, half-accusing leer, obviously meaning that the new fluid intake was coming from me! Helen always pretended she didn't notice such things."

Only over at William's could the young men relax openly together—often in the bathroom, where they enjoyed the erotic play of letting the hot water run until the room was like a sauna, then indulging in steamy sex among the vapors. "Tony taught me the trick of filling the mouth with hot water, than taking in the penis, giving it a hot flash. All this was great fun, though it also produced great bills, ruined the paint and the wallpaper, and made the downstairs neighbors complain. They said they were being dripped on."

William remembers that Tony wildly enjoyed the passive role in sex, and said he had trained himself to accommodate any partner—first by using his own fingers, then the handle of his handgrip exerciser, then a small candle, and finally a larger one. (Candles and hand lotion were regular commodities in Bambi's room.) According to William, Tony always came profusely. But as his public visibility increased and his career continued to bloom, "Tony struggled to overcome his desire for anal sex. He lost himself so fully in it that it may have been frightening, and he wanted to change that.

"I sometimes had the feeling that he was too easily influenced by other people, that his self-boundaries, his ego boundaries, were a little weak—and that he knew this, consciously or not. It was one of the reasons for his reclusiveness. He was holding on to himself."

Often, when they were in bed together, Tony would go into a kind of ritual postcoital trance, the position for which he always instigated. He would have William lie on top of him, chest to chest, fingers intertwined at their sides, and suddenly an eerie stillness would overtake him. "We would either stare into each other's eyes for long moments, or Tony would look blankly at the ceiling, or he would whisper inaudible and incomprehensible nonsense into my left ear. It was quite unlike his usual cheery self, in or out of bed. Any kind of rational talking would break it off entirely. By some tacit agreement, we never mentioned it."

There were Sunday excursions, record-buying binges at Sam Goody's (much to William's chagrin, Tony preferred the pop music of

Doris Day and Judy Garland and the jazz of Chet Baker to classical music), and occasional trips to the beach, which Tony adored. There was even one "family" spree on Cape Cod that included the "Mysterious Lady" and the "Mysterious Michaela," the ever present Helen, and Punky. Tony and William did not sleep together there.

"He loved to walk on windy beaches, throw stones at the ocean, huddle against the wind in sandy valleys hidden from passersby by brush and stunted trees," William remembers, "sometimes with erotic results." But back in town, in the real world, Tony was Helen's willing captive.

Physical communication was the only ground on which the lovers could safely meet. "The truth was that Tony and I were not going anywhere, we were not developing together. Our romance had really ended already because it had stopped growing, it had become fixed, part of what Tony would leave behind when he became a star.

"One time, the three of us were sitting in the park, and Punky came and simply lay down on the ground. Helen looked at him—I swear, this is forty years ago but I can still hear the words—and said, 'That's how I like to have a boy, underneath my feet.' It was a rather representative statement, I thought."

By mid-February, *Tea and Sympathy* had moved to the Longacre Theater, and the producers were busy trying to woo Joan Fontaine into renewing her contract, which was up on February 26. Fontaine, however, had been suffering from a painful bout of bursitis of the shoulder, and had recently missed several performances. June Allyson, Anne Baxter, Madeleine Carroll, and Viveca Lindfors were all bandied about as possible replacements, but Kazan and Robert Anderson found themselves so impressed with the work of understudy Mary Fickett that they finally gave her the much coveted role.

"Kazan was excited because I was so much closer in age to Tony than the other women had been," Fickett recalls. "He saw the play in an entirely different light, and walked me up and down in front of the marquee like an expectant father, telling me things to do."

For Tony, it was a welcome change. He and Fickett, who was also from Massachusetts, began meeting at the theater up to an hour and a half before curtain time. "It wasn't a ritual that we talked about," she remembers, "it just evolved. I would go into my dressing room and put on my electric pot of coffee, and Tony would come in with his guitar and sit on the couch and sing to me. And we would talk. We didn't talk about things that had to do with us, we talked about bigger things. That was his way, and therefore mine, of preparing for the performance. He established the kind of relationship with me that Laura and Tom had to have onstage. I really used to look forward to it.

"He was that boy. I'd seen John Kerr do it before, but Tony had a quality that was fantastic in the part—all the rawness and the hurt and the confusion he just had. I found his performance tremendously poignant. He was also a beautiful-looking young man."

One night, at the very end of the play, after Fickett had brought Tony's hand up to her open blouse with that famous closing line—*Years from now, when you talk about this, and you will, be kind*—there was a mishap backstage, and the final curtain did not come down, leaving the two stars stranded in a most compromising position. "Tony had his face looking up at me, and out of the side of his mouth he said with a clenched jaw, '*Don't* move.' I froze. Where was I to go? I could take the blouse off. Today, that doesn't sound like much, but it would've been pretty risqué if I'd suddenly thrown off all my clothes—which, in a way, I would have been more than willing to do with Tony, although that was not an aspect of our relationship. He just said to me, 'Don't move.'

"I had his left hand against my chest, and for a minute we heard nothing going on backstage. As we waited, he started to raise his right arm with such control and so slowly to touch my shoulder and my face that the audience never breathed. As he did this, we finally heard all hell breaking loose backstage, and the curtain came down. But I'll never forget that kind of incredible intuitiveness he had, that spontaneity. He took charge. He knew that he was the one who had to take charge."

Spring of 1955, legendary film director William Wyler sent his assistant, Stuart Millar, to New York to check out the hot young talent of Broadway and television. Wyler was casting for his new project, a screen version of *The Friendly Persuasion*, Jessamyn West's affectionate book of stories about conscience-torn Quakers during the Civil War, and he wanted unknowns to play the secondary roles. Millar paid a visit to *Tea and Sympathy* to check out the fledgling Perkins.

He'd already seen John Kerr in the role. "Tony's performance was more passionate, more poetical than Kerr's," Millar recalls. It wasn't much of a stretch to imagine him in the part of Josh, the troubled son who breaks away from his family's pacifist vows to fight for freedom. Millar gave Tony a script, and arranged for him to read for Wyler as soon as the director got to New York. Kerr was also under consideration, as was young actor Ray Stricklyn and the ever present James Dean, whom Wyler really wanted. Fortunately for Perkins, Dean had already starred in Elia Kazan's *East of Eden*, and was not about to take a supporting role.

John Kerr claims he was offered the part, but that his agent talked him into a two-picture deal at MGM, where he played lead roles in *Gaby* and the Vincente Minnelli production of *Tea and Sympathy*, again opposite Deborah Kerr. "I was reluctant because I loved the book of *Friendly Persuasion*," Kerr admitted forty years later. "It's better than any movie I was ever in. But that's one of the breaks."

Tony's reading took place one Sunday morning in Wyler's suite at the St. Regis Hotel. "About a half hour later, he had the part," Millar remembers. "Willie was thrilled with the reading, he saw everything instantly. It was really one of the best, if not *the* best, readings I've ever seen. Tony read two scenes, once each, and Wyler said, 'Yes, yes,' and his eyes gleamed. They chatted for a while, Tony left, and Willie said, 'Great. Take him.' No screen test, nothing."

"He was sort of lanky, like [Gary] Cooper," Wyler later recalled. "And I didn't want a fellow who was too physical. I wanted someone who looked strong in spirit."

Not everyone was so enthusiastic. Helen felt that Tony needed more stage training, and there were plans for Tony to star in a new John Van Druten play. "I had little money and was practically set for *Dancing in the Checkered Shade*," Tony recounted in 1956. "My agents were split in their decisions. New York said I should stay and do the play. Hollywood said I should come out and do the picture. It was like flipping a coin. So I took the picture and positive I had made a mistake, went from 170 to 150 worrying my way through it!"

Tony's instincts were right; the play never made it to Broadway.

Tea and Sympathy closed on June 18, 1955. "It was a very unhappy time for me," William remembers. With his own prospects glittering on the horizon, Tony became impatient with his lover. "Sometimes he would be irritable, abrupt or withdrawn, and it was not the kind of friendship where people are free to have fights with each other. Instead, Tony would close off if something went wrong, and our relationship would suddenly become one-sided."

At a rare dinner with an actor friend of William's, Tony flirted shamelessly, tauntingly, in front of his beau, and centered the conversation around his impending departure for the Coast. "I underestimated the malicious fun of which Tony was capable," William says. "He later confessed that it had just been to tease me and make me uncomfortable.

"We had already run out of things to say and do together, and we were thrown back on obligatory sex whenever we met. In my opinion, the reason for this was the lack of growth in our relationship. There really wasn't any way I could go with him where he was going, and holding the fort at home was Helen. So there was little place left for me to fit in."

Tony was traveling by train to California. William took him to the station to help him get his bags into the compartment. Then they stood and looked at each other awkwardly, trying to think of something to say.

William: "Would you like to make love again?"

Tony: "No!"

"I think we both laughed at that," William recalls. "I hope we did. Then the train moved, and away he went, without me."

7

NEW BOY IN
TOWN

ESSAMYN WEST'S *The Friendly Persuasion*, originally optioned
by director Frank Capra as a possible vehicle for Bing Crosby and
Jean Arthur, had been sitting on the shelf for ten years, no doubt
because it concerned the very uncinematic question of Quaker social conscience. But William Wyler loved the book. When Allied
Artists, previously known as Monogram Pictures (it had changed
its name in 1953 in an effort to shed its B picture reputation and
gain major studio status), signed him in early 1955, Wyler knew exactly
what he wanted to do: make the film, his first in color, starring Gary
Cooper as Jess Birdwell, the strong, silent Quaker father. Civil War
pictures were big at the time and several were under production at
other studios, most notably MGM's *Raintree County*, starring Montgomery Clift and Elizabeth Taylor. In a desperate attempt to fight the
popularity of television, the studios were trying to recapture some of
the fading glory of *Gone With the Wind*.

Wyler had originally envisioned Katharine Hepburn as Eliza Birdwell, Jess's determined wife, believing that the chemistry between the
two stars would be electric; Cooper, however, wanted to work with
newcomer Audrey Hepburn. In the meantime, Maureen O'Hara tested
and Eleanor Parker was screened, and a multitude of other actresses—
including Lucille Ball, Grace Kelly, and even Shelley Winters—were
talked about and dismissed. Finally, after Vivien Leigh declined, and

Ingrid Bergman, who was in Italy with Roberto Rossellini, decided she did not yet want to return to the States, Dorothy McGuire was hired. It was a choice Wyler would regret for the entire shoot.

He was thrilled, however, with his youngsters, who were all unknowns from New York. Aside from Tony, there was Phyllis Love, who had taken a leave of absence from Broadway's *Bus Stop* to play "Coop" 's daughter (a role she won over Susan Strasberg), and Mark Richman, a former pro football player who, like Tony, was active on television and had starred on Broadway in *End as a Man*. Of the three, only Tony had prior screen experience.

Location shooting began that August, during an intense heat wave, at the Rowland Lee Ranch, where two hundred acres of San Fernando Valley had been painstakingly transformed into 1862 southern Indiana farmland—complete with barn, cow shed, and cornfields. The cast met early every morning at the Allied studio on Sunset Boulevard to be driven to the ranch, a good hour and a half away (there was no freeway at the time).

Awed at first to be working with the legendary likes of Cooper and Wyler, Perkins soon settled down to business. "Tony was always kind of detached, somewhat imbued with himself, and frankly, not the most outgoing or warmest person in the world," Mark Richman recalls. "As an actor, he was hardworking, sincere, but he didn't go out of his way to be friendly or gracious."

Perhaps that was because all three of the young newcomers were so busy "preparing" their roles. According to Richman, "Tony was remarkable in one scene that Willie Wyler didn't shoot. We were up in Chico, California, doing some location stuff, with me on the horse leading the home guard, and where Josh has to fire the gun. They were going to do the close-up where he makes the decision to shoot and kill somebody. Tony asked to take a few minutes, and the assistant director was saying, 'Come on, we gotta move, we're losing light, c'mon, c'mon!' But Tommy Plume, an old-time second-unit director, said, 'No, no. Let's give the boy a break here. Hold on.' He was very patient. Tony got on camera, fired the gun, and he started to cry. It was very spontaneous and rich. Whatever he used for preparation, it was admirable."

At the time, Perkins claimed to have been inspired by the trendy Method technique of his young costars. But in his last recorded interview, on the American Movie Classics channel shortly before his death in 1992, a balding, emaciated Perkins dispelled, with almost rhapsodic bitterness, any lingering notion of his artistic technique: "Youth, you know, youth can do anything."

"He was more like a boy than a twenty-five-year-old," Phyllis Love remembers. "Tony connected with you in a way that was very affectionate."

No one noticed this quality more than Dorothy Jeakins, the Oscar-winning costume designer, who, like Helen Merrill, was old enough to be Tony's mother. Matronly and artistic, Jeakins was on the set constantly, working to give her creations authentic detail. On Mark Richman's Civil War uniform, for instance, she tore the jacket in one spot and stitched it together to give it a worn, lived-in look. "She was always doing things like that," the actor recalls. "She sort of became a mother figure to Tony, combing his hair, telling him how to wear it, what to wear. She was the type of person who latched on to somebody, and she latched on to Tony."

The *Friendly Persuasion* set was a happy one, despite Wyler's strained relationship with Dorothy McGuire. Phyllis Love and Tony shared a fascination with Cooper's eyes, which they both felt exuded a powerful, animal energy. Cooper, in turn, enjoyed working with the young actors, whose work he often praised.

Only once did Tony, who was soon hailed in a *Life* magazine cover story about the film as a "24-year-old copy of Cooper," rub the veteran matinee idol the wrong way. It happened one afternoon as they were sitting around between shots with Mark Richman. "Coop was warm and gracious and kindly, he liked us a lot, and Tony loved to hear him talk," Richman remembers. "Tony said, 'Coop, tell us about when you were a young actor,' and that was the only time I saw Coop angry. He said, 'Cut all this youth shit out!' Tony just fell silent. That was the only time I saw Coop get testy."

"I think he'd do well to spend a summer on a ranch," Cooper told *Life* about his up-and-coming screen son, "—it would toughen him up and he'd learn a lot from another kind of people."

Joe Hyams, one of the first Hollywood columnists to interview Perkins on the set, remembers that the press agent who introduced them made a big deal out of the fact that Tony was Osgood Perkins's son. "Tony seemed annoyed by that. He was uncomfortable with it. I had the feeling that he wanted to be known on his own, not as some-body's son."

Hitchhiking still offered Tony a defiant way to be on his own (he didn't yet know how to drive). Workday mornings, he'd hitch from the Chateau Marmont—where he'd been put up alone, probably at his request, while the rest of the cast stayed in apartments more conve-niently located in Los Feliz—down to Allied Artists at 4376 Sunset. He enjoyed telling strangers he was the stand-in for a hot new star named Anthony Perkins. "You really ought to watch for him," he'd say, "he's pretty good." Once, Tony was even picked up by Rock Hudson. (Ac-cording to Hudson's longtime friend, Mark Miller, Hudson was not impressed with the young Perkins, whose peculiar East Coast attitude and obvious intelligence annoyed him. Though they ran into each other periodically over the years, Hudson and Perkins were never close.)

"Tony thought hitchhiking was a wonderful way to know people without having to know them," Stuart Millar remembers. "I used to kid him about it. I'd say, 'You know, this kind of thing isn't going to be possible when the picture comes out.' I really felt that Tony would be lionized as soon as *Friendly Persuasion* was released. I thought he was going to be a major romantic leading man star. He turned out not to be. But I thought he had that kind of promise."

Hollywood was smaller and quieter then, still a cowtown crawling with coyotes, an occasional rattlesnake, and lots of actors. For those who wanted to keep it that way, out of the way, the Chateau Marmont was *the* hotel. A bogus Loire Valley "chateau" on L.A.'s famous Sunset Strip, the Marmont was especially popular with visiting New York the-ater folk; perfect for the car-impaired, it was within walking distance of a number of restaurants and night spots, including Schwab's drugstore, where, like Lana Turner, you might be "discovered" sitting at the soda fountain, and Googie's, the futuristic greasy hamburger joint that was the favorite hangout of Hollywood's young up-and-comers like James Dean, Jack Nicholson, and Dennis Hopper, as well as lots of down-and-outers. At the Chateau you could be self-sufficient without wheels, and could come and go as you pleased via the basement garage elevator, thereby avoiding the front desk. Garbo had been alone there, *The Day of the Locust* had been written there, and plenty of stars had trysted there. It also offered a little-known swimming pool where young stars such as Natalie Wood, Nick Adams, and Tab Hunter gathered to meet and relax among themselves. The Chateau was Hollywood bohemian, and perfect for Tony Perkins, who appreciated the quirky atmosphere and enjoyed walking the length of the Sunset Strip, from Crescent Heights to Doheny, barefoot.

"That was the center of the universe in those days," says actress Maila Nurmi, who is best remembered for her brief stint in 1954 as the curvaceous TV horror movie hostess Vampira, a Charles Addams-ish creation she later reprised in the Ed Wood cult film *Plan 9 from Outer Space*. Her other claim to fame was having a close friendship with James Dean. She and Tony became fast friends at Googie's. "Tony lived across the street from the Chateau Marmont, in the janitor's room, which was fifty dollars a month. They had no janitor at the time, so they allowed him to have it. Later, he got a little grander and had a real room upstairs. He would be on his way to work early in the morning, at four-thirty or five. I was still up all night with the last few of my cronies at Googie's. We'd all be bleary-eyed, and Tony would arrive fresh and ready to go to Allied Artists. He'd have his six prunes and his bowl of cereal, and then he'd hitchhike down Sunset."

She and Tony shared a similar iconoclastic sense of humor, and were soon linked romantically by Allied's small publicity mill, though Nurmi was married at the time to TV writer Dean Reisner. "Tony had a magnificent sense of humor," she recalls. "Usually I'm with dolts and everything lies pretty fallow, but with him I became a bright woman myself. He had a way of bringing intelligence out in you."

Tony's "dates" with the voluptuous Vampira invariably ended prematurely. "He'd always take me home by nine o'clock and say, 'Well, you know, I have to get up very early.' I wasn't ready to go home so soon. Then people would tell me they'd seen him at Schwab's at eleven. 'Not possible, he walked me home, he went right home!' 'No, he was there with a young boy.'" Tony was also romantically linked with Gary Cooper's daughter, Maria, but their "breakup" was one of the things that supposedly cooled Coop's affection for his screen son.

"It must have been very hard for Tony," reflects Nurmi. "He was so tall and skinny, he was practically anorexic! And he had lockjaw. He was so shy, his jaw would just lock whenever he was tense—which was often. His eyes would dart and he'd spit words out."

Respite came, once again, from an older woman, Dorothy Jeakins, at whose cultured Brentwood home he began hiding out on weekends. Like Helen, Jeakins, who already had two young sons, doted on Tony, and he, in turn, knew just how to respond. "She adored him," Stuart Millar says. " 'Love' would be a very strange word to use. He was young enough to be her son."

"It was a grand infatuation," confirms another friend of Jeakins's. "She never came out and said, 'I am in love with Tony,' but she'd bring him into whatever she was talking about, she would refer to him constantly. I was fascinated by Dorothy being in love with someone so much younger than she was." Tony's face and figure began appearing in many of Jeakins's costume sketches, even those unrelated to the film.

"When I was going with him," Maila Nurmi explains, "he was taking Dorothy Jeakins to public places, because she was respected and I was a disgrace. I was somebody you weren't seen publicly with. They used to call me 'Vampira, character about town.' I had too reckless a sense of humor, too adolescent. The straitlaced people looked down on that. And Tony was a social climber, overtly, admittedly."

"He loves being important," Jeakins would later be quoted in a huge *Newsweek* profile on Perkins. "His life is occupied with success."

Tony and Maila still occasionally attended the astrology parties of the *Los Angeles Times*'s zodiac columnist, Carroll Righter, but Tony's sights were now set higher. On the way to another soiree, at the Chandler mansion in Los Feliz, she remembers Tony telling her: " 'You know, when we get there, you won't see me. I'm going to leave and you won't see me all evening.' I thought he was kidding. 'No,' he said, 'I'm serious.' I asked why. 'Because there will be important people there, and I'll be with them. I'll be getting to know them.' " Maila was appalled, but a good sport.

"In a very little while he came back. I said, 'What are you doing here? Why aren't you social climbing?' He said, 'There's nobody here.' So he and I resumed playing. Tony had gone prowling around the mansion and found a fuse box, so we went up into the crawl space and unplugged the fuses, and all the lights went out! Fortunately, it was Halloween, and no one knew the difference."

William flew out to see Tony midway through the *Friendly Persuasion* shoot. "We had corresponded just enough to arrange my visit," he recalls. "I met him at the Chateau, we went to his room, and didn't know what to say to each other. We were both trying, we were still very fond of each other, but we no longer seemed to have anything in common."

They had sex—"When it was over we were both relieved"—then went for a swim in the pool. "Ironically, the radio was playing 'Love and Marriage.' To this day, when I hear that song, I see that pool, with Tony so young and beautiful and touched with genius. The rest of the short visit went very well, and we were able to go back to the way we'd been before. But I knew that was the very problem; I couldn't go *forward* with him."

Nevertheless, before William left, Tony and he made an adolescent vow: "for life, no matter what . . ." William didn't know that his lover had already been seen briefly around town with a handsome young actor named Robert Francis (who died tragically in a plane crash shortly thereafter), and more significantly, with Warner Bros.' hunky blond heartthrob, Tab Hunter, whom he'd recently met at that very same swimming pool.

Word of Tony's luminous performance in the Wyler rushes raced through Hollywood, and he was suddenly looked upon as a potential hot property. Over at Warner's, volatile James Dean had just caused a sensation in Elia Kazan's *East of Eden*, and the release of his next film, Nicholas Ray's *Rebel Without a Cause*, was already eagerly anticipated by both industry insiders and hungry young movie audiences. The disgruntled youth market, something television ignored, had unexpectedly been tapped, and suddenly the hurting studios were clamoring to get their piece of the teenage pie. By 1957, B pictures about rock and roll, delinquency, and teenage monsters of every variety would be all the rage.

Meanwhile, Paramount had bought the rights to a script called *Fear Strikes Out,* a recent episode of the dramatic television series *Climax!* that was based on the memoir by Boston Red Sox baseball star Jim Piersall, about his much publicized nervous breakdown and recovery. Championship ice skater turned actor Tab Hunter, who had starred on the show, asked Warner Bros. to buy the property for him. But despite his having just been voted Outstanding New Personality of 1955 in an audience poll conducted by the Council of Motion Pictures

Organizations, Hunter's request went unnoticed by Jack Warner. Warner hated Hunter's agent, Henry Willson, a known homosexual whose clients included Rock Hudson and Troy Donahue. "Paramount snapped it up immediately for Tony," Hunter recalls.

Shortly thereafter, in what many people believe was the beginning of a carefully orchestrated smear campaign, Hunter was exposed in the much feared *Confidential* magazine as one of Hollywood's secret "limp-wristed lads," who, in October of 1950, had attended a "swish party" set up by the LAPD "strictly for boys" and been arrested along with "two dozen of the gayest guys the vice squad had ever seen . . . charged with violating California's Penal Code, Section 647.5, which calls for the arrest of 'idle, lewd or dissolute persons.'" Police entrapment of gays was a common occurrence in the 1950s. "Tab seldom, if ever, goes to pajama parties anymore," *Confidential* gloated, "but who can blame him? After all, he learned the hard way that you can't tell *who* is wearing that nightshirt next to you. It could be an understanding chap. It could also be a cop!" The article marked the beginning of the end of what had initially been a promising film career.

Producing *Fear Strikes Out* was Alan Pakula, former assistant to Paramount production head Don Hartman. After toying with the idea of having handsome, all-American Piersall play himself, Pakula, reportedly at the recommendation of both William Wyler and Paramount executive D. A. Doran (who had produced one of Osgood Perkins's Broadway shows), settled on slim, baseball-hating Tony for the lead. It was an ironic bit of casting.

When James Dean died tragically on September 30, 1955, Perkins began to look even more appealing to Paramount. The mournful outcry of a hysterical public and the subsequent exploitive flood of James Dean merchandise and memorabilia made the dead rebel even more popular than he had been in life. What would his fans do without him?

Even more important: Who would replace him?

Probably at Tony's own instigation—he loved to spout misinformation—several movie magazines reported that Dean and Perkins had once been roommates.

"Tony was very aware of Jimmy Dean," recalls actor Jack Simmons, who had appeared with Dean on *General Electric Theater*'s "The Dark, Dark Alley," and played one of the gang members in the still-to-be-released *Rebel Without a Cause* (and was reportedly Dean's live-in lover). "In fact, I think that's what drew Tony to me and Maila. He was not trying to copy Jimmy, but something about the timing of their careers fascinated Tony. Jimmy had had a big success [*East of Eden*] when he was very young; Tony was about to have a big success with *Friendly Persuasion*, and he was young. But Jimmy's career had soared to such a height! Tony aspired to that."

Dean's popularity had been so meteoric, in fact, that it had stirred up considerable resentment within the industry; some colleagues were actually relieved at his untimely death. Rock Hudson, his costar in *Giant*, which was still in production when the fatal car crash occurred, admitted to his wife that he was ecstatic the brutal accident had eliminated one of his major competitors.

Jack Simmons remembers: "The night Jimmy Dean died, I was at a friend's apartment, and Tony showed up at the door with Maila Nurmi. They started telling me the details of Jimmy's passing. I said, 'No, no, no, that's not possible,' and went into a terrifying, shrieking, crying, crazy fit. Maila, I remember, stayed. But Tony just sort of slipped away and vanished, like he just slid under the wall-to-wall carpeting. That, of course, was a significant moment in my life.

"No one can ever be a new Jimmy Dean. Jimmy was all internal and driven, while Tony Perkins was sort of mechanical, physically plotted and contrived, although he hid it pretty well. There was no comparison." Few moviegoers would argue with that.

"I don't think it ever occurred to me that I was going to be the successor to anyone," Perkins told Richard Brown in 1992. "I don't think I thought about it for a moment."

Nevertheless, by the end of November, Perkins had signed a seven-year semiexclusive contract with Paramount, with time off for two Broadway plays. He would soon be touted in the press as "Hollywood's $15,000,000 Gamble." From today's post-*Psycho* perspective, it's hard to imagine Anthony Perkins as anything other than the boy king of creepy, but at the time of his signing, he was just another hot young property, pretty and malleable, with no distinctive public persona.

"When I was a kid, Tony was in *Tea and Sympathy* on Broadway, and he was not only a great actor at a very early age, he was a great beauty," says film director Joel Schumacher, with whom Tony became friendly in the early 1970s. "Freud said anatomy is destiny. You didn't get plucked off Broadway to become a big movie star in those days unless you had the looks. And he was extraordinary looking."

Because of his dark comeliness and his guitar playing, Perkins was likened as well to Elvis Presley, the gyrating rock-and-roll phenomenon who was at Paramount making his screen debut in *Love Me Tender*, under the auspices of producer Hal Wallis. When Perkins first arrived at the studio, comedian Jerry Lewis reportedly mistook him for Presley, engaging him in a lengthy conversation before realizing which actor-singer he was talking to. As Tony's longtime friend Stephen Paley put it, "He was kind of a thinking girl's teen idol, as opposed to Elvis Presley, who was kind of a greaser." (Later, Tony's MCA agent, Herman Citron, who also represented Alfred Hitchcock and Jimmy Stewart, would try in vain to interest Tony in starring in Harold Robbins's *A Stone for Danny Fisher* for Hal Wallis. It was eventually made as *King Creole*, a vehicle for Presley.)

With the sudden studio hype came sudden apprehension. Hollywood was a famously homophobic town, ruled by right-wing gossip columnists like Louella Parsons and Hedda Hopper—and worse. *Confidential* magazine was selling a whopping four million copies per issue in 1955, and its success had spawned a slew of equally cheesy imitations like *Hush-Hush*, *Uncensored*, and *The Low-Down*. America's puritanical bent was turning hypocritically in on itself. Careers were derailing and the public was loving every minute of it. "Everyone reads *Confidential*," Tony's friend Humphrey Bogart said. "But they deny it. They say the cook brought it into the house."

Over at MGM, where Vincente Minnelli's production of *Tea and Sympathy* was being readied for the cameras, Robert Anderson's script, creaky and evasive by today's standards, was considered too explicit. In August, the *Tribune* reported that MGM had finally "licked the problem of homosexuality in *Tea and Sympathy* by making the boy an extremely shy 'sissy.' By this simple device the studio was able to receive Production Code approval of the screen play." The same sort of sexual watering down would dampen the power of MGM's 1958 film version of Tennessee Williams's Pulitzer Prize–winning play, *Cat on a Hot Tin Roof*, among others. In retrospect, Broadway seemed like a liberal haven.

Alone in his room at the Chateau Marmont, Tony cooked on a hot plate, using unlabeled food cans as pans and plasticware from the Plush

Pup hot dog stand across the street. His hitchhiking became famous, as did his habit of walking barefoot along Sunset Boulevard and his collection of white gym socks, which were supplied daily from Paramount's wardrobe department. All this was fine for his bohemian New York image, which was just about as honest and manageable a persona for Tony Perkins to have, one he could control without too much of a stretch. To quote one fan magazine editor at the time, "We need someone to fill Dean's shoes and Perkins looks like it. He does offbeat things like Jimmy and that makes good copy."

Nevertheless, he always used the public phone in the hotel lobby for personal calls.

As for the occasional Hollywood party, he soon realized he would need a female companion younger than Jeakins and more successful than Vampira to bring on his arm.

Gwen Davis was a nineteen-year-old aspiring singer and songwriter when she met Tony Perkins at a gathering of young Hollywood hopefuls. It was a meeting that would ultimately torment her for years to come. "This extraordinary, unmistakably bright person appeared in the middle of the party," Davis recalled four decades later, "and began challenging me." He recited a line from an unnamed movie and promised to take her to lunch if she could guess the title of the film. The girl was thrilled.

"He was intellectually dazzling, physically beautiful," Davis remembers. "At twenty-four, he was already Dorian Gray, and he knew just how to work me; I went immediately to my task of identifying the quote so he would take me to lunch. I mean, Tony was being touted as the up-and-coming new teenage movie idol, the replacement for Jimmy Dean. I had just gotten out of college, and to become involved with the number one young man in Hollywood was Valhalla."

Their date, however, turned out to be just breakfast at Googie's. Even so, "Tony was mysterious, I was captivated. We talked about everything, rat-tat-tat, because he was faster and smarter than anybody. And I was right there with him." Eventually, their relationship would spur Davis to take her first stab at fiction, a Hollywood potboiler featuring Maila Nurmi, James Dean, Natalie Wood, Marlon Brando, and Tony—all thinly disguised—called *Naked in Babylon*. But for now, she was content to be enchanted by the knowing, overgrown boy.

The association had its advantages. When Davis, a complete unknown, opened at the Purple Onion on Hollywood and Sunset, Tony was there to attract the press as well as an up-and-coming young crowd that included Tab Hunter, Venetia Stevenson (the knockout daughter of director Robert Stevenson and actress Anna Lee), actor Russ Tamblyn (whom Stevenson would soon marry), and columnist Army Archerd. Suddenly, Davis's name was in the papers.

"Gwen was a lot of fun," Jack Simmons remembers, "very aggressive and a good writer." Her act included some stand-up comedy between songs. One of her best one-liners concerned the much photographed movie magazine romance between Warner contract players Natalie Wood and Tab Hunter; as Davis put it, "Natalie Wood and Tab wouldn't."

There were those who felt Davis was using Tony for publicity. "Gwen was initially my friend," Maila Nurmi says, "not of my own choosing. I never liked her, but she was someone hanging around. I *dis*liked her intensely. She was a barracuda. I mean, if you're overly aggressive, you've got to have a lot of charm. She had a marvelous sense of humor, but she didn't have charm. Nobody liked Gwen, but she was very young and fat and funny. She was also a cruel and vicious bitch."

"Tony was my first great love, my first romance," Davis maintains. "I worshiped him, wrote songs for him [including one, "First Romance," that Tony later recorded for RCA], poems to him, sent him telegrams. I didn't know he was gay. In those days everybody wasn't sleeping together. When a man didn't come on to you, it was because he respected you. In the fifties, nobody 'came out.' There wasn't even a word for it." Tony was amused and touched by Davis's affection, and unable to resist leading her on.

"She was his beard woman," Maila Nurmi says.

He always promised to call Gwen in the evening. "I would sit there and wouldn't go to the bathroom for fear that my tinkle would obscure the tingle of the telephone, sometimes until twelve or two o'clock in the morning," she recalls vividly. "He was cruel beyond measure. Then I'd fall asleep, until the phone would ring at about four o'clock in the morning." An unidentified voice—sometimes male, sometimes female— would hiss into Davis's ear that Tony was at the beach in the arms of Tab Hunter. "I'd scream, 'Stop it! Stop it!' and hang up. I didn't know who was making these poison-pen calls. Then I'd tell myself that I never wanted to see or speak to Tony again."

One time, a prankster (perhaps Tony himself) left a life-size cardboard Tony Perkins cutout, swiped from a theater lobby, on the lawn in front of Davis's apartment. Another time, after Tony had learned to drive, Davis was so upset by another round of "He's at the beach" phone calls that she went to his garage in the middle of the night and felt around in the pitch black to see if indeed his car was gone. It was. "Then the phone rang at four-thirty in the morning, and it was him, and he didn't even say hello. He just said to me, 'You know, sometimes I park my car on the street so you don't know where I am.' He was so insidiously smart. He knew just how to make me nuts."

"I don't think he was ever in love," Maila Nurmi reflects. "I don't think he was capable of it then. He couldn't have been in love with anyone because he was too deeply, deeply tense and guarded. Everything was a machination, nothing was natural with him. I'm sure he'd long since made himself invulnerable to pain. Somehow I think he had done it when his father died. I knew he wasn't contented."

But he was still good for an occasional laugh. To get back at him for being such a shameless social climber, Maila herself arranged an elaborate practical joke: "A friend of mine was in charge of renting a vacant penthouse in Jack Haley's building on Rossmore, furnished with all sorts of antiques and marble. We brought Tony there for dinner, and had a whole group of bizarre people acting as my 'employees.' I was going to show Tony that I'd finally caught a billionaire."

Tony was greeted at the front door by the "maid," a stark naked young woman with a crew cut and breasts painted like eyes. Later, Maila broke a glass in the bathroom and screamed; Tony was told she had smashed a thousand-dollar bottle of perfume. Finally, everyone sat at a long table under a crystal chandelier and ate TV dinners. "What else could we serve? It gradually dawned on Tony that it was a practical joke. One fellow even stood on his head, held himself up with one hand and masturbated with the other! We said, 'Ignore him, he does that when the moon is full'—anything to shock Tony! Because he was such a geeky farm boy."

After a grueling eighty-one-day shoot, *Friendly Persuasion* was in the can. Tony spent Thanksgiving in Los Angeles at Dorothy Jeakins's house, and was home to Helen by Christmas. But he had changed, as William was quick to note; though they both tried to pick up where they had left off, Tony's mind was elsewhere and, not surprisingly, much of his time was taken up by new obligations.

One pleasant result of his time in Hollywood was his new repertoire of imitations: Gary Cooper, dead-on; an extremely wide-eyed, innocent Dorothy McGuire, who knew *exactly* what she was doing (which was very characteristic of Tony). "He could even imitate 'Anthony Perkins,' " William says, "although few people saw him do it. He was very good at being this charming, gangling, sweet American boy, and somehow just suggesting, without actually showing it, something bizarre underneath. He could turn it on and off."

There were also new "inside" phrases, inflections, and *deflections*, he seemed to have picked up on the Coast. "On hearing that a certain gay actor had gotten married," William recalls, "he looked very thoughtful and said, 'Well, if that's what he *really* wants,' in a very doubtful voice. One would never have imagined he would do the same himself years later. When I talked about new ways to revive our friendship, he said portentously, '*That's* rich thinking.' I assumed he was copying someone he had met out there. When reminded that we had once discussed being in each other's wills, he quickly said it would be a better idea for us to pay jointly for a needy child. This seemed to me a way of getting rid of the topic, not a serious suggestion."

The two were seeing each other less, and sleeping together even less than that. What time they did spend together was usually just a few minutes before another appointment, or a long, silent walk in the park.

One day in Helen's kitchen William tried to talk seriously with Tony, but at that moment the chair he was sitting in tipped and sent him sprawling on the floor. "Tony quickly got down so that he was facing me, and put his forehead against mine," William remembers. "We were both crying now and murmuring things about being sorry. Eventually we helped each other up, wiped each other's tears.

"Helen reacted rather oddly to this new phase of all our lives. When Tony was out of town, which was more and more frequent, she and I were as good friends as ever, maybe more. She needed several part-time minions, and I was very happy to be one of them, as I really cared for her. On the other hand, when Tony was in town, she became quite unavailable and treated me like one of 'them,' the 'outsiders,' who must now be kept at a distance. I never knew whether this was her idea, or Tony's, or just something that happened."

Not long after their relationship had fizzled out, Tony decided he wanted to take back the harlequin painting he had given William their first Christmas. "I received this news through Helen," William recounts. "And I said no, it was insulting. If he wanted his painting he could call and ask for it, and come and get it. Well, the day came when he appeared at my new apartment to pick it up, and annoying as it may seem, no sooner had we said hello than we fell weeping into each other's arms and spent the afternoon in bed.

"The sexual aspect had only one more go-around. On another occasion, I was going to the theater with Helen, but Tony was in the house and we somehow found ourselves back in his bedroom. I think we would have respected ourselves more if we had let the moment pass. Helen and I went to the theater, and that was the end of that.

"The last time I saw him was backstage at either *Look Homeward, Angel* or *Greenwillow*, I forget which. I sent in my name and was ushered into his dressing room just as I had been years before. But it was now the number one dressing room for him, and we could only chat for a moment before his valet came in and said so-and-so was waiting. He admitted that he was very busy, and we shook hands. As I left, I looked back, hoping for a reminiscent smile and nod, but he was already talking to somebody else. I never saw him again, and I always found it painful to see his films."

Maila Nurmi had followed Tony back to New York in the hope of reviving her comatose career with more substantial television work, but a brutal near-rape in her small West Side apartment in early January 1956 ultimately sent her back to Hollywood. Before that unfortunate event, however, Tony invited her to dine on Fifty-sixth Street. "I knew all about Helen before I went there," Nurmi says, "because he'd sent a lovely towel set home for Christmas the first time he'd had any money. He'd told me a lot about Helen and his dog. He wanted us to get acquainted.

"She was, I believe, his mother figure, and I was perhaps a sister figure—I don't know what I was, but he wanted us acquainted. He didn't want me acquainted with Dorothy Jeakins, he wanted me acquainted with Helen. Dorothy was also a mother figure, but maybe because we were both in the same town and my name was mud in the industry, he didn't want to be associated with me there. I found Helen to be like a university librarian, and felt very much at home with her. She was austere, stern. She was obviously in love with him, and they were playing house. I liked her, and I was furious at Tony because he was so cruel to her."

As he'd done with Gwen Davis, Tony seemed to be manipulating the emotions of his older benefactress. "It was her home and she had cooked dinner, and he treated her like a housekeeper," Nurmi recalls. "He acted like I was a precious, adorable thing—a way he normally didn't treat me. He exuded love, and that was done to hurt her. She stayed cool. I'm sure she was suffering. That was the first time I was aware that he was a sadist."

Tony also offered Maila one of his paintings, which, in her haste, she left behind. "The next time I saw him I told him I forgot it, and he said, 'Well, you didn't want it so you can't have it.' I can see his point there, but the fact was I was so distressed by his treatment of Helen that I forgot it."

What Maila didn't realize was that she herself had probably been made the victim of an elaborate gag. On occasion, Tony and Helen would act as master and maid for unsuspecting guests, Helen often taking on the persona of "Gretchen, the housekeeper," and Tony treating her as such. Perhaps on some level they were both acting out the underlying dynamics of their own increasingly professional relationship with each other.

On January 25, 1956, Tony made his second appearance on NBC's *Kraft Television Theatre* in a creaky Irish family drama by Walter Macken called *Home Is the Hero*, about the conflicts that arise when a father returns home to his family after years of incarceration for killing a man in a drunken brawl. Originally a Broadway play that had bombed while Tony was in *Tea and Sympathy*, the script had been whittled down to less than an hour's playing time to make room for Cracker Barrel cheese commercials. Brian Donlevy, who had appeared with Osgood in the 1929 film *Mother's Boy*, starred as the guilt-ridden father. Tony played Willie, the drunkard's angry son.

Director William Graham remembers the cast being shocked by Donlevy's short stature and incompetence—he could not remember his

lines after so many years of working piecemeal in films. Tony, however, behaved like a gentleman in the face of Donlevy's ineptitude; it
was his presence on the show, and not Donlevy's, that was causing excitement. Tony was a hot property, and TV dramas were often populated by has-beens. Graham recalls Tony as being very quiet and
consistent in his performance, again in contrast to the likes of the late
James Dean. But unlike his performance in *Friendly Persuasion*, which
was fresh and fairly natural, Tony's performance as Willie shows off all
his worst tendencies as an actor. Speaking monotonously out of the
side of his mouth in a pinched, half-baked brogue, Tony seems to wal-
low in the strained fraudulence of his troubled-boy shtick—his own
constipated, forced brand of Method acting that would be the unfortunate trademark of many of his early films.

"I expected much more of his talent," Graham remembers. "I
thought he would really be a superstar. But he wasn't."

After *Home Is the Hero*, Tony returned to Los Angeles, where he
did two shows for CBS: *Studio One*'s "The Silent Gun" with Lloyd
Bridges (February 6), and *Front Row Center*'s "Winter Dreams" (February 19), based on the F. Scott Fitzgerald story about a young man from
the lower middle class who falls in love with an unworthy rich girl.
Piper Laurie played his fickle love interest.

"I thought he had great vitality, great energy—and I thought he was
very, very cute," recalls Laurie, who had already done a string of movies
for Universal at the time. "I loved his shoulders. He had a sexuality
about him that he never really used in the films that he did, beyond the
early ones. Later, he became so intense, kind of brittle. His intellect—he
was extremely bright—overshadowed what I perceived then as an innate sensuality."

Nevertheless, Laurie noted that "he didn't seem sure of himself at
all. He was very nervous. We both used to smoke a lot. And he used to
bite his fingernails, especially before a take. They'd bleed sometimes. It
seemed very deliberate to me. He said he needed to do it, that it helped
him in some way. [Jane had for years urged him to stop.] There was a
lot of talk that he was going to be a big star, that he had this wonderful
part ahead of him, Jimmy Piersall. But Tony carried it very nicely, he
didn't have an obvious kind of career obsession, which was refreshing
to me."

Tony had been a Piper Laurie fan since making *Friendly Persuasion*.

"While I was on location," he told *Hollywood Screen Parade* in 1957, "there wasn't much to do except go to the movies. Piper Laurie's picture, *Ain't Misbehavin'*, was playing and I got a terrific kick out of her song, 'Just a Little Love.' "

Like Gwen Davis and many other young women who would encounter Tony in Hollywood, Piper Laurie mistook his professional interest for flirtation. "He was very excited [because] I had sung in a movie, and when he heard I had the recordings at home, he asked if he could come over. So he did, and I guess I had expected an evening with an attractive young man. It *felt* like a date. But it wasn't that at all. He was just genuinely excited about the songs! He listened to 'Just a Little Love' over and over and over again. He was so excited by the idea of singing. He said, 'Oh God, I'd love to do that,' and within months he had recorded it." By the time *Friendly Persuasion* would be released at the end of the year, Tony would have a set of six 45 rpm singles on the Epic label as part of his big studio buildup.

On March 25, back in New York, Tony got the chance to sing on TV when he starred opposite Kim Stanley in the *Goodyear TV Playhouse* drama "Joey," written by his and Helen's friend, Louis Peterson. "A song was needed for me to fit into the action of the story," Tony later recalled. "I suggested 'Just a Little Love' and my idea was accepted. It worked out pretty well and I have Piper to thank for her coaching."

In "Joey," Tony was well cast as a dim-witted dishwasher whose overprotective mother (Ruth White) smells trouble when her son falls for a provocative blond ex-stripper (Stanley) who comes to work with him. "It was a rather showy part for Tony," says Peterson, who soon followed Tony to Paramount when the studio wanted to turn his script into a feature vehicle for Perkins. "He had a wonderful time working with Kim Stanley. He had a great deal of respect for her. Kim was a very difficult woman, but she was very good with him, and the scenes they had together were really quite marvelous."

Tony was impressed by Stanley's reputation as queen of the Method actresses, and gave an attentive ear to any advice she offered. Still, he could never quite bring himself to pursue the craft he had been born into with Stanley's level of seriousness. Perhaps his nonchalance about technique was a way of coping with the possibility of failure.

"I've always been afraid to audition for the Actors Studio," he admitted with seeming modesty in 1961. "They might say no."

Paramount's first showcase for their boy commodity, *The Lonely Man*, required Tony's presence back in Hollywood on March 28, 1956. More than seven months before the release of *Friendly Persuasion*, Tony was already being treated like a star. Paramount's chief hope for the financial future, the last matinee idol the studio would try to create, Perkins seemed every inch the clean-cut, all-American boy—the perfect fifties antidote to the wave of "dirty shirt" actors that had previously been in vogue. But concern about his sexuality would soon undermine the studio's faith in him.

The Lonely Man, a Western about the troubled reunion between an aging gunfighter and his son, starred Helen's friend, Jack Palance, who had received supporting actor Oscar nominations for his performances in *Sudden Fear* (1952), opposite Joan Crawford, and *Shane* (1953). Making her film debut at the last minute, after Kim Stanley proved unavailable, was newcomer Elaine Aiken, a former beauty queen from Brooklyn who, like Stanley, was a devotee of the Method. Like Tony, she was twenty-four years old and under a seven-year contract with time off for legitimate theater. But unlike Tony, whose weekly salary was $2,500 (for a ten-week total of $25,000), Aiken's total salary for her eight weeks on the picture was $8,000 (supporting actor Neville Brand got $9,000 for just three weeks of work). Shooting began on April 7 in Lone Pine, California, four and a half hours away from Hollywood by car.

Adjusting to his new role as star wasn't easy. Tony was on probation, as it were, being scrutinized and evaluated at every turn. There were reports of bad behavior: snapping at a grip who dared to sit at the cast's lunch table; getting so carried away during a staged fistfight with actor Robert Middleton that a break had to be called; leaving a crew member stranded on the remote location because Tony didn't want him riding in the star's car. Perkins emphatically denied all the incidents.

Adding to the stress was the fact that Perkins, who was not athletic at all, was required to ride horses and shoot guns like a pro. He and Jack Palance had no rapport. Gary Nelson, who was second assistant to director Henry Levin (and who, years later, would direct Tony in Disney's *The Black Hole*) remembers "a lot of tension on the set. Everybody thought it was an important picture they were making. Most of the actors were from the Method school, but it was really Palance who was the macho act. He would go off and do push-ups and run before every scene. People would stand around waiting for him to get ready, and there was a lot of tension in the air."

Humor, again often at the expense of others, was Tony's vent. "He made fun of people who were in B pictures," Maila Nurmi says. "Boy, later he was in some. When he was making *The Lonely Man*, I was living with my mother. One day the phone rang, and it was Tony, and he sounded frightened. He said, 'They're coming! They're coming! They're getting closer! I just thought I'd call you in case this is the last time I'll be able to speak to anyone.' I said, 'What?!' And he said, 'The little pig people! I'm here on the set, we're doing *The Little Pig People*, and I found out they actually exist—and they're coming!' Of course, I couldn't even have worked in *The Little Pig People* at that time, and here he was, in a high-budget film with Jack Palance, pretending to be one of these people in a sordid, minor production."

"We were kids, both of us," recalls Elaine Aiken, with whom Tony was quickly linked romantically by Paramount's publicity department. "We'd travel back and forth to New York. We'd use the same car, mine. We both enjoyed *not* enjoying Hollywood." Tony would dare Aiken to act like a star. "He would say, 'Go over to the studio head and demand such and such. Let's see if we can get it.' Most of the time we did.

"One time, when they asked if there was anything they could get me 'to make me happy'—and I didn't need anything, I was just happy to have a job—Tony said, 'Get peaches from Africa.' We got them. We'd be invited to openings and parties. We were a couple, although there was nothing physical about it."

Behind the studio's flashbulbs and fan magazine stories, Aiken knew that Tony was gay. "I don't think we ever discussed it, it didn't matter. It didn't bother me. I just wanted a friend." With Aiken, Tony could be himself. He would later be seen with Tab Hunter attending private parties at her apartment, dangerously soon after the studio had warned the two men not to appear in public together.

Because of bad weather in Lone Pine *The Lonely Man* finished shooting a week behind schedule, on May 18. The film would ultimately be re-

leased after *Fear Strikes Out*, and would do little for the careers of anyone involved, especially Aiken. She returned to New York, where she
is today considered a top Method guru. *Newsweek* called *The Lonely
Man* "an almost eerily quiet Western, which somehow manages to be
drab." When asked about the film for this book, Jack Palance couldn't
even recall it.

If Tony returned to Fifty-sixth Street, it couldn't have been for
long; makeup tests and rehearsals for his much anticipated starring
role in *Fear Strikes Out* were set for June 11. As an indication of the
studio's faith in him, Perkins was given a dressing room next to William Holden's.

Sympathetic TV director James Sheldon had been Tony's first
choice to direct the Piersall script, but Sheldon didn't feel he had sufficient experience to take on a feature film. Alan Pakula then assigned
the project to another TV director, Robert Mulligan, who had directed Tony and Kim Stanley in "Joey." Karl Malden, another familiar face, was cast as Piersall's ambitious working-class father who, in
his desire to achieve the American dream, pushes his son to the very
limits of sanity.

The writing team of Ted Berkman and Raphael Blau, who had
created the popular Ronald Reagan vehicle *Bedtime for Bonzo*, were
brought into Pakula's office to meet their new star. "Into the room
slouched this tall, skinny guy with long hair falling over his eyes, wearing glasses, stooped shouldered and shy," Berkman recalls. "My first
thought was, 'This guy's going to play a sharp, aggressive ballplayer? Al
must be out of his mind. There goes the movie.' "

Blau remembers that Perkins "was vehement that he wanted no
personal publicity at all. This was his first big role, and he was an *actor*,
not a personality. He refused to have the color of his underwear published in the papers or that sort of thing." Nevertheless, according to
Berkman, during the same meeting "the studio was already busy setting
up a date with one of the starlets to maintain the illusion that Tony was
a swinger with the ladies."

Norma Moore, who played Mary Teevan, Piersall's love interest,
would be one of Tony's most visible "dates." Pakula had cast the
twenty-one-year-old TV actress at the recommendation of director
Mark Rydell. Originally from North Carolina, Moore had worked for
two years at the Neighborhood Playhouse in New York. *Fear Strikes*

Out was her feature film debut. Though they were both living at the Chateau Marmont, the first time she met Perkins was at her screen test: the scene where Jim makes Mary dinner at her apartment after they've just met in the ballpark.

"He was wonderful at the test," Moore remembers. "He couldn't have been easier to meet and to work with, friendly and jovial and warm. We kidded around. He made it easy." But Tony's generosity toward his leading lady would not last long when the truth about his private life threatened to leak out.

Robert Mulligan put his actors through an intense monthlong rehearsal period on the actual sets where the film would be shot. They rehearsed it in sequence, without scripts, like a stage play. The only sequence that wasn't carefully planned was Tony's climactic breakdown scene on the ball field; Mulligan was saving that for the right improvisational moment during the shoot.

Filming began mid-July. Mulligan barred the real Jim Piersall from the set, not wanting any of the cast members to be influenced by him. Still, the self-promoting ballplayer phoned the set every day to find out how it was going.

It was going well, especially with the performance Mulligan was drawing out of Tony Perkins. But Moore sensed that something else was going on, beneath the surface, with the boy she was supposed to be in love with onscreen. "Tony became progressively more aloof as the filming continued," she admits. "It was kind of a shock to me. I'd thought I had this friend, you know. I remember washing his sweaters for him at the Chateau Marmont—I can't believe I did that, that was pretty bad—but he became less and less friendly as the filming went on. Was that part of his preparation? Was he distancing himself because that's the way the role went? I didn't quite understand it. I felt confused, hurt, and very disappointed."

The many publicity dates she was sent on with Tony as his "new best girl" after Elaine Aiken did little to improve their deteriorating relationship. It was just more work. "As far as going out and eating dinner, I don't think we even had that much of a date. We had a photographer there every second. It was all posed. When your every move is photographed, it's not terribly fun. The Paramount costume department even gave me the same gown that Elaine Aiken wore on her date with Tony. I thought I would die when the picture came out.

Tony never said a word; I thought he was the kind who would have noticed."

"The dates for *Modern Screen* were very structured," agrees Venetia Stevenson, who was under contract first at RKO, then at Warner's, and was soon linked in the fan magazines with both Tony and Tab Hunter. "You'd be looking your best and wearing your white fox shawl. It was part of our job to pose for pictures, but it was fun because most of the time you liked the person you were with. Tony and I were actually good friends off camera.

"There was a group of us that hung out: Diane Varsi, Dennis Hopper, Tony and myself and several others. At that time, we all considered ourselves the intellectual elite of the younger people in Hollywood. It was very much a Beat, Jack Kerouac, existentialist period. We talked a lot, and we all wrote." James Dean-ish angst was fashionable, as was paying a shrink to listen to your woes. According to Stevenson, "It was almost part of the acting."

Having arrived from New York a star, Perkins was the only contract player in their circle who was looked up to as a "real" actor. "Anybody that actually knew him liked him," Stevenson says. "He was very kind, imaginative, and fun—almost childlike. But I don't think a lot of people knew Tony. He was very introverted and shy, and he shunned a lot of the Hollywood publicity."

"Tony didn't like adulation, he didn't like recognition," Tab Hunter remembers. "He liked it from his peers. He was competitive, but only with himself. He was very, very hard on himself. He certainly knew what he wanted as an actor. He had a tremendous desire to succeed."

Tony's homosexuality and his close association with Hunter were accepted if not discussed among the contract players. "If a studio knew that a male star was gay, they would do everything to hush it up," Stevenson admits. "I don't know about Gwen Davis, but certainly we all knew that Tony was gay. Because it was a big shock to me when I heard he got married. Not Tony. He was very gay, totally gay. We were real friends, and he would sleep over at my house in the same bed. But there was never, ever any . . . well, you know. If you have a friend of the opposite sex who's gay, it's just in the air. You know what I mean?"

By Hollywood's standards, Tony was almost open about his homosexuality—honest at least among his friends—whereas Hunter had always remained silent about his own sexuality, even among his intimates at Warners. Hunter had been burned by the press, and lived in constant fear of *Confidential* magazine. Tony's young career was still untouched by scandal, but his boyish gullibility and arrogant intellect were about to get him his first taste of big-time trouble.

Finding himself suddenly caught in the cogs of the American dream factory, Tony had a lot on his mind. For the first time since his days at Brooks, he was under serious pressure to play ball. "Tony wasn't an athlete," Karl Malden remembers. "He couldn't throw a ball. They had to hire a real pro, Tommy Holmes, to go out there and teach him how to throw, and he still couldn't do it. There's a scene where we're pitching the ball back and forth in the backyard. We were told to throw it pretty hard, to be mean with each other, really vicious. And Tony gave up. He did it a couple of times and said, 'I can't. That's enough.' "

Tony's physical difficulties did not pass unsniggered at by the film crew. "There were times when he was embarrassed," director of photography Haskell Boggs says. "He was a very quiet person, not the type to cut up on the set. He was sort of strange that way."

Compounding the difficulty at a very basic, unignorable level was the fact that left-handed Tony was playing a right-handed baseball hero. To compensate for the "abnormality" there was discussion about flipping the film and printing it backward so that all the images would be instantly reversed, but the idea, which would require any onscreen signs or words to be written backward, was dropped. Instead, Tony struggled to learn how to throw with his right arm—struggled as he hadn't had to since Jane had constricted the use of his left hand at Miss Carden's School. Away from the derisive eyes of the set, he practiced tirelessly, alone on Marmont Lane. Even so, according to makeup man Karl Silvera, "He just didn't have what I call a baseball player's arm. He was a hard worker, but we used to kid him about a lot of things."

No matter how hard Tony worked to throw like a pro, the macho illusion was shattered whenever Tab Hunter came to visit him on the set, which was frequently. "Tab was a known homosexual at the time," camera operator Leonard South remembers. "I don't think Tony was, he kept to himself. But he used to have Tab come on the set two or three times a week, and they'd have lunch or something. The crew made a lot of jokes about it; they were cruel. Of course, Tony was upset. He'd go off to his dressing room, and answer them in a way that said he didn't want any more of it. If guys made cracks, he'd get upset and just walk away from them."

Norma Moore confirms that Tab Hunter "caused a lot of controversy on the set. He was very nice and friendly to us, coming by frequently, watching, and then meeting Tony afterward. I was well aware of homosexuality; it had derogatory overtones at that time. But it was nothing I ever thought of about Tony until Tab started showing up on the set. That was where the crew's antagonism came from. Tony became more and more difficult as the film went on. By the time we were in the last third or fourth of the shoot, the crew was antagonized by him. They made snide remarks about him, and he just distanced himself. He barely spoke to me by then." For Tony, it was Brooks all over again, but this time with potentially devastating consequences.

"Bob Mulligan was annoyed that Tony was such an introvert," Leonard South says. "He knew the problems and didn't like the situation with Hunter, who was in the news pretty strongly at that time. Toward the end, they [Paramount executives] told Tony to keep Tab Hunter off the set. Then he showed up on the location we were working, and they told Tony again that they didn't want any part of his coming to the set, whether it was at the studio or the location."

Nearly forty years later, Tab Hunter still denies the *Fear Strikes Out* incident: "That's bullshit, total garbage. That wouldn't happen, that wouldn't happen, that wouldn't happen." He also denies ever having heard the rumors of his alleged love relationship with Perkins.

Fledgling producer Alan Pakula was especially nervous about the possibility of a sex scandal, which could instantly topple the film and its star. Desperate, he turned to Louis Peterson, who was at Paramount working on the script for Tony's next picture, *Joey*. "Alan came and talked to me about it," Peterson admits. "He said he was afraid it was going to get into *Confidential* magazine, and he wanted me to use my good auspices to talk to Tony. I said I would not do that, I told him it was none of my business. 'You're the producer,' I said, 'if anybody should tell him, you should. You're in jeopardy, not me.' The whole thing was beginning to be discussed on the lot."

In 1979, Tony privately recounted the trouble to director Joseph Hardy while they were rehearsing the Bernard Slade play *Romantic*

Comedy. "Tony said one thing that always endeared him to me," Hardy recalls, "that when he was a rising young star at Paramount, he was seeing a great deal of another actor, they were around town together, and finally the big studio head called him in and said, 'You cannot do this anymore. We're going to make you a star, and you can't be seen around town with this guy. You've got to get a girl, you've got to stop seeing him.' Tony replied, 'But I love him!'—which left the studio head speechless—and walked out. That kind of honesty on his part, and that kind of charm, probably didn't stand him in too good stead. Which is too bad."

To squelch the leaking rumors, Paramount sent Perkins and Norma Moore on a double date with Tab Hunter and a young actress named Jan Chaney. The happy foursome were seen together and photographed at the Ice Follies, solely for the benefit of the press.

For most people of the era, it was inconceivable that an attractive young movie star could be anything other than what he was being passed off as. "I know that Tab Hunter was on the set quite a bit," Karl Malden admits, "but it never dawned on me. I don't think Tony was gay. I think he was trying to find out. He knew a lot of gays. He was intelligent enough to know the problems that arise. I think he was uncomfortable with women, afraid. When he got married, he did the right thing."

Meanwhile, people were coming at Tony from all sides. Gwen Davis, his romantic sycophant, had begun writing *Naked in Babylon*, her roman à clef about young Hollywood, in which she and Tony were gradually becoming the central characters. "I began to write as an exorcism to get rid of him, because on some level I understood that something was rotten in Denmark, that Hamlet was not a well boy." Every morning on his way to Paramount, Tony would stop by to read the latest installment while Gwen made him breakfast. "He was very excited because it was a good novel," she says.

But her last chapter, a confrontation between their characters dealing head-on with the fact that he was homosexual, couldn't have been written at a worse time for Perkins. He read it, and showed up at her apartment that night—on time, as promised.

"I have a friend who writes songs and poems and funny Valentines, and now she's going to be the most famous writer in America," he told her sweetly. "And then I read the last chapter. *Have you ever been put inside a Waring blender?!*"

"I said, 'Tony, let me off the hook. I'll burn the book, I'll destroy it. Just let me free myself. What do you want me to do?'

" 'Change the ending.'

"So I did. I changed it, and made it very vapid."

Back on the set, Tony, like Piersall, seemed almost on the verge of cracking. Bart Burns, who played Red Sox manager Joe Cronin, remembers that Tony used a real bat for the scene in which Piersall momentarily loses it and starts savagely bashing the dugout walls and benches. Tab Hunter admits that "Tony very seldom got angry, very seldom would you be able to see if something really bothered him. But when he did, he really let it go. He kept a great deal inside. I've seen him get very frustrated about things. He kept a lot inside."

Forty-eight hours before a location shoot at L.A.'s Gilmore Stadium, Bob Mulligan felt the tension had built sufficiently, that the time was right to shoot Tony's big breakdown scene, even though it had not originally been scheduled to take place during that particular game. Tony was given twenty-four hours to prepare for his showstopping moment, which would essentially be a spectacular display of spontaneous, improvised histrionics.

"It was tough for him," Karl Malden recalls. "He was really afraid of that scene because he wasn't a physical person. And that was a very physical scene. He was afraid of what he had to do, run and physically climb that fence. So he just had to let himself go and what happened happened. It rubbed him out."

According to Norma Moore, Tony was especially "serious, very intent, very nervous before shooting that—pacing, not talking to anybody, shaking his hands."

The only person he talked to was Robert Mulligan, who remembers Perkins at that point as "riding on instinct, very giving and very trusting and very brave."

The breakdown scene is remarkable for a number of reasons, not the least of which is the frightening combination of hysterical rage and terror that Tony registers as he runs out of control from base to base in a mad parody of a home run, almost crucifying himself on the chain-link fence to scream with tearful fury at Karl Malden, "Was I good enough? Answer me, Pop, did I show 'em? Was I good enough for you?" before being dragged off, kicking and screaming (and foreshadowing Norman Bates's immortal silent scream at the end of *Psycho*) by an army of uniformed jocks. For gay men at the time, the scene, which still impresses and disturbs upon repeated viewings, must have been at least a subversive acknowledgment of difference—the ultimate fantasy of gym-class defiance, and a heartrending confession of need.

"I have a feeling that Paramount was trying to re-create the kind of conflict that existed between Jimmy Dean and Raymond Massey in *East of Eden*," Perkins said deprecatingly in 1992. "I think they were just trying to give it that kind of flare and feeling."

Movie magazines claimed that Tony was hospitalized after shooting the breakdown. He was not. The only hospital Perkins visited was the set on Paramount stage 10 a week later. Actor Adam Williams, who played Piersall's psychiatrist, Dr. Brown, recalls that Tony continued to be "quite difficult" during their sensitive doctor-patient scenes. "We'd rehearsed for a week, and everything the psychiatrist asked needed a specific answer. But Tony decided he would improvise, he would give answers that were not what I was looking for. Several times I had to stop the shooting because I couldn't answer him."

During the scene where Piersall is lying on a bed after having just come out of electroshock therapy, Tony, who knew Williams had acted in the film *The Proud and the Profane* with Deborah Kerr, pulled his "doctor" down and whispered, "Was she a good kisser? Joan Fontaine's a terrible kisser!"—harking back to his days as the sexually beleaguered Tom Lee. The taunt may have been a last-ditch attempt to pass himself off as "just one of the guys" for the benefit of the crew.

Later in the script, Piersall tells Dr. Brown that he wants to continue his career, "But I don't know if I can. Everybody knows about me. Where I've been." The words easily parallel Perkins's own off-screen isolation and doubt.

In the closing scene of *Fear Strikes Out*, Piersall finds the courage to play ball again in the arms of his steadfast wife—saved, like Tom Lee, by the love of a good woman. As Tony looks at Norma Moore and tells her that he loves her, gradually beaming (a smile is never something that seems to come naturally to Tony Perkins onscreen), he has the look of someone who has just talked himself into something he's not terribly sure about. The music swells, and Tony returns to the field, well adjusted at last, conforming.

Shooting ended three days behind schedule, on August 17, 1956. Production plans for the sensitive *Joey* fell through when producer Robert Emmet Dolan left Paramount after thirteen years, taking Louis Peterson's script with him.

On August 21, an admittedly exhausted Tony Perkins was interviewed for Hedda Hopper's column. When asked if he preferred blondes or brunettes, he replied, "Blondes—but don't know why. Just do."

COG

FTER *FEAR STRIKES OUT*, Paramount almost didn't want to cast Perkins in *The Tin Star*, a Western about a young pacifist sheriff who can only earn the respect of his town by learning to fight like a man. Tony had to fight to get the part, which would give him the chance to share the screen with Henry Fonda. "The producers, Bill Perlberg and George Seaton, told someone who told someone who told someone who told me that they wouldn't have me in their picture for a million dollars," he admitted at the time. Reportedly, he marched right into their office and convinced them otherwise himself. Because of the rumors that were starting to circulate about him, Tony had to make twice the effort to keep up his guileless image for the Paramount big boys. He could no longer afford to be seen around town with the wrong people, and now he knew it.

"They're all out of work," he proclaimed of his former friends at Googie's, "and if you're seen with them, people get the idea you're out of work too."

The Tin Star was to start shooting on October 22, and Tony was due back on the eighth for riding lessons and makeup tests. He paid a quick visit to upstate New York, where Jane had been hospitalized after an automobile accident—it had happened on her birthday, September 12—then rendezvoused briefly with Helen, most likely on the Cape, before returning to California.

Some sources speculate it was there that Helen, at the instigation of the studio, tried to persuade Tony to break off his relationship with "T.H.," as Tony cryptically referred to Tab Hunter in private, for the sake of his career. Whether it was she or Perkins's lawyer, Maurice Greenbaum, who others claim had made an emergency trip to the Coast during the baseball picture, the romantic advice didn't seem to stick.

"Helen was like a mother to him," recalls Tab Hunter, who was seen visiting Fifty-sixth Street as late as 1960. "She's German and has a hard head, I'm German and have a hard head; we got along fine. She was very protective of Tony, which was good for him, to a degree. When you're in the public eye, it's nice to have someone to ward people off. But I also think you have to be exposed to all that and be able to handle it yourself."

Perhaps because his future was looking so bright, Tony became even more guarded than he had been before. Artist Don Bachardy and novelist Christopher Isherwood, well known around Los Angeles as a couple even in the 1950s, met Perkins at a party given by Gore Vidal at the Chateau Marmont and continued to socialize with him occasionally over the next few years. "He had just finished *Fear Strikes Out*, and he was very circumspect," Bachardy remembers. "He never talked queer, or in any way acknowledged his queerness to us. I suppose it was much more usual then to be secretive. Of course, he was carrying on with Tab Hunter for a long time, we were told on good authority." Be that as it may, Perkins was "always by himself" at these get-togethers.

Only in a mixed gathering, such as a party at his pal Elaine Aiken's, would Tony allow himself to be seen with "T.H." Otherwise, he would only venture out alone. Still, among the silent, invisible Hollywood gay community, T.P. and T.H. were very visible, try as they did not to be. A date with Tony and Tab was not unlike Tony's after–*Tea and Sympathy* drugstore rendezvous with William, but raised to a higher degree of paranoia. Simply catching a movie meant taking separate cars, buying separate tickets, sitting in separate seats, and leaving separately. In the late fifties, the Vista Theater was a revival house, near the remote gay neighborhood of Silverlake, that attracted a primarily male audience. It was one of the few places where T.P. and T.H. dared to go together, probably at Tony's insistence. The Vista boasted an esoteric schedule of films and Tony felt no one would bother them there. But the two young stars were still careful.

One "T & T" sighting occurred just before a screening of Jean Cocteau's *La Belle et la Bête*: T.P. marched in, looking straight ahead, and sat far down on the right-hand side. Tongues buzzed. Then T.H. entered and sat in the center, toward the back of the theater. When the lights went down, T.P. got up and went back to sit with T.H. According to one patron who witnessed the surreptitious game of musical chairs, "None of us in the theater thought that was really necessary."

Driving home, the same patron noticed Tab in his mustard-colored Ford Fairlane stopped at the light at Hollywood and Vine. There was a beep, Tab looked up, and behind him was Tony in the powder blue T-bird he had recently bought on a much publicized car-shopping spree with Venetia Stevenson (Tony would soon have his own car repainted mustard, like Tab's). The curious moviegoer followed the mustard and blue cars' intricate series of beeps and signals onto the Sunset Strip in West Hollywood. They turned right on Horn Avenue, where Tony was residing at 1127½, then onto Shoreham, where Tab lived at 9080. There the two roadsters were seen parked together under the same unassuming carport.

"I left a note on the seat of Tab's convertible," the amused "stalker" recalls, "with a drawing of two pansies intertwined. Later, a mutual friend mentioned to me how Tab lived in constant fear of *Confidential* magazine, that he was worried about another possible article. So shortly thereafter I went back to Tab's door to apologize, which I did. Tab was very cold."

For the rest of his rocky career, Hunter would be reported, in typical euphemistic Hollywood fashion, as preferring the company of dogs and horses to women. Though by the mid-seventies it would be common knowledge that he was living in Virginia with his male "secretary," the closest Hunter has ever come to "coming out" was in a 1971 profile for *Rona Barrett's Hollywood* magazine. Extolling the virtues of nature, Hunter said almost mockingly, "I can be alone in my patio with a drink in my hand and fall in love with the scent of my pine trees. If that's queer, baby, then I'm queer."

Though the men lived just a block apart, within walking distance of girlfriends Gwen Davis, who also lived on Shoreham, and Venetia Stevenson, who lived on Clark, the press never caught on to the

Hunter-Perkins affair. "That wasn't part of our consciousness," Joe Hyams claims. "The word *gay* didn't exist. We knew Rock Hudson was gay. We kidded about that because Hudson was overtly, flagrantly gay. I mean, he was predatory, he flaunted it. We all laughed when he married Phyllis Gates. There were several others that we knew about who were gay, and we kidded about them. Tony wasn't one of those. If he was gay, he did a fine job of keeping it to himself." Even so, rumors were rampant in West Hollywood of loud arguments and violence on Shoreham Drive. According to friends, Tony was the more monogamous homebody of the couple.

"Tony wasn't promiscuous," Venetia Stevenson says, "he wasn't one of those guys who would go out to bars every night. I understand that later on he was completely promiscuous. But when I knew him, he had serious relationships."

Maila Nurmi remembers differently: "Everybody in town knew that Tony was brutalizing Tab. Everybody knew it, it was common knowledge. He tore him to shreds, at a time when Tab's career had just been taken away from him and he was very emotionally insecure."

Perhaps Tony's almost schizoid flip-flopping from intellectual to insecure frustrated the cagey Hunter. "Whether he was insecure or not, I don't know," Hunter reflects, "but he came off that way. When you're a young man or woman thrown into a business like that, thrown into the public eye, you have a tendency to adopt a persona. After a while, that persona can become a part of you so that you possibly lose your individuality. That's something one has to really watch carefully. People do put up their own defense barriers, their own walls; they will go so far, and let other people go so far, but not beyond that wall. That's what Tony did, and I respect him for it."

At this point in his career, with two major movies already in the can and another about to be shot, Perkins's place in Hollywood was still hanging in the balance. Paramount had spent millions on an actor who had yet to be seen in a single major film; *Friendly Persuasion* had not yet been released, and while the inside word on Perkins was good and the advance publicity relentless, there was no telling how he would actually go over with the fickle public. After *Fear Strikes Out*, Tony must have felt the rumblings underlying the studio's confidence in him more acutely than ever.

Tony continued to rely on his boyish charm to help him navigate

the choppy political waters of Hollywood—especially in his relationship with homophobic columnist Hedda Hopper. Hopper doted on
the clean-cut, vulnerable Perkins—she would later refer to herself as his
"second mother" (though she was actually his fourth)—and he in turn
cultivated her maternal desire. As with Merrill and Jeakins, he knew
just how to work her. "I've fallen in love with the guy—and at my age,
too!" she declared. "If he didn't have a mother and would allow it, I'd
adopt him."

Mary Webster, who played Millie, Perkins's love interest in *The
Tin Star*, remembers being trapped in his dressing room one day when
Hopper suddenly showed up to interview him. A newcomer to films,
who had toured on stage with Tallulah Bankhead in *Dear Charles* and
had just made her screen debut in Jerry Lewis's first solo picture, *The
Delicate Delinquent*, Webster was understandably nervous in the presence of one of Hollywood's major power mavens. Hopper, however,
who had herself started out as an actress, ignored the girl completely,
focusing solely on her favored boy.

"I wanted to get out of there," Webster recalls. "Tony very gra-
ciously introduced us, and tried to bring me to her attention by men-
tioning some nice things about me. But her attitude was like, 'Later.' I
remember him bending over backward to help me out. But she was
obviously very much a fan of his."

Louella Parsons was also on the Perkins bandwagon. Filling in for
Parsons, who was traveling in Europe at the time, Dorothy Manners
called Tony "the boy who is coming up the fastest of any young actor
in Hollywood. . . . Not that I want to be clobbered by the loyal fans of
James Dean, but not since Jimmy has there been a young actor with the
talent and appeal of this boy."

Amid the persistent hype, *The Tin Star* began filming in the San
Fernando Valley, under the direction of veteran Western maestro Anthony Mann. For this project Perkins was paid $4,500 for each of ten
weeks, totaling $45,000, considerably more than he had been paid for
his labors on *Fear Strikes Out*. (By comparison, his seasoned costar
Henry Fonda, who had worked with Osgood Perkins and Lily Pons in
the 1935 RKO film *I Dream Too Much*, received a grand total of
$175,000.)

Every day the two stars shared a car out to the Paramount ranch,
and Tony was surprised when Fonda, who was famous for being aloof,

recounted the ongoing saga of his private life. "It was one hour out and one hour back for three weeks," Perkins said. "He paced the story to last, picking it up every morning where he'd stopped the day before." Among the subjects Fonda divulged to Tony was his current love affair with beautiful Italian aristocrat Afdera Franchetti, the woman he would soon marry. (Just a few years later, while making *Tall Story*, Tony would share a lover with Fonda's daughter, Jane.)

"Fonda gave Tony a lot of advice," makeup man Karl Silvera remembers, "which Tony really took deeply to heart. He helped Tony a great deal." Although the role of Sheriff Ben Owens, a pacifist who finds his self-respect only after learning to kill like a man, was more suited to Tony's own experience than Jim Piersall had been, the constant use of guns and riding of horses still made it a far cry from the sensitive mooning of Tom Lee. Rodd Redwing, a fifty-year-old Chickasaw Indian who had been in films since 1922, was hired to coach Tony in the drawing and firing of six-guns. Tony supposedly only got the rhythm right by practicing to a jazz recording of "Shine On, Harvest Moon."

Mickey Finn, an ex–L.A. cop turned stuntman who also had a small part in the film, taught Tony how to tumble and stage-fight. It was as intensive and trying as his experience learning to play ball, but this time, instead of withdrawing when the going got tough, Silvera recalls, "Tony became very, very good with a gun." Mary Webster recalls that while Fonda sunbathed between takes, Tony remained serious about his role, disappearing to concentrate on every upcoming shot.

Or maybe he was concentrating on something less professional. The studio may have been able to prevent Tony from receiving visits from T.H. during working hours—Webster later ran into the two having lunch together quite publicly in Beverly Hills—but it couldn't stop him from eyeing other young employees. Tom Orme, a charismatic and pretty blond Perkins look-alike who worked in the Paramount mail room, was one. Like many gay men on the lot, Perkins had the hots for the good-humored Orme, who was well aware of his own sexual appeal to both men and women, but was, unfortunately for Tony, straight as an arrow. Nevertheless, at Tony's request, Orme was transferred from the mail room to the set, where he worked as an "usher" and enjoyed watching the Perkins-Fonda duo perform.

While *The Tin Star* has stood the test of time as one of Perkins's better, more solid films, in retrospect it is fascinating to watch for all the wrong reasons. Tony comes across as a sort of fearful Jimmy Stewart—even down to his now famous Norman Bates stutter, the first inkling of what would later come out so fully under the clever eye of Alfred Hitchcock. Perkins's shiny, pouting lips and traumatized, almost cross-eyed mask of a face have rarely looked quite so fresh or sexy on-screen.

In the climactic final shoot-out, jaw dementedly set à la *Psycho*, Perkins slaps the town bully's face twice before shooting him dead with two guns at once. Reinforcing the macho Hollywood ideal, the next day Sheriff Tony stands for the first time with his arm around marriage-minded Millie as they wave good-bye to Fonda and his woman (Betsy Palmer), who are leaving town. Only after killing a man is Perkins affectionate to his starchy, schoolmarmish girl, as if he had to destroy a part of himself in order to be able to touch her. Years later, with psychoanalysis as his weapon, Tony would play sheriff to his own troubled conscience.

Meanwhile, unsure of the public's verdict on his future, Tony did everything in his power to comply with Paramount's wishes and publicity schemes. In anticipation of the release of *Friendly Persuasion* and *Fear Strikes Out*, the studio deluged the fanzines with Perkins hype. Acting the wholesome, all-American boy, at least during working hours, he said whatever they needed him to say, no matter how ludicrous. For magazines like *Motion Picture, Hollywood Screen Parade, Teen Life, Movie Life, Movie Stars Parade*, and *Movie Mirror*, he talked about everything from Mom to marriage—or, more specifically, why he *wasn't* married.

"I don't think I could act as well if I were married," Tony proclaimed in the December 1956 issue of *Motion Picture*. "I'd have to think about being married instead of acting. But you never can tell. I didn't think I would ever learn to drive a car, either, but I just did." In the same piece, Tony's "perky" date, Elaine Aiken, said, "I think the sweetest thing of all is that he doesn't treat me like a girl."

Saccharine features began sprouting up like weeds, touting Tony as Tinseltown's most eligible bachelor: TONY PERKINS—COULD YOU BE HIS BRIDE?, WOULD TONY DATE *YOU* TWICE?, SWEETHEARTS ("When a fellow, Anthony Perkins, takes his girl, Norma Moore, on a very special date—that's the way that love begins!"), and the more accurately titled WHY TONY PERKINS IS GIRL SHY.

As with Rock Hudson, who was known euphemistically in the fan magazines as "the Quiet One," and Tab Hunter, who preferred the company of four-legged beasts to women, Tony's "bachelorhood" was twisted by the press into a fantasy carrot to dangle before the dreamy eyes of gullible teenage girls. Pushing his new film, Paramount distributed ten thousand *Tin Star* badges to Tony Perkins fan clubs across the nation.

"I'm not a star," Perkins modestly told Sheilah Graham. "I thought when I got this many pictures, that I'd feel like a star, but I don't. A star is someone people go to see in a picture which isn't any good. I haven't reached that stage." Not yet.

As for marriage, he told the columnist, "I haven't got the courage. I've worked so hard for so long, I think it would be irresponsible of me to marry. . . . And when I marry I'll keep my wife in New York. Hollywood is a bad place for marriage—it's hard enough for single people."

On October 30, 1956, an invitational premiere of *Friendly Persuasion* was held at the Fox Wilshire Theatre. It was Tony's first real taste of movie stardom. The event was covered by CBS for Art Linkletter's *House Party* TV and radio shows, as well as by local broadcast stations, MGM newsreels, and foreign correspondents. Fourteen sections of bleachers were set up to seat three thousand fans, supposedly the largest bleacher accommodations ever erected for a premiere. Among the luminaries in the audience were costars Gary Cooper and Dorothy McGuire, Gregory Peck, Debbie Reynolds and Eddie Fisher, Audrey Hepburn and Mel Ferrer, Kim Novak, Jerry Lewis, Doris Day, Natalie Wood, Henry Fonda, Dorothy Malone, and Tab Hunter.

Tony "attended both the preem and the party stag," reported *Variety*'s Army Archerd, and supposedly gave his other ticket to an usherette.

The film opened two days later on November 1 at New York's Radio City Music Hall, the first Allied Artists release to be booked at the prestigious movie palace. Reviews were mixed—*Time* found the look of the film artificial ("The pastures are sometimes dyed a fluorescent green that would surely blind a cow")—but generally enthusiastic regarding Tony's performance. "Perkins scores resoundingly as the son who goes off to fight," said *Variety*, while *Cue* raved that "the find of the picture undoubtedly is talented young newcomer Anthony Perkins."

"My mother pretends she is not delighted by all this," Tony told Sheilah Graham, "but I know she is."

While Tony's career spiraled upward, Tab Hunter's continued to downslide. Nearly two years after the devastating *Confidential* exposé, even the fanzines had now turned on him. Vocal about the fact that his contract with Warners was holding him back from getting more interesting roles on television, and complaining that the studio was not supportive of his recording career, he began to get a reputation as being difficult. Jack Warner put him on suspension. The September 1957 issue of *Teen Life* even ran a piece entitled "When Tab Came Tumbling Down," that declared with almost sadistic glee, "We predict the continuing downfall of Tab Hunter. . . . America is full of good-looking young men, Mr. Hunter, and maybe some of them can act too."

In the next few years, bad press would plague Hunter—first, in 1960, a much publicized (but ultimately groundless) charge of dog beating, then in 1962 allegations that he had illegally imported objets d'art from Red China to sell in his Beverly Hills antique shop. "I never believed I was number one anything," Hunter later said of his days as a matinee idol. "I never wanted any of that glamour. . . . The thing that hurt me so much was how the press, and people in general, blew everything out of proportion."

Tony may have felt that way, too, but he would never be quite so open about his own disillusionment without the protection of a hit film, a hit show, or a family to hide behind.

For Columbia's *The Sea Wall*, his first loan-out film, Perkins received a reported $125,000, a fee much higher than any in his Paramount contract, and certainly more suitable to a star of his impending stature. The French-Italian coproduction, produced by Dino De Laurentiis, would also mark the first of many misguided European projects Tony would undertake in his search for artistic challenge and control, when the mentality of Hollywood became too confining and predictable.

One of the attractions this time was the chance to work with acclaimed French director René Clément, a documentarian who had worked as a technical consultant to Jean Cocteau on Tony's beloved *La*

Belle et la Bête. Clément, whose work bridged the gap between the old guard and the New Wave of postwar French filmmaking, had already won two Academy Awards in the best foreign language film category, one for *The Walls of Malapaga* (1949), the other for *Forbidden Games* (1952).

The Sea Wall would also team Tony for the first time with powerhouse American actress Jo Van Fleet, who had recently won an Oscar for her role as James Dean's mysterious mother in *East of Eden*. Cast this time as Tony's domineering mother, a hardworking widow who believes she can make a financial go of her Malaysian rice fields if her restless teenage kids will just stay home and help her, Van Fleet would later play a similar role with Perkins on Broadway in the phenomenally successful stage adaptation of Thomas Wolfe's novel *Look Homeward, Angel*.

Sultry Silvana Mangano, "the Italian Rita Hayworth," who was married to De Laurentiis, was cast as Tony's sister, and as his older love interest was Alida Valli, the exotic Italian beauty who had been hailed by David O. Selznick as the new Garbo a decade earlier. Richard Conte and Nehemiah Persoff were also featured.

Aside from the money and obvious prestige of the international co-production, the film would allow Tony the chance to sing on the big screen, "One Kiss from Heaven," a ditty by A. Romeo and Sam Coslow (not, unfortunately, Nino Rota, the quintessential foreign film composer, who scored the movie's incidental music). *The Sea Wall* would be shot on location in Bangkok in January and February 1957, and thereafter at the Cinecitta Studios in Rome. It would be Tony's first trip outside the United States as an adult.

"When I asked [Tony] if he was taking anyone with him to Rome," Sheilah Graham wrote in her "Hollywood" column that December, "he looked surprised and said, 'No, should I? I'll have more fun, I believe, going alone.'" That would certainly be true in Bangkok, where Tony would indulge his appetite for casual sexual encounters; but in Rome, far away from Paramount's cautious eye, Tony planned to rendezvous with T.H.

In Bangkok, the cast was put up in, as Tony described it for *Photoplay*, a "Las Vegas–type hotel . . . complete with swimming pool, air conditioning, two restaurants, thick carpets and scorpions in your shoes in the morning." But most of the location work was done 175 miles away, in a bug- and reptile-infested fishing town called Petchburi. Despite the dampness, bad food, and inclement weather, filming progressed smoothly. The strong sunlight gave everyone in the cast such deep tans that the use of makeup for the VistaVision and Technicolor cameras became unnecessary.

In his spare time Tony taped three radio broadcasts in English for the United States Information Service that were beamed by Radio Free Asia to Communist satellites throughout the Far East. Blatant U.S. propaganda, extolling the virtues of American freedom goals as opposed to the intentions of Red China and Soviet Russia, one of the broadcasts was a rock and roll record show for Asian youth, during which disc jockey Tony again managed to work in some good words about Uncle Sam. It's hard to imagine apolitical Tony pulling it off with the proper fervor, but nevertheless everything he said was translated into Chinese, Indo-Chinese, Thai, and Korean.

Friendly Persuasion was playing in Bangkok at the time—in English—but even so, Petchburi villagers would travel miles each way to see it. Thousands of miles from home, handsome American Anthony Perkins, the star of the first foreign film ever shot in Bangkok, was surrounded by fans. He told *Photoplay*, "Once I got caught on a strange street just as a movie house let out after the show. Someone recognized me, and before I knew it I was backed up against a wall, signing autographs madly, surrounded by hundreds of squealing youngsters."

Actor Nehemiah Persoff, who would later act with Perkins in the disastrous *Green Mansions*, recalls that Tony would get his per diem in cash, and casually walk the Bangkok streets with a large Coca-Cola shoulder bag full of bahts (Thai currency). "He must have had over a thousand dollars' worth of bahts in his bag," Persoff says. "It was stuffed with money." Tony would browse the shops without any apparent concern that someone might grab the provocatively open sack off his shoulder.

According to Jo Van Fleet, money wasn't the only thing Tony was casual about in Siam. Away at last from the tense puritan restrictions of Hollywood, with more money—foreign play money—than he had probably ever had before, Tony, tall and lithe and rich, became reckless with his proclivities, indulging himself in a frenzy of anonymous sex. After Tony espoused American freedom on the airwaves, in Petchburi, says Van Fleet, "the little kids would come to his door and yell, 'To-

neee, To-neee!'—because they wanted to come in and have a little
[sex]." The bahts may have had something to do with it.

One time, the actress accidentally caught her young costar outside
with two small boys. He was "feeling their butts," she remembers. "I
didn't say anything, but he turned around and saw me. So [later], when
we did *Look Homeward, Angel*, Tony came to me and said, 'You know
a lot about me, don't you. Please don't tell anybody.' " Word of
Tony's illicit involvement with numerous Thai youths would eventually circulate back in the States.

So, too, would gossip of Tony's intimate relationship with the
film's director, René Clément. The fact that Clément spoke not a
word of English, and that Tony was fluent in French, only added to
their intimacy; the two could huddle together in a language practically
all their own. Clément was exactly the kind of artist Tony fundamentally aspired to be: independent, adventuresome, and respected around
the world—able to call his own shots—an intellectual whose opinion
could silence a room. It's not hard to imagine Tony wanting to get as
close as possible to such a man, who was a far cry from the small-
minded, shortsighted actors and technicians of the Hollywood factory.

To combat the sexual hearsay that was starting to leak out, in
Rome Tony was carefully linked in the press with Natascia Mangano,
the sister of Silvana, even though it was there that he hooked up with
Tab Hunter, who had just bought out his contract with Warner Brothers and was starting to work in Europe himself. "I had to go over to do
something," Hunter recalls, "so I picked up a car in Germany and
drove to Rome, and saw him there for a while." It was assumed by
those who ran into them, like Tony's old housemate Richard Franchot, that the two men were trysting. (At the same time that he was
privately seeing Hunter, Tony was photographed welcoming the ubiquitous Rock Hudson, another of Hollywood's secretly gay stars, to the
Cinecitta Studios.)

Meanwhile, back in the States, *Fear Strikes Out* opened to rave reviews. "[Perkins] delivers a remarkably sustained performance of a sensitive young man, pushed too fast to the limits of his ability to cope
with life's pressures," *Variety* wrote. "It's an exceptional job, reflecting
rapport with the character."

"Up to this point every recent young male star has been compared
to James Dean," noted *The Hollywood Reporter*. "From now on the

standard of comparison, for acting and popularity, is likely to be Tony Perkins. . . . He is the boy that millions of women of all ages will wish fervently did live next door."

Despite the accolades, *Fear Strikes Out* did not score a home run at the box office, probably because of the incongruously serious, almost un-American, subject matter; in the minds of the moviegoing public baseball and mental illness did not mix. Jim Piersall himself thought the film version of his book was "terrible," and apparently had an intense personal aversion to the boyish man who had played him onscreen.

The twenty-ninth annual Academy Awards ceremony took place on March 27, 1957, while Perkins was still in Italy. Tony's performance in *Friendly Persuasion* had earned him a nomination in the Best Supporting Actor category, the only Oscar nomination he would ever get. Also in the running were Don Murray (*Bus Stop*), Anthony Quinn (*Lust for Life*), Mickey Rooney (*The Bold and the Brave*), and Robert Stack (*Written on the Wind*). A supreme story of disappointment—which Tony would tell, jokingly, for the rest of his life—took place the morning after, when he phoned the *Rome Daily American* to find out if he had won. A janitor answered the phone and obediently read Tony the names of the winners. Yul Brynner . . . Ingrid Bergman . . . "Best Supporting Actor won by Anthony"—the man dropped the paper, and Tony froze as his informer fumbled on the other end of the line to pick it up—"Quinn."

As the Rome shooting days dwindled and the oppressive cloud of Hollywood blew ominously nearer, Perkins's behavior took on an almost manic intensity. Nehemiah Persoff remembers Tony playing games more dangerous and uncharacteristically physical than the harmless word games he usually enjoyed on the set with coworkers. "One day at the dubbing stage, Tony and Mickey Knox [the script supervisor] played this game which scared me to death," Persoff recalls, "but it didn't seem to scare them." There was a huge hook hanging from a long, thick chain that was attached to the ceiling of the stage; Tony and Knox took turns standing against the wall, dodging the enormous hook as the other one swung it at him. "The one who flinched first was the loser," Persoff says. "But neither one of them did." Perhaps it was Tony's way of preparing himself psychologically for the insidious rigors of Tinseltown.

En route home, Tony was interviewed in London, where a sour

tone began to taint his responses. When asked to describe the Clément film, which by now had been retitled *This Bitter Earth*, Tony retorted, "In how many words?"

"Five."

"*Rose Tattoo* in the Orient," he replied fliply.

He wasn't far off. Originally intended as a prestige film, *This Angry Age*, as it was finally called in the United States, was released during the summer of 1958, without the benefit of a Broadway premiere, on a double bill with the low-budget Anita Ekberg sexploitation thriller *Screaming Mimi*—a taste of things to come.

"Film abounds in somber atmosphere and sensual situations but the story at times is out of focus," said *Variety*. "Left uncertain is why Miss Van Fleet and her family are on this unlikely location in the first place and how Perkins, who looks strictly from Midland, U.S.A., and Miss Mangano, obviously of Latino extraction, would be paired as brother and sister."

Only the *New York Times* had anything kind to say: "Some will note that the film has a flat literary quality, as did Jean Renoir's *The River* of some years back. . . . But there is considerable truth in this film, if you care to look for it."

Paramount greeted Perkins by staging a faux surprise "Welcome Home, Tony" party for the benefit of the press. Tony was photographed blowing up balloons, opening "gag gifts," and giving an elaborate thank-you speech to his studio "friends" Nick Adams, Dennis Hopper, Shirley MacLaine, Earl Holliman, and starlet Valerie Allen. The only real friend in attendance was Venetia Stevenson. (When asked about Perkins for this book, Earl Holliman couldn't remember ever having met him.)

His next film, Don Hartman's production of Eugene O'Neill's *Desire Under the Elms*, was to begin shooting on May 6, 1957, following several weeks of rehearsal. Delbert Mann, who had won an Oscar for his first feature film, *Marty*, had been signed to direct, and gorgeous Italian film star Sophia Loren had been incongruously cast (by Hartman) as O'Neill's New England heroine, Abby (her name was changed for the film to Anna). Under the guidance of her soon-to-be husband Carlo Ponti, Loren had signed a lucrative four-picture deal with Paramount, and was already being touted by the studio as "the Sizzler" and "the Roman Rocket." Apparently Eugene O'Neill himself had thought *Desire* could be improved for the screen if the girl were made a foreigner, new to American soil. Indeed, against the picture's relentlessly drab scenery, Loren gives *Desire* its only spark of life.

To play Ephraim Cabot, Tony's father in the film, Spencer Tracy had been the first choice, then Clifton Webb. Finally, with some reluctance, Hartman had settled on folksinger Burl Ives, who had recently emerged as a fine dramatic actor in Kazan's *East of Eden,* and would win an Academy Award that very year for his supporting role in William Wyler's *The Big Country.* Still, it was Loren, whose popularity had already begun to eclipse that of her Italian rivals Silvana Mangano and Gina Lollobrigida, who got top billing. (She also received the highest salary: $150,000, plus $30,000 for living expenses.) The press made much of the fact that "the Roman Rocket" would be sharing her first American screen kiss with Anthony Perkins.

Gwen Davis, still in denial about Tony's sexuality, wasn't too pleased. "I was so concerned about his being around Sophia," she remembers. "Of course, she could have chewed him up and spit him out."

Rehearsals began on Monday, April 15, in Paramount's stage 4, where the interiors of the Cabot farmhouse had been built. Except for one day of location work in the Santa Monica Mountains, the entire film was to be shot on soundstages. Much was made of the elaborate sets created by art directors Hal Pereira and Joseph MacMillan Johnson: clapboards and beams taken from demolished mansions were integrated into the farmhouse set, and New England–indigenous trees (elms and birches) were shipped in from as far away as Minnesota to lend authenticity to the exterior scenes on stage 16. To show the change of seasons, clouds were painted on an enormous backdrop in different colors that were visible only under certain lights. But despite all the attention to detail, the movie was shot in black and white, according to a Paramount press release, for "artistic" reasons (meaning money).

Just before shooting, Tony flew to New York to sing one of his new RCA 45 rpm singles on the April 28 *Ed Sullivan Show.* Among the other guests were Lena Horne, Jack Paar, and Jim Piersall. "He spent most of the afternoon curled up awkwardly backstage, watching the stage crew manipulations of sets with intense interest," Sullivan wrote in his "Little Old New York" column in the *Daily News.* "To get him to smile that night, during the rendition of a song, we posted men next to the cameras to flap their ears and do other incongruous things." (The unnamed song could appropriately have been "First Romance," the ditty Gwen Davis had written for him, but it was the more popular "Moonlight Swim" by Sylvia Dee and Ben Wiseman, which would be revived four years later by Elvis Presley in the film *Blue Hawaii*.)

"I can make a happy song sound sad," Perkins noted of his own tremulous, untrained voice.

Back on the Coast to commit O'Neill to celluloid, it didn't take long for Tony to realize he was out of his league. Not only was he pitted against two larger-than-life costars, but another imported female force of nature, Anna Magnani, who was filming George Cukor's *Wild Is the Wind* with his Oscar-winning nemesis Anthony Quinn, had her dressing room right across a Paramount street from his. Tony, it seemed, was surrounded by domineering personalities. (Even Dorothy Jeakins, known on the set as "Big Dorothy" because of her height, was doing the costumes.) Between takes, Tony urgently asked visitors, "What's wrong? What's wrong?"—so unsure was he of his performance in each shot.

One of the problems was that the Cabot father and son disliked each other offscreen as well as on. While such a dynamic may have added to the tension of their scenes together, it no doubt contributed to Tony's discomfort while working on the film. Not only was Burl Ives physically imposing and seemingly fearless, but he was also a zealous Christian who would loosen his vocal cords by thunderously reciting verses from the Bible in his dressing room.

"*Dio mio*, he is a religious man," Loren commented to Delbert Mann. "When he's not acting, he's in his dressing room praying."

Ives and Perkins could not have been less alike. "Burl Ives didn't think Tony was a strong person," makeup man Karl Silvera recalls. "Or maybe it was that he wasn't like Burl, a big, blustering athlete. Burl thought Tony was too 'nice.' I guess that's what Don Hartman saw, though. Evidently, he wanted somebody who didn't have a lot of virile strength." Silvera remembers that Tony was especially concerned about how he would look in the film, especially in the scenes where he had to be shirtless.

"This pressure can kill you," Perkins told a *Photoplay* reporter in the commissary one day. "Sophia Loren and Burl Ives are sitting in their dressing rooms relaxing, while I don't have a minute when I'm not working."

Tony knew he was no match for the voluptuous Italian star, at least not before the cameras. While he admittedly patterned his performance as Eben Cabot on Laurence Olivier's Heathcliff in *Wuthering Heights*—with, as he put it, "an added nasty streak"—he confessed that acting with Loren wasn't easy. "I felt like Charlton Heston trying to play opposite the Burning Bush in *The Ten Commandments*," he told John Knowles of *Holiday* magazine. "When there's a Burning Bush on the screen no one is going to look at me." To another publication he described Loren as "a woman who looks as if she were perfectly turned out by a machine."

"Those big tits must have frightened him," commented one close friend.

Even as late as 1967, after doing a second film with Loren (the flimsy thriller *Five Miles to Midnight*), Perkins still remembered her debut with acrimony. "Somebody told her she should get her face in the camera in every scene," he said to Earl Wilson. "I didn't like my part anyway, and all you could see of me, even in my scenes, would be the back of my head and my ears."

But he told Hedda Hopper a more ingratiating story: "Did you know we almost got married once? It was while making *Desire*. She was depressed one day and so was I. I suggested we go to Mexico and get married. But we got into an argument as to whose car we'd take—I wanted to drive mine. It was a heated battle and we ended by not going because we couldn't agree about the car." At the time, Loren was completely devoted to Carlo Ponti.

"Sophia used to have a lot of fun kidding Tony," Karl Silvera remembers. "We did a sitting in the still gallery, and Ernie Bacharach, who was the Paramount still photographer, wanted them to do some close poses and so forth. It was really funny. She teased him very much, in many ways—just about getting close to her. She was very overpowering."

The film's most crucial scene was to be shot on Wednesday, May 29: Perkins's torrid love scene in the hayloft with the world's most beautiful woman. So highly anticipated was their kiss that studio publicity even joked that the hay had to be fireproofed—because of the close proximity of the lamps, not the heat between the stars. To offset all the attention, which was causing him considerable anxiety, Tony staged a little scene of his own that day.

"He did such a strange thing," Maila Nurmi recalls with absolute clarity. "Toward the last, Gwen [Davis] came over and said, 'Tony wants you to have lunch with him at the Paramount commissary. But he and I are going to buy you a dress first.' Buy me a dress? I had plenty of clothes. 'He's given me the money,' she said. 'I'm going to take you shopping. He's told me what he thinks is right for you.'" The offer made Maila distinctly uncomfortable, but the chance to see Tony was too good to pass up.

Davis took her to Ohrbach's department store and "picked out a thing that was more suitable for June Allyson—a blue-and-white checkered gingham with a little Peter Pan collar. Frightening! Absolutely wrong for me, super conventional and demure, which I am not, by any stretch of the imagination." White polished shoes and white gloves were added to the outfit, and they went to lunch.

Tony met them at the commissary, and afterward escorted them to the stage 16 set. "My! He was nice to me," Nurmi recalls with some cynicism. "They were going to shoot the love scene, it was a closed set, and I wondered why I was watching him shoot a movie—I'd never done it before. I wasn't part of his life, I'd been out of his life for months. Suddenly, there I was. Why?"

Unbeknownst to Nurmi, Tony was using her services as an actress. After a few takes, he stopped the scene and said something to the director. "It was a hot day," Nurmi recalls. "Tony came over to me, took me to a chair, and sat me in it. 'Do you want some water?' he asked. Now, shooting had stopped for this. I later deduced what it was all about. Word got out that I was his fiancée, a socialite. I was sort of being Grace Kelly in order to pique the curiosity of Sophia Loren.

"Later, during a break, he had us all sitting in a row out in the alley—Gwen, Dorothy Jeakins, and I—and he was standing in front of us, parading, while Sophia looked on, wondering, 'What is this? Who are all these women who are adoring this man? What is his charm?' That was one of the last times I saw Tony." Since he couldn't match Loren's sexual supremacy onscreen, he tried psychologically to top it offscreen.

"His working with Sophia Loren was a *joke*," Gwen Davis says in retrospect. "The most sexual woman in the world, and poor Tony. It was not hard to overpower Tony except when you were dealing with him on a mental level. Any woman—not even worth her salt, just a sexual woman—was very intimidating to him."

Next to Loren's cool confidence, in the final film Perkins looks unquestionably ill at ease, coming across as sulky rather than sultry, and vocally pinched. When Anna (Loren) tells her lover, "Nature will beat you, Eben. You might as well confess now as later," it seems distinctly, unsettlingly relevant to something beyond the playacting. Whatever may have occurred between the stars in that artificial barn, years later Perkins would have only fond memories of the love scene, in a project he admittedly found an embarrassment.

In 1958, director Delbert Mann declared, *"Desire Under the Elms* comes to the screen, I am convinced, true to O'Neill. I am proud of it in every way, as I am sure all those who were associated with it are." By 1993, he, too, had formed a different opinion: "Tony seemed slight when matched against Sophia, who was quite powerful. I would like to have seen the picture cast differently. The chemistry, the electricity between the actors was just not quite right. It's not one of my favorite pictures."

The critics did not disagree. "Mr. Perkins . . . seems rather fragile and petulant to be the cuckolder of his sire," wrote *The New Yorker*, "and Miss Loren . . . conducts herself as if her only problem were to keep her eyes open under a most generous application of mascara." In the *Herald Tribune*, William K. Zinsser called it "a listless film . . . cold and mechanical, almost without feeling. . . . Perkins is insipid to the point of being neuter, and this pivotal role has no vigor."

Tony Perkins, the actor and the man, was slipping fast in the crushing cogs of a monstrous career machine that was beyond his control, and far from the realm of art or inspiration. But hope arrived unexpectedly. "One day as I was sitting on the set for *Desire Under the Elms*, an agent handed me a script of *Look Homeward, Angel*," he told the *New York Times* that December. "Before I even read it I knew I was going to do it. One of the reasons I had signed with Paramount was that I had found out they owned the movie rights to the book." Years before on the Cape, Helen Merrill had urged Tony to read the epic Thomas Wolfe novel about a sensitive young artist breaking away on his own.

This *Angel* was not a movie, however, but a play. Tony was about to return to his family roots, the Broadway realm of his father, where he had made a name for himself three arduous years before. For once in his life, providence seemed to be offering him a way out of a bad situation, a chance to start over.

"I feel I have a great need to go back to New York and do a play, because that's where I can learn about acting," he revealed to *McCall's*. "To be an actor in Hollywood you have to produce like a hen given feed. I'm going back. It's not really too late. I'm only twenty-five."

9

ARTIST

EING A STAR IS JUST AWFUL," Tony Perkins confessed in the September 1957 issue of *Photoplay*. The duties of stardom, which he had worked so hard to achieve, had worn thin fast. Angry and emotionally frayed, he indulged in a public farewell spree of Hollywood bashing.

"I'm not really suited to be a movie star," he told *McCall's*. "I have no confidence in myself. I'm not interested in money. I'm not good-looking. I have a hunch in my spine. I can't see worth a damn. I have a very small head. I haven't many opinions. I dislike nightclubs—the kinds of things that bring you easy publicity. I have no string of French girls. I'm not tough. I can't put on a show in public. I'm much too sensitive to be in Hollywood. I'm an ideal target."

On May 9 it had been reported in the trades that he was on the verge of signing with Broadway producer Kermit Bloomgarden for the lead in Ketti Frings's stage adaptation of *Look Homeward, Angel*, to be followed up by a Paramount film adaptation (possibly with Audrey Hepburn), the script for which had apparently already been completed by Miss Frings. With three unreleased movies in the can, Tony felt he could afford to let go of his taxing film career for a while, whether his MCA agents felt it was a wise decision or not. But before being released from the Paramount prison, he still had one stale obligation to fulfill for Don Hartman, Thornton Wilder's *The Matchmaker*, the story of a meddlesome Yonkers widow, Dolly Levi, that later served as the basis for the musical *Hello, Dolly!* Rehearsals were set for July 24.

If nothing else, the film offered Tony his first comedic role, and put him in professional contact with the kind of theater actors with whom he was desperate to connect. Originally intended as a vehicle to reteam Katharine Hepburn and Spencer Tracy, *The Matchmaker* cast was now headlined by Shirley Booth, who had won both a Tony Award and an Oscar for her performance in William Inge's *Come Back, Little Sheba*, and whom Tony had met in Los Angeles during her recent run in *Desk Set*. To Tony, Booth represented the highest order of New York artist, and he immediately began raving to the press that she was his "favorite actress." Like most East Coast actors, Booth was put up at the quirky Chateau Marmont, Tony's first Hollywood home, and he made a point of visiting her there on several occasions.

Also in the cast were talented newcomer Robert Morse, reprising his Broadway role as store clerk Barnaby Tucker, and actress Perry Wilson, who had played Tony's mother in *Fear Strikes Out* and knew him from the Cape, where she lived with her husband, Joseph Anthony, the film's director. Hal Wallis's discovery Shirley MacLaine, who had made her screen debut in Alfred Hitchcock's black comedy *The Trouble with Harry* and who had just played opposite Booth in *Hot Spell*, was cast as the pretty milliner, Irene Molloy. Booth was paid $100,000 for ten weeks' work, with Perkins a close runner-up at $75,000. MacLaine's salary was a mere $25,000 for the same number of weeks.

According to Perry Wilson, her director husband was disappointed with Perkins, finding him to be not as "deep" an actor as he obviously could have been with a bit more effort. No doubt Tony's admiration for and friendship with the film's Dolly Levi didn't help. "Shirley Booth wasn't the easiest person to be close to," Wilson says. "She was a real theater person, and didn't have a whole lot of thoughts about life in general. I don't think she was of a very deep intellect. She hadn't really thought over a lot of things that were going on in those days [namely the blacklist]." The Broadway theater had remained oddly unscathed by McCarthyism; as for Tony, Wilson believes he was just too young to be concerned. Like most people, she wasn't aware of the kind of sexual blacklisting that Tony had known since his early college days; he'd been given plenty of reason just to look out for himself.

In his myopic idolization of Booth and his yearning to be free of Hollywood, Perkins was less chummy with his younger costars. Wilson recalls that Shirley MacLaine was distinctly uncomfortable with him. *Newsweek* reported that Tony had thrown a bucket of water over her head in a rage, when an ad-lib game they were playing one day on the set—mocking other Hollywood types boasting of their sexual conquests—had gone too far. "He has a sense of humor and what seems to be the courage to do these idiotic things," MacLaine was quoted. "Or maybe he's just terribly ignorant."

Tony felt threatened by MacLaine's youthful drive, fearing he would be upstaged and humiliated yet again. "I can't stand aggressive women," he declared in a fan magazine that September.

To try to break through his reserve, on another occasion MacLaine took a movie magazine photo of Perkins that he had tacked up in his dressing room and glued it to the camera, in full view of the entire cast and crew. "I drew a mustache on it and eyebrows and earrings or something, and he got very upset," she said. "I think it's immaturish of him to be mad because I put a picture up. . . . His feelings get hurt if you step out of line." She summed it up when she told *The Saturday Evening Post,* "I've never been allowed that precious moment of seeing what Tony Perkins really is. I don't know what's an act and what isn't an act."

According to one friend, "Tony thought Shirley MacLaine was one of the meanest people he'd ever met."

The Matchmaker wrapped on September 19, 1957. "We had a party for everybody in the film at our house in Santa Monica," Perry Wilson recalls. "Shirley Booth and Shirley MacLaine and all of them came, but Tony kind of kept with my kids out by the pool more than with the grown-ups. He really dug kids a lot. He really didn't feel too comfortable around movie stars and stuff like that. I think he wished he weren't so much in the limelight, at that time."

Soon after, he left for New York, driving across country in his T-bird, to prepare himself for *Look Homeward, Angel* rehearsals. When asked about his latest film, Perkins resignedly told *Holiday* magazine, "I just don't think it's going to be very good."

The film, in fact, is not very good; it's visually lackluster and far too static. But in Tony's case, his comment is a self-fulfilling prophecy. In the title role, Shirley Booth gives a wonderful, understated, spontaneous performance, and as the youngsters, Morse and MacLaine could not be more charming. Only Perkins appears uncomfortable onscreen, though he photographs handsomely.

Fans maintain that his awkwardness is just a facet of his virginal character, Cornelius Hackle. But what can account for the discomfort the viewer feels while watching Perkins strain his way through a light adolescent monologue extolling the wonders of womanhood? Delivering the saccharine first-act speech with excruciatingly false giddiness—staring directly into the camera, in unforgiving close-up—Perkins seems to be reading cue cards, there are so many cuts: "A fine woman is the greatest work of God!" he begins, barely able to contain himself, smiling broadly, almost painfully, with a vacant, evasive look in his eyes. "I mean, really they're different from men, oh yes they are—and they're awfully mysterious, too."

Later, when Dolly Levi defends Cornelius's manhood to his boss, Mr. Vandergelder (played by Paul Ford), with the line, "By day he's your faithful, trusted clerk, but by night . . . well, he just leads a double life, that's all!"—it's hard not to interpret it in a new light relating to Perkins. Near the end of the film, in the drag sequence at the Harmonia Gardens, no one bats an eye as Perkins and Morse dance together in women's clothes, even though Tony looks more frightening than funny, tall and birdlike and sinister, like the still unborn Mother Bates.

Though the critics blandly praised *The Matchmaker*, it was an inauspicious swan song for Don Hartman, who died of a heart attack before the film was released. *Time* magazine wrote, "Tony Perkins, who seems to be trying to recapture Jimmy Stewart's lost youth, paws the ground and in that familiar marble-mouthed drawl reckons that he might try kissing a girl. . . . a highly amusing farce."

On October 11, 1957, Louella Parsons announced that Tony Perkins was the number one "star of the future," according to an exhibitor's poll, with Sophia Loren the first runner-up. Like a bad joke, she wrote: "That doesn't make Don Hartman mad because he picked them both for *Desire Under the Elms*. He says he wants to change *Look Homeward, Angel* so that Sophia could again be teamed with Tony. 'I could make her a foreign girl as I did in *Desire*.'" If Tony read the preposterous statement, it must surely have added to his relief to be back on Fifty-sixth Street.

The play *Look Homeward, Angel* had an almost equally incongruous company, composed largely of talent not from the theater, but from television. It had been adapted from Thomas Wolfe's novel by Ketti Frings, a TV writer whose one previous Broadway play, *Mr. Sycamore*, had flopped without a trace in 1942. Producer Kermit Bloomgarden initially sought the services of seasoned stage directors Moss Hart and Garson Kanin, but neither was available. Finally, in early August, television director George Roy Hill, whose credits included *A Night to Remember* and *The Helen Morgan Story*, was hired to tackle his first Broadway show. After Bette Davis withdrew because of an injury, Jo Van Fleet, with whom Hill had worked on the small screen, was signed to play Eliza Gant, her first role on the New York stage since 1953's *A Trip to Bountiful.*

Wolfe's autobiographical tale of a dreamy young man struggling to break away from his dysfunctional family (particularly Eliza, his domineering mother) would prove to be Perkins's best career move since *Friendly Persuasion.* At the time he received Ketti Frings's script, he had also been offered the role of George Willard in Christopher Sergel's adaptation of Sherwood Anderson's *Winesburg, Ohio.* Directed by *The Matchmaker's* Joseph Anthony, *Winesburg, Ohio* opened on Broadway on February 5, 1958, with an impressive cast that included Dorothy McGuire, James Whitmore, Sandra Church, and Ben Piazza (in the role Tony rejected). It closed after just thirteen performances. *Angel*, on the other hand, would go on to win both the New York Drama Critics Circle Award and the Pulitzer Prize for Best American Play of the 1957–58 season.

But it was not a natural-born hit. George Roy Hill's assistant, Virginia Raymond, who had worked with him on NBC's *Kraft Television Theatre*, remembers that the first version of Frings's play "so little resembled [the novel] that George Hill went to Los Angeles [where actors were auditioning at the Huntington Hartford Theatre] and spent three months helping Ketti Frings bring the book into the play." Frings had originally angled her version from Eliza's point of view, and had "treated [Eugene Gant] like he was just her sixteen-year-old son. That kind of struggle was going on all the time. George and Tony really brought the play to what it was, even though Miss Frings got the Pulitzer Prize."

Rehearsals began October 14. George Roy Hill remembers Perkins as a natural, untrained actor who was "ideal for the part. He had a kind of gawkiness, a blasé sensitivity that was quite remarkable. His approach was a purely pragmatic one; he'd find a way to play it, and he had no theories to get in his way. I don't know what devices he used internally, but he was always very concerned with acting as acting. His rehearsal time was spent experimenting." (At one rehearsal, Hill had Tony simulate an orgasm during the scene where he caresses his father's Carrara marble angel. "It really worked very well, but when Kermit saw it he went up the spout.")

"It was an interesting time for actors," Virginia Raymond recalls, "because the Method was just becoming what everybody wanted to do." Young Perkins fell somewhere in between the mannered style of his father's era and the new, seemingly organic style exemplified by Brando and Dean. "Mixing old styles with the Method was difficult. Jo [Van Fleet] was a huge aficionado of the Method, and Tony was very drawn to her for that."

The following year, while still in the run, Perkins admitted to *Holiday* magazine that "the single performance which influenced my own acting most was Brando's in *On the Waterfront*. . . . That's the direction I want to go in as an actor. To convey the maximum with the simplest, barest means. . . . I still have never studied acting, which manifests itself in a feeling of inadequacy." Tony was finding his boyish MO, which had always been his primary survival skill, suddenly at odds with a deeper need in himself.

Years later, on the set of Mike Nichols's *Catch-22*, Tony would tell costar Austin Pendleton that he had found Van Fleet's "Method" lacking. "He loved her," says Pendleton, who saw the show on opening night, "but he thought her work was too easily read, technical, that you could see the wheels going."

And there were a lot of wheels turning, not all of them artistic. Jo Van Fleet was as famous for her petty, conniving temper tantrums off the stage as she was for her acting on it. "Jo was nothing if not difficult," George Roy Hill admits. "She had an innate desire to create mischief. She would get into situations and then sit back and watch them progress." According to Hill, Van Fleet and the legendary Welsh actor Hugh Griffith, who played her alcoholic husband, "hated each other with a good, full hate."

"None of the cast liked her particularly," remembers Florence

Sundstrom, who played Fatty Pert in the show. "She was so self-centered and so insecure."

Part of the problem stemmed from the fact that Van Fleet disliked playing the money-grubbing virago night after night. Lenka Peterson, who replaced Frances Hyland as Laura James, Eugene's love interest, recalls that "Kermit Bloomgarden got mad at her because she wanted to be loved and her character was a bitch. Jo would always schmaltz it up, she'd get sloppy because she wanted the audience to sympathize with her, and it would dissipate her performance." Things got so bad that one night the stage manager darkened the whole house midperformance when Van Fleet willfully made a move she had promised not to. Bloomgarden refused to renew her contract in 1958, causing Van Fleet to beg the colleagues she had abused to sign a petition to keep her on board—in vain.

If Tony was bothered by Van Fleet's shenanigans, for the most part he kept it to himself. "He was so good, there wasn't anything she could do to put a hatchet in there," Florence Sundstrom says. But Rosemary Murphy, who made her Broadway debut as Perkins's stage sister Helen, maintains that working with Van Fleet was "very hard for Tony. I remember him saying one time, 'She has to have everything *her* way!' But he was very clever, and knew that out of town it was her play, but opening night on Broadway it was his play. He had the sense to hold back until the right moment—an actor's animal instinct so that she wouldn't squash him!"

Though Tony's name was the casting coup for the show, he downplayed his movie star status. By the time *Angel* reached Philadelphia's Walnut Street Theater, tickets for the Saturday, November 9 opening night had already been sold out. It was a good omen; the critics were ecstatic in their praise, comparing it with landmark dramas like *Death of a Salesman* and *A Streetcar Named Desire*. "Anthony Perkins, returning to the stage after a brief but bright spell in films, appears to be in line for a stack of awards for his sensitive portrayal of the novelist," exclaimed *Variety*. "He has a scene in the last act that hasn't been duplicated here for many seasons."

"Intensely moving drama," wrote the *Philadelphia Inquirer*. "There is nothing of the moony adolescent in Perkins' approach; nothing counterfeit in his emotions. He is not a boy to be ridiculed, but a young man to be respected. . . . Jo Van Fleet . . . gives a performance which wins applause at the end of all her major scenes." Among the people who came to see the show in tryouts were Tab Hunter and Liz Smith.

Despite its success, there was concern at the top that *Angel* still needed more Wolfe and less Frings in order to make it on Broadway. Rewrites ensued. Adding to the growing tension was the fact that the play was set to open at the Ethel Barrymore Theatre (where Perkins had made his Broadway debut just three years before) on November 28—Thanksgiving night. "Kermit Bloomgarden always wanted to open on a Thursday," Virginia Raymond recalls, "and we all said, 'Everybody's going to fall asleep after a big dinner!' But somehow there was enough Thomas Wolfe there to really impress. Nobody was more surprised than all of us."

That night, when the final curtain fell, audience and cast alike were moved to tears. Seventeen curtain calls followed. "I've been in plays that were successful after that, but I never had that tingle on an opening night," Rosemary Murphy says. "It was really electric, and partly because of Tony."

Austin Pendleton was in the audience: "All the press was there that night. There was a lot of electricity about it. The programs were gold. It was a brilliant night, and Tony was remarkable. I went to see it a couple more times while he and Jo Van Fleet were still in it. They were extraordinary together. I remember it better than things I saw a few weeks ago." Gwen Davis was also there, along with hordes of teenage fans, and, of course, Helen, Jane, and Michaela. ("[Jane] was lovely, but I didn't feel there would be a lot of affection there," noted Virginia Raymond.)

The New York critics raved. "Seldom has there been so perfect a mating of actor and character," wrote *Newsday*'s George Oppenheimer. "Judging only from this one performance, I have not the slightest hesitancy in stating, loudly and unequivocally, that Mr. Perkins is the finest young actor of our contemporary theater."

"Mr. Perkins' grave, quiet yet buoyant acting gives continuity and a future to this endearing character," declared *Times* critic Brooks Atkinson. "And Miss Frings, being honest, gives it an intimation of doom just before the curtain falls. For we know that this lad who starts off so brightly is beginning a journey that will always be tormented."

Aiding him in his quest to achieve the high theatrical standards of

Osgood Perkins was George Roy Hill, who shared with Tony, as Murphy recalls, "an almost fatherly relationship."

Tony, in fact, was nearly obsessed with Wolfe, reading the novel of *Look Homeward, Angel* between acts of the play. "I'm not doing this for glory," he told Joe Hyams. "It's a character I can identify with, but I wouldn't emulate. Wolfe was bent on self-destruction—he was an agonized man, fruitlessly searching for things he never wanted to find. He used to walk up and down the streets looking in windows for 'it,' but if he found it he would have had nothing much to write about."

In his own version of Wolfe's futile search, Tony would rise at 6 A.M. on Sunday mornings, after the exhilaration of Saturday night's performance, and drive the empty city streets—slowly, often right along the center divider—in his Thunderbird convertible. "I drive looking up, at about a forty-five-degree angle," he told *Times* writer Arthur Gelb. "You find some of the most fantastic revelations this way. The wonderful apartments with their balconies, for example. This terribly personal way of life right in the middle of everything. It keeps me interested for hours at a time."

After the play was safely ensconced as a hit, an unnamed colleague revealed that Tony had been terribly nervous and unsure of himself throughout the entire rehearsal process. "Tony's anguish was genuine. He believed everyone else would be wonderful, and he would be terrible. Part of the difficulty stemmed from the fact that few things are harder for him to do than to raise his voice in anger, and the role required it. Tony drove himself desperately, and his ultimate portrayal of Eugene Gant was something that he ripped from within himself."

When *The New Yorker* asked Perkins if there were any similarities between his own childhood and Wolfe's, he admitted, "Well, some of the characters seem right out of my family." In the act 3 confrontation scene between Eugene and Eliza, when the boy thanks his miserly mother for her "ten million hours of indifference" and "two minutes of cheap advice," it's not hard to imagine the sense memory Tony drew from to work up the emotion. "By God," Eugene tells her, "I shall spend the rest of my life getting my heart back, healing and forgetting every scar you put upon me when I was a child. The first move I ever made after the cradle was to crawl for the door. And every move I ever made since has been an effort to escape." Eliza, for her part, responds with the same rigid platitudes she has always fallen back on: "Now for Heaven's sake, spruce up, boy, spruce up! Throw your shoulders back! And smile, look pleasant! Let them know up there that you *are* somebody!"

"Ninety percent of the world has had this kind of a sudden test with their mothers," Tony said. "I felt it the first time when I left for boarding school when I was fifteen; again when I went to college and later to Hollywood. My mother didn't say to throw my shoulders back, as Eugene's mother does, but words to that effect—'Don't bite your fingernails!' "

Arthur Hill, who played his brother in the show, remembers that Tony "shattered the audience" in the death scene "because he was shattered himself." Lenka Peterson agrees: "His emotions were true; I don't think he ever faked or indicated. He always found it somehow within himself. But he was very private in his work. He never talked about it." One backstage observer commented about Perkins, "There are a lot of crossed wires in there, and I wouldn't want to tangle with them."

On some level, Perkins still felt undeserving of all the accolades and attention. According to Mario Busoni, back at Helen's Tony would still say with a "bittersweet irony, 'I have a certain boyish charm that I'm cashing in on right now.' He was not his father. He did not have the arrogance about himself that many people in the theater do."

Rosemary Murphy remembers that after each show he "always wanted to be reassured that he'd been okay." And he never missed a performance—except once when he was running a fever. (Even so, he showed up that night in the back of the theater, a muffler wrapped around his burning head, to see how his prize role would be played by his understudy, Lionel Kane. He must have been pleased when about 250 patrons—a quarter of the audience—asked for refunds upon learning of his cancellation.)

"Sometimes actors talk to me about methods and training and all of a sudden I get a terrible chill," Tony admitted with unusual candor. "I don't know what they're talking about. I'm afraid to start studying now, just as some actors are afraid of analysis—they fear it will change them. I'm really on treacherous ground."

Stars like Joan Crawford, Audrey Hepburn, William Holden, and Laurence Olivier were among the more recognizable visitors who poured into Tony's dressing room after the show—and always there were the hordes of teenage autograph hounds, reminders of his dormant obligations on the opposite coast. The fans waiting for him at the stage door were so overwhelming that he devised a secret escape route, involving various hallways, tunnels, and building underpasses, so that he could get away unseen.

Nevertheless, Charles Williamson recalls clearly that Tony "felt enormous relief to be back in New York, working there again, without the pressures of all the fan magazines. Any bitterness he felt was displayed simply by his enthusiasm for being in New York." Apparently, Perkins was angry with Louella Parsons, who, after all the care he had put into his dealings with the Hollywood gossip community, had jokingly printed in her column that he and Tab Hunter were seen together so often that fans might start getting the wrong idea. He felt stabbed in the back.

So, too, did Tony's high school chum Henry Scammell, after a backstage visit. "Tony was quite rude and hurtful to my wife," Scammell says. "He treated her sort of at arm's length, and she was very shy. He had the flu, I think. When we were leaving, he called out to me in one of these broad stage whispers which was intended to be heard by everyone, 'Henry, ditch the broad and meet me later!' My wife heard it, and I could see her just curl up." The two friends would not speak again until after Tony himself was married, fifteen years later.

When Ellery Woodworth visited Tony on behalf of Browne and Nichols to ask for a donation for a proposed Osgood Perkins Memorial Theatre, he was met with a similarly flip reception. "Well, you know, I really don't have any money," the actor told him. "The fact is I don't have anything. The people who run me own everything. They own me, and manage everything I have. I don't have any of it." Tony still handed all his money over to Jane to handle for him.

Life onstage was much more satisfactory; Tony could easily compartmentalize relationships that were born from artifice. "The reason we were such a happy company was because of Tony," Rosemary Murphy maintains. "He needed to be loved, and he needed to be wanted, and the backstage life was wonderful."

Games and practical jokes were common. During one act, Tony had almost a minute offstage in which to collect a prop pencil and notebook for his next scene; invariably the other cast members set up a race-against-the-clock obstacle course for him to run to get the items.

"Once we made him go all the way up to the second floor," Murphy recalls fondly, "to find me in an *Esquire* pose in panties, holding the pencil. He just adored that."

"One time we were both offstage for a while, and we were lying on these boxes, side by side, just talking," Lenka Peterson remembers. "Tony took my hand, and I just wanted to stay beside him forever—I was so crazy about him! When he was with you, he was totally with you. There was nothing else. And you felt like you could talk to him about anything." As he had with Mary Fickett during *Tea and Sympathy*, Tony fabricated a seductive offstage rapport with Peterson that ran seamlessly into their onstage work together.

Despite the charm he was able to exude on the opposite sex, it was tacitly known that Tony was gay. "Oh, there was no question," Murphy says. "It was a terrible shock to me, because in those days when I had a crush, I didn't want to accept that. But there was no mistaking it."

"Even in the theater, nobody would admit they were gay," Peterson confirms. "Theater people would be understanding about it, but just the same, it wasn't something that you would be blatant about. We had progressed a little bit beyond the general public, but not much. It was assumed that Tony was gay at that time. There was word that he was in love with Tab Hunter, though I never saw him."

No one remembers seeing Timmy Everett, either, the promising dancer turned actor who was getting rave reviews just two blocks away at the Music Box Theatre for his supporting role as the lonely Jewish boy in Elia Kazan's production of William Inge's *The Dark at the Top of the Stairs*, with Teresa Wright, Pat Hingle, and Eileen Heckart. Exactly when Everett and Perkins first met is unclear, but by the time their shows were both playing to packed houses, they had become romantically involved, even living together briefly before Tony left *Look Homeward, Angel* to return to Hollywood. (Coincidentally, at the same time, dancer Grover Dale, who would become one of the major loves of Tony's life, was appearing at the Winter Garden Theatre as Snowboy in the Leonard Bernstein–Stephen Sondheim musical *West Side Story*.) Company members knew about the Tony–Timmy relationship because the two men made frequent visits to each other's dressing rooms, and talked about each other. Like Tony, Timmy was a loner who did not join in group activities such as the Broadway League softball team (as Pat Hingle wisely put it, "A dancer is not necessarily a ballplayer").

"He was an outrageous young man," recalls dancer Sondra Lee, who appeared with Everett in Marc Blitzstein's musical *Reuben, Reuben*. "He had a kind of maniacal energy as a dancer." He quickly became as famous for upstaging other performers as he did for his talent and good looks.

Actress Tuesday Weld brought Everett to the attention of Elia Kazan, who cast him in the Inge play. (Weld, meanwhile, was fired from the same show before it got to New York; she would, however, go on to have a successful career in films, giving wonderful performances opposite Tony Perkins in both *Pretty Poison* and *Play It As It Lays*.) Despite all his success—he would win a Theatre World Award for *The Dark at the Top of the Stairs*, and later an Emmy for his role opposite Kim Stanley in a two-part episode of the *Ben Casey* TV series—Everett's wildly erratic behavior started to manifest itself offstage as well as on.

Though rumors of drug use had always plagued the volatile young dancer, by the time he appeared in the Kazan production, his emotions were out of control. According to company members, Everett would regularly throw tantrums in his dressing room just before the show, threatening not to go on. These emotional eruptions were usually the result of a backstage visit from Tony. "Nobody really loves me," went the hysterical, tearful refrain, into whoever's shoulders happened to be available. But invariably, at the sight of his understudy, Ed Earle, ready to go on, Everett always managed to pull it together. He never missed a performance.

Everett also had a penchant for getting violently drunk at gay bars, and the job fell to Earle to rescue him from the excesses of booze and sex. Anachronistically reckless regarding his homosexuality, Everett felt himself somehow above the danger of fifties homophobia. "He was an enormously talented young man who was quite confused," stage manager Burry Fredrik says. "[He and Tony] kept a lid on it, they certainly were not advertising [their relationship], but we were aware very definitely that something was going on. Timmy was far less stable than Tony. I think Tony had made a much better adjustment to that part of his nature, to homosexual activity." Much of Timmy's insecurity was said to stem from the fact that he was pitifully underendowed sexually.

When Tab Hunter visited New York to see Tony in *Angel* again, the two were inseparable, and consequently Timmy's backstage histrionics increased. According to record producer Ben Bagley, who later put Perkins's singing voice to good use on several of his obscure Painted Smiles LPs, Everett was "very enamored, and Anthony did not reciprocate. But he had great sympathy for anyone who felt this way. Tony felt it was a big responsibility to fall in love, that you had to be very, very careful before you entered into anything." In a desperate plea for sympathy, to get Tony's full attention, Everett finally tried to take his own life.

Maila Nurmi, who later knew Everett in Hollywood, heard the whole story. "Tony tried to drive Timmy Everett to suicide," she says. "All the gay boys were after Timmy, who was very pretty and very delightful. When Timmy had been on Broadway, he'd had a lover's quarrel with Tony—Tony had rejected him or done something to break his heart—so Timmy Everett had slashed his wrists after a matinee and was hospitalized, clinging to life, hovering near death, and calling for Tony. They told Tony, who just said, 'That's his problem.' Timmy did survive, but he eventually died of a heart attack."

"Timmy was a troubled guy," a married Perkins tersely commented years later to Fonda family biographer Peter Collier. "He was aggressive, antagonistic, soulful. He didn't leave anything out."

After the suicide attempt, Everett did not return to the show. But by the time he opened at the Morosco Theatre with Maureen Stapleton, Eli Wallach, and Suzanne Pleshette in S. N. Behrman's *The Cold Wind and the Warm* on December 8, 1958, his drug taking had become more overt. He was no longer notorious for his backstage fits, but rather for his black leather carrying case full of large vials of pills, which he popped constantly. (He later became even more seriously addicted to pills after he and his sister, Tanya Everett, opened the discotheque Il Mio in the Delmonico Hotel on Park Avenue at Fifty-ninth Street.)

Not even Everett was exempt from the conformist gossip of columnists like Dorothy Kilgallen, "the Voice of Broadway," who in May of 1958 printed that he was "wooing" Joan Crawford's daughter, Christina, and later linked him romantically with his friend Tuesday Weld. During the run of *The Dark at the Top of the Stairs*, when Everett's jealousy over Tab Hunter was at its peak, there had even been some fear that Kilgallen would blow the lid on "the T Triangle"—

Tony, Timmy, and Tab. Such a column could have destroyed all three careers in a single swoop.

Meanwhile, a lengthy profile in the March 3, 1958, issue of *Newsweek*—"Tony Perkins: Shooting Star"—served to keep the autograph hounds lapping and yapping. The piece hailed Perkins as "possibly the most gifted dramatic actor under 30 in the country."

"Everything he does is an extreme act," an unnamed colleague was quoted. "He has a small malicious streak in him. He has no friends. He wants to be accepted and he probably feels if he could be a movie star he *would* be accepted. But this is a false premise. When he grows up he'll have everything he needs for this profession. Right now he's like the beautiful dust jacket of a book with nothing between the covers. I think he ought to meet a good psychiatrist."

In his own defense, Tony said, "Hell, even *I* don't know what my real personality is, so how can anybody else? People have said that I try to create an illusion of boyishness, that I hide behind a mask to conceal my real personality. Well, that's hogwash. Anybody who has to create an illusion to live is foolish."

The article, though not the most flattering, was a huge source of publicity for Paramount's hottest property. But it must also have been a disheartening reminder for Tony that his time as *the* talented young toast of Broadway was running out.

On April 13, 1958, the twelfth annual Tony Awards were presented at the Waldorf-Astoria. *Look Homeward, Angel* had been honored with nominations in several categories, including Outstanding Play, Outstanding Dramatic Actress, and Outstanding Director. Tony, of course, had been nominated for Outstanding Dramatic Actor along with his costar, Hugh Griffith. Together they were up against some formidable competition: Ralph Bellamy for *Sunrise at Campobello*, Richard Burton for *Time Remembered*, Laurence Olivier for *The Entertainer*, Peter Ustinov for *Romanoff and Juliet*, and Emlyn Williams for *A Boy Growing Up*. Bellamy won the prize; Perkins and Griffith may have canceled each other out. *The Dark at the Top of the Stairs* tied with Dore Schary's *Sunrise at Campobello* for the Outstanding Play trophy.

Tony began to talk about future plans, of doing another stage play, possibly a musical version of the classic film Western *Destry Rides Again* (the job ultimately fell to Andy Griffith). He told Hedda Hopper that he wanted the lead in Josh Logan's proposed film of *Parrish* (a role that would ultimately go to blond, blue-eyed Troy Donahue), and in April it was announced that he would star with James Cagney in the Irish Rebellion film *Shake Hands with the Devil* (but that heroic role went to beefy young star Don Murray). Perkins expressed a wish to tackle a movie or stage version of F. Scott Fitzgerald's *This Side of Paradise* as a literary follow-up to his immersion in Wolfe.

Backstage visits from two very different directors offered Tony a choice between two divergent career paths. First, Mel Ferrer came to the theater to see if Perkins looked Latin enough to play Abel Guevez de Argensola, the brave young fugitive who finds phantom romance in the jungles of South America, in his adaptation of the W. H. Hudson novel *Green Mansions*. Ferrer's glamorous wife, Audrey Hepburn, had already agreed to be part of the package to ensure MGM's financial support. "The next week," Perkins recounted years later, "Billy Wilder stopped by my dressing room and asked if I'd star in a movie with Frank Sinatra. I told Billy I'd committed myself to Mel, and couldn't go back on my word. Well, *that* movie turned out to be *Some Like It Hot*, with Tony Curtis and Jack Lemmon."

Associates close to Perkins at the time maintain that the real reason Tony chose the jungle adventure over the drag comedy was that, after *The Matchmaker*, he did not wish to do another film in which he would be seen in women's clothes; despite the brilliance of Billy Wilder, Tony felt *Some Like It Hot* would be bad for his uncertain image, and opted instead to work with superstar Audrey Hepburn. How much his agent, Hermon Citron, advised him in this decision is not fully known, but it's clear that Tony felt the impending pressure of Hollywood, and the need to conform once again to the unforgiving standards of American malehood. Letting go of the artistic instinct that had led him back to Broadway, Perkins's conscious choice to star in the unplayable *Green Mansions* would not make his return to MGM a happy one.

"The trouble with being someone [famous] like me is that everything I do seems suspect," he complained to *Look* magazine toward the end of his run in the play. "Actually, everybody is nonconformist in some way or other, but nobody admits it."

Early that summer, George Roy Hill threw a party for the cast and their families at his house on Fire Island. Again, Tony ended up spending most of the day with the "other" kids. "He loved children," actress Bibi Osterwald recalls vividly. "Tony was not married, but other people brought their children, and Tony went out of his way to play with them. He showed my son how to fly a kite—he must have spent two hours that day teaching him how to get that kite to fly. I'll never forget that."

On the train back into town, Tony spoke wistfully of Osgood when the subject of a stabilizing family life came up among the theater folk. "Well, I don't know what that would be like, I never had that," he told Osterwald, who remembers him looking "quite sad when he said it. He wished that he'd had a good relationship with his father." With every turn of the locomotive's wheels, Tony could already feel his surrogate family and his time as an artist slipping away from him.

"Tony was always sort of sad," Lenka Peterson recalls affectionately. "He was absolutely glorious looking, intelligent and creative and talented. But I always felt that he never quite got to the level of stardom that he should have, that his work should have brought him many more rewards—like he was a little bit at war with himself, almost as if something in him said, 'I don't deserve it.' When people have a clear feeling of self-respect and approval, they move toward their goals very directly, and they usually get what they want. But Tony was a more complicated person. It might be that he was taking on the attitudes of the general public and turning them against himself. If Tony were born now, he would be freer, because the world isn't as judgmental about people like that anymore. I feel like Tony paid a high price for society's ignorance and indifference."

He gave his final performance in *Look Homeward, Angel* on June 28, 1958. That night, backstage, the cast placed shirt cardboards spelling out WE LOVE YOU TONY up the stairs and down the hall, along the route where he would run his prop race. It was an emotional evening for everyone. "Closing night, Tony didn't want to leave the theater," Rosemary Murphy remembers. "He and George Roy Hill had a very special bond. I left at midnight, but he was still there, crying and hating to leave."

His replacement was Andrew Prine, a twenty-two-year-old actor who had never been on Broadway before. Film star Miriam Hopkins took over the role of Eliza, opposite Ed Begley as the alcoholic husband. With the changes, the play lost its magic. "Mr. Prine skillfully reproduces the outlines of the original performance by Mr. Perkins," wrote Brooks Atkinson. "But . . . something illuminating has been lost. Mr. Perkins had a defenselessness and a sense of adolescent privacy that gave the drama greater poignancy." The overall performance of the new cast, claimed the critic, was "more temperate" and less true to the sprawling emotions of Thomas Wolfe. As for Tony, he disliked the performances of both the new mother and son with a proprietary intensity.

Tragically, and in true keeping with the bittersweet timbre of Wolfe, the performance of which Anthony Perkins was most proud—which, probably for the first time, he had dug deep into himself to produce, and which was quite possibly the most complete and deeply felt performance he would ever deliver, either on stage or screen—was lost forever. No videotape remains of his interpretation of Eugene Gant. The performance lives on only in the dwindling memories of the audiences who were there to witness it.

Though Tony had fully hoped to bring his performance to the screen, no film of the play was ever made. As early as April 1958, there were reports that executives at Paramount, which controlled the basic story rights, were hesitant to proceed with a motion picture adaptation because of the possibility of claims by Ketti Frings. Later, when Kermit Bloomgarden, along with the estate of Thomas Wolfe, tried to negotiate a consolidation of the rights to both the play and the novel, the studio placed the exorbitant price tag of half a million dollars on the book, when they had paid only forty thousand for it years before. In the mid-sixties, Jack Karp, former production chief at Paramount and D. A. Doran were slated to produce a film, which never materialized, and in 1969 Joshua Logan was reportedly ready to direct a movie from the script by Frings. But by then, Tony was too old to play the part he had created. *Look Homeward, Angel* has yet to make it to any screen, large or small.

Yet, oddly enough, an element of Tony's performance does live on today, in an unexpected and appropriately roundabout way. Screenwriter Joseph Stefano had seen a full rehearsal of the play at the invitation of his friend Leonard Stone, who played the role of Hugh Barton. "I remember watching this very long scene," Stefano says, "and I found my eye kept drifting over to Tony, who had nothing to do, but just kind of stood there and began to dominate the scene with his stillness. He had a look about him that was . . . I don't know. Kind of an innocence, a really pellucid innocence." Two years later, when meeting with Alfred Hitchcock to discuss the script for *Psycho*, that image of

Tony standing silently on the stage would come hauntingly back to Stefano, and would ultimately mold his conception of the film's lonely motel keeper, Norman Bates.

"Tony was truly remarkable," maintains Stefano. "There wasn't any question that I would be seeing more of him on the stage or on the screen. I felt about him the way I have felt about very few other performers."

Eugene Gant would be resurrected in Norman Bates, the horrific role that would eclipse not only Tony's last unequivocal Broadway triumph, but his very own identity as an actor and a man. Eugene Gant, whom Tony had exhumed from deep inside his young soul, would become an immortal creature that would both define and ultimately consume him as an artist.

JUNGLES AND JOCKS

ORE SCHARY, who had written *Sunrise at Campobello*, the play that had undermined *Look Homeward, Angel* at the Tony Awards, was also responsible for buying the rights to W. H. Hudson's novel *Green Mansions* as a possible vehicle for MGM's blossoming young sex siren, Elizabeth Taylor. For whatever reason, probably misgivings from studio top brass, no film was made. In 1953, it was announced that Vincente Minnelli would direct an adaptation by Alan Jay Lerner, to star either James Dean's girlfriend, Pier Angeli, or singer Yma Sumac. Again production plans were nixed. Executives were uneasy about the fantasy aspects of the story, which, in retrospect, would have been better suited to an animated film. It took the blind passion of actor Mel Ferrer, who had written a treatment while in Mexico shooting *The Sun Also Rises*, to convince MGM to finally surrender three million dollars to the project, which he intended to direct. Of course, his superstar wife, Audrey Hepburn, fresh from *Funny Face* and *Love in the Afternoon*, was included in the deal. To help her husband out, she had humbly agreed to play the impossible role of Rima, the mystical bird-girl. *Green Mansions* would be the first major setback of her sparkling career.

It seemed at the time the worst miscalculation of Tony's less luminous career as well. Having accepted the swashbuckling role of Abel under pressure—to please the perceived expectations of others (agents, the world) and not his own—he arrived in Los Angeles nervous and unhappy and missing the freedom and honesty he had discovered on the stage. He'd given up his apartment on Horn Avenue when he'd left to do *Angel* and moved into a new West Hollywood bachelor pad right below the Sunset Strip on Hammond. Being back in the self-proclaimed "entertainment capital of the world" did not hold good memories for him. To his heightened senses, returning to Tinseltown felt like a regressive step.

Nor was his triumphant return to his movie alma mater, MGM, an auspicious one. After months of applause on the boards of the Ethel Barrymore Theatre, he wasn't even recognized at the studio portal. "I went to the casting gate because that's the gate I went through when I was in *The Actress*," he told *The Saturday Evening Post* in 1960. "So I said, 'Green Mansions. I'd like to go through.' 'What's your name?' 'Tony Perkins.' 'Tony Perkins? Are you a native bearer?' 'No, I'm a featured player.' I just didn't want to say, 'I'm the star. Let me in or I'll have you fired.' 'Well,' the man said, 'you can't go through this gate.' Finally one of the casting directors walked by, and he got me in."

The inhospitable greeting offered a bitter taste of things to come, namely the inattention of his new director. Mel Ferrer was already exhausted when filming began on July 15, 1958. He had recently returned from an arduous and futile trip to South America, where he and his scouts had traveled the Orinoco River recording authentic animal sounds and looking for jungle locations—but the density and darkness of the real forests where the Hudson novel was set precluded the possibility of any shooting there. Instead, Ferrer and his men had plucked rare animals and plants from their natural habitats and sent them at considerable expense to Culver City to join their equally displaced and uncomfortable human costars on the artificial sets.

Upon returning from his grueling expedition, Ferrer had hastily appeared with Harry Belafonte and Inger Stevens in MGM's three-character nuclear disaster flick *The World, the Flesh and the Devil*, which itself proved a catastrophe at the box office. By the time he arrived on the set to direct, Ferrer was all too aware of how much his professional credibility depended on making a success of *Green Mansions*.

"There were problems of locale and casting," he admitted, "but mainly the fear of fantasy. I didn't see it as a fantasy, but a true and honest love story." He later amended that statement by saying, "This is really a story of the religion of nature. We are trying to show that God is present in everything." Everything, perhaps, but Dorothy Kingsley's hackneyed script.

Not surprisingly, Ferrer was more focused on his wife, who was worried that her square jaw would look downright fat in Cinema-Scope, than on Tony, who was at a complete loss as to how to approach the generic hero that he was being paid $125,000 to impersonate. "I don't have as much faith in myself, at least as much as I ought to in my position," he wistfully told Joe Hyams, who visited the set. "I'm a good actor if a part is in my line. Playing Eugene Gant on Broadway in *Look Homeward, Angel* was right up my alley. But I was really helped with my performance word for word, movement for movement, by George Roy Hill, the director. I didn't know how to do the part any other way. . . .

"I think I'll be good in this picture," he added, with forced optimism. "Mel Ferrer, the director, seems to know what he's doing. If he doesn't, I'm in trouble."

Two years later, Tony admitted to *The Saturday Evening Post* that he'd had "some very heated disagreements" with Ferrer, who found his persistent questions and need for guidance bothersome. At one point, Tony claimed, when the picture was running behind schedule, Ferrer actually blamed him when the studio insisted that a particular scene be dropped: "He angrily accused me of deliberately asking so many questions that we lost the scene." Adding to Ferrer's fury and paranoia was the fact that Tony had never cared for the scene in the first place.

Feeling himself once again sinking fast in the mire of the studio system, and smart enough to know that the role of Abel was eluding him, for the first time in his life Tony looked for outside help. At the suggestion of Tab Hunter, he took some private lessons with Hollywood acting guru Jeff Corey, at the modest but now famous garage studio on Cheremoya Avenue where James Dean, Jack Nicholson, and his friends Tab, Diane Varsi, and Venetia Stevenson had all studied before him.

"I had the feeling that Tony needed some reinforcement on his own," Corey remembers, "that he wasn't getting 'the hook' from Ferrer."

Just how much Corey was able to help Tony with his vaguely written role is uncertain, but Tony clearly appreciated the company of a creative and sympathetic friend—someone who might be able to help him hold on to the artistry of his craft. Corey, who knew the sexual score with Tony and had heard of his difficulties with Tab, had seen Osgood Perkins years before in *Chrysalis* and spoke glowingly of him, which pleased his pupil enormously. Tony, in turn, confessed to Jeff that he felt deprived having never known his father.

"I used to love the way Tony walked," Corey recalls fondly. "He had a very lovely grace to his movements, a kind of outdoorsman's walk that Gary Cooper and Henry Fonda also had." It was a physical elegance, Corey says, that Tony's late predecessor, James Dean, had lacked.

Back in the MGM jungle, however, the situation remained strained and Perkins felt more lost and awkward than ever. As a career move, *Green Mansions* was a crass miscalculation, a trap he now dearly regretted having stepped into. The self he had begun to uncover so profoundly and effectively on the stage was now on the verge of being suffocated again under the heavy burden of American machismo.

"He was totally miscast for that part," says actor Henry Silva, who played Kua-Ko, Tony's muscle-bound, loincloth-wearing nemesis in the film. "That part should have been played by a very physical, action-adventure guy. It had to be a tough, rugged leading man, someone physically commanding, maybe even Stewart Granger at that time. Tony was too poetic and very fragile—fragile looking, and his emotions were very soft. He was so shy.

"At that time I had been lifting weights for a number of years, working on bodybuilding before it became voguish, and I probably outweighed Tony by forty pounds. But we both had the same waist size. We had a scene in a river where Tony kills me, and he and I couldn't stop laughing because it was so ludicrous. You couldn't even call him a flyweight, you could maybe call him an air weight! He was supposed to take this knife and overpower me, and from whatever angle they shot it, it was impossible, because my arms—cold, without pumping—were about seventeen and a half inches, and I think his thighs didn't even measure that. He was very trim, and he had extraordinarily broad shoulders, almost to the point of exaggeration, because the rest of his frame was quite small. Finally, we devised something that never fully worked."

Assistant director Robert Relyea, to whom fell the thankless job of staging the fight scene, recalls that Tony's left-handedness, which "looks funny on the screen, doesn't look normal," only added to the difficulty they had pulling the whole unlikely thing off: "He looked peculiar with the knife in the 'wrong' hand."

Despite their physical differences, Tony told Hedda Hopper that his macho costar was one of his "best friends." "Tony was very young and I was very young," Silva says, "and we had a great time together. He was a very private person, but with humor I was able to get through to him." Tony may have been sexually attracted to the muscular young actor, who seemed to have all the right attributes for Hollywood, attributes Tony himself lacked.

Perkins liked Silva enough to take him along to Dorothy Jeakins's Brentwood home for lunch one day. Silva remembers noticing two dusty Oscars in one of Jeakins's closets, as well as the unmistakable affection she clearly felt toward her young man. According to the bodybuilder, "She had a hell of a big crush on him. I mean a major crush—the sun would rise and fall on him. She liked me, but I would say she was in love with him, mad about him. He wasn't as enthusiastic about her, I didn't see any sparks flying from his direction to her. But she was crazy about him."

During *Green Mansions*, Tony received a welcome visit from Helen Merrill and her darkroom assistant, Michael Smith (called "Smish" by Tony, in honor of Helen's accent), when the two drove his T-bird across country after finishing a photographic assignment at the Aspen Music Festival. Tony put them up at Dorothy Jeakins's. Needless to say, when his East Coast and West Coast "mothers" came face to face in Brentwood, things were polite but palpably tense. The distraction of Helen's new young companion did little to assuage the obvious jealousy; no great friendship was ever struck between the two competitively Tony-doting women.

Meanwhile, despite his efforts with Jeff Corey and the reassuring proximity of trusted friends, the experience of making *Green Mansions* did not improve for Perkins. He lost ten pounds during the rigorous shoot, which was clearly becoming an ordeal for him. "It was a tough picture physically," Robert Relyea confirms. "We were up to our elbows in animals. It was a nightmare technically, which put pressure on the actors." (Much to Tony's relief, a boa constrictor that had been captured and imported for a scene with him died while in the MGM zoo.)

The stress of knowing how wrong he was as Abel began to undermine Tony's already questionable confidence. "My great problem," he told *The Saturday Evening Post* in 1960, "is that I've always felt—and especially since I've become a so-called personality and a celebrity and so forth—that it was all a very exposable myth that I was somebody. I've felt that this was an absurd dishonesty . . . [that] I would be shown up as an empty, worthless nothing." As he explained to *Good Housekeeping*: "I spent a couple of years playing parts in which I was supposed to be a decisive person, but all the while I was in torment over this feeling of being a total cipher. It just about paralyzed me. And when it gets to that state, you know you want to do something about it."

His soul-searching and feelings of inadequacy became so overwhelming during the film that he finally turned to Henry Silva for help. Silva suggested Tony call Gerald Aronson, a popular Hollywood psychiatrist whose impressive roster of clients included Marlon Brando.

Tony wasted no time. "I called from the set, and I put all my hopes on the telephone call. I said, 'This is Anthony Perkins; you may have heard of me.' He said, 'No, I never have.' So I thought, 'Well, he'll never see me. I'm sunk.' But he said he would see me the following day." Thus began what would ultimately become the singularly cohesive, transforming passion of Perkins's life: psychoanalysis.

Concurrent with his newfound, fervent self-examination were his continuing duties as an escort for ambitious starlets. One such date was British beauty Joan Collins, whom Tony described as "the most gorgeous brunet I have ever seen in my life." After accompanying her to a premiere one night, Tony found himself back at her apartment on Shoreham Drive, just down the street from where T.H. had lived, where he proceeded to do something rather strange. While Collins went into her kitchen to prepare some sandwiches, Tony grabbed a pencil and frantically began writing his phone number on almost any flat surface he could find—tables, doors, even on the fridge. Then he vanished. While this incident was later chalked up, after more than a decade of therapy, to Tony's supposedly hysterical fear of women, at the time he explained it in less melodramatic, more conventional terms as merely a roundabout way of getting Collins to call him. He seemed to be both attracted and repelled by the opposite sex—attracted by the friendship of women, repelled by his role as a red-blooded heterosexual male expected to pounce and mount.

The shedding of his old skin, psychologically speaking, did not preclude the sometimes harsh banishment of people with whom he'd been friendly in the past, as Maila Nurmi remembers. The last time she saw Tony was at MGM, where she was making *Beat Generation* with Steve Cochran and Mamie Van Doren for schlock producer Albert Zugsmith. "I was a has-been, but Zugsmith hired the untouchables, people who were blackballed but still had some name value, for minimum. I was married to my second husband, and hadn't seen Tony in I don't know how long.

"We were all having lunch at the commissary, and Steve Cochran said, 'Tony Perkins is sitting at the next table.' I said, 'Oh!'—my back was to him and I thought he hadn't seen me. Then Steve said, 'He sees you,' but when I turned around, Tony was gone. He'd left." Later, Nurmi sent a friendly note to Tony over at the soundstage where he was working; she never heard from him.

The promotional campaign for MGM's unlikely jungle blockbuster was huge. Much was made of the artists Ferrer had enlisted to lend prestige to his project; the Katherine Dunham dance troupe had choreographed the native rituals; Rufino Tamayo had painted the poster for the film, a vulgar montage showing lions and tigers, Silva's beefy torso, Hepburn's soulful face, and Perkins's blank one; Heitor Villa-Lobos had composed the score; and Bronislau Kaper and Paul Francis Webster had written a "hit" theme song, "The Ballad of *Green Mansions*," for an embarrassed Tony to croon on camera (MGM released it as a single, thankfully performed by Leroy Holmes instead). There were *Green Mansions* window displays in popular department stores, spreads in dozens of major magazines, heavy radio and television advertising, and even a new edition of the Bantam book with MGM art. The movie was set to open at Radio City Music Hall, where *Friendly Persuasion* had premiered just three years before.

But perhaps most embarrassing of all was the hype surrounding Hepburn's first "sexy" role and her supposedly steamy love scenes with Perkins. AUDREY HEPBURN'S HUSBAND ORDERS ANOTHER GUY TO MAKE LOVE TO HER shouted one headline. MGM's theatrical trailer touted Hepburn as "the untouched girl of the virgin forest, worshipped and feared by savage tribes, and now loved as a woman for the first time," and "popular Anthony Perkins, as confident singing a love song as he is fighting for his life." In a vain effort to bolster Ferrer's efforts,

Hepburn told reporters, "For the first time in my career, I lost my shyness. . . . Love scenes have always been difficult for me. But with my husband directing and leading Tony and me through the emotional passages, things fell into place." In fact, the so-called love scenes were so awkward that they evoked laughter from press preview audiences.

Reviews were scathing. "For the first time Miss Hepburn is less than sparkling in a film," wrote the *Los Angeles Times*. "Perkins lurches through his role—and the forest—like a somnambulist." *Newsweek* concurred: "Tony, loping disjointedly . . . after the wispy girl, bleating out his uncertainty about her reality status, looks pretty silly." Worst of all was *Variety*'s blunt observation that "Perkins seems rather frail for his role. . . . Silva, on the other hand, gives an exciting performance, fatally damaging to Perkins, the hero, overshadowing him in their dramatic conflict."

"They put him in some awful junk," William Wyler said when *The Saturday Evening Post* asked him to comment on Tony's post–*Friendly Persuasion* film career. "Instead of carefully and jealously guarding him as a valuable property—as you would a new car even—they said, 'Quickly! Make a few pictures quick!' They've been intent on making money instead of developing Tony's talent."

Dutifully, Perkins tried to maintain some dignity in the face of unmitigated disaster. "Audrey had me all wrapped up and sold," he told his old ally Hedda Hopper. "I've never been so impressed by a girl. I didn't even want to go out when I was making that picture, it was such a pleasure looking forward to seeing her on the set every day. She's a wonderful person, sensible, spiritual, smart."

Though Perkins photographs more gloriously in *Green Mansions* than even Hepburn, who wears a fake-looking long-haired wig, it's a tough call to decide which of them is more miscast: spindly, spider-legged Tony or his prim princess of precise elocution. Neither of them displays much vitality. But taken as a piece of Hollywood kitsch, the film is noteworthy; few films are as profoundly artificial. If Perkins and Hepburn seem stiff, who can blame them? It would have been more appropriate, and certainly more believable, if Abel and Rima had simply been drawn as the cartoons they are.

After the rigors of the MGM jungle, the asphalt jungle of Manhattan seemed like a vacation. For Tony, it was good to be back home in the orderly confines of New York, with Helen's trusted and discerning ear close at hand, surrounded by the pulse of artistic activity rather than the deceptive balmy torpor of Los Angeles. In his hometown, Tony could have relative anonymity and enjoy the company of his beloved dog and cats, and numerous young men, who were easy to meet on the street or while riding his bicycle.

Television director Roger Englander, who became a close friend via Helen, recalls that Perkins had no trouble adjusting to the severe dichotomy of his very private life and the demands of celebrity: "I don't think he ever had any problems with fame. He was very duplicitous. For example, when he would have interviews with people who wanted to see him 'at home,' he would never have anybody up there at Fifty-sixth Street. He was too private. He would come to my apartment on St. Luke's Place and say that he lived there. He had a lot of publicity pictures taken there." Home at Helen's was not to be spoiled by the intrusion of uncaring interviewers or press photographers—with a few rare exceptions, like the *Look* magazine piece of June 24, 1958, which showed an almost vampy-looking Tony standing seductively just within the beaded entry to his bedroom, a photo of Judy Garland displayed prominently on the wall next to him.

Tony's animals were like his children. Once, when Englander was baby-sitting a friend's dog, "Tony felt the dog needed company. So on my birthday, Helen made dinner, and Tony presented this great covered serving dish. I opened it up, and there was this little Siamese kitten, a present to me! I was terrified of cats, but I got to love this cat, which I named Pickles. Pickles and Buffalo, the dog. Tony took great pleasure in the fact that he got me over my cat fear and gave Buffalo a friend."

Tony himself found a significant new friend during this hiatus, an elfin young actor (actually three years Tony's senior) named Arthur Teno Pollick, whom he'd met at the home of a mutual friend. "Teno," as he was called by friends and later professionally, was a native New Yorker like Tony, born and raised in Greenwich Village by a single mother, who worked at night as an office cleaning woman. Like Tony, Teno had not known his father. "He adored his mother and did everything he could for her," says actor Keene Curtis, Pollick's longtime friend. "I think he'd been a mistake."

Charming and funny and manipulatively vulnerable, Pollick had always relied heavily on the kindness of strangers. While a boy soprano in the Catholic Church, he was spotted by actress Kay Thompson *(Funny Face)*, who offered to help him escape his impoverished existence with room, board, and contacts in Los Angeles. Teno accepted. After schooling at the Los Angeles City College of Drama, he did two seasons of summer stock in Phoenix, Arizona, where, like Tony, he acted in repertory standards such as *Kiss and Tell.* When Thompson's husband finally kicked him out, Teno continued to accompany the actress to the MGM lot, where he quickly befriended everyone he met, including the equally needy Judy Garland. Pollick worked briefly as a messenger at RKO before being cast in Jerome Robbins's original 1954 production of *Peter Pan* starring Mary Martin. He played Tootles, one of the lost boys. According to Roger Englander, "It was perfect because he looked like a little boy." Pollick made his Broadway debut in the show.

Screenwriter Joan Tewkesbury, best known for her work with director Robert Altman, was one of the other children in the show. "He had this quality about him of being perpetually twelve years old," she remembers. "He was very dear with all of the lost boys, and as Tootles he was the oldest of them [he was actually a whopping twenty-four at the time]. But I remember his presence more than anything; he was like a sunbeam. He was very gentle and lived in a world of his own creation—perfect for *Peter Pan.*" (Pollick suffered a terrible emotional blow shortly thereafter when he was let go from the show for being "too old." Mary Martin even gave him the bad news herself because she didn't think the stage manager should be the one to deliver it.) At the time he met Tony, Teno was in between jobs.

"He was in love with the idea that Tony was a movie star," one close friend says. "He was very impressed with all that." Though Tony and Teno would "sort of" live together, under Helen's oddly maternal wing, life with a movie star, even one as quirky as Tony Perkins, would ultimately prove too trying for the dark-eyed lost boy.

Meanwhile, Tony invited Teno to join the makeshift bowling club he had started up with Roger Englander, director Harold Prince, designer Tony Walton, and playwright Arthur Kopit. For about a year, Englander recalls, "we each took turns cooking, and then we'd go off bowling. Ridiculous." Prince even made red bowling league shirts for the players to wear on their humble outings.

Tony Walton remembers Perkins as "very mercurial, extremely pleasant and witty, very occasionally getting into mysterious, dark moods. Mostly I remember his very up, entertaining presence. When he wasn't up, I recall being surprised, that this wasn't the Tony I was used to. One instance, he got a phone call from a fan at one of the public phones in the bowling alley, and he was irritated by that. But he was extraordinarily well mannered.

"He had what seemed to me a very easy time with his success, which a lot of people didn't have. Steve [Sondheim] always seems in agony with his triumphs. Tony seemed to take it quite comfortably in his stride. I felt he had worked out a kind of presentation copy of himself that was easy for him and easy for people to accept. I don't think I ever saw anything other than the presentation copy. Because he appeared to be, on the surface, so much less complicated than so many others of that group, I was sort of grateful for the ease of that!"

With the breakneck pace of his acting career, it was hard for Perkins to find the time to properly promote his musical recordings, *On a Rainy Afternoon* and *From My Heart*, both of which were released by RCA in 1958. "I had one big seller, *Moonlight Swim*," he said the following year, "but to be a recording star you've got to be only a recording star. I think if I had devoted myself to it, I would, you know, be as good as anybody. But it wasn't worth that much to me." Except for the original cast recording of Frank Loesser's *Greenwillow* in 1960, Tony wouldn't record another album until 1964.

He spent the holidays with Helen and Jane and Teno, then flew to Australia on New Year's Day, 1959, where he was due to start rehearsals for his next film, *On the Beach*, Stanley Kramer's star-studded adaptation of Nevil Shute's somber novel of nuclear disaster. Before departing, Tony vowed to Hedda Hopper that he would not be making another film right away. "After [*On the Beach*], it's back to the theater for me," he declared. "I don't want to be away from it for more than a year and a half."

On the Beach was perhaps the first major film to deal head-on with a subject that was on everyone's mind at the time: the threat of atomic annihilation. A far cry from the nonsense of *Green Mansions*, it was just the kind of meaningful project that Tony Perkins could not refuse. "I play a young lieutenant in the Australian navy, married and

with a baby, who has to suffer along with all the others the prospect
of dying," he told Hopper. "It's a serious and sobering story about
the possibilities of atomic war destroying civilization. It's something
that could happen."

The role of the young father was, as producer-director Stanley
Kramer put it, "the most normal thing Tony has ever done." The actor
had to prepare for his first nonneurotic, completely ordinary part in
years. "Tony had some misgivings," Kramer said, "because his wasn't
the starring role."

Nor was Perkins *the* star; Kramer had been forced to sign the
biggest names he could when the distributor, United Artists, expressed
concern that the script was too downbeat. Hence, Tony was up against
the likes of Gregory Peck, Ava Gardner, and, in his first dramatic role,
the legendary Fred Astaire—all of whom were being paid more than
Perkins for their services. The highest paid was Gardner, who received
$400,000 for fourteen weeks' work; by contrast, Tony received
$107,500 for his loan-out from Paramount, plus a bonus of $17,500
from MCA, for a grand total of $125,000.

"With a relatively small part," Tony said, "every word has to be
just right. I worked harder on this script than any other script I've ever
worked on." Not only was he responding to the call of duty inspired
by the heavy subject matter, but to the sense of duty in his character,
Peter Holmes, whose responsibility lies outside himself in caring for his
troubled young wife and their child. Like many gay men nagged by
subliminal guilt over the unconventional freedom of their hidden lives,
the structured obligations of family life seemed a seductively wholesome lure to Tony. When asked about the wedding band he had to
wear in the film, he commented wryly, "I like it so much I may get
married."

"I found him to be a very natural actor," Kramer remembers,
"who was troubled at times. About life, about coping, about being
worthwhile; he constantly bounced that around. He wanted to be
worthwhile; I don't know that he was convinced that he could do it.
He wanted to be something more than ordinary. So I encouraged him
as much as I could."

But Kramer was furious when Perkins arrived in Australia looking
emaciated. As part of his serious new self-image, thinking himself too
lazy and heavy, Tony had begun a severe regimen of dieting. An as-

cetic, however, was *not* what Kramer had had in mind for the "normal" role. "He was a strange boy," Kramer says, conceding that it "added to the performance. He was very critical, demanding of himself."

Tony's relationship with his costars was diffident at best. At the Melbourne location, Gregory Peck and his wife had rented a large old Victorian house, which, thanks to their excellent French cook, became the company's social hub; once or twice a week, Kramer, Astaire, Gardner, and other members of the cast and crew would show up for dinner. "Tony came a couple of times, but did not become a regular," Peck recalls. "He was always invited. My impression is that he preferred to be alone. Or that he was uncomfortable at those gatherings. Then, too, there was the possibility that, as a serious young actor, he was living with the thought that his character in the story was doomed to gradual death from atomic radiation, as we all were, including the whole human race. It was a heavy mood, which Tony may have carried off the set with him."

"He was terribly, terribly nice to me," said Fred Astaire, who was preoccupied at the time with dispelling the rumors linking him romantically with young dancer Barrie Chase. "He knew that I was concerned about playing my first serious part, and I used to talk to him about that. I had several scenes to play with him, and he'd give me sort of signs of encouragement when he was offscreen. I really appreciated it."

Nevertheless, when it came to matters nonprofessional, Tony's lips were sealed tight. According to Kramer, "Tony didn't talk about anything to anybody, nothing personal. He never shared. He had the defense mechanism of loneliness. He used that as a buffer, for protection.

"I never saw him in true juxtaposition to women. I don't know whether that was his way of life or what. I never pried. I mention it because that would be the only way one would judge somebody with that much talent to be defeated or brought to task or embarrassed."

Tarnished beauty Ava Gardner, who was drunk every day by noon and always up for a challenge, found herself attracted to the reclusive young star, despite long-distance visits from the current man in her life, Frank Sinatra. "Ava liked Tony, she liked him a lot," one company member says. "She thought he was sexy." Unfortunately, as Gardner wrote in her memoirs years later, Tony Perkins "was shy about everything but attacking his plate."

The one person with whom Tony tried to forge some kind of a rapport was Donna Anderson, the young actress who was making her film debut as his onscreen wife. Just nineteen years old at the time, Anderson had been put under contract as an "experiment" by Kramer, who had discovered her five years earlier performing at the American School of Dance in Hollywood. Having never worked as an actress before, she was understandably worried about performing with such a formidable cast. She met Tony her first night in Melbourne, when the two of them had dinner in her sumptuous suite at the Savoy Plaza Hotel.

"I was just crazed because I was in a suite," Anderson remembers vividly. "I came from a lower-middle-class family and had never been away from home—and Tony made a point of it, that I'd accepted the suite. Later, I found out that he had refused a suite, because he knew his own psyche, and he'd taken a small room back by the boilers instead. It made him feel comfortable. So I was uncomfortable in my suite, and he was comfortable in the boiler room." Anderson recalls that Tony had decorated his tiny room with little bead animals, horse figurines, that he could "relate to. His animals were in the window, looking out over the pipes." Tony had obviously tried to re-create the safety of his cell at Helen's, but the boiler room may have offered another advantage as well: the privacy to come and go as he pleased, unnoticed, at any dark hour of the night.

At their first dinner together, Anderson says, "Tony went out of his way to make me feel uncomfortable. While we were eating, he said, 'Oh, just pick up your tomatoes like you would if you were alone.' Well, I had just come from a family that was taught not to eat with their hands like animals, and I couldn't believe he was asking me to do that. Tony was just trying to create detail and intimacy, and I was out of my league, trying my best just to keep up. Tony was trying to bring everything down to him because he didn't want to be swept away either. That's why he chose that room."

Together, Perkins and Anderson saw the sights by chauffeured car and enjoyed meals. "We didn't have any physical intimacy," Anderson says, "but we shared almost every other part of our life." For fun, Tony enjoyed throwing fruit out the hotel window, and he spent hours teaching Anderson how to sign a proper autograph.

His relationship with Stanley Kramer was another matter. Back in the States, before shooting began, Kramer had rehearsed Perkins with care and assuaged his apprehensions about working with such a daunting cast. But on location, with the myriad difficulties that came unexpectedly with filming in that part of the world, the director's behavior did a complete about-face. In Tony's own words, Kramer suddenly became "gruff, short, sarcastic." It could have been due to Tony's unexpectedly reed-thin physique.

But Kramer's problems were considerable. Though it was January, it was midsummer in Melbourne, with a record-breaking heat wave, and bugs, particularly aggressive flies, were everywhere. During the beach scenes, a man was hired to spray huge clouds of fly repellent before each take. Interiors were shot on a makeshift soundstage constructed in a building that had formerly been used to show livestock. The structure was impossible to soundproof, a fact made worse by the proximity of the city's harness-racing track and, even closer, a Billy Graham revival tent.

Perkins frequently asked to redo takes, which did not make Kramer happy either. "I would go in and get what Kramer wanted and be fast about it," Donna Anderson remembers, "whereas Tony was playing with it more. It would take him a while to digest the part, and he manicured it a lot." The role of the young father, who had responsibilities greater than a Hollywood image to worry about, often seemed beyond his reach.

Kramer reflects that Perkins "never realized what I thought he would realize on the screen. Maybe it's because of that strange quality that makes a sex symbol. Many people achieve stardom without sex appeal. I know he was a damned talented actor. But that's the nature of the business. He always suffered in his career from being challenged on his manhood. Whatever position he took, it wasn't satisfactory."

Nor was his performance, really; Tony's version of a normal young military father is perhaps one of the most inappropriately strange performances of his career, strongly prefiguring the caricature he would later become. Peculiarly shifty eyed, painfully thin, and more grotesquely angular than ever, especially in his bedroom scenes with Anderson, his Peter Holmes has all the jaw-clenching tics and twitches that would soon be erroneously associated with Norman Bates (his performance in *Psycho* would actually be far less affected). In his opening scene, where he makes his sleepy wife some tea, it almost seems he's about to poison her. Perhaps his worst moment comes later, in the submarine, when lonely scientist Fred Astaire convinces him to stop moping and love his family while he still can; in response, a weirdly inexpressive smile breaks out on Perkins's face—*the* Perkins smile, which Hitchcock would later use so perfectly in the closing shot of *Psycho*—here possibly the result of his half-baked Method preparation. You can see Tony's mind working, struggling hard and fast to find the real emotion within himself, but his face betrays his lack of confidence in being able to fully express it. His mouth broadens in a curve, but his eyes look embarrassed, inexpressive, dead.

Perkins, with his new self-awareness, felt the role showed him in a more conventional, more appealing light. "I think I'm a little sterner, stronger than I was," he told *The Saturday Evening Post*. Shooting ended in late March, and Tony enjoyed a three-day excursion to the Great Barrier Reef before returning to the States.

On December 17, 1959, as part of United Artists' "Global Concept" promotion for the picture, *On the Beach* opened simultaneously in eighteen capital cities around the world, including Washington and Moscow. Americans were given the "soft" approach in the film's ad campaigns, unlike Europeans, who were considered more informed about the possibility of atomic warfare; even so, the controversy caused by the picture on hypocritical home turf was considerable, though the reviews were good and the box office "boffo." According to *Newsweek*, "Defense brass insists an H-bomb war would not wipe out life on earth as the movie portrays," and American military VIPs were ordered to steer clear of the film. A *New York Daily News* editorial called *On the Beach* a "defeatist movie."

Bosley Crowther of the *New York Times* hailed it as "deeply moving. . . . Mr. Kramer has brilliantly directed a strong and responsive cast. . . . The great merit of this picture, aside from its entertaining qualities, is the fact that it carries a passionate conviction that man is worth saving, after all." *On the Beach* won a Golden Globe nomination for Best Film Promoting International Understanding. Such sentiment must surely have gratified Tony, whose search to be part of something greater than himself had only just begun.

Back in New York, the affair with Teno continued, sometimes in the city, sometimes at the rustic seventeen-acre home Tony now owned, hidden away in the dunes of Cape Cod. Helen was, of course, part of that home, and according to a close friend, "She hated Teno, who was just so pretentious and stupid." The feeling was apparently mutual. Helen did, however, tolerate Jane, and occasionally, when they were all together in Wellfleet—with Michaela, of course—there was the unmistakable semblance of a big, unorthodox family. If they were not exactly happy together, they were at least used to one another's quirks.

Surprisingly, Teno and Jane hit it off; the widow Perkins seemed captivated by the young actor's pixieish good looks and hyper charms, and he was clearly taken in by her fashion sense and breezily sophisticated airs. Though they would know each other until her death from cancer in 1979, it was a relationship that would ultimately prove devastating to Teno, who would come to find out just how mysterious the "Mysterious Lady" could be.

The Cape was just about the only place where Tony could always be both himself and part of an unassuming community as well. With its wind and sand dunes, the fierce Atlantic Ocean on one side and the warmer waters of Cape Cod Bay on the other, Wellfleet offered Tony a place close to nature where he could be at peace and freely enjoy the discreet company of his ever changing "family." Hedda and Louella were nowhere in sight, and the staunch Yankee locals took pride in treating Tony no differently than they did anyone else.

Wellfleet also offered Tony proximity to Provincetown, the popular gay resort on the fist at the end of Cape Cod's flexed arm. Like Fire Island, Provincetown attracted homosexuals and artists with its remoteness and solitude and windswept beauty. Via word of mouth, the silent tribe had been congregating there since the 1920s. "It's a fabulous spot for a single girl," Tony coyly told a Hollywood reporter. "In the summer the town is full of wealthy doctors, lawyers, and psychiatrists from New York and on the weekends the young bachelors drive down from Boston." Just what kind of bachelors, Tony failed to specify.

Certainly, nothing could distract Tony from his copious reading, fishing, or copulating with handsome young men he often met in passing on the beach. For him, the freedom of the Cape was irresistible; for Teno, it was hell. "Teno would get into jealous fits," one friend says. "He was very possessive, and he could not accept a relationship with somebody like Tony, who had to be here and there, and who was hot for many other people. That was not what Teno needed." Roger

Englander confirms that Teno had a mighty jealous streak, adding, "It must be awful to be in a relationship with a movie star."

One of the people with whom Teno had to contend was a handsome teenager named Stephen Paley, whom Tony had met in the waiting room of his attorney, Maurice Greenbaum. Though it is believed by many that they were lovers, Paley emphatically denies any such involvement. "Ours was not a sexual relationship, of any form," he maintains. "Tony had a very circumspect life. He knew who he was, and he was very careful about what he did. He was not a reckless person. Relationships meant things to him." Others feel that Perkins was more fatherly, even a mentor, to his young friend. Paley and Perkins would remain close for more than thirty years.

Together they dined regularly once or twice a week, always with Helen, who became a mother figure for Paley as well. "It was never me and Tony alone, though occasionally we'd go to the movies with some of his other friends. He liked horror pictures." Paley recalls taking the subway out to Brooklyn with Tony, post-*Psycho*, to catch a showing of Roger Corman's *The Pit and the Pendulum*. Riding the trains was one of Tony's favorite ways to be recognized, even though he sometimes wore an obviously fake Groucho Marx gag nose and mustache (which only helped make him more conspicuous).

According to Paley, "The thing the general public doesn't know about him is that he was so intelligent and so funny and wry. He was much smarter than he was a good actor. His real personality was far more interesting than the character he played, that coltish, boyish juvenile. He was kind of like David Letterman in a way, cynical, with a mean streak—a mean, funny streak. He had this wonderful acerbic humor about himself. He pretended to be a loner, but he really had lots of friends. There was a dichotomy there. I mean, he was very friendly and very nice if he liked you, and if he didn't, he would keep you at arm's length until he could trust you."

When his schedule became too busy, which was often, it fell to Jane to entertain her son's young friends, many of whom she developed lasting relationships with herself. With so many other people, like Helen, running Tony's day-to-day life, Jane could remain central to his life by answering his fan mail and nurturing his admirers. When Paley was having trouble knowing what to do with his life, Tony sent him to Jane for advice.

Another bone Tony tossed her was his money. While Helen was his advisor on matters artistic and intellectual, Paley says, "Janet handled his business and paid his bills for him. I remember him telling me that he'd probably lost hundreds of thousands of dollars because of it. If he'd had a business manager he would have done much better. He never should have allowed her to do that."

"The fact that he let her handle his business says that there was a trust and a comfort," feels Jane's friend Cary Fuller. (Fuller met Jane when, as a high school student considering a career in the theater, he wrote Tony a letter—and got a response from Jane, who arranged for the two young men to meet backstage at *Look Homeward, Angel.* A staunch advocate for education, Jane had wanted Tony to "sell" Fuller on Rollins College, which he did. Fuller and Mrs. Perkins corresponded for years, and he was even at hand when she died.)

Whether Tony took his mother's financial prowess seriously or not, Cary Fuller remembers that managing her son's income was a full-time vocation for Jane: "Once she got caught in one of those scams where somebody had talked her into putting money into something— four or five thousand dollars—and she fell for it. It drove her crazy that she'd been taken, and she just couldn't deal with the fact that she hadn't realized that this was happening to her. Tony said don't worry about it, but it really bothered her. She liked to be in control of situations."

Behind the scenes, her desire to steer her son's affairs only occasionally extended to matters personal (protecting Tony was Helen's job). "I remember his mother calling me and crying for me to separate [Tony and Teno]," says Perkins's press agent, Buddy Clarke, who remembers Pollick as one of the great loves of his life. "I said, 'Lady, that's not my business.'" (Tony had been assigned to work with Clarke at Rogers & Cowan in New York. When Clarke quit, Tony went with him—he was angry at the company for giving him a cigarette lighter for Christmas when he no longer smoked.)

Press agent Eileen Lottmann, who later worked with Perkins at Allan, Foster, Ingersoll & Weber, recalls the actor's sense of integrity: when the island of Jamaica invited him down for an official weekend of sight-seeing and photo opportunities to boost tourism there, he refused, saying that they should spend their money on the hovels behind the fancy hotels rather than on wining and dining him. He'd had more than his share of empty publicity stunts.

Even so, Perkins could still invoke the ingenuous boy next door when he needed to, as author Richard Lamparski, who worked briefly at the same company in 1964, recalls. Lamparski had arranged a lunch at La Potiniere to introduce Perkins to *Variety* writer Bob B. Frederick, "a physically unattractive closety type, who was slavering over the prospect of meeting Perkins, but could not think of a reason to interview him." Lamparski decided they could discuss the recent South American Film Festival.

"I thought I was being paid to make Perkins look as good as possible," Lamparski recalls. "He seemed to think it was his right to make me as uncomfortable as he could, either correcting or contradicting everything I said." Yet when Frederick showed up, "all at once Perkins was six inches taller, fifteen years younger, and very, very shy. Fredericks drooled. I fought back the impulse to vomit. What an act!"

Too bad his boyish abilities didn't serve him quite so well in his next film.

Though Perkins had wanted the part, Joshua Logan had never seriously considered him for the lead in *Parrish*. Logan wanted to make a "discovery" for the role, and Shirley MacLaine's younger brother, Warren Beatty, had caught the director's roving eye in a stock production of *Compulsion*. Beatty had not yet appeared on the screen.

Nor had Henry Fonda's beautiful daughter Jane, who was currently working as a model while at the same time studying the Method with Lee Strasberg. Logan thought *Parrish* would be the perfect vehicle to launch both youngsters' careers; he tested them and signed them to personal contracts for *Parrish* and several follow-up films. Unfortunately, the first draft of the script was so disappointing that Logan asked Warners to give the project to another director and assign him a new property. (Delmer Daves finally directed *Parrish*, starring Troy Donahue and Connie Stevens in the roles originally intended for Beatty and Fonda.)

Tall Story was a Broadway comedy by the legendary writing team of Howard Lindsay and Russel Crouse, based on the Harold Nemerov novel, about a college basketball scandal in which the star player is bribed to let a visiting Russian team win while at the same time falling in love with a perky cheerleader. Determined to give Hank Fonda's daughter her break in films, Logan offered the role of the pom-pom girl to Jane, who, though she had seen the play and hated it, was glad to accept when Logan promised to expand her part.

Again, handsome, athletic Warren Beatty was Logan's first choice for the role of the basketball star, but Warner Bros. wasn't willing to risk the project on the shoulders of two unknowns. Logan's agent, Herman Citron, persuaded the director to cast another of his clients, the more established Tony Perkins, as the jock. At least Tony was tall enough. Though Logan would call Perkins's performance in the film "delightful," he would later admit his regret at not having used Beatty. Appropriately, the film was to be titled *The Way the Ball Bounces*.

Though the picture was intended as a vehicle for Jane Fonda, as a newcomer (and a woman) she was paid a mere $10,000 for her work, whereas the less convincingly cast Perkins received his usual loan-out fee of $125,000. *Tall Story* was a cheapy black-and-white toss-off for Joshua Logan, whose earlier films had been lavish color productions like *Picnic*, *Bus Stop*, and Rodgers and Hammerstein's *South Pacific*.

"This movie is basically a romantic comedy with a basketball background," Tony lamely told Vernon Scott when the UPI reporter mentioned that most sports films were box-office failures. "The emphasis is not on basketball, but on the characters involved." Even so, "I've been busy working out at the Warner Bros. gym, discovering what basketball is all about. I spend about an hour and a half a day dribbling, passing, shooting baskets, and going after rebounds. An hour and a half is about all I can take. It's exhausting." With the help of several USC and UCLA players, Tony managed to pull off his sports scenes with relative ease. But it was "the intricacy and science" of basketball that made it bearable for him. "It's a good game," Tony said. "Like chess in a way."

Television's *My Favorite Martian*, Ray Walston, who played Professor Leo Sullivan in the film, remembers that Tony "was on that court like he was born there. He always seemed to have an urgency in his movement. He had great ideas and he would express them to Josh in a very eager way, like a young boy wanting to please." In one crucial scene, during which his character, Ray Blent, is supposed to make a victorious long shot from the middle of the court, Tony flubbed it five takes in a row. Logan decided to let Perkins's double, a high school basketball star, take the shot for the cameras, but Tony begged for one more try—and, armpits meticulously shaved, made the basket. The heroic shot can be seen in the film.

According to Walston, Tony's offscreen relationship with nubile Jane Fonda was "a far cry" from the tentative one enacted before the cameras. "There was a reality to their relationship that did not come across in the film," he recalls. "The chemistry between the two of them [onscreen] had an awkwardness to it. The transition, however, when they were sitting offstage or in the back of a limo—where she would be cursing like a sailor, and so would he—was completely different."

Behind the scenes, Tony and Jane had a lot to talk about, namely Timmy Everett. When Everett visited Perkins on the *Tall Story* set, Tony, ever the mischief maker, introduced his ex-lover to Fonda, thinking she would be impressed by his manic theatricality (they were both Actors Studio devotees) and other "James Dean–like qualities." Indeed she was; according to published sources, the two were instantly attracted to each other and spent three torrid days in bed at Jane's apartment on Keith Avenue in West Hollywood. But Everett was tormented sexually, and he and Fonda would soon share the same psychiatrist. Later, in a replay of his suicide attempt over Tony, Everett would try to take his life because of Fonda as well.

For all the off-camera intimacy and heat, Fonda's on-camera love scenes with Perkins are remarkably limp—through no fault of her own. During the shoot, Tony asked Logan if he could coach Jane privately for the scenes, promising to take full responsibility for the direction; Logan could, of course, change anything he didn't like. Bowled over by Tony's enthusiasm, the director agreed.

"They worked very hard, devotedly in fact, on their intimate scenes," Logan wrote in his 1978 memoir. "When they showed them to me they were strangely slow and full of pregnant pauses, but apart from that quite attractive, so I filmed them as rehearsed. Unfortunately, when cut into the picture they were endless and, I think, hurt the picture almost more than the charm of the two people in those scenes helped it." Years later, Perkins's official forays into directing would often be just as miscalculated.

"Too many love scenes lack warmth and reality," Tony was quoted in Warners press material at the time. "I didn't have to do any acting when I kissed Jane for the first time. . . . I couldn't convincingly kiss a girl, if I didn't like her."

Given that statement, Tony's performance in the seduction scene is certainly bizarre. (He looks as uncomfortable and incongruous with Fonda as he does making his laughable entrance in the film, where, smiling blankly, he's carried across the Custer College campus by an army of *singing* all-American boys and girls. The opening scene would be indistinguishable from dozens of other artificial sequences in Hollywood films if Perkins weren't held aloft in the middle of it like some sort of neurasthenic trophy, a reminder of the flaw beneath the shiny surface of the 1950s American dream.)

In the love scene, to bring up the subject of sex, Perkins and Fonda talk blushingly of genetics, and, finally, of the mating habits of the fruit fly. "How would you like it if someone watched you under a microscope while you were making love?" she asks him coyly. Perkins's responses to Fonda foretell Norman Bates's to Marion Crane: the same inflections, the same darting, deeply piercing glances. He reacts twitchily to kissing her, his expression excruciatingly pained. Nothing could be less appropriate, yet this is the way Tony directed it.

If Tony had hoped for an ally in the powerful (and closeted) Logan, he must have been sorely disappointed. The two never worked together again, though Tony's press agents would occasionally try to create a buzz linking them to some project or another. Ray Walston recalls an odd incident that took place one night at a dinner party at Logan's house in Beverly Hills: "Tony was fascinated by a young actor named Horst Buchholz, and he kept saying, 'Now let's hurry with this dinner because there's a program on with Horst Buchholz acting in it, and I've got to see it.' So we pushed things and rushed the meal a bit, and went upstairs to watch this show on television.

"I watched Tony half of the time. He was fascinated with this guy. And at the end of the show, which was very dramatic, Tony actually broke down and could not control the crying. Both Josh Logan and I were being as compassionate as we could, but Tony couldn't control himself and was actually sobbing, uncontrollably, at what he had seen." Finally, Logan stepped back, and "seemed to be very reserved about the whole incident." Whether Tony had truly been moved or upset by something, or whether he was just "auditioning" for the director, no one will ever know. Logan, however, did direct young Horst Buchholz, who had been touted as "the German James Dean," in his next film, the 1961 version of Marcel Pagnol's *Fanny*.

Tony's own days of being compared to the immortal Dean were over.

Tall Story ultimately held little interest for Logan; once it was in the can, he wiped his hands clean of the whole tacky project. The critics lambasted it. "Nothing could possibly save the picture," declared *Time*, "not even the painfully personable Perkins doing his famous awkward act, not even a second-generation Fonda with a smile like her father's and legs like a chorus girl."

If Tony was worried about adding yet another disaster to his credits—his worthwhile excursion into nuclear disaster excluded—he needn't have been. Back at Paramount, Alfred Hitchcock was waiting to bring him out of the stale Hollywood closet he'd been in for so long.

11

THE BOY NEXT DOOR

ITCHY PUTS PERKINS IN TRANSVESTITE ROLE gloated a *Variety* headline in May of 1960. From the start, a year earlier, Alfred Hitchcock had had only one actor in mind for the strange role of Norman Bates, the lonely motel keeper seemingly hen-pecked by his domineering, knife-wielding mother. *Psycho's* screenwriter, Joseph Stefano, recalls: "The movie was based on a novel [by Robert Bloch], but the character in the book was very different. He was middle-aged and drank a lot, and I didn't like him, and therefore I felt no sympathy for the story at all. My first meeting with Hitchcock, I said, 'I would do something about that character. I would change him, make him younger, more appealing.' And Hitch-cock said, 'In other words, you're talking about Anthony Perkins,' and I said, 'Great!' He said, 'Well, that's who I would like to play it.' So we were right on the beam." Perkins signed on blind, without even read-ing the script, because he wanted to work with the prestigious and highly respected director. "He would have done it for nothing," Ste-fano says. "As would any of us."

"Hitchcock felt the film's secret would come out too quickly if we used a character actor [for Norman]," Perkins said in 1990. "You know, a Rod Steiger type. It didn't concern me that I was leaving what was then my domain [romantic leading man]. There weren't that many auteurs in those days. For an actor to get the crook of the finger from Hitchcock was about as high as you could get."

Making the deal even sweeter for the director was the fact that Tony owed Paramount a picture, and could be had for the low price of just $40,000, a bargain after the huge salaries Hitch had had to pay his recent stars like Cary Grant and James Stewart. *Psycho*'s whole budget, in fact, would be under a million dollars, and it would even be shot in black and white with a TV crew from *Alfred Hitchcock Presents*. This was quite a turnaround for the auteur whose last few films, with the exception of *The Wrong Man*, had all been expensive, almost top-heavy, color productions like *North by Northwest*, *Vertigo*, and *The Man Who Knew Too Much*. The advent of television news and the increasing influx of more adult and experimental foreign films had started to change audience expectations, and Hitchcock knew it. Gritty reality was creeping into the soft American consciousness, and the sixty-year-old director, who had started his Hollywood career under spectaclemeister David O. Selznick, wanted to keep up with the times.

Hitchcock also wanted to surpass the success of French director Henri-Georges Clouzot, who, in 1955, had snatched up the rights to a French suspense novel that he had also been after, *Celle Qui N'Etait Plus* (*The Woman Who Was No More*) by Pierre Boileau and Thomas Narcejac. In retaliation, Hitchcock had purchased another book by the same authors, *D'Entre les Morts* (*From Amongst the Dead*). The result was that Clouzot made the stark black-and-white chiller *Les Diaboliques*, which was an immediate success with both critics and moviegoers, and Hitchcock made the lavish *Vertigo*, which was panned by the press and failed at the box office, not to be fully appreciated as a masterpiece until more than twenty years after its initial release. Of *Les Diaboliques*, even the *Los Angeles Herald-Examiner*, Hitch's hometown paper, declared: "If director Henri-Georges Clouzot isn't the master of the suspense thriller today, then who is? True, Hitchcock is suaver; but this Frenchman is joltier, a master of timing and building almost unbearable suspense." Clouzot was treading too closely on what had for years been Hitchcock's sole territory. Now Hitchcock was ready to fight back.

"Hitch talked about being a big fan of *Les Diaboliques*," Tony Perkins confirmed. "It was one of the reasons he wanted to make *Psycho* in black and white."

Like his director, Perkins was also ready to take some chances.

Though his new part was decidedly unsavory and would require him to wear women's clothes, which he had previously been unwilling to do, after missing out on *Some Like It Hot* Tony wasn't about to make any more decisions based on fear. The experience of *Green Mansions* had been too painful. Norman Bates was clearly a career risk, but this time he wasn't going to blow it. In 1965, he admitted to critic Robin Bean that acting the homicidal transvestite was "one of the greatest gambles I've taken because if that picture hadn't worked, if the public's acceptance of the role hadn't been as complete as it was, it might have been a very disadvantageous thing for an actor to play. I discussed this question very frankly with Hitchcock. He agreed that it was a gamble . . . but he suggested that I give it a try anyway." Tony never had been happy as a romantic lead.

Meanwhile, the other roles still had to be cast. For Marion Crane, the attractive blonde who gets killed off in the first forty minutes of the film, Hitchcock wanted the biggest star he could get—for shock value, of course; the audience would never expect the female lead to be done in so fast. Eva Marie Saint, Hitchcock's femme fatale from *North by Northwest*, was under consideration, as were Piper Laurie, Hope Lange, Shirley Jones, and even Lana Turner, who had just made a spectacular comeback in Ross Hunter's glossy production of *Imitation of Life*. Finally, Hitchcock signed Janet Leigh, a popular ingenue of the 1950s who had recently proved her dramatic mettle in Orson Welles's *Touch of Evil*, for a salary of $25,000.

For Lila, Marion's intrepid sister, the names of Felicia Farr, Carolyn Jones, and Eleanor Parker were bandied about. Hitchcock eventually settled on headstrong Vera Miles, the actress he had once vowed to groom into "the new Grace Kelly." Miles, however, had proved unwilling to be molded into a "Hitchcock blond," and had pointedly nipped her obligation to Hitchcock in the bud when, at the last minute, she'd declined the starring role in *Vertigo*, which the obsessive director had tailor-made just for her. Miles still owed him a picture under her five-year personal contract, and the brittle role of Lila seemed a fitting end to their professional relationship.

When it came to "Mother" Bates, Hitchcock teased reporters with the names of Judith Anderson, who had immortally portrayed Mrs. Danvers in his *Rebecca*, and Helen Hayes—and some agents were gullible enough to suggest character actresses Una Merkel and Margaret

Hamilton for the part (that would ultimately go to one of Perkins's male friends). As Sam, Marion's boyfriend, Universal foisted Rock Hudson look-alike John Gavin on Hitch for $30,000, a price Hitchcock couldn't refuse, even though Stuart Whitman had been his first choice.

The entire Paramount production, in fact, would be shot at the industry's lowbrow "House of Horrors," Universal-International, the studio that had cranked out a series of great horror films in the 1930s (*Dracula*, *Frankenstein*, *The Mummy*), and not-so-great ones in the 1950s (*The Creature from the Black Lagoon*, *It Came from Outer Space*, *Tarantula*). Executives at Paramount were not pleased with Hitchcock's seemingly sleazy, exploitive choice of material—the Robert Bloch novel, based on the grisly crimes of Wisconsin serial killer Ed Gein, was considered shocking in 1959 (the same murders also served as the basis for Tobe Hooper's terrifying 1974 cult film, *The Texas Chainsaw Massacre*)—and claimed that all Paramount soundstages were booked, even though production there was at an all-time low. Paramount agreed to distribute the picture, but Hitch was on his own as far as getting it made. This did not faze him a bit.

"[*Psycho* was] a glorified television episode," Perkins recalled in 1990. "In those days even really good TV was the ugly stepsister of the motion picture industry. I remember running into John Cassavetes in the commissary, and he asked me what I was doing. I said, 'I'm working for Hitchcock.' He looked at me slightly askance, because the idea that somebody making as many movies as I should be doing a Hitchcock [TV show] was considered something of a comedown. When he heard it was a feature, he was somewhat quieter."

Hitchcock demanded quiet of his cast and crew as well; everyone associated with Paramount production number 9401—known fondly on the lot and in studio memos as "Wimpy," after second-unit cameraman Rex Wimpy, whose name appeared on clapboards and production sheets—was asked to keep his or her lips tightly sealed about the script's surprise ending, which, of course, hinged on Tony's character. Don Bachardy remembers: "He came down to the house for dinner one night, just by himself. It was while he was making *Psycho*, and he had promised not to give anything away, all the actors had been sworn to secrecy. We were quite teased by him to know what the secret of the film was, but he wasn't telling."

"*Psycho* is the weirdy of all time," Vera Miles told a prying Louella Parsons. "Of all the Hitchcock thrillers, this is the one that will get people right out of their chairs. I'd like to tell you the plot, but when we started to work we all had to raise our right hands and promise not to divulge one word of the story." It was only when actress Lurene Tuttle, who played the Sheriff's wife, carelessly leaked to the press that Perkins "dressed up as his own mother" in the film that gossip of the script's bizarre kinks began to circulate, starting a spate of sarcastic trade headlines. Fortunately, it happened late enough in the film's ad campaign to heighten viewer curiosity.

Photographic tests of Perkins, possibly dressed as Mrs. Bates, were shot by Hitchcock's television crew on November 11, 1959; principal filming began on the thirtieth. On Hitchcock's set crew members were required to wear shirts and ties; the formal atmosphere must surely have appealed to Tony, who, given the nature of his new role, was no doubt relieved to see the off-camera tech men kept in line by the Master. (It should be noted that before shooting began, Tony had personally telephoned trusted camera operator Leonard South, who had been there during the *Fear Strikes Out* harassment, to secure him for *Psycho*, but South, who had worked on Hitchcock's *Rear Window*, was away on location at the time and unavailable.)

Tony needn't have worried; his relationship with the great director turned out, surprisingly, to be one of the best of his career, marked from the start by mutual esteem. Both were highly intelligent men, and for Hitchcock, who was famous for deeming actors "cattle," the wit and reserve of his young star must have seemed like a breath of fresh air instead of the usual smog. "Hitchcock treated Tony with respect, never talked down to him," asserts press agent Buddy Clarke. Intellectually, at least, they were equals.

Tony later described Hitchcock as "expansive, benevolent, happy, productive," words not usually associated with the director who rigidly adhered to storyboards and blew off Victorian steam by psychologically degrading blond actresses. "When we started [*Psycho*] I had actually never met him but once," Perkins recalled in 1965, "and I was very apprehensive about making any statements about what I thought, what I felt about the character and about different scenes. But, even as the first day proceeded I could see he wanted to know what I thought and what I wanted to do and I was really very surprised by this. I kind of tentatively made a small suggestion about something I might do. He said, 'Do it.' And I later suggested changing a 'but' to an 'and.' He said, 'Go ahead.' I got to relaxing more with him and making more and more suggestions and ideas. At the end of the picture, I realized I'd worked with *the* director who had been more open to the actor's suggestions and ideas than any I'd ever worked with before, with the possible exception of William Wyler." At last he'd met a director who encouraged him to just be himself.

It was Tony's idea that Norman munch candy corn throughout the film, and the actor claimed that when he practically rewrote a speech—probably Norman's intense monologue about his mother in the famous parlor scene—and presented Hitchcock with the script page covered in black markings, the director merely asked him, "Have you given it a lot of thought? . . . All right, that's the way we'll do it."

Director Stuart Gordon (*Re-Animator*), who three decades later guided Perkins through his only foray as a vampire in the 1990 television film *Daughter of Darkness*, remembers the star speaking often and fondly of the late Hitchcock: "Tony told me about how he and Martin Balsam were rehearsing the scene in which Balsam was interrogating him, and they found that the scene worked a lot better if they overlapped the dialogue, with Balsam constantly cutting him off. Then Tony got a look at Hitchcock's storyboards and discovered that the scene was going to be shot as close-ups, which means that you cannot have any overlapping. Tony was nervous because he knew these storyboards were inviolate. So he went to Hitchcock and said, 'You know, I think you should have a look at how we're doing the scene,' and Hitchcock said, 'No, no, I'm sure it will be fine.' Tony said, 'No, I really think you'd better have a look at this.' So Hitch came and watched them do the scene; he liked what they were doing, and just tossed the storyboards in the wastebasket."

Though Tony later claimed that he and Hitchcock created Norman Bates together, the part of the repressed mama's boy held uncanny similarities with Tony's own life. In the quietly brooding dialogue he has with Marion Crane (Janet Leigh) just before the shocking shower scene, Norman haltingly tells his guest about the emptiness of his current life and his lonely childhood; when Marion asks if he sees friends, Norman replies, "Well, uh—a boy's best friend is his mother. . . . She—she had to raise me—all by herself, after my father died. I was only five and it—it must've been quite a strain for her. . . . A son is a poor substitute for a lover." If in fact Tony did not rewrite these words for better identification with the role, perhaps incorporating personal touches such as his actual age at the time of Osgood Perkins's death, the coincidence is almost too strange. Years later, in 1983, he described his childhood with his real-life mother in oddly similar terms: "She was left with a five-year-old boy and no bucks to take care of him. I think perhaps she was a little bit more controlling than she might have been if there had been a father around. . . . I think she was frightened. She did the best she could."

When Leigh's character asks Norman if he's ever considered putting his mother away "someplace," he responds vehemently, and rejects her apology. "People always mean well," he spits out. "They cluck their thick tongues and shake their heads and suggest—oh so very delicately. . . ." Popping to mind is Tony's statement of the claustrophobic days just after his father died, when he was surrounded by Osgood and Jane's meddlesome theatrical cronies who "kept hugging me and picking me up and clucking at me. I wanted to run away and I couldn't."

Later, in the film's chillingly futile wrap-up, the court psychiatrist, played by Simon Oakland, describes the mother-son relationship this way: "His mother was a clinging, demanding woman, and for years the two of them lived as if there was no one else in the world." If Tony's later confessions in *People* magazine are to be taken seriously, that line would surely have resonated with the guilt-ridden actor at the time. As Mario Busoni said of his *Psycho* performance, "That was not acting, that was Tony."

"Hitchcock would never direct an actor at all unless an actor was headed in the wrong direction," says Hilton Green, the assistant director who went on to produce both *Psycho II* and *Psycho III*. "What Hitchcock did was meet with his actors ahead of time to discuss their roles and where he wanted each character to develop and come from. Basically, he left them alone from that point on, unless they got off on the wrong track. And Tony never did." Janet Leigh confirms that Hitchcock's input was minimal, and maintains that Perkins had very little preproduction planning with the director. According to Joseph Stefano, "[Hitchcock] felt that the actors were doing their job and tended to stay out of their way. He really didn't like it if an actor needed him."

Tony's instincts for how to play Norman Bates were so right they were almost inborn. "He enhanced the role," Green says. "He brought things to it which had not been planned. A lot of his mannerisms—the hesitations, the little stuttering, and that sort of thing—that was Tony."

"Tony had a wonderful sense of humor, with a dark edge to it, which had not manifested itself in any of the movies he'd done up to that point," Stefano recalls. "He'd just had this incredible face that the camera loved, and had played kind of tender young men. The edge that he brought, especially to the scene with Janet Leigh in the parlor before he kills her, was almost comedic. He held on to his character incredibly, right up to the very end."

Indeed, Perkins even got permission from the usually detail-obsessed maestro of suspense to wear clothing of his own choice as Norman. "Tony was *so* serious about his role," wardrobe supervisor Helen Colvig noted. "I believe that impressed Mr. Hitchcock and even *touched* him." On one occasion the satisfied director surprised his eager star with an iced plate of pâté de foie gras, flown in all the way from Maxime's in Paris.

Perkins was still deep in analysis at the time, and, for once in his life, the work he was doing on himself may have helped bring out the performance that would prove to be the most personal and flawless of his entire film acting career. He told Don Bachardy and Christopher Isherwood that he was seeing a psychiatrist every day, early in the morning before going to the studio. "I felt I was a rather lopsided personality," Tony remarked in retrospect decades later, "an unfinished personality." Nothing could be truer of Norman Bates.

Though Janet Leigh remembers enjoying her screen killer's "wonderful, observing, sardonic wit," no one on the set got close to the young star. "To my knowledge, he wasn't chummy with anyone," says John Gavin, who interpreted Tony's constant shyness as "a defensive wall." Only via his usual off-camera game playing did Tony make an effort to be social. Leigh recalls participating in Scrabble and hangman, and there was a more difficult game created by Tony himself called "Essences," a sort of twenty questions in which players had to guess the identity of a literary or historical figure by asking roundabout questions that could only be answered with a yes or a no. The guessing occasionally went on for days and often got everyone in the company worked up. Wardrobe mistress Rita Riggs recalled that "[many of us] only got to know him because we could see how his mind worked through that wonderful game."

"Tony kept to himself," Hilton Green confirms. "He was an introvert actor. Hitchcock was an introvert director. If there was a key scene, Tony always wanted to know five or ten minutes before we were ready for him, and he'd go into his dressing room. How he concentrated and did that, I don't know."

Hitchcock, in fact, confided to Joseph Stefano that he found Perkins "excessively shy around women," and saved him the embarrassment of having to appear in the shower scene by hiring a double to slash the naked Marion Crane; this allowed the girl-shy boy to fly to New York in mid-December, where preparations for the stage musical *Greenwillow*, in which Tony had been signed to star, were getting under way. Forcing Perkins to do the brutal scene "just wouldn't be very nice," the director had said. (Tony's determination to return to the stage remained, despite the satisfaction of working with Hitchcock. "I always thought *Psycho* would be gripping as a play," he claimed in 1986, as preposterous as it may seem, "and would suggest to Hitch during the shooting that we should take it to Broadway afterward.")

While dressing up as Mrs. Bates was par for the course—"He seemed to have no problems with it," Gavin says—speaking in her voice was not. Tony recommended photographer Paul Jasmin, then a struggling young Hollywood actor, for the job. As a joke, on the phone Jasmin often did an old-lady character he called "Eunice Ayers," "a no-bullshit, Marjorie Main kind of gal." Everyone on the Universal lot knew about Jasmin's prank voice; Stanley Kubrick, who was at the studio directing *Spartacus*, even taped some of the silly conversations. Hitchcock had decided that if Perkins himself did the mother's voice it might give away the ending; he had considered having a real woman do it, but felt that wouldn't work either, especially in the final shot where the voice was to emanate from Tony/Norman's mind. One day, he summoned Jasmin to a soundstage to perform "Eunice Ayers" for him. He loved "her" voice. (Ultimately, Hitchcock mixed Jasmin's voice with those of two actresses, Jeanette Nolan and the late Virginia Gregg, who later did the voice-overs for Mama Bates in the two *Psycho* sequels.)

For the revelation scene in the fruit cellar with Gavin, Miles, and "Mrs. Bates," Tony didn't use his voice either. "While working [on *Psycho*], I was boning up on singing lessons for Frank Loesser's *Greenwillow* for Broadway," Tony told *The Hollywood Reporter*'s George

Christy. "And at the end of the movie when John Gavin grabs me [in full mama regalia], Hitchcock wanted me to scream as loud as I could, but I asked if I could pretend to be screaming (to save my voice), and they could dub in screams later. Hitchcock liked the silent screams so much he never added the sound."

Joseph Stefano recalls that "Tony had a sense of the character that I liked, a kind of quiet, almost like one of [Norman's] birds. His emotions were kept so much in rein." Stefano recognized that, like Norman, Tony had to be approached delicately. "He came to a party at our house that Christmas, 1959. Hitchcock was there also. I liked Tony, but I felt that you had to move very carefully with him, that he was a very private person, very intense. We had a kind of strange room down below the living room in our house at the time, in the Hollywood Hills right above the Chateau Marmont; I went down there to get something—and Tony was down there all by himself, looking at the walls which were hung with records of mine. I had been a songwriter, and he hadn't known that. He was very impressed by the fact that here were records by Eydie Gormé and Sammy Davis, Jr. He said, 'How could I not know this?' He wandered around the house on his own, which I thought was cool." Other people's homes would always fascinate Tony, whose own home was invariably the sparest of possible dwellings. Perhaps it was his own profound sense of displacement that kept him searching the details of friends' houses, looking carefully for some key or secret he felt excluded from sharing.

David Mitchell, the Tony Award–winning scenic designer, who worked on Tony's first major directorial effort, the 1970 off-Broadway production of Bruce Jay Friedman's *Steambath* (and later on his production of Mark Medoff's *The Wager*), recalls a similar incident. Perkins would frequently ride his bicycle up to Mitchell's home on West Eighty-eighth Street for meetings. There, particularly in the kitchen, "he would scan everything out. He had a tremendous kind of intensity about him that you would get on the screen, and in person he was that way too. He noticed every detail in a room, and wanted to know who and where my kids were. You could tell he was really kind of getting an idea about your life; he was curious about everything. His eyes would roam along the things that were in the hutch and on the shelves, taking it all in.

"Later on, in a meeting, we were just finishing in my studio, which was upstairs, and he said, 'Oh yes, there's just one more thing.' I thought it might have been a prop that we'd forgotten. He said, 'I noticed on Sunday that your wife had made some deviled eggs. Do you suppose there're still a few left in the kitchen?' So we went down and had deviled eggs. He was very funny about those kind of things."

As *Psycho* drew to a close, Tony began flying back and forth to New York, where rehearsals for *Greenwillow* were scheduled to start on December 30. By the time the film wrapped on February 1, 1960, nine days over schedule, he was long gone.

"With *Psycho*, suddenly I abandoned being the young leading man and became the slightly quirky, slightly nervous, tic-ridden juvenile," he claimed in his final television interview. More to the point, as Norman Bates, the touchingly humorous, murderous boy he himself had personally fleshed out and embellished on Hitchcock's easy set, Tony got typecast as himself—something he had never been allowed to be quite as completely on any of his previous films. Eventually, the twitchy character of Norman would even take on Tony's own softer, middle-aged, recovering persona, the imaginary and the real becoming inextricably entwined. For Tony the actor, the blurred distinction would be professionally debilitating.

But for now there was another challenge to face, tackling a musical on the unforgiving Broadway stage.

ICON

Tony Perkins's first (and last) Broadway musical was a fairy tale, a whimsical fantasy of love altering destiny, with music and lyrics by that brusque composer in gangster's clothing, Frank Loesser, whose previous two shows, *Guys and Dolls* and *The Most Happy Fella*, had been huge hits. It seemed an incongruous pairing.

Greenwillow was based on a wispy novel by B. J. Chute about a quaint, imaginary village resting complacently on the banks of the Meander River, where the equally quaint village folk wear capes and carry lanterns (but just when *Greenwillow* is supposed to take place is anybody's guess). Not much happens; there are two feuding ministers, one pessimistic and one optimistic, and the Briggs family has a peculiar problem: a hex causes their men to wander the earth, leaving their families behind, only occasionally returning for a visit to "plant" a new child. They are not allowed to settle down and enjoy family life like normal folk, and the curse can only be broken when a Briggs boy decides *not* to marry and *not* to spawn the next generation of wanderers.

That's where Tony came in.

Chute's novel was high on charming little moral lessons and low on dramatic conflict, but nevertheless producer Robert Willey felt sure that the simple goodness and love permeating the thin story would win over cynical New York audiences and transport them flutteringly to

Greenwillow's ageless glens. An indication of how *uneasy* an accomplishment that would be should have been obvious when Frank Loesser himself gave up trying to pen a stage adaptation and sought outside help. Finally, after several writers quit, complaining that the novel lacked sufficient drama, screenwriter Lesser Samuels (*The Silver Chalice*) agreed to coauthor the book. Hence, *Greenwillow* became mockingly known among associates as "the Evil of Two Lessers."

Casting was another problem. Producer Willey had approached Tony for the role of Gideon Briggs, the young wanderer, while he was still in *Look Homeward, Angel*, but the actor was already obligated to do the equally ethereal *Green Mansions*. Without a Gideon, the Loesser company traveled to Nashville to audition several country singers—it was unclear to everyone whether Greenwillow was meant to be an English village or somewhere, say, in Kentucky—and there was even talk of pursuing Elvis Presley for the role. Finally, they decided only a real actor could give the role style, preferably someone with marquee value, and Perkins was agreed on. "Tony never wanted to get into a hillbilly twang," musical director Abba Bogin says. "He wanted to talk the way he talked, so we centered everything round him." The script was rewritten to suit the movie star, and rehearsals delayed to accommodate his film schedule. This did not make Frank Loesser a very happy fella.

To direct, Loesser wanted someone like the legendary Moss Hart, but Perkins countered with George Roy Hill, whom he trusted from *Look Homeward, Angel*. Hill was hired, regardless of the fact that neither he nor Tony had ever done a musical before. Hill was reluctant to take the job, but did it for Tony, against his better judgment.

At rehearsals, Loesser seemed determined to make things difficult for everyone. "I had been warned about Frank," Hill remembers. "He was a screamer, and I don't like screamers, so we had a couple of set-tos that were battle royals. There were scenes that he and I were diametrically opposed over." Things got so heated between the two men that Hill quit, only to be coaxed back by the sensitive B. J. Chute. "*Greenwillow* was a good experience, but a hair-raising one. Then I went out to Hollywood [to direct *Period of Adjustment*], and I didn't come back."

According to Ben Bagley, Loesser deliberately gave Perkins odd, high keys to sing in—notes that even a well-trained singer would be hard pressed to deliver smoothly—the most difficult of which were incorporated into Tony's big solo number, "Never Will I Marry." "Frank Loesser and Tony hated each other," Bagley says. "Loesser was a wonderful man, but he was homophobic, and he knew about Anthony." If indeed Loesser was seriously disturbed by such things, *Greenwillow* was going to be quite a trial for him, given some of the backstage liaisons that would crop up during its brief run.

"Frank felt that *Greenwillow* was an opera, and he wrote the music that way," explains Billy Goldenberg, the rehearsal pianist who was hired as dance music arranger when Charles Strouse bailed out to work on *Bye, Bye Birdie.* "Tony was not a trained opera singer; he was just a person endowed with a magnificent voice."

Others were not so generous in their appraisal of the star. "That's one of the reasons we had problems with the show," one cast member recalled. "Tony wanted all the songs. And he got a lot of the songs. But he didn't have much of a voice." According to Loesser's daughter, Susan, in her book, *A Most Remarkable Fella*, Perkins "was both insecure about his singing and critical of his material. Unhappy and demanding, he did not take kindly to my father's constant coaching."

Why did Perkins want to undertake the risk and exhausting demands of live musical theater at all? "It was a sense of failure that made me want to sing on Broadway," he told the *New York Times* in February 1960, shortly before the Broadway opening. "I made some records a few years ago of very low, soft singing that I was ultimately, if not immediately, dissatisfied with. . . . I knew my voice was better than it sounded on those records."

But Perkins, no matter how hard he tried, wasn't loud enough for Loesser. He wasn't big enough in his delivery, it simply wasn't in his nature. Loesser, meanwhile, posted an antagonistic sign for all to see: LOUD IS GOOD. Perkins and Hill shared a New England reserve—an "East Hampton intellectual snobbery," as one cast member put it—that was fundamentally at odds with musical theater. The direct approach to anything had certainly never been Tony's forte. "His voice was not unpleasant," Abba Bogin says, "it was instinctively musical. My recommendation was that we shouldn't train him too well, because we might undo what little was already there."

Most demanding was Tony's showstopping solo number, "Never Will I Marry," the only song to survive the show, thanks to recordings by Judy Garland, Barbra Streisand, and Linda Ronstadt. At the time, it became an instant camp classic within the invisible gay community because fey Anthony Perkins was singing it; indeed, over the years it has proved an ironic theme song for the actor's own surprising personal life. Dark and dramatic, even bitter, yet packed with sudden high notes, the song required both flawless musicianship and a laserlike Method intensity. It was nearly too much for Tony to pull together.

"Everybody sang well except Tony Perkins," said the late Lee Cass, who played one of the villagers in the show. "I heard him sing some of those songs later—he continued to sing 'Never Will I Marry'—and it was even worse than I remembered it." (No doubt Cass was referring to the 1985 PBS special *Best of Broadway*, on which a petrified, cadaverous-looking Tony reprised the song with excruciating difficulty.)

Meanwhile, some people thought Perkins's vocal shortcomings worked. According to Stephen Sondheim, "He was fine, wonderful. One of the things that makes 'Never Will I Marry' so brilliant [on the recording] is the crack of his voice when he reaches the tenth."

George Roy Hill maintains that Tony's singing was "remarkably good. It didn't have the timbre of a real Broadway voice, but it didn't have the hard edge. It had a quality of its own. 'Never Will I Marry' was a wonderful example of that. He had some other songs that were very good, but that's the one that stretched him the most."

"He understood what the number was about," Abba Bogin points out. "He sang it far better when we were in our next-to-last week than he did on the album. He was getting much freer about singing, about opening up."

But even with coaching, Tony was never quite loud enough, and ultimately had to be miked in performance. His inability to fully deliver what Loesser wanted created considerable strain; to compensate for his vocal deficiencies, Tony overgesticulated wildly during the song, something that Loesser silently, maybe even maliciously, failed to correct. "Frank Loesser got tickled about the whole thing and never made him change," singer Maggie Task says. "When it came to lines like 'Wide my world, narrow my bed,' Tony would throw his arms open on 'narrow my bed'—which was just the opposite. Maybe he was being funny? I never figured it out."

Dancer Don Atkinson, too, remembers how Tony would "hyperextend his arms back with stiffened elbow" during the number: "He looked so strange, because he was big and had a huge arm span. I told him to at least bend his arms a bit at the elbow."

Tony wasn't the show's only casting problem. His pretty leading lady, an ex–Copa Cabana girl named Zeme North, who had made her Broadway debut in a small part in *Take Me Along*, couldn't sing Loesser's music either. In fact, she was even less loud than Tony. The chorus and orchestra were instructed to drown her out whenever she had a high note to strain for.

Although Tony respected the superior musical know-how of most of his fellow performers, the constant script and song changes tried his already frayed nerves. "Perkins felt like somebody was stabbing him or wounding him if we cut one of his numbers in the show," Bogin recalls. "He was like a child that you were taking candy away from. One time he just walked off the stage. Hill had to follow him to his dressing room, close the door, and talk to him for something like twenty minutes. Hill dealt with it best because Hill was his baby. But he wasn't always forceful enough. It was always a great job to convince him that a song was not being taken away because he didn't do it well, but because the material didn't work. You really had to treat Tony like a baby to get the best out of him. In general, I think he felt more comfortable with the other dancing boys, who were probably not all interested in girls."

In Philadelphia, where *Greenwillow* was to open on January 30, 1960, Tony chose to stay at the Warwick Hotel with the dancers rather than in the fancier Hotel Belvedere, which had been chosen for the director and stars. Don Atkinson, who was the youngest dancer in the troupe, fondly known among the boys as "Bubble Buns," remembers Tony as "probably the friendliest person in the company." Atkinson was straight, so "the gay thing was a problem; I got hit on a lot and was relatively defensive. Once Tony tried something, and I, being this boy from Ohio, just froze up. Then he just patted my cheek. But he never leaned on me again after that."

Another male dancer in the show who was heterosexual sensed something "carnivorous" in Perkins: "I always made sure I was never caught in a corner, so I would never have to make a direct rejection. With Tony I had to shift down how far I could let our friendship go, because I felt that he would inevitably make an effort to move it on to a physical level."

In the company of the other gay boys, Tony could be sexually freer. It was a time of uncharacteristic partying for him, as he needed an outlet for his musical tensions. "Tony took everybody barhopping," Atkinson recalls. "We always had gays in drag waiting at the stage door, guys in gold lamé waiting to get Tony's autograph, because every night we'd all go out, from bar to bar. They were Tony's groupies."

"One night two of them followed him right into the hotel," chorus boy Carl Nicholas observed. "I happened to be up and I thought, 'What is that loud screaming?' These two transvestites were carrying on in the lobby as if no one was there. I immediately stepped back because I didn't want Tony to see me. They were all dressed up and all screaming, and Tony was laughing and carrying on a conversation. He couldn't shake them. He was a bit promiscuous."

★Vince, an actor-dancer who was in Philadelphia at the time in another show, met Perkins at the Hotel Belvedere's Variety Club, an after-hours hangout for show folk where drinks were served right through Sunday night. He and Perkins were briefly introduced by John Kriza, lead dancer of the Ballet Theater.

"As I was getting up to leave," Vince recalls, "suddenly Perkins was right behind me. 'Where are you going?' 'I'm going home,' I said. 'I've got to work tomorrow, during the day.' He said, 'Do you want company?' Well, I was flattered, I can't say I wasn't. So we went to my suite at the Hotel Bradford.

"Let's say we went at it. But I felt totally unfulfilled. I just couldn't figure out what this gentleman wanted. Back in those days, in New York, I was totally into leather, but working I couldn't be. I never wore anything except boots—which I do remember Tony insisted I keep on while having sex. But to me, it was more voyeur sex, where he looked and I moved. We had physical contact, but nothing that exciting."

Vince had no more encounters with Perkins until both their shows were in New York. "To my surprise, I got an invitation from Tony to the opening night." After the performance, he didn't go backstage, but left a thank-you note with his number. Tony wasted no time calling. "He asked me if I had a friend, and would we like to come over, and he'd watch while we did our usual things."

This time Tony was no longer removed. "That night we really had a lot of physical contact because we were doing things that he liked, not the normal gay sex. Anything that got sloppy and messy was fine, Tony became like an animal. He loved being pissed on, and from that moment on it was 'You name it, I'll do it.' He loved eating a guy's ass after he got fucked, things like that. There was some S and M. We had sex in leather. He wore jeans. He liked inventiveness."

Even after their respective shows both bombed, Perkins and Vince continued to see each other from time to time. "He had a thing for men who were tall and thin, who had more of a coarseness than he did. There was a side to him that could become very feminine. He was never much after bodybuilders, but he used to say that he liked the way dancers 'prowled.' I mean, in the bars, you could see him watch somebody come in, and immediately, if they were his type, it was like an antenna would go up and he would stalk. He was fascinated by anything that was kinky. He started getting a reputation for what he wanted, the off-color stuff, not just getting into bed and sucking and fucking. It had to be more than that. It had to have an animal quality." According to Vince, Tony especially enjoyed it when he and his sex partners dressed up in suit and tie for the ritual of giving and receiving "golden showers."

Meanwhile, back at the theater, those who didn't know Perkins so intimately could see the company he was keeping. "Tony's demeanor was never open," says actress Ellen McCown, who replaced Zeme North just before *Greenwillow* went to New York. "He said to me once, 'I wonder why people try to get at me,' and I said, 'Well, Tony, you're like a little island with a great giant wall around it, with little peepholes in it. Naturally, everybody's going to try to climb over the wall just to see what's there!' He was very guarded. It invited aggression."

Perkins was still in analysis during *Greenwillow*. "He really wanted to overcome his sexual preference, he wanted to work out of it," McCown remembers. Part of that struggle obviously involved a great deal of sexual activity on the side, a "working out," as it were, of the problem. Since his home with Helen was out of the question as a trysting spot, Tony had subordinates book hotel rooms for him under different names, and if necessary used their vacant offices to take men for quick encounters. It was common knowledge within the company that Tony had even struck up an intense relationship with his understudy, a young dancer-actor from Pennsylvania named Grover Dale.

Tall, lithe, and pleasingly midwestern looking—facially similar to Timmy Everett, in fact—twenty-five-year-old Dale had got his start as a chorus boy in a Pittsburgh summer production of *Call Me Madame* starring Elaine Stritch. After moving to Manhattan, he joined the June Taylor dancers and quickly became a regular on the Jackie Gleason, Martha Raye, and Milton Berle television shows. After appearing in several doomed out-of-town musicals, he made his Broadway debut in the chorus of *Li'l Abner*. His role as Snowboy, one of the Jets in the 1957 Bernstein-Sondheim musical *West Side Story*, launched his career as a featured player. At the time Dale met Perkins, he was already living with *West Side Story*'s male lead, Larry Kert, at 50 West Fifty-sixth Street, where they kept separate apartments, one above the other.

"Grover was probably even more insecure than Tony was," pianist Billy Goldenberg says, "which was one of the reasons it was hard to teach him Tony's songs. I have a feeling that's probably what Tony related to. He knew this was someone with a lot of talent and a lot of fears—maybe even some of the insecurities he felt about himself, although Tony was a good deal more outgoing than Grover."

"Tony never said anything, but he was having an affair with Grover," confirms Stanley Simmons, who was the assistant to *Greenwillow* costume designer Alvin Colt, and lived next door to Perkins on Fifty-sixth Street. "Grover was very much within himself, too, involved in his own career. I don't think Tony felt comfortable at all. He was scared, a nervous wreck most of the time."

Tony Walton admits that the relationship was no secret, "but they were discreet. It wasn't a big deal. Folks were aware of it, and [Tony and Grover] didn't shove it." According to George Roy Hill, "It never seemed to get in Tony's way." Meanwhile, backstage rumors of a turbulent love triangle—Tony-Larry-Grover, Teno-Tony-Grover—were out of control.

When Ellen McCown asked Dale why he and Perkins didn't just live together, "he said, 'I don't need to be in pain because of him,' which indicated to me who was in what position in that relationship. [An almost identical remark was widely reported to have come from Tony's ex-lover, Timmy Everett.] But Grover was also trying to be bisexual." During the show, Dale reportedly dated dancer Margery Gray, who went on to marry *Fiorello!* lyricist Sheldon Harnick. Thirteen years later, after living with Tony Perkins for six, Dale would finally marry Broadway actress Anita Morris.

Opening night at Philadelphia's Shubert Theatre, Tony received a Western Union telegram from Hedda Hopper. KNOW YOU WON'T DISAPPOINT YOUR SECOND MOTHER, she wrote. YOU'VE JUST GOT TO BEAT YOUR LOOK HOMEWARD, ANGEL RECORD. This time, though, he would not be able to live up to her doting, matronly expectations. *Variety* raved that "[Anthony Perkins] makes an emphatically successful musical debut," but most other papers were not so taken with the show. "While Loesser has not stinted in supplying songs and situation numbers to brighten the tale, they do not seem able to budge *Greenwillow* out of its meandering path," said the *Philadelphia Evening Bulletin*. "The combined efforts of the cast . . . fail to get the evening into high gear."

Drastic measures were necessary to doctor the show for New York, where it was set to open at the Alvin Theater on March 3. All of Tony's "family" came to urge him on. Dorothy Jeakins attended a preview, and was immediately backstage afterward, advising him on how to improve his performance. And Helen Merrill was always there— even butting in on Jeakins's territory. "I was afraid of Merrill, frankly," Stanley Simmons says. "She was rather forbidding as a human being, and very difficult during the show—difficult about Tony and what he wore, his collars and what have you."

Accompanist and composer Billy Goldenberg, who became a close friend of Perkins, recalls Merrill fondly: "I never really knew what the relationship between Helen and Tony was, but she was very nurturing to artists and had a lot of common sense; I don't think Tony had common sense. She was the voice of reason in his life, and I think she loved him. She always put things into proportion." No doubt Tony needed that, now more than ever.

Opening night was pushed to March 8 to buy a few more days of doctoring and avoid a possible Actors Equity strike. Even so, the reviews were ultimately unfavorable. "Whatever the charm of *Greenwillow* the novel, the play is as vague in its storytelling as in its geography," wrote *Time*. "It offers lovers but no proper love story, devils but no improper temptations, and the sort of artificially flavored language that tries to be folk poetry but turns out as horrible prose. . . . It is not first-rate Loesser." Walter Kerr of the *New York Herald Tribune* agreed that

Greenwillow was "do-it-yourself folklore," but added that "few musicals have ever been given the legitimate fiery-eyed intensity that gangling Anthony Perkins, with his crooked, nervous smile, brings to his series of nonexistent problems. . . . He acts, sings, and even kicks his coltish heels with something more than abandon—with an earnestness and an honesty that are immaculately professional."

"In addition to being an impressive actor, Perkins turns out to be first-rate in his singing," Brooks Atkinson declared. " 'Summertime Love' and 'Never Will I Marry' are full of lonely beauty when he sings them."

The critic was onto something when he referred to the "lonely beauty" of Perkins's vocalizing. *Greenwillow* stands as the singularly lovely anomaly of Perkins's career, a brief moment when Tony the actor and Tony the man melded to express feelings that did not require jaw-clenching angst or a butcher knife, did not require difference. Like Tony, Gideon Briggs is a young man who has lost his traveling father, who knows the curse of his own solitary nature, but who longs for the sense of belonging, of being part of other people, that can only be found at home with family and friends—something Gideon has never had and fears he may never know. When he sings the syrupy first-act number, "The Music of Home," extolling the small joys of family life (whistling teakettles, playing children), the lyrics may be hackneyed and a little too peculiarly quaint, but Tony's voice gives them an undeniable emotion—an underlying yearning—that saves the song from banality. On the cast album, his voice, no longer in constantly shifting imitation of Tony Bennett or Sarah Vaughan, no longer smoking jacket smooth, moves the listener with its simplicity and unembellished sincerity; he makes it personal.

Later, in his duet with Ellen McCown, misappropriately titled "Gideon Briggs, I Love You," it is Tony whose singing delights and touches, not the professionally trained ingenue. When he sings repeatedly that he loves her—"there it is plain as daylight"—it's achingly direct; in no other role does Perkins make as outright, as unashamed, as joyful, or as poignant a declaration of love. And, surprisingly, it suits him. The song ends, loses its authority, when McCown belts out the same lines; after the sweet straightforwardness of Perkins's expression, her intonation sounds harsh, her delivery archly coy. They could be singing two completely different songs. Clearly, Tony identified with

Gideon, a boy torn by the opposing sentiments "home is where I belong" and "born to wander till I'm dead."

Actress Marian Mercer remembers seventeen curtain calls on opening night. "You never would have believed that it wasn't a hit," she says. "The music just carried the day."

The old adage that the show must go on still applied. On March 13, a rainy Sunday, the cast gathered in Webster Hall on East Eleventh Street (now a popular gay disco) to record the *Greenwillow* album for RCA Victor Records. Like Glynis Johns on the Broadway album of Sondheim's *A Little Night Music*, Tony had a cold that day, which explains some of his nasal tones on the LP. Otherwise, according to McCown, the recording went "very smoothly, except that some of us had to stand six or seven feet behind Tony while he was at the mike, to make it sound even on the recording. I had this blasting loud voice; Tony had a small voice. But it was very, very lyrical."

Bad reviews aside, theater parties had bought enough advance tickets just on Loesser's name to keep the show running for thirteen weeks. Tuesday, Wednesday, and Thursday nights were packed with presold parties; Friday nights, Abba Bogin recalls, "you could graze sheep in the theater—there was nobody there!" The attraction of seeing movie star Tony Perkins back onstage was not the big draw the producers had hoped it would be.

Among Perkins's colleagues who came to see the show were Fred Astaire (with Barrie Chase), Piper Laurie, and his *Tall Story* costar Ray Walston. "It wasn't that I didn't like the show," Walston relates, "but I left after the first act. I didn't know that someone would see me and go backstage to tell Tony I was out front."

Walston ran into him sometime later in a drugstore on the corner of Fifty-fifth and Seventh Avenue. "I'd never realized how tall he was, despite the fact that I'd made a film with him. Maybe it was because he was angry. He looked at me and said, 'Why didn't you come backstage? Even if you didn't like the fucking thing, why didn't you come backstage and at least say hello?!' And I couldn't answer him, just stood there looking into those brown eyes. He got what he had ordered, walked out the door, and that was it."

To hear Tony tell it, the show was an inspiring experience. "When I played in *Greenwillow*," he later said, "we'd get terrible houses—only a handful of people on some nights. I always liked that. The audience would be feeling terrible; they'd be wishing they hadn't come, because nobody else came. But I always felt I could bring them out of it. I always felt if there were five or ten people out there, I could give each one my individual attention."

One of the people Tony Perkins touched deeply was "Gloria," a wildly devoted fan who, by today's standards, would be considered a stalker. A tall, striking, well-built black woman, "Gloria" would wait for Tony in the alley or at the stage door, sometimes even outside Helen's building, wearing nothing but a (sometimes mink) coat. After she appeared one night in the dressing room and opened her coat for him, a startled Tony had to request more security at the theater.

Perkins received a Tony Award nomination for *Greenwillow*, even though by the time the ceremony took place on April 24, 1960, the show was just weeks away from closing. He was up against Jackie Gleason and Robert Morse, who had both been nominated for *Take Me Along*, and Andy Griffith for the short-lived Harold Rome musical *Destry Rides Again*. Gleason won. (Roddy McDowall, the object of so many of Perkins's boyhood jokes, won a Tony Award that night for his supporting dramatic role in *The Fighting Cock*. Tony Perkins would never be so honored.)

Greenwillow closed on May 28, after ninety-five performances. (In 1989, when Susan Loesser asked to interview Perkins about *Greenwillow* for her book, he declined. Privately, he told a friend that his "most miserable days" had been working with Frank Loesser.)

Meanwhile, Tony Perkins had bigger fish to fry. *Psycho* was set to open in New York on June 16. He told one cast member that he thought it was the best thing he'd ever done.

"No one . . . BUT NO ONE . . . will be admitted to the theater after the start of each performance of *Psycho*," declared print ads for the new Hitchcock film.

In an official bulletin sent to film exhibitors, Hitchcock insisted, "I believe this is a vital step in creating the aura of mysterious importance this unusual motion picture so richly deserves."

Unusual the film certainly was. By 1960, America had reached its apex of postwar smugness and insularity, an illusory security kept stoked by convenient frozen foods, big cars, and the proliferation of television sets. Overweight Americans could watch *My Three Sons, Bachelor Father,* and *Father Knows Best*—all top shows lauding the joys of family life—in the privacy of their own homes, or venture out to see romantic box-office favorites like Doris Day, Rock Hudson, Sandra Dee, and Elizabeth Taylor in wide-screen Technicolor splendor. Alfred Hitchcock, too, was known for high-class entertainment like *To Catch a Thief* and *Rear Window*—colorful, big-budget thrillers with stars like Cary Grant, Jimmy Stewart, and Grace Kelly—not a grimy, black-and-white shocker about a cheap motel, a shower, a toilet (*Psycho* boasts Hollywood's very first onscreen flush, which upset censors more than the murders), and a raving transvestite. *Psycho* was a subversive quickie flick that undermined American preconceptions of safety and clean surfaces as it brutally killed off its pretty leading lady and offered a boy next door who was not what he seemed. The film horrified and outraged the public.

It was also a phenomenal blockbuster.

"Anthony Perkins' intelligent performance, the best of his career, makes the picture what it is," the *Daily News* exclaimed, "which is better than it would be without him. He is seen as a lonely young man with an abnormal love for his mother. And he hates girls."

"This is a first-rate mystery thriller," wrote *The Hollywood Reporter*, "full of visual shocks and surprises which are heightened by the melodramatic realism of the production. . . . Perkins gives by far the best performance of his career."

Not everyone agreed. "One of the most vile and disgusting films ever made," one British critic declared. Nevertheless, *Psycho* rapidly became one of the biggest moneymakers of the year, at home and abroad, and remains one of the highest-earning motion pictures of all time.

After Perkins's steady string of disappointing films and the abject failure of *Greenwillow*, *Psycho* gave his career, and his ego, an unexpected and exhilarating boost. "I actually felt guilt-ridden [whenever a film did poorly]," Tony told columnist Bob Thomas. "I thought that maybe I was kidding myself, that maybe the movies just weren't my medium. That's why it's so great to be associated with something that is headed for an $18 million gross. It is the most-seen black-and-white picture of all time; only the big color epics surpass it." He added, with a verbal pat on the back, "Naturally the credit goes to Alfred Hitchcock. But I think the cast contributed to its success, too. I think *Psycho* with unknowns would have been a good hit, but I don't think it would have been the smash that it is." He was right.

The film's megasuccess surprised everyone involved, even Hitchcock himself. According to Joseph Stefano, "We didn't feel we were doing anything outstandingly different, or that it would be a kind of seminal film. And yet all of us were affected by it. The problem that we all had was that it was very difficult ever to top that. It's always difficult when you do a film that is destined someday to become a classic, and is also as phenomenally successful as *Psycho* was; you can't get that kind of smash again. Very few people do. Orson Welles never did. Hitch never had that kind of hit again." Nor did Tony.

Greenwillow died an early death, but it was not Perkins's last stab at musical comedy. As ironic as it may seem, just as *Psycho* was opening, he appeared at the Carousel Theater in Framingham, Massachusetts, for a two-week run in the Richard Adler–Jerry Ross musical *Damn Yankees* (T.H. had starred in the film version two years earlier, and Timmy Everett in the original Broadway production). A theater-in-the-round inside a large circus tent, the Carousel boasted a seating capacity of 2,800 and a hefty twenty-piece orchestra, both unusual in the typically downscale realm of summer stock. The sheer size of the theater allowed for a weekly gross that could afford film stars as headliners, paying them between five and ten thousand dollars a week, quite a lot of money in those days.

As Carousel producer Richard Earle recalls, *Damn Yankees* had originally been scheduled that season as a vehicle for Ginger Rogers, who had agreed to play Lola. When word came back from her agent that she'd decided the part wasn't big enough for a star of her magnitude, the management agreed to put her in *Annie Get Your Gun* instead. Earle had to find a new star for *Damn Yankees*.

"About that time I'd heard that *Greenwillow* might close," he remembers. "It was a Frank Loesser show, and we presumed it would run for years. Anyway, I had a funny image. I had seen *Fear Strikes Out* and had an image of Tony Perkins in a baseball uniform, and I suddenly thought, 'You know, *Damn Yankees* is about a guy who sells his soul to become the all-American hero or boy, if you will'—and that was very much the image that Tony had."

A casting agent was sent to see Perkins backstage at the Alvin, and Tony, who may have found himself suddenly with no plans (and was offered good money), agreed. If Tab Hunter could do it, so could he.

But instead of Gwen Verdon, Tony's Lola would be Cathryn Damond. Perhaps, after the Loesser fiasco, Tony hoped to find some long-lost sustenance by regressing one more step to his summer theater roots.

He arrived a week early to spend some time on the Cape. "I met him at the airport," Earle recalls clearly, "and he was just so hyper. I asked why, and he said, 'I just sneaked into a showing of my new film, and I've never seen an audience react like that. They just screamed and yelled and went crazy! It was the most exciting experience of my life just to stand there and watch them go wild.' "

Despite Perkins's sudden career blaze, Earle says, "he was a consummate professional. I did not expect him to work as hard as he did. He was an excellent technician. We were putting this show together literally in a week, and quite often we would run the dress rehearsal twice, which made everybody tired. The tent was a mess, things were scattered all over, coffee cups, and I remember seeing Tony walking around cleaning up."

Dancer Donna McKechnie, who had auditioned unsuccessfully for *Greenwillow* and would eventually go on to make a name for herself in the original cast of *A Chorus Line*, was just fifteen at the time. She spent the summer of 1960 dancing at the Carousel, and remembers Tony as "very private, but polite and gracious—and very romantic and wistful to me. I looked at him as a figure of pure romance, poetic romance. He exuded that. For a young girl, he was easy to have a crush on. We all wanted to embrace him, to protect him. I kind of fell in love with him. He could do everything." McKechnie, who later married choreographer Michael Bennett, one of the first high-profile AIDS casualties, would be part of Tony and Grover Dale's heady New York theatrical crowd in the 1970s.

Dancer William De Silva, on the other hand, "found him to be as strange as he was in *Psycho*. In the evenings, during performance, when he was not needed onstage, he would go to his dressing room, and his lights would be out. He sat in complete darkness. He was very moody. Sometimes he would talk and be friendly, other times he would just walk past you and not even say hello. His mind was somewhere else."

Richard Earle attributes that to the fact that Perkins was serious about the job at hand: "Some of the stars treated summer stock, even though they were getting substantial money, as a lark in the hinterland. He was very low-key, and certainly didn't put on any star airs."

Damn Yankees opened on the Fourth of July, and local reviews were predictably positive. The *Boston Globe* wrote, "Though his singing voice is very limited, Tony Perkins exudes boyish charm, and he is an actor of far greater powers than the role of Joe Hardy demands."

"We had dinner after the show one night at a little club," Earle remembers, "and I knew everyone there, so I could protect Tony from people who might come over and bother him. We were sitting way over in the corner.

"There was a new bandleader that night, and he suddenly got on the microphone and said, 'We have a movie star with us tonight, Tony Perkins, and I'm sure if you give him a big hand he'll come up and sing a few songs for you!' I went right under the table and started to apologize—but Tony was up on the stage! They worked out a key, he sang, and had a wonderful time." Tony told Earle afterward that he had sung impromptu with the Benny Goodman orchestra in New York just the week before coming to Framingham. Such public high jinks were unusual for Tony to indulge in, but he was feeling good, in control of his destiny, happy in the knowledge that he had finally made a comeback.

And what a comeback. As more and more people saw *Psycho*, the public's ability to differentiate between the Tony they had thought they'd seen slashing Janet Leigh in the shower and the Tony they occasionally encountered in real life became blurred. The effect was almost overnight. What had seemed a career boon quickly became a Hitchcockian nightmare of mistaken identity.

"Just after *Psycho*, he and Jane went to the supermarket one time," Michaela O'Harra recalls, "and when they came back they were giggling because there had been a bunch of teenagers there and they'd heard one of them say, 'That's Tony Perkins—and *that's* his mother!' "

Boston Globe writer Joseph P. Kahn, whose family was friendly with the Perkinses in Truro, was eleven when *Psycho* was released in 1960. "Four summers later found Tony holed up on Cape Cod, out of work and disenchanted," he wrote in a 1992 tribute to his friend. "For diversion, he and I, accompanied by my younger brother, would often drive down to Orleans to play pitch 'n' putt golf under the lights. . . . The three of us would stroll out onto the first fairway. Heads would turn. Jaws would drop. Fathers would drape an instinctive hand around the shoulders of wives and small children. . . . The sight of Tony Perkins, hair cut Norman Bates–short and shoulders bony as a turkey vulture's, freely swinging a 9-iron, was usually enough to send terrified tourists scurrying down Route 6 in search of safe haven."

Richard Earle recalls vividly the film's immediate impact at the Carousel Theater that fateful summer: "One afternoon the whole cast went down to Boston to see *Psycho*, and that night, Wednesday, I always stood at the back of the theater. It was the strangest show that evening, just all off-balance, and I couldn't understand why. Finally, I asked one of the kids in the company what was going on, and he said, 'That film is so weird, we can't look at him.' It was a subtle change, but I caught it. It was palpable. It was almost at that moment that his career did a turnaround."

Tony Perkins's thoughtful, personal performance had opened a virtual Pandora's box to the naive public, revealing a truth most weren't prepared to accept: that the boy next door had secrets as deep, and sometimes as terrible, as any of the screen's legendary madmen and creatures of the night. The suggestion that there were seething undercurrents in Hometown, USA, was almost too much for "normal" moviegoers to comprehend. The frail mama's boy with the shy smile had suddenly become an icon of America's most dreaded impulses.

THREE STRIKES, YOU'RE OUT

IDING HIGH ON *PSYCHO* MANIA, Tony bought out his Paramount contract in early 1961, two years before its option point. Now that he was big enough to freelance, he wanted to pursue projects of his own choosing as well as command the kind of fees he'd received on the three loan-out pictures he'd made. His next film, Anatole Litvak's slick soap opera, *Goodbye Again*, based on the Françoise Sagan novel *Aimez-vous Brahms?*, was shot in Paris in the fall of 1960. It marked the beginning of a new phase of his career—a second career, as it were—and introduced him to a fresh, creative scene in Europe, where movies were made by self-proclaimed intellectuals and artists rather than taciturn macho technicians. In France, the innovative *Nouvelle Vague* of filmmaking, pioneered by the likes of Claude Chabrol, Jean-Luc Godard, Roger Vadim, Louis Malle, and François Truffaut, was all the rage, and would ultimately change the way films everywhere would be viewed in the future.

Anatole Litvak was not such a director. The Russian-born Litvak had worked in Western Europe as an assistant on many classic films—he edited G. W. Pabst's 1925 Garbo vehicle, *The Joyless Street*, for instance—before finding a lucrative niche for himself in Hollywood as the director of such popular studio movies as *Sorry Wrong Number*, *The Snake Pit*, and *Anastasia*. He had seen Perkins in *Look Homeward, Angel* and been impressed. Tony was his first choice to play Sagan's callow young man who has an affair with a woman old enough to be his mother, a simpering role that would put the first post-*Psycho* nail in the coffin of Perkins's American movie career.

Cast opposite Tony in *Aimez-vous Brahms?*—or, as it was bandied about, *The Way We Are, Time on Her Hands,* and *Paula,* until Tony suggested *Goodbye Again,* "because it had been the title of one of my father's most successful stage plays"—was two-time Academy Award winner Ingrid Bergman, with whom Perkins would appear again thirteen years later in *Murder on the Orient Express.* To add some sex appeal to the film, masculine French heartthrob Yves Montand was cast as Bergman's philandering other lover.

Tony's first professional pairing with Bergman was a potentially volatile one; a competitive actress who was well aware of Perkins's quiet but intense screen presence, she felt that "he could steal it" (meaning the film). She was also famous for bedding her male costars (though at the time she was married to Swedish stage producer Lars Schmidt). When Litvak suggested that Tony and Ingrid get acquainted over dinner *chez lui,* Bergman canceled because of some emergency at home. "One day," Tony later recalled, "I ran into a woman in hair curlers on the dressing room stairs at Boulogne studio. Suddenly a voice said, 'Are you Tony Perkins?' I looked around and it was Bergman. That's how we first met."

"I hear you're pretty good," Bergman reportedly said. "I guess maybe I better watch out for you."

"I wanted to make a good impression," Tony remembered, adding, "I also wanted to remain on my feet." Apparently, "Ingrid started talking about how as an actor she always kept her ego out of it. She said how she'd done a play and she went up to someone and said, 'I understand you can be very hard to work with and are very competitive and I don't work that way.' I was grateful to her for her frankness and having the first salvo—how wonderfully air-clearing."

Nevertheless, before their first working day together, a scene in which his character, brash tyro attorney Philip Van der Besh, mimics the courtroom styles of several different nationalities of lawyers, Perkins made sure he was letter perfect. "I burned those words into my mind," he recalled. "I fired through it without a mistake and I must say that Ingrid kept looking at me all the time with a 'So *this* is the boy?' expression."

"From then on," one observer noted, "the script was never out of Ingrid's hands."

Their love scenes generated more tension. Before their first screen kiss, Bergman wanted to practice—privately. In her 1980 memoir, the actress wrote, "I took Anthony Perkins into my dressing room . . . and I said, 'For heaven's sake, kiss me!' Anthony did a double take, then he laughed and said, 'Why? What for?' I said, 'Because we've got to do it later in the film. . . .' He grinned, and understood, and said, 'Okay,' then kissed me, and said, 'That hurt? No? Good.' "

Years later, Perkins told *People* magazine that Bergman "would have welcomed an affair. Every day she invited me to her dressing room to practice a love scene. I insisted on standing near the door, which I kept open." This, too, would be chalked up to Tony's professed "hysterical blindness" when confronted by an attractive member of the opposite sex.

As for Bergman, she commented on her screen rival lovers, "[Montand and Perkins] create a wonderful contrast. Montand instinctively feels everything. He is warm and sensitive. Perkins is just the opposite type of actor."

In a letter to his friend Stephen Paley, Tony admitted that he found working with Bergman difficult, that he was never sure how he was coming across opposite her. Early in the shoot, he did something unlike him. Before filming the scene where Bergman and Montand, who have accidentally run into Philip in a nightclub, take the boy home drunk, he decided to do it actually as "stinko" as he could possibly be without falling down. It was a night shoot, so at dinner that evening with Montand, Bergman, and "Tola," as Litvak was called, Tony ate very little and consumed one full *demi-bouteille* of white wine himself. Not a drinker, he was so inebriated by the time he arrived on the set that he decided to go all the way, and drank some Scotch that Bergman had on hand. In an unusually sloppy display, he ended up lying with his head on her shoulder, rhapsodizing about the time when, as a fourteen-year-old, he woke Jane up at some ungodly hour so that they could be the first people in the theater on the opening day of *Notorious,* Bergman's second Hitchcock film. After the scene, Tony went home and was sick.

Whatever his reasons for the behavior, it broke the ice between him and his screen lover. The next time they met, Bergman asked Tony how he felt and what he remembered. "Nothing," he said.

"You don't remember what you *told* me?" she asked teasingly.

"No."

Bergman laughed, then confessed that he hadn't told her anything significant at all. Perhaps that had been Tony's intention: to create a charming illusion of intimacy and trust, thereby gaining the upper hand in their working relationship without the complications of sex. (A few weeks later Tony wrote to Paley that he'd had an anxious dream in which he and Bergman were married in a small church in Georgia, with fake squares of green grass along the aisles to make it look outdoorsy.)

With his hefty hangover lingering, Tony had to face a busy social schedule that week: first a gala for George Cukor's *Let's Make Love* starring Montand and Marilyn Monroe (Tony was not looking forward to it), and then on Wednesday the first of *two* Judy Garland concerts he would attend in Paris, accompanied by the Litvaks and novelist Françoise Sagan (he *was* looking forward to that; a serious Garland fan, Tony visited the singer backstage on both occasions).

The press was quick to link Tony romantically with the twenty-five-year-old, recently divorced Sagan, "the female Norman Mailer of the Left Bank"; he was quoted erroneously as saying, "I like her very much. And I'm tired of being a bachelor. I want to get married soon."

The reality was quite different. "You feel like she hates you for the first three weeks," he recounted. "She doesn't talk much, but it's not a case of shyness. She just sits there and soaks up everything everyone else is saying." Tony was also reported to have had "a few dates" with actress Jean Seberg.

But Tony's time in Paris was more than the usual press conferences and publicity acts; unexpectedly, he found himself accepted by a fascinating and free social circle of writers, artists, and actors from all over the world, in a city where he himself was respected as much for his talent as for his fame. In France, being "tough" wasn't so important. People seemed to have more to talk about, more on their minds than where and with whom they could be "seen." Tony's social calendar from mid-September through December read like the perfect welding of commerce and art:

September 15, he dined with Josh and Nedda Logan, who were

thrilled about Logan's new film, *Fanny*, starring Horst Buchholz (Tony hated it);

September 20, he canceled dinner with Judy Garland and her husband, Sid Luft, to accept an invitation to dine with Hitchcock and his wife, Alma Reville, at the Relais Bisson;

October 5, breakfast with Hitchcock to discuss a possible film project about the famous British escape artist Jack Shepperd, who lived in eighteenth-century London (nothing came of it);

A few days later, dinner with novelist James Jones and his wife, Gloria, at their home on the Ile St. Louis, with blacklisted director John Berry and black American writer James Baldwin, who cooked spareribs and rice (the Joneses quickly became Tony's closest friends in Paris), followed by a huge cocktail party for Paul Newman and Joanne Woodward, two of Tony's first acquaintances in Hollywood, who were in town to film *Paris Blues* (Tony was miffed when he was invited via secretary).

In late October, Tony drove out with the Hitchcocks to visit Ingrid Bergman and Lars Schmidt at their country home in La Grange aux Moines, Choisel. That night at dinner was the first real reconciliation that occurred between the "Master of Suspense" and his once leading lady since their estrangement during the filming of *Under Capricorn* in 1949. The Hitchcocks returned to Paris after dinner, but Tony stayed the night, and was put upstairs in daughter Pia Lindstrom's vacant room. All of Bergman's children were away, in fact, owing to Roberto Rossellini's request that they be educated in Italy. Their clothes hanging forlornly in the closets, their watercolors on every wall, Bergman missed them terribly. The poignance of the empty house did not go unnoticed by Tony, who was keenly attuned to the loneliness of a fractured home.

His own home in Paris was a rental, a two-story flat in the back of an elegant middle-class building near the Ecole Militaire in Les Invalides. Owned by popular gay novelist Gordon Merrick (*The Lord Won't Mind*), the apartment featured a spiral staircase that connected the living room to the bedroom and bath upstairs. (Tony did not know Merrick personally; the flat was secured through an intermediary.)

It was conveniently located just three blocks away from what quickly became Tony's favorite Parisian restaurant, Le Vert Boaccage, which he fondly called the "Tomato Tart." A small, unassuming establishment with beautiful linens, it was run by two "butch" ladies who made Tony feel right at home. The women accommodated their young American patron by keeping the kitchen stocked with a ready supply of his favorite drink, milk, a leftover from Tony's days as a tubercular child, which they always served him right away (most Parisians could hardly think of anything more atrocious to drink with their meals).

It has been speciously written that during the 1960s, Tony Perkins lived in Europe; this is only true insofar as he worked there continually through that decade. After each picture he always returned to New York. It would be easy to surmise that, for Tony, Paris offered asylum from the bigotry of "redneck" Hollywood. But being gay in France created just as much a dichotomy. As his friend Robert Hussong, who met Tony via the James Joneses during *Goodbye Again* and soon after became his agent at MCA's Paris office, explains, "France is run by the bourgeois middle class, and they are not broad-minded—all the more reason why one had to have the same sense of good taste. Tony had enormous taste and style, so he would overcome all of this wherever he was. Paris was not a refuge. He never considered Europe his home. He never thought he'd be back in Paris."

Even so, rumors persisted that Tony was a regular at the Trap and other Parisian backroom bars, as well as the convenient public pissoirs located throughout the city, sometimes with famous friends like Rudolf Nureyev. Perkins and Nureyev were introduced in New York by press agent Chris Allen at the time of the dancer's triumphant American debut in 1962, and had allegedly become sexually involved. Whereas Perkins's sex life was a mystery to many, Nureyev's promiscuity was as well known as his art. (According to one source, after a ballet performance at the old Metropolitan Opera, as Tony, Helen, and Nureyev walked along Fifth Avenue, the dancer tried to take the movie star's hand and was instantly rebuffed.)

On November 4, 1960, *Psycho* opened in Paris and became the talk of the town, much to the annoyance of the competitive Anatole Litvak. Only *La Verité*, starring the sexy Brigitte Bardot (with whom Tony would soon work), was causing as big a stir. Meanwhile, back in the States, John F. Kennedy had just been elected president; Tony wrote to Stephen Paley that he was pleased, though Lyndon Johnson appalled him.

With *Psycho*'s French release, Tony's presence in Paris was even more known. He became friendly with Leonard Bernstein, Simone Signoret, and dancer Roland Petit, and was visited on the set by James Baldwin. He socialized at the Paul Newmans' Montmartre home with Anna Magnani, and attended a cocktail party thrown by agent Irving Lazar for Richard Brooks and Jean Simmons along with Glenn Ford, Yvette Mimieux, David Lean, Daryl Zanuck, Roger Vadim, and the ubiquitous Hedda Hopper. (Zanuck offered Tony the part of a lieutenant in a war movie he was trying to persuade Federico Fellini to direct. Tony was rightly skeptical.)

Dorothy Jeakins was also in town, and camping out chez Tony. But away from Hollywood, where her friendship served him well, she quickly wore her welcome thin. "Tony thought she was a pain in the ass in Paris," Paley recalls. "She was so needy. He liked her, but all these calls would come in, and Tony was very secretive then, he wouldn't even allow her to tell people she was staying with him. She could give out the number, but she couldn't say whose number it was. He really prized his privacy at that time. He thought of himself almost as a male Garbo, he wanted to appear mysterious, kind of a loner." Indeed, despite his renewed popularity, Tony often dined in public alone, content to be seen reading a book (*The Leopard*, for instance, or E. M. Forster's *The Celestial Omnibus*), and continued to enjoy the solo experience of moviegoing. In Paris, he saw *Strangers When We Meet*, *Heller in Pink Tights*, *L'Avventura*, *Sergeant Rutledge*, and the cut version of George Cukor's *A Star Is Born*, a film that touched him with its relevance to his own experience at Paramount (perhaps it brought back bittersweet memories of first meeting William or T.H., who was then battling charges of dog cruelty in Los Angeles).

Goodbye Again finished shooting on December 14. An exhausted Tony wrote to Stephen Paley that he would probably be home by Sunday the seventeenth. The picture had been a hard one.

After Christmas at home with Helen, Teno, Stephen, Jane, and Michaela—at which time Earl Wilson reported that Perkins was considering singing on Broadway again, in either the upcoming *Carte Blanche* or David Merrick's *Subways Are for Sleeping*—a tired Tony returned to Paris briefly in January for some additional work on the film. Ingrid Bergman had been unhappy with one scene, and had demanded that it be reshot. According to Perkins, she couldn't remember her lines, and blamed her mistakes on the script, complaining repeatedly that it did not incorporate enough of Sagan's original dialogue. The scene took two full days to complete.

Goodbye Again, which opened in the spring (Paris) and summer (New York) of 1961, was as lauded in Europe as it was panned in the States. The story of an older, unmarried woman sleeping with a younger, equally unmarried man was just too much for the Puritans back home. "This sort of [relationship] has happened more than once in this country, though it has been more generally accepted in Europe than here," wrote the *New York Post*'s Archer Winsten. "Bergman's still too wholesome. Montand is too masculine to be supplanted like that. . . . And Perkins isn't the man to do it." *The New Yorker* dismissed the film as "just another soppy drama of upper-middle-class amatory woes, which not even Miss Bergman's Dior gowns and Van Cleef & Arpel jewelry can do much to redeem. . . . Mr. Perkins' callowness isn't always, I fear, the product of an art that conceals art." Several critics mentioned that they were unable to shake images of *Psycho* from their minds while watching Tony in the new film.

As usual, the *New York Times*'s Bosley Crowther came to Tony's defense: "Of the actors, Anthony Perkins not only has the most engaging role but he also plays it in the most engaging fashion and almost carries the picture by himself. . . . He ranges from boyish excitement to deep and tear-popping grief and makes it believable and cogent. It is too bad they throw the play to the woman at the end."

Though it does rank as one of the better films of Perkins's career, due in large part to Bergman's graceful and cohesive presence—and especially when compared to the mostly execrable European-made films that would follow—his performance, while sufficiently flip and moody, suffers again from a lack of sexual magnetism. Fatal to the film is the obvious fact that there is no real tension or chemistry between Bergman and Perkins; she is warm, he is cerebral, and nothing comes across. Perkins is simply not believable as a young man in the throes of first love. Bergman and Montand, on the other hand, despite their characters' unhappiness, seem more at ease together, more physically comfortable and intimate as lovers.

Nevertheless, the performance garnered Perkins an impressive number of foreign film awards, including Italy's David of Donatello trophy (which he shared with Spencer Tracy, who won for Stanley

Kramer's *Judgment at Nuremberg*), Belgium's Grand Prix International, Germany's Grosse Otto, and, most important, the Best Actor award at Cannes, where Sophia Loren was honored in the female category for her shattering performance in *Two Women*.

Psycho, for all its subtle art and miraculous box-office glory, would be less honored. While both Hitchcock and Perkins were presented the British equivalent of the Academy Award in early January of 1961, and Perkins himself given France's Victoire de Cinéma for creating Norman Bates, it was the American Oscar that the director and star coveted most of all. Hitchcock, who had been nominated four times before but had always gone home empty-handed, pretended not to care ("What do I want with another doorstop?"), but associates knew that the ongoing snub vexed him. Suspense films and thrillers, however, had always been widely considered the realm of B directors.

"Hitchy" wanted his revenge, and promised his talented stars, Perkins and Janet Leigh, an Oscar campaign that would at least win the three of them nominations. It would be Tony's first since *Friendly Persuasion,* and a chance to replenish some of his beginner's luck. Tony asked Hitchcock to hire Buddy Clarke to orchestrate the campaign, and the director was more than happy to comply.

"This COULD Be Tony's Year," Hedda Hopper declared. "This very bright young man may well take home an Oscar for his horrifying portrayal of a maniacal killer."

Psycho ultimately received nominations in four categories: direction, supporting actress (Leigh), black-and-white cinematography, and art direction. Perkins had been overlooked in favor of Trevor Howard for *Sons and Lovers,* Burt Lancaster for *Elmer Gantry,* Jack Lemmon for *The Apartment,* Laurence Olivier for *The Entertainer,* and Spencer Tracy for *Inherit the Wind.* He cabled Hitchcock, "So happy for you. Hope it goes all the way." The director, who was reportedly indignant over the treatment of his star, wired back, "I am ashamed of your fellow actors."

When the Oscars were presented at the Santa Monica Civic Auditorium on April 17, 1961, *Psycho* came away with nothing. Hitchcock lost to Billy Wilder (*The Apartment*), and Janet Leigh was defeated by another perky blond, Shirley Jones, who had been cast against type as a prostitute in *Elmer Gantry.* Neither Hitchcock nor Perkins would be nominated again, though the director would be given the condolence prize of the Irving G. Thalberg Memorial Award in 1967. In the meantime, Perkins cheered himself up by taking Roger Englander to see Judy Garland in her legendary concert at Carnegie Hall on April 2.

Professionally, Tony tried to keep the momentum going by claiming to have other projects in the works with Hitchcock. "Hitchcock has something in mind," he told Hopper. "When a director and star make a successful film together there's always a lot of stories in the newspapers about them wanting to do another together—but this time it is really legitimate."

PERKINS OFFERS HEAD TO HITCHCOCK, screamed a *Los Angeles Times* item, explaining that Tony's own newly formed company, inaccurately identified as "Wampam" Productions, was trying to get Hitchcock interested in directing a film of a Kevin J. Connell mystery novel, *The Man Who Lost His Head*, to which Perkins had secured the rights. (Would such a mocking headline have topped a story about a more masculine star like Burt Lancaster or John Wayne?) Wigwam Productions, as the corporation was actually named, not only signaled Tony's new commitment to control his own career, but gave Jane, who ran the company with the help of attorney Maurice Greenbaum, a chance to invest her son's money in a variety of stakes, including Canadian real estate and cattle brokerage.

"My lawyer came up with the suggestion we use my initials, T.P. . . . and call it Wigwam Productions and use a tepee as a symbol," Tony said flippantly of his mother's endeavor. "My initials to the public are A.P. so I said maybe we could call it APE productions and have a monkey as a symbol."

Immediately following *Psycho*, Tony was announced for a number of upcoming films: *Act One*, Joshua Logan's biopic about Moss Hart, which ultimately starred George Hamilton; George Roy Hill's impending epic *Hawaii*, which was eventually made with Max Von Sydow; *The Comancheros*, in which Perkins was to be reteamed with Gary Cooper (it was finally cast with Stuart Whitman and John Wayne); and *La Vie Morte*, a tragicomedy with Brigitte Bardot that was never made. He was also up for the title role in David Lean's *Lawrence of Arabia*, but Peter O'Toole got that, with dazzling results.

The picture Perkins most wanted to make was *Dooley*, 20th Century-Fox's proposed biography of Dr. Tom Dooley, the handsome, young, self-promotingly philanthropic doctor in Laos whose altruism had made him a national hero—who also happened to be gay. *Tea and Sympathy*'s Robert Anderson had written a script, and both George Roy Hill and Joshua Logan had expressed interest in directing. But Fox producer Martin Manulis wanted *The Apartment*'s Jack Lemmon for the title role (Pat Boone and Montgomery Clift were also serious contenders). Recovering from a changeover of regime, the studio would not commit to the costly project, which would require intensive location shooting. Dooley's family, not to mention the social climate at the time, demanded removal of all suggestion of sexuality from the script, and the film never got off the ground.

One of the more immediate rewards of *Psycho* was the $2,000 bonus Hitchcock gave Tony—which Tony, in turn, "gave" to Helen Merrill. At lunch in New York one day he said to his old friend, "If I asked you to do something without telling you what it was, would you do it?"

Without hesitation, Helen said yes.

"I want you to have your nose fixed."

Merrill, whose nose had been broken and who had never considered her face her fortune, agreed—especially after Teno Pollick, who was a big advocate of cosmetic surgery, talked her into it at home. Forever after, Helen's proboscis would be referred to among the makeshift family as the "Hitchcock Nose."

Blacklisted director Jules Dassin—whose career in Hollywood had been nipped viciously in the bud in 1951 when another director, Edward Dmytryk, named him as a Communist before the House Un-American Activities Committee—had thrived in exile. Now married to Greek actress Melina Mercouri, he had gone on to make several entertaining films, the most popular of which was undoubtedly his latest, *Never on Sunday*, the story of an intellectual boob (played by Dassin) who tries to educate a free-spirited prostitute (Mercouri). The film was a huge success outside of Greece, particularly in the United States, where audiences were taken with the Mediterranean scenery and the hit theme song by Manos Hadjidakis, which won an American Oscar.

Dassin's first choice to play the boob in that film had been Anthony Perkins, but at the time he could not afford the actor's price. After the success of *Never on Sunday*, however, MCA had new confidence in Dassin, and Herman Citron allowed Perkins to be signed for his next project, a modern-dress version of the Greek tragedy *Phaedra*, in which Tony would play Alex (think Hippolytus), the young man who has a fatal affair with his stepmother (played once again by an older woman, Mercouri). Perkins's box-office name got Dassin the proper financing, though the casting would unbalance the entire film. (Françoise Sagan had introduced Tony to the Dassins in Paris during *Goodbye Again* and the three had become fast friends. One of the things Dassin promised Tony during the *Phaedra* shoot was fresh milk daily; "Tony loved milk," Mercouri wrote in her 1971 memoir; "well no one is perfect.")

"You didn't steer Tony Perkins," remembers Robert Hussong, who was newly assigned as Perkins's agent at MCA's Paris office. "He was controlling about everything he did, and he made very intellectual decisions. Especially in those early years, his life was his business. He wanted to build security for himself, he always wanted to know that he didn't have to do a picture only for money. There had to be some other reason. His choices were not all terrific."

MCA Hollywood certainly didn't think so; later, when Perkins turned down a role in the all-star war movie *The Victors* (which ultimately starred George Hamilton and George Peppard) to do *The Trial* for Orson Welles, the company began to get nervous. "MCA Hollywood was a little concerned about that because they felt it was very important for him to make these big American pictures for his career," Hussong recalls. "But he liked Paris, he was highly admired there in the French film industry, and right from the time he did *Phaedra* we started getting very good offers. For the first time, French companies were prepared to pay an American star his American salary. He'd get two, three new scripts a week. He was probably the first American star who became a major star in his own right in Europe. He did it before Charles Bronson and Clint Eastwood."

Location shooting for *Phaedra* began in London in early July 1961, then moved to Athens, where the first taste of the chaos that would mark the whole production occurred during the filming of the ship-launching scene at the Port of Piraeus near Scaramanga. Filming was abruptly interrupted when the Niarchos Company, which owned the shipyard, ordered the film crew off the premises, claiming falsely that Dassin had no permission to film there. When the director refused to leave, dockworkers opened the sea vents and flooded the set. Perkins, Mercouri, et alia suddenly found themselves waist-deep in water, but would not move until police came. As for Dassin, he kept the cameras rolling and captured the entire incident on film (which Mercouri and the other women hid in their clothes when the shipping company wanted to confiscate evidence).

In August, the production moved again to the beautiful Greek isle of Hydra, thirty-six miles from Athens, where director Jean Negulesco had shot Sophia Loren's *Boy on a Dolphin* a few years before. On Hydra, Tony was joined by his "family": Helen, Teno, and Roger Englander, who was there to write a piece on the production for the *New York Times*. "We stayed in a whitewashed, wonderful house with very few amenities," Englander remembers. "My room had icons all around and triptychs, and it had a large cistern—almost like in *Salome*, with a wooden cover over a well—in the middle of this bedroom. So I called it the Cistern Chapel." Everyone had a private bedroom, water had to be hand-pumped, ice was supplied to keep food fresh, and electricity, which came on only in the evening, was sporadic. "The four of us *were* like a little family," Englander confirms.

"It was more than a family," Melina Mercouri recalled shortly before her death in 1994. "Because when you have a family, it's not your choice. It was Tony's privileged family."

The actress adored Perkins: "We were great friends. He was the most intelligent and the most beautiful actor that I played with. He was extremely generous, a gentleman. *Phaedra* was one of the most happy films that I made in my life because of Tony. I knew him for many years from *Phaedra*, and it was a big love, a big, big love. But really love.

"He helped me a lot. I had only made three or four films before *Phaedra*, and Tony had experience. I learned many technical things from him, about lighting and how to be on the screen for close-ups. And about life, about love. I have his photo near my bed, and every night I look at him."

So apparent was the affection between the two stars that some people wondered if their relationship was actually more than platonic. "They may or may not have had sex," one observer says. "Because he bought her very intimate presents, like ladies' panties."

Roger Englander concurs that "she was a very sexy woman. Just to talk was almost like having sex with her. She made gay men feel they weren't." Even so, Tony kept his American "family" separate on the island from his professional one. "He came not with his friends very much," Mercouri noted.

Cinematographer Jacques Natteau, who would later produce *The Champagne Murders*, Perkins's first film for director Claude Chabrol, remembers that whereas actor Raf Vallone, who played the father, frequently invited cast and crew to his villa for dinner and drinks, no one was ever invited to hang out chez Tony. Tony accepted social invitations, but never reciprocated. Likewise, at the nightly company gatherings at the local taverna, he never committed himself to sit at any one table, preferring instead to table-hop, sipping from other people's drinks along the way—yet never ordering a drink for himself, and never offering to pick up the tab. (He would later do the same in Paris at the company's *apéritifs du plateau*, Saturday gatherings at a bar or restaurant to celebrate the end of the workweek, at which colleagues would take turns picking up the bill; Tony never paid a centime, though he was always sure to attend the get-togethers.)

Natteau also recalls that Perkins never introduced Teno Pollick, but flirted quite openly with Helen Merrill, whom he occasionally brought around to the set. He continued to pretend that he wasn't "queer," even though, according to Natteau, no one in Europe would have cared.

Perhaps one of the reasons Tony kept his villa off limits was that he was having trouble keeping a lid on Teno. As he had done in Malaysia, Tony indulged in an anonymous sex spree in Greece (and Paris), which did not make his "lost boy" too happy. "Teno told me that Tony carried on with Greek boys—with *everybody*—right and left, thinking that he didn't know it," one friend says. "He said that Tony's apartment in New York had a well where the fire escape was, and even there Tony would always be carrying on outside with somebody he'd picked up."

Pollick's faithful friend Keene Curtis remembers that "Tony took Teno to Paris, but was nervous about his being there. So Teno sometimes had to stay behind when Tony went for interviews or big public things. But he understood. Tony was always careful about his career. Maybe living together would have been one step too much. But they were together a lot, and the fact that Tony would even take him to Paris was a big step."

While off camera Tony tried to keep his personal risks low, he greatly enjoyed the dangers on camera. Most precarious was Tony's shrill suicide scene in which his character drives a sports car over a cliff. The arrival of the brand-new Aston-Martin roadster caused quite a commotion on the island, which had never had a car on it before. Perkins himself had to drive it—*fast*—along a twisting donkey path high above the sea to get the shot. He later recounted how they shot the scene "with a camera bolted to the hood in front of me so I couldn't see where I was going, with Dassin crouched in one corner looking through a mirror so he could see what I was doing, with three old ladies stopping the traffic ten miles down the road. And driving at full tilt around those hairpin curves. That's the way he wanted to do it because that was the hardest and most unrealistic way to do it."

The company moved to Paris in mid-September, to shoot interiors at the Boulogne Studios, including the crucial—and then very racy—nude love scene between Perkins and his vivacious but mature movie stepmother. The scene took two days to complete. On the way to the studio the first morning, it was raining, and Dassin got the idea of splicing in shots of torrential rain running down the window panes from the rain splashing on the windows of his car.

Another dampening factor was that Perkins couldn't act the scene. Mercouri, whom Tony would later proclaim a "completely spontaneous actress," immediately picked up on his seeming frigidity and went privately to her husband and Jacques Natteau between takes. "I cannot do this with him," she complained, "there's nothing there. I can't feel anything. He's like ice." Indeed, the scene stands almost as a monument to bad casting (though many viewers at the time remember the faux sensuousness of the scene as an erotic milestone).

Phaedra wrapped in mid-October 1961. "This is one film people won't come out of with a shrug," Tony declared in November. "They may come out furious, but they won't be indifferent. . . . There are scenes and dialogue that are absolutely daring in a cinematic sense."

The press began hailing the "new," adult Tony Perkins as a "man of action" rather than the mooning adolescent he'd previously been known as. PERKINS IN MARKET FOR WIFE one headline fraudulently announced, and Tony was quoted as saying he'd "really like to get married."

If Perkins had hoped that these sexier roles would change his image, the plan backfired, at least in his unforgiving homeland. *Phaedra* was a disaster. "Dassin has reduced the age-old tragedy to a joke by miscasting Tony Perkins as the son and trying to turn him into a Great Lover," wrote *Cue*. "He has neither the physical, emotional, nor acting equipment to make an on-screen Melina Mercouri think the world well lost for love of him—particularly when her husband is played by so virile and magnetic an actor as Raf Vallone. The seduction scenes of steam-heated passion between Perkins and La Mercouri are so bad they're funny." Even *The New Yorker* admitted that Tony "occasionally causes the picture to teeter on the brink of unpremeditated comedy. Mr. Perkins' voice, manner, and appearance being those of an aging prep-school boy, it's hard to believe that a lioness like Miss Mercouri would trouble to bare her notably numerous teeth at such a quarry, or that a lion like Raf Vallone, who plays Theseus in the guise of an Onassis-like shipping magnate, would have troubled to sire him."

Most condemning of the film was the men's magazine *Esquire*: "Vallone, whose only definite trait in the film is virility, would seem much better able to satisfy the formidable sexuality of Mercouri . . . than the wispy Perkins, who becomes more fragile and epicenely contorted with each new film. He is so outmatched in every way, from breadth of shoulders to manliness of voice, that during the many, many love scenes, I had the unsettling notion that they were both in drag."

"Our judgment of the film was that we had failed," Mercouri revealed in her memoir. "It was an honest attempt, but finally it became more a bourgeois drama than a tragedy."

The real tragedy was the nail it would inexorably drive into the coffin of Perkins's U.S. film career. In *Phaedra*, his American masculinity level hit an all-time low, an impression that was heightened by his miscalculated, downright campy eye movements—meant to denote smoldering passions. When, with an archly raised eyebrow, he tells Mercouri, "We have to talk," it seems he wants to discuss something other than their illicit situation. Ironically, his scenes with handsome Raf Vallone carry more of a sexual charge. Early in the film their farewell kiss, quite naturally delivered, evokes an unusually beaming smile from Tony, and at the end, as they stand arm in arm high above the shipyard, he sounds utterly convincing and self-assured when he tenderly tells Vallone, "To me, you used to be a name in the newspaper. But here I can see you and touch you."

Perkins's effeminacy, which made him a laughingstock in the States, was seen almost as a virtue by European audiences, who appreciated his "sensitivity." *Newsweek* reported in late 1962, when *Phaedra* was released, that his popularity in France was rivaled only by that of sexy Jean-Paul Belmondo, and that in Germany he was the second most popular foreign actor to Rock Hudson. For every domestic fan letter, he received fifty from Europe. "I'm not on the top-ten list," Tony admitted. "To be a big box-office star in America, you have to have several qualities I don't have." As for his popularity on the Continent, he exclaimed, "It's a phenomenon. And nobody's more phenomenized than myself. I can make any deal now in Europe I want. In any country, I can just sit there and say I want to do this movie for that company with this producer and that director—and I'm actually turning down money."

"Ah, Tony," Melina Mercouri sighed to *Newsweek*. "He is attractive to women. He is dangerous to women. When you touch him, he goes away a little. He is an *anguille* [eel]. Vallone is a good-looking man, but Perkins. . . . Ah, I'd pick Perkins any time."

So would Anatole Litvak, who insisted that Tony take the lead in his next film, a suspense thriller called *All the Gold in the World*, written by Peter Viertel and Hugh Wheeler. Tony was reluctant to take on the role of a creepy loser who, unknown to authorities, survives a plane crash, then hides out in the Paris apartment of his estranged wife to wait for the life insurance money to kick in.

But when Sophia Loren signed on (replacing the previously announced Jeanne Moreau), Perkins accepted Litvak's offer; since *Desire under the Elms*, Loren had gone on to become a respected dramatic actress and an Academy Award winner. As with Audrey Hepburn, Tony decided it would be a smart career move to act with her again. *All the Gold in the World*, which would be shot in both English and French versions, began production on December 11 at the St. Meurice Studios in Joinville. In lame imitation of Hitchcock, Litvak refused to reveal the ending of the picture to the press.

Joining Perkins and Loren in the cast were Gig Young, Jean-Pierre Aumont, and nine-year-old Thomas Norden, who had been in *Greenwillow* and whom Tony had recommended to Litvak for the role of the boy neighbor who discovers him. Perkins took an almost paternal interest in the homesick boy's well-being, and the two spent much time together off the set.

Tony was certainly more permissive than a parent would have been. "*West Side Story* had just come out," recalls Norden (who went on to star in TV's *Flipper*), "and all I wanted to do was buy a switchblade. They sold them in Paris, and Tony took me shopping after we finished filming. He just sort of looked the other way when I bought mine. He could relate to young people, and he was sincere about it. We were friends. Anybody else was just a grown-up."

Another person with whom Tony was friendly was supermodel Ivy Nicholson, who had a small part in the film. She was madly in love with Tony. "In those days models were mute and mysterious," Perkins said in 1987. "She was outspoken, witty, very volatile. One time we had an argument, and friends of mine informed me to arm myself with a pistol when I went out because of Ivy's unrestrained temper." Later, reportedly jealous over Tony's rapport with Loren, Nicholson went to her dressing room and slashed her wrists.

"You know how human nature is," says Maila Nurmi, who heard the story right away. "Women love all the men who are bastards, men love all the women who are bitches. People love rejection, it fascinates them. And Tony knew that. He was playing that game all the time. He tried to drive people to suicide." Given Tony's elaborate game playing a few years later with the sophisticated Stephen Sondheim crowd—diversions that he and the composer would depict as downright deadly in their screenplay *The Last of Sheila*—it's not hard to fathom how Nurmi got that impression. (As for the troubled Nicholson, by the mid-1980s, after two failed marriages, she ended up penniless on San Francisco's skid row.)

Filming proceeded smoothly except for the interruption of some cameramen from NBC-TV, who arrived to shoot "candid" footage of Loren at work and at play for an upcoming special television documentary, *The World of Sophia Loren*. Orchestrated to promote Loren's already prominent position in the cinematic firmament, the show featured interviews with Litvak, Perkins, and others—all about Sophia—as well as scenes of Perkins (looking as thin as a rake) and Loren thesping for Litvak's cameras and relaxing between takes. They are shown lounging together on a bed, laughing and singing "After I'm Gone," then putting together the pieces of a puzzle, which Tony refers to as "woman's work, like sewing"—an odd comment, probably tongue in cheek, coming from a man whose only known relaxation among colleagues was playing word games and puzzles.

He looks distinctly uncomfortable during his Sophia interview, smiling stiffly and staring blankly into the camera without blinking as he spouts redundancies about his costar: "If she picks her next movies very, very carefully, she could become one of the great stars in pictures, I think." His appearance is reminiscent of an equally zombielike one he made the year before on a *Hedda Hopper's Hollywood* special, which also featured segments on Venetia Stevenson and Gloria Swanson. His lax behavior before television cameras was certainly idiosyncratic and must have concerned his promoters at MCA.

Five Miles to Midnight, as the film was titled, wrapped at the end of March 1962, but not until fifty-nine-year-old Litvak was released from the American Hospital at Neuilly after suffering a concussion when he fell from a ten-foot platform during the last shots. The movie did nothing for the careers of anyone involved. "Unbelievable and uninteresting," proclaimed *The Hollywood Reporter.* "Perkins, who is supposed to be terrifying, succeeds only in being tiresome. His characterization has no real menace, but a kind of whining mediocrity that a healthy, vital woman such as Miss Loren could easily and speedily rout."

At a screening of the film in New York, Janet Perkins commented to a friend, "I don't know what I'm going to say to Tony about this one."

Those close to Perkins and his career tried frantically to advise him on his next move. "He wouldn't listen to me," Buddy Clarke remembers. "He did three pictures in a row—one with Ingrid Bergman, one with Melina Mercouri, and one with Sophia Loren, who was younger than Tony but looked older—in each of them he played a weak, almost effeminate kind of man. Not really effeminate, but weak. When he got through with the third picture, I said, 'Tony, I'm not your manager, but I'd love to be without any fee. What I would do now would be to put you in a Western, put you in jeans, have you fuck a young girl, get the shit kicked out of you, kick the shit out of somebody in a fistfight—change your image.' He said, 'Stick to your press agenting.'

"If he had listened to me, I know his career would have been prolonged. Nobody wants to see the same person on the screen over and over and over. Particularly as you start to mature, and lose whatever it is that attracted young girls to you. He was badly managed. People took advantage of him. They saw a chance to make a buck. And Tony must have died a very rich man because he never spent three dollars on anything."

Rich or not, he was about to make another seemingly (to him) foolproof career move, as Franz Kafka's Joseph K, the ultimate victim, for that other misunderstood Hollywood genius, Orson Welles.

CHAPTER 4

THE RIGHT STUFF

O RSON WELLES, *the* director who had brought *Citizen Kane* to the screen in 1941, had long been considered box-office poison, an auteur as famous for his egocentric indulgences as for his cinematic genius. A series of films that tried to recapture the glory of *Kane* had failed to do so, and after his brilliantly chilling *Touch of Evil* received meager distribution and dashed all hope of a Hollywood comeback, Welles resorted to acting in other directors' films, mostly in Europe, to raise funds for future projects.

It was while appearing in Abel Gance's vulgar spectacle *Austerlitz*—which boasted an international cast including Jack Palance, Claudia Cardinale, Jean Marais, and opera star Anna Moffo—that Welles was approached by the father-son producing team of Michel and Alexander Salkind to direct a screen version of a literary classic, which he could choose from a list of works in the public domain they had already compiled. "They had Kafka's *The Trial* on the list, and I said I wanted to do *The Castle* because I liked it better," Welles told his chronicler, Peter Bogdanovich, "but they persuaded me to do *The Trial*. I *had* to do a book—couldn't make them do an original. . . . They thought *The Trial* was public domain, and then had to pay for it—but that's another story." It should have clued him in to the Salkinds' financial solvency. Nevertheless, despite a "lack of profound sympathy for Kafka," Welles agreed to do the picture; it would be his first complete film, free from any studio intervention, since *Kane*.

The Salkinds next approached MCA agent Robert Hussong in Paris, who arranged a meeting between Perkins and Welles to discuss the possibility of the actor playing Kafka's persecuted protagonist, Joseph K. The two met for the first time on the stairs between floors of Welles's hotel and their rapport was instant. "[Welles] paid me the great compliment of saying he would like to know whether I would make the picture because if I wasn't going to make it, he wasn't going to make it either," Tony later recounted. "I'll never know if that's the way it really would have been or not, but I prefer to take it as the truth and I will always want to believe that." The prospect of working with the director of *Citizen Kane* was too thrilling to question.

Production began on March 26, 1962, at the Boulogne Studios. Also in the cast, in cameo roles, were Jeanne Moreau, Romy Schneider, Akim Tamiroff, and Elsa Martinelli. Welles himself took the role of "the advocate" when Jackie Gleason refused to travel by air to Paris. "He's the best there is," Perkins said of his director. "He's wonderfully sure of himself and his ability without being dictatorial and autocratic about it. He's like Hitchcock in that respect, and also in the way he never needs retakes—the first is almost always the best. But he isn't inflexible."

"They were both geniuses," Hussong says. "Orson had no truck with stupid people. But he would listen to someone he respected. And he listened to Tony very carefully. They had a wonderful exchange. Tony was able to make suggestions, always keeping in mind that he was the actor. Orson never resented it because he considered the source."

Welles devised a direct, verbal shorthand—"Too neurotic" or "Not neurotic enough"—for his direction of Perkins, who by now knew only too well the kind of performance that was expected from him. On a more loquacious occasion, Welles told Perkins, "You are pinned to the wall with a thumbtack, you are like a sick moth," a description to which Tony instantly conformed.

"They were wonderful together," recalls Hussong, who occasionally accompanied the director and star to dinner. "Tony loved to hear all the gossip about the early days, and Orson was happy to talk about Rita Hayworth and William Randolph Hearst and all of those people.

He was not high on the list of favorites at that time, he couldn't get a picture together. It was the Salkinds who gave him the opportunity to work again."

But the Salkinds' promise promptly fell through when they ran out of cash. To collect Perkins's expense money, Hussong would frequently have to wait outside the producers' apartment when he was told that Mr. Salkind wasn't in. Tony, however, chose to remain oblivious of the financial woes and faithful to his dazzling boss.

Welles, no stranger to monetary chaos, rose to the occasion. When Michel Salkind informed him that there was no longer a budget to build the elaborate sets he had designed "for a special visual effect" that was to carry the bulk of the picture, the director improvised with spectacular results. From the window of his suite at the Hotel Meurice, Welles noticed the two glowing clock faces of the Gare d'Orsay, a neglected train station that had fallen into almost complete disrepair. "I went down at four in the morning and got in a taxi and went to the Gare d'Orsay and went in," Welles recounted to Bogdanovich. "And from four in the morning until dawn, I wandered around . . . and found everything I needed for the picture." Perkins described the Gare d'Orsay, which was renovated into the Musée d'Orsay in the 1980s, as a "Victorian nightmare of passageways and grillwork, dust, dirt, decay." It was perfect for Welles's vision of Kafka. (For another sequence, filmed on Mount Vesuvius near Naples, Tony and Welles almost fell into the crater trying to get a shot. The sequence was never used in the final film.)

The entire film contains not a single line of original track, and Tony credited Welles with teaching him the fine art of looping. (A superb mimic, Welles dubbed many of the voices himself, including a few of Tony's lines.) "I hated dubbing until I did *The Trial*," Perkins said, "then I realized the possibilities of it." His ability to almost instantly match the movement of his lips onscreen—often *improving* his performance with new inflections—was one of the few skills of which Tony would remain proud at the less-inspired end of his career.

Starstruck by Welles, whom he called "an unfailing optimist," Perkins sent Billy Goldenberg, who was also a fan, one of the director's cigarette butts as a souvenir. Early in the shoot, he even considered composing a book about the director, long before Peter Bogdanovich undertook *This Is Orson Welles*. To that end the actor carried a tape recorder in his coat for a week, taping everything Welles said, then transcribing it at night in the hotel. "And then I got a little worried," Perkins revealed in 1965. "We were talking one night at dinner—and I said, 'How do you feel about articles about yourself?' And Orson said, 'I hate them. I hate everything that's ever been written about me, never liked anything, it's all untrue.' So I had so much respect and admiration and real love for him that I abandoned it. And at the end of the picture I told him what I had done and he said, 'Oh, why didn't you? Why didn't you do it? I would have loved it!' So it was another chance shot."

In 1992, Perkins told interviewer Richard Brown: "We spent sixteen hours together every day, seven days a week, so there was a synthesis of people there that was very, very strong—much stronger than the movie. I think the movie's a bit of a mess."

Most critics agreed. "Kafka's somber allegory of brutal bureaucracy is lost in excessive symbolism and scenery," said *Life*. "Tony Perkins is ludicrously miscast." *Variety,* however, hailed Tony's work as his "most knowing, incisive screen performance to date," and *Newsweek* declared that "Perkins, whose great talent lies in his ability to suggest the nut next door, is twitchy enough in his movements and, at the same time, normal enough in his looks to be the perfect Kafka hero." Even so, neither publication much liked the pretentious film as a whole. Perkins's Jimmy Stewart–in–limbo performance gives the visually top-heavy film its only relief from an otherwise unrelenting gloom.

"It was so disappointing to Tony that *The Trial* didn't turn out to be a great picture," Stephen Paley recalls. "It was just one of those awful debacles."

At a special Equity screening of the film at the RKO Twenty-third Street theater in New York, actors Peter Cook and Jonathan Miller sat behind Tony, howling hysterically through the entire performance. Worse, when two reels got mixed up, no one knew the difference.

"It was a great experience," Tony told critic Robin Bean. "I wouldn't care if nobody saw that picture—I owed myself that. I would have done anything for the experience of working with Orson Welles."

When the Welles picture wrapped on June 5, 1962, Tony went immediately into preparation for his next movie, André Cayatte's *Le Glaive et la Balance,* which was to start lensing at Boulogne on June 25 before

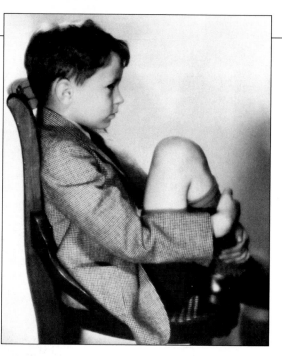

Tony, probably at age 5, photographed by Marcus Blechman. (MUSEUM OF THE CITY OF NEW YORK, THE THEATER COLLECTON)

Paul Muni *(left)* and Osgood Perkins *(right)* in the Howard Hawks classic *Scarface* (1932).

A teenage Tony during his prep school days at Browne & Nichols. (© KOBY–ANTUPIT)

Summer stock, 1950: in *Charm* with (*left to right*) Mary Diveny, Janet Gregory, and Henry Gerrard; following Anne Francis (*below*) in the conga scene from *My Sister Eileen* with Marguerite Morrissey. (COURTESY OF CHARLES WILLIAMSON)

Tony (*right*) with classmate Louis Ingram in *The Importance of Being Earnest,* Rollins College, 1953. (ROLLINS COLLEGE ARCHIVES)

With Jean Simmons and director George Cukor on the set of *The Actress*, 1953.
Tony would later downplay the fact that this was his first film. (© 1953 TURNER
ENTERTAINMENT CO. ALL RIGHTS RESERVED)

Landlady/confidante Helen Merrill, 1958, before Tony gave her the "Hitchcock nose."
(MICHAEL SMITH)

Tony with actress Mary Fickett in a publicity still for the Broadway production of *Tea and Sympathy*, 1955. (THE BILLY ROSE THEATRE COLLECTION, THE NEW YORK PUBLIC LIBRARY FOR THE PERFORMING ARTS, ASTOR, LENOX AND TILDEN FOUNDATIONS)

Painting was one of Tony's favorite pastimes on Fifty-sixth Street. (ARCHIVE PHOTOS)

On the cover of *Life* with Gary Cooper to promote *Friendly Persuasion*.

Two of Tony's first friends in Hollywood were Vampira *(left)* and Tab Hunter *(right)*.
(LEFT: ARCHIVE PHOTOS)

To dispel rumors of homosexuality, Paramount sent Tony and Tab to the Ice Follies
on a double date with actresses Jan Chaney *(left)* and Norma Moore *(right)*.
(ARCHIVE PHOTOS/DARLENE HAMMOND)

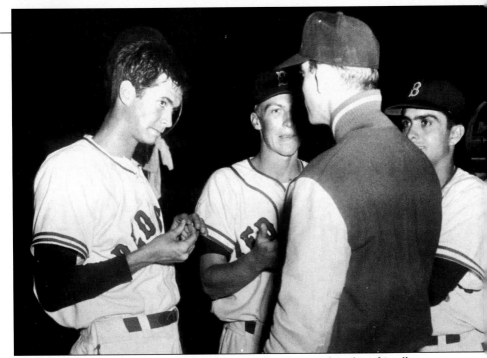

The atmosphere of *Fear Strikes Out* was less than friendly.

Tony blows off some steam by demonstrating an old college trick.

Actor Timmy Everett, with whom Tony was involved during *Look Homeward, Angel*.

Tony read the original Thomas Wolfe novel backstage during the run of *Look Homeward, Angel*. (ARCHIVE PHOTOS)

Janet Perkins and her son, 1958. (JOHN VACHON)

Alfred Hitchcock watches over Tony during the swamp scene in *Psycho* (1960). (COURTESY OF THE KOBAL COLLECTION)

Perkins strikes a pose as Norman Bates.

With Janet Leigh and Hitch outside Cabin Number One. (COURTESY OF THE ACADEMY OF MOTION PICTURE ARTS AND SCIENCES)

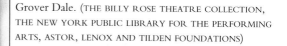
Grover Dale. (THE BILLY ROSE THEATRE COLLECTION, THE NEW YORK PUBLIC LIBRARY FOR THE PERFORMING ARTS, ASTOR, LENOX AND TILDEN FOUNDATIONS)

A boyhood dream come true: his name in lights and lights and lights....

Tony and Punky share a quiet moment on Cape Cod, 1960. (PHOTO BY STEPHEN PALEY)

With Ingrid Bergman,
another older woman,
in Anatole Litvak's
Goodbye Again (1961).
(© UNITED ARTISTS)

With Yvonne Furneaux
in Claude Chabrol's
The Champagne Murders (1967).
(© UNIVERSAL PICTURES)

With Orson Welles in Chabrol's *Ten Days' Wonder* (1970); it was their fourth film together. (COURTESY OF LAURA KAY PALMER)

Acting and directing Remak Ramsay and Sheila Wells in the road tour of Neil Simon's *The Star-Spangled Girl* (1967). (COURTESY OF REMAK RAMSAY)

The wedding party: Stephen Paley
and Janet Perkins with
the happy couple.

Tony weds
Berry Berenson
in Wellfleet,
Massachusetts,
August 1973. (PHOTO
BY STEPHEN PALEY)

Berry Perkins, wife and mother. (© CHRISTOPHER MAKOS)

The last resort: resurrecting Norman Bates
for *Psycho II* (1983).
(© UNIVERSAL CITY STUDIOS INC.)

Like father, like son: nine-year-old
Osgood Perkins as the young Norman
in *Psycho II*. (© UNIVERSAL CITY
STUDIOS INC.)

With maverick director Ken Russell on the
set of *Crimes of Passion* (1984).

(*Previous page, right*)
Perkins relaced
Anthony Hopkins as
Dr. Martin Dysart in the
Broadway production
of *Equus*, 1975.
(COURTESY OF ERIC HARRISON)

Psycho III (1986) marked
Perkins's film directorial debut.
(© UNIVERSAL CITY STUDIOS INC.
PHOTO BY BERRY BERENSON)

During a stopover in New York while on tour for *Psycho III*; the film's failure
shattered Perkins's confidence. (© CHRISTOPHER MAKOS)

moving to locations in Nice and Monte Carlo. Tony was anxious to work with Cayatte, a lawyer turned writer turned filmmaker who used the visual medium as a vehicle for his polemics against the French judicial system.

Two Are Guilty, as the film was retitled for its brief run on American turf, a mystery thriller told in flashback, was no exception; in it, Tony played one of three young men with sordid pasts (handsome Jean-Claude Brialy and Renato Salvatori were the other two) who are suspects in the kidnapping and murder of a small boy on the Riviera. No evidence exists to convict any of them, so how can justice be carried out? Who should decide, the jury—or the angry mob? The film offers no satisfactory answer. (It should be noted that while Brialy plays a sleazy real estate agent and Salvatori a ski instructor–gigolo, Tony is cast as an American with a compromising incident on his record that took place years before in a fraternity house.)

The heavy-handed message wasn't the only thing significant about the film; for *Two Are Guilty,* his first French film, Perkins was paid an unprecedented $200,000—more money than any other American actor had ever earned in a foreign film, and certainly more than Perkins himself had ever commanded, even on domestic loan-out from Paramount.

Years later, on the Elstree Studios set of Sidney Lumet's *Murder on the Orient Express,* rising costar Michael York would remember Perkins's groundbreaking work abroad with admiration. "He echoed what I tried to do," York says, "not just to have an American career, but an international, European career."

Nevertheless, *Two Are Guilty* did little to enhance Perkins's reputation. The few American critics who saw it savaged it. "For American audiences, the most important actor in the picture is Anthony Perkins," Brendan Gill wrote in *The New Yorker,* "and he is simply terrible." Once again, a project that had seemed promising intellectually—Tony called it "an art film"—ultimately proved inferior and disappointing.

During filming in the south of France, Jane and Michaela O'Harra came to visit Tony at the villa he had rented in Cannes. "Tony did a lot of films abroad," O'Harra notes, "and he was always given two first-class tickets, one for him and one for his valet or secretary or whatever. Well, he never used them, he just went business class. So he built up a lot of credit, and he gave that to us. Neither one of us could have afforded it otherwise." For the month of July, he put the women up in a house near Antibes, where Jane had spent the summer of 1925 with Osgood, long before Tony was ever born.

Robert Hussong remembers the widow Perkins well: "She had opinions and enormous influence on Tony. She was his financial adviser, not Helen, and she was zealous about his affairs. It wasn't a mummy-son relationship. She was tremendously proud of him, but I don't think that she was always sure why he was as successful as he was, of whether he merited it or not. He was far more famous than his father."

"Tony didn't have any sense of money as money," O'Harra recalls. "Once, after he had begun to make a good deal of it, we were sitting around talking about money, and he said, 'It's just like Monopoly to me.' "

Back in New York, Helen demanded that they move to larger quarters—she wanted her own space and was sick of having Tony in the little back room—so they did, just a block away to a carriage house at 137 West Fifty-fifth Street, for which Tony paid a reported $250,000. There they each had the luxury of their own floor (Tony on top, Helen underneath), and Tony could remain in the neighborhood where he was still reassuringly known as "the youngster." (He had turned thirty during *The Trial*.)

Almost immediately, Helen, whose career as a photographer was gradually falling by the wayside, opened an art gallery on the parlor floor of the renovated house as a new outlet for her combined creative, managerial, and people skills. Financed by Tony, the venture was christened the Osgood Gallery. Sideo Fromboluti, one of the painters whose work Helen showed, remembers it as "one of the most beautiful galleries in New York, with huge skylights and huge rooms." Unfortunately, the enterprise was short-lived. According to Fromboluti, "They really didn't know much about the art scene. Instead of using New York artists, they began using artists from everywhere—Israel, Bucks County—which is fine, but they didn't bring the crowds. When a New York artist has a show, he brings in a whole crowd of followers." The unprofitable Osgood closed almost a year later.

Fromboluti also remembers seeing Tony engaged in a public tiff at the gallery with a young man, probably the neglected Teno Pollick: "Later, in Wellfleet, Tony was married with children. But at the Osgood, he was quite homosexually involved, tremendously involved. He and a young person, who looked a little bit like one of della Francesca's angels, were having a heated discussion, and crying—it was all emotional between the two of them." It was an unusually open display for the normally cautious Perkins.

While Helen organized the new home and tried to make a go of her art dealership, Tony indulged his musical interests. He called *Greenwillow* accompanist Billy Goldenberg for some lessons in "popular piano." "The days I spent there were really kind of magical," Goldenberg remembers. "Helen and Tony would always fix me a wonderful lunch. I was just twenty-four years old, and Tony gave me a great sense of self-worth, which I needed at the time. I mean, here was this star who had just done *Psycho*, spending a lot of time with me, talking about a lot of things. He got to know me very quickly—he wanted to know more about me than to talk about himself. He rarely talked about himself."

Perkins and his teacher shared a love of the abstract. "We would be working on a piece of music, for example, and at the bottom would be the name of the publisher. In one case, it was Mosher Music, and Tony loved the sound of the word 'Mosher.' So that became a little joke between us. Whenever I wrote him postcards or letters from anywhere, I would sign them sometimes 'Mosher,' sometimes 'Thorg' [a *Flash Gordon*-esque character the two of them had dreamed up]. These were the strange, little, funny things that only he and I understood, that made for a friendship."

With *Harold*, a new farce by playwright Herman Raucher (who later wrote the script for the film *The Summer of '42*), Perkins was prepared to tackle his first stage comedy. Clearly intended as an about-face from his sinister screen image, *Harold* also marked Tony's first venture as a producer: Wigwam Productions was cofinancing the show along with producer Arnold Saint-Subber, scenic designer Ben Edwards, and actor Larry Blyden, who was signed to direct. Wigwam would receive 10 percent of any profits plus a weekly management fee of $500, and as the star, Tony was guaranteed a weekly salary of $2,000. *Harold* would open in New Haven on Halloween, 1962, in Washington on November 5, and finally on Broadway on November 29.

Rehearsals began October 9, with a cast that included comedian

Don Adams, Nathaniel Frey, John Fiedler, Sudie Bond, and the young Miss Joey Heatherton. But there were problems from the start, not the least of which was the overly coy script, which seemed to combine equal measures of *Pygmalion*, *Penrod*, and as one critic noted, *Snow White and the Seven Dwarfs*.

In the title role, described in Raucher's script as "the eternal adolescent," thirty-year-old Tony was cast as a virgin pushing twenty, another variation on the Fred Whitmarsh theme. The sitcom plot concerned the efforts of his dorky but colorful friends to turn Harold into a Prince Charming, enabling him to nab the society girl of his dreams. As Tony put it, "Think of Eliza Doolittle as a man and not a girl, with several Henry Higginses remodeling his character." It's hard to imagine what attracted Perkins to the project, which was hopelessly hokey even at the time; perhaps he found the character's passive malleability somehow appealing, even true.

Burry Fredrik, who had stage-managed on *The Dark at the Top of the Stairs*, also managed *Harold*. "Tony was very caring about the other actors and, of course, the outcome of the show," she recalls. "He believed he could bring the play alive, that he could make it work. But this play was simply not funny."

In New Haven, the company began to realize the play was doomed, and tension flared between Tony and actor turned director Larry Blyden, whom Tony found negligent. But there were other things on Perkins's mind, namely their next stop.

"The only time Tony was, how shall I say, *inside*, hard to draw out—preoccupied—was when we were in Washington," Herman Raucher observed. "I was in his dressing room opening night at the National Theatre, and he said, 'My father died on this stage.' I asked him if he was going to be all right, and he said, 'Yeah. I just hope *we* don't die!' "

While Tony and the rest of the cast were put up at the Jefferson Hotel, the crew stayed just a block away from the theater at the Willard, the same hotel where Osgood Perkins had died. "I'm thinking of moving to the Willard," Tony casually mentioned one day to company manager William Craver.

Craver asked why.

"It's just convenient."

The star asked Craver to arrange for him to see some of the rooms

there, and to accompany him on a tour of the hotel. Afterward, he decided not to move. But a day later, Perkins called the Willard management himself to ask if it would be possible to find out which room his
father had died in. Sadly, the Willard no longer had the twenty-five-
year-old records. (Tony never mentioned his inquiry to Craver, who
learned of it only accidentally from the hotel manager.)

Harold's Washington debut was a far cry from Susan and God; the
pans were unanimous. The Washington Post declared that the play "may
be nice enough for what it is, but since what it is is practically nothing,
this gets us no place except in and out of the National Theatre."

Tony kept up a brave face. "We're going to pull it off," he told the
same critic. "Great changes have taken place since Harold arrived in
Washington." One of the changes was that Miss Heatherton was written out of the show.

The play opened at New York's Cort Theatre as scheduled, in the
midst of a newspaper strike. That might have been a blessing in disguise. Walter Kerr, who managed to review it, called Tony's performance "schizoid. . . . Nothing against Mr. Perkins himself, of course.
He is a fine actor, with shoulders that hike nervously as though they
were suspended on puppet strings, and he can let his shirt buckle out at
the belt or shift his furtive eyes in an entirely convincing evocation of
high adolescence. I think he should stop doing it, though, at least in
plays like this one. To put so much skill into what he could have
played equally well . . . at summer camp 12 years ago reduces honest
performing to not much more than a stunt. Mr. Perkins is using genuine adroitness to prove he can ride a scooter-bike."

"I was embarrassed whenever Tony wasn't good," says Gwen
Davis, who came to see the show with her future husband, Don
Mitchell. "During Harold, I was in agony the entire time. It was simply
dreadful."

So was her reunion with the boy-man for whom she still carried
the proverbial torch. "We went backstage, and Tony stood at the sink
and washed his hands for at least six minutes. Don, who was not particularly literary, said it was like Lady Macbeth—Tony just would not
stop washing his hands with this twisting motion. Then Tony turned to
me and said, 'You look wonderful.' And he turned to Don and said,
'Are you her hairdresser?' And my guy was a real guy. Through some

cosmic mercy, this beautiful, very menschy man had come along and claimed me.

"I called Tony later and said, 'Why'd you say something that cunty?' And he said, 'Well, you just looked so good I naturally assumed he was your hairdresser.' I said, 'Tony, don't do it again.' That was the first time I talked back."

The new couple later ran into him at the opening of the musical *Fade Out, Fade In*, starring Carol Burnett. "By then I was thin and, I must say, really pretty," Davis recalls. "Tony turned to Don and said, 'She looks really beautiful. What a shame you didn't meet her years ago.' And I wanted to say to him, but didn't, 'It wouldn't have done any good because I was in love with a faggot.' I couldn't use those words, even to myself, at the time. I never stopped loving him, though I now had a real relationship. I loved him in a very different way."

Harold closed on December 15, 1962, after just twenty-six performances. Perkins's name was not the audience draw the producing teams had hoped, and the show lost an estimated $110,000 of its $125,000 investment.

Tony suddenly found himself with time on his hands. "I thought the play was very funny," he claimed. The disastrous comedy marked the beginning of what would be an amazing, unbroken string of artistic disappointments.

Next, Tony was up for the lead in *She Loves Me*, the new musical by Jerry Bock and Sheldon Harnick, about a pair of shop clerks who accidentally fall in love with each other as penpals via a lonelyhearts club (based on the movie *The Shop Around the Corner*). He lost the role. "In the end, I think Harold Prince was looking for someone a little more grounded, more lumpen," designer Tony Walton explains. "So he ended up with Dan Massey. Tony had such an obvious romantic quality that it worked against him." According to Ben Bagley, Tony extricated himself from the production voluntarily when musical star Barbara Cook, who was "in" with Prince, demanded and got top billing.

Perkins vindicated himself in 1966 when he and Cook recorded *Ben Bagley's George Gershwin Revisited*. Of the six records he made for Bagley—initially at the suggestion of Bagley's lover, Montgomery Clift, who had admired Tony's early recordings—this was the only one on which the singers were not credited alphabetically; Tony had asked

Bagley to give him a special "and Anthony Perkins" at the end of the otherwise alphabetical roster to keep his name from being right under Cook's. He and Cook were never paired on another Bagley LP.

In early 1963, Tony also wanted the lead role in an upcoming 20th Century-Fox picture called *Shock Treatment*, about an unemployed actor who goes under cover at a state mental institution to find some stolen cash. Muscular Stuart Whitman was ultimately cast in the film, which also featured Carol Lynley and Lauren Bacall.

In March of that year, Tony had his caricature in Sardi's Restaurant moved next to that of his father.

Against the advice of Herman Citron, who continued to represent him after MCA folded in 1962, Perkins accepted a role in another "art film," *The Fool Killer*, which was being produced independently for Allied Artists by Ely Landau, who had recently brought Eugene O'Neill's *Long Day's Journey into Night* to the screen. Set to direct was José Quintero, famous for his stage productions of works by O'Neill and Tennessee Williams, and for the 1961 film of Williams's novella *The Roman Spring of Mrs. Stone* starring Vivien Leigh and Warren Beatty.

Based on a novel by Helen Eustis, *The Fool Killer* is the story of a young boy in the post–Civil War South, who befriends—and runs away from his abusive family with—a strange amnesiac drifter who may or may not be an ax murderer. Quintero interviewed nearly one thousand child actors before settling on Edward Albert, the twelve-year-old son of actor Eddie Albert and actress Margo, to make his film debut as the boy. To play the postwar drifter, which was almost a disillusioned, psychologically battered extension of Josh Birdwell, the role Perkins had played in his previous Allied Artists film, *Friendly Persuasion*, Tony was offered a mere $25,000. Citron urged him to do the film for no fee at all rather than set a new low rate for his services, but so impressed was Tony by the work of Landau's coproducer, Mexican film director Servando Gonzalez, that he agreed to do the film against the wishes of his powerful agent.

A month after shooting began on location in Knoxville, Tennessee, Quintero resigned for "artistic differences," and, much to Tony's delight, was replaced by Gonzalez. Also on location, to supervise the authentic period attire, was Dorothy Jeakins, who was now more grasping of her young man than ever before. With Tony spending so much time abroad and beyond her reach, she had perhaps fallen even more desperately in love with him. Whatever the case, in response to her attentions this time, Tony fled.

"On *The Fool Killer*, he tried to escape Dorothy," confirms a close friend of the designer. "He spent an awful lot of time with Margo and her two children the way someone will do when they don't want to be alone with someone else. Dorothy was very difficult, very demanding. She was a beautiful artist, much to be admired, but kind of a pain in the neck if you got too close. Margo and her kids saw *a lot* of Tony on that picture." Now that he was professionally grown up, able to make his own decisions about his career, Tony felt hampered by Jeakins's maternal grasp. As he would soon do with Helen, too, Perkins abruptly severed the designer from his life. Though they would work together again on Mike Nichols's spectacular fiasco, *Catch-22*, their relationship basically ended with *The Fool Killer*.

The Fool Killer did little to improve his domestic star status. It was not released until 1965, and was poorly distributed. When it was re-released in 1969, probably in a desperate effort to recoup production costs, even fewer people saw it. "Young Albert is made a paper-thin storybook hero," wrote *Time*, "while Perkins, with no Hitchcock to guide him, mopes through his small starring role with an air of boyish menace that might easily be mistaken for sulking."

If Herman Citron feared that Perkins had lost his ability to command big bucks after *The Fool Killer*, he needn't have. In France Tony was still the idol of millions and via Robert Hussong an offer came through that was hard to refuse: to be the first American leading man to appear opposite French sex kitten Brigitte Bardot, in an upcoming espionage comedy titled variously *Agent 38-24-36*, *The Adorable Fool*, and *The Beautiful Bird Brain*. Tony's supply of ultraglamorous leading ladies seemed truly inexhaustible. For his role as a bumbling, unemployed British bank clerk turned Russian spy, Perkins would receive $175,000. He and "B.B." would be guided through their slapstick turns by Édouard Molinaro, the French film director who would go on to write and direct the hit gay comedy *La Cage aux Folles*.

Tony was warned that Bardot could be difficult, and gave in to her demand that the film be performed entirely in French, even though the exterior scenes were to be shot in London. "Brigitte speaks excellent English," he told Bob Thomas. "She speaks it even better than Sophia, and I think she has hidden the fact for self-protection. It allows her to be uncommunicative with Hollywood producers who want to sign her for pictures." Despite relentless offers from America, Bardot always remained firm in her refusal to become part of the Hollywood studio system. Unlike Tony, with his faulty return to Hollywood in *Green Mansions*, Bardot had the confidence to make Hollywood come begging to her, and the resolve never to budge.

In the scandalous 1983 *People* interview, in which he enumerated the scores of movie beauties who had propositioned him over the years—including Ava Gardner, Jane Fonda, and Ingrid Bergman—Perkins painted a similar picture of his relationship with Bardot, claiming that she had invited him to her penthouse and offered herself to him. "I was like an uncaged leopard," he said. "Sooner than get close to her I would have crashed through the window and fallen to the pavement ten stories below."

Robert Hussong confirms that while Tony felt quite comfortable around his older female costars, he was distinctly *un*comfortable with the young Bardot; much to her mystification, he never even shared a business dinner with her. Adding to the confusion was the fact that everyone, including Herman Citron and Bardot's agent, Olga Horstig Primuz, tacitly assumed that Perkins and the handsome Hussong were lovers (they were not).

Meanwhile, so intense was the public's fascination with Bardot that filming on the streets of London was practically impossible. In order to complete a simple shot of the two of them entering Hyde Park, their stand-ins had to be whisked away as decoys in her Rolls-Royce, while, as Tony recalled, "Brigitte and I were smuggled down through the kitchen of the Westbury Hotel and onto the floor of a taxi. . . . We were driven to a subway entrance and we rode the subway to that square. The watches were synchronized, and we went straight up and crossed the square and the men got out the cameras and started to shoot."

But Perkins enjoyed riding on the megafame of his sexy costar. According to Hussong, in Paris, where they shot the interiors, "Tony had moods where he thought it was fun to be recognized. Then he would have moods where it was very important not to be. We would go to great lengths, including disguises, to be able to go places where he wouldn't be able to go otherwise. He was great with mustaches. We always had a bottle of spirit gum in the apartment or hotel. He wore all kinds of outfits, which in a sense only attracted people to him. But he never saw it that way." (While shooting *The Trial*, for instance, Perkins liked to wait casually outside theaters where *Psycho* was showing, with the express purpose of being noticed; it cheered him up.)

Another thing that buoyed him was playing fairy godbrother to less prosperous friends. Billy Goldenberg, who had never been to Paris, received a call from Paris one morning at about 6 A.M. "Billy, can you be here tomorrow?" It was Tony.

"What?"

"I've convinced Pathé Marcone that they should bring my American musical director over here to do my record album [*Tony Perkins Sings Chansons*]."

Perkins offered Goldenberg the use of his flat, his French maid, all expenses paid. "That was what Tony loved the most," Goldenberg muses, "creating scenarios for people, and making them happy. He loved realizing the dream for somebody. I didn't know what to say, but I was on the plane for Paris the next day."

His sojourn was charmed. Mornings were spent sight-seeing; then Tony's maid, Marinette, would prepare a delicious lunch back at the flat. In the afternoons, Goldenberg would orchestrate, then go to Boulogne, where Tony was shooting, and together they would go over the songs at the end of the day. "He had a little piano in his dressing room, and we would rehearse there," Goldenberg recalls. "Brigitte would come in, usually only dressed in a bathrobe, and she would listen and tell us how good or how terrible we were." When Tony wanted some original songs for the Columbia album, he arranged a meeting at his flat with songwriter Pierre De Lanoe, who had written the popular "What Now My Love?" For Perkins, De Lanoe wrote "Abracadabra" and "C'est jouette, Paris" (which translates as "Paris Is a Gas"). Recording *Tony Perkins Sings Chansons* marked the height of Perkins's popularity in Europe.

"Tony said he lived through me," Goldenberg remembers. "Every morning at breakfast, he would have me recount every single thing I'd done the night before. 'I want to do all the things that you're doing,' he told me, 'but I can't because I'm too well-known.' He would have been mobbed almost anywhere he went." Voyeuristic curiosity about the freer lives of friends and colleagues would remain one of Tony's obsessions long after his marriage to Berry Berenson.

Mobbed he may have been, but the reality of Perkins's personal life wasn't nearly so austere. "Gerard," a struggling Parisian painter, was one of Tony's biggest crushes. Twentyish, elfin (like Teno Pollick), and endearing, Gerard spoke no English, but, according to Stephen Paley, "looked like Alain Delon with a gorgeous ass." Though they shared an apartment together in Paris, Tony and Gerard never ventured out in public without the faithful Bob Hussong accompanying them as a cover. While life in Paris was clearly more fun, in some respects it was no different than it had been in Hollywood.

Perkins was still in Paris in November 1963 when the news service reported that President John F. Kennedy had been assassinated. He walked into his apartment to find Goldenberg and Hussong looking very glum. In tribute, French television went off the air. "Tony wasn't particularly political," the composer notes, "but he loved charismatic people. I think he related more with Jackie than with Kennedy himself. He was very shaken. We all were."

Perkins was back in New York by early 1964—with Marinette, whom he had imported to keep house on Fifty-fifth Street. But her presence was not appreciated by Helen, who, without photography or an art gallery to run, felt suddenly demoted. Helen's position as Tony Perkins's official housekeeper was no longer just a game; it had become her personal and professional identity. With the advent of Marinette, Helen found herself adrift in her own home, obsolete, with little to do but field calls. Tony, of course, was oblivious; he soon brought over Gerard as well, whom Marinette already knew. Helen was left out in the cold, and surely must have been relieved when both of Tony's human imports finally decided to return to their homeland. Gerard left his lover several dark figurative paintings, which hung in Tony's bedroom for years until Berry Berenson had them removed.

A Ravishing Idiot, as the Bardot picture was called in the States, did little for the careers of either star. The most that can be said is that they look attractive in a film that may very well be the least amusing comedy ever made. "Perkins is forced to play his timid, smiling stereotype," *Variety* said, "which . . . does not get much help from the uneven scripting and direction. . . . B.B. will have to be the main selling point." She already was.

"I figured I had reached the pinnacle when I had done a film with Brigitte," Tony told reporter Bob Thomas. "How much higher could I go? So I decided it was time for me to come home. . . . I can't say I really went to Europe with any plan in mind. I went over to make one picture. The reception was so marvelous that I stayed. I didn't do it with any idea of getting a tax break. Far from it—I was paying both American and French taxes.

"It was great for me as an actor," he added. "There were opportunities I couldn't get here."

UPI reporter Vernon Scott aptly noted that while Perkins was too "baby-faced" to pass as a matinee idol back home, "in Europe he's Rock Hudson, Greg Peck and Burt Lancaster rolled into one. The unlikeliest sex symbol since Don Knotts." Alas, even that wouldn't last.

LIMBO

A FTER SEVEN ALMOST BACK-TO-BACK FILMS and one di-
sastrous play, Tony took some much needed time off. *The Fool
Killer* and *A Ravishing Idiot* had not yet been released in the
States; for all the public knew, Tony Perkins had disappeared.
RELAXED PERKINS YAWNS AT IT ALL proclaimed a *New York Times*
headline in September 1964.

"My next part must be a little pearl," he said.

On Fifty-fifth Street he contented himself with Helen's company,
his ongoing psychiatric sessions, and various sexual trysts with, among
others, a popular television actor, and Grover Dale, who was rapidly
becoming Perkins's main man. The hardworking Dale, who had just
made his screen debut as Debbie Reynolds's brother in MGM's *The
Unsinkable Molly Brown*, was still living on Fifty-sixth Street with Larry
Kert, but the relationship had amicably cooled. Tony and Grover were
often seen walking Punky around the neighborhood.

At the same time, the New York Academy of Medicine was urg-
ing physicians across the nation to regard homosexuality as a curable
illness. "The homosexual is an emotionally immature individual who
has not acquired a normal capacity to develop satisfying heterosexual
relationships," the academy said; the "condition" was simply a manifestation of fear of the opposite sex and an avoidance of adult responsibility. The report was in large part a conservative reaction to a

purported increase in "salacious" literature (building from Gore Vidal's groundbreaking gay novel *The City and the Pillar* to John Rechy's *City of Night*) and the "growing aggressiveness" of gay organizations like the Mattachine Society, which publicly rejected the mental illness label.

But the renewed backlash was primarily the work of one man, Irving Bieber, a psychoanalyst who had spearheaded a nine-year study of 106 gay men that was hyped as the largest, most extensive study of the origins of homosexuality at the time. The results, published in 1962, strongly reflected the role-playing sexism of the fifties. The study claimed that disruptions in family relationships early in life, such as divorce, contributed to a child's homosexual development, particularly if a boy was left in the care of a "domineering" mother: "A constructive, supportive, warmly related father precludes the possibility of a homosexual son; he acts as a neutralizing, protective agent should the mother make seductive or close-binding attempts." In Bieber's white-picket-fence world, a friendly dad was as clear an antidote to "perversion" as Clorox was to dirty laundry.

"Homosexual relationships are generally turbulent and shortlived," Bieber declared in the *New York Times Magazine* in 1964. "Few last more than a matter of months or a year or two. . . . To prevent childhood homosexual symptoms from developing—or possibly even to 'immunize' youngsters against them—it is necessary to consider the behavior of parents.

"We know, for instance, that mothers of male homosexuals usually behave in . . . abnormal ways. They are overly intimate with their sons. They are also excessively possessive, over-protective and inclined to discourage the son's masculine ways. . . . You don't find many homosexuals whose fathers took them on camping trips or to baseball games." Though his assertions were controversial even then, the American psychiatric community and the public at large were quick to embrace Bieber's misogynistic theories as scientific truth.

Gay men of the era, in the confusion of their guilty displacement and isolation, were ready for some answers, and Bieber's were the only ones around. In this heavy atmosphere of blame, Tony Perkins's lonely childhood with Jane seemed like a textbook case. (For that matter, so did Norman Bates's—Hollywood momism taken to the most perverse degree.) Tony's later allegations against his mother could almost have been concocted by Bieber himself.

Perkins's feelings about his father ran silent and deep. Early in his career he had almost dismissed Osgood's accomplishments and had skirted the issue of his absence, but now—certainly since his flop at the National Theatre in Washington in 1962, the same year Bieber's theories were published—Tony was more emotional whenever Osgood's memory rose up. In 1965, when Perkins was back in Paris to appear in René Clément's World War II spectacle, *Is Paris Burning?*, a tedious all-star fiasco in which he was again risibly miscast as a hayseed American soldier, he invited his blond costar, Skip Ward, who had just worked with Howard Hawks on *Red Line 7000*, to a local showing of *Scarface*.

Ward had never seen the film. "It was a terrible print," he remembers, "scratchy with French subtitles, but it was a nice thing to do on one of our afternoons off. When it was over I looked at Tony and said, 'Are you all right?' because frankly he looked like he had been crying. I said, 'Tony, what's wrong?' His eyes were red and he had a handkerchief out. 'I'm all right,' he said. 'That was my father.' "

Also fitting Perkins squarely into Bieber's psychoanalytic straitjacket as an "immature" deviant was a spate of publicity about how the "baby-faced" actor was no competition for Hollywood's more masculine leading men. NOT AGING FAST ENOUGH—PERKINS declared one article, which quoted Sophia Loren: "When I play opposite Tony he makes me look like his mother, even though I'm younger than he is."

All of this must have disturbed Tony. "I'm sick of playing unheroic, immature roles. I'm emotionally and mentally prepared to play mature parts. However, this young face of mine is holding me back." He was thirty-two years old.

In 1966, Tony put Helen in charge of finding them a new home, as Fifty-fifth Street and the surrounding area was gradually being demolished to make way for skyscrapers. What she found was a townhouse on quiet, tree-lined West Twenty-first Street, directly across from a Gothic theological seminary and its garden, in the unassuming neighborhood of Chelsea. Number 467 needed some work, had lots of light, and could be easily divided to give the odd twosome, which had now become a threesome, some privacy. In a brazen step, Perkins agreed to let Grover Dale move in. The two of them would share a bedroom and bath on the top floor, directly above the living room, dining room, and kitchen; Helen would take the basement, or garden floor, as her lair. As usual, there were no locks on any of the interior doors.

Perhaps to obscure the truth of their living arrangements, Tony decided to rent out the parlor floor, with the excuse that he wanted someone else in the house for security reasons (though it was doubtful Helen would be going anywhere). To avoid placing an advertisement, Tony informally leased the floor to stage manager William Craver for two hundred dollars a month. No actual lease was ever drawn up, but "Craver," as Tony called him, would live in the house for nearly a decade, until after the birth of Tony's first son.

Twenty-five years later, Chelsea would surpass Greenwich Village as New York's premier gay neighborhood; but for now, it was a private haven, conveniently close to the theater district, but far enough off the beaten path to be safe. "That's what I like about Chelsea," Tony told Earl Wilson in 1968. "It's more informal than the Village. You wear whatever comes to hand when you open the closet."

Helen wasted no time fixing up the place and ensconcing herself in the neighborhood. Without photography to occupy her, and with Tony spending so much time out of the country, she became more and more the meddlesome *hausfrau*. She cooked when Tony and Grover entertained—Lillian Hellman, Jerome Robbins, Elaine Stritch, and Mike Nichols were regulars for Scrabble—and she formed "the Broom Brigade," a corps of local kids recruited to clean the house and sidewalk. As usual, everyone had a nickname: "the Rabbit" lived next door, and "the Wolf" was agent Jay Wolf, who lived nearby.

In early June of 1966, Tony returned to Paris to star in the first of two projects he would do for Claude Chabrol, the director widely considered to be France's answer to Alfred Hitchcock. *Le Scandale* (*The Champagne Murders*), to be shot in both English and French versions, was being produced by Universal Pictures' new European team, which had just wrapped Charlie Chaplin's flat-footed comedy *The Countess from Hong Kong*, starring Marlon Brando and Sophia Loren.

In *The Champagne Murders*, Perkins was again unconvincingly cast as an ex-gigolo who may, or may not, be responsible for a series of fortuitous deaths within a champagne dynasty. It was Tony's own unique ambiguity that had attracted Chabrol's professional interest in him. Cast opposite Perkins in her first major role was producer Jacques Natteau's beautiful wife, Yvonne Furneaux, who had appeared in the 1959 Hammer remake of *The Mummy*, played a prostitute in Fellini's *La Dolce Vita*, and been seen (and heard) as Catherine Deneuve's oversexed sister in Roman Polanski's chilling *Repulsion*.

Relations between Tony and his screen wife, known on the set as "Tessa," Natteau's pet name for her, were not good. Imperious and insecure—and jealous of Perkins's star power—she took out her frustrations on George Skaff, a young American actor who did not speak French, by coldly snubbing him. In response, to defend Skaff, Tony tried to break Furneaux by mumbling disturbing words in her ear during their close-ups together. "He thought she was a pompous bitch," Skaff says. "She tried to hold her composure, but she almost fell apart. She'd give him a glare after the take, but she didn't dare tell him to stop." To this day, Furneaux remembers the pleasure Tony took in the discomfort of others.

Much of the film was shot on location outside of Paris at the chateau at Rosny-sur-Seine. Tony requested a room in the castle rather than a hotel suite in the city ostensibly so that he wouldn't have to travel; he told Furneaux that he could "drink in the atmosphere better" there (but the feeling within the company was that he just wanted to save the expense money). Whatever his reasons, stay at the chateau he did, entirely alone, with no servants, only his exercise equipment for company. Furneaux recalls that Perkins was constantly dieting, never hungry, yet at the nightly company dinners still managed to move from table to table pinching food from the cast and crew. "As an artist, he was an honest man," she concedes.

But personally honest he was not. Though the romance with Grover Dale was soaring back home, Perkins kept mum on the subject, even around the sympathetic George Skaff, who was also in the closet. When Tony accidentally ran into Gerard, his old Parisian flame, his only comment was that the garçon was already losing his hair (for years, Tony had been privately worried about losing his own hair, and had frequented a New York "hair-popping" salon to stimulate his follicles).

"He wasn't comfortable with himself at all," Skaff recalls. "He could express himself intellectually, but not about relationships. Only when we discussed acting would he really come alive. He had a theory that the camera revealed the soul, that it did things that were almost otherworldly."

Later, back in Los Angeles, Skaff remained friendly with the star, though Perkins was hesitant to be seen in the company of other gay men. "I'm so well known that I'm afraid to fraternize with people in the open," he complained; "I don't get to meet many people." As a favor, Skaff arranged a dinner party at the home of two very masculine gay lovers, with the caveat that the guests not put Tony "onstage," as it were, that it be a relaxed, quiet evening.

"As usual, Tony dressed in grungy jeans, very down-to-earth," Skaff remembers. "We got to the house, and *everybody* there had on ties, cologne, dressed to the nines—because they knew he was going to be there. They did everything I told them not to do. He went along with it, he was the consummate professional, but I was just sweating up a storm. I was still a bit intimidated by him because he did have an edge, he could be acerbic.

"Tony was on the floor, sitting very Ghandi-like, very humbly, and everybody stood around him, asking questions. It was really like Jesus in the temple; they were all asking stupid questions that they thought they should ask a celebrity. The evening was interminable. Finally, when we left, Tony put his arm around me and said, 'George, I've never had more fun in my life. I enjoyed your suffering so much.'

"Occasionally, I'd bump into him after he got married, and he was always friendly enough, but he always reminded me of a wary animal, a deer or something. You always wanted to keep your distance, otherwise he might dart."

Americans had trouble making sense of the cryptic *Champagne Murders*. "The eye of [Chabrol's] camera seizes upon odd juxtapositions of sound, of color and images," Vincent Canby wrote. "A close-up of Miss Furneaux's green eyes framed in deep blue eye-shadow seems to have a meaning of its own." Poorly distributed, the film crept into local theaters on the lower half of a double bill.

"It was around then that I stopped seeing Tony's movies," Stephen Paley admits. He obviously wasn't the only moviegoer who felt that way.

In New York that September, Tony took another stab at musical theater, this time for television, in Stephen Sondheim's *Evening Primrose*, which was created for ABC's *Stage 67*. Adapted by James Goldman from a short story by John Collier, it was the spooky tale of a disillusioned poet who hides out in a department store overnight, only to discover a secret nocturnal society that's been living there for years—and a pretty, lost girl, with whom he falls in love.

The story had a macabre quality that appealed to Sondheim, who had always wanted to write a horror-suspense musical (he would eventually fulfill that wish with the award-winning *Sweeney Todd*). A sort of *Romeo and Juliet in the Twilight Zone*—in which the lovers are pursued by "the dark men," menacing shadow figures who patrol the store—*Evening Primrose* was enhanced by Perkins's quirky image.

Cast as Ella, the lost girl, was Charmian Carr, who had recently been seen as the oldest Von Trapp daughter in Robert Wise's popular film of *The Sound of Music*. "Nobody had ever heard of Charmian Carr," producer Willard Levitas remembers. "[Executive producer John] Houseman said, 'Hasn't anybody seen the most successful movie?' Well, none of us would be caught dead seeing *The Sound of Music*. Anyhow, Carr was brought in from the Coast, and Stephen Sondheim was exasperated because she couldn't sing."

During "Take Me to the World," her romantic duet with Tony, which was recorded live, she wasn't able to hit the high notes. They were given to Tony, who, unlike his trial six years earlier with Loesser's "Never Will I Marry," had no trouble producing them with strength and clarity.

For Carr, *Evening Primrose* was a difficult experience, coming at a time when she was torn between her career and an impending marriage (which was delayed by the shoot). She ultimately chose to have a family, but remembers Tony's sensitivity to her predicament; he introduced her to Jane's beloved Church of Religious Science, and during a break, took her to visit the Center for Creative Living on East Forty-eighth Street. Jane's influence, it seems, went deeper than perhaps her son would ever have admitted. Six months later, Carr herself was married by a Religious Science minister.

"Anthony Perkins was very sweet," Levitas recalls. "The only time he ever showed any temper tantrum was when they took some publicity photos and he wanted me with him to look at the proofs because he was trying to play down his past from *Psycho*. He said, 'I don't want to look like Norman Bates.' He was hung up on the way he looked."

Given that, *Evening Primrose* must have disappointed Tony terribly. From the opening shots of him moving stealthily through Stern's department store (Macy's was used for the exterior), accompanied by the ominous sound of a throbbing heartbeat, he looks cagey, nervous, even crazed. It was Sondheim's fault: "I wanted the numbers to be conversational and not formalized. I told Tony not to look straight into the camera, that he should look around the edges as if he were talking to the world. And, of course, it just looked ridiculous."

Adding to the peculiarity of the performance are Perkins's occasional, inexplicable lapses into British or "mid-Atlantic" line readings, like a child pretending to act.

"It was one of the worst series ever filmed," the actor said of *Stage 67* twenty years later. "I think our project suffered somewhat from being a part of it. And it came off a little stiff because they insisted on doing it on tape instead of film."

The critics tended to agree. "[The] score as a whole proved richer in promise than in realization," said the *New York Times*. "[ABC's] experimental program series looks more and more as if it had been rushed into production without adequate opportunity for careful preparation."

Nevertheless, despite the pans, *Evening Primrose* is a small-scale success, uniquely atmospheric as a chamber piece, with laudable singing from its star. Sondheim was pleased, except with the opening number: "Everything in the store should have had a price tag on it."

A comedy by Broadway's hottest playwright, Neil Simon—whose *The Odd Couple* and *Barefoot in the Park* were running simultaneously—must have seemed like the perfect antidote to Perkins's *Psycho* image. The summer of 1966, he signed to star in the playwright's latest effort, *The Star-Spangled Girl*.

The story of two politically protesting San Francisco roommates whose solidarity is threatened when they both fall for the same Republican girl next door, *Girl* was a lame attempt to combine the volatile social temper of the sixties with the kind of situation comedy that had made Neil Simon a household name. For Tony, the chance to originate the role of a hard-driving liberal magazine editor may have seemed like his own crack at the kind of *Front Page* part that had made his father a legend. But Simon, feeling that the play was forced and thin, had actually tried to back out of the commitment after thirty or forty pages of script had been completed, only continuing at the insistence of producer Arnold Saint-Subber.

George Axelrod, whose reputation rested largely on his authorship of two popular comedies of the 1950s, *The Seven-Year Itch* and *Will Success Spoil Rock Hunter?*, was hired to direct when Gene Saks proved unavailable. As the other leftist roommate, talented young actor Richard Benjamin, who had toured in both of Simon's current hits (and had met Tony at the 1964 Buenos Aires Film Festival), was cast. And for the crucial title role—which Tony had vainly tried to convince Elaine Aiken to take—Connie Stevens, the popular blond TV personality who had risen to fame on the series *Hawaiian Eye*, was recruited to make her Broadway debut. Rehearsals were held in the decrepit upstairs studio of the Amsterdam Theater on Forty-second Street.

From the start, the press concentrated on Stevens, whose teenybopper appeal had recently intensified thanks to her love affair with Elizabeth Taylor's ex-husband, Eddie Fisher, who was constantly bringing Stevens jewelry backstage and writing love notes in lipstick on her dressing room mirror. Tony resented his costar's glitzy fame; the kind of attention he had once been the focus of as Paramount's golden boy now seemed conveniently at odds with the higher standards of the legitimate theater.

"[Stevens] had a charming personality, but she had no stage experience," Neil Simon recalls. "It wasn't her fault; if I had written a better part, we probably could have gotten a more experienced actress for it. Tony was really very generous to her during the rehearsals and during the play itself because he knew we could have done better."

When Tony tried to give Stevens notes during one show—suggestions on how she might improve her performance—the pretty star was offended. Much like her character in the play, Stevens, sensing that she was out of her league onstage, reacted with defensive bravado; her performance became progressively more strident and one-note.

Axelrod did nothing to help, and the cast quickly divided into two camps: the New Yorkers (Perkins, Simon, and Benjamin) versus the New Yorkers gone Hollywood (Stevens and Axelrod). Simon remembers: "I knew we were in trouble when, during rehearsals, Tony and Dick Benjamin would bypass George Axelrod, who was sitting in the front row, and talk to me, three rows back. They had sort of given up on him and were doing it by themselves."

"There was a lot of tension," one observer says. "Connie Stevens's love life really burned Tony's ass, the way she went off with Eddie Fisher and missed performances. They borrowed Sinatra's jet and went down to the islands somewhere, and she kept calling in—'I can't make it for the matinee, but I'll be back for the evening performance'—and the excuse was that the jet had a flat tire! Tony, of course, was the consummate professional."

Word of their differences eventually leaked out. When Earl Wilson asked Perkins if he had accused Stevens of upstaging him, the actor replied, "No, but she's accused me!" Tony claimed there was no "competitive acting" going on, but admitted that "there have been silences between us." (When asked to be interviewed for this book, Connie Stevens declined, saying that she had no fond memories of Perkins or the play.)

"If Tony respected you, he gave you everything," Simon remembers. "If he didn't, then you didn't get along."

In late December, *The Star-Spangled Girl* opened at New York's Plymouth Theater to middling reviews. Most critics pointed out what the playwright already knew: that one-third of the piece, the part of the girl, was fatally contrived and one-dimensional. But though *Girl* was heralded as Neil Simon's first flop—for years, Perkins would obstinately maintain that it was Simon's "funniest"—it managed to run for a solid year, due largely to the public's fascination with Connie Stevens.

One night, when she missed a performance, hundreds of audience members marched to the box office to demand refunds. "That made Tony happy," Ben Bagley claims. "He said, 'I'm no longer Connie Stevens, I'm no longer a sex symbol. If it was me who was out they wouldn't ask for their money back.' It was a big relief."

Yet when Tony himself came down with walking pneumonia and was hospitalized for a whole week, he managed not to miss more than four performances. "I read in *Variety* that the grosses were going down and I was sure it was because I was out," he later said. "I became so determined to do the show the doctor finally agreed and filled me up with antibiotics and let me go on. In this flying-high condition I walked onto the set and suddenly it all hit me—the lights, the audience, Oliver Smith's beautiful blue cyclorama outside the window. In my half-stoned state I just wanted to sit down and cry, 'This is so wonderful—this is my love.' "

Simon remembers Tony's "sense of dedication to the part. He had a sort of paternal feeling toward it. He never did light comedy, but he was quite good. I think he felt it was important to be able to do that as well as the *Psychos*."

Perkins's private resentment toward the audiences who had lionized him as the supreme weirdo of the silver screen began manifesting itself in subtly hostile ways. Front-row patrons often placed their white programs on the black apron of the stage, which Tony hated. In retaliation, during performances, he would occasionally move toward the apron and snatch up a sacrificial playbill, carry it around for a while, then stash it somewhere on the set, where he ultimately hid about a hundred of them.

He was also a stickler with the greedy autograph hounds who waited at the stage door every night. Signing autographs was no problem for the *Psycho* star, but if someone handed him the same program to sign twice, he would hold it up for the entire crowd to see: "No, no, no, no, no, this is your *second* one. This person has a program signed on the front, she has just handed it back to me in the middle for a second signature. I think we all know what we think of her, *don't we?*" For the unlucky fan, it was equivalent to a public hanging.

Perkins's attachment to the play became increasingly rigid, his own performance almost hysterically fixed. Actor Paul Sand, who took over Richard Benjamin's role on very short notice in the spring of 1967, remembers Perkins being obsessed with stage directions, and panic-stricken at even the slightest hint of improvisation or variation from the script. His line readings and moves were exactly the same every night.

"I was always stunned that people were laughing," Sand recalls. "I had no idea what they could have been laughing at. After every show, Tony would come tearing over to me with a note—'What did you sit down *there* for?!' And I, being from Second City [the Chicago improv group] and a 'rebel,' would say, 'Because I felt like it.' He came from the opposite school. He gave me lots—*and lots*—of notes." Even onstage during the performance, when Tony had no lines to speak, he would watch Sand and actress Sheila Wells (Connie Stevens had left because of a pregnancy) with a piercing, hawklike stare rather than involve himself in the stage business.

His understudy, William Bogert, remembers simply saying, "How are you?" to Tony in passing—to which the star snapped back, "What does *that* mean?"

"His lack of communication was extraordinary," Bogert says. "He never did anything straight-out, he always came around corners. I was amazed when he got married, surprised that he could get that close to anybody."

At the time he was "married" to Grover Dale, but still had to hide it, though his homosexuality was no secret among the company. Rumor had it that Tony frequented a house of male prostitution run by one of the dressers in an apartment on the Upper West Side—and that the blue blazer he wore in the play had come directly off the back of a trick he'd picked up one night.

According to Neil Simon, Perkins's private life "was very well guarded. The only inkling I had about it was that Tony would sometimes disappear at night. We'd be out of town with nothing to do, and Tony would say, 'I'll see you later.' We'd ask where he was going, 'Aw, I'm just going out.' I also knew that he was going to an analyst who was a friend of mine, and was trying to work things out. Personally, I think he was fighting it, that it was a great conflict in his life. Those days were very different. One was not allowed to be very open about [being gay]. Certainly, theatrically, it could be a death knell for you—especially in films."

But Tony's career in TV-ravaged Hollywood was already dead, as his new agent, the talent maverick Sue Mengers, well knew. Like Helen, Mengers was a German immigrant. She had parlayed a secretarial job at the William Morris Agency into a high-powered position with Creative Management Associates (which later became International Creative Management), had wined and dined Perkins for eight months before he agreed to employ her. "We preyed on people who were out of work," she later admitted.

Mengers's aggressiveness was notorious, and it infuriated as many people as it impressed. Tony, for one, found it a great source of amusement. Ben Bagley remembers being invited to dinner on Twenty-first Street expressly because Mengers would be there: "Tony said, 'Sue is coming and I want you to be here, because you've never met anyone as crude as this.' And I said, 'Yes, I have,' and he said, 'No, you haven't. I want you to meet her.' Well, she *was* the crudest person I'd ever met, and I didn't think that was possible. He delighted in shocking me with her. She took her shoes off after we ate, and her feet smelled to high heaven, and she dangled them in his face. I was on the same couch and got up to move because the odor was so repellent. She was enormously fat and enormously crude."

Years later, during his Broadway run in *Equus*, according to wardrobe supervisor Eric Harrison, "the only [backstage visitor] he ever got alarmed about was Sue Mengers. He used to be terrified of her coming because he said she'd eat the fucking walls, anything. He was never complimentary about her." Though Perkins and Mengers had a close friendship—she was one of the first people he would confide in about the circumstances surrounding his devastating illness—the actor was privately jealous of his agent's unladylike, ballsy fearlessness, something that he, certainly as a leading man, lacked. On some level, he resented his dependence on her, and he manifested this spite with disparaging remarks (and with a bitchy Mengers-based character in the screenplay he cowrote with Stephen Sondheim, *The Last of Sheila*).

Whatever else she may have been, Mengers was a shrewd deal maker and a lifeline for the aging fifties sweater boy. When Noel Black, a twenty-six-year-old UCLA film school graduate, needed an actor to headline his first feature—a psychological thriller based on Stephen Geller's novel *She Let Him Continue*, for which Tuesday Weld had already been signed—Mengers was quick to arrange a meeting at Joe Allen's restaurant. Black may not have been Hitchcock, Welles, or even Chabrol, but Mengers was smart enough to know that if Tony Perkins wanted to revive and prolong his domestic career, he was going to have to swing with the times and be open to a whole new generation of young, independent American filmmakers.

"At that time, Tony had not done a mainstream American movie in years, and was, in the common vernacular, considered to be hurting," Black recalls. "Any other actor would have jumped at this opportunity, and used the fact that we didn't have a good backup for him as leverage for more money. Tony did not ask for more money." He accepted their offer of $75,000, considerably less than he had been getting, requesting only that production be postponed for a month or so to let the play die its natural death.

This put more pressure on the young director. *Pretty Poison,* as the film was soon retitled, was set at the peak of summer, and was to be shot on location in verdant Great Barrington, Massachusetts; by the time Tony's run ended in August, it would almost be fall, leaving even less time to capture the right lush look before the leaves started to turn. They would have to work twice as fast.

As for Perkins, who hadn't made a movie on American soil since *Psycho* eight years before, the return seemed particularly well timed; the recent success of films like *The Graduate* and *Bonnie and Clyde* heralded a bright new wave of filmmaking on the rise in Hollywood. But *Pretty Poison* was troubled from the start. Noel Black's lack of experience inspired a swift antagonism. On the first day of shooting one of the producers walked out. "Noel knew how to set up shots," actor John Randolph remembers, "but he knew nothing about acting. Tuesday Weld was neurotic as hell. She would break down and cry. She hated the director, and she permitted that hatred to color everything she did. So Tony was dealing with a director who did not know how to talk to actors and an actress who was hysterical half the time."

Even so, Perkins gently rose to Black's defense when the tough New York crew, many of whom had worked with seasoned pros like Elia Kazan and Sidney Lumet, began giving the novice director a hard time. Black's difficulties no doubt reminded Tony of his own painful days and nights on *Fear Strikes Out.*

As usual, he kept a safe distance from his young leading lady and turned his boyish charm on older women. At the inn where the cast was put up, Tony took his meals separately in the kitchen, in the company of the elderly proprietress. During the scene where Beverly Garland, who played Tuesday Weld's bitchy mother, was "shot" by her daughter and had to fall down a flight of real stairs, chivalrous Tony offered to test the tumble himself first—in effect to choreograph it for the apprehensive actress. In his spare time, he played Frisbee and indulged his penchant for kites and gliders. "He was a lot like a kid," John Randolph says, "enamored of certain toys with a childlike quality."

Perkins was then thirty-five years old, and took pride in thinking he was probably at his physical peak. Makeup supervisor Robert Ji-ras, who later coproduced (with Dominick Dunne) the film of Mart Crowley's *The Boys in the Band*, remembers that Tony's sole cosmetic need was tinted suntan lotion. "I think it was Elizabeth Arden or Helena Rubenstein. All I had to do was shake it into his hands and he'd rub it on without even looking." Indeed, not since *Friendly Persuasion* had Perkins photographed in color with such vibrant, youthful handsomeness.

While he worried that his role as an arsonist fresh out of a mental hospital was unlikely to shake the specter of Norman Bates, the part was not without its virtuoso moments, of which Perkins was careful to take full advantage. Noel Black recalls that before Tony's long soliloquy when Weld asks him if he really murdered his aunt years before, "he was already intensely submerged in the role about a half an hour before we were ready to shoot. I could see the tears in his eyes."

With its lusciously muted color photography, its fine performances, and its subtle satire of hometown America, *Pretty Poison* ranks, after *Psycho*, as one of the best, most enduring films of Perkins's career. (It was also the picture on which Tony found Murray, a stray collie dog that he took home with him to New York.) But 20th Century-Fox, which had recently suffered a huge financial loss with the top-heavy Julie Andrews musical *Star!*, did not know quite how to market the offbeat picture. The film ended up showing at a few Greenwich Village art houses in late 1968, and quickly vanished.

But a few dissident voices, namely *The New Yorker*'s Pauline Kael and *Newsweek*'s Joseph Morgenstern, applauded the little movie, condemning Fox's foolishly timid ad campaign. "[The] most beautifully conceived and the most precise performance Perkins has ever given," wrote Kael. Unfortunately, their rescue came too late.

Years later, at a 1990 screening of the film at UCLA, Perkins joined Noel Black and John Randolph to speak briefly and answer questions from an enthusiastic young audience. Randolph noticed that he was "very serious, lacking the childlike quality that I remembered from working with him. He seemed more sad." As soon as the event was over, Tony left with his family and Stephen Paley. "He only pretended to like the movie at the screening," reveals Paley, "but in the privacy of the car, driving home, he said, 'That really was a piece of shit, so slow moving.' "

Meanwhile, in 1967, his boyish charm fading, his career stalling, Tony Perkins still didn't quite know where he fit in. The Vietnam War had spawned a generation of skeptical Americans who didn't subscribe to the placebos that had kept their parents in line. Renegade filmmakers like Martin Scorsese, Bob Rafelson, Francis Ford Coppola, Robert Altman, and even Tony's old fellow studio cog Dennis Hopper were just coming into their own. Gone were the Hitchcocks, the Welleses, the Cukors and Wylers. Hollywood, and America, was a very different place than it had been in 1955.

GAMES

ITHOUT HOLLYWOOD AS A BACKDROP for his political game playing, Perkins turned to literal game playing in Manhattan. On Halloween of 1968, for example, he was one of twenty adult theater folk (including Roddy McDowall, Lee Remick, Herbert Ross, Nora Kaye, and Mary Rodgers) who took part in the now legendary "Eleanor Clark French Memorial Treasure Hunt."

Masterminded by Tony and Stephen Sondheim a full month in advance, the game involved detailed maps, four limousines, a bag of odd props (pins, scissors, string), and a wild-goose chase all over the city in search of often elaborately staged clues, which were loosely marked by Eleanor French posters (a forgotten local politician some of whose old campaign placards Tony had discovered in his basement). The clues ranged from the almost cinematically eerie (a message written on the side of a lone bowling pin standing in an empty lane at the end of an otherwise bustling alley) to the seemingly homespun (charming Janet Perkins inviting players into a brownstone for some coffee and cake—where a message was hidden in the icing). Perkins had found in Sondheim, whose relationship with his mother was as problematic as his own, a mischievous intellectual cohort with whom he felt "absolutely compatible."

Tony's love of games had begun, obviously, with his grandmother

Mimi, and had developed over the years from the boredom of waiting around on movie sets, playing anagrams and Scrabble and hangman and Jotto with the likes of Ingrid Bergman, Janet Leigh, and Jane Fonda. By the mid-1960s, however, Tony's word games had gone a step further and taken on a darker edge, played with an almost fanatical intensity by an elite group of smart, talented movers and shakers that included Mike Nichols, Mary Ann Madden, Leonard Bernstein, and Phyllis Newman.

"The games at Mike's house were both fun and lethal," recalls André Previn, whose solo jazz piano album, *All Alone*, was one of Tony's favorites. "You'd make one stupid mistake and the whole room would look at you as if you had committed some extraordinary felony! They would actually get together in those days just to play murderous word games, all violently difficult."

Tony's easy seduction into this contrived coterie of adult Romper Roomers may have begun as early as 1965, when Mike Nichols, who was on the Coast directing his first film, *Who's Afraid of Virginia Woolf?*, imported Perkins from New York to act as the human surprise at a birthday party for his assistant, Mary Ann Madden. Madden, who later became the crossword puzzle editor at *New York* magazine, was given a box of clues that led her on a hot-cold treasure hunt of her own— "You're getting warmer, warmer . . . you're hot!"—until she found herself before a large closet which concealed Tony Perkins, whom she adored.

Or it could have started at another complex birthday surprise for Felicia Bernstein, which her husband Leonard had asked Stephen Sondheim to orchestrate. Sondheim decided to throw "a happening"—the sixties version of performance art—and recruited Perkins to help him write it, a precursor of their dramatic collaborations to come. "I don't know why I called Tony," Sondheim says, "except that we were all friends. So we wrote our takeoff on 'happenings,' and called it 'Laundro-masques.'

"The way it was set up was this: Lenny and Felicia would go out to dinner with a friend of theirs, [actor] Michael Wager. I arranged with him to say, 'Oh listen, Felicia, on the way to dinner I have to stop off at the Caffè Cino because they're having a happening there and I've got to say hello to someone.' That was the excuse."

An audiotape of droning, contrapuntal music had been prepared and a vast cast of "bohemians" assembled to lend the event the proper sophomoric authenticity. "So they go to this coffeehouse where there were about twelve tables full of Village types," Sondheim recalls, "and on the stage someone reading poetry on a stepladder with this terrible music playing—I mean, exactly what Felicia would *hate*. Then the MC came around and slipped pillowcases over everyone's head, and unbeknownst to Felicia, fifty people were hidden in the rest rooms and under the tables, everywhere. Twenty seconds later, the 'masque' was removed, and there were all her friends yelling surprise! She literally sat on the floor. I mean, people like Lillian Hellman were squashed in the men's room. We even went so far as to have cheap, off-kilter mimeographed sheets printed with the cast credits."

But the most famous game of all was Sondheim's murder game, which he had invented to cheer up actress Phyllis Newman after the out-of-town closing of Frank Loesser's last musical, *Pleasures and Palaces*. "Murder games always consisted of turning out the lights and everybody groping around and screaming," Sondheim explains. "I thought I'd invent one where people really had a certain amount of fear or suspense." The game, which required eight to sixteen players and an entire house or apartment in which to move, was tried out at the country home of choreographer Jerome Robbins (Grover Dale's mentor) before "opening" in New York on Twenty-first Street, chez Tony and Grover.

"The principle of the game is that you don't know who the murderer is going to be," Sondheim continues. "Say there are twelve people. Envelopes [denoting assigned roles in the game, as later illustrated in *The Last of Sheila*] are handed out entirely by chance. The idea is that you get sent off to various parts of the house to pick up clues, and try to get back to the one 'safe' room without being murdered on the way."

The town house lit only by votive candles, illuminating each shadowy corridor and room just enough to see, the players, including Mary Ann Madden and playwright Peter Shaffer, fanned out into the darkness in search of evidence. "By sheer coincidence," says Sondheim, "Tony picked the murderer card." This time, fate had typecast the actor, adding an ironic twist to the proceedings.

Sondheim recalls: "Peter Shaffer was sent to a bathroom to pick up his clue, which was under the sink. He picked it up, looked in the mirror, and behind him was Tony Perkins with a gun in his hand! Bang-bang, you're dead.

"When we all went to pick the 'bodies' up, Shaffer had smoked

two cigarettes—they were out on the bathroom floor next to him—
and he'd only been 'dead' for five minutes. Do you know what it is to
smoke two cigarettes in five minutes? You've really got to [suck]. He
was so terrified. I mean, of all people, Tony Perkins just a couple of
years after *Psycho*!"

The game was such a smash that Peter Shaffer asked Sondheim to
orchestrate another at the London home of his brother Anthony Shaffer (which ultimately inspired that Shaffer to write the play *Sleuth*). It
also inspired Perkins, about a year later, to come up with his own version of the game, almost identical to the Sondheim original except for
the peculiar requirement that all participants wear surgical gowns. "It
had nothing to do with *Psycho*," Sondheim says, though the significance of the flimsy garb remains unclear.

"Tony was always very good at the games, very funny and droll,"
remembers Herbert Ross. "He was so intelligent. I'm sure he felt
strongly about the fact that he was smarter than a lot of people who
were doing professionally better than he was."

For years Perkins remained part of the celebrated highbrow circle
that would regularly drop by Sondheim's Turtle Bay home for a round
of "cutthroat anagrams" or "truth games." According to Billy Goldenberg, who later composed the score for *The Last of Sheila*, "These were
roughly intellectual, sometimes very cruel games. The movie was an
extension of them. Whenever I would hear about those evenings, I was
terrified—they scared me, frankly, because there was something cruel
about them. Certainly this group of people was a really bright bunch,
no question. But they were also a competitive bunch. Power was very
important. They played truth games, where they would sit around talking about the things they feared the most in themselves and . . . it was
hitting too close to the bone for the other person's enjoyment. I didn't
feel there was any humanity in it. A lot of it is in that movie." Many of
the players were clients of the same psychoanalyst, Mildred Newman.

Truth games aside, Ben Bagley recalls that Sondheim's presence
"ruined" many a Christmas party at Tony and Grover's: "He'd take
over the whole evening. He'd go to the piano and say, 'Now I want to
show everybody why "I Got Rhythm" is a great song.' Tony became
very pretentious when he was involved with Sondheim, and I didn't
like him at that time."

Producer Howard Rosenman, who met Perkins at the composer's

home, said that Tony "made a lot of people very, very uncomfortable. He had a cool, detached way of looking at you and letting you know what a schmuck you were."

Despite the otherwise playful exterior, friends detected an undercurrent of rivalry on Twenty-first Street—especially when a wispy Brad Pitt look-alike named Christopher Makos, who was new in town from Los Angeles, showed up for an evening of board games at the Perkins residence. He had been invited by a mutual friend. "The joke was whoever lost would have to go to bed with Tony and Grover," Makos recalls. "I understood that to be a joke, but I was considerably younger than the rest of them. Of course, I lost, so I guess I was supposed to . . . you know those kind of games that rich people play. They were always looking for new people to participate."

Tony quickly became infatuated with the young newcomer, who was taken quite by surprise. "I didn't understand what it was all about," says Makos. "I thought he was basically a married man, I thought that was a relationship no one could tamper with." Many people maintain that Makos was a major factor in the final rift between Perkins and Dale, but according to Makos, "Tony and Grover's relationship, as a relationship, was over when I saw it. They seemed more like friends than what you'd call a tight relationship. I don't feel that I came between them. I was part of many things that they were both doing. I'm sure I was not the only outside person that Tony was having little affairs with. I can't speak for Grover, but these were two adult men who probably loved each other very much, and I'm sure that mini-affairs were not intrusive to the point of breaking up their relationship."

Makos was later widely perceived as having been a sort of male prostitute, owing to a suggestive entry in Andy Warhol's notorious *Diaries* dated June 6, 1983: "I love seeing the new *People* magazine with Tony Perkins on the cover, and it talked about him being gay, as if it were all in the past. Isn't that funny? . . . Left out Tab Hunter and Chris Makos, but it didn't say that he used to hire hustlers to come in through the window and pretend to be robbers. I wonder if Chris had to do that. I guess maybe he did. Chris did get wild." Unbeknownst to Tony, Makos was involved at the same time with writer Dotson Rader.

"Chris was never a 'hustler,' " says his friend, gay activist and journalist Lance Loud. "He was a hustler in a much broader sense of the

word, not a pay-for-play guy at all. He was a social creature, *always*
hustling. He was never working Tony for a permanent position in his
life. He liked him kept as a friend, and to be kept by him in a very,
very loose way. Tony did give him money, lots of money. But it was
never a set thing." Perkins also gave Makos his first camera, and photography would become the young man's vocation, as it had been
Helen's, Stephen Paley's, and would even be his future wife's.

"Frankly, what was I, twenty-something?" Makos muses. "It was
just terrific fun. Hanging out with a famous movie star, having sex with
a famous movie star—isn't that what people read about in novels? I
never fantasized about being around famous people. With Tony, it just
happened."

That was part of the problem at home: as one friend put it, "Tony
was a big star, and Grover was trying to be." After more than a decade
of hoofing in the chorus, in 1968 Dale was featured in two major
movie musicals: *Half a Sixpence* (reprising the secondary role he had
played on Broadway three years before) and *The Young Girls of Rochefort*
with Gene Kelly and Catherine Deneuve. As frustrating as it may have
been for Dale living in the shadow of a film star, his career was still
ahead of him.

Conversely, Perkins's was not. "I keep being offered boy's roles,
but I turn them down," he told one reporter. "There's something
grotesque about a man of my age playing boys on the screen." Perkins
and Dale were both looking for ways to crystallize their careers, gain
the upper hand, be in control. And for both of them, directing seemed
like the only way to go. Sondheim encouraged Tony to try it.

"Tony was incredibly brilliant and witty and gifted," Noel Black
remembers. "It was just a natural to think that he would be a fabulous
director."

His first stab at it had occurred in late December 1967, when he di-
rected himself, Remak Ramsay, and Sheila Wells in the road tour of
The Star-Spangled Girl, which had opened at the Papermill Playhouse in
New Jersey, moving on to Miami–Fort Lauderdale, Los Angeles, San
Francisco, St. Louis, and Denver (where George Hamilton took over
Tony's role in the show). Toning down the "frantic" pace of George
Axelrod's one-note Broadway production, Tony tried to steer the
show in "a much more reasonable way." The *Newark Evening News*
noted that "Perkins, who has an uncanny ability on stage to look as if

he is thinking about the problem at hand [he was], also is a director of merit."

In 1968, after flying to London to star in a quickie BBC-TV production of *The Male Animal* with Claire Bloom, he accepted an offer from Philadelphia's Playhouse in the Park to direct a stock production of Peter Ustinov's *The Unknown Soldier and His Wife: Two Acts of War Separated by a Truce for Refreshment*, which had opened (and promptly closed) on Broadway the previous fall under the command of tyrannical British director John Dexter, who would later torment Perkins during his Broadway run in Peter Shaffer's *Equus*.

Tony's first task was to cast the title role. Richard Cox, a handsome young drama student whom Helen had seen in a play at the Yale Repertory Theater, more than fit the bill; he was also a Chelsea neighbor, who could see right into the Perkins home from his family's house a block away. "One day Helen screamed out the window, 'Come over, I want you to meet someone!' " Cox recalls. It was Tony, who had noticed Cox before, found him attractive, and wanted him for the part no matter what, even though he was not yet a member of Equity (and was straight). As a union requirement, Perkins held auditions, then hired Cox anyway. For the young actor it was a big break, his first Equity job (later, Grover Dale would direct him in his first television commercial, breaking him into the TV actors union).

Cox was quickly accepted as part of the household, even joining the trio out on Cape Cod, where Tony would occasionally surprise visitors by coming down the stairs dressed as Mrs. Bates, knife and all. A teetotaler as far as alcohol was concerned, Tony now enjoyed occasionally smoking marijuana—and the kind of conversations that would arise when, say, a Thanksgiving turkey was stuffed with it.

"When I was hanging out with them, it was all one big, happy family," Cox remembers, "a salony atmosphere, people sitting around the table eating good food, talking about interesting things. There was tension later. But Helen wouldn't really talk about it."

As she had done with Tony and scores of other young artists years before, Helen took Cox under her wing. "She was like an aunt to me in those days. She's wonderful when people are just starting, sort of an Auntie Mame. She was very influential in my life, but later she wouldn't come to see me in plays and stuff, and I didn't understand why. She nurtures people, and moves on." In Tony's case, she would soon be forced to move on against her will.

Cox remembers Perkins vowing that "he wouldn't act anymore if they kept offering him *Psycho* roles. He was very intellectual, and liked experimental theatre—André Gregory's Manhattan Project, Peter Brook, and Dutch and Italian directors. He was looking for an outlet, trying to figure out a balance between that and his commercial career, which had been so big. I remember him weeping—*weeping*—at the end of the Open Theater production of *The Serpent*. But that was a world apart; he was a movie star."

As a director, Tony was intellectual as well. For instance, one of his notes to Cox during *The Unknown Soldier* was "Think of a Daumier drawing." "I didn't know who Daumier was," Cox recalls. "Tony was very cultured in music and art, and would use these images in his directing."

"A director needs a middlebrow intellect," Perkins was quoted.

Gretchen Corbett, the young actress who played the soldier's wife, remembers her director as generous and supportive, yet not at all personal, never divulging anything about his life away from the theater.

The play opened for a one-week run on August 19, and was well received by the local press. Sue Mengers even came to see it, as Richard Cox recalls. "Tony tried to set me up with her. He said she liked to meet young guys when she was traveling. She was just like everything you've ever heard about her, very loud and talked with a very truck driver kind of language." Young men aside, Mengers was surely more intent on convincing her client not to give up, just yet, on his film career.

Late December, however, found Perkins in the wilds of Wisconsin, directing Molière's comedy *The Imaginary Invalid* at the Milwaukee Repertory Theatre. Far from the critical eyes of New York, Tony could test his skills without fear.

"I honestly believe that you have only to look at the careers of those stars who've sold out to see that an increase in luxury means a corresponding decrease in ability," Tony said as he embarked on his tentative new vocation. "I deliberately shun the sybaritic life. I always remember what Marlon Brando once said: 'I've always done my best work when I've been unsettled and had no home.' Look at him now.

Marlon is the Macbethian example of the actor who accumulated too much. I don't want that to happen to me."

By 1969, Mike Nichols was considered the new Orson Welles. With *Catch-22* he became the first American director since Welles to be given complete creative control over a studio film (in this case, Paramount). It seemed only natural that Tony Perkins would work for him.

Joseph Heller's blackly humorous and immensely popular World War II novel had been tempting filmmakers like Richard Brooks, Richard Quine, and even Orson Welles since its publication in 1961, but perhaps because of the difficulty of conveying the dreamlike yet cynical tone of the book, it had never made it to the screen. Only a genius of a director could pull it off, and in Hollywood's eyes that genius was Nichols, the thirty-seven-year-old wunderkind who seemed to have the Midas touch. After an unbroken string of stage successes on Broadway, his first two films, *Who's Afraid of Virginia Woolf?* and *The Graduate*, had both been huge box-office hits, the latter earning Nichols an Academy Award for Best Director. *Catch-22* was expected to be his magnum opus. Tony had signed on without even knowing which part he would play.

Logistically and thematically, *Catch-22* was a precarious undertaking, a multimillion-dollar period epic with a delicate, complex antiwar message at its center. Just after New Year, an impressive flock of up-and-coming young stars like Jon Voight, Martin Sheen, Bob Newhart, Charles Grodin, Richard Benjamin, and Art Garfunkel flew to desolate Guaymas, Mexico, where a costly five-mile highway had been laid just to get them all to the elaborate $250,000 set, which itself consisted of a six-thousand-foot airstrip, a control tower, a mess hall, and various other buildings. No expense had been spared. A squadron of eighteen authentic B-25 planes, for example, had been acquired and made flyable at a cost of about $10,000 each.

"At that moment in time, *Catch-22* was *the* film to be in," recalls Austin Pendleton, who played the small role of Colonel Moodus. "I remember thinking it was Mike affirming Tony's career, which was perceived in some quarters to be on the slide." For his comic turn as the ineffectual Chaplain Tappman, Perkins's fee was $100,000; the film's young star, Alan Arkin, received about twice that amount.

There were problems from the start. After a week of shooting, the almost two hundred extras, all students from the University of Arizona, were busted by the Mexican police for marijuana possession and promptly deported back to the States, leaving the film's wide-screen scenes with a vast, empty, surreal look rather than the bustling backgrounds Nichols had originally envisioned. Then there was an outbreak of hepatitis in the company. Later, stunt pilot and cameraman Johnny Jordan died tragically when he fell off the back of a plane during a second-unit shoot.

The most spectacular mishap occurred during a scene that called for a full squadron landing: one of the B-25s got caught in the prop wash of the plane in front of it, and Nichols, his actors, and crew watched helplessly as the out-of-control aircraft careened toward them. "We were almost killed," screenwriter Buck Henry recalls. "Like morons, we were all right there on the runway. Everybody fell off something and got hurt trying to get out of the way of this oncoming plane. That's the kind of thing I remember Tony laughing at hysterically when it happened. It's hard not to laugh—an entire camera crew on top of each other. Tony laughed whenever something went horribly wrong."

If his reaction seemed a tad extreme, it was perhaps only representative of the excruciating boredom the entire cast was feeling, being, as Henry put it, "stranded in a craphole in the middle of Mexico, with nothing to do if you weren't working. Sometimes we would go days or weeks without actually working, which made some of us completely loony." Actors could rarely leave the location because of the physical difficulty of travel, and the off chance that they might unexpectedly be needed in a shot.

"Kvetch-22," as the production became not so affectionately known, dragged on for months, the monotony only occasionally broken by calamities and visits from writers like Nora Ephron, Penelope Gilliatt, and model-actress-photographer-reporter Candice Bergen. John Wayne also dropped in unexpectedly on his way to make a Western in nearby Durango. "If you quit early," actor-director Peter Bonerz remembers, "the only thing to look forward to was margaritas and beer. There was marijuana around, but it was smoked in private." LSD (for which actor Seth Allen had a well-known penchant, something Tony would later share) was also done off duty.

For cast members who had families with them, like Alan Arkin and

Dick Benjamin (whose wife, Paula Prentiss, was also in the film), the Mexican purgatory was somewhat more bearable. Perkins had Grover Dale there briefly, before the dancer returned to New York to choreograph his first Broadway show. The two kept a low profile.

"Tony coped very easily," Buck Henry recalls. "He was a genius at filling the time. He and Grover and Dick and Paula hung out together a lot. They would cook up bizarre practical jokes and stunts to pass the time. Tony was a master at mischief. He loved to get people confused, rattled, and sort of tipping over the edge. He was also great at games, of course, so we filled the time with complicated word games that were at best silly and at worst obscene."

One challenge was to see who could come up with the most synonyms for "pussy." Another diversion was a stoned-around-the-campfire kiss-and-tell contest in which cast members confessed their past sexual dalliances on film sets. According to Henry, "Tony had some particularly good stories to tell. They were very racy, sometimes shocking. He was always on the make, and I mean that in the best sense—in his brain, not to mention whatever other parts. [Mike Nichols's nickname for Perkins was "Pork."] He was always 'reading' circumstances, always reading your behavior. Sometimes it was easy to think you were giving a kind of performance for Tony because you were always aware of him as the Watcher, almost as the voyeur of his own experience. It was interesting to find the buttons to make him lose control."

Art Garfunkel, who made his acting debut in the film, gingerly remembers Tony as being "like an older brother watching the game we were both playing. You know how many people have said they have a third eye? One could really see that in him. He was a watcher of his own being, and he created a balanced counterpoint with the two. If the being of Tony leaned left, the watcher leaned right. It was in his body language; hips would go left, but upper torso would go right. His body language was amazingly agile and complex, things would go in different directions."

His body was the one thing over which Perkins could maintain his ascetic control. By today's harsh standards he hardly qualifies as a hunk, but in 1969 his trim, well-muscled frame caused a slight stir. Certainly none of the straight men on the film was in as good shape. But weight lifting was something gay men had long embraced, both as a sexual lure and as an obvious way to assert their oft-denied masculinity. "At that

time there weren't many of these Soloflex things around," Peter Bonerz recalls. "I was quite surprised to see this probably European chro-
mium steel contraption moved into Tony's room. I don't think anyone
else on the film was a bodybuilder or concerned about his form in that
way. Some of us played tennis or ran, but Tony was paying attention to
his muscle mass, which was very novel then."

Buck Henry describes the Perkins build as "overdeveloped from
the waist to the neck, and his shoulders were so huge that it made him
look like his head was too small. Which is what gave him that great, almost prehistoric birdlike look." Just how serious Perkins was about his
physique can best be seen in his shirtless scenes in two later films,
Chabrol's *Ten Days' Wonder* and Alan Rudolph's *Remember My Name*.
By the end of the decade, however, the actor would require padding
under his T-shirts to maintain the illusion of muscle.

On February 12, Orson Welles arrived to shoot his scenes as General Dreedle. He stepped off the plane (with Peter Bogdanovich, who
was in the midst of interviewing him for his book) wearing food-
stained clothes and without a trunk or suitcase; the military uniform
for which he was swiftly fitted became his sole outfit for the week.
"Perkins was the only one of us who had already worked with Orson," Henry recalls. "The two of them were deeply moving when
they met each other. Welles was very effusive, and it was very moving
to all of us."

Working with the great director was another matter entirely. He
arrived not having learned a single line, and not intending to. Bonerz
recalls Welles as "a diabolical, selfish, unscrupulous actor" who interrupted master shots to demand close-ups and blamed crew people
whenever he blew lines, which was often. He had only accepted the
small role to finance a project of his own. Perhaps he resented the
young Mike Nichols, who was everything Welles had once been (and
was even directing a property Welles had wanted for himself).

According to Austin Pendleton, "Mike would be about to shoot
and suddenly Orson would start to say how it *should* be done. He managed to kill all the spontaneity and edge, and made everything kind of
blunt and obvious. He didn't know anything about comedy, and he
would give these lectures about comedy to Mike Nichols, of all people.
Mike was patient with him. It was a drag."

Nevertheless, between shots the cast would sit in their canvas-backed chairs in a circle out in the desert, and at the head would sit Welles, who entertained the group with his iconoclastic opinions on every film or film director alive or dead.

"He was a raconteur nonstop for a week, and then he was gone," Garfunkel remembers. "But he loved Tony, greeted him as a dear friend. They were very sweet, two people who knew what was good about each other. Tony was the one person Orson knew and liked on the set." Both were outsiders who came from a different epoch of film-making.

Consequently, Perkins was unsure of his abilities against those of a new generation of young stars. Alan Arkin vividly recalls Perkins going into a "clench" before every take of every shot: "Just before Mike called action, Tony would almost invariably say, 'Oh, God, where did I go wrong.' Acting seemed very painful for him. It was a kind of ritual he went through, and it seemed terribly sad to me. . . . It's something I've never forgotten."

"He was very nervous," Pendleton concurs. "I think acting was an ambivalent experience for him. I was always very sad that he didn't *pursue* acting a lot more throughout his life, because he was so good."

Pendleton and Perkins were both just starting to direct, and spent a lot of time sharing their ideas. "He drew the set [from *The Imaginary Invalid*] for me in the sand, and then described this very particular way he had it lit," Pendleton recalls. "He clearly thought this was going to be a big way he'd be spending his time."

Tony spent much of his time in Guaymas contemplating other, less worldly things. Perhaps inspired by the extraordinary landscape, he proselytized the veracity of the latest mystical fads to whoever cared to listen. He was especially taken with "Bridey Murphy," the colorful, hypnosis-invoked past-life personality of a Denver housewife, and the "thoughtography" of Ted Serios, the man who could allegedly project his thoughts onto film inside a Polaroid camera (both were eventually proven to be frauds).

According to Buck Henry, "Tony believed everything, and he was determined to bring me around to some kind of belief. We had long, funny arguments during which I would dramatize this guy taking photos with his brain. Tony was *determined* to believe this. He was a cross between a metaphysician and someone with impeccable logic."

But beneath that sophisticated, boyish, contradictory exterior was a man profoundly dissatisfied with himself, anxious about his dwindling career, and isolated by pride and fear. In the strange, windswept limbo of Guaymas, Perkins began to reevaluate where he'd been and where he was going. No longer a major star, not yet a director, the remaining, humbling role of ordinary person seemed most uncertain of all. Stardom aside, he had never been ordinary. He was on the brink of a journey that would occupy the rest of his life, the search for his own humanity.

"I almost didn't talk to Tony," remembers actor-director Bob Balaban, the film's Captain Orr, "but we found ourselves alone in the dining room one day and sat down and confessed to each other that we just couldn't talk to anybody. After months of being there, it was like hell, and we were just miserably unhappy. This ennui had set in. I thought everybody else was having a great time. So it was a freeing moment for me that he should feel this way—and he was thrilled that somebody else was going through what he was going through.

"Tony had an innocent curiosity about everything, the way a baby will walk into a room and look around. Only Tony had a great mind as well, an unusual mind that was very open. He really listened and really watched.

"He confessed to me that at the beginning of his acting career he had treated people really badly, that he had always been kind of tense, didn't talk very much, and totally kept to himself. He would never be friendly with the crew, he'd just come out, do his job, and leave. He said it was because he'd been uncomfortable, he didn't realize what was expected from a movie star. He was looking back, and thought it was kind of a shame."

Years later, a harshly self-critical Perkins recalled the filming of *Catch-22* as "like going to an encounter weekend. There was no place to go, nothing to do except interrelate and coexist with others. And I just couldn't manage it. I didn't have any skills at intimacy. In New York a single person with a few bucks can devise a way of living that is tolerable. I would pretend I was living a life that was working for me— and in a sense it was—but it was a life of enormous limitations. When I was on that movie location, I realized I wanted to be more available to share my thoughts and feelings with others."

After a lifetime of dissimulation and denial, with no studio to justify it any longer, Perkins found himself emotionally bilked, spiritually stranded. Living in the Hollywood closet had left him inwardly bankrupt, and torn. Despite the fact that his live-in relationship with the ambitious Grover Dale was a role model for many other gay professionals, in 1969 it was still the love that dare not speak its name; without the proper conviction, a love affair just meant more fear. As for Grover, he was busy with a new show, a project that could at last put his name indelibly on the musical theatrical map. But while it was common knowledge that the dance world was composed largely of homosexuals, a public avowal could still stymie a career. In June of that year, the Stonewall riot in Greenwich Village would begin to galvanize the gay community in its demand for equal rights. But the popular condemnation that, to quote *Time* magazine, the "homosexual subculture . . . is, without question, shallow and unstable" would take years to soften.

Adding to Tony's sense of unsureness was the fact that his only "blood" family, Jane and Michaela, were splitting up after nearly twenty years together. "Jane did a lot for Michaela," Cary Fuller says, "but toward the end of Jane's life it was clear the two of them could not live together. It was a real falling-out." According to one relative, "Jane started having stomach troubles because she was so upset over Michaela's leaving. Apparently they had some gigantic misunderstanding. Jane felt she had been taken advantage of. It was something she really didn't like to talk about. But she was very, very hurt." The friendship would ultimately mend at the last crucial moment, but for now it only served to undermine Tony's already weak sense of security. In a supremely empathic gesture, he would buy his mother a comfortable new apartment on East Fiftieth Street.

Meanwhile, he turned to his friends, Dick Benjamin and Paula Prentiss, for help. Prentiss, an attractive comedienne whose offscreen suicide attempts had almost ended her career, not to mention her life, four years earlier, was more than happy to recommend their New York psychoanalyst, Mildred Newman, as the answer to his malaise. Perkins called her as soon as he returned home.

In fact, so persuasive was the Benjamins' enthusiasm for Newman that several people on the set, including visiting journalists Nora Ephron and Dan Greenburg, ended up going to her. (Just a year later, during the course of an interview for the *New York Times*, Perkins himself would likewise convince writer Rex Reed to give Newman a call.)

Newman and her husband, Bernard Berkowitz, also an analyst, thrived shamelessly on the word-of-mouth their celebrity clients generated, to the eventual detriment of their reputation. Tony would quickly become their most outspoken promoter.

He didn't have much else to promote. Released in June of 1970, the highly anticipated *Catch-22* was another major disappointment, the first critical and commercial flop of Mike Nichols's career, due in part to the earlier release of Robert Altman's hilarious *MASH*. The country wasn't big enough for two antiwar satires.

Perkins returned to New York in time for the March 22 opening of *Billy*, a rock musical by Ron Dante and Gene Allan audaciously based on Herman Melville's *Billy Budd*. Grover Dale had staged the show's huge musical sequences. It was a momentous occasion for Dale, who had worked for two years as assistant to the revered (and feared) Jerome Robbins. Using some of the techniques and ideas he had developed under Robbins in the show, Dale was counting on *Billy* to make his mark as a major choreographer. Tonight, he would finally come into his own.

"Grover was quite a taskmaster in rehearsals, which were very intense," assistant conductor Wally Harper remembers. "He was very into his head, very pensive, really considering every move."

Musical director Jack Lee recalls feeling certain that Dale "was in therapy because of the way he was dealing with the dance in the show. He was heavily into making sure the dance was organic, that there was a truth where it came out, how it happened. He didn't throw in dance for its own sake. Grover had great drive."

Billy closed after one performance.

Even Clive Barnes, the usually generous *Times* critic, denounced it, writing that the book (by Stephen Glassman) "reduces the Herman Melville story to the level of pulp adventure" and likening the music and lyrics to "graffiti on the wall of literature." He did, however, rave about the "brilliant" musical sequences: "Mr. Dale, in his first assignment as a Broadway choreographer, shows real talent. The dance ensembles, every one of them, displayed a vigor and gutsiness the rest of the show woefully lacked."

"The show was ahead of its time," maintains Jack Lee. "I don't think the critics knew how to take it. *Billy* dealt with things today, like gayness. Even though it was never brought up, that's what it was about—the rednecks of the world versus the innocent. I did not expect it to close so fast, because the audience response was great. The audience really loved it."

Grover Dale received the not insubstantial consolation prize of a Tony Award nomination for his work. But he still had not achieved his glory.

It was a time of change for everyone in Tony's life. Things at home were increasingly difficult. Tony had found himself at the center of a tug-of-war between Helen and Grover, who were not getting along under the same roof. Christopher Makos would often ask, "How can you be living with your boyfriend and have this other person there all the time?"

Helen's control of Tony's daily life, no longer a necessity, was slipping, and with little beyond the house itself to keep her occupied, she became increasingly nosy. She couldn't stand not knowing everything that was going on, and Grover, quite naturally, resented it. He did not trust her, and pointedly ignored her or was simply rude, as she struggled to regain her grasp. As for Tony, he remained passive as the conflict grew, choosing not to interfere. As one friend put it, "He always needed somebody to tell him what to do."

"Grover was a very selfish snot," Ben Bagley recalls. "He wanted Helen's apartment in the house—after she'd done all the work on it— to turn it into a dance studio. And Tony was a slave to Grover. It was a very destructive relationship, and Tony couldn't help himself."

Several violent arguments erupted between the lovers over getting Helen out. Grover won, and Helen, after all her years with Tony, left. "It was like throwing your mother out," says Bagley. "Grover was a shit."

"Helen was very possessive," defends Stephen Paley, "and Tony felt that he was a grown-up and wanted to have his own life. Their arrangement had been a peculiar one. It wasn't a sexual liaison and it wasn't mother–son, it was almost a *Pygmalion* in reverse. Tony just wanted out of the relationship. He kept Helen in his life, but at arm's length after that."

According to friends, he also paid her a financial settlement— ranging somewhere between fifty and one hundred thousand dollars—

that eventually enabled her to get on with her life, starting up a new and prosperous business as a literary agent. Paley maintains that "it was the greatest thing that ever happened to her."

Meanwhile, Tony was seeing Mildred Newman privately three or four times a week, at a rate of thirty-five dollars an hour, as well as participating in group sessions. He convinced Grover to go, and also urged a session on Helen. It didn't take with her. When Newman asked her why she wasn't angry about the situation with Tony, she replied simply that she had nothing to be angry about. She had already resolved not to give up on an almost twenty-year friendship.

Newman's therapeutic shtick that it was okay to love yourself without guilt and get the happiness and (mostly) the success that you naturally deserve seemed to be rubbing off on Tony. After appearing in *WUSA*, a drably liberal melodrama about Southern political corruption and bigotry (in which he played a homicidal social worker), Perkins took some decisive steps toward directing.

First, he canceled plans to star in the new Hal Prince–Stephen Sondheim stage musical *Company*, ads for which had already been published touting his name. "I had signed up to do the lead in *Company* and suddenly this specter rose up in front of me—of performing again for a year and a half—and I just dreaded it," he told Rex Reed. Perhaps the possibility of another *Greenwillow* was too much to bear. "I felt at that moment I was just getting somewhere as a director and I wanted to get out of acting. . . . That was the real moment of truth."

Sondheim recalls that "Tony thought the character of Bobby was the cipher at the center of *Company*, and would be very difficult to act. It's true. He's onstage the whole time and just reacts. It's a passive figure. That's the way Tony explained it to me, that it was difficult to play a passive part. Everybody else has all the colors." (Bobby, a thirty-five-year-old bachelor with ambiguous feelings about his impending marriage, struck many people as a veiled homosexual character—a fact that ultimately caused Tony's replacement, movie star Dean Jones, to quit the show five weeks after it opened. He was replaced by the more appropriate Larry Kert.)

"I used to be articulate, energetic, outgoing, full of life," Perkins explained to Rex Reed. "Suddenly I was depressed, dull, full of anxieties about my career. I started wondering where did it all go? And *why*? Now, after nine months in analysis, I know I want to stick with directing because it is more fulfilling to sit in an audience watching something I've created work than to be up there onstage doing it myself. If nobody knows who I am, I'm delighted. I no longer care about images."

In early November, the thirty-seven-year-old actor returned to Milwaukee to direct the American premiere of *The Burgomaster*, an obscure German play by Gert Hofmann that had been produced four times on European television. The ironic story of the moral decline of a small-town bureaucrat and the concurrent enlightenment of his boarder (who happens to be a terrorist), it was "one of those really self-conscious, serious plays, which was good for an actor like Tony," according to Chris Makos, who was brought along ostensibly to engineer the electronic sound effects he had compiled for the show. "I read it, and at the end didn't know what was going on."

"I'm old-fashioned enough to believe a play should have emotional content and plot construction, and not leave the audience puzzled about the meaning," Perkins told the *Milwaukee Journal*. "I want something that happens in life, not in abstraction."

CHAPTER

17

SUBTEXT

"I LIKED HIM INSTANTLY," playwright Bruce Jay Friedman recalls, "although I hadn't thought of him as a director. He was a little
shaky, because he started going over the script and it was almost
like he felt an obligation to suggest changes." In early 1970 Tony
had beat out several other candidates (including Broadway veteran
Bob Fosse) to direct *Steambath*, Friedman's highly anticipated new
comedy (his debut play, *Scuba Duba*, had won an Obie Award for
outstanding Off-Broadway production of 1967, and was still playing
to packed houses). An absurd black comedy about purgatory (in the
form of a decrepit steam room), God (the Puerto Rican attendant),
and the meaning of life, *Steambath* seemed like the project that would
put Perkins's name on the mainstream map as a director. It was scheduled to open on May 7 at New York's Truck and Warehouse Theatre
in the East Village.

Perkins was understandably nervous about the biggest turning
point of his career since *Look Homeward, Angel*, and felt he had to make
his mark right away. The most drastic alteration was to lighten up the
play's ending, which left the protagonist, Tandy, an ambitious writer
and the new boy in hell, disfigured and homeless on the streets of Manhattan. Instead, they decided to leave him in limbo, begging for a
chance to redeem himself.

Cast in the role was comedian Dick Shawn, though Friedman

maintains that the best reading came from actor Dane Clark, who vehemently refused the job when he heard who was directing. Clark predicted that Perkins would never allow another actor freedom in the part, an omen that would prove accurate.

About sixty actors auditioned for the role of the Puerto Rican attendant before Hector Elizondo. "I had to wait a long time," Elizondo remembers, "and then the first question they asked me, which made me laugh, was 'Are you really Spanish?' I said, 'No, I changed my name. My real name is Vic Smith. I changed it to Hector Elizondo. What are you talking about?' At which point I gave a kind of scary reading, meant to intimidate them. Tony was very quiet, withdrawn, not amused. I figured I'd blown that job."

Perkins was, in fact, infuriated, but at Friedman's insistence Elizondo was hired. So were Conrad Bain, Alan Weeks (who had appeared in the doomed *Billy*), Gabor Morea, and Tony's ex, Teno Pollick, as one of two comic gay boys (the other was played by Jere Admire, who had been in the chorus of *Greenwillow*). Grover Dale was hired to choreograph their campy dance routine, a small job he could have done with his eyes closed.

Though Teno had enjoyed a moderately successful career on television—appearing on shows like *The Eleventh Hour*, *Bonanza*, and *Gunsmoke*—he had fallen on hard times in the mid-1960s, when he suffered the first of what would become a series of debilitating kidney complications. He frequently borrowed money from Tony to pay his doctor bills. Gabor Morea remembers Teno always carrying sandwich bags full of stamps on torn-off envelope corners that his mother had collected for him from the office wastebaskets she emptied at night.

"Teno lived a lot in fantasy," says Alan Sues, who lived next door to him for a while in Los Angeles. "He was basically a sweet person who was almost a typical Hollywood story. His career had sort of stopped, and he had these fantasies all the time of what it was going to be like—and this is such a crappy business on a good day."

Steambath was expected to be a major hit, so all the actors were given Broadway contracts, which meant more money for everyone with no need to renegotiate when the play moved uptown. Because of the combination of Friedman, Perkins, Shawn, and the wonderful supporting cast composed of old pros and fresh faces, the show was already causing quite an advance buzz. Everyone went happily into rehearsals on April 7.

Tony applied some of the touchy-feely ideas he had picked up in analysis to his work, calling cast members at home to ask, "Are you comfortable? Is there anything you'd like to talk about?" (This did not go over so well, especially with some of the older actors.) Yet he kept his relationships with Pollick and Dale strictly professional during working hours, always arriving at and leaving the theater alone. Grover was not around much, making only occasional appearances to work on the gay boys' short lip-synching number.

Rehearsals went smoothly until about the third week, when Perkins began asking the actors to indulge in what one cast member describes as "sophomoric, avant-garde, textbook exercises."

"Okay, we're going to rehearse in the dark," the director would announce. "I want everyone to be another character in the play."

"Well, which one?"

"Oh, just any one you want."

He would instruct them to act out an infantile state or pretend to be crawling through honey on the floor, always with the lights out. To "find his center" at rehearsals, he stood with his great arms outstretched and assumed a Christlike pose, as if he were being crucified. Alan Weeks remembers it as "mental masturbation."

"It was like he didn't know what to do next," Gabor Morea concurs, "so he was coming up with these bizarre ideas. Everybody started getting very jittery." Tony even briefly suggested that they perform the show in the nude, a gimmick that was fashionable at the time.

For all of Perkins's awkward attempts at free-flowing openness, there was little real communication. "He never socialized with the cast," Conrad Bain says. "The minute there was a break in rehearsal he always had something urgent to do—the phone or writing a note—he didn't allow himself to just sit and shoot the breeze with the rest of us. He seemed not to be confident that he could let his guard down. And if he wasn't busy, he had this exerciser thing that he worked constantly. He'd come to the theater at night, and he'd spend twenty minutes exercising. I thought, 'Isn't there any other place he can do that?' "

Hector Elizondo, who gradually developed a rapport with the high-strung director, remembers that Tony "was trying desperately to quit Hollywood. He was unhappy with the way his career had evolved, and sensed his time was sort of passing. He wanted to have another option in this business." To Bruce Jay Friedman, Tony confessed his "greatest fear": that someday he'd end up playing piano in a roadhouse and be introduced as "Tony 'Psycho' Perkins."

"He was enormously charming," the playwright says, "but also very controlled. He always seemed to have four ideas going on in his head at once, always a subtext."

For financial and technical reasons—there was trouble fine-tuning David Mitchell's elaborate set, which sent a heavy bank of steam rolling out into the audience as soon as the curtain went up, melting hairdos in its path—*Steambath*'s opening was pushed to June 3. It just hadn't gelled yet.

Most people who saw Dick Shawn as Tandy agree that he was perfect for the part. But coming from the world of stand-up comedy, he was nervous about sustaining the flow of emotional concentration that the play required. Unfortunately, the guidance he expected from his director wasn't forthcoming. According to Elizondo, "Comedians are very tender people who need a lot of confidence, a lot of soothing. Tony couldn't give him that, so Shawn was fired." Most associates felt the move was "a major mistake."

By now it was already mid-May. Other roles were swiftly axed as well. "Tony got to a point in directing where he didn't know what else to do," Gabor Morea explains. "He started coming up with, 'Well, maybe if we eliminated *that* character, it would work.' People were let go at a moment's notice."

"I want to encourage people to do their work creatively without feeling that I should walk in and over," Perkins purported in *Show* magazine. "One rule that I made for myself was that I would never say 'do it this way.' "

Dick Shawn's vacancy was immediately filled by volatile Method actor Rip Torn, who stepped into the role on May 26, even though he was already appearing in a play in Washington, D.C. "Rip Torn had barely gotten off the plane when Tony started telling him where to stand, getting him all involved in the blocking," Friedman recalls. "Rip just wanted to *act*. He was enormously uncomfortable, and I don't think Tony was helpful. It didn't work out."

Torn was dismissed on June 4. There were reports that the exhausted actor could not memorize his lines. "I shuttled back and forth from Washington and joined the cast with only one day of rehearsal," he told the *Times*. "Last Sunday, they (the management) were cheering me but on Wednesday they were booing me. . . . I was like the soldier on the firing line and I think the generals acted a little hasty."

Backstage, "Who's the lead of the week?" became the sardonic refrain.

"It was all being done so quickly that a lot of people left with ill feeling," Morea recalls. "The whole preview period was topsy-turvy; we never knew who was going to be there or who was not. When Rip Torn left, we didn't even have notice that he was gone. Suddenly, there were just new people on the stage." Including Anthony Perkins, who had agreed to take over the lead role on short notice.

Many people felt that it had been Perkins's intention to play Tandy all along. "As a director, he was concentrated on that role," one cast member says. "There had been a so-called 'artistic difference' between Tony and Dick Shawn, who, in retrospect, was probably the most right for it. But Tony really coveted the role himself, he *wanted* to do it, and I don't blame him."

It's hard to imagine Perkins, with his trademark New England reserve, thinking he'd be able to bring the necessary hard-driven, guilt-ridden qualities to Friedman's Tandy, a New York Jew who must account to "God" for his messed-up life—including how his ex-wife's "private parts" ended up in a porno film (it's especially hard to imagine Perkins bringing much conviction to dirty humor). "I'm really doing what I wanted Dick Shawn to do," he told *Show*.

"When we realized Tony was going to take over, we all said, 'Oh, no, please don't,' " Elizondo admits. "He was about as wrong for it as you can imagine. It was too ethnic, too particular. But by that time he was too close to it, had too much energy invested in it. He was also battling other private things. He always had a feeling that he should have done something else with his life."

"I'm the first one to admit I'm not ideally suited to play the lead," the star told Rex Reed, "but if you're the director too, there's nobody around to criticize you."

The opening night was pushed again, to June 30, so that Perkins could fly to Los Angeles on the fifth to appear in his first made-for-television film, *How Awful About Allan*, for producer Aaron Spelling. During his absence, Charles Grodin took over, under the direction of

Jacques Levy, but the two did not get along, causing the producers to shut the play down temporarily until Perkins returned on the twenty-seventh.

How Awful About Allan was based on a novel by Henry Farrell, who had written *Whatever Happened to Baby Jane?* A psychological thriller about an emotionally troubled blind man who returns home from a mental institution to live with his sister and the mysterious boarder she has recently taken in—who seems to want to harm him—*Allan* co-starred Julie Harris as the sister, and Joan Hackett, who would later play a key role in *The Last of Sheila*. To save time getting into character, Tony had a pair of opaque contact lenses made at his own expense so that he would actually *be* blind during the shoot. But *Allan* was little more than the first in what would ultimately be a long line of mediocre suspense films for the actor.

He returned to the Truck and Warehouse Theatre just in time to play *Steambath*'s final three previews and prepare for opening night. If he'd been rigid before, he was now frantically so, constantly giving the other actors notes, even as late as a half hour before curtain, which was against Equity rules. When it happened with Hector Elizondo, they had words backstage. According to one cast member, "Hector said, 'Fuck you, forget it, I'm doing it in the way I want to do it,' and Tony acquiesced. Tony was a masochist. He liked punishment."

"He wouldn't stop with his picky details and meaningless little notes," Conrad Bain confirms. "I would come offstage having just done a scene with him, and he'd still be giving me directions. I didn't know what the hell he wanted. Finally one night I said, 'Look, Tony, don't give me another note for any scene I have onstage with you because there's no way you can have perspective on it.' Total silence. Snit. He never really spoke to me again after that."

Set designer David Mitchell says that Tony "had a Hamlet-like quality of indecision. He understood things in such complexity that as a director he found it difficult to simplify them. It would have been easier for him if he'd been less of an intellectual."

Nevertheless, Gabor Morea maintains that as an actor Perkins was "very giving. He was committed onstage and wanted you to look good when he was up there with you."

When *Steambath* finally opened, the reviews were mixed, most critics predictably citing Tony's performance as the major flaw. "Mr.

Perkins just isn't the soul of comedy or Friedman," Martin Gottfried wrote in *Women's Wear Daily.* "Perhaps it's because he just can't get excited about anything, and comedy is energy. Hysterical self-pity is at the core of Friedman's comic truths and Perkins is always calm. He is an introvert and the hero is an extrovert or, if you want to put it another way, Friedman's work is deep Jewish and Perkins is Wasp enough to start a nest."

"The play has been staged . . . firmly and vigorously," conceded Clive Barnes. "Mr. Perkins is fine but perhaps a little too Wasp-like. . . . On the other hand, [he] does deal very well with the central issue of Tandy's failure. . . . Perkins does express exactly his sense of inadequacy."

"Considering all the camps, cliques, backstage friction, and problems, I'm amazed we're open at all," Tony complained to Rex Reed.

Buck Henry, who saw both Rip Torn and Perkins in the role, remembers Torn's interpretation as "hilarious. Tony was less hilarious, but more Kafkaesque. I was always worried about the towel, that was my problem with the play. Of course, Rip didn't give a damn about it." Whereas Torn had performed the part stark naked except for a towel—which had occasionally slipped open, evoking horrified gasps from the audience—Tony modestly wore briefs on stage. "Tony liked the teasing aspect of it, but didn't really want the audience to be disturbed," Henry explains. By 1979, when Perkins allowed himself to appear nude onstage for a scene in Bernard Slade's *Romantic Comedy,* his feelings for the audience would no longer be quite so polite.

After the opening, his cast's attitude toward him was not so polite either. Backstage was one long dressing room that spanned the width of the theater; Tony, the star, had the left corner to himself, the other men were in the center, and the two actresses in the show shared the extreme right end of the room. "People slowly began moving their stuff closer and closer together on one end, leaving Tony on the other end all by himself," Gabor Morea recalls. "It was so cold, nobody would even say hello. You'd see him down there, getting ready for the show, looking in the mirror at what everybody else was doing. It was incredibly tense. He reacted like it was them against him."

"Tony got very paranoid," one actor says. "If he saw a group of us talking together, he would come up and say, 'Are you talking about me?' " Many of the actors began to wish the play would just close.

Perhaps to counteract the guilt brought on by the venomous back-stage atmosphere, Tony indulged in bursts of dissociative generosity; he sent the balding Morea to his hair-popping salon ("it was *too* bizarre"), and paid for acting lessons for an ambitious cabdriver he barely knew. Morea remembers feeling sorry for Perkins "because you could see the pain he was going through, and he would not ask for help. He wasn't able to do that."

But alone at Hector Elizondo's for dinner, the struggling director seemed to relax. It was clear to his host that Perkins liked "small gatherings, being with people he knew. That's when he suddenly became another Tony Perkins, animated, telling stories, whereas in public he was very cool, guarded, stiff. That was his protection. Privately, he didn't seem like any kind of movie actor. He talked about other things—the environment, love, books, art. He was starting to talk about family."

"He was in analysis and was obviously thinking about a whole different lifestyle," David Mitchell adds. "He would let things slip during conversations, and he always had questions about my kids—the way they were growing up, how they were at that age. It was well beyond politeness. He was curious."

Steambath closed on October 18, 1970, after just 127 performances. Despite the producers' high hopes, it never made it to Broadway. There was no closing night party. "Tony was greatly relieved," Gabor Morea observed, "which was unfortunate because it could have been a glorious experience. Instead, this happy, excited director turned into a caged animal in a corner."

But Perkins wanted another opportunity to prove himself. Grover had recently directed a successful production of *Pinkville*, an antiwar play by George Tabori, at the Berkshire Theater Festival. Backstage, Tony confessed to David Mitchell that he was looking for a job. Two years later, Perkins would try to team up with the designer again for a staging of *The Guardsman* at Joseph Papp's Public Theater, but the plans would fall through. By then, Tony would be taking control of his life in a very different way.

Anthony Perkins still had his fans. Abbe Miller was a fourteen-year-old Chicago girl who had seen *The Matchmaker* on TV and promptly developed a huge crush (to this day, young girls are still seduced by his image, in pictures as unlikely as *Green Mansions* and *Murder on the Orient Express*). "I had this tremendous drive, and I wanted to meet him," she recalls, "but I didn't want to be just one of these kids who puts pictures on her wall." Instead, the teenager wrote an autobiographical script about her mother, who was a substance abuser, with a perfect part for Tony: the handsome doctor who saves her in the nick of time. She sent him the script via his agent, and began phoning the Truck and Warehouse Theatre to ask the stagehands if he'd received it.

"Tony would get on the phone, and he'd put on all these voices," Miller remembers. "I'd say, 'I know who you are, and I want to know if you've read it.' He would never give me a straight answer. But I must have gotten to him because one day my mom handed me a letter from Mrs. Osgood Perkins. I thought, 'Oh, my God, who could this be?' It said, 'I am Anthony Perkins's mother. I take care of most of his mail. He has read your script and he thinks you're very talented.' "

A correspondence began between the "Mysterious Lady" and the fan; it quickly blossomed into a friendship that would last nine years, until Jane's death. As she had with Cary Fuller and others, Jane became a sort of surrogate mother for Miller, a voice of reason and constancy for a girl who had none in her life. Like Michaela, Abbe was younger, troubled, and fired with ambition. She regularly poured out her personal problems in letters, and called Jane collect every Sunday.

"Janet knew everyone in the theater," Miller says, "but they weren't lasting friends. She gravitated more toward younger people that she could nurture. She would send me checks, gifts in the mail. She sent me money. She'd say, 'Go buy yourself something frivolous.' She sent me postcards from everywhere. She saw something in me, and I wish to God I'd done something to deserve it." What Miller had done without realizing it was fill the emptiness left by Michaela's absence and Tony's indifference.

Mrs. Perkins was admirably nonjudgmental about Miller's dilemmas at home, and encouraged her to write, becoming a mentor as well as a mother to the girl. Occasionally Jane even arranged for Tony to say a few words to her on the phone. When Grover Dale wanted a recipe from a certain famous Chicago restaurant, Tony had Jane ask Abbe to track it down and call Grover with the information. Eventually, Jane even introduced the girl to her dear friend Teno Pollick, and the two began a correspondence of their own.

"Janet wasn't open about Tony's relationships," recalls Miller, who knew the score even then. "Everyone was a 'friend.' One time I asked in a letter if Tony was gay, because there was a rumor in my high school, and she blew me off, total denial. She eluded it. Instead, she wrote back how most people in the theater are gay and how there's such a stigma against homosexuality. And this was before the days of AIDS."

While Jane could meddle and manage the outskirts of her son's life all she wanted, there was nothing she could do to mollify his deteriorating life at home. Things between him and Grover had become irreparably rocky. "Anonymous," who had known Perkins years before on the staircase of the Loews Fifty-first Street movie theater, remembers running into him in 1970 at the Epicure's Kitchen on Tenth Avenue at Twenty-third Street; their tables were side by side: "He was alone, very moody, depressed because of his problems with Grover. Tony's sex life was unsatisfied, but he was still madly in love with Grover. Grover was making him very unhappy."

After one particularly bitter lovers' quarrel, Tony urgently invited Ben Bagley to dinner: "When I got there, all the way from Queens, Tony said, 'This is awful, but Grover's coming back and I can't have you here for dinner. Just tell me what to do with string beans.' He'd been in such pain when he'd called me, and when I got there he was elated because Grover was returning. Tony was looking for commitment and a lifelong relationship."

Earlier that year, Tony had recorded "I Cling to You" on *Ben Bagley's Vernon Duke Revisited*, an album that also featured cabaret star Blossom Dearie, Tammy Grimes, and the usually nonsinging voices of Rex Reed and Joan Rivers. According to Bagley, Tony, who interpreted each piece by methodically writing out his feelings about it, whispered his way through the tender song as if he were speaking it to Grover, of which he informed his lover afterward. Nevertheless, by Christmas of 1971, Dale would no longer be living on Twenty-first Street.

In the meantime, while Dale pursued his career as a choreographer, Perkins flew to England and Paris to shoot *Quelqu'un Derrière la Porte* (*Someone Behind the Door*), a quickie French suspense melodrama in which he was cast as an unscrupulous shrink who mentally manipulates an amnesiac (Charles Bronson) into murdering his wife's lover. Like

Perkins had been a decade before, Bronson was a major box-office draw in Europe, largely forgotten in his home country; now it was his name the foreign producers were banking on. When the film opened domestically late the following year, *Box Office* noted that the virile Bronson "comes off the best, displaying vulnerability and a gruff charm. Anthony Perkins, as the unethical neuro-psychiatrist, does not fare as well, failing completely to build an aura of evil."

1971 began dismally.

In February, Perkins's Truro home was robbed, and all of his precious longplaying records stolen.

Later that month a headline in the *New York Times* declared MORE HOMOSEXUALS AIDED TO BECOME HETEROSEXUAL. Therapists claimed to be enjoying a high success rate in changing their patients' sexual orientation using a combination of psychoanalysis and "behavior therapy." One of the sources, Dr. Joseph Wolpe of Temple University's Behavior Therapy Institute, explained how, to "erase their sexual interest in men, [male] patients are . . . subjected to such 'aversive' stresses as mild electric shocks when shown pictures of naked men." Other therapists believed that gay men could overcome their preference through sheer willpower, one of them even going so far as to suggest the organization of a "Homosexuals Anonymous," based on the tenets of Alcoholics Anonymous.

Such thinking was all the rage, and Mildred Newman and Bernard Berkowitz were not immune to it. That same year, they spent twenty thousand dollars of their own money to self-publish a book of their own psychobabble, the simplistically titled *How to Be Your Own Best Friend*, in which the happily married shrinks reduced the issue of homosexuality to an insidious question of positive thinking: "Analysts once thought they had little chance of changing homosexuals' preferences and had little success in that direction. But some refused to accept that and kept working with them, and we've found that a homosexual who really wants to change has a very good chance of doing so. Now we're hearing all kinds of success stories. The nature of homosexuality hasn't changed, but the way of looking at it has."

Two years later, after being acquired by Random House for sixty thousand dollars, *How to Be Your Own Best Friend* would become a national best-seller, the paperback rights alone going for almost a million dollars. Passive Tony could hardly withstand the winds of such widespread opinion.

Also in February, Perkins began work on a new production of Patrick Hamilton's classic thriller, *Angel Street*, which he had been hired to direct for Cincinnati's Playhouse in the Park that spring. Rehearsals began in New York at the McBurney YMCA on West Twenty-third Street. Despite the disappointments of *Steambath*, Tony attacked his new assignment with gusto, ordering his cast of unknowns to play the familiar characters (well remembered from the George Cukor movie *Gaslight*) as younger and more passionate. Wherever possible, he stressed the sexual tensions of the piece, even going so far as to direct actor Bill Moor, who played the murderous husband, to act as if he were suffering from a case of shingles or a sexually transmitted disease, the pain of which would intensify as the plot progressed.

Angel Street opened on April 1, just a few days before Tony's thirty-ninth birthday. Grover did not attend, having already seen a preview (which had not impressed him). Local critics were lukewarm in their praise, but Austin Pendleton, who was about to be in a show at the Playhouse himself, remembers Perkins's production as "emotionally and psychologically rich, full of atmosphere. It was just gripping, and seemed terribly fresh. I was really amazed by it." Tony returned to New York after the opening night, leaving the play to run without him for the rest of its two-month engagement.

In June, rather than go alone, Tony took Christopher Makos with him to France, where he was to do his second film for Claude Chabrol, *La Decade Prodigieuse* (*Ten Days' Wonder*) with Orson Welles and Catherine Deneuve (who was replaced shortly before filming by the less charismatic Marlene Jobert). Based on a lowbrow Ellery Queen murder mystery about a possibly homicidal young man (Perkins, of course) who is having an affair with his father's wife, *Ten Days' Wonder* was Chabrol's most ambitious project to date, boasting a budget of two million dollars.

Chabrol, intending to turn dross into gold, called his film "a Gothic opera" and planned, in typically French fashion, to downplay the plot and "make it more poetic." The result was one of Perkins's most esoteric and unwatchable films yet, which the *Los Angeles Times* said "seems like a parody of *Last Year at Marienbad*" and *The New Yorker* dismissed as "spurious and unfathomably idiotic." The most interesting

scenes in the film are those in which Perkins appears shirtless, displaying the impressive fruits of his rigid dieting and bodybuilding.

Makos says the sojourn was one of many "secret trips" they took together, always keeping a low profile, "because at that time it still wasn't
acceptable to be gay. Tony wasn't scared or paranoid, because he had
dated Tab Hunter, who was caught in all those scandals in the fifties,
which was a much harder time. Obviously, if he could withstand that,
hanging around me wasn't much."

With the camera Tony had given him, Makos took photographs of
all the people they met and visited (which formed the basis of his first
professional portfolio), but "unlike other people, Tony would never let
me take a seated portrait of him. I'd have to take snapshots, and sometimes I resented that. I don't think he wanted to use our relationship
that way. He never wanted it to seem like he was helping me too
much. One sensed that he and Grover had helped each other a lot professionally, and maybe that's why their relationship became something
else. Tony liked keeping our relationship a *relationship*."

"Chris never pursued Tony," maintains Lance Loud, who was one
of Makos's closest friends at the time, "and he never led him to believe
he was in love with him either. Chris was always very up-front. He
wanted to have his own career and maybe a friendly relationship with
Tony with some sex thrown in, but he certainly didn't want Tony to
become love stricken, which I think at one point he did a little bit.
Chris's spurning of his advances may have been one of the things that
made Tony decide to really try and go straight."

He certainly had the right analyst for it. "Most doctors treat homosexuality as aberrant behavior, and Mildred does fall into that category," her patient Joel Schumacher admitted in 1992. Even Perkins's
tight-lipped longtime pal, photographer Paul Jasmin, confessed that
"[her] purpose in life was to change his sexuality."

Though Perkins would always maintain that Newman never
pushed heterosexuality on him—explaining, shortly before his death,
that she was rather "a crusader for a wider road, for choice and limit-
lessness"—he did concede that she battered his vacillating, guilty heart
like a Jewish mother, using the old adage "How do you know unless
you've tried it?"

Reformed, Tony later condescendingly rationalized his own resistance to the opposite sex this way: "It's like someone who only does water-skiing and refuses to try snow-skiing."

Meanwhile, back in Chelsea, Tony was introduced to an attractive young fan who, unlike Chris Makos, actually *was* a hustler. Kerry X. LeBre had started out on Forty-second Street (he was there the night John Schlesinger shot *Midnight Cowboy*) and was one of the first New York rent boys to advertise in the *Village Voice* under "male modeling" and in the *Times* under "actors." His client list included celebrities like Halston, Rock Hudson, and comedian Paul Lynde.

The *Psycho* star fell into a category all his own. "I wouldn't have asked for a dime from Tony," claims LeBre, who fostered a longtime crush on the star. "In fact, even *I* was leading a double life; I never told him what I did."

LeBre recalls that Perkins, in the midst of his breakup with Dale, "was very happy to meet me, very eager to go to bed with me. He was very loving, very touchy, very physical. Very affectionate. But he made me nervous as hell. He was very intimidating just because of his size and who he was." So intimidating, in fact, that it affected LeBre's usually hot sexual performance: "The two times we tried—he wanted to, and I wanted to—I couldn't, because of who he was. As soon as we would get into bed and start doing things, in my mind I would think, 'Oh my God, *this is Tony Perkins.*' I'd met many stars, it was just *him.* He had an incredible aura about him. We were naked in bed, he was very eager, but I just couldn't do anything." Neither marijuana nor amyl nitrite ("poppers," in their original, yellow snapper prescription form), which they had both brought, helped. For Tony, who had been trying to live down his fame, it was yet another kind of disappointment.

"After the second or third time this happened," LeBre remembers, "he still didn't ask me what was wrong. I finally said, 'Hey, I can't do it with you, you're Tony Perkins. I'm sorry, I want to, but I can't.' When I told him that, there were quite a few emotions. He was hurt. I think he may have wanted to pursue something more with me because he really seemed let down by it."

But the two became friendly, talking regularly on the phone and occasionally going out to dinner. Tony frequently stopped by LeBre's apartment on West Twenty-second Street—usually on his way to or from Mildred Newman's office in Greenwich Village. When LeBre asked why he was seeing a shrink, Tony replied point blank that he "wanted to be straight."

"I thought it was kind of strange," LeBre says. "Why was he stopping to see a homosexual when he was going to a therapist to become a nonhomosexual? I got the feeling he was confused even then. But he was such a sweet man."

Perkins loved to kneel at LeBre's feet, massaging his thighs and calves. (The young Grover Dale had been known for his great-looking legs and ass.) "I heard that the reason he wanted to go straight was because Grover had," LeBre adds. "It makes sense. If he was hurt, he might want to go and do the same thing. I had the definite feeling that he was lonely. He was Tony Perkins, very recognizable on the street. There was no way he could camouflage himself. I'm sure that leads to a lonely life. People like me would want to meet him just because of who he was. After I had met him, though, it was nothing like that. I realized he really was a special person."

"Tony's acting ability was pretty amazing," Chris Makos says. "I always wondered when we were doing stuff together if he was being real or if he was using his acting ability to manipulate situations. I sometimes couldn't tell the difference.

"One time I wanted to test his talent, so I asked him, 'What can you do to show me that you really can act, that you really can bring up emotions?' So we went over to one of those bridal shops on Fourteenth Street where they sell cheap wedding gowns, and he just sat right there and cried in front of them. He did. Then I knew he could really act."

In his next film Perkins played a gay man paid by his own mother to stay married to a woman. *Play It As It Lays*, based on Joan Didion's novel of Hollywood existentialism, had all the markings of an important film: it was being produced by the brainy team of Dunne-Didion-Dunne (Dominick–Joan–John Gregory) for Universal and directed by *Diary of a Mad Housewife*'s Frank Perry, who felt so passionately about the book that he had acquired the rights to it with his own money.

Tony felt it was a project worthy of his intelligence and talent. "It's the first good picture I've done where I've played anyone my age," he said.

He was reteamed with his difficult *Pretty Poison* costar, Tuesday

Weld, who had nabbed the lead role of Maria, the cynical narrator/ model turned starlet who is recovering from a nervous breakdown. Every actress in Hollywood, from Elizabeth Ashley to Lauren Hutton, had wanted the part, but much to Frank Perry's regret, Dominick Dunne had pushed for Weld, who was a neighbor of his in Malibu. Perry had been in favor of Bonnie Bedelia. "Maria should have been anorexic," the late director said, "and Tuesday was plenty beefy."

Nor did the director want to replicate the star coupling of Noel Black's film. Though Tony would later claim that Weld had requested him for the role of B.Z., the kinky, closeted, suicidal movie producer, he had actually been the first and only choice. He wasn't even asked to test.

"Tony, at first, was not thrilled about Tuesday," Dominick Dunne remembers, "because he had done *Pretty Poison* with her, and apparently they hadn't gotten on. But I must say they got on in this movie. He was just so fucking perfect for the part. He had that sort of upper-class distance, that in-control neuroticism, which hid a vulnerability."

Perry sensed that there was a distinct parallel between Perkins and B.Z.: "He understood the character profoundly, including the destructive aspects." When a reporter later asked Tony if he had patterned his self-annihilating character on anyone he knew, he replied wryly, "You might say it's taken from life."

Also in the cast were Tammy Grimes as B.Z.'s wife (a last-minute replacement for actress Diana Lynn, who died suddenly), Ruth Ford as his mother, Tab Hunter look-alike Roger Ewing (a friend of Teno Pollick's) as his massive masseur, and newcomer Adam Roarke as Maria's husband, Carter Lang. Shooting began in Los Angeles in early December 1971, moving thereafter to locations in and around Las Vegas, Nevada.

Despite the seriousness of the project and the sophistication of everyone involved—the *Play It As It Lays* set was marked by a thick layer of East Coast snobbery—there was still some risk for Tony in tackling his first obviously gay role. Memories of Paramount troubles nagged, and he was inevitably reminded of his own fallen star in the toppled hierarchy of Hollywood.

For handsome young Adam Roarke, whose short career, like that of his character, had so far been composed of low-budget quickies like *Women of the Prehistoric Planet* and *Hell's Angels on Wheels*, Frank Perry's film was a big break. His first encounter with Anthony Perkins took place at a 7 A.M. makeup call. Roarke had arrived at 6:30 and was half made-up when he saw Perkins in the mirror, standing in the doorway behind him. There were no hellos.

"How many films have you done?" Perkins asked.

"Fourteen," said Roarke. "Why?"

"I've done thirty-five," Perkins lied, and walked away.

"He was upset that I was in makeup before him," Roarke explains, "that I had stepped out of the pecking order."

Their bumpy start, however, softened when Roarke took it upon himself to defend Tony against the crew, who as usual tried to provoke him out of his shyness, often with gay slurs directed ostensibly at his bitchy character, B.Z. (it didn't help matters when Grover Dale paid a brief visit to the Vegas location). Roarke regaled the crew with tales of how Perkins had been his commanding officer in the army, defending him in the line of fire, and so on. Tony was touched, and enjoyed the joke, always wanting to know ahead of time what the macho embellishment of the day would be.

According to Roarke, Perkins was "wound tight, coiled like a snake, always listening to hear what people were saying. If the crew laughed, his body would become even more rigid. He was very conscious of what everyone said."

Tony remained withdrawn even when the cast and crew shared pot and pills to relieve their boredom on location. "Nights there was never anything to do," Dominick Dunne recalls. "We'd all go in somebody's room and hang out and drink or smoke joints or something like that, and then just get hysterical." Adam Roarke remembers Tony stoned as being "even more cut off, almost studying you. It was as if he got high to go deeper into himself." This may have been partially due to the fact that Perkins was preoccupied with writing at the time, working long-distance on the script for *The Last of Sheila* with Stephen Sondheim.

"Tony was a very, very precise person," explains Joel Schumacher, who designed the costumes for *Play It As It Lays* and eventually went on to direct such blockbuster films as *The Client* and *Batman Forever*. "You had to be on your toes around him because he didn't suffer fools. He wasn't a lover of small talk and would cut right to the heart of every situation, every conversation. Many people found this uncomfortable."

When Perkins did come out of his shell, it was usually to spread the gospel according to Mildred Newman, passing out pamphlets of *How to Be Your Own Best Friend* to everyone on the set. Like many people at the time, Schumacher, who had recently "gotten off the needle, as they say in street terms," found *Best Friend* an eye-opener. "For me, having never been in therapy, a lost soul crashing around the freeway of life, it was the first thing I had ever read with any kind of help in it. I was dying of thirst in the desert and it was like someone threw me a Perrier. Tony was on a path. He was a searcher, very involved in what is loosely and vulgarly called New Age philosophy. That's a catchall phrase for everything. But he was dedicated until his death to making some sense out of all this."

Schumacher quickly became a client of Newman's, as did director Frank Perry. Dominick Dunne had also been persuaded to read *Best Friend*, but he "wasn't swept away by it. It was an enjoyable book. But some of the people who went to them were like zealots. She had a huge influence on Tony."

"After therapy I felt much freer and easier as a performer," Perkins claimed. "I was able to walk onto the set or into rehearsal and feel unfettered by any fears or anxieties."

Adam Roarke, however, sensed that Tony's acting "was never totally everything it could have been," that his edgy reserve curtailed his ability to fully express himself. Even an affectionate hug from Tony went only so far, no further, and was accompanied by a trademark twisted smirk rather than an outright smile.

But Frank Perry was thrilled with Tony's work: "He was the only actor I've known whose intelligence did not interfere with his talent or his ability to deliver art."

Indeed, *Play It As It Lays*, though today almost unwatchably dated, boasts what is perhaps Perkins's most mature, understated, self-assured performance in film. As the catty, closeted B.Z., Tony finally allowed himself to look middle-aged and tired, the perfect aging "queen" who's been passing as one of the guys for too long. Yet at the same time there's something relaxed in the portrayal; gone are the twitchy mannerisms, furtive glances, and tics that had characterized his Norman Bates shtick for so many years. When he curls into a fetal position in Tuesday Weld's lap after washing down a handful of Seconals with vodka, it is, as Liz Smith wrote, "a moment of shocking simplicity." When Weld's character declines his invitation to do the same, he tells her flatly, "You're still playing. Someday, you'll wake up, and you just won't feel like playing anymore."

Perkins gave sole credit for his consummate embodiment of the self-destructive B.Z. to the success of his work with Mildred Newman. In essence, *Play It As It Lays* marked Perkins's public denunciation of himself as a gay man.

Critics predicted a load of Oscar nominations for the film. *The Hollywood Reporter* hailed Perkins's performance as "his best screen work since *Psycho* . . . he and Miss Weld are electrifying together." But while Weld went on to win the award for best actress at the 1972 Venice Film Festival, Perkins was again overlooked. The film did dismally at the box office, owing in part to Universal's lack of confidence in it (the studio had wanted to tack on a happy ending) as well as the movie's undeniable disjointedness and ambiguity. Nevertheless, *Play It As It Lays* remained one of Perkins's personal favorite films. "Of his later career," Stephen Paley asserts, "that's the movie he wanted to be remembered by."

It was also, several people claim, the film on which Tony Perkins first met the woman he married.

CHAPTER 18

DEUS EX
MACHINA

ERRY BERENSON was a Perkins fan obsessed and, unlike Abbe Miller, whose only ally was the outcast "Mysterious Lady," one with the right social connections to meet just about anyone she fancied in New York.

Or in London, Paris, Rome, or Milan for that matter.

The twenty-four-year-old photographer, whose work had appeared in *Life*, *Newsweek*, *Glamour*, and most regularly in the "Boutique" pages of *Vogue*, had, like Tony, spent a lonely but privileged childhood in a series of (English, Swiss, and French) boarding schools. But she'd always had her scrapbook of "shy" Tony Perkins clippings to keep her company. Bashful herself, she needed the reassuring fantasy of Hollywood's sensitive, soft-spoken boy next door.

Berinthia Berenson, as she was born in New York in 1948, was the last spawn of a matriarchy of powerhouse women that had started with her grandmother, haute couturiere Elsa Schiaparelli. The faded theatrical glory of Osgood Perkins seemed downright cuddly compared to the dramatic past of her own illustrious line of hard-won "aristocrats."

Born in 1890 to a family of respected Roman intellectuals—her father was dean of the faculty at the University of Rome and one of her uncles was the astronomer believed to have discovered the Martian canals—Elsa Schiaparelli never knew what it meant to be oppressed by one's sex. As early as age six, she ran away from home and was said to have been found three days later leading a parade down a Roman street. Shipped off to an English boarding school at seventeen, she promptly dropped out in favor of a more bohemian existence in New York's Greenwich Village, where she wrote poetry and planned to become an artist.

In London shortly thereafter, she fell madly in love with a French theologian and lecturer, Count William de Wendt de Kerlor, and wasted no time marrying him. The couple moved back to New York, where Elsa gave birth to a daughter, Yvonne Maria Louisa Radha de Wendt de Kerlor. The count, however, soon became smitten with American dancer Isadora Duncan, and he and Elsa were divorced.

It was then, in the early 1920s, as a very *un*fashionably down-and-out single mom, supported by her own mother and living on oysters and ice cream in the Brevoort Hotel, that Schiaparelli began to come into her own. She began a period of ferocious socializing, leaving little Yvonne, whose health was poor, with a nanny (much the way Jane had left Tony with Mimi). During this time she nicknamed her daughter "Gogo" because of the child's constant complaints about her comings and (mostly) *go*ings. At age six, Gogo would be sent away to boarding school, in tacit keeping with the Schiaparelli family (and later Berenson) child-rearing policy.

Two other independent women helped "Schiap" (pronounced "Skap"), as she was called, find her destiny. First, Gabrielle Picabia, the estranged wife of surrealist painter Francis Picabia, gave Schiap entrée to a charmed and controversial circle of avant-garde artists that included Man Ray, Barone de Meyer, Edward Steichen, and Marcel Duchamp; the connections and friendships she made among them would prove pivotal in her future career. Next, Blanche Hays, another New York divorcée, who also had a daughter to raise, convinced Schiap that together as a foursome their two all-female families could live better on the Continent. They promptly set sail for Paris.

Stylish and headstrong, Schiaparelli wanted to break into the world of high fashion, but, not surprisingly, she couldn't sew a stitch. One designer with whom she applied for work even told her she'd be better off planting potatoes than designing dresses. Instead, she started designing gold jewelry, while being encouraged in her loftier pursuits by Paul Poiret. She just needed the right break, the right moment to show off her innate flair for haute couture.

Her moment came in 1927, when she asked an Armenian seam-stress, whose hand-knit peasant sweater she had admired, to knit her a similar one in black and white with a trompe l'oeil butterfly bow on the front. When Schiap herself wore it to a prestigious luncheon for the Paris fashion elite, it created an immediate buzz. High fashion, after all, was dominated at the time by the queen of tasteful understatement, Coco Chanel (who would soon dismiss her up-and-coming rival as "that Italian woman who makes dresses"). In contrast, Schiap's dra-matically artsy design was shocking. When Lord and Taylor placed an order for forty butterfly sweaters, she hired twenty more Armenian seamstresses to fulfill the store's demand, and her career was on its way. (Decades later, in Hollywood, Berry Berenson and a female friend would unsuccessfully try to emulate her grandmother's debut by mar-keting for a short time a line of pricey chenille sweaters and shawls.)

Like Alfred Hitchcock, who brought Salvador Dalí to Hollywood in 1944 to create the dream sequence for his psychological thriller *Spellbound*, Schiaparelli enlisted her surrealist friends, like Dalí and Jean Cocteau, to brainstorm on ideas for embroidery and print patterns. Dalí, for instance, dreamed up a print that made a dress look torn. Shrewdly blending fashion with art, Schiap created, among other things, ladies' hats that looked like lamb chops, and even an otter-fur bathing suit that sold at Lord and Taylor for $395 in 1956. She was the first designer to use zippers as decoration. But most noticeable and last-ing was her use of outrageous colors, like ice blue, poppy red, sun yel-low—and, above all, "Shocking," the vivid pink that became her trademark (and the name of her perfume) at a time when haute couture generally meant Chanel's dignified shades of blue, gray, and black.

"She slapped Paris," designer Yves Saint Laurent said, "she smacked it. She tortured it. She bewitched it. And it fell madly in love with her."

"I like to amuse myself," Schiaparelli explained matter-of-factly. "If I didn't, I would die."

Just three years later, in 1930, she had more than two thousand employees working for her, and by 1935 she had opened a ninety-eight-room virtual factory of style on the Place Vendôme. Hubert de Givenchy and Guy Laroche were just two of the many young design-ers who started out under Schiaparelli's professional wing as stylists.

As for Gogo, the world's first designer baby, at sixteen she traveled with her very own set of "Shocking" silk sheets, and she and her high-powered mother were the toast of both Paris and New York.

But designer sheets were no substitute for the workaholic mother she rarely saw.

School vacations somehow always managed to fall on Schiaparelli's seasonal unveilings, so at these times little Gogo was pawned off on her mother's rich friends. The famous mother and daughter rarely spent more than a few precious days together—precious to Gogo anyway.

"People quivered when she arrived at her Place Vendôme boutique," Gogo told *Vogue* magazine decades later. "She could be quite scary, even to me. She would sit imperiously on her sofa for long periods, often in silence. Mummy was a real Italian, fiery and willful."

When the Second World War broke out, Gogo was enjoying life as a London debutante, attending a constant round of chic soirees, drinking martinis and posing with lengthy cigarette holders. But that didn't stop her from volunteering to help evacuate expectant mothers from the city or becoming an ambulance driver in France for the French Army Red Cross. When the Germans invaded, the U.S. ambassador urged Gogo, who was American by birth, to leave France. Her mother agreed, and arranged for her to catch a boat in Genoa.

While crossing the Atlantic, Gogo met Robert Berenson, the handsome twenty-seven-year-old Grace Line travel executive and great-nephew of legendary art critic Bernard Berenson, and they were engaged in February of 1941.

But Schiap was adamantly against the match. "She was jealous," Gogo admitted. "I ended up eloping."

After the war, during which the couple had been separated for two years while Gogo served all over the world with the American Red Cross, the Berensons settled in New York, where Robert (or "Berry," as Gogo called him) was president of two of Aristotle Onassis's shipping companies. In 1947, they had their first child, Marisa (short for Maria Louisa, like her mother), and the following year another daughter, Berinthia, whom Gogo nicknamed "Berry Bee" to differentiate her from Robert. Onassis was the younger baby's godfather, and Diana Vreeland unofficially christened the girls the "White Star Line children," after the sister ships the *Mauretania* and the *Berengaria*.

Marisa and Berry were born into a charmed world populated by New York's high society—the Millikens, Mortimers, Cochrans, Phippses, Burdens—and European royalty like the duke ("Duky" to Gogo) and duchess of Windsor. But when Robert became a diplomat in 1958, Gogo felt the best thing to do, because of the extensive travel demanded by his job, was to send the girls away to the best boarding schools that money could buy. Thus continued the hands-off parenting legacy started by her own egotistical mother.

"I wanted them to have wholesome childhoods," Gogo claimed.

Though summers were spent together either in the Swiss Alps or on the beaches of the Riviera, the Dalmation coast or Tripoli—and winters at the family chalet in Klösters, where they were surrounded by movie industry transplants like Gene Kelly (who taught the sisters to dance), Deborah Kerr, and Irwin Shaw (both of whom had worked with Berry Bee's future mate, Anthony Perkins)—boarding schools meant separation and loneliness for the two privileged girls. They lost themselves in movie star scrapbooks, Marisa's full of images of the silver screen goddesses she longed to emulate—Audrey Hepburn, Lauren Bacall, even Jayne Mansfield—Berry's bursting with clippings and portraits of her teen heartthrob—gangly, gawky, adorably lonely Tony Perkins.

"I always had such a crush on Tony," she recalled years later. "Once when he came to live in Paris, Marisa and I went through all the phone books trying to find his number." (Oddly, it was after seeing him in Phaedra, one of his weakest roles, that Berry Bee became enamored.)

The girls were brought up religiously as Italians. At one point, Berry even attended a convent school in Paris. "I was raised as a Catholic," she told Redbook in 1974, "but there was something scary and haunting about all those black-clothed figures running up and down the halls. And there was a madhouse next door." Black must certainly have seemed strange to the granddaughter of Elsa Schiaparelli. Whatever the case, their impersonal upbringing instilled in both sisters a sense of isolation and independence.

In early 1965, Robert Berenson died at the age of fifty-one, after a long battle with cancer. Both daughters had returned to New York the Christmas before to be with him during his final days. But when their sad vigil was over, seventeen-year-old Marisa refused to go back to the constrictive life that had been arranged for her in Europe, particularly in Florence, Italy, where she had been enrolled in a school she described as being "like a concentration camp." Tall and striking, the five-foot-nine, 112-pound Marisa decided she would stay in Manhattan and work for a living as a model—but to her immediate disappointment she was rejected by the powerful Eileen Ford Agency.

"The Empress of Fifth Avenue," as longtime family friend Diana Vreeland was known, came to her rescue, featuring the beautiful drop-out conspicuously in *Vogue*, and propelling Marisa Berenson almost overnight to supermodel stardom. "She was a top model from the first photograph," Halston told Eugenia Sheppard. "She simply can't take a bad picture." Marisa's meteoric career would eventually include no less than nine *Vogue* covers, and roles in several important films.

As usual, Schiaparelli was furious. "She was horrified and didn't think that girls from good families should do modeling," Marisa recalled bitterly in 1990. "Here she was involved with fashion all her life. She wanted me to settle down with somebody respectable and do all that, whereas she had left home and started a career and was incredibly famous in her own right and did it all by herself. She certainly didn't open doors. It was more of a hindrance than anything having that kind of background."

Diana Vreeland put it more bluntly: "Marisa was uniquely beautiful and adored by men. Her grandmother was neither. It was a case of pure jealousy."

"Mummy never forgave Diana Vreeland for launching Marisa's modeling career," Gogo admitted to writer and friend Nuala Boylan in 1993. "Secretly, I think she envied Marisa's daring and gutsy decisions, like her nude portrait in *Vogue* [there would also be two spreads in *Playboy*]. Mummy called her autobiography *Shocking Life*. But what was so shocking about it? Marisa was the genuine shocker. Sometimes it was volcanic when all of us got together."

"God help you if Schiap didn't love you," says artist Harold Stevenson, a longtime confidante of all three generations of Schiaparelli–Berenson women, "because she had passions of hatred as strong as passions of love. She was extremely difficult with Marisa; they were too much alike and were always kind of head-on. But Berry was very different from Schiap, so her grandmother rather adored her. Berry's shyness and kind of natural, throwaway beauty Schiap thought were divine. In other words, Berry could do no wrong."

While big, beautiful Marisa rebelled against the family, asserting herself and her obviously full-grown sexuality, little Berry stayed instinctively on the sidelines and watched. More all-American looking than her exotic gazelle of a sister—shorter, blond, and chubby, with an upturned pug nose—Berry was the natural tomboy of the two girls. It was obvious that she could never compete with her flamboyant sibling. But winning her grandmother's admiration proved early on that her own particular brand of anticharm could attract the love and attention that was so hard to come by in her high-flying family. Like Tony, who had coped with his father's posthumous legend by adopting the exaggerated persona of a needy, innocent boy, Berry had no choice but to let her difference be her calling card. Amid glittering social crowds, her studied simplicity created an aura all its own. Tony Perkins had done the same thing years before in Hollywood.

"Berry was always the good one, the funny one, the pretty one," Marisa claimed in 1985, ". . . my mother always called me a little monkey."

"She can wear a shower curtain and look fabulous," Berry said of her sister.

While Marisa never stopped complaining that Schiap had "made life hell for me," Berry would quietly rebut that their grandmother was, actually, "very, very sweet."

Many people saw their basic differences as a veiled sort of sibling rivalry. "They were competitive, but in a weird sort of way," says photographer Peter Strongwater, who later shared studio space with Berry in New York. "Marisa so overshadowed Berry, that's why I always thought Berry clammed up and became a very private person. She really tried to be as diametrically opposite from Marisa as she could be. I mean, if Marisa would wear fourteen thousand jewels and Halstons and stuff, Berry would come in a pair of blue jeans and a suede jacket. So it was competitive, but actually a smart move. I guess it was the only move that Berry could make. I mean, she hardly ever dressed up and Marisa always came looking like she'd just stepped off a *Vogue* set."

Berry, who considered herself the ugly duckling, protested when Halston asked her to fill in for Marisa at a runway show: "Oh, no. I can't. You don't understand. I'm fat and not very pretty." But she did it anyway. By 1970, both sisters were listed among the twelve best-dressed women in fashion.

"I don't think that Berry is capable of sibling rivalry," says Joel

Schumacher, a longtime cohort of both sisters. "She would cut off her arm for Marisa. What would their rivalry be? Marisa was a great model and an actress and has an international beautiful-people life. Berry got married and stayed at home. So where would the rivalry be?"

In 1976, three years after her dream-come-true marriage to Tony Perkins, Berry told *Cosmopolitan* that she and Marisa were "so different that there's never been any serious competition, no threatening rivalry. She has always done the glamorous things. She became a model. I became a photographer. She became a film star. I married one." (This was said just as Marisa, after a string of failed romances with European gliterati, was about to throw herself into a brief and violent marriage to American millionaire Jim Randall.) Somehow, the "White Star Line children" always managed to run neck and neck.

Meanwhile, the sisters were united in their shared distance from the neglectful Gogo. "[She] is totally oblivious to what I went through growing up," Marisa confessed in 1977. "We speak of my childhood, and it's as though we were describing two different people. . . . Diana Vreeland was more family to me than mother."

Berry had earlier admitted to the *New York Times* that she saw Gogo "irregularly; sometimes two or three years go by. I really don't have that much in common with her." By the late 1960s, when both girls were based in Manhattan and working at their separate careers, they claimed to have "not even a dime" of family money at their disposal, nor any trust funds to help them make ends meet.

For Marisa, of course, money was no problem—but her complicated life as a glamour queen was, and it fell to her hefty, athletic, sensible sister to both scold and soothe her. "Berry loves her sister and has an almost motherly feeling toward her," *Vogue* editor Carrie Donovan noted in 1971. "It couldn't have been an easy role. Marisa has always been a star. . . . [Berry] was quite a chubby child. But it never occurred to Berry to be jealous." Not even when Marisa, hailed as "the Garbo of the seventies," was being glorified on movie screens all over the world in Luchino Visconti's *Death in Venice*. (The revered Visconti, an old friend of the family, had cast Marisa in his 1971 film after spotting her in *Vogue*.)

Berry had first met Carrie Donovan in London, where she'd been living with Gogo since her father's death, boring herself with secretarial courses. Finally, with some string pulling from Marisa, she'd been hired as an assistant to photographer Patrick Lichfield. During a *Vogue* shoot in Dublin, Berry and Donovan had hit it off. When Berry arrived in New York to strike out on her own as a photographer, she called Donovan, and was soon hired to shoot *Vogue* "Boutiques," the candid party and social shots that regularly appeared on the back page. No doubt her famous surname added cachet to what was otherwise an afterthought in the magazine. Everyone in New York knew her as Marisa Berenson's baby sister. It was an identity she would never fully be able to shed. A personality of her own was something money couldn't buy.

Though Berry lived in a modest railroad flat above a grocery store on Second Avenue at Fifty-eighth Street, which she and her equally well connected roommate, socialite-model-designer Lou Lou de la Falaise, had decorated themselves—their tiny kitchen was painted a deep lacquer red and the flat was strewn with seductive Turkish pillows and Indian tapestries—her family name gave her entrée to all that was exclusive and au courant in New York, from the eclectic Riverside Drive salons of Maxime McKendry (Lou Lou's mother and the wife of John McKendry, curator of the Metropolitan Museum of Art), where people like George Plimpton, Diane Von Fürstenberg, Patti Smith, and Robert Mapplethorpe were thrown together to share ideas and elegant dinners, to the decadent downtown parties of the Andy Warhol Factory.

And then there was Halston, whom Berry met through his brilliant sketch artist, Joe Eula, with whom Lou Lou had roomed before her. "It was the beginning of the seventies," Eula recalls fondly, "the beginning of the [Halston] boom, and we were all just thrown together, all different ages, all different cultures. And in came this marvelous blond, a really, really naive Cinderella. We all adored Berry."

Indeed, Berry struck many people in Halston's fast-track New York–Fire Island crowd as a wide-eyed anomaly, a wholesome wallflower who was unaffected by the drugs and rushing ambition that surrounded her. "She literally had no airs," says photographer Gerard Malanga, who at the time was the "official poet" in Halston's court. "She was always in the shadow of Marisa, but was diametrically very different from Marisa. She wanted to be very down-to-earth. She didn't brag about her background. Whatever her family history was, she really transcended all that."

Rock singer and poet Patti Smith, who met the Berenson sisters at Maxime McKendry's, remembers that Marisa tended to draw conversations to herself, while Berry was always an attentive listener. "She seemed unspoiled, uncompetitive, and really interested in what other people had to say," Smith remembers, "at a time when we were all struggling." Photographer Robert Mapplethorpe, another McKendry regular, was touched by Berry's open-mindedness and curiosity about his work, years before it ignited a national controversy.

"Marisa, of course, was the bombshell," Joe Eula observed. "But, underneath all those marvelous blond Goldilocks and that f-eleven click eye, Berry was a very beautiful gal—with a sense of humor that was, and is, just as keen as a razor's edge. And a little bit dark.

"On the surface it was all that [naïveté], but she was not unaggressive. She was a very good photographer, and she thought nothing of running around—she was madly in love with every rock star. I mean, Jim Morrison, she'd just faint at the name. And when she photographed Ryan O'Neal, she went crazy over him too. This, of course, while she was putting up pinups of Tony Perkins, the man of her dreams, on the wall of her heart."

While Marisa's love affairs with Euro-playboys like Baron David de Rothschild reaped tons of publicity, her little sister was not exactly lacking for attention. "Berry always had a coterie of beautiful young men around her," remembers actress–writer Jennifer Lee, who roomed with her for a while. "She knew everybody in fashion, and was very comfortable in the mix of gay men. Very comfortable."

Perhaps too comfortable. Without fail, almost every man Berry dated was gay. She developed a crush on Robert Mapplethorpe's lover-assistant, David Croland (they went on "double dates" with Robert and Lou Lou), and briefly attempted to out-Marisa her sister with, as Jennifer Lee recalls, "some young baby baron or prince or something who was very weak and, to me, obviously gay."

"Berry traveled in a very high homosexual group," Peter Strongwater confirms.

According to one close friend, it was no accident: "Berry had a definite penchant for homosexual men, which was kind of odd. It was just something she was into. Maybe it was a way for her to protect herself from getting hurt, being with a passive individual as opposed to an aggressive one." (Decades later, after years of living in contagiously homophobic Hollywood with Tony Perkins, Berry would deny ever

having had any knowledge of the sexual preferences of her sophisticated fashion friends—or even of her husband's early lifestyle.)

It was therefore not surprising when, in 1969, Berry got together
with Richard Bernstein, an up-and-coming young artist whom she met
at an open-house party in her loft. Not only was Bernstein's sexuality
moot, but in keeping with Berry's democratic image, he was a poor
Jewish boy from the Bronx. In other words, the type of man Marisa
wouldn't be caught dead with.

"[Being around] royalty was second nature to Berry," Bernstein recalls. "She used to say to me, 'We're invited to my godmother Jackie
[O.]'s for dinner,' and I'd say, 'Oh shit. Let's get some Chicken Delight
and go watch a movie.' They were tolerant of me."

Like the movie star who would eventually become her husband,
Bernstein was waging a psychological war with himself, struggling in
analysis to subdue his own sexual preference for men. "It was one of
those chemical things," Bernstein remembers of first meeting Berry.
"We became friends and started dating. She was a lovely, extraordinary
human being."

He saw their relationship as part of his "working goal" to "straighten
up and fly right": "I wanted to make this thing with Berry work, and
everything that I was working at—to have a relationship, a heterosexual
relationship—all worked. I was actually surprised because on our second
date we became intimate, and it was kind of wonderful.

"At that time I knew I was bisexual. I talked to Berry about it afterward, and it was okay. We were lovers. She was glowing and losing
weight. She had been a little chunky, a wallflower living in the shadow
of her glorious, glamorous sister."

Many of Berry's friends balked at their sudden romance, viewing it
as a case of unabashed opportunism on his part. "Richard was in love
with Berry, I don't know why particularly," Harold Stevenson says. "It
was kind of embarrassing for her. She was a devoted friend, and they
were very close and went around together. Richard, I suppose, thought
she was a good catch. She loved him as a friend, but she was never in
love with Richard."

According to Jennifer Lee, "Berry was in a fast track with a very
high profile group of fashion people and could introduce you to just
about anybody. Richard was very ambitious and attached himself to

something that looked on the upswing. He lost a lot of faith when they split up."

Berry rejected her friends' warnings that Richard was a hustler who was out to use her for connections. "She didn't want to know," Bernstein recalls fondly. "She was wonderful, and always loyal."

Berry, too, had her detractors. Perhaps because of her healthy, outdoorsy good looks and the fact that she was dating Bernstein, there were flimsy rumors around town that she was lesbian.

Gerard Malanga never believed it: "Berry was a sort of tomboyish person, but in a very feminine way. There was nothing butch about her. And she was very sensitive. She had the kind of emotions where she could cry when she needed to."

"Berry would touch anyone, and that was pure affection," Joe Eula clarifies. "But a dyke? No way, no how. Her third sister was really Lou Lou. They might have been close, like two kids madly in love with each other at the same age, in adoration of each other and smoking the same kind of marijuana. But a dyke? Tsk-tsk-tsk. In fact, women frightened Berry—well, aggressive women did. She loved Elsa Peretti, but she was scared to death of her." With Gogo and Marisa, Berry already had her timid hands full.

But Grandma Schiaparelli was another matter. Eula recalls an unusual dinner party at his apartment on West Fifty-fourth Street for Schiap, Gogo, and Gogo's new husband, the Marchese Gino di Cacciapuoti de Giugliano, whom she had met and married on the isle of Ischia in 1968. "We were like little kids entertaining the king and queen," he says, "scared to death—then off, one by one, in the back, to take whatever drug got us back in that room. Schiap stayed until three o'clock in the morning, Berry sitting at her feet, not in idolization, but in just adoration."

Like Tony, who needed a semblance of family he'd never had, Berry instinctively drew older women to her, bewitching them with her virginal looks and caring manner. Something she'd been denied as a child, a mother's unerring love, she intuitively knew how to give back to her elders, who had long given up on getting it from their own daughters in the chill society of Park Avenue. In fact, so winning was Berry's way with people that she soon usurped her busy sister as Diana Vreeland's favorite orphan.

"According to Berry, she had never been lonely," Richard Bernstein says. "She'd always had her mother and her grandmother and her sister to take care of. She'd always felt this responsibility and the pressure of Schiaparelli, to be the strong one as opposed to the flighty one. Marisa would always put her foot in her mouth socially, emotionally, and careerwise, but Berry was like the Mother Courage for the whole family."

"Both sisters were neglected," Joe Eula says. "But Diana adored Berry, and she was always counted in at Diana's dinner parties—a lot more so than Marisa, who was always used as an ornament. With Berry it was the 'Come on, young lady, you sit next to me, we'll protect you,' kind of thing."

Vreeland was also one of the few people who approved of the relationship with Bernstein, even when Berry photographed him nude for *New Woman* magazine. "She liked what I did for Berry," Bernstein maintains. "She saw me bring out this wonderful femininity, this twinkle in the eye. It just happened. We were lovers, and Berry was happy. I tried to inspire her, give her art history—I told her a lot about her own family [i.e., art critic Bernard Berenson], which she didn't even know. We went to old movies, and I would show her lighting and make sure she knew who all the great photographers were."

Together they traveled and took photographs. They were engaged, and even had names picked out for their future offspring. But the demands of their respective callings persisted. Richard's paintings were shown at galleries around town, while Berry waited for the next boost to her laggard career. "One year I earned ten thousand dollars," she later recalled, "and was thrilled until I realized that my expenses were eight thousand dollars."

According to Peter Strongwater, "She could have been much more ambitious considering the access she had to people. She wasn't burning up the midnight oil. She would do the shooting and kind of whine, wondering why she wasn't getting better pages or more pages. I never got the sense that she was out there looking to use people to get ahead. She wasn't a hustler, by any means."

"Berry was the worst photographer in the world," another friend says.

An impromptu Halston shoot in Strongwater's studio, arranged by Marisa, helped legitimize the winsome cameragirl's reputation. Styled by Elsa Peretti, modeled by Marisa, and shot by Berry, the session,

Strongwater says, resulted in some "great pictures for that time. It was all very loose, there was lots of wine and stuff."

Meanwhile, Fred Hughes and Andy Warhol had begun to take an interest in the Berenson–Bernstein coupling. "Andy was incredibly envious," Bernstein claims, "working his web of public relations to get into [the fashion] world." Consequently, in 1972, Warhol offered him the position of art director at *Interview* magazine, with a job for Berry taking the celebrity portraits for the cover (many of whom she was able to recruit). They began working as a team, Richard adding his trademark color airbrush strokes to her black-and-white faces. Supermodel Pat Cleveland was their first cover together, followed by Liza Minnelli (shown taking her own picture with a Mickey Mouse camera), Peter O'Toole, and others.

They also began collaborating regularly on features within the magazine—interviews with artists like Larry Rivers and James Rosenquist—with Richard doing the talking and writing, and Berry doing the shooting. She would only agree to do the talking when it came time to interview Tony Perkins, the man she had always dreamed of marrying.

As the lovers became busier and busier, they began to grow apart. Richard took several solo trips to Europe, leaving Berry alone in New York. It was during this time, she later confessed, that she "bribed" her close friend Joel Schumacher, who was doing the costumes for *Play It As It Lays*, to introduce her to Tony Perkins. Exactly where that introduction took place remains something of a mystery.

Several people, including Dominick Dunne, recall Berry arriving at the film's Nevada location, ostensibly to visit Schumacher. "It was there that Tony met Berry Berenson," Dunne asserts. "Joel and Berry were incredibly close friends, and she came out to visit him in the desert with the express purpose of meeting Tony. She had always had a crush on Tony Perkins. She was only there a couple of days, but that's where they met. She just fell in love with him."

Others, like Frank Perry, contend that it was actually in her small New York apartment, which was used as the character Maria Wyeth's bachelorette pad, that their first encounter took place (unlikely, as Tony was not needed for that scene).

But the popular and highly publicized scenario of their "magic" meeting, the one upheld by the Perkinses themselves, is that it took place early that spring at a wrap party thrown by actress Ruth Ford at her lavish apartment in the Dakota, the sinister old building on West Seventy-second Street that was made famous in the film *Rosemary's Baby*. Again, Joel Schumacher acted as the go-between when Berry, her blond hair having just been cut boyishly short by Joe Eula, arrived with Liza Minnelli. "Berry wanted to meet him, and he didn't want to meet her," Schumacher recalls.

By 1993, after nearly twenty years of being perceived by the public and press as an almost saintly Hollywood wife, Berry remembered it differently. "I really didn't want to meet him," she told *Premiere*. "It was one of those things which I preferred to keep a fantasy. But I remember walking into the dining room, and I knew he was standing behind me because he was very intense, and I turned around and there he was. I practically fainted."

"Tony was shy and didn't want to meet any new people," Schumacher maintains. "He was uncomfortable at this party the way a lot of movie stars are. I said, 'No, you're really going to like Berry, she's a fabulous person. Just relax.' And we sat down on the floor and the three of us had dinner. I did not know they were going to fall in love, get married, and have children. I did not fix them up in any way. These were two people I loved, and I wanted them to know each other, that's all."

Berry seized the opportunity to ask Perkins if he would let her interview and photograph him for *Interview*. He agreed, well aware that he would be out of town and unavailable for the next month or longer.

Tony's personal interests at the moment consisted almost solely of piano lessons, blond boys, and therapy. But Mildred Newman was determined to banish the "fear" from Tony's life, to save him from the "monosexual isolation" he had settled for.

"She was constantly provoking me about women," he said in 1992, "asking why I was repressed in that area. We had heated disagreements, knockdown arguments. I would say, 'I don't want to talk about this again today,' and she said, 'I *do* want to talk about it.' We kicked it to pieces."

Newman was relentless, and Perkins began to believe that his lifelong "bachelorhood"—not his career or his problems with Grover—was the source of his ongoing unhappiness. During one session, Newman asked him to fantasize making love to a woman, and Tony broke down. He began to cry, uncontrollably (which he could do on command). She asked him why.

"I don't know," he told her tearily. "It's so sad, so sad."

Saddest of all was the typical lack of tolerance Newman brought to any but her own conventional lifestyle. Tony was about to become one of her "success stories."

In April 1972, Perkins flew to Tucson to make an appearance as a wandering preacher in John Huston's star-studded camp Western, *The Life and Times of Judge Roy Bean*. The film starred Paul Newman, and featured an impressive roster of secondary players such as Jacqueline Bisset, Roddy McDowall, Ava Gardner, Tab Hunter, and a voluptuous young starlet named Victoria Principal, who would later make a name for herself on the hit television series *Dallas*.

Though they had no scenes together, it was the first time Tony and Tab had worked on the same set since they had dared to appear together as guest stars on an episode of the TV game show *Peter Potter's Jukebox Jury* years before. They were still friends. "If you didn't know the stories that Tab Hunter was gay, you would never have guessed," screenwriter John Milius says. "By then people were a little more tolerant. Still, we were around all these cowboys and it was a very strong heterosexual atmosphere. But everyone liked Tony and Tab."

Everyone liked nubile Victoria Principal, too, especially the straight men. "We *all* wanted her," says Milius, "and we all tried." But Principal was untouchable, a walking sexual fantasy no one could have.

No one except Tony Perkins, that is. In what he later told *People* magazine was a matter of "spontaneous combustion," Perkins enjoyed a four-day sex binge with the aspiring actress that left her grateful and impressed—impressed because he claimed he was a forty-year-old virgin. (All the men he'd slept with didn't seem to count, nor did his substantial relationship with Grover Dale. Gay sex, by prevailing standards, was viewed as nothing more than pathetic faux sex for the emotionally crippled, or something only convicts resorted to in prison.) "I tried everything I could think of," he said of his wild nights with the starlet, "because I thought I might never get another chance."

"It was, for both of us, a very special time in our lives," Principal admitted cryptically to *People*. Perkins fervently swore that after their fourth night together all of his supposed anxieties about the opposite sex had miraculously vanished, along with a "feeling of lethargy" that he claimed had plagued him for years. Almost overnight, he had become a real man.

But according to director Herbert Ross, by mid-August "he was terribly nervous, very high-strung, and not happy" when he and co-writer Stephen Sondheim arrived for a few days in the south of France for rehearsals and rewrites on *The Last of Sheila*. Perhaps it was the challenge of facing the demands of a stellar cast that included not only his pal, Richard Benjamin, but James Coburn, Dyan Cannon, James Mason, Joan Hackett, and the number one female sex symbol of the decade, Raquel Welch.

Or perhaps it was the fact that *Sheila*, with its assortment of pathetic, ruthless, "fictitious" Hollywood types, was for Tony a public skewering—a disownment—of the industry he had come to hate. "Tony had the Olympian contempt of a really smart person for the kind of skullduggery and nightmarish obviousness of the business," said film producer Howard Rosenman. "I think [Tony and Sondheim] both had a delicious time satirizing Hollywood."

Naturally, several of the cast members immediately wanted their parts enlarged. "There was fur flying at times," Dyan Cannon remembers, "but Tony was a real peacemaker. And he wasn't afraid to say no."

Originally set on a snowbound Long Island estate, *Sheila*'s puzzling plot, about a diabolical film producer (Coburn) who hosts a weeklong "truth game" for a bevy of his beholden colleagues (all of whom have jangling skeletons in their closets)—in order to find out which one of them murdered his wife—was based on the games its writers and director had enjoyed in New York. Ross and producer John Calley quickly changed the location to a luxury yacht in the Mediterranean, which they both agreed would be more fun to shoot on. Excised completely from the script was a risky scene set inside a gay club, in which the character in question (the screenwriter/closet homosexual, a dead ringer for Tony, played by Benjamin) was exposed in a pornographic film projected on the disco wall.

Left shamelessly intact, however, was the character of Christine, played by Dyan Cannon, a comic man-eating floozy openly based on Tony's (and Cannon's) foulmouthed agent, Sue Mengers. Cannon was even asked to gain some weight for the role. "They wanted me a little rounder," recalls the actress. "They wanted her sassy and a little obnoxious. It wasn't a difficult character for me to play." Most critics agreed that Cannon's hilarious performance stole the picture.

Sondheim had broached the possibility of Perkins's playing Clinton, *Sheila*'s manipulative mastermind, for which he would have been perfectly suited, but at that point in his shaky career Tony rejected the idea flat out.

Sheila was not smooth sailing. First, the yacht Ross had chartered to serve as the location sank near Mykonos on its way to Nice. Producer Sam Spiegel's cruiser, the *Malahne*, was quickly rented as a replacement, but it was shorter than the original boat, and costly sets of the cabin interiors had to be built at the local Studios La Victorine, delaying the production. Further complications arose because of inclement weather, and when the Arab terrorist group Black September threatened to bomb the set because of the number of Jews employed on the film. "The French police refused to protect us," Ross recalls. "We all had bodyguards for about ten days."

Later, when *Sheila* was close to wrapping, Raquel Welch—whom Tony confided to friends he thought was the most physically perfect woman he had ever seen—contrived to get some publicity by walking off the picture, claiming that Ross had attacked her. In turn, James Mason told reporters that Welch was the most inconsiderate actress he had ever dealt with, and the shoot ended in a blaze of animosity. "She really should have done it closer to when the picture actually opens," Tony commented cattily, "when something like that in the paper would have done the picture some good."

The Last of Sheila premiered in Cannes the following May, shortly before its domestic release. Reviews were mixed. *Variety* called it "a major disappointment . . . far from the bloody *All About Eve* predicted . . . simply a confused and cluttered demi-*Sleuth*, grossly overwritten and underplayed," adding that Richard Benjamin's gay confession scene actually drew laughter from the audience. The *New York Times*, however, hailed the script as "a dazzling technical achievement," and the Perkins–Sondheim team won the Edgar Award for Best Mystery Screenplay of 1973.

Tony refused to do any writing on his own. "I asked him to write screenplays for me several times afterward," Herbert Ross says, "but he never wanted to do it. Independent of Steve, he never felt he was good enough."

Though Perkins would work on two more (still unproduced) screen treatments with Sondheim—including a 1940s musical mystery called *The Chorus Girl Murders* for choreographer-director Michael Bennett, who wanted a vehicle for another unlikely leading man, Tommy Tune—both times he had to be coaxed. "Only when I said I would write it with him did he say yes," Sondheim notes. "He was adamant about it. My guess is that he didn't have the courage to do it by himself any more than I did."

Though basically a loner, Perkins hadn't done much on his own in his life. He had certainly never lived alone, until now. He was tired, and unsure of himself.

Dyan Cannon remembers *Sheila* as a special time for Tony, who was in the midst of radically changing his career, and his lifestyle: "He was one of the most sensitive men I've ever known, I think because he embraced so many of the male and female qualities. He never felt it was necessary to be macho, and in that, was just so attractive and so appealing. I found him to be very sexy.

"We confided things to each other. Changes were going on inside of him, and we talked about that. I felt privileged because he really let me in. Before he made the change [to heterosexuality], he was thoughtful about it. Stuff was going on. I just think it was an evolution for him. A better word is an unfoldment. He wanted to launch out into the deep, and open up to areas that frightened him. I really think he was trying to cross the barriers of fear in his life."

Tony would later be quoted as saying that his fear of "beautiful predators," as he called women, had always been so fierce he'd been blinded by hysteria at the mere sight of one. Yet producer Jerome Hellman, who had been George Roy Hill's agent in the late 1950s, remembers that Perkins used to make a big show out of it whenever an attractive female passed them on the street, turning and ogling like any "normal" guy.

Whatever the case, his fling with Victoria Principal seemed to have given him new confidence, hope for a brighter, more acceptable future.

When Tony returned from the south of France early that fall, there was a note from Berry waiting for him on Twenty-first Street, to remind him of the *Interview* piece he'd promised her. She had also left several copious, adolescently fawning messages on his answering machine. They arranged a quick series of "technical" Saturday morning meetings at his town house to prepare for the photo shoot and the actual interview, which Berry would conduct herself.

Andy Warhol, a mischief maker always on the lookout for potential drama, loved the idea of Berry doing the piece alone. She was very excited about it. But when she asked Richard to accompany her as usual, he declined, thinking he would distract her on her first assignment as a writer.

The day of the interview, Berry arrived suffering from a bad hangover. Tony made her fresh OJ and coffee, and they relaxed outside on his sundeck. Topics discussed ranged from his recent films and directorial efforts to his introduction to "poppers" (supposedly on the set of *WUSA*, to make him cry on cue), psychoanalysis, porn films, and voyeurism.

"I honestly can't say at this point in my life what it is I want," he admitted. He then recounted an incident where he had watched a friend of his have sex while hiding in the friend's bedroom closet, carefully avoiding any mention of the gender of the third party involved: "It turned me on, but then it wasn't the watching that turned me on; I wanted to be out there and *not* in the closet, out there in the room with them or just with one of them. So I cleaned up the closet instead."

When Tony mentioned that he loved to cry at the movies, Berry suggested they make a date to see a tearjerker together later that week. He agreed. "After she left, I collapsed," Tony told *Redbook* in 1974, "thinking, What have I done? What have I got myself into."

Meanwhile, Richard Bernstein tried to persuade Berry to tone down the gushing introduction she had written for her *Interview* piece, a virtual valentine to Tony Perkins in which she confessed that she had been in love with him since girlhood, devotedly keeping an adolescent scrapbook of his clippings and photographs "so that I could possess at least some part of him. In my wildest dreams never did it occur to me that one day I might actually meet him." Richard worried that Berry's ode, coyly titled "What's Tony Perkins Really Really Like?," would make her a laughingstock because of the actor's well-known reputation as a homosexual—a reputation of which she was well aware. It didn't faze her a bit.

Berry began refusing all offers of help from her fiancé, especially when it came to the follow-up meetings with Perkins. The whole project suddenly became strictly confidential. "After a while, I got real curious," Bernstein recalls, "because she was putting an awful lot of time into this. I felt like a fool."

Jennifer Lee remembers Berry raving about Tony back at the apartment: "No matter what the cost, she was going after this man. She loved him. And I really think there was more attached to it, too, than love. She saw that with Tony she'd finally be able to come out of the closet as a person."

Tony and Berry never made it to that tearjerker. As Berry recalled in 1993, they didn't need to: "We were sitting there [his place, during their final interview session], and I had a feeling it was like the last time I would ever see him, because I was beginning to feel a bit ridiculous. He put on this Italian record, and it touched a chord in me and I started to cry—hysterically! He didn't know what to do with this weeping woman."

Tony professed relief and appreciation that Berry was "not playing any girlish games. I didn't think there were any girls like that in the world. I couldn't understand why she wasn't already married."

"He fell in love with her and it was as simple as that," Joe Eula says. "It was a very, very whirlwind courtship."

Their sudden romance confused as many people as it inspired. "I never thought of Berry as a very sexual girl," Peter Strongwater recalls. "She just seemed to be almost a nonsexual person, which is why I was so taken aback by the whole Tony Perkins thing. She didn't leave behind a whole string of broken romances or boyfriends—except for Richard Bernstein, and you can make of that whatever you want."

As for Tony, he was not shy about introducing Berry to the men in his life. Christopher Makos remembers being "intimidated by her because she came from a substantial background of wealth, power, position, and I was just a kid from Southern California. I had nothing to hold up against her except my wit, and my strong male good looks at the time—which was something Berry didn't have. But she did have the same sort of haircut I had, and the same strong jawline, so it was interesting. People said that Tony had replaced my looks with her looks. We were the same type."

"If bisexuality means you can get it up with a woman, then I think Tony was," Ben Bagley asserts. "I don't think it was his sexual preference. But I think he found the right woman. I can't imagine him with any other woman. In fact, I refer to her as 'boyishly fetching' in my liner notes."

Makos agrees that Perkins probably didn't expect his orientation to change, "but I think he thought he could put mirrors up and redirect his ideas about sexuality. At least if he was having bad sex with Berry he might have children, which was a goal he had at that time. He always talked about having a conventional family eventually, because he'd already had a counter-style family with Grover and Helen and Stephen Paley. Tony was a creative person and I think he just wanted to do something else." He had also turned forty just months before, and was feeling the pressure of his own particular midlife crisis.

According to Makos, "Tony still desired having sex with men. And I think Berry was prepared for that. She was no dummy. She went after him, and when it looked like the opportunity to play out his desire to have a family, it was perfect. Perfect things just happen."

"She went after him like she went after me," adds Richard Bernstein, who, typically, was the last to learn of the affair. "But not like a vamp or a temptress, you know, just very sensitive. And egged on by her friends."

Halston teased her, "So Berry, I hear you're a star-fucker."

Finally, she had to tell Richard, who still remembers the crushing confession as if it happened yesterday. After a screening of an Andy Warhol film that they had attended with all of their friends, "Berry said, 'I have to talk to you,' so we went to her house and she dropped this bomb on me that she had slept with Tony Perkins. I couldn't believe my ears. All of a sudden I turned into an emotional child and was very mean. It was awful. I was freaking out. She said, 'But I love both of you, and I want us to be close.' I said, 'That's impossible!' "

In a rage, Bernstein told Berry the truth about her new lover, that he was just a shadow of the boys he played onscreen, a notorious gay man whose every spoken word was an act. "No," she protested, "he's going to Mildred Newman and he wants to be straight! He wants to change his life."

"She left me," Bernstein recounts, "and I thought my world was crashing down. I made very stupid attempts in the following week or so. One day I would send her the garden of Eden, a tremendous box of flowers, and the next day I would want to send her a little canary, dead in a shoe box. But I didn't. It was very painful."

So painful, in fact, that Bernstein went on a self-destructive drinking and drug binge. He ended up on Tony's doorstep, stoned out of his mind, sobbing—and carrying a knife. "Tony was very sweet under the circumstances," Bernstein says. "I was amazed he even let me in, because Berry had told him I was freaking out." He accused Perkins of misleading her, and worse, of merely picking her out of a catalogue—*Vogue*—after he had done "all the work" on her, molding her into a self-confident young woman and bringing her out from under the oppressive shadow of her sister.

"Let her make up her own mind," Tony said calmly.

"I said, 'No, no, no, you don't understand—you've probably never had any problem being with someone of your choice, be they man or woman.' I'd been cultivating this relationship for my life, and it just wasn't fair." Bernstein warned Perkins that Berry wasn't in love with him—she was just infatuated with his fake screen image.

"Don't you think I've had this problem all of my life?" Tony replied. "We should let Berry decide."

But her mind was already made up.

Shortly thereafter, the heartbroken, frantic artist tried to kill himself with an overdose of pills; he was rushed to the hospital in the nick of time by Berry and her friends Lucy Saroyan and Jennifer Lee. The next morning a distraught Berry called Tony, who immediately made an appointment for her with his personal panacea, Mildred Newman. (Richard Bernstein, too, called Newman, who he claims had ordered Berry to avoid him. "I want my patients to win," she said, advising Bernstein to go see his own analyst.)

Jennifer Lee accompanied her roommate downtown to see Newman. When the session was over, Tony was waiting for them outside, and the depressed trio went for a walk in Washington Square Park. "Berry loves him madly," Lee wrote in her 1991 memoir, *Tarnished Angel*. "I think he loves her but I can't tell for sure. It's as if he possesses her."

Twenty years later, shortly after Perkins's death from AIDS, Berry told *Premiere* magazine, "A lot of people looked at the two of us and said, 'Who are they kidding? This is never going to work.' I was so naive I couldn't figure out what they were talking about." She also denied any knowledge of her husband's lifestyle at the time. "He told me, and it just didn't register. I had been very sheltered."

"She wasn't naive," Chris Makos says. "Wasn't she going to clubs? Wasn't she involved wth her sister? Weren't they like these party girls? How can you be naive coming from that kind of background—and dating Richard Bernstein?"

"I don't think the word 'naive' is applicable," Harold Stevenson concurs. "I mean, these girls have a certain type of sophistication. But I think they were always innocent. The sophistication didn't kill the innocence."

Though Berry's fashion friends had encouraged her to pursue Perkins, once she "got" him they were less than enthused. The fact that he was a movie star was exciting, but his personality was a major disappointment. No one had expected him to be such an introvert. He didn't like parties, and didn't care about the latest fashion trends.

"He didn't fit in," Joe Eula recalls, "not even for a minute. We all loved *Psycho*, but he was not easy to get along with. I don't think Tony was very taken with the drug scene, and we were. I found him very weird. But he was, that's fact. That was his charm. I think he had engraved that in himself so deeply that he couldn't tell reality from playacting."

"He was Norman Bates," Bernstein affirms, "kind of creepy. It didn't affect Berry. But it affected all her friends. He was hard to talk to, so introverted, so much going on."

According to Peter Strongwater, "Berry and Tony were both very shy and kept very much to themselves. It was an unusual pairing. I never quite got it."

Few did.

Gradually, word of the strange affair leaked out to the press. At the invitation of Stephen Paley, who was now a record company executive, Tony and Berry went on their first public date together, attending the opening night of Liza Minnelli's sister, singer Lorna Luft, at the St. Regis Hotel. Tongues began to wag. After all these years, did Tony suddenly feel it was necessary to be seen with a beard? Was it a publicity stunt? Or was Tony *Berry's* beard? "Who's riding who?" became the joke around town.

"Tony was always looking for answers," Joel Schumacher reflected in *Premiere*. "Being a movie star did not answer the question. Being a household word did not answer the question. What usually happens for a person on a spiritual path is that he meets someone who is a master. The master comes from love. I think Tony met the master when he met Berry."

In February of 1973, about three months after the consummation of their relationship, Berry moved in with her loving disciple. She brought along her Scotty dog, Squadgi, a name she had made up herself meaning "something soft and cuddly." At least Tony liked dogs.

A RECENT HETEROSEXUAL

ERRY HAS SOME FABULOUS FRIENDS," Tony told *Women's Wear Daily* after they'd started living together, "but some of them have been reluctant to accept our relationship. It has to do with jealousy; it must. Lou Lou de la Falaise was funny. She came down and stayed with us and couldn't believe Berry could cook, much less open a jar of Cheez Whiz. Change is hard for some people to take."

His own circle was no less baffled. "I've also discovered that a lot of your friends never wanted you to change," Tony said. "Especially the image that they create for you." Perkins, it seemed, was fighting typecasting in every aspect of his life.

To make an all-around fresh start at forty, he had been trying to negotiate film-directing jobs as well, but for various reasons none of them worked out. As early as 1970, he had wanted to direct *Los Angeles 2017*, a script by Phillip Wylie that Universal owned, about twenty-first-century L.A. residents who have been driven underground by smog. But the infamous "Black Tower," Universal's ominous executive office building, opted instead to give the job to the young Steven Spielberg, who was under contract.

In 1972, ABC-TV offered Perkins the chance to direct a David Wiltse script called *Thriller*, with Noel Black on board as producer (at Tony's request), but after months of preparation, a changeover of management derailed the project. A year later, producer Robert Shaye asked him to star in and direct New Line Cinema's very first script, Richard Maltby's *Killer*, a murder mystery that boasted a puzzle for the audience to solve at the end. Pathologically unable to work (much less live) alone, Perkins again hired Black as a "consultant," but after months of planning withdrew from the project, suddenly unsure of his directorial vision.

A less risky offer came from actress Maureen Stapleton, who requested Tony to direct her upcoming summer-stock production of Neil Simon's *The Gingerbread Lady* when the show's Broadway director, Bob Moore, proved unavailable. Casting would begin in May for a nine-week tour of the New England circuit, which would allow Tony and Berry the chance to spend some time in his beloved Wellfleet.

The actor credited his years of analysis for all the changes he was making in his life, and for what he considered his ability to feel "more in charge of myself, more capable of living my life in a way I can approve of."

"I feel so much calmer now with [Berry] in my life," he told *Women's Wear Daily*. "I feel so much less compulsive, less at the mercy of things. I feel a part of feelings now."

Nevertheless, whenever Berry went out of town on her occasional photographic assignments, Tony would indulge some of the feelings he still had for boys like Chris Makos. "He was so horny one day he called Chris while I was over visiting," Lance Loud remembers. "Chris was really irritated by the fact that Tony would always be calling him from the street corner and want to come over in five minutes, never any planning. He *had* to see Chris in a few minutes, so Chris told me to hide in the bathroom. Chris was very, very discreet and never let on who it was."

Makos eventually let Loud come out, and introduced him to Perkins. "He was very, very nice," Loud recalls. "If he was embarrassed or uncomfortable around me, he never let on. He was extremely easy-going."

Loud was then the lead singer in a punk rock band called the Mumps, and in the bathroom had been trying to get his dyed-red hair to stand straight up like David Bowie's. "I was complaining about how my hair just didn't have the height that I desired, and Tony said, 'Bend over'—I mean, I was fully dressed—and I did, and he took the blow-dryer and blew-dry my hair and combed it. He'd learned on a movie set that if you wanted your hair to stand up, this was how to do it—and it worked fantastically! He really could have had a promising second career."

Meanwhile, when he got into character, his new career as a straight man went smashingly well. "He's very real and brilliant—everyone falls in love with him," Berry cooed to *WWD*. "He's the first man I've ever lived with. It's really nice to have someone to come home to, to share things with, and I really feel at home here."

A turning point came when Berry's little dog, Squadgi, ran into the street in front of the house and was fatally hit by a car. According to friends, Tony was deeply moved by Berry's tears, touched by her vulnerability and the depth of her feelings for the animal; he vowed then and there to protect her from ever being hurt that way again.

Still, marriage was not in their future—at least "not for a while," Berry told the *Times*. "I think living together is just as much fun." Even so, she began to let her photography fall to the wayside in favor of dance classes and acting lessons. "What we have today is as good as a marriage," she declared in *WWD*. "We're in love, and that's something I wouldn't lie about." She failed to mention that Gogo hated the entire situation.

In early May, just as Tony was immersing himself in *The Gingerbread Lady*, Berry dropped a bombshell on him: she was pregnant. They hadn't been trying; she said she'd been using birth control. According to Tony, "There was just no way she could get pregnant."

"There was no way we were not going to have that child," she later said.

Tony was not pleased. At forty-one, he felt he was too old to become a father—a father who might die on his kid—and was disturbed by the fact that it hadn't been his idea. "I had never even held a baby in my arms before."

Berry, of course, wept. "She could cry at the drop of a hat," one observer says. "You have never seen so many tears come out of one person in your life."

An appalled Gogo called from Ischia, begging her "degenerate" daughter to get married right away. Jane and Michaela (who had patched up their friendship) and even Sue Mengers urged Tony to do the same, though Jane was less disturbed by the unwed aspect of the pregnancy than was Michaela, who annoyed Berry with admonishments that no child should be raised without a proper father.

Suddenly everything was moving very fast. In response, Tony sheared off almost all of his hair, down to a very severe crew cut, which was then more in fashion among Manhattan gays than the casual, shaggy look he'd been sporting since *Play It As It Lays*.

Berry offered to have an abortion so that Tony wouldn't feel "backed into a corner." That seemed to ease the tension. But still, her friends had "mixed reactions" about the news of her predicament.

"There was a short period of confusion," he admitted calmly a year later. "The baby was so unexpected. I suggested that the world was changing, that in ten or fifteen years it might be nicer for a child if his parents were *not* married. It was a very good argument, but finally I wasn't totally convinced." A decade later he would remember things quite differently, saying he'd been "thrilled" at the prospect of fatherhood.

They became engaged. "I didn't feel shotgunned into it," Tony claimed. "She wanted to get married all along, but she didn't pressure me into it."

Not only did their engagement get the judgmental Gogo off her back, but her society friends "did cartwheels" when they heard the news. No doubt Mildred Newman did too. To further validate their new identity as a conventional couple, that June Tony and Berry, along with Richard Benjamin and Paula Prentiss, and several other celebrity-patients (including Rex Reed, Nora Ephron, and Neil Simon) appeared in a full-page ad in the *New York Times Book Review* extolling the life-transforming virtues of *How to Be Your Own Best Friend*, which had recently been published by Random House and needed a sales push. Accompanying their photos were testimonial quotes:

"It will change your life," Rex Reed proclaimed. "It has certainly changed mine."

". . . for people who do not love themselves enough," Richard Benjamin declared.

Berry likened the book to "a deep breath of mountain air," and Tony recalled, "On a remote movie location the cast and crew who passed around a simple mimeographed copy of this manuscript called it, simply, *THE* BOOK. Appropriate title, I'd say."

While many were appalled at the shameless snob appeal employed by the ad campaign—"I thought it was grotesque that so many of my friends lent their names to the selling of that book," Buck Henry says, "really low class"—sales soared almost overnight. *How to Be Your Own Best Friend* became an instant bible for the "me" generation, and its authors frequent guests on television talk shows, often accompanied by one or more of their famous clients. According to Tony, everyone "loved" Mildred and Bernie so much that they didn't mind being "exploited."

Less than two months after this public display, Tony and Berry would tie the matrimonial knot. "Without therapy," he later said, "I would never have done writing or directing—not to mention being a husband and the father of two sons."

His closeted double life banished for the time being, Tony appeared to be at peace with himself. Cloaked in the trappings of normalcy—a pretty bride-to-be by his side and a baby on the way—he was flooded with relief, certainly on the professional front. Cast members in that summer's *The Gingerbread Lady* were impressed by his generosity and sensitivity, and his unflappable mellowness in the face of the constant pressures of the tour.

"What was extraordinary was his total accessibility," remembers Nicholas Guest, who played the small role of Manuel. "The whole company was made to feel incredibly relaxed by his presence. It was an extremely pressured situation, moving from town to town, setting up again and again, but he was so secure that he was able to have a sense of humor about everything. He was determined to make it a great time all the way, no matter how much work was involved. It was apparently a very happy time in his life. Berry was always smiling."

Producer Charles Forsythe remembers Perkins as an "easy" director who "reminded me a little of Guthrie McClintic in that way," and Maureen Stapleton confirms that Tony's guidance was always "right on."

Even so, the newly heterosexual director was quick to surprise his cast with occasional barbs of campy humor, usually at someone else's expense. As Guest recalls, "Without batting an eye, he would look at you and say, 'Those clothes are really awful, where *did* you get those *horrible* shoes?'—with incredible timing." He may have been lampooning his fiancée's friends.

Despite the support and backstage visits of a steady stream of show business luminaries such as Walter and Carol Matthau, Harry Bela-fonte, Alan Arkin, Cyril Ritchard, Jill Clayburgh and David Rabe, and even Katharine Hepburn—and Straw Hat Awards for Best Director, Actress, and Newcomer (Lucy Saroyan)—Tony politely bowed out be-fore the end of the tour in order to get married on August 9, 1973. Berry spoke for them both when she said it was "a nice thing to do for our baby."

"I was very pleased for Tony, and hoped he'd be happy," Roger Englander remembers. "He seemed to be happy. I think in a funny way he actually did it to please his mother. Or maybe just to thumb his nose at all the little boys he'd been with. The perversity of it makes sense, in not being second-guessed. I think that was important to him." In some way it was just another strategic move in the broader game of life.

But if Tony was pulling a surprise punch to grab some much needed approval at long last, Jane still knew how to one-up him. Berry quite naturally viewed Mrs. Perkins as the kind of mother she'd never had, and Jane, in turn, tried to fulfill that role, liberally support-ing Berry's pregnancy no matter what. According to her other surro-gate daughter, Abbe Miller, "Jane thought Berry was Tony's saving grace." But when Tony himself came to her for the final approval, she cut him down fast.

"I only hope you're good enough for her."

"That put him away," remembers Gwen Davis, whom Tony later told about the incident in L.A. "He sat there and looked at me, and for the only time in our whole relationship, his eyes filled with tears. After a lifetime of not only not relating to women, but not wanting a woman in his life, he brought his mother a trophy on a tray, and she devastated him. She never acknowledged anything about him."

Berry's biological mother didn't treat Tony much better. To Gogo, he was just a modest New York boy; the fact that he happened to be a movie star certainly didn't mean much to the imperious woman for whom the yachts and balls of Euro-royalty were prosaic.

Apparently, the feeling was mutual. "He couldn't stand her very much," Englander says. "I gathered that she was a real tyrant. Once, when he was in Paris, he took her to the fanciest restaurant for dinner, and they didn't have very much to say to each other. So he said, 'You know, Orson Welles introduced me to this restaurant.' And she re-torted, 'Oh, the duke and duchess of Windsor brought me here.' "

Still, there were those among the Perkins clan who weren't convinced that his new union was the right answer to his recent unhappiness. "I always felt so sorry for Tony because, to tell you the truth, I don't think he should have gotten married," one longtime female friend admits. And comedienne Nancy Walker, who had been a big supporter of Tony's relationship with Grover Dale, was appalled at the sudden capitulation to sexual convention.

Also causing reverberations was the fact that Dale had beat Perkins to the altar by just eleven days, unexpectedly marrying buxom actress Anita Morris, whom he had met in a workshop production he was directing. After firing the leading man "so I could get out there and play the part opposite Anita," Dale added a special kiss to one of their scenes together; their first stage kiss was also their first real kiss. Like Berry, Morris was inducted into therapy with Mildred Newman.

Dale and Morris were married alfresco in West Brookville, New York, on July 29; Tony and Berry wed on August 9—both just a few short months before the American Psychiatric Association, in a major step toward greater public acceptance of gay men and lesbians, lifted its long held categorization of homosexuality as a mental illness. Many insiders felt that Dale had purposely rushed into his marriage out of a feeling of competition with his famous ex-lover. Others felt that it was Tony who had been frantically compelled to "keep up with the Dales."

"They were both approaching forty and decided that they really did not want to die not having children," one associate says. "It was a planned-out, conscious decision, a very clinical thing. They sought out their mates. I don't know if Grover got as good a deal."

Not surprisingly, many people still choose to facilely view both marriages as fraudulent "beard" unions, but the reality was in fact more complex.

"When Tony decided he wanted to have a marriage and children, it must have been an incredible struggle," says Donna McKechnie, whose marriage to choreographer Michael Bennett had also caused controversy. "Just from knowing how he worked, I'm sure he did everything with really serious intent, to the fullest. What it says to me is that he was trying to enhance his life, not change it. Because my own experience with Michael, though not the same at all, was that it had so little to do with homosexuality. The fact is we were in love. Michael made an effort, with great pain, but could not do it. And it had nothing to do with sexual persuasion. It had to do with the fear of intimacy.

"With someone like Tony Perkins, who wanted a family, I just think most people don't understand it. Unless you know all the choices in that person's life, how can you? It wasn't like Tony and Grover were ashamed of their relationship. They were from the times when they were raised. They were sophisticated men, and they were very discreet about it. People don't change that much."

Tony may have had his detractors, but so did Berry—namely her own family, none of whom were present at the small, impromptu ceremony. Buddy Clarke remembers phoning Truro to congratulate Tony; when Berry answered he said, " 'Mrs. Perkins?'—and she got hysterical. She said, 'You're the first person who's ever called me that!' "

Marisa, of course, was thrilled for her little sister, but was too busy globe-trotting to attend. She showed her support in other ways. Shortly after the marriage, in a *Newsweek* cover story called "The Girl Who Has Everything Plus"—which touted Marisa as the queen of the international jet set, among whom bisexuality and homosexuality were considered chic—the still-single glamour girl praised the proliferation of "untouchables" or openly gay men: "I, for one, have become a big fan of homosexuals. I adore them. They are talented, sensitive, refined people who make the best friends. I'd rather go out with a fag than a boring man any day."

So would Tony, who still had his pangs. While pregnant Berry was in Paris with Halston that December to attend the fashion spectacular at Versailles, Tony lingered outside the window of Chris Makos's ground-floor apartment on Waverly Place, staring in long and wistfully at his young blond lover (who often walked around his living room nude) before quietly retreating back to Twenty-first Street.

"He was a very romantic man," Makos remembers fondly. "He was always looking for a good script, and a good director. That was my take on it. I'm sure Berry was probably a good director, and her script was 'Let's Make a Family.' That's why that relationship worked so well.

"I wonder if Tony had lived longer, once that idea of family had been completed, where would he have been? Would he have gone back to the homo life? What was he doing toward the end of his life? Probably trying to take care of his health."

★   ★   ★

Tony stepped before the cameras again that fall in his first film for director Sidney Lumet. *Leaving Cheyenne*, based on the Larry McMurtry novel, not only offered Perkins the chance to work with another top-notch filmmaker, but the opportunity to do "something different from anything I've done the past ten years": to play a red-blooded Texas cowboy who competes with his best friend (Beau Bridges) for the love of a free-spirited woman (Blythe Danner) over a period of about forty years.

Clearly, this was "the kind of transitional role I need," the perfect vehicle to convey Tony's newfound masculinity and maturity to the moviegoing public. He was vocal about the fact that he was sick of playing twenty-four-year-old boys, and vowed that he would make "no more schlocky films." But Lumet had cast the unlikely Perkins because of the "Gary Cooper quality" he'd exuded in *Friendly Persuasion* seventeen years before, a quality that had long since vanished.

Shot mostly on location in Bastrop, Texas, with interiors done back in New York, *Cheyenne* was independently produced by Stephen Friedman, who had brought McMurtry's *The Last Picture Show* to the screen in 1971, under the direction of Peter Bogdanovich, with dazzling results. The combination of talent involved in *Cheyenne*, along with the script's trendy ménage à trois theme, made the project seem like another surefire hit.

But there were snarls, not the least of which was how to make the stars age effectively onscreen. After rejecting the idea of using three different sets of actors for each time sequence, Lumet had to settle on novice makeup artist Phil Leto when two previous candidates canceled. Though no one cared for Leto's work, time and budget constraints prohibited any alternative. "Bridges winds up looking like a student playing Gramps in a high school production," *Variety* later wrote, "Perkins like an emaciated Gregory Peck and Danner not unlike Perkins playing Mrs. Bates in *Psycho*."

There was also trouble with Friedman's script. According to Lumet, the whole cast quickly got the sinking feeling that they were on a "treadmill, that their characters were growing older but not going anywhere. There was no money for art."

Perkins's love scenes with Danner may have been the most self-assured of his career, due no doubt to the confidence boost of his recent marriage, but neither he nor his costars were spared the arrows of the critics when the film was released the following year as *Lovin' Molly*. Vincent Canby of the *New York Times* noted that Perkins, "who doesn't look like the young man in his early 20's he is supposed to be at the beginning, returns to his *Friendly Persuasion* mannerisms. He acts mostly with his jawbone . . . then ages in the stiff-faced manner of a person who's had too many facelifts." The critic also suggested that because the film "is so literally staged and acted . . . one begins to question the true psychological relationship between the two men. Is Molly important to each of them as herself or as a kind of sexual surrogate for the other?" It seemed Tony would never be accepted as a real man, at least onscreen.

But back in New York, he did become a father. On February 2, 1974, Osgood Robert Perkins, "the baby that couldn't wait" as Berry affectionately called him, was born, at a healthy nine pounds, twenty-two inches—and named in honor of both his parents' dads. In typically therapeutic fashion, Tony had assisted at the natural birth.

"I'm pretty calm," he told *Newsweek*. "I don't feel thrown by it."

"Darling, I've re-created you," Berry reportedly said.

Perkins credited Mildred Newman with the delivery almost as much as his wife. "Having a child was not on my agenda," he told the *Daily News*, "but a good psychotherapist is one who tries to encourage a person to find choices for himself and at a certain point I found myself with a choice. Life is so much fuller than if you're exposed to just one choice."

Stephen Sondheim was named godfather to little "Oz." "Maybe now that I'm a father they'll let me play father roles," Tony said.

Just eight weeks after the birth, the Perkins family flew to England, where Tony was slated to appear in Sidney Lumet's star-studded film of Agatha Christie's *Murder on the Orient Express*. Shot at the Elstree Studios, it was the most expensive British motion picture in years, with a cast that included Ingrid Bergman, Albert Finney, Vanessa Redgrave, Sean Connery, Jacqueline Bisset, Richard Widmark, and Lauren Bacall. Though Tony's role as McQueen, Widmark's fey male secretary, offered little challenge and no hope of image flipping, the film was too prestigious to refuse.

Lumet let Perkins "fly" with the part, only occasionally reining him in as he embellished McQueen with all his trademark stutters and nervous tics, almost in a mockery of his famous alter ego, Norman Bates. Over dinner one night, Tony proposed that Lumet direct him in a remake of the Fritz Lang thriller *M*, with Tony cast as the tormented, sympathetic child killer originally played by Peter Lorre. Lumet was intrigued, but after viewing the classic film again, quickly dismissed the idea of tampering with it.

Back in New York, Helen, now a successful literary agent, had come across a script by Russell O'Neill called *Don't Call Back*, a stage thriller about an aging actress who is held hostage in her Manhattan apartment by a gang of thugs, one of whom is her estranged son. She called producer Charles Bowden and recommended Tony as a possible director. (At the time, Grover Dale was enjoying a huge success as director of the hit Broadway musical *The Magic Show*, starring illusionist Doug Henning and Anita Morris.) Perkins had yet to make his Broadway directing bow, and this new play of psychological suspense seemed tailor-made for it. *Don't Call Back* would open July 8 for a one-week run in Falmouth, Massachusetts, before moving on to a pre-Broadway tryout at the Kennedy Center.

Popular television and radio personality Arlene Francis was brought in to star as the terrorized diva, leaving Tony to fill the other parts with unknowns. As the gang leader, O'Neill wanted handsome African American actor Lawrence-Hilton Jacobs of *Welcome Back Kotter*, but Perkins fought hard to cast against type, opting instead for the baby-faced Ernest Thomas, who would later be a regular on the series *What's Happenin'*. Thomas looked more like a good kid gone bad than a brute, a quality that appealed to Tony.

For the crucial role of the son, Tony rejected the blond and eager Dennis Christopher, who was a friend, in favor of a dark-haired young Perkins look-alike named Michael Mullins. "Tony saw the part as one he might play," Mullins remembers. "On some level he wanted to direct himself."

Perkins displayed flashes of directorial hubris, but was quick to back down if called on it. What changes he asked for in the script were usually humored. He completely altered the setting from a lavish Park Avenue duplex, which O'Neill had described in detail, to a more atmospheric unfinished apartment, eerily empty except for packing crates—even though no star the magnitude of the heroine would be caught dead in such a place. According to associate producer Morgan Holman, "We let him do it because he was a name."

The problem of his personality whenever he was off the analyst's couch persisted. "His strong point was he understood drama, he knew what to do," Holman recalls. "His weak point was he was not good in dealing with people. He was not a warm person. He was not a direct director."

Only under the influence of marijuana (he carried cigarette packs full of rolled joints) would the usually withdrawn Tony open up. Stoned, he would become overly friendly, even intimate with colleagues, then regret it later. Producer Charles Bowden, for one, got the impression that Tony was not in complete control of himself.

"The time he thought I gave my best performance was when I had been drinking," Ernest Thomas says. Surprisingly, Tony condoned it. "He said he and a few other celebrities would smoke weed when they did films, that it could open up your creativity and make you do things you didn't even know you could do. He said it kept him from being inhibited." Now, though, Perkins seemed to need it just to cope.

"I found him very nervous, very fidgety, very given to outbursts," Michael Mullins remembers. "Not emotional outbursts, but any communication you might get from him would come only after long periods of holding it back. Then all of a sudden, blah blah blah."

Perkins was fascinated with Mullins, but careful to keep his distance. Some observers interpreted his behavior as jealousy over Mullins's youth, the fact that he could still play the troubled-boy roles that had been Perkins's early specialty. Others saw it as a sexual attraction.

"It was like he wanted to manipulate me," Mullins says. "He would make suggestions, but they were always vague. He would whisper things to the other actors when he knew I could see him, then he wouldn't tell me what it was all about. I'd say, 'Tony, just *tell* me what you want. Believe me, I can give it to you, but this second-guessing is driving me crazy.' And he would say, 'Oh, just keep doing what you're doing. It's fine. Don't worry.'

"Mostly, I remember him leaning against the standing rail at the back of the theater, just intently watching everybody. Then he would give notes, and there wouldn't be any for me. He was trying to trick me into giving him the responses that he wanted. He was so closed off from his emotions, that was the only way he could do it." Tony occasionally invited Mullins to spend his free time at the beach with him and Berry and "Oz," but even during these relaxed moments, a strange silence fell between them.

Meanwhile, in rehearsals the young actor continued to feel "abandoned" by his director, almost as if Perkins got pleasure out of watching him struggle onstage. "It had to do with living in the closet," Mullins realizes in retrospect. "It's an insidious thing that happens. I was obviously gay and in the closet, so was Tony, and the fact that he didn't feel comfortable with me . . . we couldn't be more open with each other because of what that might look like. He couldn't make direct statements or say things that were simple and honest, even if it had nothing to do with either of us. He was just too frightened of what might seep out, what he might let slip."

Not surprisingly, there were miscommunications at the top as well; early in the run, Tony was unable to resist giving Arlene Francis notes between the first and second acts. Naturally, she was infuriated, and complained to Morgan Holman immediately. "I went to Tony after the show," Holman recalls, "and he acted as if he didn't understand— 'Don't they want to know what they've done wrong in the first act?' I didn't know whether it was an act or his true self, but there were times when he'd suddenly get very boyish, and you'd just want to protect him. And then he'd do something that was so hard, you'd think, 'That son of a bitch.' " Perkins privately resented the fact that the producers always sided with their lady star.

On opening night, just as she made her entrance, Arlene Francis fell down the rather steep stairs of her "duplex," quickly recovering and going on with the show. Horrified, Ernest Thomas ran backstage to find Tony, who was sitting casually with his wife. "They liked to smoke weed," Thomas says, "and they must have been buzzing at that moment. I said, 'Tony, Arlene fell!' And he just went, 'Yes'—and started laughing uncontrollably, he and Berry both! It was infectious, and the next thing I knew I was laughing too. I couldn't believe the director was laughing about this."

Henry Scammell, Tony's long-estranged school chum, was also surprised when out of the blue he and his wife were invited to Wellfleet to meet Berry and Oz. Henry hadn't seen Tony since the actor had insulted the newlywed Mrs. Scammell backstage at *Look Homeward, Angel*. Henry accepted, his wife declined.

Tony desperately wanted to know why they hadn't stayed friends. "He didn't say it directly," Scammell recalls, "but it was implied that he wondered if I had decided to end the friendship because of his sexual preference. It had nothing to do with that." When Scammell recounted the backstage incident, Tony didn't remember it, and blamed his behavior on "the curse of celebrity."

According to Morgan Holman, "Deep down Tony really wanted to be one of the guys and be loved, but there was something that just didn't work. Berry was wonderful for him in that way. As quiet and withdrawn as he was, she was very outgoing."

"You never saw two people who belonged together so much," Ernest Thomas agrees. "Berry was a big kid, a tall, gangly child. She loved that man inside and out, unconditionally. It was just good to see the way she would look at him while he was directing us, with her chin in her hand. No matter what people say about him, the bottom line is this woman loved him and he loved her and they had beautiful kids together. He said it was the best thing that ever happened to him. Her love was so overwhelming that it had swept him off his feet."

Don't Call Back received decent notices and played to packed houses, but it was a "rough" play for Falmouth's audience of older ladies, many of whom were outraged by its language and by the grueling treatment of Arlene Francis in it. The producers even received hate mail because of it.

But despite the promising start, disagreements over script changes and casting continued, and Tony abruptly dropped out, forfeiting his impending Broadway debut. The chance to appear in a new film with superstar Diana Ross had a lot to do with it. According to Michael Mullins, "he got offered *Mahogany* and jumped ship," derailing the entire tour.

While his decision threw a major monkey wrench into a lot of people's plans—Mullins, for instance, was replaced for Broadway when Len Cariou took over as director—ultimately it was a smart move for Perkins. *Don't Call Back* opened in New York on March 18, 1975, and closed after one laughed-at performance. Critic Martin Gottfried dismissed it as "exquisitely trashy," and a discouraged Arlene Francis told the *Post*, "I may never go into the theater again. It's too depressing."

Before *Mahogany* started shooting that November, however, Tony jumped at the chance to direct *The Wager*, a new comedy by young playwright Mark Medoff, whose *When You Comin' Back, Red Ryder?*

had recently won the Obie Award for Distinguished Playwriting of 1973.

The story of a dangerous bet between two college roommates—one a vicious intellectual, the other a jock—as to whether the jock can "score" with the sexy wife of their next-door neighbor, *The Wager* had been plagued by rewrites and cast changes during its recent run at the Manhattan Theatre Club, under the direction of Lynne Meadow. The new production was scheduled to open off-Broadway at the Eastside Playhouse on October 7, 1974.

Actors Kenneth Gilman and John Heard came with the show as the jock and the cuckold, and as the scheming intellectual, Kristoffer Tabori (who himself had replaced actor Bob Balaban in the original production) was left behind and replaced by Christopher Allport.

Every up-and-coming actress in New York, including Susan Sarandon and JoBeth Williams, wanted the pivotal role of the seduceable Honor, even though it had been and would continue to be the play's major flaw. Cara Duff McCormick and Margaret Whitin, two completely different types, had already essayed the underwritten part, neither of them to the satisfaction of Medoff or the producers. When Linda Cook, a perky young redhead from Atlanta, was recommended to Tony by actress Elaine Kerr, who had appeared in his production of *The Gingerbread Lady*, he hired her on the spot.

Perkins invited Cook, who had to relocate for the play, to stay on Twenty-first Street while she looked for an apartment. She arrived on his doorstep wearing only the clothes on her back, her baggage having been lost by the airline; Tony invited her in to meet Halston and "have a smoke." Feeling a mess, she declined, but on the way upstairs caught a glimpse of Halston, Berry, et alia "sitting up on a big couch that was strewn with oriental pillows and rugs, getting stoned."

According to several sources, Tony had by now become "obsessed" with marijuana—so dependent on it, in fact, that he'd had a special inhaling device made that weirdly resembled a gas mask. After the theater or therapy, he would come home and immediately pull the rubber strap over the back of his head, completely covering his nose and mouth with the mask, so that he could breathe only smoke. He was thrilled by this "natural" drug that seemed to make him so much more open to life, almost like a magical extension of his psychoanalysis. As he had done with *How to Be Your Own Best Friend*, he constantly pushed dope on sober skeptics to see how they would react to its power. Marijuana had become his new best friend.

Most intimates agree that it was the influence of Berry's haute couture crowd that got Tony deeper into pot and made him willing to experiment with other recreational drugs, like LSD and cocaine. It was certainly a far cry from the rigid bachelor of Fifty-fifth Street who used to launch into an hysterical tirade at the mere whiff of pot in his home. One of the more outward signs of his trendy new seventies excesses was a pair of silver spray-painted penny loafers, blatantly trippy fashion accessories that he often wore to the Eastside Playhouse.

Meanwhile, according to Linda Cook, "the scent of blood was in the air" from the very start of rehearsals. Management fired Chris Allport on the first day ("he just didn't come back from lunch"), and replaced him with actor Graham Beckel, who was fired the day after. Production was then shut down briefly to await the return of Kristoffer Tabori, who had already been fired once. "I'd never been in a show where so many people were getting fired," Tabori recalls. "It was ridiculous for a four-character play." For Tony, it seemed like *Steambath* all over again.

Once everyone was reassembled, however, things started to improve. "The rehearsal process was an exciting one," Ken Gilman remembers. "Tony always came to rehearsal with ideas, which is unlike a lot of directors. Even in terms of physical business, he came loaded. One of the most important things he told me was 'Play up your imperfections.' That has really stayed with me all my life as an actor."

"I felt Tony was a director I could both trust and respect," Tabori agrees. "He was phenomenally engaging, very forthcoming, very open. He had thought a lot about the play, and was with us on our journey."

Perkins felt that the best way to approach *The Wager* was as a black comedy, stressing the darker, more dangerous aspects of the illicit triangle as well as the basic humor of the situation. His cast agreed. The group quickly formed a sort of mutual admiration society. Tony, with Berry and baby always in sight (and his trusty gas mask waiting at home) was less guarded than usual.

"At one point, the guys all took him downtown to some of the peep shows on Times Square," Cook recalls. "When they got back they were all telling tales about blow-up dolls, and Tony was very open about the fact that he had only been officially straight in his own mind for a couple of years. He felt like the new kid on the block where women were concerned, and they would tell him, 'Anything you need to know, Tone, come to us. We'll straighten you out'—no pun intended. It was very relaxed.

"He was thrilled about the baby and about Berry. He loved having her as a showpiece on his arm, and was very charmed by her as a human being. There was a glow about him whenever he talked about her. He was very open to learning new stuff about men and women. I guess I didn't realize to what extent he was truly in the closet with other people because he was so open with us. I thought he had the same face with everybody. He certainly was not discreet about saying that he had only been straight for a few years—in fact, he seemed almost proud of it."

After three idyllic workweeks, Mark Medoff, who had become known for using actors as scapegoats for *The Wager*'s script deficiencies, joined the company for the final week of rehearsal. Kris Tabori warned Tony about the notoriously macho playwright's penchant for deconstructing and reconstructing struggling productions. The director didn't believe him: "It's not a problem. I'm telling you, I can handle it."

As predicted, Medoff sat in on a run-through, and the next day, as Tabori puts it, "the shit started hitting the fan." The cast disbanded temporarily while Perkins and Medoff "talked." A few days later, Tony called his actors to a secret meeting at an East Side restaurant. "He was very shaken and had lost a lot of confidence," Linda Cook says. "He conveyed that he had led us all down the wrong path."

Ken Gilman remembers Tony being "distraught. He had been instructed by the producers that they really wanted to see the play become a light, frothy comedy, as opposed to what we'd been trying to do with it. We were all very disappointed."

Back at the Playhouse, Medoff was now a constant presence at rehearsals, loudly contradicting every direction Perkins gave. "It was a terrible place to be in as an actor," Cook says, "because your allegiance is to your director. At one point backstage Tony got quite teary. He said he was afraid he was going to be fired. It didn't make you feel like you had a foundation under your feet. But Tony never put up a fight about it."

According to Tabori, Perkins "started to get cagey, reserved in judgment, coming up with very strange justifications and reversals of opinions. Everybody was retrenching." The weight of the pressure from Medoff and the producers was almost too much for Tony to bear.

Previews began on Friday, September 27, as rewrites came in fast and furious. Almost daily the play was given a new ending. And there was still uncertainty surrounding the character of Honor; neither Medoff nor Perkins seemed to have a clear picture of her. Was she a bimbo, a brain, both? Tony was at a loss regarding the motivations of the play's one female character. "He'd direct me by telling me something he'd seen in a film," Cook recalls. "He'd say, 'I saw this movie where the girl came in and went to the window, and they talked for a while, and when she turned around there were tears running down her cheeks. Do that for me.' So I would do it."

Opening night was pushed to October 21. According to Cook, "Tony took me to dinner and tried to get me drunk before the show. He kept saying, 'Have more wine, have more wine,' and I kept going, 'No, thanks.' He told me he often went on stoned on marijuana. That night, I just went on sheer instinct. It was probably the most painful acting experience of my life."

"Poor Linda was pretty piss-awful," Tabori remembers. "She didn't have any idea what she was supposed to be playing."

The audience was packed with Tony and Berry's friends, many of them—like underground film star Pat Ast, who embarrassed everyone with her nonstop cackling—from the Halston crowd. Reviews were kind. *Times* critic Clive Barnes praised Perkins for directing the piece "with the lightest possible of touches."

But the personality conflicts were not over. Just after the opening, Linda Cook was in a bar near the theater. When the bartender asked her how it was going, she replied honestly, "Well, it's been difficult because it's a play about the relationship between one woman and three men, and I'm working with a playwright who's a male chauvinist and a director who's a recent heterosexual." Word got back to management that she had called Tony Perkins "a fag," and she was asked to leave the play.

"I said, 'That's not what I said—and what's the problem? Tony's very open about it.' " Nevertheless, by the end of the week Cook was replaced by a surprise understudy no one in the cast had even known about. The other actors were appalled, and refused to go on with the new girl until Cook's contract break was resolved to her satisfaction.

"I hit the fucking ceiling," Kris Tabori remembers. "I have never been so angry in my entire life. To do this three or four days after opening night, when in fact we'd gotten away scot-free and the reviews were good—even for her. There was a trust relationship with his cast that Tony had severely violated."

Tony, as usual, was nowhere to be found. "He never called me, never talked to me, never confronted me with anything," Cook says. "At that point I wasn't surprised because he had seemed like he was in such a weak position, so unsure of himself. He had told me I had this wonderful quality that was going to make me a star—this special ability to make people laugh and cry at the same time, that sort of thing—and then he just disappeared when the stuff hit the fan."

Tabori feels that Perkins's need to succeed by being agreeable, political, was at odds with his deeper instincts: "It was a big conflict for him. He did not follow his heart, and he lost his nerve."

"He was not the person I thought he would be in terms of loyalty," Cook reflects. "We got along great at first. But just as things looked like they were teetering, instead of taking the helm, Tony jumped ship."

Mahogany again offered the escape hatch. A star vehicle for singer Diana Ross, who had recently won an Oscar nomination for her film debut in *Lady Sings the Blues*, *Mahogany* was an old-fashioned rags-to-riches woman's picture, set in the glitzy world of high fashion and updated for an African American audience. It began shooting in Chicago on November 18, 1974, under the direction of British auteur Tony Richardson.

Perkins was disappointed and furious when he realized that his role, Sean, a controlling fashion photographer who discovers Mahogany (Ross) working in a department store and turns her into a top model, had been rewritten to capitalize on his *Psycho* persona; the part, which he had researched by visiting with photographer Richard Avedon, had been made stereotypically faggier, cattier, more monstrously homophobic than originally written. Tony blamed Sue Mengers for pushing him into the project, but ever the consummate pro, went ahead with the required performance.

Indeed, Perkins is more convincing than usual as the sadistic, closeted Sean (thought, typically, it's never made exactly clear in the film what his "problem" is). Rarely has the actor's perverse brittleness been so deftly channeled; during the sadomasochistic fight scene with Mahogany's jealous beau (Billy Dee Williams), Perkins chuckles with hysterical pleasure as they wrestle together on the floor—ending up in a hateful simulation of fellatio as the macho Williams fires an empty gun into Sean's open mouth.

Though Perkins and Diana Ross got along well—according to one friend, Berry was even mildly jealous of their rapport when she later visited the set—the shoot was not an easy one. Richardson was fired in January for his alleged inability to relate to African Americans, and replaced by Motown impresario Berry Gordy, who had never directed a film before. Tensions between Gordy and Ross ran high, and Perkins resorted to drugs to keep his spirits up.

Even so, *Mahogany* set box-office records when it opened in October of 1975.

For Tony, the bitter satisfaction of being connected with a hit was further compromised by scathing reviews. *The New Yorker* noted that Perkins, with his "druggie-male-hustler mannerisms," was "all too embarrassingly convincing," and *The Advocate* wrote, "Looking more cadaverous with each film, [Perkins] plays a psychotic photographer with every facial twitch at his command. We are never let in on his ghastly secret—is he a latent homosexual or just impotent?—but then, no one really cares anyway. It's a revolting character, with Perkins chewing all the scenery in sight at his hammy worst."

Discouraged yet again by the politics and futility of acting in film, he returned to New York, where hope lay in his loving family—and on Broadway, in what Tony hoped would really be "the role of a lifetime."

20

THE ROLE OF A LIFETIME

O N OCTOBER 24, 1974, Tony and Berry attended the opening night of Peter Shaffer's *Equus* with film producer Julia Phillips, who later wrote in her memoir, *You'll Never Eat Lunch in This Town Again*, that she'd found the play "a crock of faggot shit," an opinion that had led to "a pretty heavy argument" with Tony afterward. He strenuously objected to the idea that the play had anything to do with homosexuality at all.

The dark story of a psychiatrist's intellectual and spiritual obsession with a violently disturbed boy, *Equus* was reportedly the highest-grossing drama in the history of modern theater. The esteemed British production, starring Anthony Hopkins as the troubled Dr. Dysart, under the direction of John Dexter, had stunned audiences and critics alike at Broadway's Plymouth Theater with its intense emotions and riveting language.

When producer Kermit Bloomgarden, who had produced *Look Homeward, Angel* eighteen years before, asked Perkins to replace Hopkins, whose contract was up in June, Tony adamantly did not want to do it. Finally, "on a dare" from John Dexter, he agreed to tackle the role, even though he claimed it was "one hundred percent beyond my acting muscle." Martin Dysart would be his first (and last) "classical," or verbally demanding, text-driven part; Perkins in turn would be the first American actor to play it.

"Even my own analyst approves of the play," he said, comparing Dysart's unorthodox involvement with his patient to Mildred Newman's "highly conversational approach." He alleged that most people had automatically assumed he'd be taking over the role of the troubled youth. "You can't go on looking boyish forever," he declared. "After all, I'm forty-three years old."

There were clearly aspects of Dysart, beyond the obvious psychoanalytic one, that Perkins could strongly identify with: both were men experiencing, as Tony put it, "professional menopause," and both were conventionally married but harboring deep-rooted passions that lay outside the nuptial bed. As Dysart says, comparing his own arid marriage with his patient's "sick" lust for horses, "I watch that woman knitting, night after night—a woman I haven't *kissed* in six years—and he stands in the dark for an hour, sucking the sweat off his God's hairy cheek!"

Dexter insisted that his new star not see the show again, and to minimize the chances of his being influenced by the current cast, rehearsed Perkins only with the understudies. Whereas the charismatic Anthony Hopkins (and later Richard Burton) had dressed meticulously as Dysart, Perkins, like Berry in the face of the overwhelming Marisa, took the diametrically opposite approach: he cut his hair short so that it would look grayer, stopped shaving, and bought a baggy, ninety-dollar, "indestructible" suit at Macy's to don onstage, the kind of outfit he felt the cracking doctor would wear. After each rehearsal, he simply crumpled it up.

But for Tony, the greatest challenge was to act on a grander scale than he was used to. "In my career I'd always done things thriftily," he said, echoing his psychoanalytic motto about choices; "I was good at the boxed-in, the narrow, the limited. Not the big, never the big—but the big was all that would do for this role.

"Dexter just wouldn't accept the desiccated, dried-up pod I tried to give him [the] first day of rehearsal. He dared me to be what he called 'spacious,' and a dare is one thing that can really ignite you."

A "dare" is hardly how most of Dexter's actors would describe his tactics; "scare" is more like it. The director's lacerating tongue, which regularly reduced cast members to tears, was as feared as his artistic vision was venerated. "John Dexter was a brilliant director," says actress Marian Seldes, who had first met Perkins in 1948 at a party thrown by

June Walker. "[But] he could say things that were cutting . . . like a knife going through your heart."

No one was spared. When he wanted to see the female cast members, he'd command, "Bring the slits onstage." Everything was turned into a sexual slur. "We've all heard you have a big cock, Mr. Perkins," he said during one rehearsal, "but it's not very interesting to see you looking down at it through the entire performance."

"Dexter was a flaming . . . well, he wasn't a queen, but he was a very angry homosexual," one observer says. "He humiliated Perkins like I've never seen anyone humiliated. He knew Tony's history, and that he had a wife and children, and he said things to Tony—scathing, vicious things—like I'd never heard before, or since. But Dexter could make you eight hundred feet tall as an actor, and Tony knew that."

Painfully exposed at rehearsals, Tony was more than ready to bow down to Dexter's cruel genius, no matter how abusive it got. "When the director screamed at him, Perkins never screamed back," wardrobe supervisor Eric Harrison remembers. "He took it for what it was worth. Dexter could be ruthless and very rude, but even in those tirades there was always a grain of truth. Perkins was a good actor because he looked underneath what was said, and used it constructively."

Many of his colleagues felt that the American star's peculiar brand of stiffness actually made the central thrust of the play more accessible. Actress Frances Sternhagen, who played the boy's mother, maintains that "Tony's performance was in many ways the perfect casting because there was an awkwardness to his physical appearance that really embodied what the psychiatrist was talking about, which was that he couldn't feel passion and that he envied the boy. Tony Hopkins, for example, is a very passionate person, so it was almost hard to believe when he said he couldn't feel passion. When Tony Perkins said it, you really believed there was something deeply personal about it."

Seldes agrees that Perkins's innate combination of "vulnerability and guardedness" was perfect for the role, and recalls that Tony was "obsessive about his Dysart. He could never get enough notes from the stage manager or enough comments from the cast."

Still, rising to the rare challenge of a great play and a tyrannical director did not squelch his actor's ego. According to one cast member, Perkins was "the most dichotomous person, on the one hand totally self-effacing, and on the other the biggest megalomaniac on earth." He disliked sharing his onstage laughs, and didn't take it too kindly if someone else got applause. Indeed, when Dexter later instructed him to drop his comedy points during the performance, Tony immediately set out to replace them with new ones.

"Dexter treated him rather badly," stage manager Robert Borod says, "but because of it Tony gave the performance of his life."

When Perkins opened in *Equus* on June 30, 1975, he received some of the best notices of his entire career. "Perkins is excellent," *Variety* exclaimed. "The performance has more vitality and directness now, and tends to involve the audience to a greater degree."

"Mr. Perkins has rarely been better," raved Clive Barnes, calling the performance "admirably variegated . . . capable of many shades of meaning and shifts of purpose, and perhaps true to his dramatic track record, Mr. Perkins never seems too far away from his own couch. But then one not infrequently meets psychiatrists in desperate need of psychiatric help."

The *Village Voice*, however, was not bowled over ("Perkins is a bundle of tics"), and the *Post*'s Martin Gottfried blamed Tony alone for "the draining of the play's electricity," which he felt lay in the script's alleged homosexual subtext. "Perkins seems afraid to enter the play's center ring, where its sexuality lies," the critic noted. "*Equus* is basically a devotion to pure passion. Its reference to homosexuality is unmistakable. If the psychiatrist reveals nothing of his own suppressed sexuality, he becomes merely a device in a drama of social science. There is a homosexual courtship in his treatment of the boy. Perkins refuses to play it. Indeed, his eyes seem afraid to make contact with [actor Tom] Hulce's."

The accusation enraged the star, who firmly declared in one interview that *Equus* "is not associated with homosexuality, in my opinion or the author's either. But the people who want to see that can really be quite shrill." In the same piece, Perkins cryptically added that it was "nice to be able to have alternative choices"—to *what* he didn't specify—"that's what my analysis has done for me." (The irony of all Perkins's proselytizing is that, in fact, he did *not* have any "alternative choices" in terms of how he could comfortably live his life in society's eyes.)

Still, despite his newfound expansiveness, he spent most of his time offstage just like the old Tony, alone in his dressing room, pumping hand weights incessantly. Between the two shows on matinee days, he literally wouldn't engage in any conversation at all; when approached, he would gingerly touch his throat and shake his head no. The performances were too important to him.

"He didn't seem to have much of a life," one observer says. "I'm not even sure he had that much to say to his wife." Instead, he lived vicariously through gossip, begging company members like a child to "tell me, tell me, tell me"; if the gossip was good, he'd pump his handgrips faster.

After the show, there were visits from celebrities like Audrey Hepburn, William Holden, and Stephanie Powers, which thrilled the actor. Conspicuously absent was Tony's mother, Jane, who never attended, perhaps because he never invited her. "He was constantly saying, 'My mother wouldn't like this' or 'My mother would loathe all of this,' " Eric Harrison recalls, "particularly the scene where the girl takes her clothes off. He said his mother didn't approve of most of his performances anyway, especially in films." But faithful Helen Merrill was there—much more frequently than Berry, who was pregnant again— and often with baby Osgood in tow.

Also back in Tony's life was Kerry LeBre, who was now supporting himself by selling drugs. An occasional toke from a joint had been enough to satisfy Tony when they had first met, but now "he *wanted* pot," and bought it by the ounce in his dressing room after the post-curtain visitors had gone. Linda Cook, who attended a performance, "wondered if he was very stoned" onstage. One source remembers there being nights "when he seemed high, very jittery," which led to speculation about cocaine use.

"He always smoked marijuana before he went out at night after the show," Harrison affirms. To the press, Perkins claimed that he had no need to "unwind" after the play, that he rushed right home to his wife and son by eleven-thirty. But Harrison recalls that Perkins was familiar with all the gay bars in the theater district—"especially the hustler ones," such as the Haymarket, O'Neill's Yard, and Fiesta—and "used to go to some black leather bar, which he thought was very interesting. He always tried to take me."

Perkins gave hints and sent signals, but was never completely forthright about what he was "into." Mostly he just liked to watch. Harrison accompanied him to a couple of bars where "he'd look around and say, 'Is there anything decent here?'—that's as direct as he would ever be. But I never saw him go off with anybody. He was very discreet. The only thing I noticed was if he talked about large black gentlemen, those exercise presses in his hands would start going very fast, and he'd snigger."

"I think he had sexual problems," another company member says. "We had six or eight incredibly beautiful men who played the horses, and Tony stayed far away to make sure he would have no desire. He stayed in his dressing room."

The star received an unexpected blow to his ego that December when he was asked to step down so that famed Shakespearean actor Richard Burton, who had suddenly become available, could take over as Dysart for a special limited engagement. Not only was Burton classically trained (and Welsh), he was also a world-class celebrity because of his amorous association with Elizabeth Taylor, whom he had recently remarried. Adding insult to injury was the fact that Burton's contract stipulated that he repeat the role in the upcoming film of *Equus*, under the direction of Sidney Lumet, who wanted a real Brit for the part (and thought Perkins was too young for it anyway, though he never actually saw Perkins in the show).

Burton's ten-week run, which would begin on February 15, 1976, was announced in the trades on Christmas Eve Day. "Well, I've learned one thing in this business," Tony told the rest of the cast one day as he allowed himself to relax in the greenroom: "The bigger the hit, the bigger the shit."

He was reportedly agreeable when management offered him a $25,000 settlement, but his agents held out for a more vindicating $40,000. If he was upset, he never showed it. The good boy had grown into a perfect gentleman, and Perkins was photographed greeting Burton backstage at the Plymouth Theater with a smile.

"The producers just baldly asked Tony to leave," Frances Sternhagen recalls. "He was hurt, and yet he understood what was happening. If somebody else had been playing the part at that time, they would have asked that person to leave too. Because indeed, when Richard Burton came in, the crowds just flocked." To cash in on the stellar turn, ticket prices were raised.

The Saturday before Burton was to start, management asked Perkins if he would mind giving up that day's matinee so that Mr.

Elizabeth Taylor could get one performance under his belt before his official debut. Perkins calmly agreed, which, according to one insider, "he didn't have to." When the announcement was made that Richard Burton would be giving the performance, the applause was so thunderous that the show was delayed for several minutes until the audience settled down.

But Burton, who had not been on the Broadway stage since Alexander Cohen's 1964 production of *Hamlet*, was rusty. "That matinee," Borod recalls, "I heard lines from every show he'd ever done—Shakespeare, whatever—he never stopped talking, and didn't always say lines from the play, but he got through it and the audience adored it."

Burton's gold mine, of course, was his unmistakable, sonorous voice, but he was privately terrified of the stage and kept a crib sheet with all his lines on Dysart's clipboard. There were times, too, when he want on tanked, and according to Sternhagen, "just couldn't do it at all. The drink had really gone to his brain."

Yet Burton had an undeniable charisma, and was ultimately rewarded with a special Tony Award. He may have looked wasted and used, but he could do no wrong, even when he did. "There was a strength there that Perkins didn't have," Robert Borod says. "Not physical strength, inside strength. And, of course, Tony carried along a lot of baggage with that image that he had to fight."

"No, I didn't go and see Burton do it," Perkins told one reporter. "I think I was afraid I might have seen something in his performance that I missed."

Instead, according to one source, he took a much needed bachelor vacation to Morocco (where he indulged his taste for drugs and boys), but not until after Berry had given birth, on February 9, to another son. Much to the amazement of just about everyone, she christened him "Elvis"—supposedly meaning "beautiful face," *not* the King of Rock and Roll—a name that made "Osgood" seem almost ordinary by comparison. This time Halston was crowned godfather.

When *Post* writer Jerry Tallmer asked Tony if Elvis had been an "accident" too, the actor responded, "Absolutely." Then he added, "Actually this is the third conception. We lost one—before Osgood. So really *that* was the accident. So it's inaccurate to identify this third one as an accident. We thought Osgood would like a companion." Tony's slip about a first miscarriage, which neither he nor Berry had ever mentioned in print before, would indicate that they had indeed known each other, perhaps secretly, before their allegedly "accidental" meeting at Ruth Ford's.

In March, Burton's engagement was extended for two extra weeks, to run through May 8, while another comparably high-powered star was sought to take his place. After Gregory Peck, Charlton Heston, and Jack Lemmon all said no, the producers shamelessly asked Perkins to come back. He accepted, defeated by the lack of any alternatives.

The only other job he'd had was one he'd pursued himself, an embarrassing stint on March 14 as guest host of the popular television show *Saturday Night Live*. Despite the fact that the series still boasted its talented original cast—Gilda Radner, John Belushi, Laraine Newman, Jane Curtin, and Dan Aykroyd (who would later be a close friend and neighbor of Tony and Berry's in L.A.)—the writing of this particular episode was more pointless and juvenile than usual. Most memorable, but also predictable, was Tony's "Norman Bates School of Motel Management" skit, a satire of quick-diploma TV ads in which spokesperson Norman alternates with Mother by holding a newspaper over his mouth and speaking in a lame falsetto. He fares much better in another sketch as a bow-tied psychiatrist who cheers up his patient (Curtin) by forcing her to sing show tunes.

Perkins returned to *Equus* on May 11. "I used to think that if you were a star, you were treated like a star," Marian Seldes says. "Apparently that's not so. I admired Tony very much for putting that all somewhere else in his mind and coming back to the play when it needed him. I think he wanted to work on the part some more."

John Dexter had been on best behavior while Burton was in the show; the Welshman had threatened to walk if Dexter abused or threatened to fire anyone without his approval. But "the day Burton left and Tony came back in," remembers actor Keith McDermott, the blond Tab Hunter look-alike who now played the boy, "Dexter was horrible and very cruel to some of us—especially me. And I felt that Tony, as the star of the show, could have protected us and protected himself. He did neither."

If anything, Perkins now seemed almost to masochistically enjoy the humiliation that Dexter dealt, as if it were a relief to have tangible manifestation of the scorn the management had already shown him. "He seemed to embrace the role of victim rather easily," McDermott says. "I can still see him, his head bowed, with a sort of half smile on his face and an eyebrow raised, as John Dexter was insulting him in front of all of us.

"I liked Tony a lot personally. He spoke to me as a peer and I felt very comfortable with him. But I didn't like acting with him as much as I liked acting with Richard Burton. He was the opposite of Burton, who was unpredictable in a good way, fiery. Tony did the same performance every night, like clockwork. He was robotic. He would do strange things onstage. In one scene he would shake his head no whenever he said yes, and nod yes whenever he said no. I never knew what it was about. But he did it every single time."

Actor Page Johnson, who played McDermott's father, confirms that Perkins was always "*exactly* the same. God knew what Burton would do. He'd say, 'I'll bet you a cup of coffee I can put a Welsh ballad into the show today'—and he would! Tony was always wonderful, but I used to say to him, 'Go for it! Surprise me. Strike out once in a while, fall down—*do* something.' He never would. He was very insecure, unaware of what an untapped talent he had."

Perkins's self-confidence was further undermined when *Times* writer John Corry asked Marian Seldes, in her first New York interview, to compare him as an actor with Burton. Flustered, the actress used the word "quixotic" to describe the volatile Burton, and "predictable" to describe Tony, which she immediately tried to retract in favor of "reliable" or . . . It was too late.

After seeing the piece, Tony confronted her at the theater that night and asked her point-blank if she had really used that word. She admitted that she had, but in a longer sentence, that it had not been meant as a criticism of his work.

"I'm sorry," she said.

"It's no good being sorry," he snapped. "I have to go out there and play this part and everyone in the audience will be thinking, 'He's predictable.' " He refused to accept her apology, and the faux pas placed a freeze on their friendship that would not thaw for some time.

Kevin Sessums, who later played the boy opposite Perkins for two weeks at Philadelphia's Playhouse in the Park, says the star performed "in a void. There was not a lot of connection. He had his way of doing it, and you had to follow along. That rigidity was his way of controlling things." Tony also continued his directorial penchant for giving post-performance notes to just about everyone in the cast. According to McDermott, they were "notes by innuendo," always roundabout and evasive and useless.

Instead of discussing things up front, Tony liked to play oblique games with his young male costars. "Let's watch each other," he would tell McDermott, "and come up with one word that's not good, not bad, to describe each other's performance." Several days later, as they were onstage during the first act, Perkins whispered out of the side of his mouth, "Poised." McDermott had no idea what he was talking about, then remembered. "It was exactly the word I would have used to describe him," he says. Though the voyeuristic game made the actor feel "trapped," unsure of how to respond, Perkins seemed to delight in keeping him off balance.

Perkins seemed to be constantly testing himself, tempting himself. Berry's former roommate, Jennifer Lee, who stayed on Twenty-first Street for a few days that spring, relates this peculiar encounter in her autobiography: "One afternoon, I'm taking a shower and Tony walks into the bathroom and begins to shave. He's just got briefs on and I'm standing behind a foggy, but see-through, shower curtain. We're alone in the house. I try to act cool, as if this is nothing, but I know Tony feels my discomfort. . . . I wonder if Tony wants some sort of approval or reaction from me. He's obviously preening and very nearly naked. Maybe because he's gay and has only limited experience with women, he feels he has to prove something. Or it could be just plain exhibition-ism. Maybe he just likes to show off his taut and sinewy body. What-ever it is, I don't like it. And he keeps on shaving—for what seems an eternity."

Tony didn't exactly try to hide his sexuality at the theater. With other gay cast members, he would proudly bring out photos of his family, then, in the same breath, inquire about the most sordid intima-cies. He begged Kevin Sessums "to tell him gay stories. I was openly gay, and the minute he found that out, he wanted to know everything I did the night before. He liked to live vicariously, because I don't think he was acting on those impulses at that point in his life. He loved his kids a lot, and he talked about them a lot.

"Once I made something up just to shut him up. I wondered if I told him a sexual escapade, would it make his performance any differ-ent—and he *was* a little more animated that night."

At the same time, he advocated heterosexuality and family life to whoever would listen, like Terence Burk, the *Equus* horse "captain," who discussed his bisexuality with Tony: "I had started to date a woman, and Tony was very supportive. He said, 'Explore it completely and just find out more about yourself, because we can all follow direc-tions if we really put our mind to it and want to.' He told me that lov-ing Berry and getting married gave him something he'd never had before, a home life he'd never experienced."

"She was his sanity with those children," Eric Harrison affirms. "He said when she had Osgood, it was the greatest blessing, and that with Elvis he'd been twice blessed—that it made up for all those years of fritting away with nothing. In fact, he told me he wished he'd met her before."

Not everyone got such a rosy picture. When a curious Keith Mc-Dermott asked Tony about his marriage, the star admitted, "Well, I ac-cepted seventy percent happiness."

Offstage, Tony tried to live as "normal" a life as possible. He and Berry made themselves a visible, accessible part of the Chelsea com-munity. For instance, when their baby-sitter, a teenage girl from down the block, found herself with no date for her senior prom, they recruited a young actor to escort her to the dance. And they were fre-quent users of the little neighborhood park around the corner on Tenth Avenue, which was perfect for outings and picnics with the boys. On one occasion, Diana Vreeland was directed to the park, where her onetime protégée was now draped with a baby sling rather than the latest Halston, and saddled down with toys and a tricycle rather than a camera and tripod.

"To all of their friends, they always had an extraordinarily open house, even though they had Osgood and Elvis," Joel Schumacher re-members. "There was always room. Marisa would stay there, I would stay there. Marisa went through some bad times between divorces and between movies. There always seemed to be somebody sleeping in the bed in the basement, one or two of us, or somebody on the sofa.

"It was a center of warmth and kindness and great food. They had big Christmas dinners, birthday parties for everybody. Both of them cooked, and there were a lot of interesting friends helping out. There were gypsies, tramps, and thieves running through the house, it was a salon of bohemian artistic crazy people. They were good parents, but certainly were not the Joneses in any way, shape, or form. They were Tony and Berry."

Back at the theater, degraded by Dexter and the *Equus* management, Perkins occasionally affected a grand, pretentious air in front of "little people." When Sue Mengers arranged for him to meet with a young director named William Richert, who wanted Perkins for a sinister role in his first feature film, *Winter Kills*, Tony played hard to get, and stalled by inviting him to *Equus*. "Tony gave an incredible performance," Richert recalls.

Afterward, in his dressing room, the star sat at his mirror removing his makeup. "You know, there's a scene in the second act where I usually get a laugh," Perkins said. "I didn't get one tonight. Why do you suppose that is?"

Richert had no idea. "I felt like I was being quizzed. He wanted to see whether or not I was a director. Then, suddenly, he stood up and walked out of the dressing room. I ran after him, down the hall and around a corner, and we were out on the stage of the theater, in this boxing ring–like set. 'I love the theater,' he said. 'Don't you?' Then he turned on his heels really fast and just walked off, with no exit line, nothing. As he passed through the door, he said over his shoulder, 'Call Sue Mengers Monday morning,' and I got him."

Equus closed at the Plymouth Theatre on September 11, 1976, and reopened at the Helen Hayes Theatre (where *Don't Call Back* had died) on October 5.

Berry flew to Los Angeles at the end of November to be matron of honor at Marisa's lavish wedding to handsome airplane-parts millionaire Jim Randall. Dressed by Halston in "Shocking" pink chiffon, Berry wept for the cameras (there were photographers and television crews even at the altar) as she made her way down the aisle, which was set up under a large tent in the garden of her sister's new Beverly Hills home. Reporters and columnists had been carefully sprinkled throughout the guest list, which included George Hamilton, Liza Minnelli, Barry Diller and Diane Von Fürstenberg, Andy Warhol, Anjelica Huston, Harold Stevenson—and the Marchese and Marchesa Gino Cacciapuoti, who had been absent from Berry's wedding. The event received national magazine coverage. Sixteen turbulent months later, however, Marisa's marriage, unlike that of her baby sister, would be over.

On February 13, 1977, as a concession to his limp film career, Tony took four weeks off from *Equus* to shoot his scenes for *Winter Kills*. He was replaced during that time by the show's esteemed London star, Alec McCowen.

Winter Kills, based on the Richard Condon novel, boasted a promising cast—Jeff Bridges, Dorothy Malone, John Huston, and Elizabeth Taylor (in a much publicized, uncredited, nonspeaking cameo)—but the film, a trendily paranoid satire of a bizarre presidential assassination plot, would prove more notable as the first single film production in movie history to file for bankruptcy. In March, unions pulled the crew right off the MGM soundstage where Richert was in the middle of shooting a scene with Tony Perkins and Jeff Bridges.

Perkins, who had suffered his share of professional embarrassment, told the novice director, "Never mind, we'll have lunch. Look straight ahead and keep smiling." As they marched past hordes of onlookers— "the entire lot," Richert recalls—Tony recounted how Orson Welles, in a similar situation, had simply hoisted the camera onto his shoulders and continued shooting sans crew. "Tony was heroic," the director remembers. *Winter Kills* would not be completed until 1979.

Earlier that month, Tony's ex-lover Timmy Everett had died, reportedly in his sleep from heart failure, though it was actually the result of a drug overdose. Few people outside of the New York theater even remembered the troubled actor, and if Tony had been at all upset by the news, no one knew it.

None of this deterred Berry Berenson from making her screen debut in *Winter Kills* as a pretty morgue attendant who shows Bridges the body of his murdered girlfriend with a droll "Don't touch"—a possible hint of the surprising dark humor that so attracted Tony to her.

Berry had been taking acting lessons steadily for three years, even while she was pregnant, at the West Fifty-sixth Street studio of thespian guru Wynn Handman (almost directly across from Tony and Helen's old digs). "It was therapeutic and relaxing," she told *Women's Wear Daily.* "And it was better than lugging around heavy photography equipment."

Perhaps at her suggestion, Tony even filled in as a substitute teacher when Handman was out of town. Actress Sylvia Miles recalls Berry and a classmate rehearsing a scene for Tony at their home on Twenty-first Street; when baby Elvis started crying, "nobody paid any attention," and they just kept acting. Tony claimed his wife was "wonderfully talented." She would soon be put to the test.

The experience of *Equus* was not without its pay-off. In mid-1977, Perkins was unexpectedly offered the lead in *Remember My Name*, a new film by hip young screenwriter–director Alan Rudolph, protégé of independent pioneer Robert Altman. Perkins had not immediately leaped to Rudolph's mind for the role of a construction worker with two wives—one of whom, just out of prison, is stalking him. But Rudolph's wife had happened to catch Perkins in *Equus*, and suggested him to her husband. He and Altman, who was acting as producer, both thought it was a great idea.

Perkins agreed via phone to do it. Once again, the chance to work under the auspices of an auteur like Altman—whose films, such as *MASH, McCabe and Mrs. Miller*, and *Nashville*, had created a whole new style of naturalistic, incisive, and distinctly American filmmaking—was irresistible to the actor who had once been stamped a carbon copy of James Dean and was now viewed mainly as a has-been.

At a meeting in Altman's New York office, Tony asked Alan Rudolph who was going to play the second wife (Geraldine Chaplin was already cast as the convict). No actress had been secured. Tony promptly suggested Berry.

"Is she an actress?" Rudolph asked.

"Well, she's acted," Tony said. "She wants to be. And Marisa Berenson's her sister."

Rudolph felt that "if Tony was comfortable with her, there was something that might come out of it that I wouldn't have to guide. He was very, very excited."

So was she. "I never thought it would happen that I'd be in a film with Tony Perkins," she exclaimed.

Shooting would start in mid-October in Los Angeles, leaving plenty of time for Perkins to prepare his dilettante wife for her first major screen role. It also gave Berry time to find a suitable home for them in Hollywood; after waking up one morning to find two men dead on the sidewalk across the street from their town house, she no longer wanted to raise her children in New York. She made several trips to the Coast before settling on a Laurel Canyon rental.

According to one person close to the Perkinses at the time, Berry saw the move to L.A. as a chance to maneuver Tony away from his old friends, whom she outwardly professed to like but privately felt threatened by. That same source claims that she was just as "hungry for the spotlight" as her famous sister, but wanted people, especially her husband, to think differently. Whatever the case may have been, the move to the Coast, a place that Tony had always despised, was clearly a strike at independence for Berry, a step toward reestablishing an identity of her own after subduing so much of her personality for her role as wife and mother.

Tony decided that if his wife intended to become a star, she needed the kind of stage experience he'd had as a novice. He took it upon himself to give it to her, quickly arranging with producer Charles Forsythe (*The Gingerbread Lady*) for the two of them to appear that August at the Cape Playhouse in Dennis, Massachusetts, in John Van Druten's dated romantic comedy *The Voice of the Turtle*. Tony would also direct. When his run in *Equus* ended in early June (he was replaced by another brutally typecast American, *Star Trek*'s Leonard Nimoy), the Perkinses left Manhattan for the peaceful dunes of Truro and the footlights of summer stock.

Rehearsals began July 25 in Carleton Hall, just a few yards from the Playhouse, to which the famous couple commuted thirty miles every day from Wellfleet. They arrived claiming to know all their lines, but the one-week rehearsal period was kept strictly off-limits to *any* visitors, a harsh restriction that locals were quick to note.

For Berry's stage debut, Tony demanded that the Playhouse stage designers, Helen Pond and Herbert Senn, a local couple, build an unusually elaborate set with troublesome effects such as rain falling outside the windows of Berry's "apartment." Though the designers were more than happy to comply with his "vision," the rain went largely unnoticed by audiences.

Tony was surely aware of the significance of the Gertrude Lawrence Dressing Room, which was to be his wife's for their stint at the Playhouse; he purposely brought along a pair of vintage green silk pajamas that had belonged to his father, Osgood Perkins, to wear in the show. Perhaps in some way he hoped to pay homage to his father's farewell in *Susan and God.*

As for Berry, who was erroneously described in one local paper as an "ex–Revlon model," she came equipped with costumes by Joel Schumacher, lingerie and period terry-cloth robe by Fernando Sanchez, and makeup by celebrity cosmetician Way Bandy. "I haven't done much photography or modeling since I had the children," she modestly told one reporter. "Being a mother is a full-time job. But now I am coming out again."

In the play, Berry was cast as the central character, Sally Middleton, an aspiring actress in 1940s New York who falls in love with a soldier on leave (Perkins) when he is stranded at her apartment after her best friend (played by Jean DeBaer) dumps him for another man. The breezy situation comedy, which had run for a whopping 1,500 performances in 1943, seemed simple enough, but no matter how much uninhibiting marijuana the director and his star smoked together, timing and props and lines and nuances were too much for the beautiful amateur to pull together all at once. After three or four days of frustratingly slow rehearsals, Tony gave up, handing the directing reins over to Charles Forsythe.

Despite the difficulties and the pressure, Perkins's demeanor was never less than gentlemanly. "He was a very understanding, very calm person," Cape Playhouse superintendent Annie Walker recalls. "There were no diva fits, nothing like that. He was calm, methodical: 'This is what I need, this is what we have to do.' "

Uncharacteristically, it was by all accounts Berry who was the temperamental diva of the little show. Charming offstage, especially in the eyes of the local men, at the theater she was extremely needy, and vocal about her needs, constantly making petty complaints about her tea not being hot enough or the flowers in her dressing room not being fresh. The smallest details would set her off. She was obviously hysterical about her approaching performance, and Tony acted as her buffer, always there the instant she raised her voice, always able to calm her down behind the closed dressing-room door.

"They were very reclusive," property assistant Rory Murphy recalls. "You didn't see them much. It was pretty intense for Berry. She was justifiably nervous. She wasn't bad, she just wasn't very interesting."

Observers felt sorry for Tony, always having to apologize for his wife's mood swings.

"I kept thinking their lifestyle was getting in their way," Helen Pond recalls.

Most likely Berry hadn't wanted to do the play in the first place. Backstage, she was audibly more concerned about their next project, anxious to get on with the Rudolph film, which she talked about constantly. Perhaps she felt bored by having to do the Cape Playhouse at all.

She shouldn't have. Though she looked gorgeous entering a room, and appeared to have all the charisma of a Hollywood actress offstage, onstage she had surprisingly little presence or poise. When *Turtle* opened on August 1, even the local critics, usually kind, couldn't deny it. "Her aspiring is tiring," said one.

Another wrote: "It was obvious that she has no previous acting experience, and I can only hope that she did not spend a great deal of time and money taking those [acting] lessons. Miss Berenson is quite attractive and probably takes great pictures, but her movements are wooden, her delivery monotonous and her performance as exciting as a glass of warm root beer." The same critic called Tony's performance "typically low key and gentle," adding that he "managed not to obliterate his wife completely from the stage, something that could have been done quite easily."

There were other mishaps too. For one performance, someone had sabotaged the costumes, slashing Jean DeBaer's, and cutting out the buttocks on Osgood Perkins's pajamas, so that when Tony wore them onstage, he mooned the audience. Another night, Berry walked into a wall while carrying a tray.

Marisa Berenson caused a major stir when she flew in on a private jet to see her sister perform. Berry told the *Boston Globe* that she and Marisa were "mulling over the idea" of starring in a movie or play together. "Marisa always wanted me to act," she claimed. "Somehow I always hesitated—until now."

Interestingly, Berry was embarking on her new career just as her sister, once hailed by the press as the "Garbo of the Seventies," was becoming a movie industry joke. Ever since director Stanley Kubrick had cut almost all of her dialogue from the period epic *Barry Lyndon*, in which she had starred with Ryan O'Neal, Marisa's reputation as a potential actress had not been the same. She was still, however, the prime candidate to star in Allan Carr's proposed film of the life of actress Vivien Leigh.

After eight stressful performances, none of which was much fun for the Perkinses, *The Voice of the Turtle* went to Ogunquit, Maine, for a final painful week. A few months later, interviewed by her husband for *Interview*, Berry admitted that she'd found some of the reviews "very spiteful. I mean, that girl who said that my performance was just about as exciting as warm root beer—at first, it stunned me, of course, one's ego always wants people to love one—but then I thought she was probably right."

Before heading West to set up house in dreaded Hollywood, Tony took one last stab at *Equus*, commuting daily from New York to Philadelphia for a two-week stint that began on August 29. Colleagues noticed that he seemed even more jittery than before, and rumors of cocaine use continued.

During one performance, though, he had ample reason to be nervous when a strange young man in the audience came up onstage and sat down next to him on the circular cast bench. "This guy was convinced that Tony was his shrink," Kevin Sessums recalls. "The audience thought he was just part of the play, and Tony thought this was *it*, that he was going to be killed or something. You could see in his face that he was scared to death, but he didn't stop the performance, he kept right on going. Finally the stage manager came and escorted the guy off. Afterward, Tony was really upset, very shaken. But he never broke character. It was very odd."

His final performance as Dr. Martin Dysart took place on September 10, 1977. It was a wrenching night for the emotionally battered actor. "After his last performance, he put his arms around me and said, 'I can't stay, it's too much for me. I'll get in touch with you,' " Eric Harrison remembers. "Two or three months later I got a great, heart-rending letter from him." So, too, did Marian Seldes, with whom Tony had been so angry.

Equus marked the end of an era for Anthony Perkins. No future role onstage, and certainly none onscreen, would ever challenge him again the way the tortured, self-examining psychiatrist had. No role would be as utterly satisfying, except that of husband and father.

21

THE BLACK
HOLE

I'M ONE OF THOSE GUYS WHO CHANGES HIS LIFE," Tony said of his role as Neil Curry, the blue-collar builder with a shady past in *Remember My Name*. "I'm an architect in New York, but then I run to California and hide out as a construction worker. That's when I meet Berry, and we get married."

As for her role as Barbara, his beer-drinking, Kmart-shopping wife, the socialite who had grown up in New York, London, Paris, and Ischia drew on her own recent experience as a humble wife and mother: "I feel that I understand middle-class. I've been there."

But she didn't seem to want to stay there. Jennifer Lee, who had also migrated to L.A. at the time, recalls being struck by Berry's new-found ambition: "Berry was living in Laurel Canyon with Tony and the kids, looking fabulous, with a gorgeous new haircut—doing a lot of dope, I might add—and she's in that movie. She thought this was her moment. She had the husband, the kids, and now she was going to become a star."

"For three years I've been completely glued to the children," Berry told *Women's Wear Daily*. "If I was thinking then about making movies, I never admitted it to myself."

"I'm basically quite shy," she said. Later, when her own face graced the cover of *Interview* as a plug for the movie, she admitted, "It always astonishes me when somebody thinks of me as a person."

"Berry was always friends of the stars, always surrounded by them, always holding up the mirror," Jennifer Lee says. "I think she's really got a lot of anger about that."

Tony, her best press agent, kept her buoyed. "I want Berry to have an acting career," he told *WWD*. "She deserves it and she can do it."

But he still had doubts about whether *he* could do it. Robert Altman recalls the actor being "very nervous about [the film]. He was doing double duty, worrying about himself and his wife. And I think the blue-collar aspect of it worried him. I told him, 'You don't have to be born with a hammer in your hand to take on that situation. This guy's got a strange past.'"

After Tony's first day before the camera, Alan Rudolph invited him to attend the dailies in Altman's office with the rest of the cast and crew. He refused. "I never went with Hitchcock or Orson Welles," he told the young director. "I don't go to dailies." Rudolph insisted that Perkins come to at least see what the film was all about. Perkins finally agreed—but not until the following night, when he wouldn't be in any of the scenes screened.

Even so, immediately after seeing the rushes Perkins tried to quit. "Everybody's so good in this film, it's not like acting," he told Rudolph. "I'm wrong for this. I can't be in it."

"What are you talking about?"

"Geraldine [Chaplin] and Berry are amazing. It's not the kind of acting that I've wasted so much of my life on. What I've been doing is all fake; this is real, and I'm totally wrong for it." He offered to buy his way out.

"If you quit, then I quit," Rudolph told him.

Close to tears, Tony agreed to stay on, and to attend the nightly rushes. "From that moment on, he became our number one cheerleader," Rudolph recalls. "Everyone loved him. Geraldine just adored him. He went from being insecure to being the most stabilizing factor in our film." Tony just needed to be reassured that he belonged.

"I didn't worry about [Berry] from the first day on," he told the *Los Angeles Times*. "I realized very quickly the person I should be worrying about was myself."

If he was trying to protect his wife from critical eyes, he needn't have bothered; both Altman and Rudolph were pleased with her performance. According to Rudolph, "She had an instinct for it. She was less self-conscious than any of us. I thought the whole performance of Tony and Berry together was seamless, yet they were playing against what their life was. No one knows what secrets they brought to it."

Berry liked Rudolph's reliance on improvisation and simply played her scenes "as if I was myself in that situation." Tony noted that while his script was heavily marked with notes, his wife's was clean: "I realized I was in the hands of a nonseasoned professional."

To bring out the same natural quality in his own performance, Perkins did something he hadn't done since *Goodbye Again*. For the reunion/seduction scene where he and Geraldine Chaplin get drunk in a bar before going to bed, Tony asked the propman to get him some real booze.

"He was drinking for real, and we did it in just two takes," Rudolph recalls clearly. "It wasn't acting, it was *meta*-acting. There was nothing unprofessional about it; they were both amazing. The exit from the bar was the last thing we did before lunch, and Tony was getting pale. Finally he said, 'Did you get what you need? Do you want us to do it again?' I said no. So he got up from the table, grabbed a trash can, barely made it outside, and vomited. He spent lunch lying down somewhere, then he was fine. He continually added that something extra."

A similar example of his extraordinary physical self-control occurred during the filming of *Winter Kills*. In the confrontation scene where Jeff Bridges hits Perkins with a rubber blackjack to get him to talk, the young actor really did strike a blow to Tony's arm, not realizing how painful—and dangerous—it was. "Tony screamed as if he had broken his arm, it was for real," William Richert recalls. "During that whole scene he was actually experiencing excruciating pain. But instead of blowing it, he used it. Afterward, Jeff was mortified, and so was I. We were all concerned. But Tony didn't make a lot out of it."

Later, on location in Paris shooting *Twice a Woman* for director George Sluizer (who went on to make both the Dutch and American versions of *The Vanishing*), Perkins showed up for work with a terrible flu. Sluizer remembers being amazed at the actor's bodily control: "He would keep the sweat in for the length of a take, forty or fifty seconds, then as soon as I said 'cut' it would just pour out of his skin like a fountain."

The publicity mill began to grind for *Remember My Name*. "Spurred on by acclaim, Berry has big hopes for her movie career," *Us* magazine declared. "It may not be long before she outshines sister Marisa."

The *New York Post*'s Page Six reported that Marisa's baby sister was so talented Robert Altman had "expanded her part and raised her billing from sixth to third." ICM agent Michael Black, Sue Mengers's protégé, took Berry on as a client, and there was talk for an iota of a second that she and Tony would star together in a Western. But the only thing Western Berry would ever be in were her cowboy boots (and even that wouldn't last after she told *Vogue* in 1978 that she was worried her walk was "getting too butch").

Off-camera, the Perkinses persisted in playing up their humdrum, just-ordinary-folks image. "[They] live in a comfortable house off one of the canyons," Roderick Mann wrote in the *Los Angeles Times*, "drive around in an old, two-seater Thunderbird and avoid the lush movie-star life as though contact with it might somehow cause gossip."

But there was gossip anyway. "To me, when I knew them in New York, they were in love and very together," Jennifer Lee says. "When they moved to L.A., something happened. It felt like they had very separate lives. She started feeling her own identity and her own power. They were very removed from one another."

There were rumors that a heterosexual musician, a "real man," was trying to sweep Berry off her muted feet, becoming the first serious threat to her five-year-old marriage. And, as usual, there were plenty of Tony sightings in adult bookstores and gay bars, and along Santa Monica Boulevard, where L.A.'s male hustlers still loiter. According to a former employee of Le Sex Shoppe on Ventura Boulevard, Tony Perkins wandered in one afternoon wearing a felt hat and a scarf, and acted quite casual as he checked out the gay magazine and book section. Before leaving, however, he approached the young men behind the counter, and in a camp Gary Cooper drawl said, "Boys, you're runnin' a nice, clean shop here. No fist-fuckin', no B and D. Nope. Just a nice, clean shop. Keep up the good work"—in essence, making a joke out of his own self-consciousness.

"Perkins and Berenson are a dull, distracted duo as the harried pair," the *Washington Post* wrote after *Remember My Name* opened in 1978. Many critics were perplexed by the apparent miscasting of the Perkinses as lower-middle-class suburbanites. Janet Maslin called

Tony-as-construction-worker "just a matter of poor judgment," and Michael Sragow wrote that Berry, "by the way she talks, must have landed in the L.A. suburbs via Bryn Mawr." Her performance, called "amateurishly flat" by one critic and "tirelessly vacant" by another, proved a total loss, generating little interest in her as a Hollywood commodity. Indeed, on-screen she looks strangely devoid of any emotion, expressionless until the final turnaround scene in which the abandoned Barbara angrily sits in front of the TV with a cigarette and a beer, suddenly transformed into the same kind of jailhouse toughie that stole her husband.

Berry told reporters she was hoping to return to photography. "I'd like to think I'll always have something to fall back on," she said. With the flop of the film, she reportedly ended her affair and retreated back to the safety of her marriage. (She would make one last foray onto the big screen as the pool manager in Paul Schrader's 1982 remake of *Cat People*.)

The quirky *Remember My Name*, which Columbia Pictures refused to distribute in the States, was, like all of Tony's more artistic undertakings, relegated to the domestic art house circuit. Though there was still talk of his directing his first feature film—*Freeway*, based on the Deanne Barkley novel—that project vanished along with plans for the Western vehicle.

Next, Perkins was set to star in *The Survivors of Buffalo Creek*, a two-hour dramatic television special based on the true story of a dam that burst in West Virginia in 1972, killing more than a hundred people and traumatizing the rest, resulting in a multimillion-dollar lawsuit. The only name in an ensemble of unknown actors, he had been cast by *Play It As It Lays* director Frank Perry as the survivors' compassionate attorney, the first lawyer ever to sue on the grounds of irreparable "psychic impairment." Unfortunately, fear of legal action caused NBC to pull the plug on production at the last minute. The cast, which had already assembled at the actual site, was handsomely paid off; Tony came away (from what could have been one of his stronger roles) with about fifty thousand dollars.

A less dynamic offer followed to play the "villain" to America's sweetheart, Mary Tyler Moore, in the CBS-TV film *First You Cry*, based on newswoman Betty Rollin's book about her experience with breast cancer. Perkins told UPI's Vernon Scott that it was "quite an honor" to costar with the immensely popular Moore, who was also the film's producer. Rehearsals began in L.A. in early February 1978, before location shooting in snowy New York.

"The part of Mary's husband definitely suits me," he said. As Rollin's stoic, workaholic husband—a lonely man who can't express his feelings at all, much less deal with his wife's emotional needs after her mastectomy—Perkins gave a surprisingly subtle and compelling performance.

"Working with Tony was interesting because he was more internally motivated and controlled than probably any actor I've worked with," director George Schaefer recalls. "He was wide open to direction and to suggestions in rehearsal. But over and above everything we discussed, I felt there was something inside him that had laid out a ground plan for his performance, which he never lost. He paced the emotional involvement and exposed the vulnerability of the character very, very carefully."

Schaefer encouraged his actors to improvise, which pleased Perkins, but terrified Mary Tyler Moore, who was used to the prescribed demands of a weekly series. The perky sitcom star, for whom *First You Cry* was a major career stretch, remembers Perkins as a generous actor who "wanted not to be obvious" in his role, and acted "without artifice." Though their hours on the film did not permit much socializing, the two stars respected each other's talent and reputation.

"He was a charming person, a very keen actor who seemed to love his work," Moore says. "I remember him talking about his son a lot. He was just a nice guy, and not what I had expected at all. I had expected him to be arch and very sophisticated and stylish—and I'm sure he was all those things—but that's not what you most remembered about him."

First You Cry wrapped in Los Angeles on March 16. "This is the first time I've been in Hollywood and not lived in a hotel," Perkins told Vernon Scott, adding that he wasn't sure how long he and his family would stay. "Now Berry's had a lot more offers for work," he lied. "It's only fair after four years of looking after the kids that she had some time on her own to do the kind of work she enjoys."

Many of Tony's old bachelor friends didn't even know that he had made the move West. "He had suddenly disappeared from my life, and I was very sad about it," recalls Billy Goldenberg, who was by now a successful film-score composer. "I ran into him at Ma Maison one day. Orson Welles was at the back of the restaurant, and Tony came in to see him. We smiled at each other, and it was very difficult for me. It was like we were looking at each other and trying to recapture another time. I tried almost too hard to appear friendly. Tony was nice enough. His wife was there, he introduced me—very distant, both of them. I don't think she even knew who I was, frankly.

"Maybe that was a part of his life he was having some trouble with, and he wanted to change. God knows he did. I'm just sorry he eliminated a few of us. Maybe he needed to."

But some couldn't be eliminated, like the tenacious Teno Pollick, whose acting career had fallen on hard times (except for a bit part in Robert Wise's *The Hindenburg*) after a botched kidney operation that left him in constant pain and unable to work (his surgeon had operated on the wrong kidney). Having signed a waiver before the procedure, Pollick was unable to sue for malpractice. Instead, he became addicted to painkillers and booze, and was in constant need of money, which Tony was occasionally good for.

"Teno had two heart bypass operations," his friend Keene Curtis says, "and four or five more kidney operations. His whole front was just a mass of scars. The pain got worse and worse, and so did his depression." After his first relapse, Berry was the first person to appear at his bedside in the hospital.

Tony and Berry's new circle of friends seemed to include a lot of charity cases. "When you were friendly with them, you were like waifs who would drop by," Jennifer Lee recalls. "You would bask in the glory of Tony and Berry—everybody would—bask in their goodness, in their magic, whatever. The family-ness of it all."

According to Joel Schumacher, "Berry, like a lot of European children, was sent away to boarding schools, and we know about Tony's life. They made a home together. And strangely enough, most of the people there, like me, were stray dogs."

"You would never see a fight between them," Lee says. "You'd almost be relieved to see somebody throw a glass across the room or something. Berry was a crier. If there were problems, she would stuff it, keep it in, or cry. I really don't think she dealt with problems." As for Tony, "He loved to make people squirm, especially the girlfriends, the little waifs who would come by without families, without boyfriends, without careers, who were struggling for all of the above, and who needed kindness more than anything. He was so withholding. If you were pouring out your heart and soul, Berry would listen, and he'd just walk away. We were all threats to him."

Perkins's longtime pal, Bob Hussong, who was now also in L.A., was often invited up to Tony and Berry's for family-oriented events such as Thanksgiving or Christmas. But he usually declined: "It was okay to be a bachelor, but it wasn't okay really to infringe upon certain situations, even with them, if your [male] lover of ten years was going to come with you. It was never said, but I felt that. So I didn't go to those things."

"That was true even if you were heterosexual there," Jennifer Lee adds. "You weren't allowed to be whole. Some people require you to be a mess. It's controlling and it makes their life look terrific."

Marisa Berenson was no exception. When her marriage to Jim Randall ended and she was dropped from Allan Carr's Vivien Leigh project (Randall was coproducer), she, too, came crying to Berry and Tony, and according to Lee "was made to feel just as inadequate in that household as the next person. That was their hold. To tell you the truth, I think it was very mean. We all needed to be embraced and nurtured. It was scary to be around—mean, not loving."

Tony and Berry were among the first to call when actor Ken Gilman, a neighbor in Laurel Canyon, got divorced. "They didn't take sides," Gilman fondly recalls. "They just wanted me to know that they were there if I needed somebody to talk to, that they understood some of the things that had gone down. I think that really said a lot about the two of them." Likewise in 1981, when Jennifer Lee's troubled boyfriend, comedian Richard Pryor, broke down during a performance at the Hollywood Palladium, the Perkinses instantly appeared backstage.

Jacques Natteau and Yvonne Furneaux were shocked when Tony and Berry dropped by their Hollywood Hills home for a visit; it had been just a little more than a decade since *The Champagne Murders*, but Perkins looked "a hundred years old," an emaciated Peter Pan whose behavior was equally as off-putting. According to Furneaux, he seemed distracted and extremely hyper as he dashed around the house, intently taking stock of every object "as if someone had stolen it from him."

"In ten years, he had become a skeleton," Natteau says, "no longer connecting, losing his hair." His aged appearance and bizarre conduct were probably the results of amphetamine abuse, as Tony had found it increasingly necessary to fog pain and seem "up" at all times in Hollywood.

To make conversation, Furneaux commented to Berry that Tony "should be playing Hamlet."

"Oh no, no, no," Berry replied. "He couldn't do that."

The Champagne Murders costar George Skaff ran into Tony and Berry at Bob Hussong's, "but I never met his kids, and he never asked me up to his home. He was more restrained. He certainly wouldn't discuss cruising or anything like that. Maybe an arched eyebrow if somebody attractive passed us or something. But nothing like the Tony I knew before. I just figured he'd settled into heterosexuality, the married-man syndrome."

In May 1978, Tony returned to France, this time with his wife and kids, to play the obsessively law-upholding Inspector Javert in Sir Lew Grade's television version of Victor Hugo's classic, *Les Misérables*. In Seurlat, where they were put up, they ran into Ken Gilman, who remembers Tony "was really enjoying himself as a family man. It made a big difference in his life in terms of coming to grips with the idea that he was only getting certain types of roles. He was very devoted to the kids."

"Most of our friends are people who can enjoy children and play with them," Tony told *Vogue*. "They realize that children are human beings." Sounding not unlike a fundamentalist Christian, he surmised in *Interview* that "since the shipwrecked, dope-heavy last ten years, I think there's a possibility that the family might come back into its former position of strength." His wife agreed.

When *Les Misérables* aired on CBS later that year, critics praised the lavish production values more than the acting. The *New York Times* wrote that Perkins "has a few speeches about how the laws of society must be observed, but the rest of his performance is restricted to looking exceedingly grim while dressed in forbidding black costumes."

In early June Marisa Berenson suffered a severe concussion and numerous facial lacerations after a devastating car accident in Brazil, where she was filming *Killer Fish*, a quickie thriller with Margaux Hemingway and Karen Black—a far cry from the days when her beauty graced only the films of directors like Luchino Visconti and Bob Fosse. Her companion in the crash, Alex Ponti, the producer son of Carlo Ponti, sustained a concussion as well, but Marisa had to undergo emergency plastic surgery and follow-up procedures that lasted an ex-cruciating eight weeks.

When Berry and her husband were interviewed that October at the first annual San Diego Film Festival, where *Remember My Name* was being screened, Berry, the happily married wife–mother–movie star, remarked that her unfortunate sister was still struggling "to recover emotionally from the terrible year she's had."

It was Robert Altman who put Tony in touch with a little-known Dutch director named George Sluizer, who desperately wanted him for the lead in *Twice a Woman*, a low-budget melodrama about lesbianism and murder. John Cassavetes had already rejected the role of a drama critic whose ex-wife shacks up with a teenage girl whom he promptly beds. Perkins didn't like the script—the lesbian aspect made him un-comfortable—but when Sluizer signed Swedish actress Bibi Andersson, who was famous for her work with Ingmar Bergman, as the wife, he accepted.

It was not a lucrative deal. Sluizer's budget of $750,000 precluded American movie star salaries, and Perkins only got about a quarter of the fee that ICM's Michael Black, who now represented both Per-kinses, requested. When Sluizer met him at the airport in Holland in the smallest car imaginable, a French Citroën, Perkins laughed. "He ac-cepted the fact that it was not Hollywood," Sluizer says. "He was not a person who complained about everything he didn't have."

The frustration came out in other ways. Tony played sadistic little games with his director, doing things just off-camera that threatened to break the continuity of a shot—crawling under a bed or suddenly put-ting his glasses on—until the *exact* moment that the camera reached him, at which point he'd be on his mark instantly, in character. "It was a power game," Sluizer explains. "He was trying to test me, and we didn't have time to play those games. He was a very easy actor techni-cally, he knew the camera, but I wanted to get him more involved." Sluizer had little success convincing the star to drop the *Psycho* manner-isms that had become his professional crutch.

Tony's first explicit nude lovemaking scene, with nubile model turned actress Sandra Dumas, didn't help. "Just baring his shoulders was dangerous for him because he was rather skinny and looked bony," Sluizer recalls. "Americans are very body conscious. His T-shirts were re-inforced, he had pads under them." Adding to Perkins's panic was the fact that the shapely Dumas was anxious to get the scene over with. Too young to be awed by his past career, she embarrassed him in front of the entire company, referring to him as "the old bastard" and impatiently urg-ing him on.

The love scene was scheduled for the morning, but at the last minute Tony refused to do it, pulling Sluizer aside for a private confer-ence that lasted from nine in the morning through lunch, leaving the bored crew waiting in the next room. He harangued the director vi-ciously for hours—"Why do you want this scene? What is your fuck-ing problem? Are you a sex pervert?!" According to Sluizer, "He was trying to break me down emotionally, playing the psychoanalyst, wait-ing until I was just as vulnerable as he would be in the scene. I have a very strong will and don't get pushed easily into a corner, but finally I got irritated and raised my voice—and I was so hyped that a tear started to come out of my eye. When he saw that, he said, 'Okay, let's shoot *now*.' Only when he had twisted me like this was he able to do what he'd thought he couldn't do. He did his best, and I knew it was diffi-cult for him. Emotionally, the scene was not faked." When it was over, Perkins lay motionless, desperately holding Dumas, unable to move for a good half hour.

Off-camera, it was clear to everyone that the star was infatuated with the director's seventeen-year-old son. "Tony was a little bit in love," Sluizer admits, "but very proper about it. He had double feel-ings." Even the boy was aware of the crush, and would jokingly tell his father, "If he's not on the set tomorrow, he's with me!"

Though the script's lesbian theme made him uneasy, Tony im-bued his own character with gay undertones, meticulously turning up the collars on his wardrobe, which at the time was a signal of homo-sexuality among Dutch men. With the distinguished Bibi Andersson, he again played director, giving her notes between takes in an attempt to rigidly manipulate her responses. Andersson did not appreciate his unsolicited advice, and pointedly ignored it.

"This doesn't make sense," Perkins tells Andersson in the film, using the embarrassing mid-Atlantic accent he affected for all his classical or European roles. "You're no lesbian."

"Don't worry. You produced two children. That makes you some kind of a stud."

Though the dialogue holds some ironic parallels with his own life, Andersson's defiant sexuality seems less threatening in the face of the clearly gay Perkins than it might have with a more conventionally masculine actor. Likewise, the film's bloody denouement is no surprise given Tony's familiar twitches and darting glances. When the dreary *Twice a Woman* opened ephemerally in the United States in May of 1980, critics rightly dismissed it as a piece of ersatz Bergman.

But things seemed to be looking up for Perkins back in Los Angeles when he was cast in Walt Disney's multimillion-dollar science fiction epic, *The Black Hole*, the studio's bald attempt to cash in on the *Star Wars* phenomenon. No expense was spared as *Hole* started principal photography on October 11, 1978, utilizing all four of Disney's Burbank soundstages simultaneously. Guards were posted outside the closed sets, and the entire undertaking was veiled in secrecy in an obvious attempt to generate some publicity.

Unfortunately, neither an extensive merchandise blitz (including an Anthony Perkins doll) nor heaps of hype could save *The Black Hole* from falling into one. "Despite a title that manages to be at once sexist and racist," *The Hollywood Reporter* wrote, "*The Black Hole* is far from controversial. . . . In the current spate of space age sci-fiers, this entry is easily the drabbest and most derivative."

It did nothing to erase the public's perception of Tony Perkins as a horror movie has-been. And he hadn't even made a real horror movie yet.

In early 1979, Gore Vidal contacted Tony to discuss his starring in a six-hour miniseries on the life of Abraham Lincoln. Watching Perkins's performance as Inspector Javert in *Les Misérables*, Vidal had been struck by Perkins's "eerie resemblance" to the president, and started negotiations with producer Norman Lear and NBC. Perkins was interested, but owing to scheduling difficulties the project fell through. Vidal then suggested *Lincoln* as a stage vehicle, but fearing the separation from his family that a theatrical tour would require, Tony declined.

January found Perkins in Toronto shooting *Double Negative*, a thriller loosely based on Ross Macdonald's novel *The Three Roads*. The movie was basically a tax write-off of its production company, and Tony was paid almost $150,000 for a little over a week's work. Not surprisingly, he was cast as a debauched blackmailer.

According to director George Bloomfield, Perkins "had a ball" with the "kinky" aspects of the character: "He brought a tremendous amount to it. I suspect that Tony was a person who had a very free-flowing fantasy life, which he drew on." For one sex scene, Tony suggested that he and his female partner both wear sunglasses in bed. Bloomfield objected because he wanted the eyes to be visible, but Perkins got his way; his eyes are seen reflected in the woman's lenses.

"He liked to improvise," costar Susan Clark remembers. "He was very alive and always able to find some quirk in the character. But the man himself was very private, very mischievous. He would throw a line one way in rehearsal—then do a different inflection to see if you were really listening during the take."

Assuming his role as de facto successor to horror star Vincent Price (another closeted gay actor), Perkins hosted *The Horror Show*, a CBS-TV anthology of "60 Magical Years of Movie Monsters, Madmen and Creatures of the Night," which aired on February 6. Kicking off the program with writer Richard Schickel's assertion that horror "is basically un-American," he introduced the shower scene from *Psycho* with the simpleminded statement that Hitchcock's shocker marked the dissolution of the American family. A month later, on March 7, Perkins was on hand to introduce the shower scene again on the American Film Institute's Tribute to Alfred Hitchcock.

He flew to Ireland in June to portray another generic madman in the pitifully titled *ffolkes* with Roger Moore, and there was talk of his playing Soviet informer Alger Hiss for a British miniseries. Then it was announced that he would return to Broadway in Bernard Slade's new play, *Romantic Comedy*. Producer Morton Gottlieb, who had tried vainly in 1975 to sign Perkins for Slade's smash hit *Same Time, Next Year*, had sent him the new script while he was shooting overseas. Anxious to stop his run of dud movies, Tony immediately called Berry, who had just enrolled Osgood and Elvis in school in L.A.; she agreed to make the haul back to Chelsea if it would give

Tony's career the boost it needed. There weren't any films in her immediate future.

In mid-August, just in time to miss her sister's stage debut at the Beverly Hills Playhouse, Berry started the drive cross-country to meet her husband in Cape Cod—where Michaela O'Harra was watching over Janet Perkins, who had been hospitalized in Hyannis with breast cancer.

Marisa Berenson opened in William Saroyan's *The Time of Your Life* on August 24, 1979, the same night that Osgood Perkins's eighty-four-year-old widow died.

Jane had known she'd been ill for about a year. "She'd gone in for a general physical, feeling fine," recalls O'Harra, who had been living in Truro full-time. "But they checked her breasts and found out that she . . . So I stayed with her all that winter in New York, and then took her up to the Cape. I say 'take' because we always owned cars and I did all the driving, she didn't drive. She didn't need 'taking care of.' She was never in any pain, really. Totally ambulatory. But none of us wanted her to be alone after she found out."

Tony's cousin Stephanie remembers the last time she saw Jane: "She showed me how on one of her breasts, the nipple wouldn't come out like the other one would, and she was scared. She was going back to have it examined." Jane had taken estrogen when she'd gone through menopause. "She was one of the pioneers in that too," Stephanie says. "It kept her very young and vital—she used to bring her slant board to do sit-ups when she'd visit me at age seventy-eight—but I'm scared to death of estrogen because of what happened to her."

According to O'Harra, "We never knew that death was imminent. So Tony didn't even come." Jane was hospitalized not for cancer, but because she had come down with pneumonia.

Tony and Berry and the boys didn't arrive until just a couple of weeks before she passed away. But Cary Fuller was there, and a distraught Abbe Miller called frequently. One time, Tony answered the phone, and refused to acknowledge his mother's young friend, trying to convince Miller that he was someone else. "That was the only time I got pissed at him," Miller recalls. "He was no longer my hero. I said, 'I want to know about your mom. C'mon, she's like a mom to me too,' and he warmed up. He finally responded, only because I forced him to.

I asked if she was dying. He said, 'Yes, she is. But she's lost her hearing, Abbe, she can't talk to you.' I said, 'Well, then just do me a favor? Hug her for me.' "

"Until the very end Jane thought that Religious Science could still help her through it," Cary Fuller observed. "But this was just a battle she couldn't fight."

No one was at Jane's side when she passed on. Tony received a phone call from the hospital, and in turn called Michaela. "She's gone," he said.

"She really died very happily," O'Harra maintains, "because she loved children, and when Tony married and had the two kids she was just delighted. She was crazy about children—anything young." Abbe Miller claims her name was the last thing Janet Perkins uttered before she died.

A small memorial party was held on Jane's birthday, September 12, in the apartment Tony had bought for her at 230 East Fiftieth Street. Fuller remembers that "Berry was much more broken up than Tony. He just didn't show it." Only after seeing for himself how deeply Fuller cared for Jane did Tony begin to cotton to the young man, who, like Abbe, had once been just been a dogged fan. Only since her illness had Tony allowed himself to become at all close to his mother again.

"Berry had a lot to do with it," Miller says. "She loved Janet, and Janet adored her."

Back in Hollywood, sickly Teno Pollick was shocked by the news of Jane's death, but not nearly as shocked as he was to learn that she had left him nothing. At his hospital bedside she had promised to bequeath him a considerable amount of money. According to Keene Curtis, "She told Teno when he was ill that he'd never have to worry, that she'd make sure everything was taken care of, that he would be in her will. Well, he wasn't. She wrote him off like that.

"Teno felt very betrayed by her. He felt that she'd planned the whole thing just to protect her son, keeping Teno under control by promising him a lot of money, with no intention of giving it to him. She left it all to Tony. Maybe she thought Teno wasn't worth anything after the operation, so why bother. Teno said the press might start making connections if she left him anything, and she didn't want that. She was protecting her son. He felt she'd conned him like everybody else had been conning him his whole life." The trauma caused by Jane's double-dealing only contributed to Pollick's relentless downward spiral.

"Tony's mother was always a big bone of contention," Jennifer Lee remembers. "She loomed very large. When she died, everyone sighed a huge sigh of relief."

REVENGE

"CASTING TONY IN *ROMANTIC COMEDY* was a process of elimination," director Joseph Hardy recalls. "He wasn't our first choice, I have to admit." Top choice had been Michael Caine, who said no when Universal-Mirisch Productions would not guarantee him the lead in the film version. Rugged Sean Connery had also been considered, but there were scheduling problems. Morton Gottlieb, at least, was pleased when Perkins signed on; he'd known the actor since *Tea and Sympathy*.

"He was very grateful he'd been cast," Hardy says, "because it was his chance to play a straightforward leading man. Eccentric and unpleasant and so forth, but still a romantic leading man."

After Blythe Danner and Lynn Redgrave were discussed for the female lead (Berry's name did not come up), Hardy suggested film star Mia Farrow. Recently divorced from conductor André Previn, Farrow had returned to the States after a decade of living in England. Though she had not acted on an American stage since her 1964 appearance in an off-Broadway production of *The Importance of Being Earnest*, she had performed for two seasons with the Royal Shakespeare Company in London. Producers were hesitant to hire the thirty-four-year-old actress best known for her fey charm, but Hardy knew she had the inner strength to pull off a Broadway debut.

"It was an odd thing that happened," playwright Bernard Slade remembers, "because we were doing a romantic comedy, and suddenly we had Norman Bates and *Rosemary's Baby* onstage."

After tryouts in Boston, *Romantic Comedy* was to open in New York at the Ethel Barrymore Theatre, where the youthful Perkins had found success in both *Tea and Sympathy* and *Look Homeward, Angel.* This time, however, he demanded top billing in the show, and the ground-floor star dressing room (which Jo Van Fleet had occupied years before), leaving Farrow, who had more costume changes, to walk up a flight of stairs to hers. Both demands struck colleagues as harsh; it was customary for a male star to allow the female lead to have first billing. But to return to the Barrymore as *the* star was a promise Tony had made to himself during *Look Homeward, Angel*—and it was one that he intended to keep. He might never be back.

Farrow didn't mind; not used to having a private dressing room anyway (it was not the norm in England), she invited costar Holly Palance (daughter of Jack), with whom she had several friends in common, to share hers. "I don't think Tony was very comfortable with that," Palance recalls. "Sometimes I had the sense that he thought we were talking about him. He seemed to be very insecure, and really needing tremendous validation."

Conversely, Perkins told *Playbill* that he was "more stable" and "not quite as driven" as he had been when he was first starting out in the business. "I'm not anxious to hit the top and stay there," he claimed. "I guess I've discovered that the *person* is more important than the career." As for his relationship with Farrow, he reportedly pulled an Ingrid Bergman on her the first day of rehearsal: "I said, 'Look, Mia, I don't have any ego. Nothing you can say or do is going to put me off or make me uptight.' She said, 'Oh, I'm the same way.' We've never had so much as a sharp look."

Costume designer Jane Greenwood remembers Perkins being absorbed with what his character, Jason Carmichael, a sophisticated New York playwright who falls in love with his lady writing partner, would wear onstage. "He was very sure about what he wanted," the designer says, "whereas Mia Farrow was very vague. We talked about him having a very splendid dressing gown, and he said, 'Oh, yes, I think it should be *unusual*.' He was very slim and lithe and well-moving, and he chose clothes that reflected that." According to Greenwood, the robe that was eventually made for him was indeed fit for a star, made of "a rather elaborate brocade, very well tailored, really quite splendid. I was surprised that he was willing to wear such a flamboyant dressing gown." Anything to upstage Farrow as his mousy love interest, Phoebe Craddock.

Farrow remembers Tony being "very open" at the start of rehearsals, but as the Broadway premiere approached, they both decided that Hardy's arch, drawing room–style direction was leaving audiences cold. "We wanted it to be more true, more human, less mannered," Farrow says. Together, the two stars struggled to go their own way with the piece in time for the New York opening.

Hardy concedes that *Romantic Comedy* "ended up playing very well, but Mia and Tony canceled each other out because their personalities were too similar. Mia was perfect for the role, wonderful and shy, yet with strength underneath. Tony had that same sort of shyness and vulnerability. So the two were at odds sometimes. Whereas if Michael Caine or somebody gruffer, less vulnerable than Tony, had played it, the show probably would have been more successful and certain of its accents."

But it's doubtful whether Caine, or any other major star, would have consented as readily as Perkins to playing the scene in act 1 where he meets Phoebe for the first time and mistakes her for his masseuse, without wearing a single stitch of clothing. It is written in the script that Jason be "totally nude" at this crucial moment, with an addendum that the actor playing him need only *appear* to be nude by careful holding of Jason's portable massage table or staging it so that he is partially concealed behind a chair. Fitness addict Perkins would have none of that, and was adamant about showing off his hard-won physique in toto—regardless of the fact that, according to Hardy, he was not entirely pleased with how his forty-seven-year-old body looked: "He would say things like, 'Oh, I wish I were twenty years younger!' Yet he had absolutely no compunctions about doing the scene."

"Tony had no problem with it at all," stage manager Warren Crane confirms. "Which is unfortunate because he should have had a problem with it. I mean, it was not attractive."

For Boston, "the bare-ierre scene," as it became known, had Perkins enter and turn upstage to face Farrow, putting the massage table down in front of him, so that while Farrow's view of his genitalia was obstructed, the audience got a full view of his bare ass. "Tony was very athletic, he had an incredibly muscular body," Crane says. "But he was painfully thin. So what you saw were all these muscles on this very tall, thin frame, and in between his legs you saw these two pendulous balls hanging down. For middle-aged women who came—I mean, the play was aimed at those people—it was distasteful. But Tony loved the shock value of it, and Joe Hardy was also caught up in it. Tony was one of the first stars to do something like that. I think it was a mistake."

For New York, the nude scene was modified so that Perkins hid his backside from the audience with the carry-on massage table, giving Farrow a full frontal view (she, of course, at that point in the play, had to turn immediately away in embarrassment). When the *Post* asked Tony how his kids reacted to seeing their father nude onstage, he replied, "Oh, they've seen me walking around the house all the time with my clothes off. . . . Nudity is the last thing they'd ask about."

On October 15, *Romantic Comedy* opened at Boston's Colonial Theatre (where Tony's father had seen *Ben-Hur* as a tot), and was well received by the press. "Perkins and Farrow are ideally cast," *Variety* wrote. "He is wiry and stinging, she is vulnerable yet resilient, and Slade keeps their relationship on a tipping scale."

Yet Perkins, whose performance never varied, grew quickly bored with the frothy show, and began to make increasingly "eccentric" suggestions at rehearsal, which Hardy invariably dismissed. "None of them were any good," the director maintains. "Sometimes they were bizarre. Tony was volatile, to say the least. He got nervous and demanding at times."

During his scenes with actor Greg Mullavey, who was cast as Farrow's estranged husband, Tony proposed that they play it as if their characters had met before (the script indicates they have not), and had had a homosexual love affair. Mullavey simply ignored the suggestion.

But the proposal may have had a deeper relevance for Perkins, who was intensely jealous of Mullavey's success on the television series *Mary Hartman, Mary Hartman* and of the hearty applause Mullavey received at the nightly curtain call. At one performance, Perkins abruptly walked off the stage during their scene together, leaving the TV star stranded. "I had to improvise, and I got really pissed at him," Mullavey recalls. "After the show, I laid into him—'If you ever do that again, I'll come and knock the shit out of you.'" As usual, Tony claimed total innocence. "He said he'd thought he had an exit. I didn't believe him. But he followed me all the way up to my dressing room to apologize. He was very intellectual in his approach to life, and he loved to manipulate circumstances and people. Maybe he'd just been thinking, 'What would happen if I walked off here? What would happen if I simply disappeared for a few moments?' "

The passive-aggressive dichotomy continued offstage. Every night, while walking by himself from the Colonial Theatre to the Ritz Hotel, where he was staying, Perkins would visit Somewhere, a gay bar with a clientele of drag queens, drug pushers, and very young boys. There, he would position himself carefully in the shadows—with the pin spotlights illuminating just his piercing eyes—to watch the comings and goings and dealings of the crowd. Employees were seen introducing him to various youths.

Back in the safety of his dressing room, Tony loved to talk about sex and what he'd seen the night before. According to Warren Crane, "In the same breath, in the same conversation, he'd say, 'No, no, I know what you're thinking, but I never fool around. Ever since I've been married I do not fool around.' He was so silly that you didn't believe him for a minute. He would tell you about his marriage right on the tail of telling you about going to the bar with all the drag queens."

Joe Hardy remembers how Perkins loved to gossip "and be wicked about other people. He wasn't dishonest about his past or his sexuality, but he wasn't dishonest about how much he loved his kids either. He was very happy to be married because he was very happy to have the children. What his relationship was with Berry, I have no idea, we never got into it."

When the show moved to New York, Berry Perkins was not around much, except on matinee days, when she and the boys often met Tony for dinner between shows. One observer describes Berry as being "on a different wavelength too. I don't know how much real personal contact they had. She seemed like she was in another space. I don't know whether she took things or whether she had just developed this as a defense mechanism, but she was always kind of vague, not there. Maybe it was because she didn't share the theatrical life. He talked very glowingly of her, but he also spent a lot of time away working." Perkins confessed to one cast member that he had left Berry on more than one occasion—the other way around would seem more believable—but that the two of them would never divorce.

"Everyone in New York City knows that Tony Perkins's marriage is just a front," Berry's old friend, Halston, was quoted. "He still has male lovers. . . . Tony couldn't settle down with another guy because he's insecure and craves kinky affairs, not a genuine or lasting relationship. Tony isn't exactly Norman Bates, but he's awfully kinky."

However mysterious their marriage may have seemed to outside eyes, no one doubted Perkins's affection for his two boys, who were always at the theater with him on matinee days (as opposed to Farrow's seven children, all of whom were backstage with her every day). "Mia's kids were just heaven, all little ladies and gentlemen, while Tony's kids were no-neck monsters," Crane recalls. "Mia was obviously a wonderful mother, and Tony was obviously a fuckup as a father. Those boys were just uncontrolled. They'd never been taught anything, discipline-wise." (Later, in Laurel Canyon, the boys would be known as the terrors of Woodrow Wilson Drive.)

Perhaps because of his growing disdain for the play, Tony would send Oz and Elvis out on the stage to play just before curtain time. "They'd start moving props, pick stuff up, get into everything," Crane remembers. "Finally, I had to tell him to keep them off the stage. He knew they were brats. They were very spoiled. And the whole family was very into analysis. Tony and Berry had both been in analysis, and even the kids were put into analysis when they were very young. Tony thought therapy would cure anything."

Romantic Comedy opened on November 8, 1979. The reviews were mixed, and Tony took it hard. Distraught, he turned to his old confidante, Helen Merrill, phoning her at 7 A.M. with the write-ups.

Most critics were pleasantly surprised by Farrow's performance, while finding fault with Perkins's. *New York* magazine's John Simon, for instance, found her "vastly superior to Anthony Perkins, who desperately lacks charisma, especially toward the middle of the play, where he is hell-bent on (poorly) imitating Noel Coward's strangulated comic underplaying. From Perkins, it somehow sounds nasty, sickly, senile—not so much deadpan as bedpan. What it may come down to is lack of virility, of simple masculine craving: I never felt that this Jason wanted Phoebe half as much as a good crease in his pants."

"A rear view of Mr. Perkins, nude . . . looks like a selection from the anatomical studies of Thomas Eakins," *Voice* critic Michael Feingold wrote, astutely noting that "*Romantic Comedy* would make much more sense if both collaboraters were men, and the thing the hero was running away from was his own sexual identity problem. One does not spend 14 years running away from Mia Farrow."

In the same publication, columnist Arthur Bell hailed Perkins and Farrow as "better than I've ever seen them. But romantic comedy actors who disrobe on stage should make certain their asses aren't flabby. Tony could do with some toning."

According to Greg Mullavey, Tony was "devastated" by one particularly brutal attack on his Modigliani physique: "We'd stopped at a newsstand, and he was standing there reading, just blanched white, all the color drained from his face, as if the life had gone out of him. He'd never expected a review to malign or castigate his body. In Boston he had weights in his dressing room. He was extremely diligent about trying to look like he was in shape."

Despite the pans and petty jibes, the curious combination of Perkins and Farrow drew in the crowds, especially when Farrow began dating filmmaker Woody Allen, whose limousine became a nightly sight outside the Barrymore Theatre. By the following April *Romantic Comedy* had fully paid back its initial investment and was turning a hefty profit. With the show on its feet, Joe Hardy left, trusting his cast to continue acting like professionals. But Tony was bored and angry, and according to Bernard Slade, "his performance became more extreme, I think just to amuse himself."

He retreated more and more into an impenetrable funk. On matinee days, he would not speak to colleagues at all between shows—"just point to his throat and mouth words," Mullavey says, "a signal that he really just wanted to be left alone"—and after every performance, he continued his penchant for giving the other actors, including Farrow, notes for improvement. Farrow admits that his notes could be "annoying," but after taking them to heart, she soon learned to ignore them (though she maintains he did it "for the good of the show").

"Sometimes he was perverse onstage," Holly Palance remembers. During one matinee, Perkins spoke with an English accent for an entire act, then dropped it. And by the eighth or ninth month of the run, he had taken to wearing sunglasses onstage during the third act (*Romantic Comedy* is set completely indoors). Palance, who was only featured in the first and second acts, sometimes watched the last act from the stalls. She was shocked when Perkins asked her during a curtain call how long she had been doing that: "How in the world did he know I was out there? I was in the last row. What that meant was that he was watching the stalls, and spending quite a lot of time trying to figure out who was there. That was the reason for the sunglasses, so that neither the audience nor the other actors could see what he was doing. I was very taken aback."

As Slade observed, "He was extremely bright, but somewhat paranoid about people being out to get him"—and he could be Machiavellian in his struggle to gain what he perceived as the upper hand. "When Mia was sick," the playwright recalls, "he phoned her that night and told her how wonderful the understudy had been, how she'd got laughs where he hadn't known there were any. Mia, who's not very vain about her work, had a delayed reaction."

It was no secret among the company that Tony smoked a lot of marijuana; many colleagues thought his weird ideas came to him while he was under the influence.

"Unlike so many other things that get more complicated as you go along, acting seems to get easier," Perkins purported in *Playbill*. "At least it gets easier for me. I've learned to peel away the layers rather than add them. It's a matter of simplifying, not relying on tricks, ticks and gimmicks."

But rely he did on the meerschaum pipe he kept in his dressing room, filled with what Crane remembers as "Maui Wowee or something. He would always ask me if I wanted a toke, and I would always say no. But one night I was going to the opening of a new disco, the Bond, and I made the mistake of telling him, so he said, 'Tonight you *must* have some.' I took two puffs from this pipe, and I'm telling you, by the time I got out of the theater I was ten feet off the ground. I don't know where he got that grass, but it was something incredible."

Once, he invited Farrow and Palance to smoke a joint with him backstage and play the Truth Game by getting stoned and confessing their true feelings about one another. "Mia and I both said we didn't want to do it," Palance recalls. "Then he said, 'Okay, I'll go first,' and he proceeded to tell us exactly what he felt about us. I don't remember what he said to Mia, but I know what he said to me: 'You don't know who you are. You have no idea that you're beautiful. You haven't relaxed into who you are.' He told me I needed to reveal more of myself in my work. I shrugged it off and defended myself. But years later, I

feel that Tony *did* know things like that, he just had a very odd, con-
frontational way of going about it.

"I thought of him as a lonely person, unreachable, unknowable in a
lot of ways. There was a sadness about him, and it was always nice to
see Berry and the kids with him because he sort of came alive in a different way when they were there. I think he felt fuller, more connected. He had a tendency to manipulate people, but not when they
were around. He was happy when they were there. Calmer."

But he continued to be restless when they weren't. After his
phoned-in performance, he could be found almost nightly at the Haymarket, the infamous gay bar just down the street that was a virtual
meat track for strippers and male hustlers. Stage manager Crane, in
whom Tony confided his secret wanderings, remembers: "At the Haymarket one night he met a guy who was the manager of a hot porn star
at the time—Lance something—who was appearing there. Tony told
me that the manager took him down to the dressing room to meet this
kid. It was one room for all the strippers, four or five of them. 'Oh, it
was wonderful,' Tony told me, 'they were all naked. It was so beautiful
and sexy'—but, of course, he didn't do anything. The manager said
that for a hundred bucks he could have the client for the night. I said,
'Of course you did it,' and he said, 'No, no, no. You know I don't do
that now.' But he was thrilled, he couldn't wait to tell me about the
naked guys, how well-hung they were and the whole thing. I mean, he
was so into it."

On another occasion, one of the Haymarket hustlers came to the
stage door and demanded to see Perkins backstage. After the performance, Tony did see him, and according to one source, the youth "was
in Tony's dressing room for a long time before coming out. I don't
know what went on, but he was certainly there for money." It could
have been the same young man who another observer had seen waiting
for Perkins at the stage door every night for two weeks. Finally, Tony
had gone right up to him—"We're going home, where do you
live?"—and whisked his young admirer off in a cab.

"He swore to me that since he had married Berry and had the kids
he'd had absolutely no homosexual experiences," Warren Crane recalls. "He said that marriage had been his salvation. I'm not sure I quite
believe that because the last week he was in the show, the bartenders
from the Haymarket all came to a performance—I guess he invited

them—plus a lot of the hustlers from the bar. They all came in a group of about ten guys. It was a pretty raunchy crowd."

Romantic Comedy's box office dropped drastically when Perkins and Farrow left on September 16, 1980, and were replaced by Keith Baxter and *Room 222*'s Karen Valentine. Tony would not be back on Broadway again.

Two highly homophobic Hollywood films were released in 1980: William Friedkin's *Cruising* and Gordon Willis's *Windows*, both thrillers in which the gay antiheroes—in *Cruising* a gay man, in *Windows* a lesbian—are literally homicidal with misery. Gay rights activists had fought long and hard for mainstream visibility, but the film industry, which had created Tony Perkins, was still unable to offer anything other than the negative stereotypes that reinforced the public's fear and loathing (this despite the fact that a large percentage of the Hollywood workforce has always been composed of male and female homosexuals). Twenty-five years after Tony had first stepped off the train in Los Angeles, little had actually changed.

The pervading paranoia and denial of Hollywood inevitably seeped into the very private lives of its stars, and the Perkinses were certainly no exception. Christopher Isherwood and Don Bachardy, who hadn't seen Perkins since 1959, ran into him again when he returned to Los Angeles, at a huge party at Sue Mengers's for Gore Vidal. "We approached Perkins, who was standing by himself, and he suddenly looked panic-stricken," Bachardy recalls. "He looked around the room for his wife and children, and kind of bid them to him before he would say even a word to us. It wasn't until he had the children in front of him that he whispered, 'My life is different.' He was treating us rather like the Popes of Queerdom, and he'd lapsed—or maybe he thought we were going to talk some sort of dirty fag talk to him, so he had to be sure that we knew about his new standard.

"Of course we'd heard he'd married. And so what, you know? I thought that was just awfully odd behavior for him. I do feel that he was a victim of psychoanalysis. Did he honestly think that marriage to Berry Berenson could make him a heterosexual?"

Perkins's career hit an all-time slump in 1981, when his most exciting prospect was a series of television commercials for aftershave lotion for airplay only in Japan, where even the most has-been American film stars were still revered (though Paul Newman, Telly Savalas, and Tatum O'Neal had also been signed by ICM to plug products there). Tony spent a lot of time at home, practicing his keyboard, and waiting for the phone to ring.

Or food shopping at the Arrow Market just down the hill on Santa Monica Boulevard. That's where *Greenwillow*'s Ellen McCown, who was now also living in the area, ran into him again. It had been twenty years. "One of the clerks at the market told me he came in there a lot," she recalls, "so I promised myself that if I ever saw him I was going to come up behind him and call him Gideon, which was his name in the show." One afternoon McCown did just that, but to her surprise and disappointment, Perkins just froze and did not turn around. When she approached him, "he pulled himself up like he had hardly ever known me. I was really put off by it."

But not nearly as put off as she was by his appearance. "He looked ancient," she says. "He had aged very strangely. He was still extremely thin, as thin as he was when he was boyish, but his face had kind of shriveled up. You know how people get leathery from the sun? It was amazing, because in *Greenwillow* he was just as young and virile-looking as anybody.

"But the sad thing to me was that before I spoke to him, I'd been watching, and he was really cruising the boy clerks in the store, flirting very animatedly. He may have been afraid that I'd seen that."

Around this time Michael Black arranged for Tony to sing "Never Will I Marry," his song from *Greenwillow*, on *Best of Broadway*, a TV special for the Entertainment Channel that would bring together more than twenty major stars of the musical theater—including Ethel Merman, Robert Morse, and Mary Martin—performing the show-stopping numbers they had originated on Broadway. "We had called Michael Black because we wanted Alexis Smith to do 'Could I Leave You' from *Follies*," producer Iris Merlis recalls. "We got a call back from him saying Tony Perkins would like to do the show too. It hadn't occurred to us, but it was a great idea. So we said sure."

Rehearsals and taping took place in January 1982, at the La Mirada Civic Theater, about forty miles south of Los Angeles. Everyone would be singing in his original key, before a live audience. "It had been a while since he'd done the show on Broadway," director Rob Iscove remembers. "Just vocalizing and getting the chops up to be able to compete in an arena like that was nervous-making. But Tony was never temperamental. You could see that he was struggling with himself, trying to get himself to do it."

The song had been difficult for Perkins twenty-two years earlier; now it was practically impossible. According to executive producer Michael Brandman, "His voice had obviously lowered in the interim. The key was higher than he felt comfortable with, and you could see him visibly straining his way through it." At one point in the dress rehearsal, he was having such trouble that Robert Morse, who was there to do a number from the hit Loesser musical *How to Succeed in Business Without Really Trying*, had to coax him through it.

Afterward, Perkins tried to quit. "I can't do this," he told the producers. "I don't *want* to do this."

"He was scared," recalls Merlis, who, after conferring with Brandman, kindly agreed to let him go, despite the fact that a lot of time and expense had already been put into his orchestration and billing.

No sooner had they released him from his obligation than he changed his mind again—probably because they hadn't put up a satisfactory fight—and decided that he *did* want to sing on the show after all. But the day of the actual performance, one observer says, "Tony was very frightened, and was looking for Valium." Someone on the staff accommodated him, and thus sedated, he went on.

Sadly, his farewell rendition of "Never Will I Marry" is one of the most horrific performances of his career. Looking wasted and gaunt— his sunken eyes shocked open with fear, mouth grotesquely twisted— he can barely carry the downbeat tune. His high notes, which could easily have been transposed down for him, sound like screams for help. According to musical director Bob Rosengarden, "You could *see* it was painful. He just looked like a fish out of water."

So desperate was Perkins's need to stake his claim on the forgotten show that he was willing to humiliate himself before what would ultimately be hundreds of thousands of viewers. Yet backstage, amid all the egos, he still behaved like the good little boy. "There was something so ingenuous about him," Michael Brandman recalls. "He wanted to be liked and didn't want to make any waves." Perhaps fortuitously, the Entertainment Channel folded, delaying the broadcast of *Best of Broadway* for three years. It finally aired on PBS in 1985.

Meanwhile, back on the home front, with Marisa's life once again on the upswing—she had recently appeared in the controversial TV film *Playing for Time* with Vanessa Redgrave, and was about to marry successful trial lawyer Richard Golub—Berry decided it was time to take a stab at yet another career, one more in keeping with her illustrious background. With the help of Lynn Lemoyne, a close female friend and former partner of designer Carlos Arias, she formed the L. B. Trading Post label, and began designing a line of expensive, Native American–inspired chenille sweaters and shawls.

"It's difficult to be an actress in this town," she told the *Los Angeles Times*, "so I've been looking for something to do. I've been around fashion all my life, so it's nice to be on the other side. It's also easy to get in to talk to people."

After being in business just a few months, the women had peddled their $200 to $450 retail knitwear to Henri Bendel and Barney's in New York, and had a personal customer list that included Halston, Liza Minnelli, Rod and Alana Stewart, and, naturally, Tony Perkins and Marisa Berenson. But, says one friend, "they did well for about five minutes."

Berry also drew her cherubic sons, now aged eight and six, into the fashion business as models for Calvin Klein Actionwear ads that were shot on locations as far away as Mexico and Greece. "Calvin's been a friend for years, but that's not how they got the job," she said. "My friend Paul Jasmin suggested them to photographer Bruce Weber, who hired them sight unseen. Now, they have their own bank accounts."

Tony left for Florida in May, where he had been asked to accept an honorary doctor of humane letters degree from Rollins College, the school which had almost expelled him thirty years before. This was not the first invitation; he'd always politely declined. Now, however, he had nothing else to do, and nothing to lose. The return visit would be his first, and his last—and one that Rollins's faculty and students would not easily forget.

The commencement ceremony was scheduled to take place on Sunday, May 23, in the Enyart-Alumni Field House. Perkins was expected to arrive in Winter Park on Friday, the twenty-first, for a press conference and student question-and-answer session in the old Annie Russell Theatre. On Saturday he was to be guest of honor, along with writer-in-residence Sloan Wilson (who was also getting a degree), at a lavish dinner at the home of President Thaddeus Seymour. But first, Tony flew to Daytona Beach to enjoy a few days of fun in the sun.

The day of the Anthony Perkins press conference arrived, and by one-thirty that afternoon the Annie Russell was filled to capacity with local TV, radio, and newspaper reporters as well as hordes of students and faculty and staff, all of whom were eager to hear what the big-time Hollywood alumnus would have to say.

Tony, however, was not prompt. In fact, he was nowhere to be found.

Two hours later, just as the students were starting to get annoyed and the tea sandwiches were turning stale, Tony Perkins careened up in a rented car and, unable to find a convenient parking space, drove onto the curb and parked on the lawn outside the auditorium. He walked in wearing dirty jeans, athletic shoes, a black T-shirt, and sunglasses, looking tired and disheveled, with several days' growth on his face. "Here I am," he said.

The entrance did not go over well with the welcoming committee. According to Dean of Students Steve Neilson, who was in charge of publicity for the event, Perkins "appeared a little disoriented. He didn't seem to be completely sober. He was either on medication or under the influence of some drug or alcohol. He was kind of stumbling around a lot."

Perkins seemed nervous, even distraught, and before taking his place onstage, he insisted on making several phone calls to Daytona, where he claimed he had left his wallet. It later turned out that he was actually trying to find his "friend," a handsome young actor he had met at the beach and with whom he had spent the last few days. Faculty members would later refer to the youth as the "Palomino Stallion."

"His behavior was not, let us say, academic," one theater arts professor put it.

Perkins at last proceeded to give his speech, which addressed not only the demands of a theatrical career, the state of the Hollywood actor, and his association with Norman Bates, and also so-called family values, specifically how drastically his own life had changed since he'd been married and had children. "I don't remember being overly inspired," Steve Neilson says.

But the students were enthralled. "He was very pragmatic,"

remembers Joseph Nassif, who was there to guest direct a stage production in honor of the Annie Russell Theatre's fiftieth anniversary. "He said that to have an acting career you must give up everything for it—starve, suffer, bleed for it. At that point, he was not happy with his career. He didn't say it, but you could see there was a bitter frustration over the fact that nothing of any consequence was really happening for him. He was in a low spot. He was making preparations for another *Psycho*, but it sounded like that was not happy. There wasn't any twinkle. It was more like, 'Here I go again. It's all I've got.' He was very honest in saying don't go into this business."

When a student suggested that his father, Osgood Perkins, must have helped him break into the industry, Tony stated adamantly, "No. My father never got me *any* job." Asked if he would accept an invitation to come and guest direct a play at the Annie Russell, he replied that he would have to weigh the idea because he didn't like to leave his family.

Immediately after the reception, Perkins drove back to Daytona to pick up the Palomino Stallion.

When a small group of Rollins staffers arrived the next morning at Winter Park's staid Park Plaza Hotel to escort Tony to another function, they encountered a bellboy coming downstairs with a shocked expression on his face. Word quickly spread that the movie star's deluxe bed was not only occupied by a tall, blond, twenty-something hunk, but that his room was strewn with leather wear and a variety of kinky sexual aids.

All was not totally debauched, however. Before the big dinner that evening, Tony paid a special visit to his old mentor, Howard Bailey, who was ill and hospitalized, and unable to attend the president's party. Bailey's star pupil sat casually on the floor at his teacher's feet, where he spent three hours talking to him—more about his two boys than anything else. Bailey was deeply touched, and Tony surely enjoyed visiting the longtime ally who was old enough to be his father. He certainly was not looking forward to the evening's festivities.

The grand dinner was held alfresco at tables for four arranged carefully around President Seymour's large swimming pool. Tony was placed at a table with Joseph Nassif, Jeanette McKean, the wealthy widow of late Rollins president Hugh McKean, and Lydia Dorsett, the widow of theater arts professor Wilbur Dorsett, with whom Tony had corresponded over the years.

"He seemed quite ill," Mrs. Dorsett remembers. "Sitting at the table, he had a tremendous array of pills that he spread out in front of his plate. He kept picking at them. And he kept asking me about my husband, who had died the year before. It seemed rather strange to me. His questions were . . . well, he seemed obsessed with *how* my husband had died, if dying had bothered him. Tony's mind was obviously not on the dinner, or even the degree that he was getting the next day. He seemed very far away from it all. And he looked dreadful." (Some people speculate that Perkins already knew he was seriously ill at this time, but it's unlikely; real concern about AIDS didn't start until Rock Hudson passed away in 1985. The pills Mrs. Dorsett saw were probably vitamins, though some of them may well have been recreational goodies to help the guest of honor through the night.)

But the real faux pas occurred when Perkins leaned over to Mrs. McKean, the patron dowager of Florida, and asked, "Have you got a joint?" A blanket of quiet shock immediately fell over the table. The proper Southern lady had no idea what he was talking about, so Tony repeated the question, this time to Mrs. Dorsett, who was likewise unable to help him out.

"I thought maybe he was joking," Joe Nassif recalls. "It was done with such a wonderful humor. He was very polite, though he did dwell on Wilbur Dorsett."

Despite the unorthodox nature of Tony's request, after the meal an attending student was quickly enlisted to escort the star to the proverbial campus weed dealer. Mission accomplished, Perkins then invited his athletic young escort to join him in his hotel room, but the youth politely declined.

If by now the Rollins administration was worried about what Perkins's deportment would be on Sunday, in front of nearly a thousand graduating youngsters and their parents, they needn't have been. According to Nassif, "The next day he looked like a Philadelphia lawyer. He was talking and dealing with people on a whole different performance level." Everyone who had seen Perkins the previous two days agreed that the actor, dressed pristinely for the ceremony in a blue blazer and khaki pants, was today playing the role of obedient student to the hilt.

President Seymour's speech, which breezed over Tony's rise from theater arts major to international star, ended ironically with Laura's curtain line from *Tea and Sympathy*: "Years from now, when you talk about this—and you will—be kind."

Immediately after the reception, Tony split, though he had been asked to stay and give some more seminars and acting classes. He had no intention of giving either—nor of donating any funds to the Annie Russell Theatre (which, of course, had been the motivation behind bestowing on him an honorary degree). Perkins was not known for his generosity with money; he was cheap, and he was angry—the pain and fear of years ago still lingered. At least now he had finally thrown some of that discomfort back in the administration's hypocritical faces. (Today, Rollins College is in the process of setting up an Anthony Perkins Scholarship.)

As he was checking out of the Park Plaza, the Palomino Stallion appeared at the top of the stairs wearing just shorts and a T-shirt. "How am I supposed to get back to Daytona?" he yelled down.

"The same way you got here," Tony said, and left.

CHAPTER 23

LEFT IN THE DARK

IN EARLY 1982, *Smokey and the Bandit III* was one of Universal's top-priority projects. The other big title in development was *Psycho II.* Executive producer Bernard Schwartz was hesitant to add a numeric title to the Hitchcock legacy, but when marketing experts assured him it would sell, he went ahead and hired thirty-three-year-old Australian director Richard Franklin to complete the concept. In turn, Franklin asked screenwriter Tom Holland to bang out a script good enough to lure the original Norman Bates back to the motel.

"We couldn't do a *Psycho* without Tony," says Hilton Green, who was put in charge of production. "We knew that no one else could play Norman Bates."

So did Perkins, whose time to play hard-to-get seemed finally to have arrived. His performance in the original *Psycho* had long been a part of film and pop iconography; now perhaps he could enjoy the kind of professional respect that had always been reserved for stars like Paul Newman and Marlon Brando, contemporaries of his who had somehow always managed to be above him, better than him.

Michael Black began negotiations by claiming that under no circumstances would his client consider doing a sequel. When Schwartz persisted, Black asked for no less than a million dollars (which, by 1982, was not an uncommon fee for a major star).

The budget for *Psycho II*, however, was only about five million dollars. "I wanted Tony," Schwartz recalls, "but those kind of numbers would have destroyed the whole movie." He countered by bluffing that there were other actors at ICM, like Christopher Walken, who were up for the part.

His price down, Perkins tried to offer his services as director as part of the package, but Universal was adamantly against the idea. Unable to bend the situation, the actor agreed to reprise the role that had caused him so much grief over the past twenty-two years. "It wasn't like he was in demand and had five or six roles lined up," Hilton Green says. "I think that had a lot to do with it."

Sue Mengers, for one, begged him not to do it. But as Michael Black recalled, Tony was resigned: "Face it, gang: I *am* Norman Bates."

According to director Richard Franklin, "Tony felt Norman had adversely influenced his life and career, but his feelings of anger had mellowed to compassion."

"They could have made *Psycho II* without me," Perkins said modestly at the time. Claiming to be impressed by "the authenticity of the script," which had Norman returning home after twenty-two years in an asylum, Tony told the press that more than anything it was the chance to play a newly rehabilitated, self-aware Bates that really appealed to him. "The work Norman did with a compassionate psychiatrist has given him a lot of information about himself," he explained. "Now he knows he has the potential for being dangerous. But he's still very trusting. . . . He's good-hearted, really, and generous of spirit." He could have been talking about himself on the analyst's couch.

Psycho II would bring back Vera Miles as Lila, now bent on avenging her sister's murder. But this time around, the "straight" Norman would also have a younger female love interest. Hilton Green shrewdly thought Janet Leigh's real-life daughter, Jamie Lee Curtis, would be "tremendous" in the role, but Richard Franklin was torn between actresses Lisa Eilbacher and Meg Tilly. (Kathleen Turner, with whom Tony would soon star in the X-rated *Crimes of Passion,* and Carrie Fisher were also interested.) Tony urged Franklin to go with the winsome Tilly, who had recently appeared in the horror film *One Dark Night.* He would later regret having made the suggestion.

Using Richard Anobile's frame-by-frame picture book, *Alfred*

Hitchcock's "Psycho," as a bible, the sets of the Bates Motel and Gothic house on the hill were painstakingly reconstructed, using many of the original props and set decorations. "To see Tony standing on the original set, to see it all re-created, was a very eerie feeling," cinematographer Dean Cundey recalls. Principal photography began in late June without any rehearsal.

For Perkins rehearsal didn't matter. According to Hilton Green, even after twenty-plus years, "You could never direct him when he played Norman because no one knew Norman any better than Tony Perkins."

Foremost on Perkins's mind was his appearance. Concerned about his trademark thinness, which had become exaggerated with age and drug use, he requested that his T-shirts in the film be padded, to give his torso a beefier, more youthful look. Unfortunately, the padding did not photograph well; after seeing the dailies, the actor joked that it looked like he had "six English muffins" stuffed down his shirt. He also commented that an overhead shot of him and Robert Loggia, who played Norman's shrink, looked like "two men talking with boot polish on their heads." Perkins had recently begun to develop a bald spot, which privately distressed him.

Otherwise, he greatly enjoyed his importance in the making of the sequel, and basked in the deference of the crew, who bombarded him with questions about Hitchcock. *Psycho II* made him feel not just like a star, but like a living part of film history.

Which was what led to the trouble with Meg Tilly. As a child growing up in Victoria, British Columbia, Tilly had been prohibited from watching television; her parents wouldn't even allow one in the house. Consequently, she had never seen the original *Psycho*, and was completely unaware of Tony's relevance to the sequel. Though Perkins had wanted her in the film, his opinion changed, quickly and violently, when he overheard her saying to someone on the set, "So how come everyone keeps treating Tony like he's the star of this film?"

"He didn't like Meg Tilly, and he took off on her," one observer recalls. "He tried to get her fired. I think when he realized it was going to be a good picture, and that she was good in it, he wanted it all to himself. She was very young at the time, and I remember her dissolving into tears and crying."

A cast member confirms that Perkins "made it rough" on Tilly, but Hilton Green, who admits there was a "personality conflict," says they never seriously considered firing the actress. "He had problems with her from a professional standpoint; I don't know why because she did a very good job. But that was Tony; he'd get going every so often on things." No doubt part of Tony's problem was the fact that Tilly's film career was on the upswing while his own had reached a peculiar dead end.

At the same time, Perkins declared to the press that being a husband and father made him less concerned with his career: "I guess most of my ambitions now are concentrated on my family. Staying married constructively and creatively is a career in itself. . . . Now, I just like to know my lines and come to the set with a tremendous amount of enthusiasm for that day's work."

While most cast members agree that Perkins was "up" on the set, especially whenever the Universal Studios Tour trams passed by, full of gawking sightseers—Tony always made a point of smiling and waving to his public—they also couldn't help but notice his attachment to his young stand-in, a tall, dark actor named Kurt Paul. No one knows exactly where Perkins met Paul, but the youth, who struck many people as needy and volatile, acted as Perkins's unofficial personal assistant, even staying for a time at Perkins's new home on Seattle Drive.

"Kurt seemed like a total parasite to me," one observer says, "somebody who had a resemblance to Tony and had found his gravy train and attached himself to Tony's star. He was creepy. It seemed like they were very close, which made me shy away from Tony."

Perkins's behavior toward Paul seemed almost fatherly, but according to another person who was on the set, "Tony had some kind of thing going with his stand-in, and it was ugly. Tony was always kidding him—*viciously* kidding him—about being gay, and I don't think the guy was. It was not pleasant. He would deliberately try to piss this kid off, verbally attack him for being gay, when the guy wasn't. I never got the sense that they were lovers, but there was something there, a lot of tension. Tony was [verbally] beating him up."

Such extremes of behavior may have been caused by Perkins's increasing drug use; a perfect gentleman on the set, clean and sober during working hours, at home it was a different story. "Tony did everything," Jennifer Lee recalls. "He even dropped acid. I thought he was really strange for that reason.

"You'd go to parties at their house and Tony would be in the corner with all the gay boys, and Berry with all the straight girlfriends, except for the odd bisexual girl. It was strange. They were so *gay*, which is fine. But it was always weird to think that he was her husband. You were in their house and it was like being in a gay disco."

Richard Franklin and his wife socialized with Tony and Berry on several occasions. One night, in the car after an Yves Montand concert at the Greek Theater, Franklin played a tape of Jerry Goldsmith's rough theme music for Norman. The sad melody moved Tony to tears, and he confessed that he'd been living with Norman for so long, it was wonderful to hear the misunderstood boy next door presented sympathetically at last.

Another time, when Franklin's wife made a worried comment about the possibility of getting a "Norman Bates" from her baby-sitting agency, Tony quickly corrected her: "But Norman would be very good with children."

Indeed, Tony's two boys were his pride and joy, often joining their father on the set. He even allowed eight-year-old Osgood, who seemed to have inherited his father's piercing gaze, to make his screen debut as the prepubescent Norman, seen only in flashbacks. But he did not hang around for his son's scenes, fearing he would distract the boy. (Years later, the grown-up Oz would appear in several films, including Fred Schepisi's award-winning *Six Degrees of Separation* and Mike Nichols's *Wolf*.)

Joe Hyams, who had first met Perkins on the set of *Friendly Persuasion*, interviewed him again on *Psycho II*: "It seemed to me, just on the surface, that Tony had become more withdrawn. In the beginning, he was very open, almost despite the shyness there was a quality of wanting to be liked. With the passing years he seemed to have become a bit closed off, and that may well have been because of celebrity."

His newfound status as a living legend aside, Tony still wanted to direct, and as a concession Franklin incorporated some of his star's visual ideas into the final film. Tom Holland, who went on to direct successful shockers such as *Fright Night*, *Child's Play*, and *The Temp*, remembers Perkins's directorial sense as "not very commercial. It was an art film sensibility, intellectual, like those movies he did in the early sixties with Melina Mercouri and Orson Welles."

On his days off, Perkins was often sighted roaming the memorabilia shops on Hollywood Boulevard. In Backlot Books, he bought several vintage posters of his old films, including the risible *Green Mansions*. When collector Sabin Gray asked him why he didn't own them already, Perkins replied that when he was young he'd thought these things would be around forever; now he realized they were worth money. Ironically, the living Norman could not find the poster for *Psycho*.

"I never look backwards, you know," the actor told entertainment writer Aljean Harmetz. "I made my first movie over thirty years ago. Without *Psycho*, who's to say if I would have endured."

Psycho II finished shooting in early August. In October, Tony flew to New York to glide arm in arm with Janet Leigh across the stage of Radio City Music Hall for Alexander Cohen's celebrity-studded TV special, *Night of 100 Stars*. You would have missed them in a blink, but Perkins no doubt considered it good publicity for his upcoming return as Norman Bates. The stint was otherwise remarkable only for what happened *off*screen: Tony spent the entire trip to and from the East Coast vainly propositioning one of the show's other stars, a young blond actor who had been acclaimed for his Broadway role as a physically challenged Englishman.

One can only imagine what went on when Perkins flew to Australia in early 1983 to star as a tormented, alcoholic minister in the obscure period miniseries *For the Term of His Natural Life*. Shortly thereafter, he walked through *The Sins of Dorian Gray*, another piece of television fare also filmed abroad, which substituted a beautiful, seemingly ageless fashion model (Belinda Bauer) for the decadent homosexual of Oscar Wilde's original story. Perkins was arbitrarily thrown in as Henry Lord (as opposed to Wilde's Lord Henry), an amoral fashion impresario, and gave the kind of robotically arch performance that was quickly becoming his calling card.

In early June, *Psycho II* opened across the nation and was the month's biggest box-office smash, topped only by another sequel, *Return of the Jedi*. Reviews were mixed, but surprisingly favorable. "The best way to enjoy *Psycho II*," Andrew Sarris wrote, "is to think of it not as a stylistic echo of the Hitchcock original, but as a welcome reminder of how much *Psycho* owed to Tony Perkins in the first place. . . . His Norman Bates has taken on a life of his own."

A flurry of parties honored the event. Tony and Berry and the boys were flown to New York for the opening there, and put up in the Pierre Hotel. The night of the premiere, Broadway north of Times Square was filled with people, and traffic was stopped for two blocks around the theater. Berry invited designer Fernando Sanchez, and Harold Stevenson and his companion, to join her and the family at the screening. They all sat together in a row. "The only person who seemed illogical there was Tony," Stevenson recalls.

Afterward, there was a big bash at Studio 54, which had been decorated for "Norman Bates Night." Tony and Richard Franklin cut a huge cake in the shape of the *Psycho* house, and Hitchcock's daughter, Patricia, who had appeared in the original film, thanked everyone for being reverential to her father's memory. Andy Warhol showed up, and Stephen Sondheim phoned in his congratulations.

"I guess *Psycho II* will make a lot of money this summer," Warhol wrote in his infamous diary, adding an anecdote to illustrate how Tony was still up to his old tricks: Chris Makos, who had recently visited the Perkinses in L.A. "said that when Berry went into the other room Tony started pointing to Chris's crotch and saying, 'I'd like to see you,' and all Chris could say was, 'All right, Norman.' I never really liked Tony because he treated me badly once when he was with Tab Hunter."

To hype the film abroad, Tony agreed to embark on a grueling two-month promotional tour starting in Germany and moving on to Sweden, Denmark, France, Spain, Italy, Australia, and finally Japan, where he would meet up with his family. Then he would return to Europe for the U.K. premiere, before flying down to push the film in Brazil. He left on June 15, 1983.

But just before that he appeared on the cover of *People* magazine, standing proudly before the *Psycho* house, with Mrs. Bates's eerie silhouette in the window beyond. TONY PERKINS OF PSYCHO II, the cover headline read. The text continued below, "Like the mama's boy he plays, he was scared of women (even Fonda & Bardot), until a good wife turned his life around." What lay inside the magazine shocked everyone who knew him more than anything he'd ever done onscreen.

"Psycho II," as the article was titled, had little to do with the film; it was all about Tony, and the bizarre similarities between him and his alter ego, Norman Bates. Strangely forthcoming, Tony had told writer Brad Darrach about his lonely childhood, his all-pervasive guilt over his father's sudden death, and his (self-described) isolated relationship with his "strong-willed, dominant" mother. After laying out this simplistic psychological blueprint, which would have thrilled Dr. Irving Bieber, Tony confessed that for years "I had wild fantasies, but my erotic experience was mostly solitary. Along the way I'd had homosexual encounters, but that kind of sex always felt unreal to me and unsatisfying. And I had never had sex with a woman—the very thought of it terrified me." (Men who had known him laughed at the bald statement of denial.)

But what sent his family and friends into a collective paroxysm of outrage were the allegations of sexual molestation and the blame that he laid on the late Janet Rane Perkins. "She was constantly touching me and caressing me," Tony revealed. "Not realizing what effect she was having, she would touch me all over, even stroking the inside of my thighs right up to my crotch." He claimed that he had "completely repressed what my mother was doing—blanked it out. For years—until just a few years before she died in 1979—I really believed that all through my childhood my mother never touched me in an affectionate way."

Everyone was horrified. "None of us liked it," Tony's cousin Stephanie recalls. "In fact, I was just furious. Everybody loved Jane so much that we were all incensed." The Rane family's traditional Waspishness, however, kept any of them from voicing their disgust. They maintain that if anyone had fondled young Tony, it was probably one of Osgood's imported maids rather than upright Janet. Accompanying the piece was a photo of Tony at age three, sitting on a lawn with a small dog and a young woman *mis*identified as his mother. The girl in the picture was actually one of Osgood and Janet's many French housekeepers.

Michaela O'Harra was in South Africa researching a novel when she received the article in the mail. "It was a ridiculous story," she scoffs. "I was, of course, horrified. But it made Tony look worse than it did her. It made them both look like monsters. The whole thing was incomprehensible to me, and to anyone who knew either of them."

Stephen Paley was enraged ("It wasn't that way at all"), and Abbe Miller still thinks Tony "made a lot of it up for publicity."

Indeed, the interview had gone on for eleven hours before Perkins, no doubt under the influence of something, volunteered the incestuous revelation about Jane.

According to Gwen Davis, "The whole *People* interview was a public attempt at suicide. He did it himself, it wasn't the magazine. It was worse than strange. He outed himself. Even my son said at the time, 'How can he do that to his children?' " When Davis called Tony to ask him about it, his response was, "Well, I figured they would have found it out if I hadn't said it."

But he had no regrets. Years later, on the Cape, he told Henry Scammell that he felt good about the confession: "I managed to get something out in the open so I no longer have to look over my shoulder at it. It was just the right thing to have done."

It's highly doubtful that Berry or the boys shared his enthusiasm for the exposé. They were left at home to deal with the embarrassing aftermath as Tony flew off to promote his big new film. The boys, especially, had schoolmates to contend with.

"I get a lot of attention in airport lounges," Tony told one interviewer.

Executive producer Bernard Schwartz accompanied Perkins for most of the European tour. In Paris, the actor took Schwartz on a grand, sentimental tour of his old haunts. "There was something about that time in his life that was meaningful," Schwartz recalls with affection, "you could see it in his eyes. When we were in Rome, he spent a lot of time lying on his back by a fountain, hoping no one would see him, just in a reverie. He loved his kids, loved his wife, but they were the only things of real substance that belonged to him, that he controlled. It seemed to me that Tony was always fighting to survive in this business."

On August 3, during a stopover in London, Perkins was interviewed live on the stage of the National Film Theatre by British critic Ian Johnstone. Exhausted from the tour, and probably high for the event, his behavior was less than highbrow. Before the interview, clips from the original *Psycho* were shown. During the shower scene, which still stuns audiences into silence with its stark brutality, Tony sat in the back of the theater, laughing hysterically and a little too loudly. He later explained that Hitchcock had considered *Psycho* "a comedy." For the rest of the evening, he appeared disoriented, unable to remember which anecdotes he had and had not told the London audience, and stopping constantly for reassurance.

He returned to California with the paranoid delusion that the U.S. critics had "vilified" *Psycho II* in his absence. Richard Franklin remembers him being quite upset, when, in fact, everyone involved had gotten off pretty easily for tampering with a classic.

That September, Perkins took part in an Anglo-American television film called *The Glory Boys*, based on a thriller by Gerald Seymour, costarring Rod Steiger and Joanna Lumley. Upset by the fact that Steiger had a much larger trailer than he did—it was a stipulation of Steiger's contract that his female lover be accommodated on the set, whereas Tony was solo—Perkins complained constantly to director Michael Ferguson that the burly actor was stepping on his lines and stealing his scenes. Steiger, in turn, warned Ferguson that Perkins was on drugs.

But obedient Tony had already politely asked the director for permission to take speed (which he claimed improved his sexual prowess) before each take. As strange as it seemed, Ferguson did not object since the amphetamines helped produce the nervous tension, the twitches and tics, that "Tony recognized as being his trademark . . . part of what he was selling."

Speed also kept the already thin Perkins even thinner. Next to his family—he passed around photos of them constantly, always declaring his love for Berry, even though he was guilt-ridden over the fact that he hadn't written to her for weeks—his svelte fifty-one-year-old figure was the asset of which he appeared to be most proud.

Perkins flew home for the holidays, returning to England to complete filming on Sunday, January 29, 1984. As he walked casually through the Nothing to Declare exit at London's Heathrow Airport, authorities pulled him aside and searched him: eight grams of marijuana were found in a small pipe, and three "spots" of LSD discovered in a vitamin bottle. Police did not reveal how they had been tipped off. (Two weeks earlier, Linda McCartney, wife of Beatle Paul McCartney, had also been arrested in the airport for marijuana possession.) The actor was released on bail after being ordered to appear in court on February 2.

Perkins felt humiliated by the arrest. Yorkshire TV's defense tried to claim that the location shooting of *The Glory Boys* had put him under severe duress, but the star pleaded guilty, adding humbly, "I accept the responsibility for my actions." He was fined the British equivalent of $142. It was his first arrest and conviction, and would, unfortunately, not be his last.

Outside the court, he told reporters, "I have never claimed to be a perfect person and, of course, the imperfections of a man in the public eye will always be under closer scrutiny than the imperfections of the man in the street."

Returning to the set, Perkins shrugged for his colleagues and gave them a big, sheepish grin. He couldn't have done it better in summer stock.

Back home, he agreed to collaborate again with Stephen Sondheim on a treatment for a murder mystery miniseries for Home Box Office. *Crimes and Variations* was set in the demimonde of New York socialites, and followed the intricate twists of a single unsolved crime through the different eyes of its various characters. Perkins and Sondheim carefully orchestrated the plot to unfold suspensefully over a period of seven days, the first episode being a full hour long, the next five just thirty minutes each, with the denouement another full hour. As of 1996, their ingenious seventy-five page outline has yet to be produced.

Marisa Berenson was getting into writing as well, with a glossy fashion and makeup guide called *Dressing Up*, for which Berry took all of the portraits of her sister, again in the Manhattan studio of Peter Strongwater, where she had got her start so many years before. It was through Marisa that Tony met Al Lowman, her handsome young literary agent. "We hit it off instantly," Lowman recalls. "He had a lightning fast mind, which I do too, and he could change subjects within the scope of one sentence, almost like a great jazz poet."

But Tony couldn't liven the beat of his sluggish career. Lowman, who spent several days visiting the Perkinses in L.A. remembers some "heartbreaking moments in their home. Tony always picked up the phone immediately, and it would be like the deal of the century. He would have these long conversations with Michael Black, whom he called 'honey,' and nothing would come of it. There was never a great movie role. I saw that this was a man who was really at the end of the line in terms of the movie world. So that gave me confidence."

Lowman broached the possibility of Perkins writing his own full-scale autobiography, and Tony seemed to like the idea. They even came up with the provocative working title *Everyone Has a Secret Life*, but as soon as the agent began to generate some interest in the project, Tony shied away, with the excuse that he didn't think his children could handle it. Given what he had already revealed to the press about their grandmother—perhaps there *had* been some angry fallout at home after the *People* revelations—it seemed unlikely. But it was enough for him merely to know that people were still curious.

Perkins was likewise flattered when Catherine Wyler asked to interview him for *Directed by William Wyler*, a documentary film she was putting together about her father. Tony arrived at Wyler's Beverly Hills home—"loped in on foot," Catherine recalls, "as if he had walked there"—and spoke briefly for the camera about *Friendly Persuasion*. Unfortunately, unable to sell the film at its original ninety-minute length, Ms. Wyler was forced to edit it down to one hour, concentrating on her father's MGM films. Tony was furious when he realized that he and *Friendly Persuasion* had been completely cut out. He didn't realize that *Detective Story*'s Kirk Douglas, and a special interview with Steven Spielberg, had also been sacrificed. Ms. Wyler wrote Perkins a long letter explaining what had happened, and *Directed by William Wyler* went on to win an Emmy Award without him.

Tony leaped at the chance to play another psycho, this time a deranged psychiatrist posing as a shoe salesman to lure women into his grasp, for Ken Russell, the visionary director of *Women in Love*, *Tommy*, and *Altered States*. The salacious *Crimes of Passion* would not only team Perkins with the kind of seditious auteur in whom he always placed high hopes, but it offered a controversial script by Barry Sandler, whose recent *Making Love* had reaped lots of publicity as the first Hollywood film to deal directly with homosexuality. Add Kathleen Turner, the dynamic star of *Body Heat* and *Romancing the Stone*, and *Crimes of Passion* seemed sure to be a sexy box-office smash.

New World Pictures was certainly counting on it. The studio, best known for its cheap exploitation films like *Piranha* and *Children of the Corn*, was sinking an unheard-of seven million dollars into *Crimes*, hoping to break into the big time with its first major film.

According to Sandler, *Crimes of Passion* was less a thriller than an exploration of "the psychology of sexuality" and "the fear that comes with it . . . the confrontation of strong-willed characters who've assumed facades to hide a lot of pain." Case in point was Turner's dual role as Joanna/China Blue, a successful businesswoman by day who gets her kicks as a street hooker by night, attracting the obsessive Peter Shayne (Perkins) along the way.

Sandler had seen Perkins in *Equus*, and was pleased with the casting. But when he met with Tony on Seattle Drive to discuss the part, the actor immediately suggested that they change Shayne to a preacher instead of a shrink, to illuminate the hypocrisy of the many then-popular televangelists, who were always caught saying one thing and doing another. "Tony took out this huge Bible and began coming up with passages that Shayne could use," Sandler recalls. "You could't get much crazier than this character, but Tony did."

Perkins virtually reconceived the entire role—with the blessing of Ken Russell, who, in his 1989 autobiography, called him "one of the most dedicated actors I've ever worked with . . . to the extent of taking [the role] home to bed with him" (Tony literally slept in Shayne's grungy clerical clothes). Everything—from Shayne's folding pulpit, to the creepy chains and crosses he wore around his neck, to his crown of thorns and the final horrific transvestism (reminiscent of *Psycho*)—was Tony's own creation. He even "worked slavishly" with the art director to decorate the walls of Shayne's sleazy hotel room with clippings from pornographic magazines.

"Tony really connected with the themes of the film," Sandler says. "It wasn't like he had to dig that deep. In all likelihood, Shayne was just a further extension of who he was." Only when Perkins suggested that Shayne should walk around with an organ grinder's monkey on his shoulder did Sandler put his foot down. Tony then suggested a chihuahua, but the writer felt a campy little dog would reduce the reverend to a conglomeration of cartoonlike gimmicks.

Perkins later came up with an even more outrageous inspiration. When Russell's longtime lover, writer Vivian Jolly, announced that she wanted to get married (they already had a daughter), Tony raised his hand and asked, "Why don't *I* marry you?" For a few bucks, he explained, he could order a certificate by mail pronouncing him a bona fide minister of the Universal Life Church, with authority to preside over births, deaths, and marriages (producer Donald Borchers had found the ad in a motorcycle magazine).

Russell, of course, loved the idea and contrived to turn the ceremony into a publicity stunt for the film so that New World Pictures would foot the bill. Wanting a nautical theme for his nuptials, Russell chose the *Queen Mary* ocean liner, now permanently docked in Long Beach, as the wedding chapel (it had previously served as the top-heavy liner in *The Poseidon Adventure*). The studio approved, and arranged for the cast and a bevy of other New World celebrities, paparazzi, and *Entertainment Tonight* cameras to be there.

On Sunday, June 10, Russell and Jolly walked down the aisle, accompanied by their flower-girl daughter, toward Anthony Perkins, who was dressed pristinely in white for this mockery of a marriage just as he had been for his own knot tying. After reading extracts from works by Wordsworth and Thomas Hardy, minister Perkins pedestrianly pronounced them man and wife. They kissed, then danced their way back down the aisle to Ted Heath's "Bow Bells Swinging the Broadway Melody."

Filming was just as bizarre. "Tony had an interesting way of acting," recalls David DeCoteau, the production's craft services or "doughnut boy." "Then I realized that he was on amyl nitrite for each scene." Again, it was Perkins's idea that Shayne use "poppers," a drug usually inhaled to add an extra "rush" to orgasm. "He was very open about his use of amyl," DeCoteau says. "That's how he worked, how he got the intensity. Not exactly a Lee Strasberg technique, but it seemed to be effective for him.

"When we were shooting on Hollywood Boulevard, cars were driving by, and it took about a minute and a half to lock up traffic so we could get a decent sound take. One time Tony exploded and said, 'God damn it! Fucking cars! Forget it! I want to shoot the fucking thing *now*! I'm into it, let's do it!' He'd found the moment in his psyche, he was ready to roll with it, and he'd had to wait. That's tough on an actor, especially in a role that requires sweat and ranting and raving."

Despite the chemical enhancement, Perkins managed to impress everyone on the set with his staunch professionalism. DeCoteau, to whom Perkins "took a liking," remembers when they shot the final scene in which the demented reverend breaks into Joanna's picture-perfect apartment: "Right before he crashed through her door, he was talking to me out in the hallway, just having this casual conversation. I said, 'Tony, they're rolling sound, I can hear the slate. Let me leave you alone so you can get into it,' and he went, 'Honey, I've been in Actors Equity for thirty years, I don't *need* any time to prepare.' Ken Russell yelled, 'Action!' and Tony just ran right to the door and screamed, 'Last rites!' It was very funny." (It was Perkins's idea, too, that Shayne sing the Judy Garland song "Get Happy" later in the scene, when he tortures Joanna with a maniacal ditty at the piano. His horrifically shrill rendition, clearly a furious parody of his own youthful Garland impersonations, would later be attacked by critics.)

"Conversations with Tony were very brief because he didn't seem to have one consistent train of thought," DeCoteau says. "He was all over the place. But he was into one thing: he loved to talk about sex a lot. He was very open about that, always winking and hinting at stuff, nonstop." Before shooting the sequence in which Shayne stands looking through a sex shop peephole while he masturbates a metal dildo, Tony tapped DeCoteau on the shoulder and asked, "Why don't you stand on the other side of the peephole and expose yourself so that glaze in my eyes will be for real?"

Part of DeCoteau's job was to clean the stars' dressing rooms at the end of the day. One evening, after everyone had left, the doughnut boy was tidying up Perkins's dressing room when he heard the door close behind him. He turned around and was stunned to see Tony standing there in his Jockey underwear, his pants down around his ankles, his shirt unbuttoned and almost falling off.

"Not a bad body for a man of fifty, huh David?"

"Yes, Tony," DeCoteau replied and continued working. "Tony could have just walked up and grabbed me or slapped my ass, but he didn't. He never got cozy, he always did it from across the stage, or across a table or room."

Yet whenever Berry and the boys came to visit him on the set, "he was like a totally different guy. Very straight, very cool, very fatherly—just a whole different side of him. It was really almost a split personality thing. Nobody knew how to predict him."

"I didn't know to what extent he had closed off that part of his life, and I didn't feel comfortable pursuing that with him," says Barry Sandler, who was openly gay, and as such, a pioneer figure in the industry. "We never got into any heavy discussions about gay life. It was always clear to me that he had a very good marriage with Berry, and that he loved her and the kids."

As for his offscreen relationship with Kathleen Turner, whom he had to lust after on-screen, Perkins later claimed, "We had an excellent time. By the time I was working with Kathleen, I was already in a frame of mind to enjoy her not only as an actress, but as a woman as well. She had her then-fiancé around quite a bit at the time, and my wife was lurking in the wings as well, so we were well chaperoned by our respective spouses and spouses-to-be."

Perkins also had Kurt Paul on the payroll again. Though Paul had been officially negotiated as his lighting double and personal assistant by Michael Black (at Tony's request), the relationship between Perkins and his young look-alike continued to puzzle most observers. David DeCoteau remembers that while Paul physically resembled Perkins, he was even "stranger than Tony, quirky and weird," yet "very heterosexual. He seemed to be close with Tony, but when it came to Tony's whole gay side, Kurt disconnected. We all thought that if Tony were to have an assistant, it would be some pretty gay boy, but no."

"He was very involved in Tony's life," another observer says, "and made it very clear to everybody else on the set just how important he was. To us, he was the stand-in; to him, he was this big-deal guy."

With its graphic depiction of the seamy side of contemporary urban American life—peep shows, sadomasochism, blow-up dolls, and blow jobs—*Crimes of Passion* was given an X rating by the Motion Picture Association of America. Though Ken Russell protested that "nothing happens in this film that I haven't seen on British television frequently," after three recuts, the film was still denied the more commercially viable R rating.

Russell was enraged by the puritanical censorship of the MPAA. "You can be as violent as you want in his country," he told *Variety*, "but you talk about sex and everyone reaches for their chastity belts." As a prime example of the hypocrisy, he cited Spielberg's family-oriented megahit *Raiders of the Lost Ark* as an obscene "hymn to violence."

"We're dealing with disturbing circumstances in the film—a

prostitute and a paranoid, and possibly insane, minister," Kathleen Turner was quoted. "If it's cut any more, it will probably be too watered down."

Though he himself performed many of the lewd acts in the film, Perkins made no public statements at the time of the controversy.

Finally, after a fifth cut—which removed a rather lengthy scene in which Turner ravishes a cop anally with his nightstick—*Crimes* was granted an R rating for domestic release, allowing Russell an unrated version for distribution overseas.

"It's an extraordinary film," Perkins then declared to the *Los Angeles Times*. "And it will jolt people. . . . So I've told New World Pictures that I'll do all I can to help the picture. The fact is, I'm still on the high I got from working with Ken."

Crimes was poorly received when it opened in October of 1984. Most critics dismissed Perkins's fever-pitch performance as just another variation on Norman Bates—indeed, it does seem an older, more desperate version of the once timid mama's boy—but *Newsweek*'s Jack Kroll noted that "the battles between Turner and Perkins have a real ferocity," and the *Village Voice* described his Reverend Shayne this way: "matted with sweat, he seems to be simmering in his own sexual juices, his steel-gray glasses beading up from the hot fluids. Perkins uses his pointed nose to punctuate his mad harangues, and his tongue scoops the air as if to lap up its poisons. When Turner spits in his face, he mechanically transfers the spittle to his hand and then licks it off; he'll taste anything." These graphic details came from Tony's own experience.

"We all had very high hopes, and we were all disappointed when the film didn't do better," Barry Sandler recalls. "We felt that it would have been more successful if it had been Ken's cut that was released. In the end we were proven right, because when it came out on video in the unrated version, it was a big hit."

Tony did the TV talk show circuit to plug the sinking film. In L.A., he was squeezed onto *The Tonight Show* between Michelle Lee and Brooke Shields. When guest host Joan Rivers questioned him about all his "affairs" with leading ladies like Victoria Principal, he warned her to "be careful . . . because my beautiful young wife is sitting in the greenroom, and she'll come out here and arm wrestle you to the floor!"

In New York, when the sardonic David Letterman asked him if the excised cop-sex sequence had contained "a lot of nudity," Tony smirked and replied in his best stoned intellectual mode, "It seems to me there can only be a certain amount of nudity, no?"—at which he and Letterman burst into private laughter, leaving the rest of America at home in the dark.

SOMETHING TO
HIDE

T HIS IS THE ROLE I've been waiting for all my life," Perkins told
the L.A.-based writing team of Morton Thaw and Edward Robak
after reading their new stage play *Together*, about the stormy relationship between playwright Eugene O'Neill and his third and final wife, Carlotta. Bursting with melodrama and psychological
darkness, it was the best script he had been offered since *Equus*.

The playwrights themselves had sent it to him that fall.
"O'Neill was always just on the edge of madness, and this appealed to
Tony," Morton Thaw recalls. "He was haunted by his family; Tony
identified with that. There's a hell of a lot of fireworks between Car-
lotta and O'Neill, and the dramatic possibilities were enormous for
him." Tony asked to turn the play over to his theatrical agent, Lionel
Larner, who then presented it to producers Michael Frazier and Roger
Stevens as a package with Perkins as star.

"There was a physical thing about Tony and a personality characteristic that I thought was ideally suited to O'Neill," Frazier says, "that
kind of dark, brooding, multilayered quality that you see in photographs of the playwright. Helen Merrill thought it would be wonderful
for him, but wondered if he'd really want to spend that much time
away from his family." Tony claimed he was prepared to commit to a
two-year Broadway run.

Meanwhile, back in Los Angeles, a cold reading of *Together* was arranged at the Pasadena mansion of producer-director Alvin Stanley. Popular television actress Lois Nettleton, who had been nominated for a Tony Award for her role in the Broadway revival of Sidney Howard's *They Knew What They Wanted*—and for whom *Together* had been written—read Carlotta. Barney Martin and Rue McClanahan read the roles of an Irish cabdriver and his wife, a couple to contrast with the fiery O'Neills. Berry and several friends and agents were invited to attend.

The actors, none of whom had ever met before, sat on chairs, with scripts in hand. Nettleton remembers being impressed by how "free and open" Perkins was: "He was very communicative, very passionate—he threw himself into it. In a way it was like we were already in rehearsal. In the very emotional parts, we touched each other. In fact, at the end a couple of people had tears in their eyes. Everyone was terribly moved by it."

According to Thaw, "Tony rose to real dramatic heights at the reading. Afterward, he came up to Ed and me and said it had gone exactly as he'd hoped. He was eager to get started with it. For him, this was a sure Tony Award because of what he could bring to the role."

The producers, however, wanted a bigger name than Lois Nettleton to star opposite Perkins. Audrey Hepburn, his *Green Mansions* costar, was their first choice for Carlotta, though the writers considered it an "absurd piece of casting," doubting whether Hepburn could convincingly portray O'Neill's shrewish wife. Jane Fonda, Faye Dunaway, and even Zoe Caldwell, who looked old enough to be Tony's mother, were all subsequently discussed. (Again, Berry's name never came up.)

As haggling continued, Tony took time out to host a PBS television broadcast of the Gounod opera *Faust*, about a man who sells his soul to the devil in return for a brief spell of renewed youth. Then he got an offer he almost refused: to reprise Norman Bates yet again in *Psycho III*. It was not a bad joke, though it sounded like one. The new *Psycho* script, by Charles Edward Pogue, who had penned the recent remake of *The Fly*, had Norman now running the reopened Bates Motel and involved in a romance with a suicidal nun. No amount of money could entice Tony to do it.

Except one: let him direct as well as star, and he'd do it for the acting price alone. Universal was reluctant to allow Perkins to use the potential moneymaker as a vehicle for his directorial bow, but they also knew that without him they wouldn't have a *Psycho III*. When he vowed to bring the film in on time, within its $8.4 million budget, the studio begrudgingly consented. Norman Bates would direct himself.

"*Affinity* is the word I used to pry my way into the Black Tower [Universal Pictures]," Perkins told the *Los Angeles Times*. "I was worried about letting Norman's future fall into the hands of someone not all that familiar with the material."

When Universal rejected his idea to film *Psycho III* entirely in black and white like the Hitchcock original, Perkins shrewdly hired Bruce Surtees—the cinematographer who had shot the Clint Eastwood thrillers *Play Misty for Me* and *Tightrope*—to give his movie the film noir atmosphere he wanted. Joel and Ethan Coen's recent tongue-in-cheek hit *Blood Simple* was Tony's inspiration, and he demanded that everyone involved in *Psycho III* attend a screening of the film. He even had the studio track down the little-known composer of *Blood Simple*'s score, Carter Burwell.

To play Maureen, the troubled young nun who finds herself hiding out at the Bates Motel, Perkins wasted no time casting Diana Scarwid, who had been nominated for an Academy Award for her supporting role in Richard Donner's *Inside Moves* and had been praised as Christina Crawford in the otherwise derided film of *Mommie Dearest*. More recently, she had appeared as the lesbian hairdresser in Mike Nichols's *Silkwood*. As Duane Duke, a dangerous drifter who takes a temporary job at the motel, Perkins hired rugged newcomer Jeff Fahey. And as Tracy, the brittle reporter who suspects Norman may still have a few screws loose, Tony signed Roberta Maxwell, with whom he had worked briefly in *Equus* ten years before, against the wishes of studio honchos, who wanted a younger actress for the part.

Tony's double, Kurt Paul, was again hired, but this time, Tony told reporter Roderick Mann, "He'll actually learn the lines and know the role. That way I'll be able to see how it all looks. Kurt's going to be a big help. . . . There's a bit of Norman in him too." Tony also hired Berry to shoot the ad campaign for the film.

By the time filming began on June 28, 1985, the director was fully prepared, with Hitchcockian storyboards and high spirits. Unlike his prickly forays into stage directing, behind the camera Tony was the perfect gentleman. "He was very much an actor's director," Jeff Fahey recalls. "It was his first time directing, and he was under a lot of pressure. All the eyes of the Black Tower were upon him, so he had his hands full. But still, he was right in there with us. He made me feel very comfortable, and allowed me to bring whatever I wanted to the table."

Diana Scarwid agrees that "he wasn't dictatorial in his approach at all, which I think was just a reflection of him as a human being. We both realized our characters were two lost souls, wanting to help each other with their capacity to love. I think we saw that in each other as people also."

Indeed, Perkins behaved with an almost paternal protectiveness toward his cast, all of whom he showered regularly with words of encouragement and trust (only privately, to Bruce Surtees, did he gripe about the performances that were displeasing him). Crisp and friendly at all times, he was quietly determined to bring the film in under budget, making sure not to give the MCA suits any ammo to use against him.

In his office on the Universal lot, Tony answered all fan mail personally and autographed photos himself. Amazingly, letters still arrived for him from all over the world (in one, from India, a woman wrote foretelling his death, but his secretary threw it away before he could see it). Whenever the Universal Studios tour trams passed while they were shooting, Tony ordered cast and crew alike, "All right, everybody wave. Every one of those people is a potential butt in a seat."

Carter Burwell, who visited the set several times, remembers how Perkins "seemed to enjoy working within the system, even though as a person he was so much more intelligent and individual than most people in the industry. Lew Wasserman would come up to him in the commissary and say, 'Hey, Tony.' He was very comfortable in the role of Hollywood actor. I don't think it would even have occurred to him to direct an independent film." Yet those had always been the kind of films he most admired.

His deep and recurrent sense of inadequacy kept the new director compliant. Though screenwriter Charles Pogue maintains "it was always his goal to see Norman as sympathetic," Perkins put up no fight when the studio demanded that he gore-enhance the murder sequences to appeal to a jaded teenage audience. Carter Burwell watched him "directing people throwing blood on the glass of a phone booth, and saying, 'Oh, a little more there! Yeah, splatter it this way!'—he seemed to be getting as much enjoyment out of it as he could." It was Perkins's own idea, for instance, to have the Sheriff (Hugh Gillin) unknowingly pop a bloody ice cube into his mouth and suck on it during the expository scene where a corpse is nearly discovered in the motel ice chest. Though Gillin objected to the juvenile gag, Tony persuaded him to do it "just for fun," saying that he probably wouldn't use the take anyway. (That's the take he used.)

While Universal upped the violence quota wherever possible—and tacked a gimmicky shock ending onto the final film—executives were adamant about toning down the sex scene involving Duane Duke and a local tramp that could have been lifted right out of *Crimes of Passion*. "Tony really wanted to make that a way-out sequence," Hilton Green recalls, "wild and sexual and all of that, but the studio didn't want that type of picture."

Actor Jeff Fahey didn't want to shoot the scene either because Tony "wanted me to do some things that I wasn't up for—like strutting around naked."

"That was all Tony," Green says.

But Perkins did compromise with Fahey, using the actor's idea to carefully hold a lamp in front of his crotch, thereby casting an even stranger light on the (Shayne-like) porn-covered walls of the motel room. "It turned out great," Fahey maintains. "Tony was very giving."

As for directing himself, it appeared to be second nature for Perkins; he amazed the rest of the cast with his ability to instantly "click" in and out of Norman—even his body language would automatically transform. Tony and Norman seemed almost to be two personalities sharing the same body.

Equally curious was Tony/Norman look-alike Kurt Paul, whose self-importance and delusions of grandeur continued to strike everyone on the set. According to several observers, he seemed to perceive himself as one of the stars, and bragged constantly about how Tony was going to help his acting career. Even Diana Scarwid recalls that "he was probably more like Norman than Norman."

Men's costumer Brian O'Dowd, who had worked with Tony on the first sequel, was another dead ringer for Norman. Tall, thin, and openly gay, the British-born O'Dowd had come to Los Angeles to be a photographer—an irresistible bent for Tony—taking candid shots of movie stars for the little-known *Hollywood Studio Magazine*. Tony generously posed for him several times.

"Brian used to tell me that he had a great time with Perkins, that he was good 'company' and that they had lots of 'fun' together," says Eric Harrison, who was now living in Los Angeles. "They'd go out together. Brian *always* referred to 'Tony and I.' That made me wonder a great deal." By the time they worked together again two years later on *Lucky Stiff*, Perkins's second directorial effort, O'Dowd would already be noticeably weak from AIDS. His death in early 1990, shortly before the public exposure of Perkins's own HIV status, would be the major factor to propel Tony into AIDS volunteer work.

Meanwhile, Tony received a surprise visit on the set from Howard and Jenelle Bailey, who were taking a vacation from Rollins College. Though Perkins was delighted to see Bailey again—it would be their last meeting—both the professor and his wife couldn't help but notice the actor's withered appearance. "I don't know whether he was just in the part of Bates, but there was a really haunted look about him," Mrs. Bailey recalls. "The face was just *gaunt*. But he was very kind to Howard, as usual."

Perhaps because of how drawn he looked, especially next to the much younger Scarwid, Tony was worried about the love scenes. Consequently, he and Carter Burwell came to heads over the Norman-Maureen theme music; Perkins was concerned that audiences would laugh if the score was too overtly romantic. Similarly, when Burwell, who was a fan of Tony's *On a Rainy Afternoon* LP, tried to coax him to sing in the film during a scene where Norman plays "Beautiful Dreamer" at the piano, he refused. "I thought it would be really touching and tried to twist his arm," Burwell says, "but he was too shy, too insecure about his voice." (His gruesome performance on *Best of Broadway* had just aired in May.) Perkins didn't even want his own piano playing on the final sound track, and had a professional pianist rerecord the source music for the scene.

With its dreamlike photography and cutting, *Psycho III* is a definite improvement over the harshly lit, flat surfaces of the first sequel. But Tony's directorial bow did not win him any new fans when it opened on July 4, 1986. "Perkins has directed himself in a curiously robotlike rhythm, as if his line readings were being paced by a metronome," Andrew Sarris wrote, calling the film as a whole "a purely cerebral achievement, blessed with intelligence but not with inspiration."

"Perkins . . . turns in his worst job in the series," the *Chicago Tri-*

bune declaimed, "nervously belting out lines . . . as if he were doing a bad *Saturday Night Live* Norman Bates skit."

"We thought the film would do better than it did," Hilton Green admits. "Tony did a very good job, but he brought out the darker side too much. This was a heavier picture than the other *Psycho*s, and the audience didn't accept it."

Universal quickly canceled plans for *Psycho IV*, which Perkins and Charles Pogue had already outlined, and which Tony was expecting to direct. In their treatment, described by Pogue as "a very, very black comedy," Norman was to escape from the asylum with a girl, only to end up back at the Bates Motel—now being run as a mystery weekend attraction where the Bates crimes are reenacted. Naturally, the fake Norman quits, allowing the real Norman to step in.

"The studio read it and didn't want to do it," Green recalls. "Tony felt very strongly that it was the best one. But I didn't think so. It was too much of the same thing." There would eventually be a *Psycho IV*, but one so mechanical and drab, no one would care.

According to Stephen Paley, Tony was "deeply, deeply shaken by the failure of *Psycho III*. That was the first time I ever saw him in a real funk. He'd been expecting the success of the second film. But audiences had been very disappointed by *Psycho II*, and by *III* they didn't want to get burned again. He thought it was his fault, that he hadn't directed it right." Buck Henry maintains that Perkins's *Psycho* sequel "was the only one that looked like a pro did it, but he told me he'd just *hated* directing, and I found that very sad. I would have thought he was a natural."

He nevertheless traveled extensively to promote *Psycho III*, taking the film to be screened at Cannes, and attending the Ghent Festival of Film Fantastique—where he donned the mask of a spoiled American movie star, demanding a hairdresser midway through an interview with a prominent Belgian film critic, and flaunting himself fearlessly in the local gay disco. How much drugs were responsible for his extreme behavior is anybody's guess.

In transit for two nights in New York, he took time out to record "All My Friends Have Gone to California" for Ben Bagley; the little-known Kander and Ebb song, from an aborted musical about street people, was supposedly written from the point of view of a male hustler. The two friends dined together that night at the

Plaza Hotel Oak Room, "and we talked about hustlers," Bagley recalls. "Tony said he was tempted sometimes, but he would never do
anything to hurt Berry. He told me he *wasn't* fucking around, but
obviously he must have been." (It was later reported in the tabloids
that Perkins kept a secret room at the Chateau Marmont as a place to
take his play-for-pay boys.)

"There is no real security in life," Perkins told a reporter after the
failure of *Psycho III*, "but I am still married."

Back in the States, *Together* was ready to get under way. Vivian Mata-
lon had been assigned to direct, and the Kennedy Center was preparing
to book the play for a five- or six-week pre-Broadway run.

But suddenly, Tony wasn't so sure about it. He wanted only to direct it now, which would mean less time for him on the East Coast and
would not require him to uproot his family. According to Morton
Thaw, "He thought a whole career was opening up for him in Hollywood directing motion pictures."

Bolstering Perkins's confidence was the fact that he had just left
ICM, where he'd been floundering for years, to be represented by the
Gersh Agency, where agent Ron Bernstein had been assigned to pitch
him as a director. "It was his last gasp for a career," Bernstein says.
"*Psycho III* was pretty good, but it hadn't resulted in much interest in
him as a director. He turned down *D.O.A.* at Disney for the right reasons. Certainly no one was offering him stuff that Sydney Pollack
wanted to do, but he got scripts. There just weren't bushels of them.
Psycho was the curse and the blessing of his career."

Michael Frazier and Roger Stevens did *not* want Tony to direct *Together*, and the deal collapsed, leaving the playwrights without a backer.
"Tony had the potential to be a great actor," Thaw holds. "Our play
would have regained him some of the luster that he'd had early in his
career. It was another lost opportunity for him. And it certainly loused
us up."

Tony would be back. But first, he flew off to Paris to appear as Tal-
leyrand in the ABC miniseries *Napoleon and Josephine*, starring Armand
Assante and Jacqueline Bisset. Affecting yet another half-assed accent—
"It's hard to identify," he told *TV Guide*, "but it's definitely not
French"—his arch performance was little more than a rehash of his

Javert from *Les Misérables*. When it aired in 1987, the three-part tele-film plummeted farther down the ratings with each installment.

Charles Williamson happened to be in Paris at the time with his partner, Tucker Fleming, and they arranged to meet Tony for a drink at the Cafe Flore. Afterward, the three of them planned to visit African American actor Gordon Heath, who had starred in Elia Kazan's 1945 production of the controversial racial melodrama *Deep Are the Roots*. Williamson arrived before his lover, and Tony expressed high curiosity about meeting Heath, who had left the States for a more accepting life in Europe, where he now lived openly with another man. The two old friends chatted pleasantly until Fleming arrived, at which point Perkins abruptly rose and announced that he had to leave.

Was it still too uncomfortable for him to be faced with a committed gay couple who had been together longer than he'd been married? Or now, more than ever, did Tony Perkins have something to hide?

RUMORS

OCK HUDSON'S DEATH FROM AIDS had shocked the world on October 2, 1985, sending a tidal wave of panic through Hollywood. Industry insiders, fueled by the tabloids, fumed with outrage that the star, knowing secretly that he was HIV positive, had allowed himself to kiss actress Linda Evans on the mouth for a love scene on the popular television series *Dynasty*. Suddenly, actors were fearful and suspicious of their colleagues' private sexual practices; no one knew exactly how the deadly disease was spread.

A month after Hudson's demise, the American Federation of Television and Radio Artists (AFTRA) announced that members "should and do have the right to refuse contact with anyone whom they believe may have any communicable disease," and the Screen Actors Guild stoked the growing alarm by declaring openmouthed kissing a possible health hazard, requiring that actors be warned in advance of such scenes. Gay actors found themselves more terrified of exposure than ever before, many fearing the emergence of a de facto blacklist.

"I think a member of that lovely euphemism—'a high-risk group'— has an obligation to refuse to do kissing scenes," said conservative Charlton Heston.

An epidemic of nasty rumors followed, and by 1987 many celebrities—including Burt Reynolds, Richard Pryor, and Isabelle Adjani— were forced to issue public statements declaring that they did *not* have the disease. Tony Perkins, who had always been noticeably thin, simply lay low with his family, tucked safely away among the fragrant eucalyptus trees and marijuana plants of Laurel Canyon.

In May 1987, he flew to Colorado for five days to replace the indisposed Roddy McDowall in a low-budget horror flick called *Shadow of Death* (fulfilling his 1950 yearbook prophecy that one day he would find success as understudy to the fey child star whom he had mocked so well in the corridors of Browne and Nichols). Already in production in an abandoned sugar plant turned studio twenty miles outside of Denver, the film starred beefy football hero Lyle Alzado as the ghost of a convicted serial killer who has come back to terrorize a movie company filming in the prison where he was executed. Perkins had the comic relief role of the movie-within-the-movie's pretentious director.

"We were shocked that he took the part," remembers director Robert Kirk, who was making his feature debut. "My perception of him was that he was much bigger than our movie." The two first met in Perkins's trailer the morning after he arrived. Kirk was immediately struck by the deep, even tone of the actor's skin. "He was very tanned when he got there, and had very specific makeup requirements. He told the makeup people exactly what color base he wanted to wear, which made him look even more tanned. He was extremely thin, but didn't seem unhealthy—though he seemed to be making a great effort to *be* healthy; he always had Evian water with him and tried to eat healthy things."

In terms of acting, there wasn't much to discuss. When Kirk, at a loss, perfunctorily asked the star what he thought his character's relationship was with Sharon Fox, the leading lady in the prison film, Tony simply replied, "Oh, he's fucking her."

"I knew then he had the right attitude about it," Kirk says.

The cast, composed mostly of local talent, was still expecting Roddy McDowall when Anthony Perkins walked onto the set. The fact that his shots suddenly took top priority, and that he did not hang around to deliver other actors' off-camera lines, created some resentment. According to actor Clayton Rohner, "He was a bit of a joke around the set because we never saw him and he seemed so disinterested. He was just a ghost." On several occasions, Perkins schoolmarmishly chided the young cast, especially the good-looking Rohner, for their lack of professionalism. (He later went out of his way to bad-mouth Rohner to agent Phil Gersh, whom they shared.)

But he was kind to Lannie Garrett, a local cabaret performer who was making her screen debut as the buxom Sharon Fox, especially when she expressed her admiration for his wife, whom she had idolized as a girl after seeing her in *Vogue*. "He was really surprised because most people didn't remember who Berry Berenson was," Garrett recalls. "He talked about how beautiful she was when they met, and how proud he was of his boys, and he showed me a picture of them." (But it was not Berry who accompanied Tony to Denver; it was Kurt Paul—"an eerie match for him," according to scriptwriter Rex Hauck—who doubled as Tony for the grisly death scene in the electric chair.)

Perkins spoke vaguely to Kirk of an upcoming TV pilot, and was, surprisingly, already preparing to take his second stab at film direct-ing—this time a pitch-black comedy of family life called *Mr. Christmas Dinner*. The experience of *Psycho III* had been "so discouraging," he later explained lamely to Richard Brown, "that I thought, 'Well, I'm going to try this again.' "

Mr. Christmas Dinner was the perversely comic tale of a lonely, fat young man who is miraculously pursued by a beautiful woman at a ski resort, only to discover that her interest in him is purely culinary: she wants to bring him home to her inbred, cannibalistic family as their holiday dinner. "The script had a black edge to it that I thought would interest Tony's wicked, black sense of the world," agent Ron Bernstein remembers. "He was not particularly eager to do this movie. But there wasn't a lot going on."

If Perkins was anything less than thrilled with the silly script by Pat Proft, cowriter of the hugely popular *The Naked Gun*, the producers at New Line Cinema never knew it; Tony bowled them over at prelimi-nary meetings with his enthusiasm and wit, promising them a sophisti-cated, light "British" farce along the lines of Hitchcock's *The Trouble with Harry*. They agreed to take him on, mostly for name value, despite the fact that there were mixed feelings about *Psycho III*. Certainly his fee of $150,000—*his* demand, not Bernstein's—was a record-breaker for the small independent company, which had never spent more than two million dollars on a picture, and survived mainly on revenue from its popular *Nightmare on Elm Street* series.

Perkins had only two demands after price, the first being that they hire costume supervisor Brian O'Dowd, who, Tony was not ashamed to tell one producer, had AIDS, little money, and needed help (not unlike the always struggling Teno Pollick). The other request was that his driver be someone *young* (who, presumably, wouldn't object to his daily pot smoking to and from the set). Little did he know they would supply him with a girl chauffeur instead of a boy.

Executives quickly began to notice that Perkins's directorial ideas were not what they had expected. Coming from a studio background, his first thought was to make the low-budget movie *look* like a low-budget movie—campy and cheap, like a 1940s Monogram picture, complete with shaking set walls—but the producers rightly didn't think audiences would get his references to film history. Worse, according to Pat Proft, "Tony had a tendency to go too much into the dark aspects" of the script, playing up the grotesque, inbred family angle more than had been anticipated. "He had an affinity for the bizarre," producer Gerald Olson concurs.

When shooting began on November 30, 1987, Perkins's behavior proved just as eccentric as his ideas, due no doubt in part to the pot smoking—and according to some people, acid dropping—he did in private during working hours. "After lunch he was out there," one observer recalls. "He would get a little convoluted."

"I had always heard that he'd done vast amounts of LSD," says Ron Bernstein, "and that may have caused some synapses to not be firing right. He always seemed odd. You would talk, and there'd be a long pause before he would reply. He would just stare at you, which was very unsettling."

Costume designer Georgia Gresham recalls Tony being hopelessly distracted during meetings: "One time when we were trying to show him some dresses, he was in front of the mirror looking at himself and sort of fussing the whole time. You *couldn't* get his attention away from the mirror. I finally decided I wouldn't have any more meetings with him in front of mirrors."

According to New Line chairperson Sara Risher, Perkins was very fashion conscious and "he could be bitchy. I remember an outfit I wore, which in retrospect was pretty hideous, and Tony saying, 'Ooooh. And what do we call *that*?'—and it was just, you know, my new skirt and sweater. I almost never wore it again."

Indeed, Perkins seemed almost more concerned with his appearance than the work at hand. Wearing his trademark oversize corduroy pants, expensive down vest (to protect his lungs from the cold), Day-Glo glasses strap, and intentionally mismatched socks, he always came to the set looking chicly theatrical—and deeply tanned.

Film editor Michael Knue, whom Tony cast as the organist in the opening wedding scene, remembers the director wildly advocating a specific tanning cosmetic: " 'Doll,' he said, 'I never go out of the house without this shade of pancake makeup'—and he proceeded to open this jar and put some on my face! He said, 'It makes you look slightly tanned and *much* healthier,' and he encouraged me to use it every day! That was the wonderful thing about Tony, you never knew if he was serious or putting you on, and there was always a little bit of both."

Despite his preoccupation with his looks, as well as his specially prepared macrobiotic-looking meals, his daily naps, his endless proselytizing for Marianne Williamson—the immensely popular "Bitch for God" who had replaced Louise Hay as the gay and AIDS communities' spiritual guru of choice with her inspiring mix of psychoanalysis and spiritualism (perhaps the natural progression for Tony from Jane's Religious Science and Mildred Newman)—and his close friendship with O'Dowd (whose low energy level caused talk), no one at the time suspected that Tony Perkins might have been ill. He was very thin, but very energetic (probably because of the portable espresso machine he took with him everywhere, even to meetings). More than anything, it was important to Tony to seem *up* and to present a tirelessly optimistic front at all times.

Again, his cast of unknown actors adored him, especially Dan Aykroyd's wife, Donna Dixon, who played the man-eating vixen in a camp style perfectly suited to Tony's vision (Aykroyd and Dixon, it turned out, were neighbors of Tony and Berry's in Laurel Canyon). Young actress Barbara Howard remembers with awe how Perkins "would compare us all to actors from the silent movies, and drew on his knowledge of film, which spanned generations." Steven and Phillip Ross, teenage twin brothers who played deranged members of the inbred family, liked Tony so much that they didn't mind when he plied them with lewd questions about whether they bathed together or had the same size penis.

One crew member recalls that "he had a parade of younger boys visiting him, on and off the set—just a parade of guys." And there was a particularly comely boom man about whom Tony couldn't help but make constant lascivious comments.

Perkins also exhibited a strong need to talk about his "double life" and how he had conquered it via psychoanalysis. "I think he was trying to convince himself that he had overcome it," producer Gerald Olson says. "He was driven by all kinds of things, and you could see that just under the surface. I know that his family was his big concern. He loved his kids tremendously, and wanted to make sure they were okay. That may have been his motivation for doing the movie."

Sue Mengers later revealed that Perkins "wanted to take care of his family. So if a piece of garbage came up, he would do it rather than wait and see if something better came along."

He already knew he was running out of time.

Meanwhile, the producers were not pleased with the footage; what had started as a straightforward, traditional, Bob Hope type of romantic comedy had suddenly turned too dark, too macabre, too *sick* with the introduction of the incestuous, flesh-eating family. After dailies one evening, when someone commented that the picture might offend audiences in Middle America, Tony lashed out: "Well, where's the line? How do we know where that line is? We don't know where the line is until we've *crossed* it. Once we've done that, we can back away."

"He didn't have the whole thing under control," producer Derek Power claims. "He was very uncertain, which was surprising for someone who'd been on as many movies as he had. Tony allowed himself to be talked out of things by the cast. He wasn't able to sustain the original concept that he'd conveyed to us verbally."

New Line's worst fears were confirmed when *Mr. Christmas Dinner* previewed in Century City in the spring of 1988. "The first fifteen minutes really worked," Ron Bernstein recalls. "Then, slowly, all of the movie's energy and air leaked out of it, and at the end the audience was dead silent. It was pretty awful. Tony was embarrassed and somewhat humiliated by the film. He didn't trust himself, and he blamed himself for a lot of things that he shouldn't have. Some people, like Sidney Lumet, recover from flops, let them roll off their back, while other people are stopped dead in their tracks. Tony was paralyzed by it."

As Sara Risher put it, "He wasn't confident as a director. He was always very intense and had strong opinions, but I guess he didn't feel comfortable enforcing them."

New Line demanded that additional footage be shot to make the film more slapstick and action-packed. According to one observer, from that point on Perkins, again deeply shaken, "only went through the motions. His enthusiasm waned when it looked like the film was not going to be a success." Returning to the location in Valencia, California, just beyond the San Fernando Valley, he commented glumly to his driver that it looked "like a place where you'd dump bodies that are never found."

His drug use increased to fog the pain. A particularly telling run-in occurred with Deborah Moore, the New Line producer who was put in charge of the reshoots. According to production designer C. J. Strawn, "He was admiring her green eye shadow, going on and on about her 'gorgeous' green eye shadow—and she didn't even have any eye shadow on. He was *really* stoned that day."

Retitled *Lucky Stiff*, the film premiered fleetingly in January of 1989, and was immediately relegated to videocassette. Even then, one reviewer dismissed it as "painfully unfunny." Watching the film, one wonders how a man who could trade spars with Welles, Nichols, and Sondheim could have directed something so thoroughly undistinguished.

"It was exhaustive," Perkins told the *San Francisco Chronicle* of his second foray behind the camera. "I was put through the wringer. But it was a wringer of joy." When asked if New Line had exerted too much influence over the project, he replied, "Did the pope tell Michelangelo what to make green or blue?"

That same year, actor Bob Balaban of *Catch-22* made his directorial debut with *Parents*, a black comedy about suburban cannibalism starring Mary Beth Hurt, Randy Quaid, and Sandy Dennis. Vastly superior to the Perkins film, *Parents* is everything that *Mr. Christmas Dinner* should have been: disturbing, suspenseful, piercingly satirical, and visually rich—in short, intelligent. To appease the imagined world at large, Perkins had subjugated his own considerable intelligence and sensitivity one too many times.

"If he'd really pursued the career that might have been, he'd be right up there with Mike Nichols and Steven Spielberg," Billy Goldenberg maintains. "He had just as much acumen as any of them. Whatever was stopping him was something inside him." All the therapy in the world didn't seem to have helped.

In 1988, literary agent Al Lowman decided to go ahead with an unauthorized biography of Perkins, and enlisted writer Ellis Amburn to begin the interviewing process. But when word of the project reached Tony's ears, Lowman received a call from the star's attorney, Maurice Greenbaum. "Tony was furious," recalls Lowman, who decided to back off rather than sacrifice their friendship.

On March 22, Tony's name appeared in *The Hollywood Reporter* along with those of ninety-one other stars who had played gay or bisexual roles in film—including Buck Henry, Melina Mercouri, Robert Redford, and Meryl Streep—in a full-page ad sponsored by producer Jerry Wheeler and the Hemdale Releasing Corporation, who were having trouble finding actors willing to play the two male lovers in their production of Patricia Nell Warren's novel, *The Front Runner.* "MYTH," stated the ad, " 'If I play a gay role, I'll never work in this town again.' " But by now the real fear had become prejudice against people with AIDS.

A few weeks after his fifty-sixth birthday, Perkins left for London and Budapest to star in the forty-first screen adaptation of Robert Louis Stevenson's *Dr. Jekyll and Mr. Hyde,* following in the footsteps of actors such as John Barrymore, Fredric March, and Spencer Tracy. This new version, however, was under the direction of Gerard Kikoine, whose previous work had been primarily soft- and hard-core porno flicks. Tony was thrilled with the money; for ten weeks' labor he would receive $660,000.

"The size of the part is tremendously important," he told one reporter.

The tale of an upstanding doctor who leads a deadly double life by night had been updated for a salacious audience. Resembling a cane-hobbling (tanned) George Hamilton by day, as the nocturnal Hyde, Perkins was given, as he put it himself, a "slightly Iggy Pop/David Byrne look"; red eyed, pale skinned, and spiky haired, clothed in chic contemporary fashions, he looks like a postpunk rocker prowling the after-hours streets. In a lurid bordello scene, shot and edited very much like an MTV video, Perkins even got to simulate masturbation while watching a rent boy and girl go at it.

But most "relevant," Tony said, was "the wholly believable suggestion that Dr. Jekyll was fooling around with cocaine," freebasing the drug instead of drinking some hokey magic potion topped by dry ice vapors. The film, he added, demonstrates how "a wealthy, well-educated man can get into the same trouble that a ghetto youth might."

When it was released in theaters as *Edge of Sanity* just after his fifty-seventh birthday—with the lead ad line *"Anthony Perkins hasn't been himself lately"*—critics began to take pity on the veteran actor. *The Hollywood Reporter* noted that "playing movie madmen has evidently taken its toll on Perkins, because all the facial tics, grimaces and wiggling eyebrows he brings to the classic role wind up looking like a second-rate comic's impersonation of Anthony Perkins. . . . His performance is very corny and sometimes quite sad. Perkins is a genuinely talented actor who must now parody his own past." He was really parodying the figure he had become.

To promote the movie, Tony was interviewed by *New York Post* writer Martin Burden, who noticed that "in his hotel suite 13 bottles of vitamins were lined up. His regimen includes 14 pills in the morning, 10 at lunch, a dozen at dinner."

"I'm interested in health and nutrition," Perkins told Burden, "but I don't cling desperately to them." The interview ends with a telling game of cat and mouse:

"Has [Perkins] gone a day without taking the pills? 'Not recently. But I'm not devoted to them.'

"But you don't go a day without them? 'That's because I have them with me.'

"And why do you have them with you? 'Because I don't go a day without them.' " Pause. " 'I tell you, I have a sense of humor about it.' "

ABC's satirical detective series *Sledgehammer* (on which Kurt Paul had done a turn as a Norman Bates–type character) was wicked enough to appeal to Tony, who had arranged a lunch with the show's creator, Alan Spencer. He had told Spencer, who was a *Psycho* fan, that he'd always envied actors on live situation comedies such as *The Mary Tyler Moore Show*, and wondered if there was some way to tailor the sitcom format to suit his image. He had no qualms, he said, about spoofing himself.

The result was *The Ghost Writer*, a "family" show about a Stephen King–like novelist whose work, it turns out, is not fiction at all, but simply a reflection of his spooky home life (the walking skeleton of his late wife, for instance, is a regular visitor). Touted as television's first "scarecom," the script was rejected by the major networks with the old complaint that it was too "dark." The fledgling Fox network then snatched it up.

Much of the show's humor was to be derived from the supernatural special effects, all of which were to be executed before the live audience, as in Broadway's popular musical *Phantom of the Opera* (with its falling chandelier), rather than via camera tricks. To that end an elaborate and costly set was constructed to carry out the technical feats. Tony again got Kurt Paul the small role of a gravedigger (which was ultimately cut), and brought the ailing Brian O'Dowd on board to do the costumes.

"Brian was in love with Tony, completely," recalls Josh Miller, who played Tony's teenage son on the show. "I think he probably knew more about Tony than anybody." As for the ubiquitous Kurt Paul, Miller, like most people, got the distinct impression that Tony was "a father figure" to him. In turn, "Kurt took care of Tony's property, watched over him. He was very ambitious, but his personality was unpredictable. He seemed to have quite a high level of emotion. I never knew if he was talking to me or to someone in the air." (After Perkins's death, Paul would be seen selling items that had supposedly belonged to Tony—clothes, books, a lamp—at the Rosebowl Flea Market in Pasadena.)

As usual, Perkins maintained a positive front despite the ever changing Fox regime's ambivalence about the show and the disinterested direction of Alan Rafkin. Alan Spencer was furious over the executives' constant tinkering and toning down of his script, which had originally presented a portrait of a decidedly perverse nuclear family (the fourteen-year-old son, for instance, smoked a pipe and was supposed to be having an affair with the big-busted housekeeper). With dogged optimism, Perkins told Spencer that *The Ghost Writer* would be the perfect vehicle to bring him back to the theater, and suggested that they rework it as a stage play he could take on the road. Mercifully, nothing came of the idea.

The Ghost Writer was so unfunny it's almost hard to believe it aired

a year later on August 22, 1990. "It was appalling," Ron Bernstein remembers. "Tony wasn't very good, and I don't think he was terribly
happy with it."

But Tony did seem to like performing for a live audience. Berry,
Dan Aykroyd, and Donna Dixon were there for the taping, and the response to his entrance, at least in the studio, was enthusiastic. The *Psycho* star still had his fans.

"How about an autograph, Norman?"

"Well, I would if that were my name. . . ."

The pilot was not picked up.

In the spring of 1989, Austin Pendleton offered Tony the part of F.
Scott Fitzgerald in a revival of Tennessee Williams's play *Clothes for a
Summer Hotel*, which was being produced that summer at the
Williamstown (Massachusetts) Theater Festival. "Word came back
from his agent that he was unable to do it," Pendleton recalls, "but
please to keep him in mind for other things because he really wanted to
do some stage work. He was so interested, in fact, that we rearranged
the dates." He was still unavailable.

According to Ron Bernstein, "There was always talk of plays, but
none of it ever seemed to crystallize. He didn't have a burning desire to
do *Falstaff* or anything like that. Nor did I particularly get the sense that
Tony was really part of the Hollywood scene out here."

Scandal struck again on Sunday, June 26. On his way back from Cer-
nobbio, Italy, where he and seven other Hollywood stars (including
Jean Simmons, Joan Fontaine, and Rod Steiger) had received lifetime
achievement awards at a gala benefit for the Variety Children's Club
Lifeline Fund, Perkins was arrested a second time in Great Britain for
smuggling 1.3 grams of homegrown marijuana into the country.

Apparently, he'd arranged to have just enough pot for three or four
joints mailed from Seattle Drive to his hotel, to coincide with his
check-in. Unfortunately, hotel staff had delivered the package to another guest named Perkins, who opened the small aluminum foil
packet containing the drugs. Detectives were waiting for the actor
when he arrived, and he was fined the equivalent of $310. He admitted
having grown the marijuana in his own backyard.

A tabloid story shortly thereafter claimed that Perkins's "addiction" to drugs had begun with medication prescribed to help him overcome his deep depression at being typecast as America's favorite psycho. "My wife saved me once from drugs and depression," Tony was quoted, "and she can do it again."

Back on Cape Cod, he sheepishly admitted to Henry Scammell, with his best Norman Bates stutter: "Well, I do like chemicals—but nothing addictive. I'm very careful. I take nothing that's going to create a craving."

Scammell noticed at the same time that Tony seemed to take "a more motherly than fatherly" attitude toward his children. "I often thought he sounded like his mother used to. He was concerned about Osgood's weight, and he asked me on several different visits if I thought Osgood was fat, which I did not. I sensed in Osgood a rage toward his father. He was just steaming mad."

The parent-child aspect of CBS-TV's *Daughter of Darkness* was what induced Tony to take on his first vampire role, an undead prince who is reunited with his innocent American daughter when she arrives in Bucharest to tell him of her (mortal) mother's death. The other attraction was the two hundred thousand dollars he would get for a four-week shot. That he admired Stuart Gordon, the director whose gory *Re-Animator* had become an instant cult classic in the horror genre, didn't hurt.

"Tony wanted the vampire to be very human," Gordon recalls. "He did not want it to be just your stock Bela Lugosi vampire routine. There was very much an Anne Rice–like sadness about this vampire, a sense that he was doomed and had seen all the people he had loved die. Tony brought a lot of heart to it. Many people regard horror films as junk, but Tony didn't see it that way at all."

When shooting began that August in Budapest (substituting for Bucharest), Perkins rarely left his hotel room when he wasn't needed on the set. "He struck me as a man who was carrying a kind of burden with him," screenwriter Andrew Laskos remembers. "There was a grim facade to his manner, which wasn't the case at all once you started talking to him. It was as if with the years something had hardened in him, yet occasionally an almost boyish enthusiasm would surprise you. He seemed to have come to terms with the fact that he was a gun for hire in Hollywood."

Producer Harry Chandler observed, too, that "Tony was not Mr.

Personality, but perhaps his reclusiveness was less a personality trait than a health need to sleep or take care of his body in a way that we weren't aware of."

As always Perkins was the consummate professional on the set, always willing to do another take, never complaining, even when they were shooting in a drafty castle (where he had to be chained to the cold stone floor) or in a rainy cemetery at two o'clock in the morning. The same could hardly be said for his screen daughter, Mia Sara, who'd starred at age sixteen opposite Matthew Broderick in *Ferris Bueller's Day Off*. Suffering with a bad cold, she was tired and irritable and didn't get on with the director, whom she found "passive-aggressive."

"She was very volatile," Gordon recalls. "Tony would just tell her, 'You're wonderful You're doing this scene brilliantly.' He never criticized or put anybody down, he was always emphasizing the positive, encouraging people. That's how he cooled her down."

Mia Sara remembers her vampire father as "refreshingly genteel, almost courtly." To cheer her up they would sing Rodgers and Hart songs together between takes (Perkins was surprised that someone her age knew the lyrics). Typically, Tony talked constantly about his boys, and "was always telling me to have children right away."

At first, she had been taken aback by how gaunt he was: "It crossed my mind [that he might have AIDS] because he was so thin and was so into the *Course in Miracles*. He carried the book with him everywhere he went. Later, I wasn't surprised."

"What is so amazing in retrospect is that he must have known he was sick during the whole shoot," Stuart Gordon reflects, "and he never, ever let on that there was any kind of problem. He never complained about the hours. He was the ultimate pro.

"When we got into postproduction, it turned out that he was also an absolute genius at looping his lines. He would redo scenes better than he had when we shot them, always in perfect synch—and he always nailed it the first time. 'My idea of hell when you die is they make you loop your entire life,' he told me. I hope he never had to do that."

Despite its corny title, *Daughter of Darkness* offers one of the better performances of Perkins's final years. As the compassionate bloodsucker who has led a double life, he gives a restrained, surprisingly touching interpretation, especially in his scenes with Sara. "My love for [your mother] was always at war with my real nature," he tells her. "I could never be with her when the hunger was upon me."

When a reporter asked him if it was frustrating being offered nothing but horror movie roles, Perkins replied, "I guess if I were a single man without a family, without a support system, without teenage children and a beautiful young wife, I'd be more unhappy." *Daughter of Darkness* aired in late January 1990.

That same month, Brian O'Dowd passed away. Tony was at his side. It was not generally known that the actor was one of O'Dowd's constant caregivers, even paying some of his medical bills, and taking in his dog after O'Dowd died. Not since the birth of his sons had Tony been so profoundly moved by an experience.

And then the unthinkable happened.

FINAL EXPOSURE

P SYCHO STAR BATTLING AIDS VIRUS screamed a *National Enquirer* headline on March 27, 1990. ANTHONY PERKINS IN DESPERATE BID TO SAVE HIS LIFE.

For the actor who had spent decades dodging publicity yet longing to be in the spotlight, the terrible announcement, noticeable at a passing glance and just within arm's reach in every supermarket and convenience store across the complacent United States, must have seemed a wrenchingly vicious joke.

Especially since he and Berry claimed they'd had no idea.

Bob Hussong, for one, phoned him right away: "I said, 'Surely it isn't true. Why don't you refute this—my God, deny it?' Tony said, 'Well, I'm having some tests done, and I can't deny what might be true.' A week later I called him, and he confirmed it. It was very, very hard for him to talk about."

The tabloid reported that Perkins had for some time already been a regular patient of Dr. Joel Weisman, a Sherman Oaks AIDS "specialist." But according to Tony and Berry, he hadn't known about his HIV status until the *Enquirer* article forced him to verify it. A lab technician must have illegally tested his blood for HIV, they claimed, after Perkins had been to a doctor to see what could be done about his Bell's palsy, a debilitating facial paralysis often brought on by the herpes simplex virus, that had affected the right side of his mouth; obviously, the results had then been sold to the *Enquirer*.

"I was devastated," Berry later recalled. "I couldn't believe it. And then I immediately thought, 'What about me? What about my children?' " Over the next two years, she would be tested four times; thankfully, neither she nor her boys had been infected. "I don't understand this disease at all," she said. AIDS caregiver was not a role she had anticipated playing.

The tabloid also alleged that Perkins was "still plugged into the gay community," and that during a recent stopover in Paris had telephoned two gay hot lines. It revealed, too, that the Perkinses had been active in the Hollywood AIDS movement for more than a year (no mention of Brian O'Dowd), recently attending a fund-raiser at the trendy City Restaurant where, according to one "eyewitness," Tony appeared "very thin and not healthy at all. Actually, he looked kind of scary. One minute he'd be talking to someone and the next minute he'd be dancing around like Isadora Duncan."

"Having seen him in the office, I didn't connect the dots," Ron Bernstein remembers. "But I was at the grocery on Saturday and started thumbing through the *Enquirer*, and I was quite startled. I walked in to Phil [Gersh] on Monday and said, 'What's the story?' And he said, 'Oh, it's not true.' I said, 'Phil, if it's not true there would have been a very big lawsuit.' " (After Perkins's death, Gersh would be sued by Bexy Communications for signing the actor to host a show titled *Heartstoppers . . . Horror at the Movies* while allegedly knowing full well that the star's health was in jeopardy. The suit would also charge that the agent hid the fact that Perkins had refused to let a production doctor confer with his personal physician for a proposed insurance examination for an upcoming film called *The Mummy*.)

Privately, Tony asked his friend Dennis Christopher to investigate various doctors and alternative therapies. "I knew his HIV positivity meant some kind of failure to Tony," Christopher later recounted in a touching speech at the actor's memorial service.

As Tony, heavy with guilt, sank rapidly into a deeper and deeper depression, Marianne Williamson urged him to join a support group, but he refused, fearing he would not get any more work if word got out that the tabloid rumors were true. Very few of Perkins's friends were even told.

He and Berry began to deny that anything was wrong. When a distraught Billy Goldenberg called to offer his support, Tony told him the story was false and proceeded to engage his old friend in "quite a warm conversation," their first in years.

"I heard that he was ill with the tabloid—with crap," says Gwen Davis, who still phoned Tony every holiday and birthday. "I wanted to be there for him. I called him and he said, 'I'm great!' I called Berry: 'Oh, he's fine.' "

They quickly went public with their denial, inviting *Hello!*, the British equivalent of *People* magazine, into their home for Tony's fifty-eighth birthday celebration. It was a sham more painful than anything Paramount had ever dreamed up. Looking like a tanned cadaver, Tony posed for a series of "candid" photos with Berry and the boys—playing Ping-Pong, opening gifts, dueling with cake frosting–coated electric mixing beaters. The frozen smiles on their faces, and the HAPPY BIRTH-DAY TONY balloons, only added to the chill of the most horrific mise-en-scène of Perkins's career.

Hello! noted the star's "slim" figure, which Perkins explained was due to his healthy diet: "When you get to be my age you want to make sure you don't eat too many sugars and processed foods, so when Berry bakes, which she does for all our birthdays, she tries to make the cakes as sensibly as possible.

"I've been slender since I was a child," he added. "I could fatten up if I was willing to eat processed foods and sweets but I'm not willing to do that . . . so although I may seem excessively thin right now, I just don't eat fattening foods. People tell me I should eat more hot fudge sundaes but that just doesn't appeal to me."

In the same article, Tony admitted that he delivered food once a week to homebound AIDS patients, but when asked point-blank about the recent headlines, he replied evasively: "I'm in excellent health right now and I'm going to continue to try to keep that way. Of course, if I could gain weight, as we said before, that would probably be a way to keep such speculations at bay, but I just don't believe in being heavy for the sake of being heavy, just to please people's visions of how they think I should look." After a lifetime spent lying to protect his false image, now he had to maintain that image at all costs to protect his family.

Tony Perkins wasn't the only star being hounded by the tabloid press. After the posthumous exposé of Malcolm Forbes's homosexuality in a March issue of the gay publication *OutWeek*, a rash of similar "out-ings" had begun sweeping the supermarket rags in an odd marriage of sleaze journalism and new gay politics. Richard Chamberlain, John Travolta, Kristy McNichol, and Chastity Bono were just a few of the celebrities accused of allegedly being closet gays. Many people likened the sudden epidemic of "outings"—which *Us* magazine called "Holly-wood's newest media sport"—to the witch-hunts of the McCarthy era. Indeed, it didn't seem so different from the muckraking of *Confidential* decades before.

But times had changed, and needed to change more. With AIDS decimating the entertainment industry as well as the homosexual com-munity, gay activists idealized their rich and famous brothers and sisters as role models, powerful potential allies in the fight against AIDS and homophobia. Unfortunately, with the major exception of Elizabeth Taylor, Hollywood in general was slow to take a stand on the disease, which was still seen as a moral rather than a medical issue.

Gossip columnist Liz Smith called outing "disgusting. It's created a mean-spirited slum of gossip that never existed. It makes homosexuals look bitchy and low. . . . These fringe groups of gay radicals use the same fascistic methods to attack people the same way they were at-tacked—like a scorpion eating itself."

Popular gay novelist Armistead Maupin disagreed: "Duplicity is the greatest crime of all in the midst of an epidemic, because it perpet-uates the very thing that has created our problems: the idea that homo-sexuality is a dirty little secret."

"At first it's scandalous," admitted Michelangelo Signorile, the gay activist and author credited with starting the whole outing craze, "but then society changes."

Looking back today, Signorile sees the impact already: "It would be very difficult right now for a Hollywood star, relatively big, to be as actively gay as a Rock Hudson. It's harder for them to maintain the closet today because the media has dropped its guard. There's been a breakdown, the rules have changed. It used to be easier to be closeted because there was less you could do. Now, there's such a great openly gay world out there, you're going to want to be part of it." (By early May of 1990, MCA, which had produced the *Psycho* sequels, became the first entertainment company to extend health insurance coverage to same-sex partners of its employees.)

Despite their public refutations, on Sunday, May 20, Tony and Berry cohosted a celebrity art and photography auction at the Ace Gallery on Wilshire Boulevard to benefit Project Angel Food, the food delivery service for people with AIDS that had been founded by Marianne Williamson. Perkins helped raise more than $540,000 as he auctioned off works by Robert Mapplethorpe, David Hockney, Herb Ritts, George Hurrell, Roy Lichtenstein, and even Berry Berenson. Associates at Project Angel Food who knew Tony during his volunteer hours driving around town say he was like a changed person at those times: friendly and kind, even happy.

There was little other work to do in the wake of the *Enquirer* revelation. An announcement that Tony was to replace Peter O'Toole in a remake of *The Pit and the Pendulum* never came to fruition. And other than a forgettable cameo in *I'm Dangerous Tonight*, a cable television film directed by Tobe Hooper (*The Texas Chainsaw Massacre*), Perkins had no choice but to reprise his most famous role one last time.

Psycho IV: The Beginning was being produced by MCA Television Entertainment, again under the auspices of Hilton Green, for domestic broadcast on the Showtime Cable Network and theatrical release overseas. Though its title sounded parodic, the film boasted a script by Joseph Stefano, who had penned the Hitchcock original. It was not, though, a sequel to *Psycho III*, but rather a prequel, in which a now happily married Norman (wed to his institution shrink, no less) looks back on the troubled childhood (specifically his relationship with his seductive/sadistic mom) that had led him to become a homicidal transvestite. It was perfect fare for the talk-show generation of TV fans, with the added thrill that Norman was fighting his old "urges"—and he might even try to kill his beautiful young wife.

Because of the *Enquirer* piece, there was naturally some concern about hiring Perkins. Before production began, Hilton Green had a private conversation with the actor: "I said, 'If it's true, we've got to know,' and he said, 'Absolutely not, it's not true.' I said, 'I'll buy that,' and we went on." According to Green, the tabloid story alone was not enough to warrant a hefty physical examination.

"Hilton told me that Tony had passed the examination for insurance," Joseph Stefano recalls, "so I assumed that the stories were not true. I'm not sure that anybody would've insured an actor who was HIV positive, although they're probably doing it all over the place."

Surprisingly, Tony again professed a desire to direct Norman's story, but after the failure of *Psycho III*, the studio flatly rejected the idea. To give the impression of enterprise and hope, Perkins suggested to *Psycho II*'s Richard Franklin that they codirect the new installment together, which never came to anything, then informally propositioned director Stuart Gordon as well. Universal finally hired Mick Garris, who at the time had only one feature film to his credit, *Critters II*.

"I told Tony that he was going to stretch for this part," Stefano says, "because here was a man who was not fresh out of an institution, but one who had changed, married. . . . He liked the idea that this Norman was on his way to recovery rather than sent spinning again by an incident."

Filming began that summer, not on the back lot in Universal City, but at the just opened, chaotic Universal Studios theme park in Orlando, Florida, where the *Psycho* house and motel had been reconstructed perilously close (for the camera) to one of the other main tourist attractions, Mel's Diner from George Lucas's *American Graffiti*. Having Tony Perkins on site was just one more convenient grand-opening gimmick. "We were as much a park attraction as we were a motion picture," notes Garris, who remembers that Tony's spirits seemed high (they always did for the Black Tower). "There were times when he was a little tired, but this was a nearly sixty-year-old man."

One instance when Perkins seemed less than enthusiastic occurred when Garris suggested he play this Norman less "campy" than the previous two. "At the word 'campy,' Tony kind of galvanized," Garris recalls. "He said, 'Well, what do you mean by *campy*?' and we went into a ten- or fifteen-minute discussion about what the term *camp* meant. I just didn't want him playing it bigger than life as in *Psycho III*, that's all."

Would that he had; *Psycho IV* proved pallid in every way, especially in the crucial casting of pretty, British-accented Olivia Hussey as the young Mrs. Bates, a role to which she was incapable of bringing any menace. "Nobody else in the cast really came up to Tony's level," Stefano maintains. "Some of the scenes that he had by himself where he's talking on the telephone are remarkable in their intensity."

Tony didn't hang around for the wrap party; he returned to Los Angeles as soon as shooting was finished. Actress Donna Mitchell, who played Norman's compassionate wife in the film, remembers that the actor became teary when talking about his family, as if he knew he would be leaving them soon.

That November, when entertainment writer Kay Gardella asked Perkins about his own traumatic past (as opposed to Norman's), he replied, "Maybe when I was a bachelor and living a solitary life in New York, things bothered me. But now that I'm married and have a family, I have my own identity. It's different." He was off to Paris, he claimed, to do a film titled *The Antidote*. No such film has ever surfaced. Perhaps it was just one of Tony's last in-jokes.

On December 27, 1990, just after his favorite holiday, Perkins was in New York to transfer the Twenty-first Street town house into his 1990 trust. He had to put things in order for his wife and sons.

At this point, whenever friends like Paul Jasmin asked him about his film offers, his response was a resigned, "You don't even want to know." *Naked Target*, for instance, was a comic thriller shot in Madrid, with Perkins in a cameo role as an insane, one-eyed, one-armed truck driver. The star, Clayton Rohner, whose experience with Perkins on *Destroyer* (*Shadow of Death*) had been less than amicable, expected the worst when the veteran actor arrived in Spain. But this time, because they were the only two English-speaking people around, they got along fine. "I couldn't believe it was the same guy," Rohner says.

Perkins regularly read to the young actor from the *Course in Miracles*, which he still carried everywhere, and expounded on the health benefits of drinking water. He also went off on several tirades against the Spaniards, "cruel boys" whose machismo he detested. Rohner noticed that Tony, who had been thin before, was even thinner now.

Back in L.A., Perkins desperately wanted to replace Michael Crawford in the West Coast stage production of Andrew Lloyd Webber's *Phantom of the Opera*—and to that end he learned three songs from the show for his upcoming audition. When actor Robert Guillaume got the part, Tony felt sure he'd been rejected because of his diagnosis, and was deeply hurt to realize that people actually thought he might be ill.

Theatrical agent Lionel Larner lunched with him at Trumps one day. "I wasn't aware that he was ill," Larner claims, "but at lunch, which was very pleasant and chatty, he brought out a lot of pills. I must have reacted to them because he dismissed them by saying, 'Vitamins.' Since so many people in California are nutrition crazy, I assumed it was true.

"Then he said to me, 'Lionel, do you think I look thin?' And I said, very matter-of-factly, 'You've always been thin,' and he accepted that. It was only when I left that I thought about the vitamins and the question. Then it did cross my mind."

On Friday, September 5, 1991, Teno Pollick was found dead in his bathtub from an overdose of pills and wine. Several suicide notes had been left for significant people, none for Tony. Keene Curtis found several photos of Tony and Teno together in Morocco and Paris during happier times, and offered them to the star, who was glad to accept them. Perkins, however, did not attend Teno's small memorial service a few weeks later.

On September 8, Hollywood was shocked again when handsome, forty-one-year-old actor Brad Davis died of complications from AIDS at his home in Studio City. His wife, casting director Susan Bluestein, told the press that her husband had known he was HIV positive since 1985, but had decided to keep it a secret for fear of losing work.

"When Tony heard about Brad Davis, I'm sure he was concerned," Berry later said. "I knew Brad well. We were in acting school together. It broke my heart that he wasn't able to share it."

It was quickly revealed that Davis had written a proposal for a book about his six years of hiding, a brutal excerpt from which was released to the press: "I make my money in an industry that professes to care very much about the fight against AIDS—that gives umpteen benefits and charity affairs with proceeds going to research and care. But in actual fact, if an actor is even rumored to have HIV he gets no support on an individual basis. He does not work."

During the last two years of his life, Perkins would be admitted to Midway Hospital twice, both times under an alias. Not surprisingly, the AIDS masquerade became even harder then. To protect the anonymity of her husband, Berry chose to visit him only under heavy disguise— usually a wig, bright lipstick, and too much makeup. On one occasion, when she arrived with an equally camouflaged female friend, Tony looked up from his bed, and not recognizing either of them, groaned, "Don't tell me—social workers." (Despite the sad charades she was forced to endure as a Hollywood wife, Berry, the only nurturer to emerge from her family of fashion divas, had been primed for caregiving by motherhood, as well as her experience nursing her father during his fight with cancer.)

At the end of September, Dr. Irving Bieber, who had caused so much anguish with his domineering mother–absent father theory of "curable" homosexuality, died of natural causes at the age of sixty-two. In November, basketball hero "Magic" Johnson revealed that he had contracted HIV through heterosexual contact, giving the disease a much needed, if hypocritical, veneer of respectability. Director Tony Richardson and actor Larry Kert would also be among the year's AIDS casualties.

Ron Bernstein remembers clearly a conference Tony Perkins called at the Gersh Agency that December: "It was one of those meetings when somebody's career isn't going well and they want to sit down and talk to everybody in the agency, see what's going on. I thought he looked so awful. He had that look of people who are dying, whether they're dying of AIDS or cancer or liver disease, and it was frightening. He was vague and rambled and didn't seem in the moment. It was painful to watch. He was talking about what we could do for him, et cetera, and looking at him I just thought, 'What can anybody do?' "

Shortly thereafter, in a last-ditch attempt to get some make-believe steam going, Perkins left Gersh for the William Morris Agency.

"Why is it today's actors look like male hookers?" Tony was quoted at the time. "Alec Baldwin, Richard Grieco, Kiefer Sutherland . . . They look like they haven't slept for days—except maybe for money. And the other actors—James Woods, Gary Oldman, Stallone—they look like they're pimps. How did Tinseltown get so ugly?" It had always been ugly.

"The last time I saw Tony was in Gelson's Supermarket with his wife," recalls Venetia Stevenson, who had run into him on and off over the years. "I didn't recognize him. Then I recognized *her*, and he really looked bad. He was wearing a hat, and looked much older than he should have.

"I think he saw me, but I just had the feeling . . . he had that look like he didn't want to be talked to or recognized. Especially since everybody had heard how sick he was for such a long time, even before the *Enquirer*. He just looked very old. And he used to be so attractive when I was most friendly with him."

★   ★   ★

1992 began with a frenetic scramble for activity.

Morton Thaw and Ed Robak had kindly suggested Perkins to their new producer, Curtis Roberts, as a possible director for *Together*, which was still struggling to get off the ground. Tony jumped at the opportunity—he still loved the play—but begged off the possibility of starring in it as well, claiming that he was now too old.

The playwrights met with him again at his home. "We did not know he was ill," Thaw says. "After the several years that had gone by, we just thought that he'd aged and was slimmer. He said, 'Fellas, when you're past the age of fifty, it's good to drink a lot of water. It's good for the prostate.' He was animated, alive, but very thin."

Perkins began working on the familiar script, which had once held so much promise for him, that January. According to Curtis Roberts, "he was very knowledgeable, and had very good ideas as a director and as a writer. He knew exactly where he was going with the play." The playwrights, however, recall Tony as being "very protective" of the script: "Anytime we made any changes in dialogue, he was immediately very unhappy—he was appalled. He wanted it back the way it was."

On February 18, an announcement went out that *Together* would premiere in Chicago in April, before heading to Broadway. Lois Nettleton was still set to play Carlotta, and would be joined by David Selby as O'Neill, with Georgia Engel and Warren Berlinger as the secondary couple.

But Tony suddenly postponed rehearsals until July when two offers for film work came along: *A Demon in My View*, a German horror film in which he was cast as a mannequin-fondling serial killer, and *In the Deep Woods*, a quickie CBS television film, again about a serial murderer (thankfully not played by him), which was to start shooting in San Diego that spring. Desperate to work—to be known to be working—Tony agreed to do the TV movie for close to scale pay.

"He didn't look particularly healthy," cinematographer James Glennon observed, "he looked tired. But he still had a glint in his eye, and he saw and overheard *everything*. The crew liked him. They showed him a lot of respect. They were young, he was a piece of film history, and they didn't want to miss anything he said."

Director Charles Correll remembers that despite the late-night shoots, Tony, who looked "gaunt and frail," made no special demands on the schedule (his only complaint was that he found his young costar, Rosanna Arquette, too "shrieky"). But his acting was even more like clockwork than usual, as Correll recalls: "When I'd tell him what reaction I wanted for a scene, he'd say a number, like '79B,' just under his breath. This went on for quite a while. I'd say something, and he'd go, '159D.' So finally I asked him what he was doing; he said that over the years as an actor, he had categorized, on four-by-five note cards, every single possible reaction to every situation you could possibly be in—he had each reaction filed on a note card with a number, and he was the only one in the world who had it memorized! I actually did believe him when he told me that. He'd been around so long it was certainly feasible." Tony was clearly trying to amuse himself under less than optimum circumstances. *In the Deep Woods* would not air until almost a month after his death.

Meanwhile, his sixtieth birthday was approaching. Berry arranged to give her husband an elaborate surprise party in New York, at the vast Central Park West apartment of Michael Marsh, the husband of one of her old school friends. Practically everyone that Tony had ever known was invited, and each person was asked to contribute a personal photo taken of or with Tony; together these pictures of a life would compose a huge scrapbook of memories, which Berry and the boys would present to him at the apex of the celebration.

Unfortunately, as April 4 neared, Tony was on the phone in L.A. one day with a friend who accidentally slipped, "See you in New York"; the surprise was ruined. But Tony kept mum, and went along with his wife's plan.

About 150 people from their dual worlds of show business and fashion—Helen, Marisa, Michaela, Mike Nichols, George Roy Hill, Ruth Ford, Ben Edwards, Jane Greenwood, Bob Hussong, Sue Mengers, Lou Lou de la Falaise, Susan Sarandon and Tim Robbins, Diane Von Fürstenberg, Jerome Hellman, Carol Mallory, Stephen Sondheim—gathered that night to surprise the *Psycho* star. The event was no mere birthday party; it was more an impromptu *This Is Your Life*, a chance for all his friends to say good-bye. Disposable cameras were passed out for the occasion.

Hush.

Then Tony entered, and instantly feigned overwhelming surprise. But amid the excitement, a tacit moment of realization hit everyone in the room: this man was dying. Still, according to one guest, "he played the role of happy host most convincingly." For Berry, the party was a generous last gesture to the man with whom, for better or worse, she had made a steady home for nearly twenty years.

Ruth Ford remembers Tony talking a lot that night about work, that he was impatient to get on with it. And as she was leaving, Berry gave Ford what seemed, even then, like an especially meaningful farewell hug.

"Don't believe everything you read," the birthday boy said cryptically to one departing guest.

"Tony looked great and seemed to be in good spirits," Michaela O'Harra remembers. "It was a very happy occasion. I don't know how many people there knew about it [his illness]. I'm sure that some did. Berry put up a great front, until well past the time that he died."

But as thrilled as Berry was about the party, the gathering precipitated a need in her to let more people in on their secret, to stop the hiding. Too many old friends had mentioned how gaunt Tony looked.

"I said to him, 'Look, I'm going to share this with a few close friends that I trust because otherwise I'm going to go crazy,'" she recounted later. "I'm not that good an actress. I told Tony I can't play this charade. I just can't. He would be fine about me telling one or two people, but then he'd say, 'Oh, you're telling too many.'" (According to one source, Tony absolutely forbade her from letting Marisa know.)

As he'd done with *People* nine years earlier, "outing" himself before they "outed" him, Tony decided the time had come to tell all. Inspired in part by the fact that Marianne Williamson's *Return to Love* had hit the best-seller lists, he contacted literary agent Al Lowman and told him he was ready to write his memoirs: "I want to do it because I'm old enough to be able to narrate an entire life, and young enough to still be able to promote it." He was no longer worried about what his sons would think.

Lowman remembers noticing "how little hair" Perkins now had. "It had gone totally gray and sparse. I thought it was just age. But to make the connection with AIDS, I didn't go that far." In retrospect, however, the agent recalls Tony "grilling" him heatedly about his knowledge of AIDS as early as 1985, after *Rolling Stone* published a series of articles on the disease.

With the working title "Apropos of Nothing" (one of Tony's

favorite meaningless phrases), Lowman began shopping the proposed book around to all the major New York publishers, and claims that offers quickly started at five hundred thousand dollars, escalating into the millions. Perkins's only response to the enthusiastic figures was a sardonic joke: "Well, I guess they'll give me a hundred thousand bucks for every dick I say I sucked." Lowman tried to convince him otherwise: "It was Tony's own obsessive interest in sexuality that was at work here because that was not the kind of book I wanted to represent."

Again, once there was serious interest, Tony begged off, claiming he had a television deal with the Turner Network that was going to occupy all his "creative energies" that summer (indeed, he was working on an idea for a pilot with Stephen Paley). "I always thought he had the wrong idea about me, the publishing industry, and the public," Lowman regrets.

In June, Perkins met with young, openly gay film director Gus Van Sant, who was having trouble casting the role of the Countess, a flamboyant drag queen, in his upcoming motion picture of Tom Robbins's best-selling novel *Even Cowgirls Get the Blues*. The part had already been offered to both John Hurt and Peter O'Toole, neither of whom was available. Perkins really wanted to do it.

"Tony's idea was to have the character be very serious about himself, not a send-up, which I thought was a good tack," Van Sant recalls. "I thought he would look great as a sort of Halston character rather than a drag queen." Tony agreed, and everything seemed to be set.

In July, Perkins again postponed rehearsals for *Together*, allegedly because British horror movie impresario Harry Alan Towers had offered him six figures to do a film in September—and he couldn't possibly turn down the fee. "He had to have been preparing for his death," producer Curtis Roberts reflects, "because he told me that he had made sure his family was well provided for if anything happened to him."

Perkins insisted his delay with the play was just temporary.

When Berry began showing up at AIDS benefits by herself, tongues began to wag that her husband was seriously ill. Bob Hussong ran into her that month at a fund-raiser for Project Angel Food: "I rushed up to her and asked, 'Where's Tony?' She said, 'Well, you know, he's working.' "

"Never, never did he mention that he was ill," says Curtis Roberts, who was on the phone with him almost every day. "I just thought he'd always been emaciatingly thin. His energy factor appeared to be fine right to the very end. I saw him just four weeks before his death, when he'd come to New York to meet with one of the actors, and even then I thought he'd just aged badly."

In New York, he was interviewed by Richard Brown for the American Movie Channel's *Reflections on the Silver Screen* series. When Brown asked him what was the most satisfying aspect of his long career, Perkins replied, "The fact that I'm still here. . . . The fact that I'm still working, still alive, and still productive means more to me than anything."

Very few people beyond the Perkinses' tight inner circle—which included Dennis Christopher, Paul Jasmin, David Kessler (the head of Project Angel Food), and Marianne Williamson—had any real idea how far Tony's health had deteriorated. Even Stephen Paley, who had known the actor for more than thirty years, was excluded.

When Tony called him in August, Paley hadn't heard from him in over a month, an unusually long time for them to go without speaking. Paley had assumed his friend had been in Cape Cod or off filming in Europe.

"No, I've been here. I've been laying low."

"Tony, you sound awful. What's the matter?"

"Well, I don't think I have to tell you what the problem is, do I?"

"It's not what I think. . . ."

"What do you think?"

"You're not sick. Are you?"

"Yes," he said. "I wanted to tell you myself before you heard it from anyone else or before you read it." And he began to cry. "Will you come see me?"

"He became very depressed and very unlike himself," Berry Perkins later recalled of those tense months. "He felt like he had messed up our lives, and we kept telling him it was okay. I mean, it would have messed up our lives if he'd had a heart attack, like his dad did. . . . At least we got a chance to say good-bye."

Eric Harrison ran into the actor in the parking lot at Gelson's and was shocked at his appearance: "There was a change in his face, a terrible haunted look. He looked like a ghost. He ran over and embraced me, and kind of wept on my shoulder. He said, 'I can't say too much because it's all too awful, isn't it. Don't be judgmental.' I told him I was beyond the point of being judgmental to anybody.

"Then he said, 'Just remember that one needs all the love one can find, that's the most important thing—not the finger that's pointed, but the love that somebody can give you.' Those were his parting words to me, and off he went."

Before the end of August, Tony was hospitalized for the second time. It was a turning point for his family. Berry later told *Premiere* magazine that "we made a very conscious decision, the boys and I, that we could either go through it completely alone in this house—just the four of us—and be really sad, or we could invite our close friends in to share this grief with us." They chose the latter option.

As the calls went out, the house on Seattle Drive, which had for two years stood like a leafy retreat from the world, gradually came back to life as old friends like Mike Nichols (who flew in from New York), Roddy McDowall, Michael Black, Sue Mengers, Richard Benjamin and Paula Prentiss (who drove up every morning from the flats of Beverly Hills to see if Tony needed anything), stopped by to say hello—and good-bye—sharing memories, laughter, and the unavoidable tears.

Even as he suffered, Tony still acted the voyeur, watching himself and his body's transformations as if from across the room, referring to his illness as his "great adventure." "He would say to me, 'This is very, very interesting,'" Dick Benjamin recalled. "He was not shying away from it. He was looking right at it, as it happened—right directly at it. And because he was looking into the eye of this, it gave us the courage to be there also."

"It was great," Berry later said. "For two weeks before he died we had this liveathon of people who would come up and sleep on the floor of his room and curl up on couches and bring food, and he finally *got* how much people cared about him. It was a really nice thing for Tony to realize that people were willing to have a pajama party at his bedside. He was not a big pajama party kind of person—he didn't grow up with groups of people who had fun together."

"Forty years above the title," he would tell friends when he was hurt, not well, dealing with a lot. "Find some others who are still around, forty years above the title."

By September, too weak to do the British horror film he had committed to, Tony got out of the deal and was replaced by Tony Curtis. He then got on the phone to Curtis Roberts and, at long last, set a definite rehearsal date for *Together*: October 8. The producer recalls that Tony sounded "very positive" about it. The playwrights were thrilled.

But his blood count deteriorated. "How'm I doing?" he would ask David Kessler.

"You're doing just fine."

"I think I am," he'd invariably say.

On Saturday, September 5, he took a turn for the worse. The next morning, Stephen Paley was summoned to the house: "Tony was really bad, and I thought he was going to die. I held his hand. He was in bed with tubes coming out of his nose and all that stuff, and was having trouble breathing. Then he was just kind of out of it."

Berry, with him every moment, would lay her head on his shoulder and just lie next to him. She slept on a cot she had placed beside his sickbed.

By Tuesday, Tony had suddenly improved: "As soon as I came in," Paley recalls, "I could hear him laughing from the bedroom." Marianne Williamson had phoned from Paris, and miraculously, Tony had somehow risen to the occasion to talk with her. After that, his spirits held for another day or two. Then, according to Paley, "he kind of lapsed into a coma again."

At one point, prostrate in bed, surrounded by friends, Tony momentarily popped out of it, looked around, and asked, "What's going on here? What is this, a death watch?" Everyone in the room broke up laughing. But it was the last laugh.

"Toward the end he was tired and depressed," his wife later told the press. "He didn't want anybody to see him. He couldn't stand up. A friend or two would come and he would say, 'I'm ready to go,' and they would say, 'It's O.K., why don't you?' But he was just holding on, holding on for the boys and me."

Curtis Roberts called on Friday, then again on Saturday, to discuss the play: "I was told he was out jogging, he was out shopping. I was told that by the housekeeper the morning of his death." Likewise, Gus Van Sant had no idea there was anything amiss; he still thought Perkins was going to play the Countess.

In retrospect, Morton Thaw feels that "Tony loved *Together* and must have known it was going to be his last project. Maybe in a sense he was holding on to life with it. He knew he was dying, and this was his way to hold on as long as possible."

He lost his grip on Saturday the twelfth. That morning Berry called Paley, asking urgently if he knew a priest. "She just wanted a priest, I don't know why. I got Father Terrance Sweeney to come over. He administered last rites even though Tony wasn't a Catholic. Berry wanted it. Then I came over myself at about two o'clock."

"Do you want to be alone with him?" Berry asked.

Paley sat alone with his old friend, talking to him, for about thirty minutes. "I don't think he could hear me. Maybe he could. He was just, like, gasping for breath. Have you ever seen anyone in that state? It's horrible."

Two nurses were there, and David Kessler and Dennis Christopher. Berry stood holding the boys outside Tony's room, the three of them weeping for their husband and father—the man who had kept up such a brave face for them for so long—mourning the end of their family life as they had known it.

By three-thirty that afternoon, Anthony Perkins was dead.

Roddy McDowall just happened to show up with a gift copy of *Double Exposure*, his new book of photographs, for Tony. Producer Howard Rosenman also dropped by, and unknowingly began to chat with the corpse before reality gradually hit.

Tab Hunter even rang from his home in New Mexico: "Tony had been on my mind a great deal, and I couldn't get him off my mind. All of a sudden, I was in the market and I saw the *Enquirer* [another article had just come out] saying that Tony wasn't well. I picked up the phone and called, and he had died that same afternoon."

As befit a movie star, Perkins's home was surrounded by photographers and reporters—even a helicopter hovering overhead—all waiting to get a glimpse of the grieving widow, or better yet, the body.

"I remembered that photograph of Marilyn Monroe dead on a slab," Paley says, "and I was so afraid that one of those people would do that to Tony that I offered to go with the body to the mortuary. As I was leaving, Dan Aykroyd said, 'I'll go with you.' " They escorted their friend together.

That night, the biggest, brightest full moon in a quarter century rose in the sky. It was Jane Perkins's birthday.

GOODBYE AGAIN

THE FULL IMPACT of what had happened would not hit Berry Perkins until the family-oriented holidays of Thanksgiving and Christmas came around again. In the meantime, she kept busy, cleaning up, taking condolence calls, making arrangements for the cremation. Her sister and her mother flew in from Paris to be at her side.

Just three days after her husband's death, on Tuesday the fifteenth, she steeled herself to meet the press. "He simply never wanted anyone to know," she explained to the reporters who had gathered at her home. "He figured if anyone knew they'd never give him work again."

She admitted that Tony had been hospitalized twice, "once as an outpatient, and we went under another name. I literally asked myself, 'Who am I today?' It was weird. You lose all sense of reality. You can't even be yourself in a situation like this. You're signing 'Mrs. Smith' or whatever. You think that this man has spent his entire life giving people so much pleasure in show business, and this is his reward. He can't even be himself at the end."

The tabloids, she went on, had been hunting them "like vultures," following their housekeeper to the market or home at the end of the day. Pointedly not wanting to echo the kind of anger that Brad Davis had expressed, she nevertheless added, "Now people say, 'Oh, if only I had known I'd have given [Tony] work.' I'm not sure I buy that."

She spoke, too, of Tony the simple man who had cherished his home in Cape Cod, where he was "treated like a private person," and even in L.A., where "he could spend days and days alone in this house, never want to get out, just putter around. He loved it."

When asked how she thought her husband had contracted the disease, Mrs. Perkins became suddenly inarticulate. She shook her head and replied, faltering: "No. We don't really know. No. It's not worth it." Twenty years of marriage to a Hollywood actor had forced the once open-minded Berry into a closet as well.

"I was saddened when he died," one colleague says, "but it was like he had died years before. It's hideous to die of AIDS, but Tony had gone long before that as far as I was concerned."

The next day, by chance, Ron Bernstein saw Berry in town shopping for a handbag. "I don't know why I expected her to be home grieving. I was somewhat startled to see her buying an alligator or crocodile bag. But why not? Here she was talking to the shopkeeper over the price of this bag. I was very sad. I felt that somehow life had been cruel to him."

"I've read these stories about the disturbing psychological problems Tony had as a child," Paul Jasmin was quoted shortly thereafter, "but you never saw them in that family. . . . There was such love and such warmth, always. The Perkins home was where you came for family love. They're probably the happiest family I've known out here."

Dominick Dunne remembers seeing the couple in an airport lounge just months before the end: "Berry came in with the dog to see Tony off. They weren't aware that I was there yet. He was flying to New York, and I believe he was ill then. There was a deep affection between them. They had this huge dog that was pulling her [probably Brian O'Dowd's]—it was a real sense of marriage between them. They enjoyed each other. Whatever they had, it was wonderful. I mean, it was a *real* family."

"I believe that Tony, in his search for truth and beauty, found Berry," Joel Schumacher maintains. "He was looking for love, and he found love, because she *is* love. If you know her and you're in her presence, you will know love, you will feel love, and you will be love. And you will love her. It's impossible to be in the same room with Berry Perkins and not love her and feel love. It's impossible. So I think that on Tony's great journey he found his quest."

"You're only as sick as your secrets," Berry told *Premiere* on the first anniversary of her husband's death. "It's a relief to everybody to put everything out on the table and realize there's nothing wrong with any of it."

On Friday, September 18, MCA took out a full page in *Daily Variety*: "Anthony Perkins, 1932–1992," read the words underneath a smiling portrait taken by his wife. "You will be missed."

His memorial service the next day, presided over by Marianne Williamson, attracted an amazing throng of stars and moguls, despite the fact that Tony had not worked with a major director in almost a decade (and had not made a major film in longer than that). Mixed in with old friends like Helen, Grover Dale, and Anita Morris were power brokers like David Geffen, Sandy Gallin, and Barry Diller. Janet Leigh, Buck Henry, and producer John Foreman, himself in the last stages of AIDS, were also there. Sophia Loren wept quietly by herself, while Dan Aykroyd acted as usher and parked cars.

Between fond remembrances spoken by friends old and new, some of Tony's favorite recordings were played over the loudspeakers: "Amazing Grace" by Hubert Laws, Chick Corea, and Quincy Jones; "More Than You Know" by André Previn; "Somewhere" by Aretha Franklin; Ernest Gold's "Waltzing Matilda" from *On the Beach*; Dimitri Tiomkin's "Thee I Love" from *Friendy Persuasion*; and Ennio Morricone's theme from *The Red Tent*, which had heralded the Perkins-Berenson marriage nineteen years before.

Elvis's godmother and Berry's longtime friend, writer Nuala Boylan, spoke of the "laughter and certainty" of [Tony and Berry's] love. "In a world of ambiguities," she said, paraphrasing the famous line from *The Bridges of Madison County*, "this kind of certainty comes only once, no matter how many lifetimes we lead."

"Tony and Berry," rhapsodized actor Dennis Christopher, who had known Perkins for twenty years. "Well, you all know. People talk about Camelot being lost. Well, it wasn't. It had just moved to Chelsea. So, what about the flip side? If there was one, I never heard it."

"He's the first man I ever said 'I love you' to," Dick Benjamin attested. "And he said it to me. And because it was Tony, I know it was the truth. And I love him." Mike Nichols, Stephen Paley, David Kessler, John Ryan, and screenwriter Charles Dennis also spoke.

The service, which lasted a good two and a half hours, "was quite unusual, special," *Psycho II* producer Bernard Schwartz recalls. "I'd never seen anything like it. Marisa Berenson sang. We all sang together, everyone held hands—and there were literally maybe a hundred and fifty guests. It was the most spiritual experience."

Some were embarrassed by it.

Others wondered what David Geffen was doing there. (The memorial also served as a fund-raiser for Project Angel Food, to which Berry had been elected a member of the board just three days before Tony died.)

Still others felt long excluded from the little family.

"That Tony never fulfilled himself is a tragedy," says Gwen Davis, who regrets that his fear of exposure prevented her from having the chance to say goodbye to her clever friend. (She had not been invited to his surprise party.) "He never did anything optimum," she muses. "And yet he was optimum. My husband, who was an athlete, used to say, 'You're only as good as the game.' Tony was as good as the game. But he never found out what the game was."

Perhaps he knew all too well what it was.

As he lay dying at home, guarded until the very last possible moment by the members of his ragtag, diverse, deeply devoted clan—"his privileged family," as Melina Mercouri remembered their close circle during *Phaedra*—he prepared a statement, which he dictated to his sons, for release upon his death: "I chose not to go public because, to misquote *Casablanca*, 'I'm not much at being noble, but it doesn't take much to see that the problems of one old actor don't amount to a hill of beans in this crazy world.'

"There are many who believe that this disease is God's vengeance, but I believe it was sent to teach people how to love and understand and have compassion for each other. I have learned more about love, selflessness, and human understanding from the people I have met in this great adventure in the world of AIDS than I ever did in the cutthroat, competitive world in which I spent my life."

Tony's private game had always been to keep them guessing, to stay one step ahead, to appear to be everything to everybody.

He had done it again.

BIBLIOGRAPHY

ALEXANDER, PAUL. *Boulevard of Broken Dreams: The Life, Times, and Legend of James Dean.* New York: Viking, 1994.

ANDEREGG, MICHAEL A. *William Wyler.* Boston: Twayne, 1979.

ANDERSEN, CHRISTOPHER. *Citizen Jane: The Turbulent Life of Jane Fonda.* New York: Henry Holt, 1990.

ANOBILE, RICHARD J., ED. *Alfred Hitchcock's "Psycho."* New York: Avon, 1974.

BERGAN, RONALD. *Anthony Perkins: A Haunted Life.* London: Little, Brown, 1995.

BERGMAN, INGRID, AND ALAN BURGESS. *My Story.* New York: Delacorte, 1980.

BURKHART, JEFF, AND BRUCE STUART. *First Choice.* New York: Crown, 1994.

COLACELLO, BOB. *Holy Terror: Andy Warhol Close Up.* New York: HarperCollins, 1990.

COLLIER, PETER. *The Fondas.* New York: Putnam & Sons, 1991.

CURTIN, KAIER. *"We Can Always Call Them Bulgarians": The Emergence of Lesbians and Gay Men on the American Stage.* Boston: Alyson, 1987.

DYNES, WAYNE R., ED. *Encyclopedia of Homosexuality*. New York: Garland, 1990.

FADERMAN, LILLIAN. *Odd Girls and Twilight Lovers: A History of Lesbian Life in Twentieth-Century America*. New York: Penguin, 1992.

FARBER, STEPHEN, AND MARC GREEN. *Hollywood on the Couch: A Candid Look at the Overheated Love Affair Between Psychiatrists and Moviemakers*. New York: William Morrow, 1993.

FREEDLAND, MICHAEL. *Jane Fonda: A Biography*. New York: St. Martin's, 1988.

HACKETT, PAT, ED. *The Andy Warhol Diaries*. New York: Warner, 1989.

HARRIS, JED. *A Dance on the High Wire: Recollections of a Time and a Temperament*. New York: Crown, 1979.

HARRIS, JED. *The Curse of Genius*. Boston: Little, Brown, 1984.

HUDSON, ROCK, AND SARA DAVIDSON. *Rock Hudson: His Story*. New York: William Morrow, 1986.

HYAMS, JOE, WITH JAY HYAMS. *James Dean: Little Boy Lost*. New York: Warner, 1992.

KATZ, EPHRAIM. *The Film Encyclopedia*. New York: Harper & Row, 1990.

KATZ, JONATHAN NED. *Gay American History: Lesbians and Gay Men in the U.S.A.* Rev. ed. New York: Meridian, 1992.

KAZAN, ELIA. *A Life*. New York: Alfred A. Knopf, 1988.

KELLY, KEVIN. *One Singular Sensation: The Michael Bennett Story*. New York: Doubleday, 1990.

KIERNAN, THOMAS. *Jane: An Intimate Biography*. New York: Putnam & Sons, 1973.

LAMPARSKI, RICHARD. *Whatever Became of . . . ?* Fifth Series. New York: Crown, 1974.

LEAMER, LAURENCE. *As Time Goes By: The Life of Ingrid Bergman*. New York: Harper & Row, 1986.

LEAMING, BARBARA. *Orson Welles*. New York: Viking, 1983.

LEE, JENNIFER. *Tarnished Angel: A Memoir*. New York: Thunder's Mouth, 1991.

LOESSER, SUSAN. *A Most Remarkable Fella*. New York: Donald I. Fine, 1993.

LOGAN, JOSHUA. *Movie Stars, Real People, and Me*. New York: Delacorte, 1978.

MADSEN, AXEL. *William Wyler: The Authorized Biography*. New York: Thomas Y. Crowell, 1973.

MCBRIDE, JOSEPH. *Orson Welles*. New York: Viking, 1972.

MCGILLIGAN, PATRICK. *George Cukor: A Double Life*. New York: HarperPerennial, 1992.

MERCOURI, MELINA. *I Was Born Greek*. Garden City, N.Y.: Doubleday, 1971.

MORRISROE, PATRICIA. *Mapplethorpe*. New York: Random House, 1995.

NEWMAN, MILDRED, AND BERNARD BERKOWITZ, WITH JEAN OWEN. *How to Be Your Own Best Friend*. New York: Random House, 1971.

OPPENHEIMER, JERRY, AND JACK VITEK. *Idol: Rock Hudson, The True Story of an American Film Hero*. New York: Villard, 1986.

PALMER, LAURA KAY. *Osgood and Anthony Perkins: A Comprehensive History of Their Work in Theatre, Film, and Other Media, with Credits and an Annotated Bibliography*. Jefferson, N.C.: McFarland, 1991.

PARKER, JOHN. *Five for Hollywood*. New York: Carol, 1991.

REBELLO, STEPHEN. *Alfred Hitchcock and the Making of "Psycho."* New York: Dembner, 1990.

RUSSELL, KEN. *A British Picture: An Autobiography*. London: William Heinemann, 1989.

RUSSO, VITO. *The Celluloid Closet: Homosexuality in the Movies*. New York: Harper & Row, 1981.

SELDES, MARIAN. *The Bright Lights*. Boston: Houghton Mifflin, 1978.

SPOTO, DONALD. *The Dark Side of Genius: The Life of Alfred Hitchcock.* New York: Ballantine, 1984.

SWINDELL, LARRY. *The Last Hero: A Biography of Gary Cooper.* New York: Doubleday, 1980.

TARABORRELLI, J. RANDY. *Call Her Miss Ross.* New York: Birch Lane, 1989.

TIMMONS, STUART. *The Trouble with Harry Hay, Founder of the Modern Gay Movement.* Boston: Alyson, 1990.

Tony Perkins Story, The. Fawcett, 1957.

WALKER, ALEXANDER. *Audrey: Her Real Story.* New York: St. Martin's, 1994.

WELLES, ORSON, AND PETER BOGDANOVICH. *This Is Orson Welles.* New York: HarperCollins, 1992.

WEST, JESSAMYN. *To See the Dream.* New York: Harcourt, Brace, 1956.

WOODWARD, IAN. *Audrey Hepburn.* New York: St. Martin's, 1984.

ZADAN, CRAIG. *Sondheim & Co.* New York: Macmillan, 1974.

INDEX